PUBLIC FINANCE IN THEORY AND PRACTICE

PUBLIC FINANCE IN THEORY AND PRACTICE

Fifth Edition

Richard A. Musgrave

H. H. Burbank Professor of Political Economy, Emeritus
Harvard University

Adjunct Professor of Economics
University of California at Santa Cruz

Peggy B. Musgrave

Professor of Economics
University of California at Santa Cruz

McGRAW-HILL BOOK COMPANY

New York St. Louis San Francisco Auckland Bogotá Caracas Colorado Springs
Hamburg Lisbon London Madrid Mexico Milan Montreal New Delhi Oklahoma City
Panama Paris San Juan São Paulo Singapore Sydney Tokyo Toronto

PUBLIC FINANCE IN THEORY AND PRACTICE

INTERNATIONAL EDITION 1989

567890 KKP AGA 943

This book was set in Times Roman by the College Composition Unit
in cooperation with Arcata Graphics/Kingsport.
The editor was Scott D. Stratford;
the designer was Rafael Hernandez;
Project supervision was done by The Total Book.
New drawings were done by Fine Line Illustrations, Inc.

Library of Congress Cataloging–in–Publication Data

Musgrave, Richard Abel, (date).
Public finance in theory and practice / Richard A.
    Musgrave, Peggy B. Musgrave. — 5th ed.
    p. cm.
    Bibliography: p.
    Includes index.
    ISBN 0–07–044127–8   ISBN 0–07–044128–6 (pbk.)
    1. Finance, Public–United States. I. Musgrave, Peggy B.
II. Title.
HJ257.2.M87 1989   88–13317
336.73–dc19

When ordering this title use ISBN 0-07-100227-8

Printed in Singapore

About the Authors

Richard A. Musgrave is H. H. Burbank Professor, Emeritus, at Harvard University and adjunct professor of economics at the University of California, Santa Cruz. After undergraduate work at Heidelberg University, he came to the United States in 1933 and received his Ph.D. from Harvard University. Having served at the Federal Reserve Board during the 1940s, he taught at the University of Michigan, Johns Hopkins, and Princeton before returning to Harvard in 1964. Professor Musgrave has authored numerous volumes and papers in the fields of public finance and fiscal policy. Named Distinguished Fellow of the American Economic Association and Honorary President of the International Institute of Public Finance, he has been elected to the National Academy of Science, and has been a recipient of the Frank A. Seidman Distinguished Award in Political Economics and of honorary doctorate degrees.

Peggy B. Musgrave is a professor of economics at the University of California, Santa Cruz. She received her undergraduate training at Cambridge University, a Master's degree at American University, and a Ph.D. at Johns Hopkins University, specializing in international aspects of public finance. Professor Musgrave has worked with the International Tax Program of Harvard Law School and has consulted with the World Bank, the U.S. Treasury Department, the Senate Foreign Relations Committee, and the United Nations. She is the author of many books and journal articles dealing with various international aspects of public finance. Her current teaching interests include public finance, cost-benefit analysis, law and economics, and women in the economy. Dr. Musgrave is currently involved in research and writing on international tax coordination.

Contents

Preface
to the
Fifth Edition

Public finances, in both theory and practice, do not stand still, and much has changed since the first appearance of this text. Consumption has emerged as a rival to income in defining the base of personal taxation. Growing attention has been given in tax theory to deadweight loss and to effects upon growth, while the distribution of the tax burden has come to be of less concern. New perspectives on fiscal federalism have appeared, reconsidering the federal role and its relation to state and local finances. Developments in the theory of public choice have addressed the political process by which fiscal decisions are reached. Upheavals in macro theory have called for a reexamination of the fiscal role in stabilization, and increased attention has been placed on its international dimension.

Fiscal institutions, as well, have been in a process of change. Public sector growth slowed down in the eighties, with rising defense outlays limiting the scope of civilian programs. Massive deficits in the federal budget emerged following tax cuts in the early eighties, with repercussions on the trade balance and a sharp growth in the federal debt. The 1986 legislation brought into being some of the earlier goals of tax reformers by broadening the base of the income tax, though much still remains to be done. In turn, bracket rates were reduced at the upper end, moving the schedule away from progression and towards a flat-rate tax. Reform of the corporation tax also traded rate reduction for a broadening of the base. Generally speaking, attitudes moved towards a more critical view of the public sector, with legislation to limit budget growth at the state and local level.

These and other developments have been accounted for in the new edition. Many pages have been rewritten and others have been extensively reworked. At the same time, the basic features of our approach have been retained. We have held on to the view that a productive study of public finances calls for a recognition of the close interaction between institutional and theoretical concerns, without sacrificing the one for the other. We have also continued to cover a wide range of fiscal problems, thereby permitting the material to be adapted to the special interests and concerns of particular courses.

Finally, and most important, this text continues to reflect our premise that the public sector has an important and constructive role to perform rather than being, as has increasingly come to be the view, an unfortunate interference in the market. Though powerful as an instrument of social organization, the market cannot perform all the functions that need to be met to achieve the economic and social goals of a democratic society. To accomplish that task, a partnership with the public sector is needed, and this is precisely why an efficient conduct of the public sector is of such importance. It is our hope that this fifth edition of our text will make some contribution to that goal.

We would like to express our thanks for the many useful comments and suggestions provided by colleagues who reviewed this text during the course of its development, especially to James Alm, University of Colorado; Joseph J. Cordes, George Washington University; Richard F. Dye, Lake Forest College; Ruth Shen, San Francisco State University; and Jeffrey Wolcowitz, Harvard University.

Our thanks are also due to Carol Marks and Brian Tyler for reading the manuscript and to Ann Bennett for once more doing the typing chores. In particular we wish to thank Kate Scheinman, our project supervisor, for her patient and helpful guidance through the editorial process.

Richard A. Musgrave

Peggy B. Musgrave

Excerpt from the Preface to the First Edition

Choosing a title for a book is like naming a product. It must describe the basic service which it renders, yet one wishes to differentiate one's own brand. *Public Finance* does the former and *Theory and Practice* serves the latter purpose.

On one side there is the vast array of fiscal institutions—tax systems, expenditure programs, budget procedures, stabilization instruments, debt issues, levels of government, Congress, the Executive, city halls, and the voters. On the other, there is the endless stream of issues arising in the operation of these institutions. How big a share of GNP should be included in the public sector and how should the choice of public expenditures be determined? What taxes are to be chosen and who really bears their burden? How should fiscal functions be divided among levels of government? How can a high level of employment be reconciled with stable prices? Pursuit of these issues leads from one end of economic analysis to the other. Our study, therefore, must combine a thorough understanding of fiscal institutions with a careful analysis of the economic principles which underlie budget policy.

As a study in public policy, this volume deals with many of the central economic and social issues of our time. They are issues which call for resolution by public policy because, like it or not, they cannot be handled adequately through a decentralized market. The existence of externalities, concern for adjustments in the distribution of income and wealth, as well as the maintenance of high employment and price level stability all pose issues which require political processes for their resolution. A public sector is needed to make society work and the problem is how to do this in a framework of individual freedom and justice.

Given the central role of the political process in fiscal decisions, the study of public finance thus reaches beyond the sphere of economics narrowly defined and into what might otherwise be considered matters of political science and philosophy. Recognizing the importance of these overlaps, we have not shied away from such problems but have tried to meet them where they arise. *Making the fiscal system work is, after all, a large part of making democracy function.*

Richard A. Musgrave

Peggy B. Musgrave

PUBLIC FINANCE IN THEORY AND PRACTICE

Part One

What the Public Sector Is About

Chapter 1

Fiscal Functions: An Overview*

A. **Introduction:** *Subject of Study; Modes of Analysis; Need for Public Sector; Major Functions.* B. **The Allocation Function:** *Social Goods and Market Failure; Public Provision for Social Goods; National and Local Social Goods; Public Provision versus Public Production.* C. **The Distribution Function:** *Determinants of Distribution; How Income Should Be Distributed; Fiscal Instruments of Distribution Policy.* D. **The Stabilization Function:** *Need for Stabilization Policy; Instruments of Stabilization Policy.* E. **Coordination of Budget Functions. F. Summary.**

A. INTRODUCTION

In the United States economy of today, over 20 percent of GNP is purchased by government; total government expenditures including transfers equal 35 percent thereof and tax revenue absorbs over 30 percent of GNP. Though sizable, this government participation falls short of that in other developed economies, especially those in Western Europe, where the governmental share of economic activity is frequently over 50 percent. Beyond the budgetary function, public policy influ-

*Reader's Guide to Chapter 1: This chapter is designed to give the general setting to the fiscal problem, thereby taking a sweeping view of the issues to be considered in detail later on. You may therefore be left with many questions. But don't worry. They will be cleared up (it is hoped) as you proceed.

ences the course of economic activity through monetary, regulatory, and other devices. Public enterprise also plays a major role in most European countries, though it is of limited importance in the United States. The modern "capitalist" economy is thus a thoroughly mixed system in which public and private sector forces interact in an integral fashion. The economic system, in fact, is neither public nor private, but involves a mix of both sectors.

Subject of Study

This book deals with the economics of the public sector as that sector operates in a mixed system. Its operation includes not only financing but has broad bearing on the level and allocation of resource use, the distribution of income, and the level of economic activity. Although our subject matter is traditionally referred to as public finance, the book thus deals with the real as well as the financial aspects of the problem. Moreover, we cannot deal with "public" economics only. Since the public sector operates in interaction with the private, both sectors enter the analysis. Not only do the effects of expenditure and tax policies depend upon the reaction of the private sector, but the need for fiscal measures is determined by how the private sector would perform in their absence.

Notwithstanding this broad view, we will not deal with the entire range of economic policy but limit ourselves to that part which operates through the *revenue* and *expenditure* measures of the public budget. Other aspects, such as the regulation of competition through the courts, the operation of public enterprise, and the conduct of monetary policy, are only minor budget items, but of great importance as instruments of economic policy. Yet, we will deal with them only where they are associated with the economics of budget policy. The term "public sector" as used here thus refers to the budgetary sector of public policy only.

Modes of Analysis

In an analysis of the public sector, various types of questions may be asked. They include the following:

1. What criteria should be applied when one is judging the merit of various budget policies?
2. What are the responses of the private sector to various fiscal measures, such as tax and expenditure changes?
3. What are the social, political, and historical forces which have shaped the present fiscal institutions and which have determined the formulation of contemporary fiscal policy?

Question 1 requires a "normative" perspective—i.e., a type of economic analysis that deals with how things *should* be done—and asks how the quality of fiscal institutions and policies can be evaluated and how their performance can be improved. The answer requires setting standards of "good" performance. Corresponding to the analysis of efficient behavior of households and firms in the private sector, defining such standards calls for a type of economics which is referred to as "welfare economics" in professional jargon. Its application to the public sector is more difficult, however, because the objectives of fiscal policy are not given but must be determined through the political process. Moreover, objectives of efficiency in resource use must be supplemented by considerations of equity and distributional justice, thus enlarging the sphere of normative analysis.

Question 2 must be asked if the outcome of alternative policies is to be traced. If the merits of a corporation profits tax or of a sales tax are to be judged, one must know who will bear the final burden, the answer to which in turn depends on how the private sector responds to the imposition of such taxes. Or if aggregate demand is to be increased, one must know what the effects of the reduction in taxes or increase in public expenditures will be, effects which once more depend upon the magnitude and speed of responses by consumers and firms in the private sector. Analyzing the effects of fiscal measures thus involves what has been referred to as "positive" economics—i.e., the type of economic analysis which deals with predicting, on the basis of empirical analysis, how firms and consumers will respond to economic changes and with testing such predictions empirically.

Question 3 likewise involves a "positive" approach, asking in this case why the fiscal behavior of governments is what it is. This is not only a matter of economics but also includes a wide range of historical, political, and social factors. How do interest groups try to affect the fiscal process, and how do legislators respond to interest-group pressures? How are the fiscal preferences of voters determined by their income and their social and demographic characteristics, and how does the political process, in fact, serve to reflect their preferences?

Need for Public Sector

From the normative view, why is it that a public sector is required? If one starts with the premises generally accepted in our society that (1) the composition of output should be in line with the preferences of individual consumers and that (2) there is a preference for decentralized decision making, why may not the entire economy be left to the private sector? Or, putting it differently, why is it that in a supposedly private enterprise economy, a substantial part of the economy is subject to some form of government direction rather than left to the "invisible hand" of market forces?

In part, the prevalence of government may reflect the presence of political and social ideologies which depart from the premises of consumer choice and decentralized decision making. But this is only a minor part of the story. More important, there is the fact that the market mechanism alone cannot perform all economic functions. Public policy is needed to guide, correct, and supplement it in certain respects. It is important to realize this fact, since it implies that the proper size of the public sector is, to a significant degree, a technical rather than an ideological issue. A variety of reasons explain why such is the case, including the following:

1. The claim that the market mechanism leads to efficient resource use (i.e., produces what consumers want most and does so in the cheapest way) is based on the condition of competitive factor and product markets. Thus, there must be no obstacles to free entry and consumers and producers must have full market knowledge. Government regulation or other measures may be needed to secure these conditions.

2. They may also be needed where competition is inefficient due to decreasing cost.

3. More generally, the contractual arrangements and exchanges needed for mar-

ket operation cannot exist without the protection and enforcement of a governmentally provided legal structure.

4.   Even if the legal structure is provided and barriers to competition are removed, the production or consumption characteristics of certain goods are such that they cannot be provided for through the market. Problems of "externalities" arise which lead to "market failure" and require correction by the public sector, either by way of budgetary provisions, subsidy, or tax penalty.

5.   Social values may require adjustments in the distribution of income and wealth which results from the market system and from the transmission of property rights through inheritance.

6.   The market system, especially in a highly developed financial economy, does not necessarily bring high employment, price level stability, and the socially desired rate of economic growth. Public policy is needed to secure these objectives. As the events of the eighties have shown, this is the case especially in an open economy subject to international repercussions.

7.   Public and private points of view on the rate of discount used in the valuation of future (relative to present) consumption may differ.

As we will see later, items 4 through 6 are of particular importance in evaluating budget policy.

To argue that these limitations of the market mechanism call for corrective or compensating measures of public policy does not prove, of course, that any policy measure which is undertaken will in fact improve the performance of the economic system. Public policy, no less than private policy, can err and be inefficient, and the basic purpose of our study of public finance is precisely that of exploring how the effectiveness of policy formulation and application can be improved.

Major Functions

Although particular tax or expenditure measures affect the economy in many ways and may be designed to serve a variety of purposes, several more or less distinct policy objectives may be set forth. They include:

1.   The provision for social goods, or the process by which total resource use is divided between private and social goods and by which the mix of social goods is chosen. This provision may be termed the *allocation function* of budget policy. Regulatory policies, which may also be considered a part of the allocation function, are not included here because they are not primarily a problem of budget policy.

2.   Adjustment of the distribution of income and wealth to ensure conformance with what society considers a "fair" or "just" state of distribution, here referred to as the *distribution function*.

3.   The use of budget policy as a means of maintaining high employment, a reasonable degree of price level stability, and an appropriate rate of economic growth, with allowances for effects on trade and on the balance of payments. We refer to all these objectives as the *stabilization function*.

While these policy objectives differ, any one tax or expenditure measure is likely to affect more than one objective. As will be noted presently, the problem, therefore, is how to design budget policy so that the pursuit of one goal does not void that of another.

B.   THE ALLOCATION FUNCTION

We begin with the allocation function and the proposition that certain goods—referred to here as *social,* or public, as distinct from *private* goods—cannot be provided for through the market system, i.e., by transactions between individual consumers and producers. In some cases the market fails entirely, while in others it can function only in an inefficient way. Why is this the case?

Social Goods and Market Failure

The basic reason for market failure in the provision of social goods is not that the need for such goods is felt collectively whereas that for private goods is felt individually. While peoples' preferences are influenced by their social environment, in the last resort wants and preferences are experienced by individuals and not by society as a whole. Moreover, both social and private goods are included in their preference maps. Just as I can rank my preferences among housing and backyard facilities, so I may also rank my preferences among my private yard and my use of public parks. Rather, the difference arises because the benefits to which social goods give rise are not limited to one particular consumer who purchases the good, as is the case for private goods, but become available to others as well.

If I consume a hamburger or wear a pair of shoes, these particular products will not be available to other individuals. My and their consumption stand in a rival relationship. But now consider measures to reduce air pollution. If a given improvement in air quality is obtained, the resulting gain will be available to all who breathe. In other words, consumption of such products by various individuals is "nonrival" in the sense that one person's partaking of benefits does not reduce the benefits available to others. This has important implications for how consumers behave and how the two types of goods are to be provided.

The market mechanism is well suited for the provision of private goods. It is based on exchange, and exchange can occur only where there is an exclusive title to the property which is to be exchanged. In fact, the market system may be viewed as a giant auction where consumers bid for products and producers sell to the highest bidders. Thus the market furnishes a signaling system whereby producers are guided by consumer demands. For goods such as hamburgers or pairs of shoes this is an efficient mechanism. Nothing is lost and much is gained when consumers are excluded unless they pay. Application of the exclusion principle tends to be an efficient solution.

But such is not the case with respect to social goods. Here it would be inefficient to exclude any one consumer from partaking in the benefits, since such participation does not reduce consumption by anyone else. The application of exclusion would thus be undesirable even if it were readily feasible. Given such conditions, the benefits from social goods are not vested in the property rights of particular individuals, and the market cannot function. With benefits available to all, consumers will not voluntarily offer payments to the suppliers of such goods. I will benefit as much from the consumption of others as from my own, and with thousands or millions of other consumers present, my payment will be only an insignificant part of the total. Hence, no voluntary payment is made, especially where many consumers are involved. The linkage between producer and consumer is broken and the government must step in to provide for such goods.

A need for public provision may arise even in situations where consumption is rival, so that exclusion would be appropriate. Such is the case because exclusion may be impossible or prohibitively expensive. Thus, space on a crowded city intersection is scarce, but a mechanism of charging each passing car is hardly feasible. Once more, government must step in when the market cannot deal with the situation.

Public Provision for Social Goods

The problem, then, is how the government should determine how much of such goods is to be provided. Refusal of voluntary payment by consumers is not the basic difficulty. The problem could be solved readily if the task were merely one of sending the tax collector to consumers to whom the benefits of social goods accrue. But matters are not this simple. The difficulty lies in deciding the type and quality of a social good that should be supplied to begin with and how much a particular consumer should be asked to pay. It may be reasonable to rule that the individual should pay for the benefits received, as in the case of private goods, but this does not solve the problem; the difficulty lies in finding out how these benefits are valued by the recipient.

Just as individual consumers have no reason to offer voluntary payments to the private producer, so they have no reason to reveal to the government how highly they value the public service. If I am only one member in a large group of consumers, the total supply available to me is not affected significantly by my own contribution. Consumers have no reason to step forward and declare what the service is truly worth to them individually unless they are assured that others will do the same. Placing tax contributions on a voluntary basis would therefore be to no avail. People will prefer to enjoy as free riders what is provided by others. A different technique is needed by which the supply of social goods and the cost allocation thereof can be determined.

This is where the political process must enter the picture as a substitute for the market mechanism. Voting by ballot must be resorted to in place of voting by dollar bids. Since voters know that they will be subject to the voting decision (whether by simple majority or some other voting rule), they will find it in their interest to vote such that the outcome will fall closer to their own preferences. Decision making by voting becomes a substitute for preference revelation through the market, and the collection of cost shares thus decided upon must be implemented via the tax system. As shown later, taxation generates efficiency costs or deadweight losses which do not arise in a market for private goods. The result of the vote, moreover, will not please everyone but it can only hope to approximate an efficient solution. It will do so more or less perfectly, depending on the efficiency of the voting process and the homogeneity of the community's preferences in the matter.

National and Local Social Goods

Although social goods are available equally to those concerned, their benefits may be spatially limited. Thus, the benefits from national defense accrue nationwide while those from streetlights are of concern only to local residents. This suggests that the nature of social goods has some interesting bearing on the issue of fiscal federalism—centralization or decentralization. As we will see later, a good case can be made for letting national public services be provided by national government and local public services by local government.[1]

Public Provision versus Public Production

Before considering how such public provision is to be arranged, we must draw a clear distinction between public *provision* for social goods, as the term is used here, and public *production*. These are two distinct and indeed unrelated concepts which should not be confused with one another.

Private goods may be produced and sold to private buyers either by private firms, as is normally done, or by public enterprises, such as public power and transportation authorities or the nationalized British coal industry. Social goods, such as spaceships or military hardware, similarly may be produced by private firms and sold to government; or they may be produced directly under public management, as are services rendered by civil servants or municipal enterprises. If we say that social goods are *provided* publicly, we mean that they are financed through the budget and made available free of direct charge. How they are *produced* does not matter. When looking at the public sector in the national accounts, we will see that the cost of such provision is divided about equally between compensation paid to public employees (whose output may be viewed as public production) and outputs purchased from private firms.[2] Public production of private goods which are then sold in the market plays only a very limited role in the U.S. system.

C. THE DISTRIBUTION FUNCTION

The allocation function, concerned with the provision of social goods, inevitably departs from the market process but nevertheless poses the type of problem with which economic analysis has traditionally been concerned, i.e., the efficient use of resources given a prevailing distribution of income and pattern of consumer preferences. The issue of distribution is more difficult to handle. Yet, distribution issues are a major (frequently *the* major) point of controversy in the budget debate. In particular, they play a key role in determining tax and transfer policies.

Determinants of Distribution

In the absence of policy adjustments, the distribution of income and wealth depends first of all on the distribution of factor endowments, including personal earnings abilities and the ownership of accumulated and inherited wealth. The distribution of income, based on this distribution of factor endowments, is then determined by the process of factor pricing, which in a competitive market sets factor returns equal to the value of the marginal product. The distribution of in-

[1] See p. 446.
[2] See p. 17.

come among individuals thus depends on their factor endowments and the prices which they fetch in the market.

This distribution of income may or may not be in line with what society considers fair or just. A distinction must be drawn between (1) the principle that efficient factor use requires factor inputs to be valued in line with competitive factor pricing and (2) the proposition that the distribution of income among families should be fixed by the market process. Principle 1 is an economic rule that must be observed if there is to be efficient use of resources, whether in a market economy or in a planned economy. Proposition 2 is a different matter. For one thing, factor prices as determined in the market may not correspond with the competitive norm. But even if all factor prices, including wages and other returns to personal services were determined competitively, the resulting pattern of distribution might not be acceptable. It typically involves a substantial degree of inequality, especially in the distribution of capital income; and though views on distributive justice differ, most would agree that some adjustments are required, if only to provide an adequate floor at the bottom of the scale. Such adjustments, however, may involve efficiency costs, and the costs must be allowed for in designing distribution policies.

How Income Should Be Distributed

Economics helps to determine what constitutes an efficient use of resources, based on a given pattern of distribution and effective demand. But there is the further question of what constitutes a fair or just state of distribution. Modern economic analysis has steered shy of this problem. The essence of modern welfare economics has been to define economic efficiency in terms which exclude distributional considerations. A change in economic conditions is said to be efficient (i.e., to improve welfare) if and only if the position of some person, say A, is improved without that of anyone else, including B and C, being worsened. This criterion, which may be qualified and amended in various ways, cannot be applied to a redistributional measure which by definition improves A's position at the expense of B's and C's. While the "someone gains, no one loses" rule has served well in assessing the efficiency of markets and of certain aspects of public policy, it contributes little to solving the basic social issues of fair distribution.

The answer to the question of fair distribution involves considerations of social philosophy and value judgment. Philosophers have come up with a variety of answers, including the view that persons have the right to the fruits derived from their particular endowments, that distribution should be arranged so as to maximize total happiness or satisfaction, and that distribution should meet certain standards of equity, which, in a limiting case, may be egalitarian. The choice among these criteria is not simple, nor is it easy to translate any one criterion into the corresponding "correct" pattern of distribution. We will encounter these difficulties when dealing with redistribution policy again in interpreting the widely accepted proposition that people should be taxed in line with their "ability to pay."

There are two major problems involved in the translation of a justice rule into an actual state of income distribution. First, it is difficult or impossible to compare the levels of utility which various individuals derive from their income. There is no simple way of adding up utilities, so that criteria based on such comparisons are not operational. This limitation has led people to think in terms of social evaluation rather than subjective utility measurement. The other difficulty arises from the fact that the size of the pie which is available for distribution is not unrelated to how it is to be distributed. As noted before, redistribution policies may involve an efficiency cost which must be taken into account when one is deciding on the extent to which equity objectives should be pursued.

Notwithstanding these difficulties, however, distributional considerations remain an important issue of public policy. Attention appears to be shifting from the traditional concern with relative income positions, with the overall state of equality, and with excessive income at the top of the scale, to adequacy of income at the lower end. Thus the current discussion emphasizes prevention of poverty, setting what is considered a tolerable cutoff line or floor at the lower end rather than putting a ceiling at the top, as was once a major concern. This, as we will see, has important bearing on the design of tax structure.

Fiscal Instruments of Distribution Policy

Among various fiscal devices, redistribution is implemented most directly by (1) a tax-transfer scheme, combining progressive taxation of high-income with a subsidy to low-income households.[3] Alternatively, redistribution may be implemented by (2) progressive taxes used to finance public services, especially those such as public housing, which particularly benefit low-income households. Finally, redistribution may be achieved by (3) a combination of taxes on goods purchased largely by high-income consumers with subsidies to other goods which are used chiefly by low-income consumers.

In choosing among alternative policy instruments, allowance must be made for resulting deadweight losses or efficiency costs, i.e., costs which arise as consumer or producer choices are interfered with. Redistribution via an income tax–transfer mechanism has the advantage that it does not interfere with particular consumption or production choices. However, even this mechanism is not without its "efficiency cost," since the choice between income and leisure will be distorted. As we will see later, an optimal solution might call for a complex mix of taxes and subsidies. However, we will disregard this for the time being and think of the function of the distribution branch as being met by a set of direct income taxes and transfers.

While redistribution inevitably involves an efficiency cost, this consequence by itself establishes no conclusive case against such policies. It merely tells us that (1) any given distributional change should be accomplished at the least efficiency cost and (2) a need exists for balancing conflicting equity and efficiency objectives. An optimally conducted policy must allow for both concerns.

D. THE STABILIZATION FUNCTION

Having dealt with the role of budget policy in matters of allocation and distribution, we must now note its bearing on the macro performance of the economy, i.e.,

---

[3] A *progressive tax* is defined as one in which the ratio of tax to income rises with income.

on targets such as high employment, a reasonable degree of price level stability, soundness of foreign accounts, and an acceptable rate of economic growth.

Need for Stabilization Policy

Achievement of these targets does not come about automatically but requires policy guidance. Without it, the economy tends to be subject to substantial fluctuations and may suffer from sustained periods of unemployment or inflation. To make matters worse, unemployment and inflation—as we have painfully learned in the 1970s—may exist at the same time. With growing international interdependence, forces of instability may be transmitted from one country to another, which further complicates the problem.

The overall level of employment and prices in the economy depends upon the level of aggregate demand, relative to potential or capacity output valued at prevailing prices. The level of demand is a function of the spending decisions of millions of consumers, corporate managers, financial investors, and unincorporated operators. These decisions in turn depend upon many factors, such as past and present income, wealth position, credit availability, and expectations. In any one period, the level of expenditures may be insufficient to secure full employment of labor and other resources. For various reasons, including the fact that wages and prices tend to be downward rigid, there is no ready mechanism by which such employment will restore itself automatically. Expansionary measures to raise aggregate demand are then needed. At other times, expenditures may exceed the available output under conditions of high employment and thus may cause inflation. In such situations, restrictive measures are needed to reduce demand. Furthermore, just as deficient demand may generate further deficiency, so may an increase in prices generate a further price rise, leading to renewed inflation. In neither case is there an automatic adjustment process which ensures that the economy is promptly returned to high employment and stability. Changing expectations introduce a dynamic force which may prove a source of growth as well as of system instability and decline.

Instruments of Stabilization Policy

Policy instruments available to deal with these problems involve both monetary and fiscal measures, and their interaction is of great importance.

Monetary Instruments   While the market mechanism, if it functions well, may be relied upon to determine the allocation of resources among private goods, it cannot by itself regulate the proper money supply. As Walter Bagehot pointed out a century ago, "Money does not control itself." If left to its own devices, the banking system will not generate precisely that money supply which is compatible with economic stability, but will—in response to the credit demands of the market—accentuate prevailing tendencies to fluctuation. Therefore, the money supply must be controlled by the central banking system and be adjusted to the needs of the economy in terms of both short-run stability and longer-run growth. Monetary policy—including the devices of reserve requirements, discount rates, and open market policy—is thus an indispensable component of stabilization policy. Expanding the money supply will tend to increase liquidity, reduce interest rates, and thereby increase the level of demand, with monetary restriction working in the opposite direction.

Fiscal Instruments Fiscal policy as well has a direct bearing on the level of demand. Raising public expenditures will be expansionary as demand is increased, initially in the public sector and then transmitted to the private market. Tax reduction, similarly, may be expansionary as taxpayers are left with a higher level of income and may be expected to spend more. Changes in the level of deficit thus play an important role. At the same time, much will depend on how the deficit is financed. If accompanied by an easy monetary policy, the expansionary effects of deficit finance will be greater as the deficit can be met by increased credit. If matched by tight money, placing the additional debt will call for an increase in the rate of interest and thus have a restrictive effect on market transactions. Moreover, effects upon international capital flows, as the American economy has seen in the 1980s, are again of major importance.

E. COORDINATION OF BUDGET FUNCTIONS

As noted before, budget policy involves a number of distinct objectives, but these overlap in practice, thereby complicating an efficient policy design, i.e., a design which does justice to its diverse goals.

Suppose first that the public wishes an increased supply of public services. Increased taxes are needed to pay for these, which leads in turn, to the question of how they should be distributed. Depending on what taxes are used, taxation may well change the distribution of income that remains available for private use. Hence some voters may favor (reject) the proposed change in public services because they like (dislike) the associated change in distribution rather than because they like (or dislike) the public service. Ideally, the two issues would be separated: Society would provide for what is considered a fair state of distribution and then adjust the financing of public services in line with the benefits which taxpayers derive therefrom. Because this two-step procedure is difficult to accomplish, decisions on the provision of public services tend to be mixed with and distorted by distributional considerations. Similar reasoning also applies in the reverse direction, when the supply of public services and hence taxes are to be reduced.

Next suppose that society wishes to shift distribution in the direction of greater (lesser) equality. Such a shift may be accomplished by using progressive (regressive) taxes to finance transfers to lower (higher) incomes. But it may also be done by increasing (reducing) the supply of public services of particular value to low (high) income groups. This, however, interferes with the pattern of public services which consumers want to obtain at a given distribution of income. Once more, one policy objective may be implemented such that it interferes with another.

Finally, consider the role of fiscal policy in stabilization. Suppose that a more (less) expansionary policy is needed. This may be accomplished by raising (lowering) outlays on public services or by reducing (raising) the level of taxation. In the former case the allocation objective of fiscal policy is interfered with, whereas in the latter it is not. However, in the latter case there is the further question of how changes in the level of taxation are to be implemented. For stabilization measures to be neutral regarding both allocation and distribution goals, proportional changes in the level of tax rates might offer the appropriate solution.

As we will see in the course of this study, there are many exceptions which call for qualification of the simple rules just given. Nevertheless, it is important to keep in mind that there are distinct policy objectives and policy should try to minimize conflicts among them.

F. SUMMARY

This chapter, being itself in the form of a summary, can hardly be summarized further. However, the main ideas presented are these:

   1. Modern so-called capitalist economies are in fact mixed economies, with one-third or more of economic activity occurring in the public sector.

   2. For purposes of this book, the term public sector is used to refer to the parts of governmental economic policy which find their expression in budgetary (expenditure and revenue) measures.

   3. Three major types of budgetary activity are distinguished, namely, (a) the public provision of certain goods and services, referred to as "social goods"; (b) adjustment in the state of distribution of income and wealth; and (c) measures to deal with unemployment, inflation, and inadequate economic growth.

   4. In discussing the provision of social goods (the allocation function), reference is made to goods and services which must be paid for through budgetary finance. Whether the production of these goods is by a public agency or whether the goods and services are purchased from private firms is a different matter.

   5. Provision for social goods poses problems which differ from those which arise in connection with private goods. Since social goods are nonrival in consumption, consumer preferences are not revealed by consumer bidding in the market. Therefore a political process and budgetary finance are required.

   6. The pattern of distribution which results from the existing pattern of factor endowments and their sale in the market is not necessarily one which society considers as fair. Distributional adjustments may be called for, and tax and transfer policies offer an effective means of implementing them, thus calling for a distribution function in budget policy.

   7. Tax and expenditure policies affect aggregate demand and the level of economic activity. Their conduct has important bearing on maintaining economic stability, including high employment and control of inflation. Hence, the stabilization function enters as the third budgetary concern.

   8. A major problem is how to conduct fiscal policy so that its major objects—including allocation, distribution, and stabilization aspects—can be met at the same time.

FURTHER READINGS

Colm, G.: *Essays in Public Finance and Fiscal Policy,* New York: Oxford, 1955, chap. 1.
Mills, G. B. and J. Palmer (eds.): *Federal Budget Policy in the 1980s,* Washington, D.C.: Urban Institute, 1984.
Musgrave, R. A.: *The Theory of Public Finance,* New York: McGraw-Hill, 1959, chaps. 1, 2.
Phelps, E. (ed.): *Private Wants and Public Needs,* rev. ed., New York: Norton, 1965.
Pigou, A. C.: *A Study in Public Finance,* London: Macmillan, 1928, part I.
Stigler, G. F.: *The Citizen and the State,* Chicago: University of Chicago Press, 1975, chaps. 1, 2, 5.

Chapter 2

Public Sector in the Economic Accounts*

A. **Public Sector in the Circular Flow:** *Income and Expenditure Flows; Factor and Product Flows.* **B. Public Sector in the National Income Account:** *Public Sector in GNP; Public Sector in National Income; Public Sector in Personal Income; Public Sector in Disposable Income.*

It will be evident from the preceding review that the functions of the public sector differ from those of private households or firms. At the same time, both sectors interact and are linked in the overall economic process. This is shown here first with regard to the functional interdependence of public and private income and expenditure streams in the "circular flow" of the economy and then with regard to the location of public sector magnitudes in the national income and product accounts.

A. PUBLIC SECTOR IN THE CIRCULAR FLOW

The interdependence of public and private flows is illustrated in Figure 2-1, which

Reader's Guide to Chapter 2: For a more detailed discussion, see "The U.S. National Income and Product Accounts," *Survey of Current Business,* July 1987, vol. 67, no. 7, and later issues.

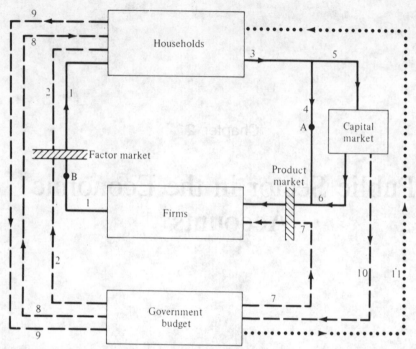

FIGURE 2-1. The public sector in the economy.

presents a highly simplified picture of the circular flow of income and expenditure in the economy. We disregard business saving and the foreign sector and assume that all tax revenue derives from the income tax. A more detailed view of tax flows is given in a subsequent chapter.[1]

Income and Expenditure Flows

The solid lines of Figure 2-1 show income and expenditure flows in the private sector; the broken lines show public sector flows. Suppose first that there is no public sector. Moving clockwise along the solid lines, we note how households obtain income through the sale of factors in the factor market (line 1), which is then spent (line 4) or saved (line 5). Saving in turn finances investment expenditure (line 6).[2] Lines 4 and 6, combining the purchases of products in the product market, give rise to the receipts of firms, which in turn are used for the purchase of factor services.

   When the government is introduced, we note that factors are bought by the public sector (line 2) as well as by the private sector and that output of private firms is purchased by government (line 7) as well as by private buyers. In addition to

---

[1] See p. 213.

[2] In taking an ex post view of the economy, this circular-flow presentation (similar to the GNP accounts for any past year) establishes an identity between saving and investment. For a discussion of what happens when some sectors of the economy wish to invest more or less than others intend to save, see p. 501.

factor and product purchases, the government also makes transfer payments (line 8). Government revenue in turn is derived from imposing taxes (line 9) and from borrowing (line 10).

As this diagram shows, the private and public sector flows are closely intertwined. Note especially that the public sector participates as a buyer in both the factor and the product markets. Its operations are thus an integral part of the pricing system. This is why it is necessary, in designing fiscal policies, to allow for how the private sector will respond. Imposition of a tax at one point in the system—for instance, at point A or point B—may lead to responses which will shift the burden to a quite different point. Moreover, the government not only diverts private income to public use, but through factor and product purchases also contributes to the income flow to households. It is thus misleading to think of the public sector as being "superimposed" on the private sector. Rather, they are both integral and interacting parts of what in fact is a mixed economic system.

It is hardly necessary to note that Figure 2-1 gives a highly simplified view of public and private sector interaction. By showing flows at a given level of income we have disregarded the effects of fiscal policies on the level of employment, as well as on productivity growth. All this will be taken up in more detail in Part Seven of this text.

Factor and Product Flows

Instead of viewing Figure 2-1 in terms of income and expenditure flows, one may interpret it as showing the real flows of factor inputs and product outputs. Reversing the arrows and moving now in a counterclockwise direction, we find that lines 1 and 2 show the flow of factor inputs into the private and public sectors, respectively, while lines 4, 6, and 7 show the flow of firm outputs to private and government buyers, respectively.[3] We must now add dotted line 11 to show the flow of public goods and services which are provided free of direct charge to the consumer. This flow, which bypasses the product market, is financed not through sales proceeds but through taxation or through borrowing. Note also that the goods and services which government thus provides (line 11) are only in part produced by government (based on the factor inputs of line 2); the remainder is privately produced and sold to government, as shown in line 7.

B. PUBLIC SECTOR IN THE NATIONAL INCOME ACCOUNTS

Since the national income accounts offer the most comprehensive frame of reference in which to view the economy, it is helpful to understand the role of government items in these accounts. This is shown in Table 2-1 for 1986. For this purpose, federal, state, and local governments are combined into one public sector.

---

[3] Since public sector sales (the role of public enterprise) are quite small in the U.S. economy, this item has been omitted in Figure 2-1. We may think of government enterprises as included under private firms.

TABLE 2-1
Composition and Uses of U.S. GNP for 1986
(In Billions of Dollars)*

	Major Items		
1.	Personal consumption expenditures		2,768
2.	Gross private domestic investment		684
3.	Net exports		– 105
4.	GOVERNMENT PURCHASES		864
5.	Wage payments	396	
6.	Purchases from firms	468	
7.	GNP		4,206
8.	– Capital consumption allowances		455
9.	Net national product		3,751
10.	– INDIRECT BUSINESS TAXES		349
11.	+ SUBSIDIES LESS SURPLUS OF GOVERNMENT ENTERPRISE		11
12.	– Other		29
13.	National income		3,385
14.	– CORPORATION PROFITS TAX		83
15.	– CONTRIBUTIONS TO SOCIAL INSURANCE		376
16.	+ GOVERNMENT TRANSFERS TO PERSON		491
17.	+ Other		69
18.	Personal income		3,486
19.	– PERSONAL TAX PAYMENTS		514
20.	Disposable personal income		2,972
21.	– Personal outlays		2,858
22.	Personal savings		114

*Government items are shown in capital letters. Line 18 includes interest paid by government to persons.
Source: U.S. Department of Commerce, *Survey of Current Business,* February 1987.

Public Sector in GNP

The gross national product may be looked upon as the aggregate of expenditures on currently produced output. Government contributes to these expenditures through its purchases of goods and services.

Total Share   As shown in item 4 of Table 2-1, government purchases are a major component of the GNP, with 20 percent of total output purchased by government. Looked at from the other end, these 20 percent of goods and services are not paid for directly when received by users but are provided free of direct charge and are paid for indirectly through the government budget. While not all these goods can be strictly classified as social goods (as we used the term in Chapter 1), we may nevertheless record the fact that over one-quarter of total output is based on budgetary provision.

In examining how this provision fits into the economic structure, we now inquire how government purchases are divided between (1) purchases of factors and purchases of products, (2) provision for consumption and provision for investment, and (3) provision to consumers and provision to firms.

Purchase of Factors versus Purchase of Products The first distinction does not appear directly in the national income accounts but is approximated in Table 2-1 by equating governmental factor purchases with public sector wage payments. Such payments to employees of government departments and schools amounted to approximately one-half of total government purchases, the remainder being the purchases of products from private firms. Thus government assumes the role of producer for about one-half the goods and services which it provides through the budget.

Provision for Consumption versus Investment The second distinction is between consumption and capital formation. While the private component of GNP is broken down by consumption and gross capital formation (lines 1 and 2 of Table 2-1), no such distinction is drawn in the recording of government purchases. Yet, government capital formation, including highways, structures, and defense equipment, is an important part of the investment process. Item 2 thus understates total capital formation in the economy.

Provision to Consumers versus Provision to Firms The division of publicly provided goods and services between final goods supplied to consumers and "intermediate goods" supplied to firms does not lend itself readily to statistical determination. A substantial part of highway expenditures, of municipal services, and of developmental outlays are in the intermediate good category, i.e., they are grants which reduce the cost of production for private firms rather than provide services which go directly to the private consumer. At least part of education outlays also belong in this category. Some intermediate goods are of the current service type (police protection for plants), whereas others are of the investment type (roads). Excluding defense, it may well be that one-third or more of total purchases are of the intermediate type.

Public Sector in National Income

In moving from GNP to *net national product* (line 9 of Table 2-1), we find that depreciation or capital consumption allowances are deducted.[4] Moving on to *national income,* we further deduct indirect business taxes (line 10).[5] Indirect busi-

---

[4] To obtain a proper figure of net output, depreciation on government as well as on privately held assets should be deducted, but in fact the national income accounts do not allow for this.

[5] There are two difficulties with this treatment:

    a. In the United States national income accounts, as prepared by the Department of Commerce, indirect business taxes include property tax receipts, about half of which are derived from owner-occupied residences and should not be included in this part of the accounts. Rather, these taxes should be deducted along with income tax when moving from personal to disposable income.

    b. While it is customary in the U.S. accounts to think of factor shares as shares in national income, it may be preferable to focus on net national product, thus including indirect taxes as part of gross factor earnings.

ness taxes, such as sales taxes, are deducted because they reduce the amount available for disbursement to factors, with national income defined as the sum of factor incomes. For similar reasons, subsidies to business firms are added, the impact being the same as that of negative taxes (line 11).

National income, shown in line 13, reflects the total of private factor earnings. This may be broken down into income derived from, or "originating in," the government and the private sector. The bulk of income originating in government is in the form of wages and salaries paid by government; as shown in line 5 of the table, such payments in 1987 equaled 12 percent of national income.

Public Sector in Personal Income

Moving from national to personal income, we again encounter a number of government items, of which some divert from, and others add to, income available at the personal level.

First, the corporation profits tax (line 14) is deducted, followed by social security contributions (line 15), including contributions by both employers and employees. Government transfer payments (line 16) are then added. They largely involve social security payments with veterans' benefits and public assistance being the next most important items. Finally, government interest payments to persons are included in personal income, thus being treated as a transfer and not as a component of national income.[6]

Personal income, in turn, may be broken down into the part received from payments by government and the part received from private disbursements. For 1986, the government share (equal to government wages plus interest and transfers to persons minus social insurance contributions) was 17 percent. Reflecting the important role of transfer payments, this is a substantially larger share than that of national income originating in the public sector.

Public Sector in Disposable Income

In moving to disposable income, we must deduct personal tax payments (line 19). They amount to 15 percent of personal income and are accounted for largely by the federal individual income tax. Moving on to the uses of disposable income (line 20), no further budget items appear, since all taxes have been deducted in advance and since public enterprise sales to consumers are included in consumption, along with private sales. Disposable income as defined in the accounts, however, falls short of a person's real income. In addition to the cash earnings that are reflected in an individual's disposable income, real income also includes the free provision of public services by government. If such real income were included on the income side, public services would become an important item of income use.

---

[6] While this may be considered appropriate, imputed interest on public capital goods (e.g., roads) *should* be included in GNP and national income but in fact is disregarded.

Chapter 3

Fiscal Institutions*

A. Survey of United States Fiscal Structure: *Expenditures; Receipts; Intergovernmental Grants.* **B. The Constitutional Framework:** *Federal Powers and Limitations; State Powers under Federal Constitution; State Constitutions, Tax Limitations, and Local Powers.* **C. Implementation of Expenditure Policy:** *Executive Budget; Congressional Budget Process; Execution of Budget Program; Audit.* **D. Implementation of Tax Policy:** *Legislation; Administration.* **E. Other Aspects of Implementation:** *Stabilization Policy; Trust Funds; Debt Management.* **F. Summary.**

The economic rationale for fiscal policy is one thing and the existing set of fiscal institutions is another. These institutions, like other aspects of political and social organization, are the product of a multiplicity of historical forces, not necessarily well suited to perform the normative tasks set forth in Chapter 1. Yet they must be drawn upon to do the job, and they must be adapted to its changing tasks.

A. SURVEY OF UNITED STATES FISCAL STRUCTURE

The fiscal structure of the United States is set forth in Tables 3-1 through 3-3.

*Reader's Guide to Chapter 3: Here we follow the preceding survey of fiscal *issues* and the public sector's place in the economy with a broad sketch of fiscal *institutions*—federal, state, and local. These introductory chapters will provide the setting for the analysis to come.

Expenditures

Part I of Table 3-1 shows how expenditures at each level of government are distributed by major functions. The table applies to 1983, the last year for which a complete pattern is available. The big items at the federal level include social insurance at 32 percent, defense with 29 percent, and interest with 14 percent, accounting in all for 75 percent of the total. The biggest items at the state level are education, welfare, social security, and transportation. By far the dominant function at the local level is education. Part II shows how expenditures, in total and by functions, are distributed by levels of government. Beginning with total expenditures, federal outlays account for 60 percent, followed by local expenditures of 22 percent and state expenditures of 18 percent. Defense is entirely and social security is largely federal. Expenditures on welfare and transportation are made largely at the state level, while education and policy are largely local functions.

Turning finally to the ratio of expenditures to GNP, we find that the overall ratio stood at 36 percent with 23 percent at the federal and 13 percent at the state plus local level. By 1987, these ratios had remained essentially unchanged. While the level of expenditures (including predominantly national defense) rose, so did GNP.

Receipts

Table 3-2 gives a similar picture for receipts. Beginning again with Part I of the table, we note that the federal government relies largely on direct taxes, including the individual income tax and the payroll taxes as the major sources of revenue

TABLE 3-1

Expenditures by Functions and Levels of Government, Fiscal 1983*

	I DISTRIBUTION BY FUNCTION AT EACH LEVEL				II DISTRIBUTION BY LEVEL OF EACH FUNCTION			
Function	Federal	State	Local	All	Federal	State	Local	All
1. Defense	29.1	—	—	17.6	100.0	—	—	100
2. Interest	13.7	4.9	4.5	10.2	81.9	8.3	9.8	100
3. Human resources	39.9	68.5	59.4	49.3	49.1	24.3	26.6	100
4. Education	1.7	19.9	41.6	13.6	7.3	25.5	67.2	100
5. Welfare	3.2	19.9	4.9	6.5	29.8	53.5	16.7	100
6. Health	1.5	8.8	8.4	4.3	21.4	35.7	42.9	100
7. Housing	1.3	—	2.8	1.4	55.6	—	44.4	100
8. Social insurance	32.2	19.9	1.7	23.3	83.5	14.8	1.7	100
9. Transportation	0.5	9.3	6.9	3.5	8.9	46.7	44.4	100
10. Natural resources	6.1	2.7	0.3	4.2	87.3	10.9	1.8	100
11. Police	0.3	1.3	5.0	1.5	10.0	15.0	75.0	100
12. Other	10.3	13.2	23.7	13.9	45.5	16.8	37.7	100
13. Total	100.0	100.0	100.0	100.0	60.5	17.4	22.1	100

*Expenditures to the public, with intergovernmental grants accounted for at the recipient level. Includes goods and service expenditures and transfers.

Source: Tax Foundation, *Facts and Figures on Government Finance*, 23d ed., 1986, Washington, D.C., p. a,8.

TABLE 3-2
Tax Receipts of Type and Level of Government, 1983*

	I DISTRIBUTION BY TAXES AT EACH LEVEL				II DISTRIBUTION OF TAXES BY LEVELS			
Source	Federal	State	Local	All	Federal	State	Local	All
1. Property	—	1.1	46.0	7.8	—	3.4	96.6	100
2. Individual income	42.7	17.9	2.7	30.1	84.0	14.5	1.5	100
3. Corporation	5.5	4.7	0.5	4.5	72.5	25.5	2.0	100
4. Death and gift	9.0	1.1	—	0.8	66.7	33.3	—	100
5. Sales and excise	6.5	32.3	9.1	13.3	29.6	59.2	11.2	100
6. Payroll	29.0	27.7	3.7	23.2	74.0	23.4	2.6	100
7. Other	15.4	20.7	38.0	20.3	39.2	24.4	16.4	100
Total	100.0	100.0	100.0	100.0	62.0	25.0	13.0	100

*Own receipt from the public. Intergovernmental grants are not included.
Source: Tax Foundation, Facts and Figures on Government Finance, 23d ed., 1986, Washington, D.C., p. a13.

while the corporation income tax and excises contribute with a lesser weight. The state tax system relies heavily on sales and excise taxes, including the general sales tax and gasoline taxes, as well as other product taxes. The local government financing places heavy reliance on the property tax. Turning to Part II, we note that 62 percent of all tax receipts go to the federal government, 25 percent to the state, and 13 percent to the local level. Also, we see that income tax and payroll tax revenue is largely federal, sales tax revenue largely state, and property tax revenue largely local.

Intergovernmental Grants

Having surveyed the pattern of expenditures and receipts from the public, we must now note the flow of intergovernmental grants, the third remaining component of our fiscal structure. The structure of such grants is shown in Table 3-3. Note that local governments are the major grant recipient, with such grants amounting to about two-thirds of its own revenue. The corresponding weight at the state level is one-third. Note also that states are the major grantor, with grants flowing to local government, followed by the federal government with grants directed primarily to the states. More will be said about this pattern when examining fiscal federalism later on.[1]

B. THE CONSTITUTIONAL FRAMEWORK

The fiscal framework of the United States is deeply embedded in the federalist spirit of its Constitution. Whereas a unitary government need not have its taxing and spending powers specified in the constitution, a federation by necessity must have them so specified. Indeed, fiscal arrangements—the assignment of taxing and

[1] See p. 461.

TABLE 3-3
Flow of Intergovernmental Grants and Receipts, 1984
(In Billions of Dollars)

	Federal	State	Local
Receipts of grants			
From federal government	—	76.1	20.9
From state government	—	—	105.8
From local government	—	5.3	—
Grant Receipts as percentage of own revenue	—	32.6%	64.5%
Rendering of grants			
To federal government	—	—	—
To state government	76.1	—	5.3
To local government	20.9	105.8	—

Source: *Significant Features of Fiscal Federalism,* Advisory Commission on Intergovernmental Relations, Washington, D.C., 1986.

spending powers—are at the very core of the contract between the constituent governments (the states in the United States and Australia, the provinces in Canada, or the *Länder* in the German Federal Republic) which combine to form the federation. Even though the central government necessarily must have fiscal powers, the composing units retain a sovereign right to conduct fiscal transactions of their own.

This is the spirit in which the fiscal provisions of the U.S. Constitution were written. Prior to the adoption of the Constitution, the Continental Congress was without taxing powers; the Revolutionary War was financed by taxing the Colonies and by borrowing. In no small part the Constitutional Convention of 1787 was called to deal with the financial aftermath of the war. The war debt had to be serviced and financial resources were needed to conduct the business of the future federal government. Fiscal arrangements were thus a major problem confronting the Convention.

Federal Powers and Limitations

The fiscal powers of the federal government were laid down in a series of specific constitutional provisions which came to be further defined by judicial interpretations given to certain other provisions not exclusively aimed at fiscal matters. The major provisions which are specifically fiscal include:

1. The granting of taxing powers
2. The uniformity rule
3. The apportionment rule
4. The prohibition of export taxes

What has been the significance of these provisions and how have they been modified since their inception?

Taxing Powers and Expenditure Functions   The general enabling statute for federal taxing powers is contained in Article 1, Section 8, of the Constitution, which provides that "the Congress shall have power to levy and collect Taxes,

Duties, Imposts and Excises, to pay the Debts and provide for the Common Defense and General Welfare of the United States.'' By including the general welfare as a legitimate objective of federal finance, the Constitution refrains from setting specific limits to the federal government's expenditure function. Interpretation of the term general welfare was left to the Congress and the courts, and it has come to be interpreted in an extremely broad sense. The general welfare is understood to cover not only general objectives, such as national defense or the administration of justice, but also highly selective programs aimed at particular regions or population groups, such as aid to Appalachia, grants-in-aid, and transfer payments. Thus, taxation for the finance of almost any type of expenditure program seems to be within the powers of the federal government.

Should the general welfare be understood to justify the use of taxation for regulatory purposes as well as for the financing of expenditures? The courts at times disallowed such use, but the later trend has been toward permitting regulatory objectives. In all, the taxation and expenditure powers granted by Article 1, Section 8, of the Constitution are broad and general, subject only to certain specific limitations and judicial constraints.

Uniformity Rule　The first specific limitation imposed by the Constitution is the uniformity rule given in Article 1, Section 8. The rule requires that ''all Duties, Imposts and Excises shall be uniform throughout the United States.'' Thus, excises on tobacco or automotive products must be applied at the same rate in all states; (if this condition is satisfied, they are permissible,) even though their revenue impact will differ greatly among the states, depending on where particular industries are located.[2] Uniformity, in other words, means uniform application of the statute, not of the amount of revenue collected from each state.

The uniformity rule has therefore imposed no significant limitation on the development of the federal tax structure on a nationwide basis. On the contrary, it contributed to the development of an equitable system by requiring equal treatment of taxpayers in equal position, independent of their place of residence. Similarly, it is also in accord with the efficiency rule that arbitrary interference with the location of industry—such as would be caused by regionally differentiated taxes—should be avoided. Nor does the uniformity rule interfere with the use of taxes as a tool of general stabilization policy, since tax rates may be raised and lowered on a nationwide basis as required.

The only respect in which the uniformity rule may interfere with the freedom of fiscal policy is in the use of the taxing power to deal with regional problems of economic development. Thus, a lower rate of manufacturer's tax on automobile production in West Virginia or Mississippi might serve to encourage automobile production in these states and help develop these particular regions, which could not be done under the uniformity rule.

Although the Constitution relates the uniformity rule to ''Duties, Imposts and

---

[2] Note that we are speaking here of the initial impact or place of *collection* and not of the place of *incidence*. Tobacco excises are collected in Virginia and automotive excises are collected in Michigan, whereas neither is collected in Nevada. Yet the burden of both taxes will be spread among all three states, depending on their share in cigarette and automotive consumption.

Excises,'' thereby excluding "direct taxes," this stipulation was not meant to invite the use of direct taxes on a regionally differentiated basis.[3] Indeed, the framers of the Constitution did not visualize federal use of direct taxes, which at that time were thought of primarily in terms of the property tax. Nor is it likely that the courts would permit a regionally differentiated use of the income tax under the Sixteenth Amendment.

Apportionment Rule and the Sixteenth Amendment   Whereas the uniformity rule proved to be a generally sound constraint in the development of a rational nationwide tax structure, the apportionment rule imposed a barrier which later on was to prove unacceptable. By demanding that "no capitation, or other direct tax shall be levied, unless in Proportion to the Census or Enumeration herein before directed to be taken," Section 9 of Article 1 in effect required all such taxes to be head taxes. Thus, tax rates would vary among states in inverse proportion to their per capita tax base. The rates of property tax, for instance, would have to be twice as high in state A as in state B if the per capita property tax base in A were one-half that in B. Adopted initially as a tradeoff which offered the wealthier states a tax assurance in return for their willingness to accept a small number of representatives in the Congress, the need for such assurance did not materialize for over a century, during which time federal revenue needs were met by the proceeds of indirect taxes, especially customs duties.

The apportionment clause did not bite until much later, when the federal government came to be confronted with the need for income taxation. The development of a national federal income tax would not have been possible if the apportionment rule had been held by the courts to apply to such a tax. The rate schedule, even if proportional within states, would have had to differ between states, being higher for those states with lower per capita income, which would have been incompatible with the principle of equal treatment of taxpayers with equal capacity on a nationwide basis and would have imposed a regressive pattern of rates on an interstate basis. Under these conditions, a modern income tax could not have been developed; and even though the original intent of the clause was to protect the wealthy against the poor states, its application in the modern setting would have been to prevent progressive (or even proportional) taxation at the federal level and thus to protect the wealthy against the poor taxpayer.

The question was therefore whether the income tax should be considered a "Duty, Impost or Excise" under the uniformity rule or a "capitation or other direct tax" under the apportionment clause. When the first federal income tax was held valid in 1880, the court chose to interpret it as an excise, but the opposite view was taken in 1895, when the second attempt at income taxation was held unconstitutional as an unapportioned direct tax. While it seems evident, in economic terminology, that the income tax is a direct tax, it is less clear which interpretation was the correct one on constitutional grounds. However this may be, the die was cast in the 1895 decision. Given the rising revenue needs of the federal government, especially in response to the potential need for war finance, the problem was resolved

---

[3] For a discussion of the economic distinction between direct and indirect taxes, see p. 215.

in 1913 by the Sixteenth Amendment. It states that "Congress shall have power to levy and collect taxes on incomes, from whatever source derived, without apportionment among the several states, and without regard to census or enumeration," thus clearing the way for a uniform and nationwide income tax. Such a tax was introduced in 1913 and was destined to become the mainstay of the federal revenue structure, as noted before.

But even though federal *income* taxation has been totally freed from the shackles of the apportionment rule, the rule might retain some future significance were additional taxes, such as a federal net worth tax or property tax, to be considered. Such a tax could be held to be in the nature of an income tax and thus be validated under the Sixteenth Amendment; but until the matter is decided, the skeleton of the apportionment rule continues to haunt the tax lawyer's closet.

Export Taxes Article 1, Section 9, of the Constitution also prohibits the levying of export taxes. Reflecting the desire of the Southern states to protect their interest in cotton exports, this limitation did not prove a major factor in later years. However, it is interesting to note in connection with the potential use of tax policy to affect the balance of payments that there is no corresponding prohibition of export subsidies.

Judicial Constraints In addition, certain other constitutional provisions have proved relevant to the federal taxing powers.

1. The Supreme Court has interpreted the federal system, with its "dual sovereignty" of federal and state governments, as implying that the federal government must not tax the instrumentalities of the state and local governments. Accordingly, interest on securities issued by such governments was held exempt from federal income tax and sales to such governments were held not to be subject to federal excise taxes. Although originally exempted on similar grounds, salaries of state and local government employees are generally subject to federal income tax. Whereas the income tax statute continues to exempt interest on state and municipal bonds, the powers granted by the Sixteenth Amendment have recently been reinterpreted by the Court as overruling the immunity doctrine as applied to the income tax.

2. Under the due process clause, provided in the Fifth Amendment to the Constitution and comprising part of the Bill of Rights, the federal government is constrained from depriving people of "life, liberty or property without due process of law." As applied to taxation, this means that taxes must not be arbitrary. Classification and differentiation are allowed, but they must be "reasonable."[4] The due process clause has not been interpreted, however, as placing an upper limit on permissible tax rates. At the same time, the taxpayer is protected by being given the right of judicial appeal.

Conclusion As this brief survey suggests, it can hardly be said that the development of the federal tax structure has been hampered greatly by constitutional provisions. The uniformity rule has been a wholesome constraint and the apportionment rule has been effectively overruled by the Sixteenth Amendment; in addition, it has become increasingly apparent that taxation can be used for regulatory

[4] See p. 29.

purposes. However, a new constitutional amendment to limit the level of federal taxation and to require a balanced budget is now under consideration.[5]

State Powers under Federal Constitution

Whereas the federal government had to be granted basic taxing powers by the Constitution, the states did not need this provision. Taxing power of the states is vested in their sovereign rights as constituent members of the federation and retained by them under the residual power doctrine. The Constitution, however, imposes certain restrictions on the taxing power of the states, partly through specific provisions and partly again through judicial application of other clauses of the Constitution to tax matters.

General Limitations   Among various general limitations, the following four are of major importance:

1. In Article 1, Section 10, of the Constitution, the states are prohibited specifically from imposing taxes not only on exports (which prohibition also applies to the federal government) but on imports as well. The purpose, of course, was to place the regulation of foreign commerce exclusively under the authority of the federal government.

2. The immunity doctrine, which forbids federal taxation of state and local instrumentalities, also applies in reverse. States may not tax the instrumentalities of the federal government. Thus, interest on federal securities is exempted from state income taxes. State excises cannot be levied on sales to the federal government, and federally owned property cannot be subjected to property tax. Yet salaries paid by the federal government are subject to state income tax. As in the case of federal taxation, the question of what constitutes an "instrumentality" of state and local governments is not defined by the Constitution, and judicial interpretation remains in flux.

3. The Fourteenth Amendment, extending the due process clause of the Fifth Amendment to state legislation, holds that a state must not "deny to any person within its jurisdiction the equal protection of the laws." This clause has been interpreted as a prohibition against "arbitrary" classification and sets some limits (though loosely defined) on the extent to which states may discriminate among various categories of taxpayers.

4. The Fourteenth Amendment has also been interpreted as granting the taxpayer the right of appeal against arbitrary acts of state or local tax administration, similar to its application at the federal level.

Interstate Commerce   Most significant and interesting to the economist are the provisions relating to interstate commerce and to the nondiscriminatory treatment of residents of other states. These provisions dealt, almost 200 years earlier, with essentially the same problems currently faced in the debate on fiscal integration of the Common Market countries. Among various provisions which are relevant in this connection, the following should be noted:

1. The due process clause is interpreted to limit a state's taxing power to its own jurisdiction.

2. The equal protection clause is interpreted as prohibiting discrimination against out-of-state citizens. Residents and nonresidents must be treated equally. This

[5] See p. 105.

nondiscrimination rule, however, does not apply to out-of-state corporations not subject to protection within the state.

3. Article VI, Section 8, delegates to the federal government the power "to regulate commerce with foreign nations, and among the several states." This clause has been interpreted as prohibiting states from using their taxing powers so as to interfere with the flow of foreign and interstate commerce. Imports from other states or exports to other states cannot be subject to discriminatory taxes. Thus, the character of the United States as a large area without internal trade barriers but common external tariffs is assured. At the same time, this does not ensure neutrality of state taxation with regard to industrial location, because location may be influenced by differential rates of excise or profit taxes.[6]

4. The same clause is applied to regulate the taxation of businesses engaging in interstate commerce. Taxes on gross receipts or profits can be imposed by the various states involved, but the total tax base must be allocated among them on a "reasonable" basis. There has been considerable debate about what constitutes reasonable allocation, and the entire issue continues to be controversial.[7]

Right to Education and School Finance   Although the states in general have wide freedom in designing fiscal measures, a series of cases in the 1970s have challenged the system for funding the public schools. The bulk of the funds for public elementary and secondary education comes from the local property tax. Since the property tax base varies among school districts, children in low-base districts may be disadvantaged. Starting in 1971 with the decision of California's Supreme Court in *Serrano v. Priest*,[8] a number of state courts and lower federal courts have found the existing scheme for funding the public schools unconstitutional. The California Supreme Court in *Serrano v. Priest* held that the "right to an education in public schools is a fundamental interest which cannot be conditioned on wealth." Judicial opinions in these cases referred to both the equal protection clause of the U.S. Constitution and to the pertinent provisions of the relevant state constitution. However, primary emphasis in most of these early cases was placed upon the federal, not the state, constitution.

Those who hoped that the educational finance decisions would bring immediate change to the system of local government finance were disappointed by the U.S. Supreme Court's 1972 decision in *San Antonio Independent School District v. Rodriguez*.[9] In a 5 to 4 decision, the Supreme Court held that the Texas system for funding its public schools did not violate the equal protection clause of the Fourteenth Amendment to the U.S. Constitution. The basis of the Court's opinion seems sufficiently broad to validate the existing financial systems of most, if not all, of the states.

The *Rodriguez* decision did not foreclose arguments that the system of educational finance of a particular state violates the provisions of that state's constitution. Since *Rodriguez*, the Supreme Court of New Jersey has held that New Jersey's scheme of public school finance was unconstitutional under the New Jersey

[6] See p. 469.
[7] See p. 29.
[8] 5 Cal. 3d 584 (1971).
[9] 411 U.S. 1 (1972).

constitution[10] and a number of states have followed, while litigation continues in others.

Even though the U.S. Supreme Court has refused to lay down a strict rule, state constitutions are interpreted increasingly as calling for equal educational opportunity and independence of education finance from the local property tax base. These rulings are being implemented very slowly, but in time they may give rise to a substantial restructuring of state-local finance and the role of the property tax.

There remains the broader question of whether these rulings on education might be extended to other expenditures of local government. If so, the line of thought initiated by the educational finance cases could come to have a substantial impact upon existing fiscal arrangements for other services as well. However, most legal experts do not expect such change in the near future.

Coordination This new perspective aside, we conclude that the constitutional framework (as broadened by the Sixteenth Amendment) has left almost complete freedom for development of the fiscal structure. There is no assignment of particular expenditure functions to the various levels, nor is there a prescription (apart from customs duties on foreign imports and taxes on exports) about what taxes should be used by the various levels of government.

Although little or no coordination among the fiscal systems of the various levels of government is provided for, the Constitution has been successful in barring direct interference of state taxation with the development and functioning of the U.S. economy over a large free-trade area. At the federal level, the uniformity rule prohibits regional discrimination in levying excise taxes. At the state level, interference with interstate trade through customs or export duties is prohibited.

In short, the constitutional framework ensures the absence of trade barriers in the sense of internal import duties as well as uniform external duties, but it does not attempt to equalize the fiscal structures of the states or to preclude all tax-induced interference with internal commodity or capital flows. Since state and local tax rates have been relatively low, adverse effects on economic efficiency have not been serious and have received less attention than those encountered in the European Common Market, where the conflict is greater since it stems from much larger differentials in national tax structures. Yet the basic problems are the same. Although we may find that fiscal decentralization has its attractions, it also has its efficiency costs.

State Constitutions, Tax Limitations, and Local Powers

State taxation operates under constraints imposed by state constitutions in addition to these federal constraints. These limitations differ in nature and in degree of detail. In some states, the tax structure is defined in detail, whereas in others, constitutional provisions deal with specific matters, such as debt limitations or prohibition of progressive tax rates. In recent years various states have adopted constitutional amendments to limit the growth of tax revenue in relation to the growth of state personal income or to other factors. Nearly twenty states now im-

---

[10] 62 N.J. 473 (1973).

pose overall fiscal limits, either by constitutional or statutory provisions.[11] The power of the legislature to raise taxes by a simple majority is thereby limited, as is the ability of the states to benefit from built-in, especially inflation-induced, revenue gains.

The fiscal powers of local government are granted by the states, since local government has no sovereign powers of its own. By the same token, the federal limitations on the taxing powers of the states also apply to the derived powers of the local governments. Moreover, led by the passage of Proposition 13 in California, state limitations have been placed on the growth of local property tax revenue and now apply in over thirty states. Even though the limitations are formally creatures of the state, it can hardly be said that local governments are without political strength of their own. Their fiscal powers may be "derived" only in the constitutional sense, but in reality they have grown beyond this, and local governments, especially those of the larger cities, have become full-fledged partners on the fiscal scene. The intergovernmental problem of the United States, therefore, is very much a triangular federal-state-local affair.

C. IMPLEMENTATION OF EXPENDITURE POLICY

We now turn to the governmental system by which the fiscal program is planned, legislated, and executed. Focus will be on federal operations, since they are much the largest, but more or less similar procedures are followed by states and localities. The three groups involved in the federal fiscal process are (1) the voters, (2) the President and the executive branch, and (3) Congress. Our concern here is with the latter two, leaving the voters for more detailed consideration in Chapter 7.

The central instrument of expenditure policy is the budget. The four steps involved in the budget cycle are (1) formulation of the President's budget by the executive branch, (2) appraisal of the President's budget by Congress and budget legislation, (3) the execution of this legislation by the executive branch, and (4) auditing by the General Accounting Office (GAO). In this chapter, we briefly consider these four functions as parts of the decision-making and administrative process.

Executive Budget

The President, with the help of the Office of Management and Budget (OMB), prepares the budget and presents it to Congress in January of each year. This budget covers the coming fiscal year, running from October 1 to September 30. The lengthy process of budget preparation begins with the setting of guidelines by the executive branch. In consultation with other agencies, such as the Treasury and the Council of Economic Advisers, implications of the budget plan for tax policy and stabilization are allowed for. The resulting guidelines then become the basis for budget requests by the various departments of government. The requests are then scrutinized by OMB in a series of budget hearings and brought into line with the

---

[11] See A.C.I.R., *Significant Features of Fiscal Federalism,* 1985–86 edition, Washington, D.C., 1986, p. 145.

President's wishes. The budget thus comes as close to being a statement of administration policy and an economic plan as is possible in our governmental system.

Congressional Budget Process

The budget must be submitted to Congress by January 3 of each year, where it is received by the Congressional Budget Committee. As provided by the budget reform legislation of 1974, this committee, flanked by corresponding committees in the House and Senate, is responsible for expediting the congressional budget process. The corresponding House and Senate committees follow a common schedule, beginning with the preparation of a "concurrent resolution" on the budget. Each committee must report its version of the resolution to its house by April 15. This resolution is to set the overall level of expenditures for the coming fiscal years as well as to provide a breakdown among major functional categories and to determine the required level of revenue. By May 15, the legislative process on the resolution must be completed, including the conference to reconcile the difference between the two resolutions. Then, trying to stay within the limits set by the budget resolution, Congress acts (or is supposed to act) on the appropriation bills, finishing shortly after Labor Day. In the time remaining before the start of the new fiscal year on October 1, Congress passes a second concurrent resolution on the budget in which it reaffirms its earlier decisions or revises them. In the latter case, a reconciliation bill that carries out the dictates of the resolution—including cuts in appropriation bills already enacted—must be passed before the start of the new fiscal year.

To help Congress follow this expeditious and exacting budget schedule, a Congressional Budget Office was established to provide Congress with technical and staff assistance, thereby greatly strengthening the ability of Congress to analyze the administration's proposals and to design its own budget. Unlike the case in the parliamentary system, in which the legislature accepts the government's budget as a matter of course or the government falls, the President's budget is no more than a recommendation to Congress. Congress may legislate as it wishes, and the full impact of political forces comes into play. Much depends on the strength which the President can muster in Congress and on the pressure which can be imposed by the President's threatening to veto appropriation bills.

The Congressional Budget and Impoundment Control Act of 1974 was a valiant attempt at budget reform, but much remains to be achieved. Congress so far has not been able to keep up with the exacting schedule prescribed by that legislation, with a large part of appropriation bills left for passage until after the new fiscal year has started. Moreover, the reconciliation process has assumed a much larger role than had been anticipated.[12]

To deal with the deficit problem which emerged after the tax reduction of 1981, the Balanced Budget and Emergency Control Act (Gramm-Rudman-Hollings Act) of 1986 was introduced, designed to secure a balanced budget by 1991, a setting to be examined further later on when fiscal policy is discussed.[13]

---

[12] For a description of the budget process, see *Budget of the United States,* Fiscal Year 1988, p. 6b-1. See also Allen Schick, *Crisis of the Budget Process,* American Enterprise Institute, Washington, D.C., 1986.

[13] See p. 106.

Execution of Budget Programs

After the budget is enacted and a department has received its appropriation and authority to spend, it may proceed to do so, but execution of the programs remains under the supervision of OMB. While expenditures must be in line with congressional legislation, the executive branch has some flexibility in timing. However, the 1974 legislation specified that once legislated by Congress, programs cannot be dropped by executive decision.

Audit

The final step in the budget cycle is the accounting and auditing function. This function is performed by the General Accounting Office, an independent agency outside the Executive Office and responsible directly to Congress. In this way Congress can ensure that the funds have been expended in line with congressional intent and that no irregularities occur.

D. IMPLEMENTATION OF TAX POLICY

Two aspects of tax policy need to be considered. One is the formulation of tax laws and the other is the all-important matter of tax administration.

Legislation

Whereas expenditure legislation is required annually to provide appropriations, whether for new or for existing programs, this need not be the case with respect to tax policy. The existing tax structure provides a continual if fluctuating flow of revenue without further legislative action being taken. Action may be taken, however, to adjust overall revenue to changing expenditure requirements and economic conditions. There may also be structural reforms to deal with taxation effects on the private sector and to adjust the distribution of the tax burden.

The major concern of tax reformers has been the need to improve the equity of the tax structure so as to make it comply more nearly with prevailing views of what constitutes a fair distribution of the tax burden and with the effects of taxation upon the functioning of the economy. Tax reform is therefore always a popular topic for discussion, but it tends to be handled in a discontinuous fashion. Major structural changes occur once or twice a decade, when political and other circumstances are ripe for ''reform.'' Such changes occurred in 1954, 1962–64, 1969–70, and especially in 1986. Typically, these were years that followed major changes in administration.

Tax policy proposals originate at both the executive and the congressional levels. At the executive level, a number of agencies are involved, depending on the nature of the proposal. Administration proposals for reform of the tax structure are the primary responsibility of the Treasury Department, its Office of Tax Analysis, and Tax Legislative Counsel. The work draws on a large staff of tax experts, economists, and lawyers, and it is a continuing process. Many tax economists, in and out of government, are consulted and participate in this work. Eventually, usually after a year or more of preparation, the program emerges and is presented to the President for consideration. Thus, presentation of the President's reform proposal in May 1985 was preceded by a comprehensive staff study involving a large group of fiscal economists in its preparation.[14] After the presidential decisions are made, the final program is formulated and presented to the Congress in a tax message.

At the congressional level, a key role is played by the staff of the Joint Committee on Taxation, working in close relation with the congressional leadership. The President's tax message is initially presented to the Ways and Means Committee of the House, not to the Senate. This is done because according to Article 1, Section 7, of the Constitution, "All bills for revenue raising shall originate in the House of Representatives." After receiving the administration's recommendations or (at other times) on its own initiative, the Ways and Means Committee holds hearings. These typically begin with a presentation by the Secretary of the Treasury, followed by testimony from outside groups, such as industry representatives, unions, and other organizations. Apart from the Treasury, which is to represent the national interest, the bulk of the testimony is given by interest groups, with only occasional presentations by experts or individuals representing the public interest at large. After the hearings are completed, the bill is formulated in executive session, sessions which are now open to the public. Frequently, the committee bills bear little resemblance to the original administration plan. The bill is then reported out and after limited discussion, which is usually subject only to amendments approved by the Ways and Means Committee, it is passed by the House.

The bill is then sent to the Finance Committee of the Senate, where the same procedures, including a Treasury response to the House bill and extensive hearings, are repeated. Although the Senate legislation is based on the House bill, the Finance committee is free to make changes or substitute its own proposals. The bill is then considered on the Senate floor, where it is discussed extensively, without limitations on amendments. After being voted on by the Senate, the bill is sent to Conference Committee where differences between the House version and the Senate version are ironed out. The bill is then returned to both houses, passed, and sent to the President for signature.

Notwithstanding the constitutional prerogative of the House to introduce tax legislation, the Senate Finance Committee has come to play a major role in tax policy. As noted before, both the Ways and Means Committee and the Senate Finance Committee are assisted in their complex task by the staff of the Treasury Department. Many committee members serve for lengthy periods and thus acquire considerable technical expertise. However, they are subject to a great deal of political pressure, and vested interests are built up which render action on reform exceedingly difficult to obtain.

As is the case with expenditure policy, the President may propose, but the power to act rests with Congress. Indeed, the balance of power over tax policy lies very much on the congressional side. Congress may disregard the administration's wishes and substitute its own proposals. Moreover, the committees may act on their own, without administration initiative. Underlying a latent hostility between Congress and the Treasury Department (independent of party lines) is the congres-

---

[14] See *The President's Tax Proposals to the Congress for Fairness, Growth, and Simplicity,* May 1985, and *Tax Reform for Fairness, Simplicity, and Economic Growth,* The Treasury Department Report to the President, November 1984.

sional feeling that revenue legislation is a constitutional prerogative of Congress and not really in the domain of the executive.

Administration

The tax laws, as defined by past revenue acts, are assembled in the Internal Revenue Code. This code, prepared by the legal staff of the Internal Revenue Service (IRS), interprets the revenue acts in their detailed application to a vast range of complex situations. Regulations are issued and codified on a continual basis to guide both taxpayers and tax officials in the administration of the law. The IRS staff engaged in this task includes some 60,000 tax agents, operating in sixty district offices throughout the country. The 1988 budget for IRS (collection of taxes) amounts to $5 billion, a great deal of money but below 1 percent of the revenue collected.

Although tax payments in the United States are based on the taxpayer's own declaration rather than on official assessment, the returns (about 120 million in all) must nevertheless be checked and audited. Procedures involved in examining and auditing tax returns are currently being revolutionized by the use of computers, but a large and highly trained staff remains necessary to assess the additional information. In recent years there has been increasing concern with practices of tax evasion and the complexity of the law, which complicate the administrative task of enforcement.

A final function in the taxing process is performed by the tax courts, to which the taxpayer may turn with complaints. The prosecution staff of the Internal Revenue Service in turn may enforce the tax law through criminal charges in the regular system of the federal courts.

E. OTHER ASPECTS OF IMPLEMENTATION

In addition to expenditure and tax policy, further issues of implementation arise with regard to stabilization policy, trust funds, and debt management.

Stabilization Policy

The important role of fiscal policy in economic stabilization has been noted when dealing with the various functions of budget policy. Indeed, the executive is charged with the responsibility for stabilization policy under the Employment Act of 1946, which called upon the President to "promote maximum employment, production and purchasing power," and, as added by the amendment of 1953, to promote "a dollar of stable value," to develop the policies needed for these objectives, and to report thereon to the Congress annually in the President's Economic Report. In this connection, the act established the Council of Economic Advisers to the Executive and the Joint Economic Committee at the congressional level.

The Council of Economic Advisers, including a chairperson, two additional members, and a large staff, is to assist the President in the preparation of the Economic Report. Designed to play a key role in formulating the broader economic guidelines for stabilization policy as well as to deal with other aspects of the government's economic program, the actual role and influence of the Council has differed with various administrations, each administration having, in the end, its own style of policy formulation.

At the congressional level, the Council of Economic Advisers is matched by the Joint Economic Committee. This committee receives the President's Economic Report in late January, after the State of the Union Message and the budget message have been submitted. In past years, this committee and its work have been of great value in furthering an intelligent approach to economic policy in fiscal and other areas and in raising the level of congressional economic policy discussion. However, the committee has declined in importance in recent years, with the Congressional Budget Committee and its expert staff in the Congressional Budget Office taking the lead.

Trust Funds

Whereas revenue and expenditure legislation are generally separated, with tax revenue accruing to the government's General Fund, they are linked in the case of the trust funds, which therefore carry a special role in the fiscal system. Total trust fund receipts for fiscal year 1988 are estimated at $257 billion, or nearly one-half the total budget receipts. In addition, there are off-budget trust funds (Social Security) with receipts of $242 billion.

The role of these trust funds and the merit of linking particular receipts and expenditures in this fashion will be considered later. Here we need only note that trust fund expenditures are not subject to annual appropriations but are made by each trust fund according to the rules set by Congress for its operations.

Debt Management

Finally, the role of debt management should be noted. The responsibility for debt management, vested in the Treasury Department, is twofold. One function is to carry out the debt transactions necessitated by a current budget deficit or surplus, involving either an increase or a decrease in the total debt. Even though the budget may be balanced over the fiscal year as a whole, the flow of tax receipts and expenditures is not synchronized on a monthly basis, so that intermediate debt financing is required. A further function, and much more important in volume, takes the form of vast refunding operations. They must be undertaken as maturing debt instruments are replaced by new issues of varying maturities and other characteristics. This operation is carried out by the Debt Management Division of the Treasury, with the assistance of the Federal Reserve Bank of New York.

The function of debt management is essentially an executive one and does not involve direct congressional participation. However, Congress has legislated certain restrictions with which debt managers must comply, including an interest ceiling and the provision that debt obligations may not be issued at a price below their maturing value. Also, Congress imposes a ceiling on the total debt which the Treasury is allowed to incur. This ceiling is used by Congress as an additional device to control the level of expenditures, even though expenditure programs have been authorized previously by congressional legislation.

Even though debt management, narrowly defined, is an executive responsibility, the terms at which debt can be placed depend greatly on the monetary policy pursued by the Federal Reserve System. The Board of Governors is thus an important and equal partner to the Treasury in managing the public debt.[15]

F. SUMMARY

This review of federal fiscal institutions, although sketchy, suffices to show that the fiscal machinery is highly complex and slow-moving. Many functions appear in triplicate, at the executive, House, and Senate levels, and coordinating them is cumbersome and not readily responsive to changing situations. Yet much of this is the reflection of our executive system of government and of the bicameral organization of Congress. The expenditure and taxing process, which is at the heart of the governmental operation, can hardly be exempted from the constraints which this system imposes. At the same time, better coordination could be obtained and a higher degree of flexibility should be possible without disturbing the basic balance provided by our constitutional system.

Regarding the federalist nature of our fiscal system, the major factors to be kept in mind are these:

1. The United States fiscal structure is decentralized, with 60 percent of expenditures to the public made at the federal level, 18 percent at the state level, and 22 percent at the local level. Revenues from the public are more centralized, with shares of 59, 24, and 16 percent, respectively. The difference reflects the importance of grants from higher to lower levels of government.

2. The levels of government differ in their expenditure structures, with defense and human resources programs of major importance at the federal, highway expenditures at the state, and education expenditures at the local levels.

3. A similarly sharp difference exists in the composition of the revenue structure, with the federal level characterized by income, the state level by sales, and the local level by property taxes.

4. Transfers from the federal to the state and from the state to the local level play an important role in the fiscal system.

Fiscal affairs are conducted within a framework provided by the U.S. Constitution. The major constitutional provisions are:

5. The Constitution requires federal taxes to be uniform in all states and originally called for direct taxes to be proportioned among states on a per capita basis. The uniformity requirement is still in effect but raises no problem with regard to national taxes; the apportionment requirement, however, has been largely eliminated by the Sixteenth, or Income Tax, Amendment.

6. The Constitution does not lay down explicit rules with regard to federal expenditure policy but authorizes the government to provide "for the common defense and general welfare of the United States."

7. The Constitution prohibits states from imposing custom duties and export taxes and requires state taxation to comply with its due process and equal protection clauses.

8. Recently it has been argued that the equal protection clause requires states

[15] See p. 556.

to provide equal education services to all citizens. This requirement, which would cut across local differentials, is still in process of adjudication.

9.   Localities are the creatures of the states and their fiscal powers derive from state constitutions.

Implementation of expenditure policy has been examined for the federal level. Both the executive and legislative branches have an important role to play:

10.   The primary responsibility for budget preparation rests with the executive. The budget (fiscal) year runs from October 1 to September 30. The budget is presented to the Congress in January and legislation thereon is to be completed by October 1.

11.   Congress may adopt or change the President's budget as it wishes, with budget legislation emerging as a highly political process.

12.   Congressional legislation in 1974 provided for a streamlined and coordinated congressional budget procedure which is designed to strengthen the role of the Congress in the budget process.

The implementation of tax policy follows a similar pattern:

13.   Proposals for tax legislation are made by the Treasury and are submitted to the House Ways and Means Committee, where all tax legislation must originate. After a vote by the House, they are passed on to the Senate Finance committee and after a vote on the Senate floor, the two bills are reconciled in Conference Committee.

14.   Tax administration is conducted by the Bureau of Internal Revenue, in line with the detailed provisions of the Internal Revenue Code.

15.   Debt management is conducted by the Treasury Department.

SOURCES OF FISCAL DATA

The major sources for fiscal data are as follows:

Budget of the United States Government, latest year. The budget gives detailed information on federal expenditures, past and proposed.

Department of Commerce, *Survey of Current Business*, monthly. The July issue of each year gives detailed data on government finance, national income account basis.

Economic Report of the President, latest year. The Report gives convenient summary data on expenditures and receipts, national income account basis.

Significant Features of Fiscal Federalism. Advisory Commission on Intergovernmental Relations, Washington, D.C., 1986.

Tax Foundation, *Facts and Figures on Government Finance*, 23d ed., 1986. This annual volume gives detailed data on state and local finances.

U.S. Treasury Department, *Bulletin*, monthly. This publication gives detailed data on current tax revenue.

Part Two

Allocation, Distribution, and Public Choice

Chapter 4

Public Provision for Social Goods*

A. **Social Goods and Market Failure:** *Market for Private Goods; Market Failure due to Nonrival Consumption; Market Failure due to Nonexcludability; Combined Causes of Market Failure; Summary.* B. **Provision for Social Goods:** *Comparison with Private Goods; Budgetary Provision.* C. **Mixed Goods:** *Externalities of Private Goods; Bargaining in the Small Group; Market Provision of Nonrival Goods; Congestion; Spatial Limitation of Benefits; Substitutability among Goods.* D. **Giving as a Social Good.** E. **Merit Goods.** F. **Summary.**

The theory of social, or public, goods provides a rationale for the allocation function of budget policy. Although difficult to resolve, it is of central importance to the economics of the public sector, just as the theories of the consumer household and of the firm are at the core of private sector economics.

Our task in this chapter, therefore, is to extend the economic principle of efficient resource use to the public sector. Some believe this to be a hopeless task and hold that the determination of budget policy is a matter of politics only, not amenable to economic analysis, a view that is unduly pessimistic. Budget policy has a

*Reader's Guide to Chapter 4: This chapter explores the nature of social goods and the resulting problem of resource allocation through the budget. With more technical aspects left to Chapter 5, this is one of the most important sections of our volume.

difficult task and will hardly realize a perfect solution. But not all feasible policies are equally good. Efficiency of resource use, here as in the private sector, is a matter of degree, and economic analysis can help us in seeking the best answer. The task is to design a mechanism for the provision of social goods which operating in a democratic setting will be as efficient as is feasible. The politics of fiscal policy and the inefficiencies which may ensue are considered in Chapter 7.

A. SOCIAL GOODS AND MARKET FAILURE

The market economy, when certain conditions are met, serves to secure an efficient use of resources in providing for private goods. Consumers must bid for what they wish to buy and must thus reveal their preferences to producers. Producers, in trying to maximize their profits, will produce what consumers want to buy and will do so at least cost. Competition will ensure that the mix of goods produced corresponds to consumers' preferences. This view, of course, is a highly idealized picture of the market system. In reality, various difficulties arise. Markets may be imperfectly competitive, production may be subject to decreasing cost, consumers may lack sufficient information or be misled by advertising, and so forth. For these reasons, the market mechanism is not as ideal a provider of private goods as it might be. But even so, it does a good job and a better one than can be done otherwise.

At the same time, the market cannot solve the entire economic problem. First, and most important in the present context, it cannot function effectively if there are "externalities," by which we mean situations where consumption benefits are shared and cannot be limited to particular consumers, or where economic activity results in social costs which are not paid for by the producer or the consumer who causes them. Second, the market can respond only to the effective demands of consumers as determined by the prevailing state of income distribution, but society must also judge whether this is the distribution it wants. Third, there are problems of unemployment, inflation, and economic growth which do not take care of themselves automatically. As was shown in Chapter 1, these are the three major areas where budget policy comes into play. This chapter deals with the first, or allocation, aspect.

Market for Private Goods

The market can function only in a situation where the "exclusion principle" applies, i.e., where A's consumption is made contingent on A's paying the price, while B, who does not pay, is excluded. Exchange cannot occur without property rights, and property rights require exclusion. Given such exclusion, the market can function as an auction system. The consumer must bid for the product, thereby revealing preferences to the producer, and the producer, under the pressures of competition, is guided by such signals to produce what consumers want. At least, such is the outcome with a well-functioning market.

This process can function in a market for private goods—for food, clothing, housing, automobiles, and millions of other marketable private goods—because the benefits derived therefrom flow to the particular consumer who pays for them. Thus, benefits are internalized and consumption is *rival*. A hamburger eaten by A cannot be eaten by B. At the same time, the nature of the goods is such that exclusion is readily feasible. The goods are handed over when the price is paid, but not before. But market failure occurs and budgetary provision is needed if consumption is nonrival and exclusion is inappropriate or inapplicable.

Market Failure due to Nonrival Consumption

Exclusion is inappropriate in the case of social goods because their consumption is *nonrival*. That is, they are goods such that A's partaking of the consumption benefits does not reduce the benefits derived by all others. The same benefits are available to all and without mutual interference. Therefore it would be inefficient to apply exclusion even if this could readily be done. Since A's partaking in the consumption benefits does not hurt B, the exclusion of A would be inefficient. Efficient resource use requires that price equal marginal cost, but in this case marginal cost (the cost of admitting an additional user) is zero, and so should be the price.

Consider, for example, benefits provided by national defense or by measures to prevent air pollution. Exclusion would be impossible and moreover inefficient, since A's partaking does not hurt B. Or take the case of a bridge which is not crowded, so A's crossing will not interfere with that of B. Charging a toll would be quite feasible, but so long as the bridge is not heavily used, the charge would be inefficient since it would curtail use of the bridge, the marginal cost of which is zero. Or consider the case of a broadcast, which with the use of jamming can be made available only to those listeners who rent clearing devices. Again, the jamming would be inefficient since A's reception does not interfere with B's. Exclusion *can* be applied but *should not* be, because consumption is nonrival. Since the marginal cost to previous users of adding an additional consumer is zero, no admission price should be charged.

But even though the marginal cost of admitting additional users is zero, the cost of providing the facility is not. This cost must be covered somehow, and it must be determined how large a facility should be provided. With exclusion inappropriate, even if feasible, the task cannot be performed through the usual market mode of sale to individual consumers. Provision through the market cannot function and a political process of budget determination becomes necessary, a process which permits consumers to express their preferences through the political process and also obliges them to contribute.

Market Failure due to Nonexcludability

A second instance of market failure arises where consumption is rival but exclusion though appropriate is not feasible. Whereas most goods which are rival in consumption also lend themselves to exclusion, some rival goods may not do so. Consider, for example, travel on a crowded cross-Manhattan street during rush hours. The use of the available space is distinctly rival and exclusion (the auctioning off or sale of the available space) would be efficient and should be applied. The reason is that use of crowded space would then go to those who value it most and who are willing to offer the highest price. But such exclusion would be impossible or too costly to be administered.[1] We are dealing with a situation in which exclusion should but cannot be applied. Here the difficulty of applying exclusion is *the* cause of market failure. Public provision is required until techniques can be found to apply exclusion.

Think once more of why absence of exclusion causes market failure. If partaking in consumption is not made contingent on payment, people are not forced to reveal their preferences in bidding for social goods. Such, at least, is the case if the number of participants is large. Since the total level of provision will not be affected significantly by any one person, the individual consumer will find it in his or her interest to share as a "free rider" in the provision made by others. With all consumers acting in this fashion, there is no effective demand for the goods. The auction system of the market breaks down, and once more a different method of provision is needed.

Combined Causes of Market Failure

Although the features of nonrival consumption and nonexcludability need not go together, they frequently do. In these instances—for example, air purification, national defense, streetlights—exclusion both *cannot* and *should not* be applied. Since these are situations where both causes of market failure overlap, it may be futile to ask which is *the* basic cause. However, the nonrival nature of consumption might be considered as such, since it renders exclusion undesirable (inefficient) even if technically feasible.

Summary

The previous distinctions may be summarized as follows, classifying goods into four cases, according to their consumption and excludability characteristics:

Consumption	Exclusion	
	Feasible	Not Feasible
Rival	1	2
Nonrival	3	4

Characteristics of case 1 depict the clear-cut private-good case, combining rival consumption with excludability. This is where provision through the market is both feasible and efficient. In all other cases, market failure occurs. For the setting reflected in case 2, market failure is due to nonexcludability or high costs of exclusion, whereas for the setting of case 3 it is due to nonrival consumption. In the fourth case, both impediments are present. If we applied the term social good to all situations of market failure, cases 2, 3, and 4 would all be included. It is custom-

[1] As suggested by Prof. William Vickrey of Columbia University, electronic devices may eventually be developed which record the passage of vehicles through intersections and permit the imposition of corresponding charges, adjusted to differ for rush hours and slack periods. Such charges may then be billed to the vehicle owner via a computer, and the costs of crowding city streets may thus be internalized.

ary, however, to reserve the term for cases 3 and 4 only, i.e., situations of nonrival consumption. These situations, to be sure, are similar to case 2 in that provision is made without exclusion. Hence the market fails and budgetary provision is called for. But they differ from case 2 because the existence of nonrival consumption changes the conditions of efficient resource use from those applicable where consumption is rival.

B.   PROVISION FOR SOCIAL GOODS

The nonrival nature of social-good consumption has important bearing on (1) what constitutes efficient resource allocation, i.e., allocation of resources to produce at least cost what consumers want most, and (2) the procedure by which their provision is to be achieved.[2] These implications will now be examined more carefully.

Comparison with Private Goods

To explore problem 1, it is helpful to compare the familiar demand and supply diagram for private goods with a corresponding construction for social goods as they would compare in a hypothetical market setting. The latter, as we will see presently, is unrealistic, but it is nevertheless useful in noting essential differences between the two situations. The left side of Figure 4-1 shows the well-known market for a private good. D_A and D_B are A's and B's demand curves, based on a given distribution of income and prices for other goods. The aggregate market demand curve D_{A+B} is obtained by *horizontal* addition of D_A and D_B, adding the quantities which A and B purchase at any given price. SS is the supply schedule, and equilibrium is determined at E, the intersection of market demand and supply. Price equals OC and output OH, with OF purchased by A and OG by B, where $OF + OG = OH$.

The right side of the figure shows a corresponding pattern for a social good. We assume for this purpose that consumers are willing to reveal their marginal evaluations of the social good—say, weather forecasting installations—it being understood that daily reports will be available free of charge. As before D_A and D_B are A's and B's respective demand curves, subject to the same conditions of given incomes and prices for other goods. Since it is unrealistic to assume that consumers volunteer their preferences, such curves have been referred to as "pseudo-demand curves." But suppose for argument's sake that consumer preferences are revealed. The critical difference from the private-good case then arises in that the market demand curve D_{A+B} is obtained by *vertical* addition of D_A and D_B, with D_{A+B} showing the sum of the prices which A and B are willing to pay for any given amount.[3] This follows because both consume the same amount and each is assumed to offer a price equal to his or her true evaluation of the mar-

---

[2] As noted previously, the term "provision" as used here refers to the choice and payment process rather than to whether the products or services are *produced* by government (such as the services of civil servants) or by private firms (such as private construction companies which are contracted to build public roads). See p. 9.

[3] This vertical addition of the demand curves for social goods was first presented by Howard R. Bowen in *Toward Social Economy,* New York: Rinehart, 1948, p.177.

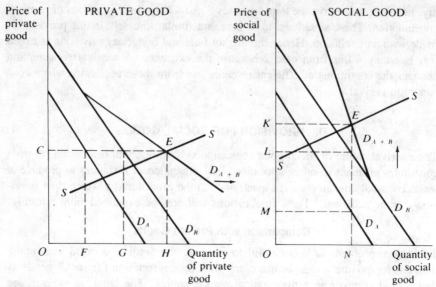

FIGURE 4-1   Demand for private and social goods.

ginal unit. The price available to cover the cost of the service equals the sum of prices paid by each. *SS* is again the supply schedule, showing marginal cost (chargeable to A and B combined) for various outputs of the social good. The level of output corresponding to equilibrium output *OH* in the private-good case now equals *ON*, which is the quantity consumed by both A and B. The combined price equals *OK*, but the price paid by A is *OM* whereas that paid by B is *OL*, where *OM* + *OL* = *OK*.

Returning to the case of the private good, we see that the vertical distance under each individual's demand curve reflects the marginal benefit which derives from its consumption. At equilibrium *E*, both the marginal benefit derived by A in consuming *OF* and the marginal benefit derived by B in consuming *OG* equals marginal cost *HE*. This is an efficient solution because marginal benefit equals marginal cost for each consumer. If output falls short of *OH*, marginal benefit exceeds marginal cost and individuals will be willing to pay more than is needed to cover cost. Net benefits will be gained by expanding output so long as the marginal benefit exceeds the marginal cost of so doing, and net benefits are therefore maximized by producing *OH* units, at which point marginal benefit equals marginal cost. Welfare losses would occur were output expanded beyond *OH*, for marginal cost would thereby exceed marginal benefits.

Now compare this solution with that for social goods. The vertical distance under each individual's demand curve again reflects the marginal benefits obtained. Since both share in the consumption of the same supply, the marginal benefit generated by any given supply is obtained by vertical addition. Thus the equilibrium point *E* now reflects the equality between the *sum* of the marginal benefits and the marginal cost of the social good. If output falls short of *ON*, it will again be advantageous to expand because the sum of the marginal benefits exceeds cost, whereas an output in excess of *ON* would imply welfare losses, since marginal costs outweigh the summed marginal benefits.[4]

Thus the two cases are analogous but with the important difference that for the private good, efficiency requires equality of marginal benefit derived by *each* individual with marginal cost, whereas in the case of the social good, the marginal benefits derived by the two consumers differ and it is the sum of the marginal benefits (or marginal rates of substitution) that should equal marginal cost. This is the rule established by Professor Samuelson in his pathbreaking articles of the late 1950s and is explored further in the next chapter.[5]

Figure 4-1 also shows how application of the same pricing rule—where the price payable by each consumer equals the individual's marginal benefit—yields different results for social goods than it does for private goods. In the private-good case, A and B pay the same price but purchase different amounts, whereas in the social-good case, they purchase the same amount but pay different prices. Yet in both cases, the same pricing rule is applied. Each consumer pays a single price for successive units of the good purchased, with the price equal to the marginal benefit that the purchaser derives.

---

[4] A somewhat different way of presenting the case of the social good, first used by the Swedish economist Erik Lindahl, views the sharing of costs by two customers of the social good as a supply-demand relationship.

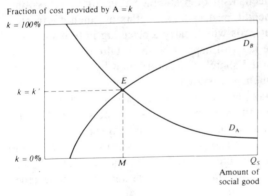

Fraction of cost provided by A = *k*

k = *100%*

D_B

E

k = *k'*

D_A

k = *0%*

M Q_S

Amount of
social good

The vertical axis measures *K* or the fraction of unit cost contributed by A. Given the unit cost *C* and assuming it to be constant, *kC* is the price paid by A, and D_A is his demand schedule for the social good *S*. Since B's price equals $(1 - k)C$, and since both share the same quantity of *S*, B's demand curve drawn with regard to *k* is given by D_B. Individual A may then look upon D_B as showing the price at which various quantities of *S* are available to him, i.e., as a supply schedule for the social good which confronts him. B similarly may regard D_A as his supply curve. The fraction of the price which both are willing to pay [*k* for A and $(1 - k)$ for B] adds to *1* at the intersection of D_A and D_B, at output *OM*. For application of this approach to a bargaining situation with small numbers, see p. 65. See Erik Lindahl, "Just Taxation: A Positive Solution," in Richard A. Musgrave and Alan Peacock (eds.): *Classics in the Theory of Public Finance*, International Economic Association, London: Macmillan, 1985, pp. 168–177. See also J. G. Head, "Lindahl's Theory of the Budget," *Finanzarchiv*, Band 23, Heft 3, October 1964, pp. 421–454.

[5] See p. 68.

Budgetary Provision

Although the presentation of Figure 4-1 is helpful in bringing out the difference in efficiency conditions, it is misleading if taken to suggest that the provision of social goods might be implemented by a market mechanism of demand and supply, with equilibrium at E as in the case of the private good. This interpretation implies that the consumers will bid as they would for private goods and thus overlooks the crucial fact that social goods are typically nonrival in consumption, and that exclusion is not feasible. Because of these factors, consumer preferences for such goods (the value which they assign to successive marginal units of consumption) will not be revealed voluntarily. Since the number of participants is usually large, any one contribution will make little difference in total provision. Knowing this, consumers will find it in their interest to act as free riders. The pseudo-demand curves of Figure 4-1 are not revealed. They do not come into play and the market mechanism cannot function.

A political process must therefore be used (1) to obtain revelation of preferences (i.e., to tell the government what social goods should be provided) and (2) to furnish it with the fiscal resources needed to pay for them. This is done through voting on tax and expenditure decisions. Individuals, knowing that they must comply with the majority decision, will find it in their best interest to vote for that solution which will move the outcome closer to their own desires, and in this way they will be induced to reveal their preferences. It is this mandatory nature of the budget decision which induces preference revelation and permits the provision of social goods to be determined.

To serve as an efficient mechanism of preference revelation, the voting process should link tax and expenditure decisions. Voters are then confronted with a choice among budget proposals which carry a price tag in terms of their own tax contribution. This price tag will depend on the total cost for the community as a whole as well as on the share to be contributed by others. Voters' choices are thus contingent on their own knowledge that others must also contribute in line with the adopted tax plan. Ideally, voters will support a tax price which reflects their marginal benefit evaluation, but as will be seen in Chapter 7, this ideal solution is not achieved in practice. Tax and expenditure votes are typically taken apart from each other. The political mechanism is imperfect and can only approximate what would be the optimal budget choice. But the political mechanism is the best (or only) technique available and must be designed and used as well as it can be.

As will be shown in Chapter 7, various voting rules may be designed. Majority rule, under certain assumptions regarding preference structures, may be expected to arrive at the position of the median voter. Other more complex voting rules may yield more satisfactory results. In a representative democracy, the problem is complicated further because most decisions are not made by referenda voting. Rather, the individual voters choose representatives who offer programs, with final decisions made by a representative body such as the Congress. Various hypotheses have advanced why such a process will bias the outcome in favor of overexpanding the public sector, an intriguing issue to be considered at a later point.

C. MIXED GOODS

Throughout the preceding discussion, a sharp distinction was drawn between private goods, such as hamburgers, the benefits of which are wholly internalized (rival), and others, such as air purification, the benefits of which are wholly external (nonrival). This polarized view is helpful for understanding the essential difference between private and social goods, but it is not realistic. In reality, mixed situations of various kinds arise.

Externalities of Private Goods

Such is the case wherever private consumption or production activities generate externalities.

External Benefits Suppose, for instance, that A derives benefits from being inoculated against polio, but so do many others for whom the number of potential carriers, and hence the danger of infection, is reduced. Or by getting educated, A not only derives personal benefits but also makes it possible for others to enjoy association with a more educated community. Since large numbers of other consumers may be affected, bargaining does not work and a budgetary process will again be needed to secure preference revelation. But the correct budgetary intervention in this case will not involve full budgetary provision; rather, it will take the form of subsidy to private purchases.

This is shown in Figure 4-2, where D_P represents the market demand schedule, obtained by *horizontal* addition of demands for the private benefits which individuals derive from inoculation or from their education. Now let D_x be a supplementary schedule reflecting the evaluation (or, as noted above, pseudo-demand) by others for the external benefits generated by these activities, e.g., the reduced risk of contagion or the pleasure of a more educated society. The D_x schedule is obtained

FIGURE 4-2 Adjustment for external benefits.

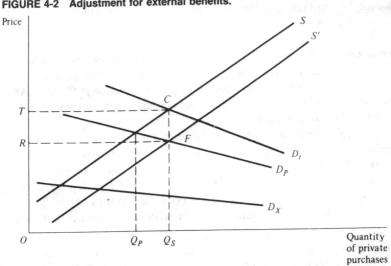

by *vertical* addition of individual demand curves for such benefits. Adding D_P and D_x vertically, D_t is obtained to reflect total benefits, including both the D_p and D_x components. Given this situation, the private market will result in equilibrium output OQ_p, since only the market demand schedule D_p is backed by voluntary purchases. But this is inefficient since the optimal output is at Q_s, where external or social benefits are allowed for as well.

In order to expand output from OQ_p to OQ_s, the government should pay a subsidy[6] equal to D_x. Such a subsidy raises the market demand confronting the supplier from D_p to D_t and output will be extended to OQ_s. Consumers pay a net price of OR, with the subsidy contributing the difference RT. The total cost of the subsidy equals $RTCF$ and is paid for out of the budget, financed by taxes on A and B imposed in line with the principles that were discussed in the preceding section. Alternatively, the subsidy may be given to the producer, lowering his net supply schedule to S'.

All this would be simple enough if D_X and hence the required level of subsidy were known, but such is usually not the case. Thus, the evaluation of the external benefits—and the determination of the proper rate of subsidy—poses problems of preference revelation similar to those which arise with social goods. Resolution through the political process is again called for.

The polar case of social goods, examined earlier, may thus be extended into a band of cases involving goods in which internal benefits to the individual consumer are increasingly supplemented by external benefits. At the one extreme of the purely private good, the distance FC in Figure 4-2 becomes zero, as D_S is the same as D_P and no subsidy is needed. At the other extreme of the purely social good, D_S becomes equal to D_X and the subsidy pays the entire price, i.e., benefits are wholly external. The good becomes a pure social good and is entirely provided for through the budget. In between, we have the cases of mixed goods, to be financed by a mix of private payments and of subsidies. The tax-expenditure theory of the preceding chapter may thus be restated more generally as a tax-subsidy theory, with subsidies ranking from 0 to 100 percent. Whereas the use of such subsidies is limited in practice, the frequent occurrence of external benefits suggests that a wider use might be in order.

External Costs   The phenomenon of benefit externalities has its counterpart in external costs. Private consumption or production activities may generate costs which are not "internalized" and not paid for by consumers or producers. As a result, costs are imposed on society which are not accounted for, and the activity in question tends to be overextended.

This is shown in Figure 4-3, where D is market demand for a private good. S_p is the supply schedule, reflecting the firms' internal or private costs, with output equal to OM and price equal to OR. An efficient solution, however, calls for inclusion of external costs as given by S_e. To secure output at ON with price equal to OT, the government may impose a tax on the producer equal to $EO = TF$, thus raising the supply schedule to S_t, reflecting both private and social cost. Equilib-

---

[6] Rather than varying the per unit subsidy in line with D_s, the efficient outcome may also be obtained by granting a constant unit subsidy equal to FC, thus dropping the s schedule to s'.

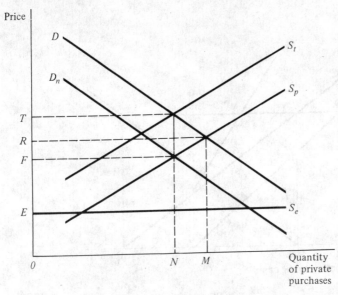

FIGURE 4-3   Adjustment for external costs.

rium output is now at *ON*. Alternatively, the tax may be imposed on the consumer, dropping the net demand schedule to D_n.

Whereas the case of external benefits was shown to call for a subsidy, that of external cost calls for a penalty tax, which leads to the problem of how to deal with social "bads," such as pollution and environmental damage.

Bargaining in the Small Group

Our preceding argument has been that a political process is needed to deal with social goods or bads because voluntary payments and preference revelation will not be forthcoming in the absence of exclusion. The reason is that any one individual will not consider it worth his or her while to pay, because with large numbers involved, individual contributions will not significantly affect the total supply. Individuals find it in their interest to act as free riders. Similarly, they will not act to prevent external costs. This difficulty is less of a problem when few people are involved. Individuals will now find it worthwhile to contribute and to bargain, since individual contributions now significantly affect their own position and that of others.

External Benefits   Whereas provision for social goods occurs predominantly in a large-number setting, external benefits may accrue in situations in which only small-number conditions are involved. Neighbors, for example, may get together in a mutual effort for tree spraying, municipalities may join in building a common garbage-disposal plant, or national governments may cooperate in undertaking joint ventures, such as NATO. Moreover, budgetary decisions are typically made not by referenda which involve a large number of voters but by bargaining among elected representatives. The small-number case is thus worth considering.

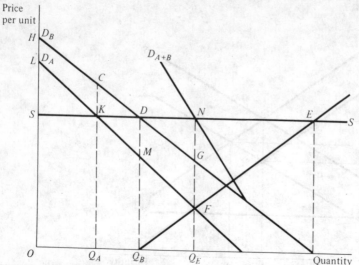

FIGURE 4-4 The small-number case.

Figure 4-4 depicts a situation where two consumers share in the benefit of a social good.[7] The provision may be paid for by A or B but the quantities provided are available equally to both. D_A and D_B are A's and B's demand schedules for the social good and SS is the supply schedule. D_{A+B} is the aggregate demand schedule, obtained by vertical addition of D_A and D_B. Up to output OQ_E, the maximum prices which A and B would be willing to offer, as shown by D_{A+B}, add to more than cost. This suggests that output will be bid up to OQ_E, where D_{A+B}, intersects SS at N. Both A and B pay a price equal to their marginal evaluation, $Q_E F$ and $Q_E G$, respectively. All this only repeats the story of Figure 4-1.

Another way of viewing the process is as follows: Since B's offers are given along D_B, we may deduct D_B from SS so as to obtain $Q_B E$, which now reflects the supply schedule at which various levels of output are available to A. Moving along D_A to its intersection with $Q_B E$ at F, A will then purchase output OQ_E, at price $Q_E F$. Thus equilibrium is established at quantity OQ_E, with A contributing $Q_E F$ and B contributing $Q_E G = FN$.

This process leads to an efficient solution, but there is little reason to assume that our two consumers will behave in this fashion. Both parties may attempt to get a better deal by offering prices below the maximum shown by their respective demand schedules. Each will learn to allow for the effects of his or her actions on the other and follow strategic behavior. They may engage in all-or-nothing bargaining rather than undertake marginal adjustments along their demand schedules. How then may we expect the bargaining to proceed? Consider B's position. If Mr. A were not present, Ms. B would purchase OQ_B. But she may not do so if she allows for A's reaction. Suppose that she expects A to purchase OQ_A if she purchases nothing, but to purchase nothing if she purchases OQ_B. Given these alternatives,

---

[7] For a diagram similar to Figure 4-4, see James M. Buchanan, *The Demand and Supply of Public Goods*, Chicago: Rand McNally, 1968.

she will decide to purchase nothing, since her gain from A's purchase of OQ_A (measured by the area OQ_ACH) exceeds the gain from her own purchase of OQ_B (measured by the area of SHD).[8] Similarly, A will not be eager to purchase OQ_A, since this may deter B from purchasing OQ_B, and his gain from his own purchase of OQ_A (measured by SLK) falls short of his gain from her purchase of OQ_B (measured by $OLMQ_B$). Eventually, someone will move and there will be responses, but it is uncertain what the result will be. Output may reach OQ_B and proceed to OQ_E or may fall short thereof. The cost share in the final quantity may be divided (or, putting it differently, the gains in consumer surplus may be distributed) in different ways. Whereas B stands to gain more from efficient provision if both contribute along their maximum offer (or demand) curves, it does not follow that she will push the bargain to OQ_E if she can get a lower price at some smaller output. The outcome will depend on the bargaining strength and skills of the two parties.

Bargaining, whether over private or social goods, need not have an efficient outcome. Whereas increasing the number of participants leads to a competitive solution in the private-good case, such will not be the result where social goods are concerned. Although bargaining imperfections are reduced, individuals will have no further reason to reveal their preferences and make their contributions. One difficulty replaces another and a political process becomes necessary to solve the problem.

External Costs Similar reasoning applies to the case of external costs. An airplane flying at night over a city, or a chimney causing air pollution, may impose external costs on many people. Yet it is impracticable for each of them to negotiate with the offender. "Transaction costs" to use the commonly applied term, are too high. But such may not be so in the small number case. Suppose rancher R raises cattle which stray onto farmer F's land and damage her crop. In the absence of any regulation, F will find it worthwhile to erect a fence or to offer R a bribe to curtail his herd. F will do so up to the point where her marginal gain from reduced crop damage equals her marginal cost of damage payment; and R will concur up to the point where his marginal loss from reducing the herd equals his marginal gain from damage receipt. Thereby an efficient solution is reached without public intervention. Moreover, the outcome will be the same, as far as reduction in the herd is concerned, whether (1) there are no rules and F has to pay R to desist, or whether (2) the law protects F so that R must pay F to secure permission to let the cattle graze. This equivalence is referred to as Coase's Law and has become of central importance in recent developments, applying economic thinking to legal issues.[9] But though the herd reduction will be the same under both solutions, the

---

[8] B's gain from purchasing OQ_B at price OS is measured by her consumer surplus of SHD, arrived at by deducting her cost, or $OSDQ_B$. Her gain in consumer surplus derived from A's provision of OQ_A equals $OHCQ_A$, since there is no cost to be deducted.

Note also that the result of $OHCQ_A > SHD$, although correct for Figure 4-4 as drawn, need not always hold. Thus, if D_B is shifted sufficiently far to the right, the triangle corresponding to SHD may come to exceed $OHCQ_A$, and B may find it worthwhile to purchase an output corresponding to OQ_B even if this deters A from making a purchase.

[9] See R. H. Coase, The Problem of Social Cost, 3 *J. Law & Economics*, 7–44 (1960). Also see R. Cooter and T. Ulen, *Law and Economics*, Scott, Foresman and Co., Glenview, Ill., 1986.

two cases differ in distributional terms. R will be better off if the law entitles him to let his cattle graze and F will better off if the law protects her crop. Bargaining may be relied upon to secure a settlement but the legal system in establishing distributive justice must still decide where the entitlement should be placed. Note moreover that, as in the case of external benefits, bargaining need not bring about an efficient solution but may be biased in favor of R or F, depending upon their respective bargaining strengths and skills.

Nevertheless, there is an interesting link as well as difference between the way in which the problem of externalities enters into fiscal and legal reasoning. Whereas the former typically addresses the role of external benefits as viewed in a large-number setting, the latter typically deals with external costs as viewed in a small-number context.

Market Provision of Nonrival Goods

It has also been suggested that under certain circumstances the market is capable of generating an efficient provision of social goods without involving a budgetary process. Suppose that there are goods which are social in that consumption is nonrival. At the same time, suppose that exclusion is possible. A monopoly supplier may then provide the good to various consumers at differentiated prices, exacting for successive units the maximum amount which each consumer is willing to pay. The supplier thus appropriates the consumer surplus derived by the buyer, but an efficient outcome ensues since at the margin the price paid equals the benefit derived. All this, however, assumes that exclusion can be enforced and that the necessary information is available to the supplier, both of which are rather unlikely conditions.

Congestion

Another case of mixed goods, also of special importance in relation to local finance, arises where goods are not truly nonrival in consumption even though they are consumed in equal amounts by all members of a particular group. As more users are added, the quality of service received by all users from a given installation declines. Thus, the quality of instruction received by the individual student from a single teacher may decline as the size of the class increases, or previously empty streets may become crowded as traffic increases.

Demand schedules are still added vertically, but the marginal cost of adding an additional consumer is no longer zero. It now becomes appropriate to charge a fee, and there is the additional problem of determining how large the size of the group should be. Once more, we will take up this problem later on when we discuss local finance.[10]

Spatial Limitation of Benefits

When speaking of social goods as "being available to all," we do not mean that the world population, or even the entire population of one country, is to be included. The spatial benefit area is limited for most social goods, and the members of the group are thus confined to the residents of that area. This restriction does not

[10] See p. 447.

change the nature of the preceding argument. A group which is sufficiently large to require provision for social goods by political process need not be all-inclusive. Street lights in San Francisco are a social good to residents of that city but a private good to Bostonians. At the same time, this feature of spatial limitation of benefits is central to the application of social-goods theory to local government. This being a major topic in its own right, consideration is postponed once more until the issues of fiscal federalism are examined.[11]

Substitutability Among Goods

There are some wants which may be satisfied either through the purchase of private goods or through the provision of social goods. Thus the need for protection may be met by private locks for each house or by police protection for the entire city block. If the first route is taken, provision may be left to the market, whereas if the second is taken, budgetary provision is needed. In situations where this option exists, a choice must then be made between the two modes. Since the private mode has the advantage of permitting individuals to consume different amounts, the social-goods mode, if it is to be preferred, must more than outweigh this advantage by offering a lower cost per user.[12]

D.   GIVING AS A SOCIAL GOOD

The problem of social goods, by its very nature, has immediate application to the government's provision of goods and services. But it is also of interest in relation to transfers. Taxing and rendering transfer payments may be viewed simply as a process of taking by those who benefit. But this is not the entire story. To the extent that A's giving to B is based on A's desire to see B's position improved (rather than to derive pleasure from own-giving), A will derive equal satisfaction from similar giving by C or D. Giving thus generates externalities not only for the recipient but also for others who see his position improved. Giving thereby assumes social good characteristics which call for budgetary implementation. In practice, it is, of course, difficult to distinguish between the taking and giving aspects of majority-based redistribution, but both elements are present. The rise of the welfare state over the past fifty years may well be interpreted as involving increased readiness to give as well as to take.

E.   MERIT GOODS

In concluding this survey of the problems posed by social goods, we once more turn to their basic nature, this time focusing on the way in which wants for such goods are generated and on the nature of "merit goods."

---

[11] See James Buchanan, "An Economic Theory of Clubs," *Economica*, February 1965.
[12] See Carl S. Shoup and John Head, "Public Goods, Private Goods and Ambiguous Goods," *Economic Journal*, September 1969.

The Premise of Individualistic Evaluation

Our distinction between private and social goods was based on certain technical characteristics of social goods, i.e., the nonrival nature of consumption and the inapplicability of exclusion. It did not depend on a difference in psychological attitudes or in social philosophy regarding the two types of goods. Utilities derived from social as well as private goods are experienced by individuals and included in their preference systems. The same individualistic psychology was applied to both types of goods.

The premise that all wants (private or social) are experienced by individuals rather than group entities is quite compatible with the notion that individuals do not live in isolation but in association with others. Human beings are social animals, and A's preferences will be affected by those of B and C. Dominant tastes and cultural values influence individual preferences and in turn are determined by them. Fashions are a pervasive factor in molding tastes, and not only with regard to clothing. To say that wants are experienced individually, therefore, is not to deny the existence of social interaction. Nor can it be argued that social goods differ from private goods because they satisfy the more noble aims of life.

Furthermore, the proposition that wants are experienced individually does not exclude altruism. If A is a socially minded person, he or she will derive satisfaction not only from his or her own consumption but also from consumption by B; or B, who is selfish, may enjoy only his or her own consumption. Utilities are interdependent and this fact broadens the range over which the economics of social goods applies. But granting all this, what matters here is that satisfaction is experienced in the last resort by A and B individually and not by a mysterious third entity called A + B.

Finally, we recognize that the quality of wants may differ. Some are concerned with the noble and others with quite ordinary aspects of life. But this does not bear on the distinction between private and social goods. The wants to be satisfied may be noble or base in either case: social goods may carry high cultural or aesthetic values, such as music education or the protection of natural beauty, or they may relate to everyday needs, such as roads and fire protection. Similarly, private goods may satisfy cultural needs, such as harpsichord recordings, or everyday needs, such as bubblegum. Clearly, no distinction between private and social goods can be drawn on this basis.

Communal Wants

The premise of wants, based on the needs and preferences of individuals, appeals to widely held values of Western culture. It also permits one to conduct the analysis of public provision within the same economic framework that applies to the analysis of private goods. The concept of communal needs, on the other hand, is hard to interpret and does not fit such analysis. Moreover, it carries the frightening implications of dictatorial abuse. Yet the concept of community also has its tradition in Western culture, from the Greeks through the Middle Ages and to date, and should be given at least brief consideration.

The central proposition to be examined is that there exists a community interest as such, an interest which is attributable to the community as a whole and which does not involve a "mere" addition, vertical or horizontal, of individual interests. This community interest then is said to give rise to communal wants, wants which are generated by and pertain to the welfare of the group as a whole. This raises two basic questions: one is to whom and how is the community interest revealed, and the other is over what range of needs should the community concept be applied.

Some observers would view the structure of communal wants as being revealed through a senate of sages, as in Plato, or a political leader who, as was once believed in Maoist China, transmits his "insights" to the people. The people, after an initial period of compulsion, come to accept these values as their own, thus removing the distinction between private and collective wants. This tenet is clearly inconsistent with our views of democracy; nor can it be defended by arguing that "in the end," all preferences are socially conditioned. Social and environmental influences, to be sure, are pervasive, but there remains a considerable degree of freedom (unless suppressed) in individual responses thereto.

Merit Goods

A more attractive interpretation is that by virtue of sustained association and mutual sympathy, people come to develop common concerns. A group of people share an historical experience or cultural tradition with which they identify, thereby establishing a common bond. Individuals will not only defend their home but will join others in defending their territory or in protecting their countryside. Such common interests and values may give rise to common wants—i.e., wants which individuals feel obliged to support as members of the community. These obligations may be accepted as falling outside the freedom of individual choice which ordinarily applies.

Not all situations which at first sight appear to involve such common preferences fall within this category. Thus individual choice may be limited in situations such as these:

1. Interference is needed to guide children or the mentally disabled.
2. Provision for certain services such as education may be imposed to expand information on available options, without continuance of that interference after the information is gained.
3. Corrective action may be needed when consumer choice is based on false advertising.
4. Government subsidies to goods with external benefits do not involve interference with individual choice but permit such choice to be made more efficiently.
5. Budgetary decisions by majority rule inevitably involve interference with minority preferences. Such violations are the inevitable if unfortunate by-product of a process basically designed to implement individual preferences.

In situations such as these, society undertakes to correct for failures in the process by which individual choice is implemented effectively. Moving closer to the case of merit goods, let us consider the case of giving in kind. An individual donor may choose to give in kind rather than in cash, because he or she considers certain uses by the recipient as meritorious. Or taxpayers may prefer social programs which provide in-kind aid, such as food stamps or low-cost housing, over cash grants. Supporters of the program feel that such uses are felt to be meritorious. As noted below, this may also enter into what is considered a fair state of distribution.

But acceptance of constraints on individual choice may extend beyond the act of giving and budgetary supports. Individuals as members of their society may feel obliged to share certain costs (e.g., for maintaining the Lincoln Memorial) or to accept certain priorities in the use of their own funds because this is called for as a matter of respect for community values. This consideration may apply to the provision of what we have called social as well as private goods. Similar considerations may hold for the case of social bads, or demerit goods, e.g., prostitution. The concept of merit or demerit goods, to be sure, must be viewed with caution because it may serve as a vehicle for totalitarian rule. Yet such common values and concerns do exist in a cohesive society and their existence may place some limitation on the conventional doctrine of individual choice.

F. SUMMARY

This chapter has examined the characteristics of social goods and why they must be provided for through the budgetary process.

1.   Private goods are goods the consumption benefits of which are limited to a particular consumer. Thus consumption by A is rival to consumption by B. Social or public goods are goods the benefits of which are available in a nonrival fashion, such that A's partaking in the benefits does not interfere with B's.

2.   A competitive market can secure efficient resource use in the provision of private goods, but market failure occurs in that of social goods.

3.   Given their large number, individual consumers will not bid for social goods but will act as free riders.

4.   With consumption nonrival, exclusion would be inefficient even where possible.

5.   To seek efficient provision of social goods, a political process of budget determination is needed.

6.   Efficient provision of social goods involves vertical rather than horizontal addition of individual pseudo-demand schedules.

7.   Between the extremes of purely private and purely social goods, various mixed cases are noted.

8.   Such mixed cases include private goods which generate benefit or cost externalities, calling for correction by subsidies or taxes.

9.   Other mixed cases arise in the context of crowding or in situations where particular needs may be met by alternative modes of public or private provision.

10.   Whereas the theory of both social and private goods is based on the premise of consumer sovereignty, the role of community preferences and of merit goods is noted.

FURTHER READING

Arrow, K. J.: "Political and Economic Evaluation of Social Effects and Externalities," in J. Margolis (ed.): *The Analysis of Public Output*, National Bureau of Economic Research, New York: Columbia, University Press, 1970.

Buchanan, J. M.: *The Demand and Supply of Public Goods*, Chicago: Rand-McNally, 1968.

Head, J. G.: *Public Goods and Public Welfare*, Durham, N.C.: Duke, 1974, chap. 1.

Also see references in Chapter 5.

Chapter 5

Social Goods Considered Further*

A. Meaning of Efficiency. B. Efficient Provision of Private Goods. C. Efficient Provision of Social Goods. D. Social-Goods Allocation in the Budget. E. Allocation or Distribution: Which Comes First? F. Summary.

We now resume the discussion of Section B of the preceding chapter, with a closer look at the theory of social goods. In Figure 4-1, we compared efficient provision for social and for private goods. To simplify, this was done by comparing a market for private goods with a pseudo-market for social goods, each viewed in a separate partial-equilibrium setting and based on the assumption that the demand for public goods would be revealed. We now allow for interdependence between the production and consumption of private and of social goods and consider how an omniscient referee (aware of how individuals value social goods) would resolve the problem in general-equilibrium terms. We begin with a brief look at what is meant by efficient resource use. This is followed by a parallel view of the problem as applied first to private and then to social goods.

*Reader's Guide to Chapter 5. This chapter reexamines the preceding discussion of social goods at a more technical level. Readers less interested therein may proceed directly to Chapter 6.

A. MEANING OF EFFICIENCY

Economics, as one learns in the first college class on the subject, deals with the efficient use of resources in best satisfying consumer wants. If the economy consisted of one consumer only, the meaning of efficiency would be quite simple. Robinson Crusoe would survey the resources available to him and the technologies at his disposal in transforming these resources into goods. Given his preferences among goods, he would then proceed to produce in such a way and with such a mix of output as would maximize his satisfaction. In so doing, he would act efficiently. But the real-world problem is more difficult. The economic process must serve not one but many consumers, and various outcomes will differ in their distributional implications. Hence, we need a more careful definition of what is meant by "efficient" resource use.

To separate the problem of efficient allocation from that of distribution, economists have come up with a narrower concept of efficiency. Named *Pareto efficiency* after the Italian economist who proposed it, the definition is as follows: A given economic arrangement is efficient if there can be no rearrangement which will leave someone better off without worsening the position of others. Thus, it is impossible in this situation to change the method of production, the mix of goods produced, or the size of the public sector in a way which would help A without hurting B and C. If, on the other hand, such a change is possible, then the prevailing arrangement is inefficient and an efficiency gain can be had by making the change.[1] This definition, so far as it goes, is quite reasonable. Provided only that envy is ruled out or overlooked, most people would agree that a change which helps A without hurting B and C is efficient. Moreover, this approach permits one to separate the concept of efficient resource use from the more controversial problem of distribution, a topic to be dealt with in Chapter 6.

B. EFFICIENT PROVISION OF PRIVATE GOODS

In discussing efficient resource use, we begin with the more familiar case of private goods. This approach also permits us to see exactly how the case of social goods differs. Suppose there exists an omniscient planner who has all the relevant information, including knowledge of the stock of available resources, the state of technology, and the preferences of consumers. The planner is then asked to determine how resources are to be used efficiently, allowing for all possible states of distribution.

Efficiency Rules Economists have laid down certain conditions which must be met if the solution is to be efficient. To state the problem in simple terms, we

---

[1] As always happens, this principle has come to be qualified and has been made subject to various interpretations. The discussion has turned especially around the topic of compensation. Some say that for an arrangement to be efficient, compensation must be made, while others say that it is enough to conclude that compensation could be made. Consider a rearrangement under which a gain to A is worth $100, and the loss to B is valued at $90. If A compensates B, B's position is unchanged, but there remains a gain to A of $10. For purposes of our discussion, we assume that B is compensated.

consider an economy with two consumers, A and B, and two products, X and Y. These conditions must then be met:

1. Efficiency requires that any given amount of X should be produced in such a way as to permit the largest possible amount of Y to be produced at the same time, and vice versa. The best available technology should be used. If one technique permits production of 100 units of X and 80 units of Y and another permits 100 units of X combined with only 50 units of Y, the former method is obviously to be preferred.

2. The "marginal rate of substitution" in consumption between goods X and Y must be the same for consumers A and B. By this we mean that the rate at which A and B will be willing to trade the last unit of X for additional units of Y should be the same. If A is willing to give 1 unit of X for 3 units of Y and B will give 4 units of Y for 1 unit of X, it will be to the advantage of both to exchange, with A increasing consumption of Y and B consuming more of X until equality of the marginal rates of substitution is restored.[2]

3. The marginal rate of substitution of X for Y in consumption should be the same as their marginal rate of transformation in production. The latter is defined as the additional units of X that can be produced if production of Y is reduced by 1 unit. Thus, if the marginal rate of substitution in consumption is 3 X for 2 Y while the marginal rate of transformation in production is 3 X for 1 Y, it will be desirable to increase the output of X and to reduce that of Y until the two ratios are equalized.

If these conditions are met (as well as some others not specified here), resource allocation will be efficient in the Pareto sense.

Finding the Set of Efficient Solutions   The steps to be followed in tracing out the efficient solution may be summarized briefly. To facilitate matters, we consider again an economy with two private goods, X and Y, and two consumers, A and B. The first step is to construct the production possibility frontier CD in Figure 5-1. With output of private good X measured vertically and that of Y measured horizontally, CD shows the best possible combinations of both that can be produced. If all resources are put into X, the largest possible output of X equals OC; and if all resources are put into Y, the largest possible output equals OD. If OE of X is produced, the largest possible output of Y equals OF, and so forth. The slope of CD thus reflects the marginal rate of substitution in production between X and Y.[3] As previously noted in condition 1, it is obviously desirable to produce any given output of X so as to supplement it by the largest possible output of Y, and vice versa. Just how this is done need not concern us here in detail, since this part of the problem is the same for both the private and the social-good cases.

The second step is to determine how the output at any one point on CD should be divided between A and B. Suppose that the output mix indicated by point Z is produced, involving OE of X and OF of Y. To show how this output may be divided between A and B, we consider the "box diagram" encompassed by $OEZF$. Beginning at O as origin, i_{a1}, i_{a2}, i_{a3} are consumer A's indifference curves, showing

---

[2] The underlying reasoning is that a consumer's marginal rate of substitution of X and Y declines as more X and less Y are consumed. Put differently, consumption of both X and Y is subject to decreasing marginal utility.

[3] Drawing the production possibility curve CD concave to the origin implies that both X and Y are produced under conditions of increasing cost.

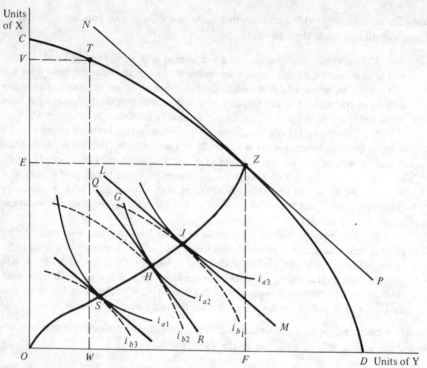

FIGURE 5-1   Efficient output of private goods and their assignment.

A's preferences for X and Y. The curves are constructed so that while moving down any one curve, A remains equally well off, with more of Y being traded for less of X. At the same time, A will be better off when moving from a lower to a higher i (indifference) curve, say from i_{a1} to i_{a2}.

We next draw a similar pattern of indifference curves for B, but now we choose Z as the origin. That is to say, B's take of Y is measured by moving left along ZE, and B's take of X is measured by moving down along ZF. Various successively higher indifference curves for B are shown as i_{b1}, i_{b2}, and so on. It can now be shown that the best possible solutions all lie along the "contract curve" OZ, which traces out the tangency points of the two sets of indifference curves. If the initial position is at G, movement to J will improve A's position without hurting B, just as movement to H will improve B's position without hurting A. By landing somewhere between H and J, the gain will be divided between the two. By following the rule that a gain to A without a loss to B (and vice versa) is an improvement, the efficient solutions must fall along OZ. Since these are the points at which the two sets of indifference curves are tangent, and since the slope of the indifference curves equals the MRS (marginal rate of substitution in consumption), it also follows that at each point on OZ the MRSs for A and B are equal. This reflects condition 2 above.

But not all points on OZ can qualify as efficient solutions. To do so, they must also meet our third condition, i.e., that the rate of substitution in consumption equals the rate of transformation in production. Otherwise, as we have noted, a welfare gain may be achieved by changing the output mix. In Figure 5-1 this third condition is met by a point such as J where the tangent LM is parallel to the tangent NP, drawn to the production possibility curve at Z. It is not met at H, where QR is not parallel to NP. Depending on the shape of the indifference curves for A and B, there may be several points on the contract curve which meet this condition or there may be none. Suppose that there are two such efficient points, J and S. Point J will be better for A and S for B, but they both reflect efficient solutions.

Having recorded them, the planner will search for efficient solutions on all other output mixes or points on CD. For each of these points (say, T) he can draw a new "box" (such as $OVTW$), derive a new contract curve, and find the new efficient solutions.[4] After this has been done for all points on CD, the planner can assemble and compare all the efficient solutions.

To do so, he may plot them as shown in Figure 5-2. The vertical axis measures utility rankings for A and the horizontal axis measures such rankings for B.[5] Plotting all the efficient points with reference to their rankings for A and B, we arrive at a utility frontier such as UU', where each point corresponds to an efficient combination of output mix and its divisions between A and B.[6] Thus point S' on the frontier may correspond to point S in Figure 5-1 with A's utility level given by i_{a1} and B's by i_{b3}. Point J' in turn may reflect point J, with A's level at i_{a3} and B's at i_{b1}. Moving down the frontier from U to U', we find that the utility level of A declines while that of B rises, but at each utility ranking for A, UU' records the highest achievable ranking for B, and vice versa. The best possible points thus lie on the frontier, with points outside the frontier unattainable and points inside inferior.

Choice of Optimum   Whereas the rules of Pareto efficiency guide us to the frontier, the choice among the "best" points traced by this frontier involves a tradeoff between gains for A and losses for B, or vice versa. As we move from J' to S', A's welfare declines and B's rises, and vice versa. The choice is one of distribution and must be made on the basis of a social welfare function, expressing an ordering by which society assigns relative values to levels of welfare experienced by A and B. Assuming these assignments to be known, we may express them by the social indifference curves i_{s1}, i_{s2}, and so on, where each curve shows mixes of welfare derived by A and B that from society's point of view are equally "good."

---

[4] Note that in moving from output mix Z to output mix T, the origin for A's set of indifference curves stays at O and that for B shifts from Z to T. B's indifference curves must therefore be redrawn so as to have their origin at T. This does not involve a change in preferences but merely a replotting.

[5] Reference is to utility rankings rather than to absolute levels. As we move up the vertical axis, we move from lower to higher levels of welfare for A, reflecting the levels inherent in the successive indifference curves i_{a1}, i_{a2}, and so on in Figure 5-1. This formulation avoids the difficulties inherent in assigning cardinal utility values.

[6] Derivation of the utility frontier may also be visualized as follows. Returning to the contract curve OZ of Figure 5-1, we may plot A's and B's utility rankings for all points on OZ in a diagram similar to Figure 5-2 and thus arrive at a utility frontier pertaining to output mix Z. A similar utility frontier may be drawn for all other output points from C to D in Figure 5-1. We may then draw an "envelope curve" which for any utility ranking of A picks the best position for B made available by any of the output-specific frontiers. It is this envelope curve which is reflected by UU' in Figure 5-2. Any one output-specific frontier may be reflected once, more than once, or not at all on UU', depending on how many efficient solutions it contains.

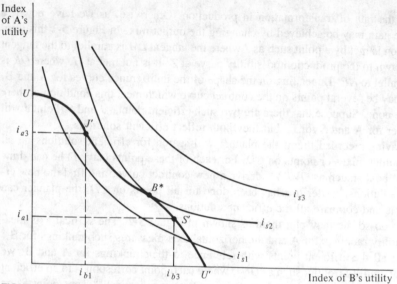

FIGURE 5-2 The distribution choice.

The gain to B which results when moving down any social indifference curve i_s is considered just offset by the resulting loss to A. The point of tangency of the utility frontier with the highest possible social indifference curve is at B*. This is the "bliss point," the best of all possible solutions. As a point on the utility frontier, it meets both requirements of Pareto efficiency, i.e., that the marginal rates of substitution in consumption be the same for both A and B and that they equal the marginal rate of transformation in production. As a point on the highest possible social indifference curve, it meets the further condition of social welfare maximization through optimal distribution. Provided that the social welfare function as reflected in the pattern of the i_s curves is given to the planner this best of all solutions can be determined via simultaneous determination of output mix and its distribution among A and B.

Allocation through the Market Having stated the problem in terms of an omniscient planner to whom all information is given, we must now recognize that such a planner does not exist. It is fortunate, therefore, that the efficient solutions of Figure 5-1 can also be obtained by the functioning of a competitive market system. Producers guided by their desire to maximize profits will adopt the least-cost method of production, thus meeting condition 1. Moreover, they will produce products which consumers want most, as indicated by the price which the products fetch in the market. Consumers, in turn, will allocate their respective budgets among products so as to equate their marginal rates of substitution with their price ratios, thus meeting condition 2. Consumers will do so because if the price of X is twice the price of Y while their level of satisfaction would be unchanged by replacing consumption of 1 unit of X by less than 2 units of Y, they will choose to purchase and consume more Y and less X until the marginal rate of substitution of Y for X is equal to the price ratio. The same prices are paid by all consumers, but depending on their tastes and incomes, they consume different amounts. In trying to maximize profits, sellers equate marginal cost with marginal revenue, which under conditions of competition also equates marginal cost with price or average revenue. Thus condition 3 is met as well. Without spelling out the details, we can thus see that the market mechanism, acting as an auctioning system and functioning through competitive pricing, secures an efficient use of resources. Even socialist planners (provided that they wish to adapt their output mix to consumer wants) will find it helpful to play the competitive game or to advise their computers to do so in order to obtain efficient results.

Solving the problem through the instrument of a market mechanism has the great advantage of inducing consumers to reveal their preferences and of inducing producers to meet them, thus providing a solution without the use of a hypothetical and all-knowing planner. This is the magic of the "invisible hand," which, as noted first by Adam Smith, permits a decentralized and competitive market system to secure efficient allocation. However, for the market mechanism to operate, there must be an initial given distribution of money income. Returning to Figure 5-2, we note that each of the points on the utility frontier corresponds to the solution reached by the competitive market (and the pricing rule which it implies) on the basis of a given distribution of income. The quality of the solution, therefore, depends on the appropriateness of the prevailing distribution.

C. EFFICIENT PROVISION OF SOCIAL GOODS

We now consider the preceding problem in a situation where both social and private goods are produced. To simplify, we include only one social good S and one private good X. Proceeding as before, we again begin with a general model in which an omniscient planner, to whom all the information is given, is charged with determining the efficient set of solutions. The solution, as first developed by Professor Samuelson, is quite analogous to that previously developed for the efficient allocation of private goods, yet it differs in important respects.[7]

Efficiency Rules Returning to the efficiency rules previously stated in connection with private goods, we see no change with regard to condition 1. Construction of the production possibility frontier poses the same problem as before. But conditions 2 and 3 will change. Since different consumers may not consume the same amount of private goods, their marginal rates of substitution of social for private goods may differ. Since the marginal rate of transformation is the same for all, it is no longer possible that the two rates of substitution should be equal for all consumers. Instead, efficiency now calls for equality between the marginal rate of transformation in production and the *sum* of consumers' marginal rates of substitution in consumption. The solution may again be traced out in a number of steps.

[7] For the initial presentation of this solution see Paul A. Samuelson, "The Pure Theory of Public Expenditures," *Review of Economics and Statistics,* November 1954, pp. 387–389; and Paul A. Samuelson, "Diagrammatic Exposition of a Theory of Public Expenditures," *Review of Economics and Statistics,* November 1955, pp. 350–356.

Finding the Set of Efficient Solutions   Turning now to Figure 5-3, the production possibility curve DC in the upper part of the figure again records the mixes of X and S that may be produced with available resources. The axes on the middle section of the figure show the amounts of X and S consumed by A, and the axes on the lower part give the corresponding picture for B. Since both consume the same amount of S, both will be at the same point on the horizontal axis, but they may consume different amounts of X and be at different points on the vertical axis. These points are related, however, by the condition that the amounts of X consumed by A and B must equal the total output of X. To illustrate, suppose that A is at G in the middle panel, consuming OF of S and FG of X. We know from the upper panel that the efficient output mix which includes OF of S also includes FE of X. Since FG is consumed by A, the amount left for B equals $FE - FG = FH$, placing B at point H in the lower panel of the figure.

We now choose a particular level of welfare for A, say that indicated by A's indifference curve i_{a2} in the middle panel. We have seen that if A is at G, then B will be at H in the lower panel. Next, let us move along i_{a2} to such points as P, T, and V. Following the same reasoning, we find that this places B at L, Z, and K. As A travels along i_{a2} from W to the left, B travels to the left along ULK. Since all points along i_{a2} are equally good for A, welfare is maximized by choosing that point which leaves B best off. This is at L, where ULK is tangent to B's indifference curve i_{b4}. This is the highest curve which B can reach while staying on LZK. If A is to be at indifference level i_{a1}, the best solution is thus that which leaves A and B at P and L, respectively, with total output, including ON of S and NM of X, divided between A and B so that A receives NP and B receives NL.

We may now repeat the procedure for other utility levels for A, such as i_{a1} or i_{a3} in the middle panel. For each of these, we arrive at a new locus of B's position in the lower panel (corresponding to ULK) and a new optimum (corresponding to L). In this way, we arrive at a set of solutions corresponding to various levels of welfare for A and B. All these are efficient in the Pareto sense and meet the condition of equality between the sum of the marginal rates of substitution in consumption and the marginal rate of transformation in production.

Looking back, we note that the steps involved in planning for efficient allocation have run parallel for the cases of private and of social goods. However, the efficiency conditions differ because of the nonrival nature of social-goods consumption.

Choice of Optimum   The welfare levels achieved by A and B under the various efficient solutions may now again be recorded on a utility frontier similar to that shown in Figure 5-2. Given the social welfare function we again obtain the pattern of i_s curves where each curve shows mixes of welfare derived by A and B (now form the consumption of private and of social goods) which from society's point of view are equally "good." B* then emerges as the best of all possible solutions. Once more this solution simultaneously determines the output mix between S and X and the division of X among A and B. Since both consume the same amount of S, no further assignment is needed.

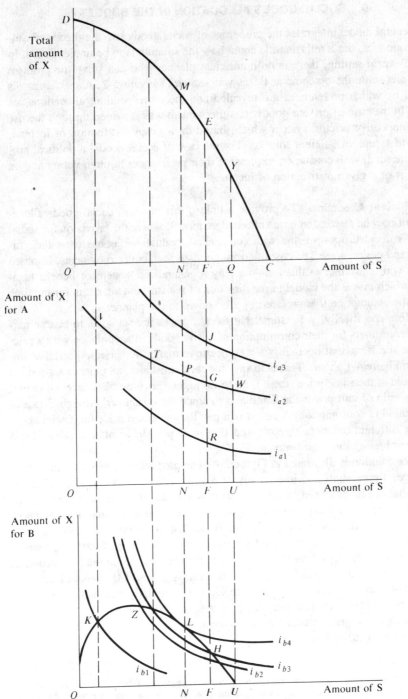

FIGURE 5-3 Social and private goods in general equilibrium.

D. SOCIAL-GOODS ALLOCATION IN THE BUDGET

This general model integrates the properties of social goods into the theory of welfare economics, but it tells us little about how the solution is to be implemented. In the real-world setting, there is no omniscient planner who can solve the problem for us and settle the outcome at B* as was shown in Figure 5-2. A mechanism is needed by which preferences are revealed and the corresponding allocations are made. In the case of private goods, this mechanism was provided through the use of a competitive pricing system which, based on a given distribution of income, serves to secure an efficient solution. For the case of social goods, a political process is needed, with consumers expressing their preferences through voting and on the basis of a given distribution of income.

Efficient Allocation   To provide a link to this process, social-goods allocation will now be restated in terms of a budget model, where the provision for social goods is decided upon in line with consumers' evaluations as based on their incomes and preferences. The cost of social goods is then covered by taxes, imposed in line with consumer evaluation—i.e., by a generalized system of benefit taxation—which moves the model in the direction of realism, but we retain for the time being the assumption that preferences are known to the planner.

More specifically, we assume that the tax prices are set so as to charge particular consumers for their consumption of social goods in accordance with a pricing rule similar to that operating in a competitive market for private goods, as implied in Figure 4-1 above. That is to say, for each consumer, all units of a good are to be sold at the same price (there is to be no higher price on intramarginal units), and the ratio of unit prices for X and S is to equal the consumer's marginal rate of substitution in consumption. A and B will pay the same unit price for X while consuming different amounts thereof, and they will pay different unit prices for S while consuming the same amount.

The solution is illustrated in Figure 5-4. The production possibility line CD in the upper figure shows various mixes of S (the social good) and X (the private good) that can be produced and that are available to the economy as a whole.[8] The middle figure shows the position of consumer A and the lower that of B. Suppose that income is divided between A and B so that A receives a share equal to OM/OC of potential private-good output OC and B receives ON/OC, where $OM + ON = OC$. The broken line MV will then record the optimal allocation of A's income between X and S at varying price ratios. It traces the point of tangency of a set of price lines anchored at M with successive indifference curves. Given the price ratio OM/OP, for instance, A's preferred position will be at Q, where MP is tangent to the highest attainable indifference curve i_{a2}. The broken curve NW traces a similar price line for B.

---

[8] The assumption of a linear transformation schedule is necessary if the pricing rule here specified is to result in the necessary equality of tax revenue and cost. Allowing for increasing cost and a concave schedule, our pricing rule yields excess revenue, because intramarginal units of the social good can then be produced at a lower opportunity cost as measured in terms of private goods. Hence a more complex formula or a rebating of the excess revenue would be needed.

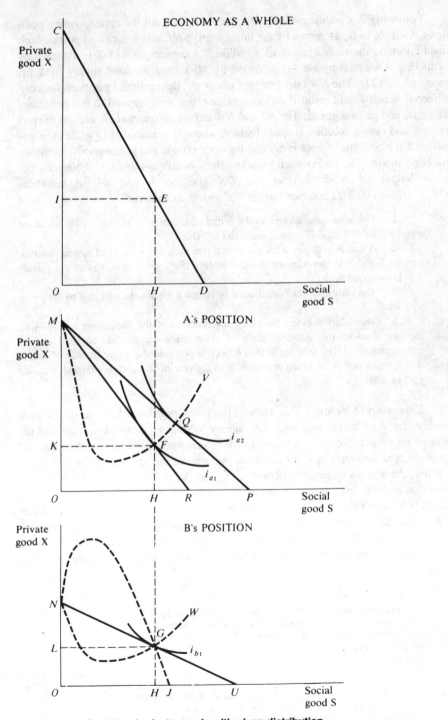

FIGURE 5-4 Social and private goods with given distribution.

Following A's positions along MV, we may trace out the corresponding positions available to B, as shown by the broken curve NJ. At each pair of points, both must consume the same amount of S, while B's consumption of X is obtained by deducting A's consumption (as recorded by MV) from the total supply of X (as recorded by CD). The NW curve in turn traces out the preferred positions for consumer B which would result if different price ratios were applied to B's purchases of social and private goods. The NJ and NW curves intersect at G, and the correct pricing and output solution is thus obtained where B is placed at G while A is positioned at F and total output is divided between private and social goods, as shown by E on the production possibility curve. Both consume OH of S, while private-good output OI is divided so that OK goes to A and OL to B where $OK + OL = OI$. This solution has the following characteristics:

1.   The solution conforms to the initial distribution of income, with A's share equal to OM / OC and B's share equal to ON / OC.
2.   A and B both pay a tax price such that each one's marginal rate of substitution for S and X in consumption is equal to each one's price ratio, so that our pricing rule is complied with.[9]
3.   The combined tax contribution of A and B equals the cost of S to the group as a whole.[10]
4.   The solution meets the efficiency criterion of the Samuelson model—i.e., that the sum of the marginal rates of substitution equals the marginal rate of transformation.[11] The solution E thus reflects a point on the utility frontier of Figure 5-2, it being that point which corresponds to a given income distribution and specified pricing rule.

Extension to Voting   This view of the fiscal problem takes one step toward reality, since an initial distribution of money income is assumed to exist and tax shares are determined on that basis. But it remains unsatisfactory in that it is still implemented through a planner to whom preferences are known. In the real-world setting, there is no omniscient planner to whom the preferences of Figure 5-4 are revealed and who can derive an optimal solution therefrom. Nor is the case of realism helped by substituting an assumption of *voluntary* bidding. As was noted earlier in our discussion of Figure 4-1, this solution breaks down with a large number of voters, where the free-rider problem arises. To provide an operational view of the budget, the model must thus be extended to incorporate a theory of the voting process.

---

[9] Note in Figure 5-4 that the unit price for private good X or P_X is the same for both A and B, but the unit price for S differs. A's price ratio P_S^A / P_X as given by price line MR equals OM / OR. Since A's price line is tangent to the indifference curve at F, the price ratio equals the marginal rate of substitution in consumption. The same holds for B's ratio P_S^B / P_X equal to ON / OU, with price line NU again tangent to the indifference curve i_{b1} at G.

[10] The amount of tax paid by A, or T_A, equals P_S^A / OH. Given $P_S^A / P_X = OM / OR$ and setting $P_X = 1$, we have $P_S^A = OM / OR$ and $T_A = (OM / OR)OH$. Since $OM / OR = KM / KF = KM / OH$, we obtain $T_A = KM$. Arguing similarly for B, we obtain $T_B = LN$. Since $OM + ON = OC$ and by construction of NW we know that $OL + OK = OI$, it follows that $T_A + T_B = IC$.

For the group as a whole, the price ratio is given by $P_S / P_X = OC / OD$. Setting $P_x = 1$, we have $P_S = OC / OD$, with the cost of supply OH of S equal to $(OC / OD)OH$, which again reduces to IC. See, however, footnote 8 above.

[11] This follows because $(OM / OR) + (ON / OU) = (KM / OH) + (LN / OH) = IC / OH$.

More specifically, the task is to devise a voting system which is effective in securing preference revelation and an efficient system of tax-expenditure determination. The solution should approximate an efficient pricing rule, such as that shown in Figure 5-4.[12] Through the voting process, the pseudo-demand schedules of the earlier discussion tend to be revealed, the budget size determined, and the tax price applied. This is the best we can do, although as will be shown in Chapter 7, the voting process by its very nature cannot bring about a perfect result. Except for a society where preferences are so homogeneous as to permit unanimity, some voters will remain dissatisfied. Yet some procedures will do better than others and the task is to find the best approximation.

E. ALLOCATION OR DISTRIBUTION: WHICH COMES FIRST?

Voting on the provision of social goods and assignment of their cost through taxes presumes the distribution of income to be given, just as did the solution of private-goods allocation through the market mechanism. This presumption suggests a policy sequence of first setting the ''correct'' state of distribution via tax transfer policies and then determining the allocation of resources to the provision of social goods.

At closer consideration, however, such a procedure becomes questionable. The way in which resources are used in the provision of public or private goods will affect factor and product prices and thus have a bearing on how real income is distributed in the market. Thus both the allocation and distribution aspects of budget policy must be determined simultaneously in a general-equilibrium system. Although efficient resource use and ''just'' distribution pose distinct policy problems, an omniscient budget planner would resolve them simultaneously.

But this is not a feasible procedure in practice. Here the political process by which preferences for social goods are revealed must be conducted on the basis of a given distribution. Such being the case, there is much to be said for distinguishing measures of redistribution from those which allocate resources to public use. Lest this is done, the efficient provision of public services tends to be distorted by distributional considerations, and vice versa. The two-step procedure thus remains a useful (if not perfect) model.[13]

F. SUMMARY

This chapter has followed up the preceding discussion of social goods with a closer look at the underlying theoretical formulation, based on the economic concept of efficiency.

---

[12] To be efficient, the pricing rule used to solicit preference revelation must equate each consumer's rate of substitution with his or her price ratio at the *margin*. But it is not required that the intramarginal units be sold at the same price. Charging higher prices for intramarginal units of the social good would tax away ''consumer surplus.'' Thus more than one efficient pricing rule is available. Among them, that one should be used which best permits implementation through the voting process.

[13] See p. 6 above.

1. Efficient resource use occurs when there is no possibility of making a change which helps one person without hurting anyone else. There are many efficient solutions to the allocation problem, each reflecting a different state of distribution among consumers.

2. Efficient resource use in the case of private goods requires the marginal rates of substitution in consumption to be the same for all consumers and equal to the marginal rate of transformation in production.

3. This result from step 2 can be achieved through a competitive market where consumers reveal their preferences by bidding for goods.

4. In such a market, all consumers would pay the same price but consume different amounts, depending upon their income and their preferences. A market demand schedule is obtained by horizontal addition of individual demand schedules.

In the case of social goods, the solution to the problem differs for the following reasons:

5. Since such goods are nonrival in consumption, the same amount is consumed by all. Efficient resource use now requires the *sum* of the marginal rates of substitution in consumption to equal the marginal rate of transformation in production.

6. An omniscient planner, to whom all preferences are known, can thus arrive at an allocation of resources to the production of private and of social goods and at a distribution of private goods among consumers which is optimal. Such a solution is optimal both in the sense of meeting the efficiency conditions of Pareto optimality and of satisfying the distributional norms of the given social welfare function.

7. This solution, however, is not operational. A political process or voting system, based on a given distribution of money income, is needed to induce the revelation of preferences. The voting process, it is hoped, approximates an efficient solution. But this solution, like that of a competitive market for the allocation of private goods, is optimal only if the underlying distribution of money income is also the correct one.

8. The allocation choice also affects distribution, so that corrective adjustments in distribution cannot be independent of the allocation choice. Nevertheless, a separation of functions remains necessary as a practical solution.

FURTHER READINGS

For the seminal statement of modern social-goods theory, see:

Samuelson, P.A.: "The Pure Theory of Public Expenditures," *Review of Economics and Statistics,* November 1954, pp. 386–389; and "Diagrammatic Exposition of a Theory of Public Expenditures," *Review of Economics and Statistics,* November 1955, pp. 350–356. Both articles are reproduced in R. W. Houghton (ed.): *Public Finance,* Baltimore: Penguin, 1970. Also see Samuelson, P. A.: "Pure Theory of Public Expenditures and Taxation," in J. Margolis and H. Guitton (eds.): *Public Economics,* New York: St. Martin's, 1969.

For early contributions to the modern approach, see:

Wicksell, K., and E. Lindahl: Excerpts of writings in R. A. Musgrave and A. Peacock (eds.): *Classics in the Theory of Public Finance,* New York: Macmillan, 1958.

For the current state of social-goods theory, see:

Oakland, W. H.: "The Theory of Social Goods," in A. Auerbach and M. Feldstein (eds.): *Handbook of Public Finance,* vol. II, Amsterdam: North Holland, 1988.

Chapter 6

Equity in Distribution*

A. Does Equity Belong in Economics?: *Determinants of Distribution; Distribution as a Policy Issue.* **B. Approaches to Distributive Justice:** *Alternative Views; Endowment-Based Criteria; Utilitarian Criteria; Egalitarian Criteria; Categorical Equity; Mixed Solutions; Equity among Generations.* **C. Limits to Redistribution:** *The Size of the Pie; Efficiency Costs.* **D. Summary.**

Throughout the preceding chapters we have emphasized that the optimal use of scarce resources involves two basic issues. The first is to secure efficient satisfaction of demands that arise from a given state of distribution. Defined in terms of Pareto efficiency—the proposition that there is a welfare gain when the position of any one individual is improved without hurting that of another—this objective is generally accepted as a policy goal. Only jealousy is ruled out thereby. But there is also a second objective: how to secure a state of just or fair distribution. Since there exists an efficient solution corresponding to each and every state of welfare distri-

---

*Reader's Guide to Chapter 6: The theory of optimal distribution, considered in this chapter, poses problems not usually dealt with in the study of public finance. Yet the questions raised must be faced up to in designing budget policy. Moreover, criteria of distributive justice, though philosophically based, are constrained in application by economic considerations, so that the two perspectives must be joined.

bution, a question remains: Which state should be chosen as equitable or just? Here the concept of Pareto efficiency helps little, if at all. The problem of distribution is one of evaluating a change in which someone gains while someone else loses. It is one of designing the pattern of i_s curves of Figure 5-2.[1]

As shown in that connection, the choice of the best or just solution might be found by postulating a "social welfare function," i.e., a set of rankings in which social weights are given to gains by some and losses by others. Given such a function, technical economics can grind out the answer, as illustrated by the tangency solution B* of Figure 5-2. But there remains the more basic problem of what shape this set of values (or the social welfare function) should take. In the end, one cannot avoid the question of what should be considered a fair or just state of distribution.

A. DOES EQUITY BELONG IN ECONOMICS?

Over the past fifty years, economists have increasingly held that a theory of just or equitable distribution is not within the purview of economics but should be left to philosophers, poets, and politicians. Indeed, when talking about the "theory of distribution," economists have traditionally referred to the theory of factor pricing and the division of national income among returns to land, labor, and capital. This theory of factor shares plays an essential role in economic analysis, but its significance lies mainly in the area of efficient allocation. For resource use to be efficient, factors of production must be applied so as to equate the value of their marginal product in all uses, a condition which holds in a socialist as well as in a capitalist society. But the theory of efficient factor use by itself is not a theory of distributive justice. For one thing, the proposition that factor allocation should be based on efficient factor pricing does not require that the final distribution of income among individuals be set equal to the proceeds from sales of their factor services in the market. The two can be separated by intervention of the distribution branch of the budget. For another thing, the ultimate concern of justice in distribution is with distribution among individuals or families and not among groups of factors. Factor shares are only loosely related to the interfamily distribution of income. While it is true that capital income accrues more largely to high-income families and wage income more largely to low-income families, there are important exceptions to the rule. The problem of distribution among individuals or families must thus be addressed directly.

Determinants of Distribution

In the market economy, the distribution of income is determined by the sale of factor services. It thus depends upon the distribution of factor endowments. With regard to labor income, this distribution involves the distribution of abilities to earn such income, as well as the desire to do so. With regard to capital income, it involves the distribution of wealth as determined by inheritance, marriage patterns, and lifetime saving. The distribution of labor and capital endowments is linked by investment in education, which in turn affects the wage rate which a person can command.

[1] See p. 64.

Given the distribution of endowments, the distribution of income depends further on factor prices. In a competitive market, these prices equal the value of the factor's marginal product. As such, they depend upon a wide set of variables, including factor supplies, technology, and the preferences of consumers. In many instances, however, returns are determined in imperfect markets where institutional factors, such as conventional salary structures, family connections, social status, sex, race, and so forth, play a significant role. As a result, the returns to various jobs may differ in line with status considerations rather than marginal product, and who gets the job may depend upon connections rather than superior productivity. Moreover, marriage patterns and bequests are important factors in determining the distribution of family money income.

The distribution of income, as generated by the above forces, shows a substantial degree of inequality, which may be seen by comparing the percentage of income that accrues to various percentages of households as ranked by their income. Thus, below 5 percent of money income in the United States accrues to the 20 percent of families with the lowest incomes, whereas the income share received by the successively high quintiles of family groups is 11, 17, 24, and 43 percent, respectively. As among various forms of income, the distribution of capital income is less equal than that of wage and salary income.[2] So is the distribution of wealth. The top quintile of households are estimated to own 80 percent of marketable wealth and about two-thirds of wealth if pension rights (including Social Security) are allowed for.[3] Moreover, recent decades have shown a tendency for distributional inequality to increase. How does this pattern, which is found in fairly similar form in most advanced countries, relate to what might be considered a fair or just state of distribution?

Distribution as a Policy Issue

By posing this question, the focus shifts from distribution as a market outcome to distribution as a policy issue. Although people will differ on the policies to be pursued, it is evident that distribution problems have been, are, and will continue to be a vital factor in politics and policy determination.

That such is true is most apparent when it comes to the design of tax and transfer policies, but also evident is the fact that almost all policy measures, even those not immediately concerned with distributional objectives, have distributional repercussions. Thus an inflationary situation may call for a restrictive policy so as to reduce aggregate demand. Its distributional effects will differ, depending on whether the demand reduction is obtained by increasing sales taxes or income taxes, by reducing various types of public expenditure programs, or by applying monetary restriction. Policies aimed at increasing the flow of international trade will have different distributional implications, depending on which tariffs are reduced. Antitrust measures designed to render markets more efficient will affect the income of capital and labor in particular industries as well as the real income of

[2] For distribution of money income, see *Statistical Abstract of the United States*, U.S. Bureau of the Census, 1987, p. 437. Data are for 1985.

[3] See E. Wolff and M. Murley, "Long Term Trends in U.S. Wealth Inequalities," New York: Starr Center, New York University, 1988.

consumers of their products. Public investment programs, such as regional development or road construction, will affect the economic welfare of various population groups and hence the patterns of distribution. Public pricing policies, such as the pricing of publicly operated subways, similarly will affect the real income of subway riders, and so forth.

Policy design thus inevitably involves distributional judgments, but standard economic analysis unfortunately does not tell us what state of distribution should be our goal, i.e., what the criteria for distributional justice and fairness should be. As just noted, this final question tends to be considered as out of bounds for economists, whose job is taken to address efficiency issues only. But given the close bearing of distributional issues on questions of economic policy and their major or even dominant weight in economic politics, economists who are concerned with public policy can hardly detach their thinking from equity issues. They can be required only to distinguish such issues from efficiency considerations, especially with respect to the application of economics to the problems of public finance, an integral part of which is the function of our "distribution branch." The efficiency-based analysis of the preceding chapter must therefore be followed by at least a brief consideration of what constitutes just or equitable distribution. Otherwise, our normative view of public-sector theory cannot be complete.

B.   APPROACHES TO DISTRIBUTIVE JUSTICE

If a choice is to be made between alternative criteria for just distribution, their implications must be understood. We first view this problem on the assumption that (1) the utility which individuals derive from their income is known and comparable, and (2) the amount of goods or total income available for distribution is fixed. Both these assumptions are reconsidered later on.

Alternative Views

Among possible criteria for what constitutes a just state of distribution, the following may be considered:

1. Endowment-based criteria.
   a   Keep what you can earn in the market.
   b   Keep what you could earn in a competitive market.
   c   Keep labor ("earned") income only.
   d   Keep what you could earn in a competitive market, given equal positions at the start.
2. Utilitarian criteria.
   a   Total welfare is maximized.
   b   Average welfare is maximized.
3. Egalitarian criteria.
   a   Welfare is equalized.
   b   Welfare of the lowest group is maximized.
   c   Categorical equity calls for provision in kind.
4. Mixed criteria.
   a   Welfare floor is set with the endowment rule applicable above it.
   b   Distribution is adjusted to maximize welfare in line with social welfare weights.

In choosing among these criteria on a self-interested basis, high-income persons will find 1a in their best interest, while having to be altruistic in supporting the other options. Low-income persons will choose 3b. However, this is not the only way to consider the choice. An alternative perspective is offered by the philosopher's view of the problem as one of social contract. People placed in what the philosophers call the "state of nature" consider what should govern the relationship among persons in a just society, including the distribution of economic welfare.[4] Depending on how social justice is viewed, this may mean that people are entitled to keep what they earn as suggested by endowment-based criteria, that reason calls for maximizing welfare as the utilitarians suggest, or that some form of equal treatment is called for by egalitarian criteria. What can be said for the various views and what are their implications?

Endowment-Based Criteria

Theorists of the social contract formulated the problem in terms of certain rights and duties to which all members of society are both entitled and committed, but they differed in their views on the content of the contract. Natural-law philosophers such as Hobbes and Locke, writing in the second half of the seventeenth century and following what are here referred to as endowment-based criteria, postulated a person's innate right to the fruits of his or her labor, thereby giving ethical support to distribution by factor endowment and the pricing of factors in the market. A similar view among modern philosophers is taken by Robert Nozick.[5]

This principle of entitlement may be stated without qualification, as in 1a, or it may be limited to such earnings as can be obtained in a competitive market, as in 1b. Claims to monopoly profits would then not be legitimate, nor would claims to wage or salary incomes in excess of marginal product. Still another possibility, 1c, is to apply the endowment principle only to an "earned" wage or salary but not to capital income. This may be proper because in line with Locke's thinking natural resources are held "in common" or simply because it is held that earning wages involves disutility of work whereas drawing interest does not. Some such consideration was applied by the classical British economists when they argued that "unearned" or capital income should be taxed more heavily than wage income.

A modern version, 1d, of the endowment approach sanctions only such inequality as would remain if all people were given an equal position at the start. In line with a radical interpretation of the free enterprise system, this means acceptance of such inequalities as result from innate differences in earning ability, in preferences between income and leisure, and in thrift. In contrast, inequalities that arise from inheritance, different educational opportunities, or family status would not be acceptable. It might indeed be argued that this constraint on inequality is called for by the logic of a pure "enterprise" system.[6]

---

[4] See Earnest Barker (ed.): *The Social Contract*, London: Oxford, 1946.

[5] See Robert Nozick, *Anarchy, State and Utopia*, New York: Basic Books, 1974, chap. 7.

[6] For an eloquent expression of this spirit, see Henry Simons, "A Positive Program for Laissez-Faire: Some Proposals for a Liberal Economic Policy," in *Economic Policy for a Free Society*, Chicago: University of Chicago Press, 1967.

Utilitarian Criteria

As distinct from supporters of these endowment-based criteria, other social philosophers rejected innate inequality in ability as a legitimate source of differences in economic well-being. The existence of such inequalities is recognized, but they should not be permitted to determine the state of distribution. To be born with a high- or low-ability level is not due to the will or action of the particular individual. Like social status, this accident of birth is considered as lacking ethical sanction as a basis for distribution. According to this view, some other principle of assignment must be sought.

Fixed Total Income   One answer was given by the utilitarians, such as Bentham, who would have income distributed so as to achieve the greatest sum total of happiness, an objective which they thought would appeal to "all reasonable men."[7] With respect to the division of a given total pie, A should be given more income than B if A's "utility level," or ability to derive happiness from personal income, is higher. Only if we assume that the marginal income utility schedules for all individuals are the same and are declining will an equal distribution of income be called for. The maximum satisfaction view, therefore, may or may not lead to an egalitarian solution.

This is illustrated in Figure 6-1. In each diagram, income is measured along the horizontal axis, while the vertical axis records the marginal utility of income, i.e., the increment in total utility which results as another dollar is added to income. The area under the curve thus measures the total utility derived at various income levels. To bypass the difficulty which arises because the utility of initial dollars may well be infinite, we consider the distribution of income above a certain minimum level OM. We assume, for the time being, that the utility of income can be measured in "utils" and that a utility comparison among various individuals is possible. The difficulties involved in these assumptions will be considered presently. We assume further that after providing each with OM, total income available for assignment between A and B is fixed at MT, an assumption to be reconsidered presently.

In the upper part of the figure, we postulate that two individuals, A and B, have the same marginal utility schedules. To maximize total satisfaction, this income will then be divided equally between A and B so that A receives MC and B receives MD, with $MC + MD = MT$. The marginal utilities of A and B are set equal at OF, as are their total utilities, reflected by $MCGH$ and $MDKL$, respectively.[8] In the lower part of the figure, we assume that A's marginal utility schedule, beyond the minimum income level OM, lies above B's. A, in other words, has a higher capacity to derive additional utility from income above OM. Assuming again a total income MT to be available for distribution, total utility is now maximized by assigning the larger amount MK to A and the smaller amount

---

[7] See J. Bentham, *The Principles of Morals and Legislation*, New York: Macmillan, 1948, chap. 1.

[8] It is easy to see that the sum of utilities is maximized by equating marginal utilities. As long as more income is assigned to A than to B, A's marginal utility will be lower. Total utility is therefore increased by transferring income from A to B until marginal utilities and (given the same utility schedules) incomes are equalized.

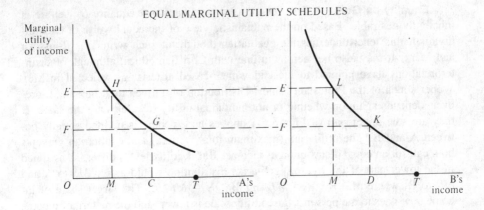

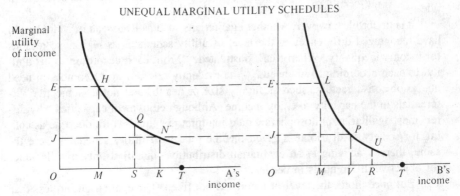

FIGURE 6-1   Patterns of distribution.

MV to B, where *MK* + *MV* = *MT*. Marginal utilities are equated at *OJ*, and A's total utility, or *MKNH*, now exceeds B's, or *MVPL*. Having a higher-lying utility schedule, A is better off for two reasons: A not only derives greater utility from the same income but, in addition, receives a larger income share.

Variable Total Income   Figure 6-1 has proceeded on the assumption that total income available for distribution remains unchanged thereby. As adverse effects are allowed for, maximizing welfare, as utilitarians from Bentham on have stressed, may well fall short of equal distribution and do so even if we assume the shape of utility schedules of all individuals to be the same. Moreover, as noted below, allowance must be made for deadweight losses which arise in the process of redistribution.

Egalitarian Criteria

Viewing the problem in terms of maximum welfare (whether total or average) is a somewhat artificial construction. Society, after all, consists of individuals, not of a sum of individuals or of an average individual. This being so, why should all reasonable men agree to maximize *total* welfare? Is not the essential problem of distribution one of relative position among individuals and should not equality of position be the goal? This is the focus of the egalitarian formulation.

Equality as Goal   A first version (3a) postulates that equality of welfare is inherently desirable. Based on the humanistic view of the equal worth of each individual, this tenet underlies the egalitarian thought of such writers as Rousseau and Marx. It may also be seen as in line with Christian ethics, although other interpretations have pointed to the endowment-based criteria, as reflected in Max Weber's idea of the Protestant Ethic.[9] Distribution of a given total income, moreover, depends again on whether or not individual utility schedules are the same. If they are, the upper part of Figure 6-1 applies and income is divided equally between A and B. The utilitarian (maximum total welfare) and egalitarian precepts both call for an equal distribution of income. But if utility levels differ, as assumed in the lower part of the figure, egalitarian distribution would assign MS to A and MR to B, where $MS + MR = MT$ and $MSQH = MRUL$. The larger share of income now goes to the person whose utility scale is lower, and the pattern of income inequality becomes opposite to that achieved under the maximum total satisfaction rule.

It is doubtful, however, whether egalitarians such as Rousseau or Marx would have recognized differences in the level of utility schedules as legitimate reasons for income inequality. When Marx postulated, "From each according to his ability, to each according to his need,"[10] he evidently referred to differences in need due to objective factors, such as family size or health, and not to subjective differentials in the capacity to enjoy income. Although enjoyment capacities may differ, most egalitarian philosophers would interpret the equal-worth doctrine as calling for society to distribute a given income total as if utility schedules were the same, thereby arriving at an egalitarian distribution, qualified only by allowance for objective differentials in need.

But once more, the level of income is not fixed. The egalitarian, no less than the utilitarian, must again allow for effects of income distribution upon the level of earnings. Taxing H in order to transfer to L may reduce the income available for distribution. If carried too far, a further rise in the tax on H may not only narrow the gap between H and L but also lessen the position of both.[11] The egalitarian rule carried to an extreme thus runs into difficulty, unless equality is valued so highly as to offset a decline in average levels.

Maximizing the Lowest Income   This difficulty is avoided by setting distribution policy such as to maximize income at the bottom of the scale. This rule, as suggested by Rawls, permits income inequality to the extent that it contributes to a higher level of income at the bottom.[12] If carried beyond a certain point, a further increase in tax rates reduces yield, thus becoming counterproductive in permitting transfers to lower-income recipients.

---

[9] See Max Weber, *The Protestant Ethic and the Spirit of Capitalism*, trans., Talcott Parsons, New York: Scribner's, 1958.

[10] See Karl Marx, "Critique of the Gotha Program," in P. C. Tucker (ed.): *The Marx-Engels Reader*, New York: Norton, 1972, p. 388. In the same context Marx notes that incentive considerations do not permit application of this norm under socialism, it being attainable only in the final state of communism.

[11] See pp. 83, 284.

[12] See John Rawls, *A Theory of Justice*, Cambridge, Mass.: Harvard University Press, 1972.

Rawls obtains such a solution from his rule of fairness by which individuals are placed into an "initial position" where they do not know what their earnings potentials will be. They then render an "impartial" choice as to what the state of distribution should be. Knowing that equalization will reduce the level of income available for distribution but not knowing what their own position on the income scale will be, they will stop short of demanding equalization. Assuming people to be highly risk averse, they will vote for that degree of redistribution which maximizes the lowest income, thus arriving at the above result. The scope of desirable redistribution thereby becomes dependent on the degree of risk aversion.

Categorical Equity

Still another approach to equity in distribution, also concerned with entitlement to minimum levels, defines the latter not in terms of income but in terms of specific consumption items. Thus the floor may be defined as a minimum supply of food, clothing, and shelter. The cost of these items might then be taken to set the minimum income, or provision might be made in kind. This is a perspective to be noted further below when the role of giving is considered. Referred to as "categorical equity," it may be taken to link the merit-good approach to that of distributive justice.[13] That approach thus helps to explain the prevalence of public policies that offer in-kind support such as low-cost housing or that subsidize products bought by them such as the food-stamp plan.

Mixed Solutions

Whereas the premises underlying these various approaches may be explored and their consequences may be examined, choosing among them hardly permits a unique answer. The basic question of whether the design of the good society can be determined by "reason" or whether "values" must be chosen remains unresolved, a matter to be rethought as civilization proceeds.

It should also be noted that in practice the various approaches need not be implemented in pure form but more likely will be combined. Thus it may be held that equity calls for ensuring that no one suffers poverty, but that an endowment-based approach should be applied once this objective is met. Such a compromise view (combined perhaps with some recognition of the equality-at-the-start interpretation of the endowment criteria) most nearly approximates the emerging mores on distribution. A few years ago it was argued in the *Economic Report of the President* that "those who produce more should be rewarded more; and no individual or household should be forced to fall below some minimum standard of consumption regardless of production potential."[14] Put differently, it is held that the endowment-based approach, with entitlement to market earnings, should apply but that the resulting degree of inequality is to be limited by setting a floor to the share derived at the bottom of the scale. Or some qualification of the endowment approach might be extended further up the scale, in line with criteria 4b above.

---

[13] See p. 55.
[14] See, for instance, *Economic Report of the President*, Washington, D.C.: Government Printing Office, 1974.

Equity among Generations

Those now living may affect the welfare of future generations in various ways. Thus advances in science and technology made by this generation will be at the disposal of the next. Similarly, the capital stock accumulated by the present generation is bequeathed as a legacy to the next one. In many ways the present generation thus benefits the future one. But dissaving, exploitation of irreplaceable natural resources and destruction of the environment place a burden upon the future. All these relationships—the asymmetrical fact that the present can affect the future but not vice versa—pose questions of "intergeneration equity" to which we shall return later when discussing social security finance and public debt. Now we only note that introduction of a time dimension further adds to the complexities of the distribution problem.[15]

C. LIMITS TO REDISTRIBUTION

The preceding discussion has focused on the basic question of what constitutes a just state of distribution. The problem of practical policy is more limited. The issue is not so much how to establish a fair society and its de novo state of *dis*tribution, but to consider whether and how to address the problem of *re*distribution. The question is to what extent and how the existing state of distribution—as determined by the market and prevailing social institutions—is to be amended. To some extent this may be accomplished by way of voluntary giving, but such transfers carry minor weight as compared with policies of redistribution decided upon by the budget process. Such policies will then be met by the responses of individuals who stand to lose or gain in the process. This in turn may affect the size of the pie available for redistribution and impose costs which must be allowed for.

The Size of the Pie

Redistribution as noted throughout this discussion involves costs as well as benefits, and both must be considered. Policies to redistribute, to begin with, can shrink the size of the pie available for distribution. This is shown here with regard to effects on labor supply, but similar problems arise with regard to possible effects on saving, investment, and economic growth. Consider two individuals, H with high and L with low earnings capacity. To simplify, suppose L's earnings capacity is, in fact, zero. In the absence of intervention, H has a substantial positive income and L has none. Now a tax is imposed on H and a transfer is paid to L. As a result of the tax, the net wage rate of H (the return in goods which H can obtain for selling leisure) is reduced. Initially H may respond by working more (H's labor supply schedule slopes backward over a range of high wage rates), but thereafter a further increase in the tax rate will induce H to retain more leisure—that is, to work less. As a result, the revenue obtainable from a given tax is not unlimited. As the tax rate is increased further, revenue will rise for some time until a point is reached beyond which further increases in the tax rate will result in declining revenue and

---

[15] See pp. 202 and 552 below.

hence in a reduction in funds available for transfer to L.[16] This relationship is illustrated by the following table, showing H's response to rising rates of tax with a wage rate of $10.

Tax Rate (Percentage) (I)	H's Hours Worked (II)	H's Income Before Tax (Dollars) (III)	Tax Revenue from H Transferred to L (Dollars) (IV)	H's Income After Tax (Dollars) (V)	L's Income (Dollars) (VI)
0	6.0	60.0	0	60.0	0
15	7.0	70.0	10.5	59.5	10.5
30	5.0	50.0	15.0	35.0	15.0
50	2.5	25.0	12.5	12.5	12.5
80	1.0	10.0	8.0	2.0	8.0
100	0	0	0	0	0

As the tax is introduced, H increases his working hours initially so as to recoup some of the lost income. He does so until a tax rate of 15 percent is reached, above which his working hours will be reduced. In moving from 15 percent to 30 percent, revenue still rises as the increase in tax rate more than offsets the decline in the taxable base, but as the tax rate is increased still further, revenue begins to fall. Whereas the goal of maximin would be served by stopping at 30 percent, a 50 percent rate would be needed for full equalization.

Efficiency Costs

The potential scope for redistribution may thus be limited because a further increase in tax rates eventually hits a revenue ceiling. But this is not the entire story. There is another and more subtle cost to redistribution which becomes effective from the outset. This arises because withdrawing one dollar of income tax from H leaves H with a welfare loss in excess thereof, and because receipt by L also imposes a deadweight loss that must be taken into account. As noted below, this factor poses a major problem in the design of welfare programs.[17]

The fact that the donor loses more than the recipient gains, however, does not mean that the transaction must involve a social loss. Much depends on the weight to be attributed per dollar of loss and per dollar of gain, so that a low-income gain of 90¢ may, as placed under a social weight, more than outweigh a loss of $1.10 higher up.

The nature of the efficiency-equity tradeoff is illustrated in Figure 6-2 for an economy containing two persons, A and B. As shown previously in Figure 5-2, the vertical and horizontal axes measure A's and B's utility levels, with utility rising when moving from O to C or from O to D. CD is the utility frontier as derived earlier in Figure 5-2, and $i_{s1}, i_{s2}, i_{s3}, \ldots$ are social indifference curves reflecting the

---

[16] See also p. 284 below.
[17] See p. 189.

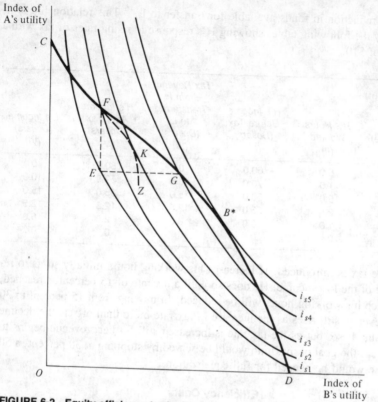

FIGURE 6-2   Equity-efficiency tradeoff.

distributive judgment of the community. B^* is the bliss point, reflecting the best of all possible solutions.

If prevailing arrangements place the economy at E, movement to points between F and G on the utility frontier is efficient (Pareto-optimal), since at least one gains and none loses. But the Pareto criterion of efficiency does not tell us how to choose among points between F and G. From the social point of view, however, G is best, since it reaches the highest possible social indifference curve, i_{s4}. Now suppose that the functioning of the market leads to point F. Given the i_s curves of Figure 6-2, a social gain results by moving from F to B^*, raising social welfare from i_{s2} to i_{s5}. This gain results even though A loses, so that the move is not sanctioned by the criterion of Pareto efficiency. Moreover, moving to a point off the utility frontier, such as K, may be superior from the social point of view to remaining at F. Introduction of a social welfare function, as reflected in $i_{s1}, i_{s2}, \ldots$ thus suggests a broadened concept of efficiency, i.e., one by which the outcome is assessed and ranked in terms of social welfare weights.

To see how this bears on the efficiency cost of redistribution, we might imagine CBD to trace the utility frontier as it would look if redistribution could be achieved without an efficiency cost. But given this cost, and beginning at F, the actually available frontier may be given by the dotted line FKZ. By moving from F

to K (but not farther!), redistribution still pays in social welfare terms, but the gain is less (involving a shift from i_{s2} to i_{s3} only) than it would be without an efficiency cost of redistribution. Although society may thus accept some efficiency loss to obtain an equity gain, distributional adjustments should be made so as to minimize this cost. This is considered further when the efficiency cost of various types of taxes is compared.[18]

D. SUMMARY

The problem of just distribution, along with that of efficiency, is an essential part of the broader problem of optimal resource use.

    1. The distribution of income as determined in the market depends on the distribution of factor endowments and the prices which the services of these factors will fetch.

    2. This process has important bearing on efficient resource use, but it does not constitute a theory of distributive justice.

    3. The distribution as determined by factor incomes need not coincide with what is considered socially desirable, thus calling for adjustment by fiscal and other policy measures.

Various approaches to distributive justice have been distinguished, and their implications for the distribution of income have been considered.

    4. Endowment-based views sanction the distribution of income as determined by factor ownership and returns.

    5. Utilitarian views call for a distribution of welfare so as to maximize total satisfaction. An equal distribution of income is required if individuals are assumed to have similar utility functions.

    6. Egalitarian views would distribute income so as to equalize the welfare position of all individuals, or so as to maximize that of the lowest.

    7. Equity considerations may be applied across generations as well as across individuals.

Redistribution policy is subject to certain limitations, which must be allowed for in policy design.

    8. The higher-income person, in response to being taxed, may substitute leisure for income, thus setting a limit to the feasible scope of redistribution.

    9. Redistribution policies involve an efficiency cost which must be taken into account.

FURTHER READINGS

For diverse classics in the literature on distributive justice, see:

Bentham, J.: *The Principles of Morals and Legislation,* L. Lafleur (ed.): New York: Hafner Press, chaps. 1–4.

Locke, J.: *Second Treatise of Government,* chap. V, Mentor Book Revised Edition, Peter Laslett (ed.): New York: New American Library, 1960, pp. 327–344.

[18] See p. 277.

Marx, K.: "Critique of the Gotha Program," in L. Feuer (ed.): *Marx and Engels: Basic Writings*, New York: Doubleday, 1959, pp. 112–132.

For more recent writings, see:

Phelps, E. S. (ed.): *Economic Justice*, Baltimore: Penguin, 1973. (A volume of important readings in the field.)

Rawls, J.: *A Theory of Justice*, Cambridge, Mass.: Harvard, 1972, part 1.

Tobin, J.: "On Limiting the Domain of Inequality," *Journal of Law and Economics*, October 1970; reprinted in Phelps, op. cit.

Chapter 7

Public Choice and Fiscal Politics*

A. Direct Democracy: *Why Vote?; Voting Rules; Majority Rule and the Median Voter; Voting Paradox; Fiscal Choices; Alternative Voting Rules; Role of Strategy.* **B. Representative Democracy:** *The Role of Politicians; Parties, Platforms, and Coalitions.* **C. The Leviathan Hypothesis:** *Voting Bias; Monopoly Government; Campaign Financing; A Political Business Cycle; Budget Limitations.* **D. Classes and Interest Groups:** *The Marxist Model; Multiple Groupings.* **E. Summary.**

We have noted repeatedly that budget determination involves a political rather than a market process. The purpose of this chapter is to consider this political process more closely. How are the individual's views on fiscal matters expressed and how are they translated into political action? How do various voting rules work out, and what is the role of parties and coalitions? Does the decision process reflect the wishes of the public or does government impose its own will? What built-in biases are there in budgetary decisions? Although traditionally these matters have been

---

*Reader's Guide to Chapter 7: Since the political process is at the heart of budget determination, fiscal theory must transgress the traditional bounds of economics and invade the adjacent domain of political theory, which is precisely what is done in this chapter, and some fascinating problems are encountered in the process. The more hidebound economics majors may skip this chapter. Others should enjoy it.

considered in the domain of political science rather than of economics, both disciplines must be drawn upon in dealing with budget determination.

A. DIRECT DEMOCRACY

Once more our story begins with the individual consumer who is the final beneficiary of public services and whose consumption of private goods is reduced when resources are transferred to the public sector. The key question is how preferences on the matter can be expressed and implemented. Decisions may be reached in the small group by a process of negotiation and bargaining. Each individual's contribution is sufficiently important to the individual and to others for them to enter into a bargaining process. Negotiation among the parties may lead to an agreement on what supply of social goods should be provided and on who contributes how much. In the real-world setting, this situation is approximated by the town meeting in a small village, or by compacts between nations, states, or municipalities designed to carry out common projects, whether they are a dump shared by various municipalities, the St. Lawrence Seaway undertaken jointly by the United States and Canada, the Atlantic Alliance, or a peace-keeping mission financed by the United Nations. In these small-number cases, some bargaining solution will be reached, although, as noted before, the outcome may not be efficient. But such bargaining solutions are not feasible where large numbers are involved. Here the contribution of any one individual acting alone is too small to make a difference, and numbers are so large as to make negotiation unmanageable. "Transaction costs," a widely used if murky term, are too high. Individual preferences must now be translated into budgetary decision through a political process, involving the individual's preferences as recorded by voting and the response of those political parties or leaders to whom the voter delegates the final decision.

Leaving the issue of delegation until later, we begin with a simplified setting of "direct democracy," i.e., a system where fiscal decisions are made by referendum among individual voters. Voters know that the group decision reached by voting will be binding on them. Therefore, they will vote so as to move the decision in a direction more compatible with their own tastes.

Why Vote?

At the very outset, a puzzling question must be raised: Why should the rational voter bother to participate in the voting process? A rational voter knows that there is only a negligible probability that his or her vote will affect the outcome, i.e., swing the balance at the margin of an otherwise 50/50 vote. Therefore, why bother to walk to the voting booth? Some people may vote because they do not realize how unlikely it is that their individual votes will decide the outcome. Others will vote because they believe that their action will encourage others to do so as well. But these are not very convincing explanations. More likely, people vote out of a sense of responsibility which they accept by membership in a democratic society. Such action may not reflect a narrowly defined act of "rational behavior" but, happily, human action is not limited to that premise.

Voting Rules

Next, specific voting rules must be defined. They involve (1) the distribution of votes, and (2) the rules by which the winning vote is determined.

In the modern (post-eighteenth century) view of democracy, it is generally agreed that each person should be given one vote. As distinct from Plato's Republic, where decisions are made by the intellectual elite, the views of all citizens are to be given equal weight. Thus our mores combine a radically egalitarian standard of "one person, one vote" in politics with a nonegalitarian distribution of "dollar votes" in the economic sphere. But though the principle of uniform vote distribution is hardly debated in the context of modern democracies, the specifics of voter eligibility are still in flux. Swiss women were allowed the right to vote for the Federal Assembly only recently, but some cantons still exclude them. Eighteen-year-olds are now eligible to vote in the United States, whereas previously they were not. In some countries extra voting rights are retained by special groups (e.g., British university representation up to 1948), and so forth.

Next, a particular voting rule must be chosen. The most commonly used rule is that of *simple majority*. Each individual has one vote, the yeas and nays are counted, and the simple majority wins. Where more than two alternatives are considered, they must be voted upon by successive elimination among surviving pairs. The U.S. Congress and other legislatures follow this rule of majority vote except in particular circumstances, such as a constitutional change or the overriding of a presidential veto or impeachment, where a *qualified majority* (usually two-thirds) is called for. Fiscal (tax and expenditure) decisions are generally made by simple majority vote. As noted below, other voting rules may be designed but we begin with the simplest and most widely used case of majority rule.

Majority Rule and the Median Voter

Voting under majority rule is illustrated in Figure 7-1. Suppose that there are three levels of budget activity to choose from—large (A), medium (B), and small (C). To simplify exposition, assume that there are three voters only, X, Y, and Z, the same reasoning being applicable to the large-number case. Finally, we assume that the cost will be spread equally among them.

Suppose, further, that X is a large-budget person who prefers A to B to C; Y is a small-budget person who prefers C to B to A; and Z is a moderate-budget person who prefers B to C to A. Z is the median voter, i.e., the voter who is at the midpoint of the size scale. This pattern is plotted as case I in Figure 7-1, where 1 is the highest and 3 is the lowest rank. Since more than two issues are involved, successive pairs must be voted upon. Beginning with A versus B, we find that B wins because both Y and Z prefer B to A, and only X prefers A to B. Matching B with C, B is again the winner. The same holds if we begin with A versus C followed by C versus B, or with C versus B followed by B versus A. In all instances B will win. As shown in the figure, all individual preferences, if plotted, show a single-peaked pattern, and the sequence of pairing does not matter. Voter Z, who prefers the median alternative and who is referred to as the "median voter," wins. This simple voting model is the one typically used in designing empirical studies of fiscal decision making, and some of its applications are examined at the end of this chapter.

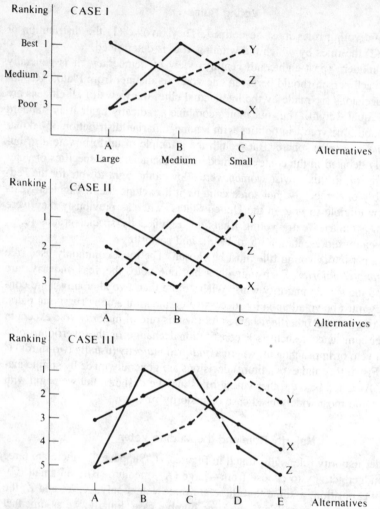

FIGURE 7-1   Preference patterns and majority rule.
(Voters X, Y, Z; alternatives A, B, C, D, and E.)

Voting Paradox

In considering the quality of various voting rules, we note a number of requirements including that (1) the outcome should be nonarbitrary, (2) it should be representative of voter preferences, and (3) it should not be disturbed by strategic behavior. We begin with the requirement that the outcome not be arbitrary—i.e., it should not depend on the sequence in which pairs of issues are put to the vote. This problem arises especially under majority rule. As just noted, nonarbitrariness results if all patterns are single-peaked, as in case I and also in case III. The preferences of all three individuals follow a cone pattern, with the peak reached at different points in the scale, and with the win going to the median peak.

But now suppose that Y has extreme tastes and prefers C to A to B. That is to say, Y prefers both extremes to the middle solution. As plotted in case II, Y's is a multiple-peaked pattern. The final result in this case depends on the sequence in which the issues are paired. Beginning with A versus B, we find that A wins over B, and in turn C wins over A; thus C is the winner. However, if we begin with B versus C, then A wins; and if we begin with A versus C, then B wins. This "voting paradox," noted first by Condorcet in the eighteenth century and more recently explored by Professor Arrow, comes as a shock to one's faith in electoral democracy. Fortunately, the paradox does not imply that majority rule *cannot* work. Rather, the conclusion is that for majority rule to give nonarbitrary results, the preference structure of individuals must be typically single-peaked.[1]

Moreover, this possibility of arbitrariness does not occur under other voting systems such as plurality or point voting, to which we will turn shortly.[2] Since no pairing of issues is needed, the issue of voting sequence does not arise. Draws may still occur, but they narrow the choice and may be resolved by runoffs among the highest-ranking alternatives. But, as we will see later, there are other disadvantages to plurality or point voting. It is useful, therefore, to inquire whether the voting paradox is likely to arise in majority decisions on fiscal issues.

Fiscal Choices

The voting paradox of majority rule will not arise if preference patterns are single-peaked, i.e., if there is an absence of voters with "extremist" preference patterns. The question then is whether fiscal choices will tend to be of this single-peaked type.

Variable Size of Budget The answer depends on the type of choice under consideration. As the simplest case, suppose that the budget contains only one type of public expenditure, that successive units are provided at constant cost for the group,[3] and that the cost is to be spread equally among all. With three consumers, each bears a "head tax" equal to one-third of total cost. The problem is only to determine the desired amount.

In this situation, there is good reason to expect that preferences will be single-peaked and of the case III variety. Provided the public good is useful to the consumer, he or she will prefer some budget size to both larger and small sizes. The principle is the same as with private goods. If apples cost 25 cents a pound, the consumer will choose to purchase a given number, say 5 pounds rather than 4 or 6.

This is shown in Figure 7-2, where private goods are measured on the horizontal axis and social goods on the vertical axis. Suppose that a certain consumer's

---

[1] See Kenneth J. Arrow, *Social Choice and Individual Values*, New York: Wiley, 1951, where it is more generally argued that it is impossible to devise a social ordering which meets certain requirements of consistency. Among them Arrow includes the requirement that the outcome not be affected by the dropping out of a nonwinning alternative. This requirement is not met by plurality or point voting, but its validity for fiscal choices (as distinct from scoring athletic contests) is not evident. See also J. M. Buchanan and G. Tullock, *The Calculus of Consent*, Ann Arbor: University of Michigan Press, 1962, pp. 323–340.

[2] See p. 94.

[3] The following reasoning remains unchanged if we assume that conditions of increasing cost prevail. Preference patterns will then peak at a smaller budget, but they will still be single-peaked.

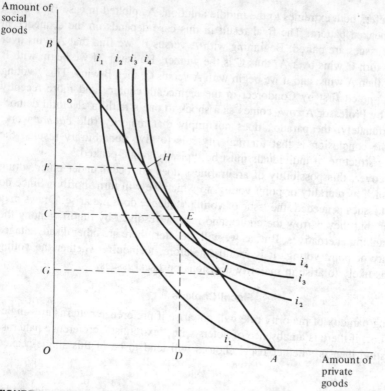

FIGURE 7-2   Choice of private and social goods.

intake of private goods in the absence of social goods equals OA. She is thus located at A on indifference curve i_1. Now the choice of a social good is offered, and the tax price charged to her is shown by the price line AB, the price ratio of social to private goods available to her being OB/OA. Her preferred point—the peak of her ranking schedule in Figure 7-1—will be at E on her highest feasible indifference curve i_4, with OC of social and OD of private goods being consumed. Further expansion of the budget size to OF, or reduction to OG, will place her at H or J on indifference curves i_3 and i_2, respectively, and will leave her in less satisfactory positions. Preference schedules being single-peaked, majority rule will lead to the same solution, independent of the sequence in which the issues are paired. The voting paradox does not arise.

Moreover, the budget size selected by majority vote will be that preferred by the median voter. Ranking voters in case III of Figure 7-1 in terms of preferred budget size, we find that Z is the median voter and his preferred budget (alternative C) wins. Above him is the large-budget group and below him the small-budget group, both of equal size. Standing in the middle, he can cast the decisive vote. Although the majority decision will thus please voters at the center of the preference scale, it does not follow that it is the best or most efficient choice. If intensity of feeling is allowed for, the large-budget people might gain more from substitution of a large budget than the middle- and small-budget people lose, or vice versa. In this simple case at least, majority rule does not allow for intensity of feeling, and this restriction is a major disadvantage. But, as shown below, intensity of feeling is not excluded as a determinant of the outcome under majority rule provided that the formation of coalitions and logrolling are taken into account.

Variable Tax Price Will preferences remain single-peaked if we replace the head tax by more realistic types of taxation? Suppose that finance is by proportional income tax. Here, the price per unit of public service differs among consumers with different incomes. As the budget expands, the tax rate goes up, but the unit price of the public service to any one taxpayer (assuming again constant costs) remains unchanged. The conclusion, therefore, is the same as under the head tax. Preferences remain single-peaked.

If the income tax is progressive, the answer depends on how rates are increased as the budget expands. If all liabilities are raised by the same percentage (i.e., all bracket rates go up by the same percentage), the price per unit of public service again remains unchanged for the individual taxpayer. The earlier conclusion still holds. But suppose that bracket rates are raised by equal percentage points. This increase will make the rate structure less progressive. The share contributed by people with lower incomes will rise. A 10 percent increase in the budget or quantity of public services will raise their taxes by more than 10 percent, and they will now have to pay a higher price per unit of public service. The reverse will apply to people with high incomes. For low-income people, preferences among budget sizes will remain single-peaked, although the peak will be at a smaller budget. High-income people will prefer a larger budget, but the impact on their preference structure is more complex.

More important, no general conclusion can be drawn if the change in tax shares changes directions as the budget expands. For instance, a rising budget may first raise and then lower the share of high-income taxpayers. As a result, they find that their unit cost for public services is highest for a medium-sized budget. Consequently, a V-shaped or multiple-preference pattern may emerge similar to that of Y in case II, thereby introducing the voting paradox and rendering majority rule arbitrary.

Variable Expenditure Mix Even though the level of expenditures on identical parks may be ranked numerically, the choice between types of parks, or between parks and fire protection, is a different matter. If we think of projects A to C in Figure 7-1 as a lineup among alternative outlays of a given amount on parks (A), fire protection (B), and roads (C), no presumption for single-peakedness can be derived from the preference function of the individual consumer. There is no obvious ordering (such as holds for different budget sizes), and all depends on how the choices are lined up. Only if tastes among consumers are highly homogeneous will there be an ordering for which all preference rankings are single-peaked.

In all, the nature of fiscal choices—especially choices among various budget mixes—is not such that single-peaked preferences may be readily assumed to exist. However, the contingency of arbitrariness may be reduced by combining issues which as a bundle permit decisions to be reached, even though this may not be possible over single issues. As we will see presently, it is the function of the politician to identify and present such bundles or political programs.

Alternative Voting Rules

Even if conditions are such that majority rule can be made to work without arbitrary results, it still remains necessary to evaluate the "quality" of the outcome under the various voting rules. By this we mean how close the resulting solution, including level and mix of goods provided for and the assignment of costs, comes to reflect the actual preferences of the voters. We have noted before that decision by vote is not an ideal solution, since mandatory application of the outcome (the resulting combination of services and tax prices) will leave some voters dissatisfied. Voters whose preferences diverge from that of the group may be left either with better terms than they would have been willing to accept or with worse terms. In the latter case, they must submit to a consumption pattern (mix of private and social goods) which is not to their liking. Nevertheless, not all solutions will be equally defective in these respects, and various voting rules must be compared from this point of view.

The obvious way to protect the minority, of course, would be to substitute the requirement of unanimous consent for majority rule. If only those expenditure-tax propositions are undertaken which command unanimous consent, no individual will be forced to accept projects which he or she does not value. But this gain would be obtained at an intolerable cost, because the granting of a universal veto would tend to block provision for public goods entirely. It is unlikely that any of the proposed expenditure-tax packages would receive unanimous consent, the more so because it is not feasible to consider an infinite number of combinations. In the end the resulting loss to the majority would far outweigh the gain to the last holdout among the minority. A voting rule with mandatory enforcement of the outcome is needed, therefore, to induce the revelation of preferences,[4] and if some are hurt or benefit less while others benefit more in the process, this fact is a disadvantage which must be accepted. The more closely bunched the peaks of the individual preference patterns are, the more the result will approximate a unanimous vote and the less will be the disadvantage which the minority must suffer. Some degree of preference homogeneity is needed for democracy to function.

Majority and unanimity, however, are not the only possible voting rules. Other options are available and their quality may be compared. Under *plurality voting*, each voter ranks the issues in order of preference. If there are ten issues, one point is assigned to the top choice and ten points to the lowest-ranked choice, the choices are added across voters, and that issue wins which has received the lowest number of points. Or variants of this approach may be used, whereby the top-ranking contenders in the first round are then rematched in a runoff, and so forth. The outcome under the plurality rule is the same as under majority vote if there are

---

[4] This necessity was recognized by Knut Wicksell, the great Swedish economist who first developed this approach. Whereas the unanimity rule would be ideal, "approximate unanimity" or a qualified majority must be sufficient. For excerpts from Wicksell, see R. A. Musgrave and A. Peacock (eds.): *Classics in the Theory of Public Finance,* New York: Macmillan, 1958, p. 87.

only two issues, but it may well differ if more alternatives are involved. Another possibility is a system of *point voting*. Here, the voter is given a number of points which may be allocated among the various alternatives as the voter wishes. Thus, one may give all points to a top choice, or distribute them among the alternatives. The alternative receiving the largest number of points wins. The result now depends on the intensity of feeling, and the outcome of point voting may well differ from that obtained under majority or plurality.

In comparing the quality of the various voting rules, let us assume first that all voters record their true preferences, without regard for the attitude of others. In other words, let us suppose that no "voting strategy" (a concept to which we will presently return) is applied. In this case, it is readily seen that point voting is the best approach, followed by plurality and majority voting in that order. Under majority rule, voters (in the absence of coalitions and logrolling) can express only their rankings between pairs of issues as they come up; they cannot give expression to their strengths of preference, nor can they relate issues appearing in different pairs. Under the plurality rule, they can relate all issues to one another at the same time, but this relation can again be expressed in terms of ranking only. A voter may rank alternative B first, A second, and C third, but the difference between B and A may be large while that between A and C is small, or vice versa.

Intensity of preferences is directly allowed for under point voting. In the extreme case, a voter may give all points to B and none to A or C. Suppose, for instance, that each voter is allotted 10 points and that within the rankings of case I above, the distribution of points is as follows:

Choice	VOTER X		VOTER Y		VOTER Z	
	Rank	Points	Rank	Points	Rank	Points
A	1	5	3	1	3	1
B	2	3	2	3	1	5
C	3	2	1	6	2	4

The majority rule would let B win. Under plurality, where the rankings are added, B receives the low score and is again the winner. Under point voting, the highest and winning score goes to C. This solution is more representative of how the voters feel and makes a case for some form of point voting.

Role of Strategy

The quality of various voting rules may thus be ranked, provided that voting strategy is not used. But in the real world, voting strategy *is* important. Because of this, B and C may not be the winners. Voters (like speculators in the stock market) will take into account how others will vote and will not throw away their votes on issues which cannot win, even though they prefer them. They may rather settle for their second choice, so as to avoid ending up with the third. Voter X may thus overstate her preference for A, giving it all 10 points, thereby making A, which she prefers to C, the winner under point voting. Others may use similar strategies, and the outcome then comes to depend on political skills. Moreover, the scope for strategy differs with the various voting rules. Inasmuch as the outcome depends on the particular preference structure, this dilemma results: the better the rule in the absence of strategy (i.e., the more sensitive the voting rule to intensities of preference), the greater tends to be the scope which it leaves for the use of strategy. Thus, a compromise must be drawn between these various aspects, and in the end a cruder system less open to manipulation, such as majority voting, may be the better choice. However, interesting work is now in process aimed at developing voting rules which offer an incentive to reveal true preferences.[5]

B. REPRESENTATIVE DEMOCRACY

Our discussion must now be made more realistic by discarding the assumption that individual voters participate directly in the decision process. Whereas the degree of direct participation differs among countries, it is usually only at the local level that fiscal decisions are made in referendum style. Rather, they are delegated to members of Congress or other legislative representatives who seek election as nominees of political parties. How does this affect the decision-making process, and to what extent will the preferences of individual voters be reflected in the final decisions?

The Role of Politicians

We begin with the role of the politician and the process of representation.

Vote Maximization with Given Preferences One view of this role, which is of particular interest to the economist, draws an analogy between the firm's competition for consumers in the market and the politician's competition for voters in the political arena. Just as economic competition, under certain assumptions, guides producers to supply in line with preferences of consumers, so does political competition under certain assumptions guide representatives to act in line with the interests of the voters.

This model, as developed in detail by Anthony Downs, offers an intriguing interpretation of the democratic process.[6] Analogous with the economists' precept of "homo econominicus" is the assumption that political action is rational, with both politicians and voters acting in their self-interest. The politician's objective is to maximize votes so as to stay in power. The voter's objective is to maximize the net benefits which he or she derives from the fiscal operation, i.e., the excess of benefits derived from government expenditures over the voter's tax costs. People will thus cast their votes for those who will best represent their interests, and politicians will offer programs and support legislation which best meet the interests of their constituents. Politicians who come closest to so doing will receive the most votes and hence gain or retain political power. In this way, the politician's competition for votes resembles the producer's competition for consumers and the preferences of voters are served in the process.

---

[5] G. Tullock and N. Tideman, "A New and Superior Principle of Public Choice," *Journal of Political Economy*, December 1976.

[6] Joseph A. Schumpeter, *Capitalism, Socialism and Democracy*, New York: Harper, 1950, p. 282; and Anthony Downs, *An Economic Theory of Democracy*, New York: Harper & Row, 1956 (see especially chaps. 4 and 10). See also H. Bowen, "The Interpretation of Voting in the Allocation of Resources," *Quarterly Journal of Economics*, 1943.

Leadership and Preference Formation What has just been described is not, however, the entire story. The role of the politician in the context of representative democracy may transcend that of implementing a given set of voter preferences. Political leadership may also exert an influence on preference patterns and thereby on the legislative outcome. Such leadership endeavors to advance its view of the public interest and thereby may depart from vote maximization, thus risking defeat. The market analogy of the preceding section thus requires qualification.

Parties, Platforms, and Coalitions

We next turn to the groupings of voters which the politicians represent and how they interact.

Parties and Interest Groups Patterns of representation may differ, depending on the political system and its constitutional setting. Thus representation in the Senate involves grouping of voters by states, while representation in Congress groups residents of smaller voting districts within states. Representatives in turn typically seek election not only as individuals but also in the context of political parties and their platforms. These platforms in turn are geared to appeal to particular groups of voters. Putting it differently, organization by interest groups helps to expedite the political process as it reduces the need for contact between representatives and individual voters.

Viewed this way, the role of interest groups, and their reflection in political parties, performs a useful function in the democratic process. These interest groups may extend across many dimensions. Recipients of high and low incomes will differ in their views regarding progressive taxation and welfare payments. Age groups may differ in their views of social security problems or of education. Various regions may differ with regard to the location of public projects, patterns of economic development, or trade policy. Ideological differences may enter in attitudes toward the size of the budget, measures of redistribution, or regulation. Group representation thus economizes on the need to deal with the preference of individual voters. At the same time, the preferences of individual voters may coincide with regard to some but conflict with regard to other issues, thus complicating the politician's task to form a winning coalition.

Platforms and Coalitions Under majority rule, successful political leadership must take a position on combinations of issues so as to obtain a program which is acceptable to a majority. Except for referendum voting, issues are not considered in isolation but are typically combined in packages or party platforms. Coalitions are formed which combine voters with congenial views on a set of issues. Policies which would lose if considered separately may win if considered in combination.

Winning Coalitions In forming winning coalitions, intensity of preferences comes to be accounted for, even though a majority rule applies. This is illustrated in Table 7-1. We assume that there are three voters and two issues, each of which contains a pair of options. Issue 1 offers a choice between options A and B and issue 2 offers a choice between options C and D. Decision is by majority vote, but to indicate the strength of consumer preferences, numbers are used to serve as an

TABLE 7-1
Preferences and Party Platforms

	VOTER			
Issues	X	Y	Z	Total Points
Issue 1: option A	1	51	60	112
option B	99	49	40	188
Issue 2: option C	51	52	20	123
option D	49	48	80	177
Combination of A and C	52	103	80	235
Combination of B and D	148	97	120	365

index of the relative value which the voter attributes to various options. Each voter is given 100 points for each issue to divide between the two options. For issue 1, voter X considers option B ninety-nine times as valuable as option A; for issue 2, he or she considers option C slightly more desirable than D; and so forth.

Now a majority vote is taken on issue 1. Option A, being preferrred by Y and Z, wins. The outcome is inefficient in that the aggregate valuation of option B (as measured by the point total) exceeds that of A. If vote buying were permitted, X could pay Y to vote for B and both would gain. In fact, X would retain a net gain even after compensating Z. Similar considerations apply to issue 2, where C wins even though D carries the higher point total. But buying and selling of votes is not permitted. Instead, X and Z may make an agreement whereby X will vote for option D in issue 2 and Z will vote for option B in issue 1, leaving both with a gain across both issues. Much the same is accomplished by politicians through the design of party platforms which allow for the intensity of voter preferences. Thus party P_1 may offer a platform combining issues A and C while P_2 offers a platform combining issues B and D. X and Z will prefer the latter platform and P_2 will win. The formation of platforms and coalitions may thus lead to superior results because it allows the intensity of preferences to enter the choice, and it does so even though majority voting rather than point voting is used.

Successful politicians (or statesmen) are thus those who can find winning combinations, and for this they must consider the intensity of preferences. As voters' preferences change, they must keep abreast of such changes and spot the development of new groupings which make for potential winners. It is this ability which at the political level may be compared with the sense for profit possibilities which guides the successful entrepreneur in the marketplace.

Logrolling The view of the bargaining process among interest groups just described appears to contradict the ill repute in which logrolling is held. What then distinguishes the preceding case of coalition forming and its constructive result from the detrimental type of logrolling? The answer, it appears, lies in the comprehensiveness of the coalition-forming process. As noted previously for the case of direct democracy, "transaction costs" may be too high to explore all feasible combinations. Interactions among interest groups and their representatives thus has the advantage of reducing the final decision process to small numbers, thereby overcoming the free-rider problem. But small numbers also carry the disadvantage of permitting monopolistic practices in an imperfect market, thereby distorting outcomes. Fortunately, however, periodic elections provide an opportunity for correction. Policies to be sustained must approximate the preferences of the majority, if not at once then in the course of time.

C. THE LEVIATHAN HYPOTHESIS

The theory of representative democracy, as described in the preceding section, has been subjected to severe criticism. The theory, like that of perfect markets, establishes a normative model which does not necessarily reflect its real application. Thus, markets can function efficiently only if consumers are well-informed, if competition prevails, if prices are flexible, if no externalities are to be dealt with, and so forth. Not all these conditions prevail, and situations arise where markets do not work as the normative model suggests. Much the same holds for the model of fiscal democracy presented in the preceding pages. For the system to function efficiently, voters must be informed, the vying for votes on the part of politicians must be competitive, the formation of party platforms must be based on broad coalitions, voting systems must be sensitive to preferences, distortion through strategic behavior must be minimized, and so forth. In reality, these conditions are rarely met. Defects in the fiscal process must thus be considered and have been viewed from a variety of perspectives. Marxist critics as noted below have seen the fiscal process as an instrument of class struggle, shaped by the diverse interests of capital and labor. In recent years, conservative critics have viewed the growth of the public sector as expressing a systematic bias in the fiscal system toward overexpansion. A modern Leviathan is said to arise and threaten free institutions.[7] Leaving the record of public sector growth and its economic determinants to the following chapter, we here consider the reasons why such bias is said to prevail. These reasons are found to lodge in both the voting process and the way in which the agents of government (bureaucrats and politicians) impose their own wishes on the public.

Voting Bias

As we have seen in our earlier analysis, social goods and goods the benefits of which are largely external will be in undersupply without public provision. This leaves open the question of whether the scope of public provision will be deficient or excessive, given our institutional setting. We take this to mean whether it is above or below what would be provided in line with consumer evaluation.

Cost to Minority One basic plank of the overexpansion hypothesis is that majority voting by its very nature will result in oversupply.[8] While only 51 percent

---

[7] See James M. Buchanan, *The Limits of Liberty*, Chicago: University of Chicago Press, 1975, chap. 9. For tax restraints to check such abuse, see G. Brennan and J. Buchanan, *The Power to Tax*, New York: Cambridge University Press, 1980.

[8] See James Buchanan and Gordon Tullock, *The Calculus of Consent*, Ann Arbor: University of Michigan Press, 1962, chap. 10.

of the voters may join in legislating a particular program which meets their interest, the tax cost is borne by all the members of the group. Assuming finance by a head tax, the cost to the majority will be only 51 percent of the total and the majority will disregard the 49 percent borne by the others who have no interest in the project. Oversupply thus results because the majority will consider only that part of the cost which *it* must bear.

Such may indeed be the case, but we should also note that opponents of projects do not consider the loss of benefits to proponents as projects are denied. To establish a general bias toward overexpansion, it must be shown that proponents are in a better position to organize than are opponents; or that proponents, feeling strongly about their project, find it more worth their while to spend money and effort to secure a majority vote. Perhaps so, but a distortion may arise in either direction and the a priori conclusion of excess bias is at best a shaky one.[9]

Underestimation of Tax Burden   A further cause of oversupply is the fact that voters tend to underestimate the cost of taxation which they actually bear. Voters are seen to support expenditure legislation without being fully aware that an opportunity cost is involved, or they may assume that the cost will be borne by someone else. This will particularly be the tendency if taxes are invisible. Thus an increase in property or income tax is felt more directly and therefore meets more opposition than an increase in indirect taxes, especially if such taxes are added to cost at earlier stages of production rather than appear as an addition on the retail bill. The less visible the taxes, the more likely it is that expenditures will be considered costless and that overexpansion will result. Under conditions of deficit finance in particular, an increase in expenditures seems costless.

Similar considerations apply when tax revenue rises due not to a legislated rate hike but to an automatic increase. Such built-in revenue gain may come about due to economic growth and inflation and may permit additional outlays which might not have been agreed to if a tax increase had to be condoned by specific legislation. Indexing of the income tax has eliminated this problem.[10]

Fiscal illusion exists, but once more the argument has two sides. While taxpayers may underestimate their burden, they may also underestimate expenditure benefits. Benefits which one derives from private purchases are visible and ratified by the purchase price. If I want my car repaired I must pay the garage, which tells me the value of benefits derived, but the roads are there for me to enjoy, like sunshine, and I may take their benefit for granted. Moreover, it has also been argued that the political process leaves a deficiency in the provision for social goods because the consumer-voter is subject to intensive advertising pressures from the producers of private goods, so that his or her perceived needs are distorted in the latter's favor.[11] This may well be the case, but it should also be noted that private producers who produce public goods (whether the defense or construction industry

---

[9] See R. A. Musgrave, "Excess Bias and the Nature of Budget Growth," *Journal of Public Economics,* vol. 28, 1985, pp. 287–308.

[10] See pp. 326, 361.

[11] See John Kenneth Galbraith, *The Affluent Society,* Boston: Houghton-Mifflin, 1958, p. 261.

or teacher unions) spend much effort and funds to persuade legislators and voters that their services are needed. As usual, there is a cross-current of forces and the net effect is by no means evident.

Deficit Finance A vote to raise expenditures when matched by a vote to raise taxes carries a visible opportunity cost to the taxpayer. But this is not the case if the additional outlays are to be deficit-financed. Voters will tend to overlook the future cost of debt service and view the increase in programs as being more or less costless. Thus deficit finance, even though it may at times be needed for purposes of stabilization, tends to expand the budget.[12] Surplus finance by the same token generates a curbing effect.

Public Employee Voting Overexpansion, finally, is said to result because public employees as voters support large budgets simply because they create jobs for them, and quite independent of the benefits derived from public services. Perhaps so, but it may also be held that employees of firms which produce goods sold to private consumers vote with the opposite interest in mind. Moreover, it may be noted that recent decades of public sector expansion have been associated with a declining share of the public sector in total employment.

Monopoly Government

Voting bias is not the only cause, so the critics argue, which leads to overexpansion of the budget. ''Bureaucrats'' and politicians also contribute thereto. They do not serve to implement the wishes of the voter, as the theory of representative government assumes, but strive to impose their own will. They find it in their interest to expand the budget and they are in a position to do so.

Bureaucrats Consider first the case of bureaucrats, the term now commonly applied to government officials and employees, a group which in an earlier social climate was referred to more kindly as civil servants. The bureaucrats' central objective, so the argument postulates, is to maximize the size of their bureaus, so as to raise their salaries or extend their power.

The empire-building bureaucrat will submit a budget request which (1) asks for more funds than needed to perform a given function, (2) overstates the benefits to be derived from a given level of services, and (3) inflates the total in anticipation of expected cutbacks. The granting agency may be duped by these tactics, but an excessive level of activity may result even if such cheating is ruled out. Thus it has been postulated that the sponsor of an activity, who decides on the budget request, will accept any proposal, provided only that ''the project is worth the money'' in the sense that total benefits do not fall short of total costs. The bureaucrat will then propose the largest budget compatible with this condition. As shown in Figure 7-3, this budget will be in excess of the efficient level.[13]

DD' in Figure 7-3 represents the sponsor's marginal evaluation of successive

---

[12] See p. 499.
[13] For this approach and the argument given in Figure 7-3, see W. A. Niskanen, *Bureaucracy and Representative Government*, Chicago: Aldine, 1974, chap. 5.

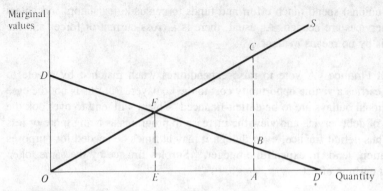

FIGURE 7-3 Maximizing behavior of bureaucrats.

units of service, and OS gives the marginal costs of providing them. At output OA, the *total* benefit, or area $ODBA$, matches total costs, or area OCA. For lower levels of outlay, benefits exceed costs, and for higher levels costs exceed benefits.[14] Service level OA and the corresponding budget of OCA are thus the largest which the sponsor will grant, and this is the budget which the bureau head will offer. This budget, however, exceeds the efficient budget output OE and expenditure level OFE, the level at which *marginal* costs and benefits are equal. While budget additions involving quantities from OE to OA still appear worthwhile to the grantor, since total benefits continue to exceed total costs, extension beyond OE is inefficient. Beyond that point each successive unit costs more than the benefits it yields are worth.

How realistic is the model of Figure 7-3? Will the grantor be that naive and will the typical bureau head in fact maximize bureau size? Or may other motivations enter, such as to serve the public interest and to expedite efficiency? While self-interest may well be a factor, it is hardly a fair reading of human nature to postulate that it is the only mode. Moreover, even if the bureau head intends to maximize his or her bureau, he or she may not be free to do so. Budgetary requests are examined within the department before they are presented to the Office of Management and Budget (OMB). They must then pass OMB scrutiny before they go to the Congress, where they must further pass congressional judgment. Although this procedure is not perfect, it does impose a constraint which the model of Figure 7-3 overlooks. The bureau head is hardly in a monopoly-like situation, free to impose an all-or-nothing offer. It may even be to his or her advantage to establish a reputation for prudence.

In all, the monopoly bureau provides an interesting analogy to the private sector, but it does not tell the entire story. Viewed from a different perspective, public employees function as civil servants who fulfill an important task in society. They

[14] To derive point A we may redraw Figure 7-3 in terms of total benefit and total cost curves. They will both be upward-sloping, with the benefit curve initially above the cost curve and rising at a decreasing rate, while the cost curve rises at an increasing rate. The output corresponding to OA is reached where the benefit curve intersects the cost curve and total benefits begin to fall below total costs; and the output corresponding to OE is reached where the vertical distance between total benefits and total costs (the excess of benefits over costs) is largest.

are needed (1) to provide technical expertise in the design of programs, so as to enable decision makers (the elected representatives) to make intelligent choices; and (2) to implement and operate programs once they are enacted. In this role, they provide an element of continuity to the governmental process and introduce a sense of rationality into its operation. Their services are crucial to the functioning of the modern state and to the design as well as implementation of public policy.[15]

At the same time, civil servants not only function as aids to elected representatives but they themselves affect the outcome. In the conduct of government, as anywhere else, knowledge is power. Public programs are complex and elected officials may have neither the time nor the expertise to analyze them. That branch of the government which is backed by technical experts is thus at a great advantage. Moreover, in rendering advice, the technician can hardly avoid (and may not wish to avoid) introduction of his or her own policy judgments, thereby influencing policy outcome.[16]

Politicians Similar considerations are applied to the role of the politician. According to the theory of representative democracy the politician functions as an entrepreneur who endeavors to maximize votes so as to stay in power. He or she does so by promoting the provision of a bundle of public services which reflects the wishes of the voters. Thereby the politician serves the interest of the voter, just as the profit-maximizing entrepreneur serves the interest of consumers. Critics hold that the politician, like the bureaucrat, wishes to maximize the size of the budget. The politician does so because a larger budget serves his or her interest, whether to gain in power, influence, or (indirectly or by way of kickbacks) in income. Given this objective, the politician will not present a program which maximizes votes. Instead, he or she will advocate the largest possible program which can still secure a majority,[17] and this budget may well exceed that desired by the median voter. This is shown in Figure 7-4, where the budget size is measured on the horizontal axis and net benefits (excess of benefits over tax price) are measured on the vertical axis.

The *OA, OB, . . . ,OE* curves then record the net gains or losses which various voters A, B, C, D, and E will derive from various budget sizes, it being assumed that a given tax burden distribution applies. Under unrestrained voting, where voters are presented with all available options, budget size *OM* will win, reflecting the preference of the median voter, or C. But the largest budget for which a majority

---

[15] Arguing along these lines, the great sociologist Max Weber viewed the growth of civil service as crucial to the development of the modern state and the spreading of a rationally rather than traditionally based mode of political action. See H. H. Gerth and C. Wright Mills, *From Max Weber,* New York: Oxford University Press, 1972, chap. 8, pp. 196–245. The role of the civil servant as trustee of the public interest, with special application to budget policy, was stressed by Gerhard Colm, *Essays in Public Finance and Fiscal Policy,* New York: Oxford University Press, 1955.

[16] One of the most interesting developments in recent years has been the growth of technical staff at the service of Congress, thus counterbalancing the technical assistance previously available only on the executive side. As a result, the ability of Congress to deal critically with executive proposals has been greatly enhanced and presidential power has been reduced. See p. 32.

[17] See Mackay, R. and Weaver, C., "Monopoly Bureaus and Fiscal Outcomes: Deductive Models and Implications for Reform," in G. Tullock and R. Wagner (eds.): *Policy Analysis and Deductive Reasoning,* New York: Heath, 1978.

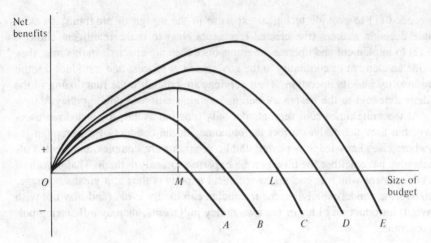

FIGURE 7-4   Net benefit curves and agenda setting.

can still be achieved is given at *OL*. This budget size will have the support of D and E, who would be willing to vote for even larger budgets since at L their net gain is still positive. Budget size *OL* will also have the support of C, who stands to gain from budget expansion up to that level. The politician thus permits voters to choose only among budgets of *OL* or larger, and *OL* wins.

Once more we are left with the question of whether politicians do in fact have the power to constrain the voters' choice in this fashion, or whether their power to do so is limited by the loss of votes to rival politicians with more attractive platforms. Given the guarantee of free and periodic elections, it would seem that gross departures from the preferences of the voters cannot be sustained for long and that corrections will occur. The "tax revolt" of the late seventies is a case in point. A distinction must be drawn also between politicians imposing their will upon the public and political leadership which sets directions of public policy. The latter may enrich the democratic process rather than impede its performance.

Campaign Financing

It remains to note the role of campaign financing as a distorting factor in the fiscal decision process. Although given relatively little attention in the body of literature reviewed in this section, it is surely a major source of bias in the system. With the rise of media campaigning, campaign costs—and with them the importance of political contributions—have vastly increased. The recent rise of single-issue-oriented PACs (political action committees) and their lobbying activities has further added to the dependence of political candidates on the support of well-funded interest groups. With vast sums spent to commit legislators in key committees such as Ways and Means and to rally voter support, independent leadership and nonpartisan judgment have become increasingly difficult. These pressures bear on tax and expenditure policy alike, and little is known about whether more funds are spent to promote expansion or restriction of the public sector. It is evident, however, that an efficient setting of tax and expenditure structures is impeded. Reform of campaign finance is thus a priority item.

A Political Business Cycle

The view of government as manipulating the public rather than implementing its wishes bears not only on the size of government but also on the conduct of macro policy. The hypothesis here is that policy makers realize the importance of economic conditions for election success and therefore conduct macro policy so as to create favorable conditions at election time.

Considerable empirical work has been done to explore the relationship between election outcomes and economic variables.[18] Specifically, attempts have been made to establish the extent to which the outcome of presidential and congressional elections depends on economic variables such as unemployment, inflation, and changes in real income. The question here is whether the party in power will be blamed for poor economic performance and rewarded for success. One would expect this to be the case, but the results of such analysis depend on how the problem is formulated. Thus, it matters a great deal how much of a response lag is allowed for (does only the record of the election year matter, or does the voter have a longer memory?) and just how the index of economic performance is defined.

However this may be, politicians will expect favorable economic conditions to have beneficial election effects, and they may therefore be expected to time policy actions accordingly. That is to say, elections will be preceded by expansionary policies to stimulate employment or by structural measures (say, farm policies) to please particular sections of the electorate. In this way, government may generate a politically based business cycle.[19]

Budget Limitations

The view that our political process overextends the public sector has generated proposals for rule changes which will render expansion more difficult. Whereas state legislation to limit the fiscal powers of local government is nothing new, such practice greatly gained in momentum during the seventies, especially the late seventies after California's "tax revolt" led to the passage of Proposition 13. This series of amendments, moreover, was extended to also limit the fiscal powers of state legislatures, and more recently introduction of an amendment to the U.S. Constitution has been under consideration by the Congress.

State-Local Level The tax revolt of the late seventies, as signaled by California's Proposition 13, was above all a protest against the property tax. Even though property taxation had risen less rapidly during the sixties and early seventies than most other state and local taxes, inflation shifted an increasing share of the tax burden from business to residential real estate. Rapidly rising real estate values, moreover, had increased property tax liabilities relative to income, thus leaving the taxpayer with the perception of an increased tax burden. California's Proposition

---

[18] See, for instance, Ray C. Fair, "The Effects of Economic Events on Votes for Presidents," *The Review of Economics and Statistics,* vol. 2, May 1978.

[19] See for instance William D. Nordhaus, "The Political Business Cycle," *Review of Economic Studies,* vol. 42, 1975; and Duncan MacRae, "A Political Model of the Business Cycle," *Journal of Political Economy,* vol. 85, 1977. For a review of this literature and an analytical foundation see Bruno S. Frey, *Modern Political Economy,* Oxford: Martin Robertson, 1978.

13 rolled back assessed values and limited future increase to 2 percent a year while imposing a rate ceiling of 1 percent. In addition, a two-thirds majority was required for other taxes to be increased. Under California's Proposition 4, passed in 1979, an expenditure limit was imposed on the state budget, restricting the inflation adjusted growth of state expenditures to that of population. Since then, adoption of legal checks to fiscal expansion has grown widely. Nearly twenty states imposed constitutional limitations on the growth of state finances, and most states also limit the permissible increase in property taxation. The implications of these changes for state and local finances are still emerging and their impact will be considered later, when state and local finances are examined.[20]

Federal Level   The U.S. Constitution, as noted earlier, does not impose an overall limitation on the taxing and spending powers of the federal government. Limitations on taxing power apply to permissible types of taxes and the preservation of due process only, whereas expenditures are limited only by the requirement that they must serve the public welfare. Congressional legislation on fiscal matters proceeds under the ordinary rule of absolute majority, with only a two-thirds majority required to override presidential vetoes. There is no constitutional provision requiring a balanced budget or limiting the public debt.

In recent years, various constitutional amendments have been proposed to limit the fiscal powers of the government. To become law, they must be passed by a two-thirds majority in both houses and must be ratified by three-fourths of the states. The leading amendment, as passed by the House in 1982, contained two major provisions. First, the Congress would be required to plan for a balanced budget. That is to say, revenue estimates (as based on the average income of the preceding three years) must match planned expenditures. A three-fifths majority would be required for a planned deficit, and a simple majority for a planned surplus. Second, tax receipts would not be permitted to grow more rapidly than national income. A more rapid increase would require endorsement by a simple majority of all members in both houses of Congress.[21] While the amendment drive has bogged down as unrealistic in face of the large deficits during the 1980s, it remains on the agenda for potential action.

In the meantime, Congress has attempted to deal with the problem by legislation rather than by constitutional amendment. Thus the Balanced Budget Act of 1986 (also referred to as the Gramm-Rudman-Hollings Act) established targets for deficit reduction leading to balance by 1991, requiring across-the-board expenditure cuts lest other action be taken. It remains to be seen whether this goal will be reached.

D.   CLASSES AND INTEREST GROUPS

The critique of the democratic model, outlined in the preceding sections, derives largely from an analysis of the behavior of single individuals, whether they are

---

[20] See p. 492.
[21] See *Balanced Budget-Tax Limitation Constitutional Amendment*, Committee of the Judiciary, U.S. Senate, July 10, 1981. Also see p. 31 for a further discussion of budgeting.

voters, officials, or politicians. An alternative approach emphasizes that individual action is constrained by membership in classes and groups, so that the fiscal process is seen as a matter of group interaction.[22]

The Marxist Model

Such an alternative approach is in line with the Marxist view, whereby the state (prior to the revolution) is to be seen as an instrument by which the ruling (capitalist) class exploits the subjugated (working) class. Actions of the state must be interpreted as part of the class struggle, which transcends the political as well as the individual sphere of social relations.

Fiscal history may be seen in this perspective.[23] In the Middle Ages, the feudal lord extracted payments in cash or kind from his serfs to sustain his rule and the military establishment needed to maintain or improve his position. Thus it was in the interest of the ruling class to have as strong and rich a state as possible. With the rise of democratic government, the ruling class lost its tight control over the state, and power went increasingly to popular majorities who shifted the costs of maintaining the state to the hitherto ruling class. As a result, the ruling class changed its view of the state. Its interests were now served better by a weak state, and it thus came to favor small budgets, low taxes, and general noninterference with the private sector. Marx in turn advocated a highly progressive income tax, listed in the *Communist Manifesto* as one of the means to hasten the breakdown of the capitalist system.[24]

More recently, Marxist writers have emphasized the interdependence between "monopoly capital" and the fiscal state. The need to absorb surplus output is said to call for expanding public outlays, especially on defense; and a rising level of transfer payments is seen as necessary to maintain social peace. At the same time, monopoly capital is said to oppose the necessary financing, thus creating a fiscal crisis of the state.[25]

This view of fiscal politics reflects the Marxist framework in which the social process is seen in terms of class struggle. It is not surprising, then, that tax and expenditure decisions will be a major instrument of that struggle. Dissatisfaction with taxation has indeed been a major factor in the history of revolutions, and redistributive fiscal measures have to a degree expropriated the "capitalist class." But by the same token, the role of budgetary activity may change from a means of struggle to a tool of social accommodation once a less divisive view of society is taken. Budget policy then becomes an instrument of gradual reform and cooperation. Looking back at the history of the last century, we see that there can be little doubt that fiscal action played a key role in this growth of social cohesion. Indeed, the rise of the modern welfare state, with its emphasis on transfers and progressive taxation, has placed the public budget at the hub of the social system. The recent

---

[22] See R. A. Musgrave, "Theories of Fiscal Crisis," in Henry J. Aaron and Michael J. Boskin (eds.): *The Economics of Taxation,* Washington, D.C.: Brookings Institution, 1980.

[23] See Rudolf Goldscheid, "A Sociological Approach to Public Finance" (translated from the German, 1925), in Richard A. Musgrave and Alan Peacock (eds.): *Classics in the Theory of Public Finance,* New York: Macmillan, 1958.

[24] See *A Handbook of Marxism,* New York: International Publishers, 1935, p. 46.

[25] See James O'Connor, *The Fiscal Crisis of the State,* New York: St. Martin's, 1973.

shift of political attitudes and critique of the welfare state in turn have focused on a critique of its fiscal components.

Multiple Groupings

Although the fiscal process as an instrument of class struggle is too partial a view, fiscal interest groups are a powerful factor. The structure of groupings, however, is multidimensional, cutting across the Marxist categories of class. Capital and labor in the construction industry will combine to promote highway programs, while capital and labor in the defense industry will combine in favor of defense. Consumers receiving both wage and capital income will combine to support programs the benefits of which they value highly. Thus, the actual interest structure is much more complex than a simple division into capital and labor would suggest.

A similar picture may be drawn with respect to taxation. Various taxpayer groups organize to represent their interests, and the congressional tax committees are under great pressure from such groups, whether it be the oil industry arguing for depletion allowances, the real estate lobby wanting faster depreciation, governors advocating exemption of interest, or university representatives calling for deductibility of tuition payments. Consumers of product X will combine in opposing its taxation, whether their income is derived from capital or from labor; and they will be joined by both workers and capitalists deriving their income from the production of X. The distinction between capital and labor income becomes relevant, however, when it comes to the treatment of the two income sources under the income tax. But even here alignment by income level, independent of source, is as or more important.

By offering a well-organized reflection of voter concerns, interest groups can make a constructive contribution. But they also distort. Some groups are organized more easily than others,[26] and some have more financial resources to press their views; and automatic development of a neatly balanced structure of countervailing power cannot be relied upon. It is thus important for a public policy to develop an institutional setting in which a more balanced representation of group interests prevails.[27]

However this may be, a realistic view of the fiscal system must take account of the strategic role of multiple interest groups, economic, demographic, and regional. A positive theory of fiscal behavior centered on the interaction of interest groups and their impact on fiscal institutions and decisions may well be more realistic than those based on preferences of individual voters, or on their disregard by self-interested bureaucrats.

E. SUMMARY

Because preferences for social goods are not revealed except in the small-number case, budgetary determination based on a voting process is needed.

---

[26] See Mancur Olson, *The Logic of Collective Action*, Cambridge, Mass.: Harvard, 1965.

[27] John R. Commons and his school have argued for a system of public representation based on groups rather than territorially selected delegates. See John R. Commons, *Economics of Collective Action*, New York: Macmillan, 1940. Related views, going back to scholastic philosophers such as Thomas Aquinas, were developed in the encyclical *Rerum Novarum*, issued by Pope Leo XIII, May 15, 1891.

     1.   Majority voting may lead to arbitrary decisions, which will depend on the sequence in which issues are paired.

     2.   If preferences are single-peaked, the median voter wins.

     3.   As applied to various fiscal choices, the voting process is simplest when deciding the size of the budget for a single social good and with a fixed tax assignment. The problem becomes more difficult if budget composition and tax structure are allowed to vary.

     4.   Plurality and point voting lead to more representative outcomes, as intensity of preferences comes to be reflected. But use of voting strategy may interfere with efficient outcomes.

A system of representative democracy has been examined, and these features have been noted:

     5.   Politicians may be thought of as maximizing votes by providing popular options, thereby complying with the preferences of the voters.

     6.   But politicians may also exert leadership by guiding such preferences.

     7.   Fiscal representation is based on a structure of interest groups, reflecting a wide variety of characteristics and concerns.

     8.   By combining issues and platforms, majority voting may come to reflect intensity of preferences.

     9.   Vote trading, if broadly based, may improve the efficiency of the outcome, but logrolling between a subsector of interested parties leads to inefficiency.

     10.   Delegation of decision making to elected representatives introduces small-number bargaining at the final level of decision making, thereby helping to overcome the free-rider problem.

     11.   Voting outcomes tend to be imperfect, but periodic free elections provide correction, requiring governmental policy to approximate the preferences of the voters.

Critics of this model have pointed to a built-in bias in the fiscal process:

     12.   The budget is said to be overexpanded due to bias in the working of majority rule and deficiencies in the voting process.

     13.   This bias is said to be accentuated by the role of bureaucrats and politicians who serve their own interest by expanding the budget.

     14.   Various devices may be applied to limit the size of the budget, including constitutional amendments and legislative constraints.

Classes and interest groups as well as individual voters enter into fiscal decision making.

     15.   According to the Marxist view, the main division is between capital and labor, and the struggle over fiscal issues may be seen as reflecting a struggle between these two classes.

     16.   Viewed more broadly, the structure of fiscal interest groups becomes multidimensional, including groupings by income, industry, age, and region, with group formations frequently cutting across capital and labor.

FURTHER READINGS

For general background on the theory of social choice, see:

Arrow, K.: *Social Choice and Individual Values*, 2d ed., New York: Wiley, 1951.

Inman, R. P.: "Markets, Government and the 'New' Political Economy," in A. Auerbach and M. Feldstein (eds.): *Handbook of Public Economics,* vol. II, Amsterdam: North Holland 1986.

Mueller, D.: *Public Choice,* Cambridge, England: Cambridge University Press, 1979.

With regard to the proposition that the budgetary process leads to over-expansion, see:

Borcherding, T. (ed.): *Budgets and Bureaucrats,* Durham, N.C.: University of North Carolina Press, 1977.

Buchanan, J. M.: *The Limits of Liberty,* Chicago: University of Chicago Press, 1975, chap. 9.

Buchanan, J. M. and G. Brennan: *The Power to Tax,* Cambridge, England: Cambridge University Press, 1980.

Musgrave, R. A.: "The Leviathan Cometh; Or Does He?" in H. Ladd and T. Tideman (eds.): *Tax and Expenditure Limitations,* Washington, D.C.: The Urban Institute, 1981.

For a sociological view of the public sector, see:

Musgrave, R.A.: "Theories of Fiscal Crisis," in H. J. Aaron and M. J. Boskin (eds.): *The Economics of Taxation,* Washington, D.C.: Brookings, 1980.

O'Connor, J.: *The Fiscal Crisis of the State,* New York: St. Martins, 1973.

For the debate over constitutional budget limitations, see:

Congressional Budget Office, *Balancing the Federal Budget and Limiting Federal Spending: Constitutional and Statutory Approaches,* Washington, D.C.: U.S. Government Printing Office, 1982.

McKenzie, R. B. (ed.): *Constitutional Economics,* Lexington, Mass.: Heritage Foundation and Lexington Books, 1984.

Moore, W. S. and R. Penner (eds.): *The Constitution and the Budget,* Washington, D.C.: American Enterprise Institute, 1980.

Part Three

Expenditure
Structure and Policy

Chapter 8

Public Expenditures:
Structure and Growth*

A. Public Expenditure Growth, 1890–1990: *Absolute Growth; Growth in Relation to GNP.* **B. Growth by Type of Expenditure:** *By Level of Government; Defense versus Civilian Expenditures; Purchases versus Transfer Payments; Changing Composition of Civilian Expenditures.* **C. International Comparison. D. Causes of Expenditure Growth:** *Expenditures on Goods and Services; Changing Scope of Transfers; Availability of Tax Handles; Threshold Effects and War Finance; Political and Social Factors.* **E. Summary.**

We now turn to a series of chapters dealing with public expenditure structure and the policy issues involved in designing expenditure programs. To set the stage, this chapter examines the size of the public sector in the U.S. economy and surveys its growth. The concept of the public sector, as we have seen previously, may be interpreted in various ways. It may be conceived as reflecting budgetary transactions, public enterprise, public regulation, and similar concerns. All these policies are of significance, but our focus here is on budgetary activity. A detailed view of how

---

Reader's Guide to Chapter 8: This chapter provides the background for the subsequent study of expenditure policy. We examine the size of the public sector as viewed from various perspectives and explore the pattern of expenditure growth and its causes—easy reading, but important for an understanding of where the public sector has been and where it is going.

the public sector fits into GNP, given in Chapter 2, need not be reviewed here. We thus proceed directly to the record of public expenditure growth.

A. PUBLIC EXPENDITURE GROWTH

Writing in the 1880s, the German economist Adolph Wagner advanced his "law of rising public expenditures." He felt, perhaps in anticipation of trends to be realized fifty to a hundred years later, that the development of modern industrial society would give rise to increasing political "pressure for social progress" and call for increased allowance for "social consideration" in the conduct of industry. In consequence, continual expansion of the public sector and its share in the economy should be expected.[1] Has this law been borne out over the years, and just how should it be defined?

Absolute Growth

Public expenditures, not surprisingly, have risen vastly in dollar terms. As shown in Table 8-1, line 1, such expenditures (including all levels of government) have increased by a multiple of nearly 2000 over the past ninety years. But this is not a meaningful way of looking at expenditure growth. Prices over the same period (line 13) rose by a multiple of 13, so that the multiple in terms of constant dollars (line 2) drops to 135. Also, population (line 12) more than tripled, so that the constant dollar multiple, measured on a per capita basis (line 3), falls to 33.

Growth in Relation to GNP

Allowance for population and price changes are obvious corrections, but they are not enough. One must also note that there has been a vast increase in productivity over the period, leading to a nearly sixfold rise in per capita income in constant dollars. There is every reason to expect that part of this gain should have been spent on the goods and services provided by the public sector. In other words, focus should be on the share of government in total expenditures, with the law of rising public expenditures defined in terms of a rising public sector *share*.

Expenditure-to-GNP Ratio   Beginning with the most global measure, we find that the ratio of public expenditures (all levels of government) to GNP rose from 6 to 35 percent over our nearly ninety-year period, with a nearly sixfold increase by the relative size of the public sector. This leaves us with a substantial increase, but by no means so drastic a rise as is suggested by the record of growth in total dollar terms.[2]

The path of overall expenditure growth, as measured by the ratio of total public expenditures to GNP, is shown in line 4 of Table 8-1 and is further plotted in

---

[1] See the relevant passages from A. Wagner in Richard A. Musgrave and Alan Peacock (eds.), *Classics in the Theory of Public Finance*, New York: Macmillan, 1958, pp. 1–16. Also see chap. 3 in Richard A. Musgrave, *Fiscal Systems*, New Haven: Yale University Press, 1969.

[2] In arriving at this ratio, the same deflator is applied to both GNP and government expenditures. Since the cost of public services has risen faster than the general price level, this multiple overstates the rise of the public share in real terms.

TABLE 8-1

Growth of Government Expenditures in the United States*

	1890	1902	1913	1922	1929	1940	1950	1960	1970	1980	1987
Total expenditures											
1. Current dollars (billions)	0.8	1.6	3.2	9.3	10.7	20.4	70.3	151.2	332.9	953.0	1,550.0
2. 1985 dollars (billions)	10.9	18.7	33.5	69.8	75.2	158.3	298.4	492.4	825.8	1,211.0	1,476.0
3. Per capita, 1985 dollars	17.3	23.6	34.5	63.6	616.0	1,196.0	1,960.0	2,718.0	4,024.0	5,133.5	5,721.0
4. As percentage of GNP	6.1	8.0	7.8	12.5	10.4	20.4	24.4	29.4	32.8	35.1	35.0
By type, percentage of GNP											
5. Purchases	n.a.†	n.a.	n.a.	n.a.	8.6	14.2	13.5	19.5	21.8	19.4	21.1
6. Transfers	n.a.	n.a.	n.a.	n.a.	1.8	6.2	10.9	5.9	11.3	15.7	13.3
By function, percentage of GNP											
7. Civilian	5.0	5.8	6.8	10.7	9.2	18.1	19.4	20.6	25.2	29.9	28.3
8. Defense	1.5	1.5	1.0	2.9	1.2	2.3	5.0	8.8	7.6	5.2	6.7
By level of government, percentage of Total											
9. Federal	n.a.	34.5	30.2	40.3	31.5	49.3	63.7	64.3	62.5	66.2	64.5
10. State	n.a.	10.8	11.6	13.4	16.8	22.3	18.2	16.5	19.4	19.7 ⎫ 35.5
11. Local	n.a.	54.8	58.3	46.4	51.7	28.4	18.1	19.1	18.1	14.2 ⎭
Related statistics											
12. Population (millions)	63	79	97	110	122	132	152	181	205	227	258
13. Price index (1985 = 100)	8.0	8.5	9.8	7.8	13.0	11.6	21.4	27.7	37.7	76.8	105.5
14. GNP, current dollars (billions)	13	20	41	74	103	100	288	515	1,015.5	2,732	4,500

*Line 8 includes military activities, civil defense, and foreign military assistance. Lines 9 to 11 include grants at the grantor level.

†n. a.: not available.

Sources: Lines 1 and 5, 1890–1922: Richard A. Musgrave and J. M. Culbertson, "The Growth of Public Expenditures in the United States," *National Tax Journal, June 1953;* and U.S. Bureau of the Census, *Historical Statistics of the United States, 1960.* For later years, see *Economic Report of the President, 1987,* and *Survey of Current Business,* July 1987 and earlier years.

Figure 8-1. With years selected so as to avoid wartime peaks, we note a 2.4 percentage point growth in the U.S. ratio from 1890 to 1913, and a rise of 7.5 points from 1913 to 1929. This was followed by a 10 percent increase in the depression years of the 1930s and the post–World War II adjustment. The rise continued in the 1960s and 1970s but at a declining rate, reaching a constant ratio in the 1980s. Even though the rate of increase has varied by subperiods, it is evident that Wagner's law of a rising expenditure share was borne out if we take the longer sweep, though at a slowing rate, and has come to a halt in recent years.

Expenditure Elasticity   Another view of the same development is taken in Table 8-2, where the data of Table 8-1 are recast in terms of expenditure elasticities. The table shows the GNP elasticity of total and civilian expenditures over selected years. We note that both elasticities were substantially above unity on through the 1960s, reflecting the rising expenditure to GNP ratios. However, we also note that the elasticity fell in recent decades. The table also shows the economy's marginal propensity to spend in the public sector, defined as the increase in expenditures as a percent of the increase in GNP. While the marginal propensity to spend on civilian outlays moved up on through the 1970s, this tendency was reversed during the 1980s.

B. GROWTH BY TYPE OF EXPENDITURE

To explain the growth in the overall expenditure share in GNP it is helpful to consider a breakdown by expenditure categories.

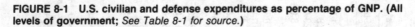

FIGURE 8-1   U.S. civilian and defense expenditures as percentage of GNP. (All levels of government; *See Table 8-1 for source.***)**

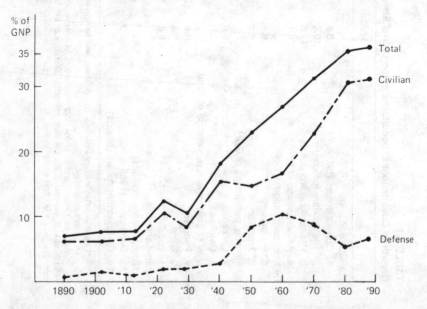

TABLE 8-2
Expenditure Elasticities and Propensities
(All Levels of Government)

	GNP ELASTICITY*		MARGINAL PROPENSITY†	
	Total	*Civilian*	*Total*	*Civilian*
1890–1929	1.7	1.8	10.9	9.0
1929–1950	2.9	2.2	30.4	18.4
1950–1970	1.6	1.8	35.9	26.5
1970–1980	1.1	1.2	34.6	30.7
1980–1987	1.1	1.0	36.6	27.5

*Ratio of percentage rise in public expenditures to percentage rise in GNP.
†Increase in public expenditures as percentage of increase in GNP.
Sources: Same as Table 8-1.

By Level of Government

As shown in lines 9 through 11 of Table 8-1, the trend over the century was toward increased expenditure centralization. Although the federal share in 1929 was about the same as at the beginning of the century, the depression decade of the thirties brought a substantial step-up. The same happened during the forties, with the federal share emerging substantially above its pre–World War II level. Since 1950, however, the federal share has been fairly stable. Also note that the rising federal share was accompanied by a decline in the local and a gain in the state share. As we will see later, these ratios tend to overstate the shift toward centralization, because intergovernmental grants are included at the grantor level. Given the increasing importance of such grants in the 1960s and 1970s, centralization as measured by shares in expenditures to the public has been less pronounced.

Defense versus Civilian Expenditures

Has expenditure growth been driven by rising expenditures for defense or by civilian expenditures as well? The ratios for the two shares are shown in lines 7 and 8 of Table 8-1 and are plotted in Figure 8-2. We note that for our ninety-year period the civilian expenditure ratio has increased somewhat faster than the defense ratio, but both have risen substantially. However, the pattern by subperiods differs sharply. The rise in the civilian ratio explained almost the entire increase for 1890 to 1940, whereas from 1940 to 1950 the defense ratio rose sharply while the civilian ratio showed little change. From 1960 to 1980 the defense ratio actually fell, while the civilian ratio rose sharply, a trend which came to a halt and was slightly reversed in the 1980s.

Although such comparisons have their shortcomings, it is evident that expenditure growth has not been primarily a matter of rising defense expenditures. Viewed over the longer run, the civilian expenditure ratio has been the driving force. As against a ratio of 9 percent in the pre-Depression year 1929, it stood at about 23 percent of GNP in 1970 and had risen to nearly 28 percent by 1978.

Purchase versus Transfer Payments

Table 8-1, lines 5 and 6, shows a further breakdown of U.S. expenditure growth, this time between purchases and transfers (including interest). We find that both

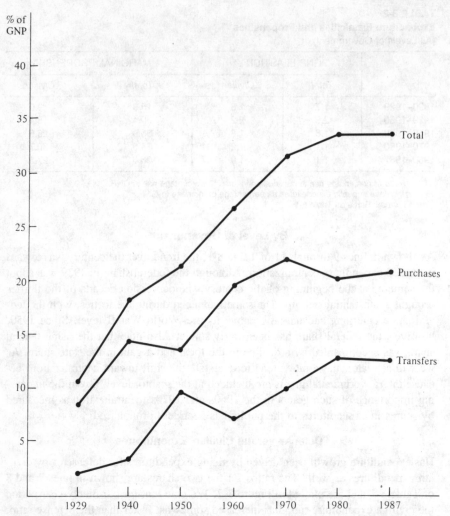

FIGURE 8-2   U.S. purchase and transfer expenditures as percentage of GNP. (All levels of government.)

purchases and transfers have contributed to the rising expenditure share but the transfer share has been of increasing importance since the 1930s. Reflecting the rise of social security and the growing importance of welfare payments, transfer payments have accounted for three-quarters of the growth in the civilian expenditure ratio since that time. Over the decade of the 1960s, the purchase ratio showed little change, and during the 1970s it declined. Taking the overall picture, we see that the role of the "distribution branch" thus expanded while that of the "allocation branch" declined.

Changing Composition of Civilian Expenditures

It remains to take a closer look at the growth of particular functions in the expenditure total. We continue to combine all levels of government for purposes of this

TABLE 8-3
Changing Structure of Government Expenditures*
(All Levels of Government)

	1902	1927	1940	1950	1960	1970	1980	1985
As percentage of total expenditures								
1. Defense-related	20.8	11.8	11.8	36.0	38.0	28.2	18.0	18.5
2. Civilian	79.2	88.2	88.2	64.0	62.0	71.8	82.0	81.5
3. Total	100.0	100.0	100.0	100.0	100.0	100.0	100.0	100.0
As percentage of civilian expenditures								
4. Social welfare	9.0	7.5	16.3	16.3	29.1	34.7	48.0	46.2
5. Education	22.4	25.5	18.2	22.9	22.3	24.8	20.7	18.5
6. Civil safety	14.7	10.9	6.4	5.9	7.6	7.2	3.7	4.3
7. Economic development	18.9	26.3	34.2	23.9	19.6	14.8	10.8	11.3
8. Transportation	17.1	23.6	16.5	10.7	11.7	8.1	5.7	5.5
9. Other	1.8	2.7	17.7	13.2	7.9	6.7	5.1	4.8
10. General government	15.2	6.0	4.8	3.7	8.9	9.5	4.3	3.8
11. Interest	8.4	15.3	10.0	11.5	8.9	6.6	7.4	12.1
12. Foreign relations and aid	0.3	0.2	0.1	10.0	2.6	1.2	0.2	0.5
13. Miscellaneous	11.1	8.3	9.8	5.9	0.9	1.2	1.2	3.4
14. Total	100.0	100.0	100.0	100.0	100.0	100.0	100.0	100.0
As percentage of GNP								
15. Defense-related	1.5	1.2	2.1	8.3	10.3	9.1	5.9	6.4
16. Civilian	5.8	9.2	15.5	14.8	16.7	23.1	27.3	28.5
17. Social welfare	0.5	0.7	2.5	2.4	4.9	8.0	13.1	13.1
18. Education	1.3	2.3	2.8	3.4	3.7	5.7	5.6	5.2
19. Civil safety	0.9	1.0	1.0	0.9	1.3	1.7	1.0	1.2
20. Economic development	1.0	2.4	5.4	3.5	3.3	3.5	2.9	2.9
21. Transportation	1.0	2.2	2.6	1.6	2.0	1.9	1.5	1.5
22. Other	0.1	0.2	2.8	1.9	1.3	1.6	1.4	1.5
23. General government	0.9	0.5	0.7	0.5	1.5	2.2	1.2	1.2
24. Interest	0.5	1.4	1.6	1.7	1.5	1.5	2.0	3.4
25. Foreign relations and aid	†	†	†	1.5	0.4	0.3	0.2	0.3
26. Miscellaneous	0.6	0.8	1.5	0.9	†	0.3	1.2	1.1
27. Total	7.3	10.4	17.6	23.1	27.0	32.2	27.3	34.9

*Includes general and trust fund expenditures. Detail may not add to total because of rounding. *Defense-related:* Includes military assistance abroad and veterans' benefits and services. *Social welfare:* Includes social security and welfare, health and hospitals, unemployment insurance, and housing and community development. *Civil safety:* Includes sanitation, fire and police, and recreation. *Transportation:* For 1902–1950 excludes state and local nonhighway transportation, which is included in miscellaneous. *Other economic development:* Includes space, natural resources, agriculture, and net subsidy to Postal Service. *General government:* For 1902–1950 this item is classified as "General Control." *Foreign relations and aid:* Excludes military assistance which is included in "Defense-related."

†Less than 0.05.

Sources: 1902–1950: U.S. Bureau of the Census, *Historical Statistics of the United States, calendar years, p. 723. 1960:* U.S. Department of Commerce, *National Income Accounts, 1929–1965. 1970:* U.S. Department of Commerce, *Survey of Current Business,* July 1974. 1980: U.S. Department of Commerce, *Survey of Current Business,* July 1982. 1985: U.S. Department of Commerce, *Survey of Current Business,* July 1987.

discussion. Whereas changes in the composition of expenditures had an important bearing on the division of total expenditures by levels of government, this aspect will be considered later on.[3]

The broad outlines of this development are shown in Table 8-3. Lines 1 and 2 show the division of total expenditures between defense-related and civilian outlays. As noted before, the rise in total expenditures (except for the 1940s) was fueled by the civilian component up to 1927, a sharply rising defense share in the 1940s, and once more a rising civilian share in the 1960s and 1970s, with a reversal of this trend appearing in the 1980s.

Turning now to the changing composition of the civilian expenditure structure, we note that the most striking feature is the rising trend in the share of social welfare expenditures (line 4), and particularly its dramatic upturn in the 1960s and 1970s. Primarily, this reflects the expansion of social security, but other welfare payments are also included. The share of education in total civilian expenditures (line 5) has remained more or less constant over the long run but has dropped in the seventies and eighties. The transportation share (line 8) showed a sharp rise in the 1920s, when the development of the automobile had its major impact on highway needs, but has followed a downward trend since then. Development expenditures other than transportation (line 9) have shown a decline since 1940, while the category of general government (including a variety of administrative functions) has been a minor item in modern budgets. Other categories, shown in lines 10 to 13, follow a fluctuating pattern.

The same picture is repeated in lines 15 to 27, giving this time the expenditure-GNP ratios for the various functions. Since the ratio of total civilian expenditures to GNP rose sharply (line 27), the expenditure-GNP ratio for most subitems (such as education) also showed a substantial increase relative to GNP.

C. INTERNATIONAL COMPARISON

A comparison with long-run expenditure growth in other countries shows a similar pattern, and a comparison for the 1960s and 1970s among OECD countries is given in Table 8-4. It will be seen that the expenditure-to-GNP ratio has generally risen over the past twenty years, with expenditure to GNP elasticities mostly well above 1. However, the U.S. elasticity has been at the lower end of the scale and the U.S. expenditure share in GNP has remained below that of most European countries.

D. CAUSES OF EXPENDITURE GROWTH

In the preceding chapter, we have examined the hypothesis that the growth of the budget share in GNP reflects a malfunctioning of the political system, a pervasive bias toward excess budgets. As an alternative approach, we now consider possible causes which might have led to a rising share and done so in line with changing economic needs and preferences of consumers.

---

[3] See p. 475.

TABLE 8-4
Expenditure Growth in OECD Countries

	EXPENDITURES AS PERCENTAGE OF GDP*		EXPENDITURE ELASTICITY WITH REGARD TO GDP
	1960	1982	1960–1982
Australia	22.1	36.3	1.19
France	34.6	56.7	1.12
Germany	32.5	49.4	1.25
Italy	36.1	53.7	1.19
Japan	33.7	34.2	1.32
Sweden	31.1	67.3	1.35
United Kingdom	32.6	47.4	1.15
United States	27.6	37.6	1.13

*Note that expenditures are shown as percentages of gross domestic product rather than gross national product and are thus not strictly comparable with the ratios used in the preceding pages.
Source: See *The Role of the Public Sector,* OECD, Spring 1985, p. 29.

Expenditures on Goods and Services

In addressing underlying causes of expenditure growth, a distinction should be drawn between expenditures on goods and services and on transfers, since rather different factors enter in these two cases.

Growth of Per Capita Income Consider first the proposition that the efficient product mix between private and social goods changes as per capita income rises, and this change involves a rising share of social goods. If so, this would suggest that efficient budget policy calls for a rising ratio of government *purchases* (and civilian purchases in particular) to GNP, as plotted in Figure 8-1.

The rise in per capita income, seen in the historical context, records the development of the economy from an agricultural and low-income state to an industrial and high-income state. It would be surprising if in the course of this development, the output of social goods (assuming it to be determined efficiently) should remain constant. To put it differently, the demand for such goods can hardly be expected to have an income elasticity of zero. At the same time, there is no particular reason to expect that this elasticity should be just unity, thereby leaving the public purchase share unchanged as per capita income rises. As we have seen, this share has increased considerably. Including government purchases for civilian purposes only, the U.S. elasticity (ratio of percentage increase in per capita expenditures to percentage increase in per capita GNP) over recent decades has ranged between 1.0 and 2.0.

Beginning with the public provision of *consumer goods,* Ernst Engel pointed out over a century ago that the composition of consumer budgets changes as family income increases. A smaller share comes to be spent on certain goods, such as food or work clothing, and a larger share on others, such as fur coats. As average income increases, similar changes in the consumption pattern for the economy as a whole may be expected to occur. Is there any reason to foresee that in the dynamics of consumer budgeting, social consumer goods will exhibit a higher income elasticity than do private goods?

At first sight, the opposite may be expected. One thinks of government services as related to basic needs, such as safety, elementary education, and basic sanitation, which seem more like necessities than luxuries. Further consideration suggests, however, that there are other public services, such as higher education or improved health services, which move within reach as income rises above poverty levels. Also, there are items such as parks, marinas, high-speed highways, and space exploration, which (at present levels of income) are of the luxury type. Some of these reflect the rising tendency for government to render services which are complementary to luxury-type private goods. In all, speculation on the point does not lead to any clear-cut hypothesis about what might be expected: the government share in consumption may well rise and fall over successive phases of income growth.

The relationship is more discernible with regard to public provision for *capital goods*. In the earlier stages of economic development, a particular need exists for the creation of overhead capital, such as roads, harbors, and power installations. Many of these items are such that the benefits are largely external, or they require large amounts of capital the returns on which are spread over a long period of time, and thus do not lend themselves readily to private provision. Hence, there is reason to expect that the public share in the provision for capital goods should be larger at the earlier stages of development. As these basic facilities are built up and capital markets are developed, the path is cleared for capital formation of the manufacturing type to go into place and for industrial development in the private sector to occur. Accordingly, one would expect the public share in capital formation to decline over time.

The law of expenditure growth thus seems to be reversed. But again there are countervailing trends. Industrial development generates problems of its own, such as urban blight and congestion, which then call for a rising level of public investment. Such investment, being of a more or less remedial sort, aims at meeting social diseconomies generated by the private sector. Moreover, as income rises, an increasing share of investment is directed at "human investment" and the finance of education has been primarily a public function. On balance, it is again difficult to forecast what the trend should be, and chances are that periods of rising and of declining share may alternate.

Technical Change   Next we note that technological change may significantly affect the share of social goods in an efficient product mix. Technological change in particular has a major bearing on the development of the expenditure share. As technology changes, so do the processes of production and the product mix which it is efficient to produce. These changes in technology may be such that they increase or decrease the relative importance of goods whose benefits are largely external, and which must therefore be provided by government.

Consider the invention of the internal combustion engine and the resulting rise of the automobile industry. This development generated a vast increase in the demand for travel and for highways, making for a larger public sector operation than was called for in the horse-and-buggy and steam-engine eras. As we noted already, the consequence has been especially burdensome for state finances. Changes in weapons technology, similarly, greatly increased the cost of military outlays, an equipment-intensive military establishment being more costly than a manpower-intensive one, especially if soldiers are conscripted rather than paid going wages. Moreover, as obsolescence is speeded up by technological change, the cost of replacement increases.

Future technological changes are difficult to predict, but chances are that the course of space technology—e.g., whether space stations will prove to be social or private goods—will be among the most important factors in determining the share of public purchases over the next century.

Population Change   Population changes may also be a major determinant of the public expenditure share. Changes in the rate of population growth generate changes in age distribution, and this trend is reflected in expenditures for education as well as care for the aged.[4] The baby boom of the postwar period has resulted in a vastly higher school and college enrollment, thus placing a major burden on state and local finances. If the more recent population trends continue, education needs will give way to demands for housing facilities; and as the population bulge moves up further in the age scale, the major fiscal problem fifty or sixty years hence may well be that of support for the aged.

In addition to these conditions, the need for public services is influenced by factors such as population mobility, leading to the growth of new cities and resulting in demands for additional municipal facilities.

Relative Costs of Public Services   In explaining the rising ratio of expenditures to GNP, we may also note that the cost of public services has risen relative to that of private goods. This increase, especially in recent years, may have reflected differential rates of inflation. The more rapid rate of inflation in the price of inputs or goods purchased by the public sector resulted in an increase in the nominal expenditure-to-GNP ratio well ahead of that recorded by the deflated ratio. But differential responses to inflation are not the only factor. Over the longer run, the nature of publicly provided goods and services may be such as to render these components of GNP less receptive to technological progress than is the case for private goods, thus raising their cost relative to that of private goods.[5]

Public services will become more costly, but it does not follow that the share of public expenditure for GNP must rise. As the relative price of public goods rises, consumers will substitute private goods. Thus the outcome will depend on

---

[4] Leaving aside the effects of population growth on age structure and therefore on the public expenditure share, an additional and intriguing implication of population growth may be noted. Suppose that goods and services provided by government were indeed of the polar social-good type as discussed in Chapter 4, with consumption wholly nonrival. Population growth would then reduce the per capita cost of a given level of public services. Depending mainly on price elasticity of demand, this might increase or reduce outlays on public services and thereby affect the expenditure-to-GNP ratio.

[5] See D. F. Bradford, R. A. Malt, and W. E. Oates, "The Rising Cost of Local Public Services: Some Evidence and Reflections," *National Tax Journal,* June 1969, pp. 185–202; and W. Baumol, "Macroeconomics of Unbalanced Growth: The Anatomy of Urban Crisis," *American Economic Review,* June 1967, pp. 415–426.

the elasticities of demand for public and for private goods. Only if demand is inelastic can we predict that the public share will increase.

Urbanization   It has been suggested, finally, that the process of urbanization and resulting congestion has increased the need for infrastructure and for public services. Needs arise which call for public provision and which are not present in a rural setting where economic units are more self-contained.

Conclusion   All the factors just discussed suggest that there are good reasons for the public expenditure share to change over time. The desired mix of goods changes with rising income. Moreover, there are exogenous factors, such as technological and demographic changes, which have major bearing on what constitutes the "proper" level of public services relative to GNP. Although these factors do not add up to a clear presumption in favor of a rising share, considerations such as these show that much may be done to analyze expenditure growth in terms of economic change as distinct from malfunction of the political system.

Changing Scope of Transfers

The preceding discussion has related to the share of public purchases or the role of social goods in the efficient product mix. It remains to consider the role of transfers. Although transfers were relatively unimportant up to the thirties, since then about one-half the rise in the share of civilian expenditures in GNP has been due to the growth of transfers. The major factor in this development has been the rise of old-age insurance. This program developed, initially at least, not as a means of adjusting the distribution of income but rather as a means of providing old-age security on a self-financing basis. Since then, the system has moved away from this principle and now involves a considerable degree of redistribution. In addition, there are transfer programs—such as welfare payments—which are pointed directly at equalizing the size distribution of income. Moreover, distributional measures do not appear only in the transfer section of the expenditure budget but are also present in purchase programs aimed at the provision for social goods and services to low-income groups.

Nevertheless, is there reason to expect the role of redistributive transfers to increase with rising per capita income? As the level of per capita income rises, the need for, and scope of, redistributional measures may be affected in two ways.

For one thing, the need for redistribution (given society's views on the desirability of equality) depends on the prevailing state of distribution prior to adjustment. If income inequality decreases as per capita income rises, less extensive redistribution measures are needed. Actually, this change has not occurred to any considerable degree. The size distribution of income has been surprisingly stable over the years, with only a slight tendency toward greater equality.

For another thing, the case for redistribution may change as income rises, depending on how the objective of redistribution policy is defined. If the objective is to adjust family incomes so as to achieve a given relative income distribution, an increase in the average level of income leaves the need for redistribution unchanged. The situation differs if the objective is to set a tolerable minimum level determined in absolute terms, such as the cost of meeting minimum nutrition requirements. In this case, the need for redistribution falls as average income rises. But again, if the minimum level is defined as a function of average income, say one-third thereof, the need for redistribution once more remains unchanged as income rises. A reading of U.S. social philosophy would suggest that concern is with minimum levels rather than a generalized state of relative shares, but it also appears that the minimum is set in relation to the average rather than in absolute terms. Hence, one might expect the scope of redistribution (income transfers as a percentage of GNP) to remain constant.

This is illustrated in Table 8-5 for a simple three-family case. Policy I is to give an income to A (the poor family) equal to 50 percent of the average, to B (the middle family) equal to the average, and to leave C (the rich family) with 150 percent of the average. Policy II is to give A a minimum income of $2,500 as defined in absolute terms, while leaving the relative positions of B and C unchanged. Policy III provides A with an income equal to 50 percent of the average but again avoids redistribution between B and C. Thus the tax on B and C in policies II and III is assessed on a proportional basis. In the lower part of the table, the same policies are repeated for a higher level of earnings. We see that the scope of redistribution (the level of transfers in relation to the level of total earnings) does not change for policies I and III but declines for II as we move from the low-income to the high-income case.

A further change in the appropriate scope of redistribution may result from demographic factors. A declining rate of population growth is reflected in an aging population, thus calling for increased provision for the aged. But, even though the growth of old-age security payments (OASI) in the United States began in a phase of aging population, it was followed by two decades of accelerated population

TABLE 8-5
Redistribution Policies*

	FAMILY			TRANSFER BUDGET	
	A	B	C	Total	As Percentage of Earnings
Low level					
Earnings	1,000	4,000	10,000		
Transfers (+) and taxes (−)					
Policy I	+ 1,500	+ 1,000	− 2,500	2,500	16.6
Policy II	+ 1,500	− 428	− 1,072	1,500	10.0
Policy III	+ 1,500	− 428	− 1,072	1,500	10.0
High level					
Earnings	3,000	12,000	30,000		
Transfers (+) and taxes (−)					
Policy I	+ 4,500	+ 3,000	− 7,500	7,500	16.6
Policy II	0	0	0	0	0
Policy III	+ 4,500	− 1,284	− 3,216	4,500	10.0

*For explanation, see text.

growth. Now that the rate of population growth is on the decline, the turn of the twentieth century will bring a sharp increase in the ratio of retired to working-age population and with it a rise in the ratio of old-age benefit payments to GNP.[6]

Although these factors are of interest, they do not adequately explain the phenomenon of sharply rising welfare and transfer payments both in the United States and in other countries. This development, it appears, must be explained primarily in terms of social and political change, including growing political pressures for "forced" redistribution ("taking") as well as use of the budgetary mechanism in providing for voluntary or semivoluntary redistributional measures ("giving").[7]

Availability of Tax Handles

So far, we have looked primarily at changing needs for public expenditures as the economy develops. Parallel to that, we also find a changing ability to finance such expenditures. In the typical low-income economy, it is much more difficult to impose and collect taxes than in the advanced economy. Not only are the skills and facilities of tax administration less developed, but the structure of the economy is such that it affords fewer and less adequate "handles" on which to attach taxes. The features of economic organization which lend themselves to income taxation are absent. Income is typically derived from self-employment and such wage income as exists is typically paid by small establishments. This makes income taxation much more difficult than in the modern economy, where earned income is largely in the form of wages and salaries and people work in large-scale establishments which readily permit the withholding of income taxes. To make matters worse for the less-developed countries (and this is relevant for profit as well as income taxation), accounting practices are not adequately developed to permit effective determination of taxable income and efficient auditing procedures.

Nor are matters much better with regard to sales taxation. Retail taxes are made difficult by the existence of small and nonpermanent retail outlets, and even excises at the producer level are not readily applied in a situation where the market is divided among many small suppliers. One feasible source of revenue collection is imports and exports, which explains why the tax and expenditure ratio to GNP among low-income economies with high trade involvement is usually larger than in economies which do not have this convenient tax handle.

These difficulties do not exist, or exist to a much smaller degree, in highly developed countries, where effective income, profit, and sales taxation is feasible. In spite of the fact that taxation in highly developed countries must adapt itself to an extremely complex financial and industrial structure, these complications can usually be solved, provided that there is the necessary political determination to deal with them. The rise of the income tax to its dominant position would never have been possible without the development of the modern economy with its pecuniary institutions and forms of organization.[8] The relative absence of adequate tax handles in low-income countries, in turn, is a major force in explaining why

---

[6] See p. 55.

[7] See p. 195.

[8] For a development of this theme see Joseph A. Schumpeter, "The Crisis of the Tax State," *International Economic Papers*, No. 4, New York: Macmillan, 1954, p. 538.

their tax-GNP ratios are lower, and this quite apart from sociological or cultural characteristics which are said to create an aversion to tax collection in low-income countries.

Threshold Effects and War Finance

A further hypothesis regarding the rising ratio of expenditures to GNP runs as follows: Voters have a basic resistance to raising taxes, but after taxes have been increased, they grow to accept them and do not insist on reducing them to their former level. National emergencies, particularly war, may cause a temporary but compelling increase in the need for public expenditures, for which voters are willing to overcome the old "tax threshold" and to accept an increase in the level of taxation which they would otherwise resist. After the emergency has passed, they are willing to retain the new level of taxation, or in any case a level substantially above that tolerated previously. Hence, new civilian public expenditures can be accommodated which otherwise would not have been provided for.

This fact is of particular importance in connection with war finance. War expenditures first displace private outlays and then are displaced by nonemergency public outlays. Since the aftermath of war is typically accompanied by social upheaval and change, the revenue windfall coincides with a change in preferences and political powers which raise the effectively desired level of civilian public expenditures. The resulting increase is thus attributable to both social and political change on one side and the availability of excess revenue at prevailing rates of tax on the other.[9]

Testing this theory for the United States, we find the pattern shown in Table 8-6. We note that the overall expenditure ratio rose sharply during both world wars and fell off sharply thereafter. We also note that the ratio for defense-related expenditures remains above prewar levels. All these facts are in line with the threshold hypothesis. However, the pattern of civilian expenditures may also be taken to reflect the normal rise of the expenditure ratio as shown in Figure 8-1, to be interrupted only by war periods. The threshold theory, while interesting, cannot be taken to give a conclusive explanation of the growth of the public expenditure ratio, at least in the United States. The table also shows that the Vietnam war did not result in a sharp increase in the expenditure ratio comparable to that of previous wars. Indeed, there was no significant wartime increase in the level of taxation.

Political and Social Factors

It remains to note the importance of political and social change as determinants of expenditure growth. Over the past century, there have been vast changes in social philosophy as well as shifts in the balance of political power among various sectors of the population. They all have had a deep effect not only on what individuals consider to be the desirable size of the public sector, but also on the force with which the views of various groups make themselves felt in the political decision process.

[9] This approach is developed in Alan T. Peacock and Jack Wiseman, *The Growth of Public Expenditures in the United Kingdom,* Princeton, N.J.: National Bureau of Economic Research, Princeton University, 1961.

TABLE 8-6
United States Public Expenditures in War Years*
(As Percentage of GNP; All Levels of Government)

	Fiscal Year	Total	Defense-related	Civilian
	1913	8.0	1.1	6.9
World War I	1919	29.4	17.7	11.7
	1922	12.1	1.9	10.2
	1938	19.1	1.8	17.3
World War II	1945	46.1	39.2	6.9
	1948	22.3	7.4	14.9
Korean War	1953	30.9	15.4	15.5
	1955	29.1	11.9	17.2
	1965	27.6	8.5	19.1
Vietnam war	1969	34.3	9.9	24.4
	1971	33.1	8.1	25.0
	1987	34.4	6.7	27.7

*Military includes defense expenditures and veterans' benefits and services. Figures are based on budget and census rather than national income accounts data.
Sources: 1913–1969: *Facts and Figures on Government Finance,* 16th ed., New York: Tax Foundation, 1971. 1971: Based on *Budget of the United States Government, Fiscal Year 1974.* 1987: See Table 8-1.

Quite possibly, the effect of these developments—particularly the rise of transfer payments as a by-product of the incipient welfare state—outweighed factors of fiscal bias as were noted in the preceding chapter. But more likely, they combined with these factors in shaping the actual course of events. Whatever the influence of these particular forces, it is evident that their combined result was a substantial rise in the share of the public sector in GNP.

E. SUMMARY

The public sector share in total economic activity has risen over the years.

1. The growth rate of public expenditures differs, depending on how it is viewed, i.e., in dollar terms, in real terms, on a per capita basis, or as a percentage of GNP.

2. Total public expenditures as a percentage of GNP have shown a more or less steady upward trend since the end of the nineteenth century, and especially over the past forty years.

3. This process applies not only to public expenditures as a whole but also to the defense and nondefense components separately.

4. The increase in the civilian expenditure share has been fueled largely by the rise of social security and welfare programs.

5. The increase in the expenditure-to-GNP ratio has leveled off in the 1970s and ceased in the 1980s. Whereas expansion of civilian expenditures had been the driving force in the 1960s and 1970s, defense expenditures assumed this role in the 1980s.

6. The U.S. ratio of public expenditures to GNP is below that of most West European countries.

Turning to the causes of expenditure growth, we note various factors other than those examined in the preceding chapter:

7. Consumer demand for public services may be income-elastic, so that public services are in the nature of luxury goods, claiming a rising proportion of expenditure as per capita income increases.

8. Depending on the state of a country's economic development, the structure of capital formation may be such as to require more or less public investment.

9. Demography and technology have been major factors in the changing public expenditure share.

10. Changing attitudes, social structures, and political forces may have been behind the rising share of transfers and redistribution-oriented programs.

11. The occurrence of periods of war finance, with a sharp rise in the budget share for war purposes, may have served to raise the threshold of what are considered acceptable levels of taxation and subsequent civilian outlays.

FURTHER READINGS

Beck, Morris: *Government Spending: Trends and Issues,* New York: Praeger, 1981.

Borcherding, T. E.: "One Hundred Years of Public Spending, 1870–1970," in T. E. Borcherding (ed.): *Budgets and Bureaucrats,* Durham, N.C.: Duke University, 1977.

Kendrick, M. S.: *A Century and a Half of Federal Expenditures,* Occasional Papers 48, New York: National Bureau of Economic Research, 1955.

Wagner, A.: "Three Extracts on Public Finance," in Richard A. Musgrave and Alan Peacock (eds.): *Classics in the Theory of Public Finance,* New York: Macmillan, 1958, pp. 1–16.

Chapter 9

Expenditure Evaluation: Principles*

A. **Decision Rules:** *Divisible Projects; Lumpy Projects; Summary.* B. **Fundamentals of Project Evaluation:** *Consumer Surplus; Net Benefit of Projects.* C. **Types of Benefits and Costs:** *Real versus Pecuniary; Types of Real Benefits.* D. **Measurement of Benefits and Costs:** *Valuation of Intangible Items; Shadow Pricing of Market Items; Cost Effectiveness Analysis.* E. **Assigning Weights in Project Selection:** *Multiple Objectives; Sectoral Allocation of Police.* F. **Efficiency and Equity Once More:** *When Are Projects Efficient?; Distributional Considerations.* G. **Discounting and the Cost of Capital:** *Importance of Discounting; Choice of Discount Rate: (1) Private Rate; Choice of Discount Rate: (2) Social Rate; Opportunity Cost of Capital; Further Problems; Current Practice.* H. **Risk and Economic Change:** *Risk; Dynamic Aspects.* I. **Summary.**

In our earlier discussion of social goods, we examined how provision for such goods may be determined, how it might be related to consumer choice, and how the political process enters in solving the problem. We now turn to a more limited, if more practical, view of expenditure determination.

*Reader's Guide to Chapter 9: Here we present the theoretical framework of cost-benefit analysis, an aspect of public finance on which there has been much lively discussion since the sixties. Eminently practical in application, it nevertheless involves some knotty theoretical problems. As discussed in Section G, they arise especially in connection with discounting.

Sound expenditure decisions, whether made by the legislator or the executive, require detailed information regarding the merits of alternative projects. The technician can perform an important service in providing this information. Our task is to explore the general methodology which has been developed to make these decisions.

In recent years this analysis has become one of the most lively branches of fiscal economics at both the practical and the analytical levels. Actually, it has a long history, beginning with the evaluation of federal expenditures in the field of navigation undertaken by the Corps of Engineers. The Flood Control Act of 1936 lent further impetus to cost-benefit analysis in the realm of water resource projects, and in 1950 general principles and rules were set out by an interagency committee concerned with the evaluation of various river basin projects.[1] Following a period of rapidly developing interest and research in cost-benefit analysis, especially in the Department of Defense, a planning-programming-budgeting (PPB) system which called for application of evaluation procedures was introduced in 1965 to apply to all federal departments. Although this early enthusiasm has since abated, these procedures remain of importance. Along with applications of cost-benefit analysis to particular situations, they will be examined in the next chapter. First, the underlying principles will be considered.

A. DECISION RULES

Project evaluation, like all issues in allocation economics, involves determination of the ways in which the most efficient use can be made of scarce resources. In its simplest form, the issue is how to determine the *composition* of the budget of a given size or how to allocate a total of given funds among alternative projects. There is also the more complex question of determining the appropriate *size* of the budget. Further complications arise when projects are not divisible but in lumpy form. In taking a first look at these various situations, we assume that benefits and costs are known. The identification and measurement of costs and benefits are considered in later sections of this chapter.

Divisible Projects

We begin with a setting in which all projects are finely divisible, i.e., may be increased or decreased by small amounts. As will be noted later, this is not a very realistic assumption, but it permits us to bring out the basic rationale of project selection.

Budget Size Fixed Suppose that the budget director is to advise the legislature—either Congress or a city council—how best to allocate a given sum, say $1 billion, between two expenditure projects, X and Y. The problem may be likened to that of the head of a consumer household who must allocate the family budget. First, the director must determine the cost C involved in providing each service and

---

[1] Inter-Agency River Basin Committee (Subcommittee on Costs and Budgets), *Proposed Practices for Economic Analysis of River Basin Projects,* Washington, D.C., Government Printing Office, 1950.

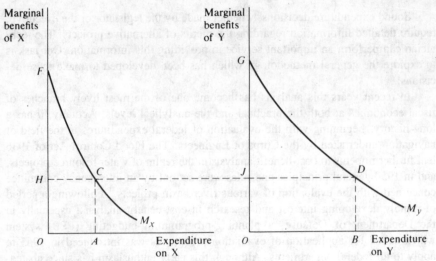

FIGURE 9-1   Expenditure allocation with fixed budget.

the benefit B to be derived therefrom. Then outlays must be allocated between X and Y so as to derive the greatest total benefit from the budget, i.e., to maximize the sum of net benefits (ΣNB) or the excess of total benefits over costs $\Sigma(B - C)$. With ΣC given by the size of the budget, the task is simply to maximize ΣB.

This is shown in Figure 9-1, where the M_x and M_y schedules show the value of the marginal benefit (additions to total benefits) derived from spending successive dollars on X and Y. The opportunity cost of spending a dollar on X is the loss of benefits due to not spending it on Y. Total expenditures should therefore be distributed between X and Y so that the benefit derived from spending the last dollar on X will equate that derived from spending the last dollar on Y. Thus OA is spent on X and OB on Y such that $AC = BD$, and $OA + OB$ equals total permissible outlays. By equating the benefits derived from the marginal dollars on X and Y, we maximize the sum of total benefits derived from X (as measured by the area $OFCA$) and from Y (as measured by the area $OGDB$).

Budget Size Variable   A more global view of budgeting indicates that the problem is not simply one of dividing up a budget of given size but also one of determining the size of the budget itself. The government must thereby decide how resources are to be divided between private and public use. We must therefore drop the assumption of a fixed budget and reconsider project choices along with determination of total budget outlays. Within the fixed budget, the opportunity cost of pursuing one public project consists of the benefit lost by not pursuing another public project. But in the open budget the opportunity cost of public projects must be redefined as the lost benefits from private projects which are forgone because resources are transferred to public use.

The task now is to maximize $\Sigma(B - C)$, including benefits and costs of both public and private projects. This condition is met by equating marginal benefits for

TABLE 9-1
Project Choice with Lumpy Projects and Fixed Budget

Project	Costs* C	Benefits B	Net Benefits B − C	B/C	B/C Ranking
I	200	400	200	2.0	2
II	145	175	30	1.2	5
III	80	104	24	1.3	4
IV	50	125	75	2.5	1
V	300	420	120	1.4	3
VI	305	330	25	1.1	6
VII	125	100	− 25	0.8	7

*Costs, benefits, and net benefits are in thousands of dollars.

the last dollar spent on alternative public and private projects. Public projects are expanded and private projects are restricted until the benefit from the last dollar spent in either sector is the same. Interpreting X as "the" public project and Y as "the" private project, we find that the solution of Figure 9-1 again applies. Given perfect markets, the marginal benefit from spending $1 in the private sector or *BD* equals $1, and the same must hold on the public side. Thus public expenditures are extended until the last dollar spent yields a dollar's worth of benefits.

Lumpy Projects

We have assumed so far that expenditures may be divided finely between projects X and Y, so that benefits may be equated for the marginal dollar spent on each. Where we deal with the allocation of funds between broad expenditure categories, this marginal approach is more or less applicable. But when it comes to specific allocation within departments, choices must be made among particular projects which are indivisible, involve lump-sum amounts, or are not smoothly expandable. If a choice has to be made between a road connecting cities X and Y and another connecting X and Z, where the X to Y distance is twice the X to Z distance, no marginal adjustment is possible.[2]

Budget Size Fixed We begin once more with the fixed budget case. Suppose that we have $700,000 to spend, say, on alternative highway projects, and that we may choose among projects I to VII, as shown in Table 9-1. The cost of each project is measured by the dollar amount required. The benefit valuation gives the total benefit for each project. Returning to Figure 9-1, we find that the total benefit for a project, involving cost *OA*, corresponds to the area *OACF*.

In dealing with this case, let us consider various decision rules. Let rule 1 require us to rank projects in line with their benefit-cost ratio and move down the

---

[2] This situation contrasts with one involving the building of, say, a penetration road into an undeveloped area, which may be expanded by small increments.

line until inclusion of a further project would exceed the budget constraint.[3] We then choose projects IV, I, V, and III. Total cost is $630,000, benefits are $1,049,000, net benefits equal $419,000, and $70,000 of the available budget is left. As an alternative, let rule 2 call for that mix of projects which yields the largest net benefit. By trying various combinations, we find that net benefits are maximized by choosing IV, I, V, and II. Here total cost is $695,000, benefits are $1,120,000, and net benefits equal $425,000. An amount of $50,000 remains unspent. Rule 3, finally, might be to minimize the amount left over, subject only to the constraint that projects must have a benefit-cost ratio in excess of 1. In this case, the choice is for I, II, IV, and VI, with a cost of $700,000, benefits of $1,030,000, and net benefits of $313,000. Nothing is left over.

Comparing the merits of the three rules, we find it is evident that both 1 and 2 are superior to 3, since both buy more benefits at a smaller cost. The choice between 1 and 2 is more difficult. Rule 1 is reasonable, because it calls for selection of projects which yield the highest return per dollar of the constrained resource, the available budget. Rule 2 offends this principle by choosing project II over III. Yet by moving from rule 1 to rule 2, additional benefits of $71,000 are bought at an additional cost of $65,000. Net benefits rise by $6,000, and even though the *marginal* benefit-cost ratio is only 1.09, this may still be considered a paying proposition. Rule 2 will clearly be preferred if we interpret the fixed budget case rigidly so as to consider turned-back funds as worthless. Taking a broader view and allowing for a possible transfer to another budget, we note that rule 2 will be superior only if other budgets cannot offer projects with a benefit-cost ratio above 1.09.

Budget Size Variable If there is no fixed limit to the budget size, the problem is once more one of weighing public against private uses of resources. Since we are now dealing with lumpy projects, this can no longer be done by balancing the benefits derived from marginal outlays on both uses. We now proceed by the rule that a public project is worth undertaking so long as the benefits derived therefrom exceed its costs. The justification for the rule is that the cost of spending n dollars in the public sector is the loss of n dollars of benefits, a loss which results from not spending n dollars in the private sector. The rule may be stated by saying that a project should be undertaken so long as $(B - C) > 0$.

Summary

The appropriate decision rules for selection of projects thus differ, depending on whether the budget is variable or fixed and whether the projects are divisible or not. The following rules apply:

---

[3] It has also been noted that the use of cost-benefit *ratios* may lead to arbitrary results where it is uncertain whether certain consequences should be viewed as reducing benefits or as adding to cost. This difficulty does not arise when computing net benefits by deducting costs from gross benefits. Where B/C ratios are used, arbitrariness should be avoided by including only the constrained resource (the dollar cost) in the denominator, with all other outcomes included in the definition of benefits. In evaluating projects, it is the return on this constrained resource that must be compared.

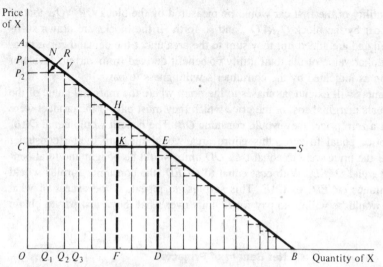

FIGURE 9-2 Project benefit and consumer surplus.

    1. *Fixed budget, divisible projects:* Distribute funds among projects so that marginal benefits are equal.

    2. *Variable budget, divisible projects:* Extend all projects until the marginal benefits equal 1, i.e., the net benefit becomes zero.

    3. *Fixed budget, lumpy projects:* Choose the project mix that maximizes net benefits, subject to qualifications noted above.

    4. *Variable budget, lumpy projects:* Choose all projects with positive net benefits.

In practice, the combination of lumpy projects and limited budgets is the most typical setting, so that rule 3 should apply. To establish the proper rank order, this means that all possible projects should be considered and compared. More likely than not, comparison will be more limited and projects will be chosen simply because the B/C ratio is above 1.

B. FUNDAMENTALS OF PROJECT EVALUATION

The problem of project evaluation is linked closely to that of consumer surplus and the change therein.

Consumer Surplus

This linkage is shown in Figure 9-2.[4] Suppose that the demand curve for a given product, say automobiles, is given by *AB*. The demand curve shows the maximum amounts which consumers are willing to pay for successive automobiles. Thus they would be willing to pay a price of P_1 for the first car, of P_2 for the second, and so

---

    [4] Note that Figure 9-2 differs from Figure 9-1. Whereas Figure 9-1 related marginal product benefits to expenditures, Figure 9-2 relates price (or marginal benefits) to quantity bought.

forth. The utility of the first car would be measured by the block OP_1NQ_1, that of the second car by the block Q_1RVQ_2, and so forth. If the blocks are drawn sufficiently small and are added up, they sum to the area under the demand curve measuring the dollar value of the total utility or benefit derived from various levels of consumption as indicated by the consumer's willingness to pay.

Consumers will extend purchases to the point where the marginal value of the last unit equals marginal cost or the price which they must pay. If the product were available at a zero price, they would consume OB. The benefit would equal OAB, and with price equal to zero, this entire area would measure their "consumer surplus." If the price were to equal OC, OD units would be bought and total benefits would equal $OAED$. With cost equal to $OCED$, the consumer surplus would be $OAED$ minus $OCED$, or CAE. This surplus, to repeat, is the excess of what consumers would be willing to pay for D units over what they must pay to obtain them.[5]

Net Benefit of Projects

We can now apply the concept of consumer surplus to measuring the benefit derived from a public project. The demand for the services of the project is again given by AB, and the project is introduced with a unit cost of OC. Returning to the tabulation of benefits and costs in Table 9-1, suppose that we have an indivisible project of size OF. Total benefits as recorded in the table correspond to area $OAHF$, with AB reflecting the vertically added "demand curves" of the consumers.[6] Total costs correspond to area $OCKF$, and net benefits, equal to consumer surplus, correspond to $CAHK$. Project choice in the fixed budget maximizes the sum of these consumer surplus areas. For divisible projects, provision should be carried to OD, the point where marginal evaluation equals marginal cost, i.e., the marginal gain in consumer surplus becomes zero and total surplus, equal to CAE, is maximized.

---

[5] Two complications to be allowed for in a more detailed analysis should be noted.

    a. If AB in Figure 9-2 reflects the consumer demand curve prior to introduction of the project, the triangle CAE somewhat overstates the gain in consumer surplus which results. This is the case because the increase in quantity from O to OD, as determined by moving along AB, reflects two responses. The reduction in price (1) induces the consumer to substitute cars for other products, even if his real income is unchanged. But the reduction in price also (2) results in an increase in the consumer's real income, thus inducing him to buy more cars. Since our measure of consumer surplus should reflect 1 only, more precise measurement calls for a "compensated" demand curve in which real income is held constant. This compensated demand curve swivels from A to the left of B, thus resulting in a smaller quantity and a reduced consumer surplus.

    b. Since the public service diverts demand from other products, does not this result in a loss of consumer surplus somewhere else in the system, and should not this loss be offset against the gain in consumer surplus from the service? The answer is no. Change in consumer surplus in "secondary markets" must be accounted for only to the extent that it reflects a change in cost. If marginal cost in the secondary market is constant, a leftward shift in the demand curve for the product does not call for a correction, since it is already allowed for in the way in which the demand curve for the service is derived.

[6] See p. 45.

C.   TYPES OF BENEFITS AND COSTS

In identifying various types of benefits and costs, these major categories may be distinguished:

Benefits and costs may be *real* or *pecuniary*
Real benefits and costs may be:
  Direct or *indirect*
  Tangible or *intangible*
  Final or *intermediate*
  Inside or *outside*

Illustrations of various types of benefits and costs are given in Table 9-2.

TABLE 9-2
Illustrations of Project Benefits and Costs*

		Benefits	Costs
		IRRIGATION PROJECT	
Real			
Direct	tangible	Increased farm output	Cost of pipes
	intangible	Beautification of area	Loss of wilderness
Indirect	tangible	Reduced soil erosion	Diversion of water
	intangible	Preservation of rural society	Destruction of wildlife
Pecuniary		Higher real income of farm equipment industry	
		MOON SHOT PROJECT	
Real			
Direct	tangible	As yet unknown	Cost of inputs
	intangible	Joy of exploration	Pollution of universe
Indirect	tangible	Technical progress generated	
	intangible	Gain in world prestige	
Pecuniary		Relative increase in land values at Cape Kennedy	
		EDUCATION PROJECT	
Real			
Direct	tangible	Increased future earnings	Cost of teachers' salaries, cost of buildings and books
	intangible	Enriched life	Forgone leisure time
Indirect	tangible	Reduced costs of crime prevention	
	intangible	More intelligent electorate	
Pecuniary		Relative increase in teachers' incomes	

*The benefits and costs noted in the table are merely illustrative for each project and not intended to be comprehensive.

Real versus Pecuniary

The most important distinction is that between real and pecuniary aspects. Real benefits are the benefits derived by the final consumers of the public project. They reflect an addition to the community's welfare, to be balanced against the real cost of resource withdrawal from other uses. Pecuniary benefits and costs come about because of changes in relative prices which occur as the economy adjusts itself to the provision of the public service and the pattern of resource demand changes. As a result, gains or losses accrue to some individuals but are offet by losses or gains which are experienced by others. They do not reflect net gains or costs to society as a whole.

As labor is hired and a road is constructed, the wage rates for construction workers may rise because the relative scarcity of their skills is increased. At the same time, increased taxes needed to pay for the road may result in reduced amounts for other services, and a loss of income elsewhere in the system. Such pecuniary changes do not reflect net gains or losses to society because they are matched by offsetting losses or gains. They must be distinguished from real costs and benefits which do. The latter must be allowed for and pecuniary changes should not enter into the evaluation. Such at least is the case unless distributional weights are to be attached to the particular gains or losses which accrue to various individuals, or unless such changes occur outside the jurisdiction within which the project is evaluated.

Types of Real Benefits

As noted before, all real benefits should be allowed for in cost-benefit analysis, but various types of benefits may be distinguished.

Direct versus Indirect Real benefits and costs may be direct or indirect or, which is the same, primary or secondary. Direct benefits and costs are those related closely to the main project objective, whereas indirect benefits are in the nature of by-products. This distinction has a common-sense meaning but cannot be defined rigorously. The most useful interpretation is in terms of legislative intent. Thus, a river development program may have flood control as its immediate objective but may also have important bearing on the supply of power, on irrigation, or on soil erosion in adjacent areas. Development of defense technology, while aimed primarily at increased defense capacity, may have important side-effects on improving technology in the private sector. The space program may be undertaken primarily to explore the stars, but it may also lead to gains in defense technology or technological improvements in the automobile industry. An education program may be directed primarily at raising the earning power of the student but it may also reduce the need to combat delinquency. In all these cases, indirect or secondary results may be distinguished from the direct or primary objective. Obviously, the former should be included along with the latter in assessing project benefits. Tracing of the more indirect benefits may be difficult, but they should be included.

Tangible versus Intangible The term "tangible" is applied to benefits and costs which can be valued in the market, whereas others which cannot are referred to as "intangible." Social goods and social costs, as shown in Chapter 4, typically fall into the category of intangible. Thus, the beautification of an area which may result from an irrigation project is an intangible benefit, whereas the increased farm output is tangible. Moreover, intangible features may arise with regard to certain benefits or costs, such as health or loss of life which are private in nature but which cannot be readily assessed in money terms. Even though intangible costs and benefits are more difficult to measure, they should nevertheless be included in the analysis.

Intermediate versus Final Another significant distinction is between projects which furnish benefits to consumers directly (since they involve the provision of final goods) and projects which enter into the production of other goods and are thus of an intermediate type. A particular project may in fact provide for both types of goods. Thus weather forecasts may be considered as a consumer good for those who plan an outing, as well as an intermediate good in servicing aviation.

Inside versus Outside A final distinction is between benefits and costs which accrue inside the jurisdiction in which the project is undertaken and others which accrue outside. Thus, flood-control measures undertaken on the Connecticut River by Vermont may not only be helpful in Vermont but also prevent floods farther down in the state of Connecticut. The former benefits are internal and the latter are external. They constitute a "spillover" from one jurisdiction to another. Both benefits should be included in assessing the project, but interstate cooperation is needed to do so. This is a matter which we will pursue further when dealing with the economics of fiscal federalism.[7]

D. MEASUREMENT OF BENEFITS AND COSTS

In Section A the principle of project selection was introduced, based on the simplifying assumption that the dollar value of benefits and costs is known. We must now take a more careful look at the problem of measurement. We consider for the time being the valuation of costs and benefits "when they occur,"[8] leaving the question of their valuation over time by discounting for later consideration. The question of measurement would be simple if all values could be observed in terms of market prices. But such is not the case. Costs and benefits are frequently in intangible form, and even where market prices are observable these may be in need of adjustment because markets are not perfect and distortions must be allowed for.

Valuation of Intangible Items

We begin with the valuation of intangible (nonmarket) items, a problem which must be solved for many public projects before cost-benefit analysis can be applied to them.

---

[7] See p. 452.
[8] See R. Layard (ed.): *Cost-Benefit Analysis*, Baltimore: Penguin, 1972, p. 117.

Social Benefits and Costs   Project benefits may be essentially intangible, as with the case of national defense, or both tangible and intangible benefits may result. Thus, education yields intangible benefits via cultural enrichment and improved functioning of the democratic process. At the same time, there is a tangible benefit of increased earning power. Similarly, costs may be partly tangible (e.g., the cost of the resource input into the construction of a superhighway) and partly intangible (e.g., the resulting damage to the beauty of a wilderness area).

Wherever intangible benefits and costs are involved, measurement takes us back to the central problem of social-good evaluation. The value of such benefits and costs cannot be derived readily from market prices, and a political process is needed to determine them. Voters must decide how much they value clean air or water or the protection afforded by an addition to national defense. Cost-benefit analysis is no substitute for this process; it is only a way of choosing among projects *after* the value of a benefit has been determined. Thus it is most easily applied in those areas where benefits are tangible and there is least need for public provision to begin with.

Intangible Private Benefits or Costs   Related problems arise in connection with benefits and costs which are private in nature (the problem not being one of externalities) but which do not lend themselves to market evaluation. If the government undertakes a cancer research project with resulting reduction in suffering, how can the benefits be valued? How should one evaluate the cost of death and injury which result from highway accidents? What about the benefits of crime prevention? The benefits and costs of some of the most important public projects may encounter these more or less insoluble difficulties of evaluation. Yet they must be faced before the mechanisms of benefit-cost analysis can be applied.

In certain cases, indirect valuation methods of a more or less satisfactory nature may be applied to these intangible items and economists have shown considerable ingenuity in developing such procedures. This is illustrated by the following cases:

     1. Highways enter as an intermediate good in the services of the trucking industry. As the highway is improved, the cost of trucking falls and so should the prices charged by the trucking firms. The reduced charge to truck users may then serve as a basis for estimating the capital value of the road.

     2. Highway improvement, similarly, will reduce travel costs for individuals, and time saved thereby offers a basis on which to measure the benefit obtained. The personal value of time, in turn, may be derived by observing the differential prices paid for under systems of transportation involving differences in travel time.[9]

---

[9] Let the cost per trip by the faster mode of transportation, A, be $C_A = a_A + bT_A + M_A$, and for the slower mode, B, be

$C_B = a_B + bT_B + M_B$,

where a = inherent pleasure (displeasure) of travel

    T = time per trip

    b = value of time

    M = other travel costs per trip

Then the cost differential between the two modes is $\Delta C = (a_A - a_B) + b\Delta T + \Delta M$.

It is further postulated that the relative probability P_A of using the A rather than the B mode is a function of the cost differential, or

$$\frac{P_A}{1 - P_A} = f(\Delta C) = f(a + b\Delta T + \Delta M)$$

3. A school program aimed at reducing absenteeism will be reflected in reduced delinquency and thus save costs of law enforcement. Other gains may be measured in terms of increased earnings due to improved training.

4. A medical program may result in reducing the death rate from a particular disease. The resulting benefit (or at least part thereof) may be measured by the loss of earnings which is avoided thereby.

5. The value of a park may be measured by the travel-related and other costs which visitors are willing to undergo.[10]

6. The value of a noise-abatement program for aircraft may be measured by the observed increase in property values adjoining airports.

In these and other forms, "hedonistic prices" may be observed and costs foregone may be observed and used to approximate the market value of apparently intangible project benefits.

Shadow Pricing of Market Items

Returning to projects whose tangible costs and benefits are recorded directly in the market via sale or purchase, no such difficulties arise, provided we deal with competitive markets. In this case, the tangible benefit is measured by the price which the public service fetches in the market, or the price at which a similar service is purchased by consumers from private suppliers. The cost is similarly measured by the price which the government must pay for the product (if the government purchases it from private firms) or by the cost which it must incur (the factor prices which it must pay) if it undertakes the production itself. The cost thus determined will measure the opportunity cost incurred in forgoing the alternative private use of resources.

Monopoly Matters are more difficult, however, in the case of imperfect markets. Here market prices of outputs do not reflect true resource costs and adjustments are needed. Such adjusted values are referred to as "shadow prices." Thus, rental incomes or monopoly profits should not be counted. Suppose that the market cost of a given product is $1 million but that in a competitive market it would have cost only $900,000, equal to the marginal resource cost of its production. The social opportunity cost in this case is $900,000, not $1 million, even though the government pays the higher price. The profit of $100,000 is a pecuniary gain to the monopolist, but not a real resource cost to society.[11]

A problem of shadow pricing may also arise in competitive markets where the transfer of a factor to public use raises its price in private use, and the question arises about the price (before or after reduction in private activity) at which the opportunity cost should be measured. A midway value offers a reasonable approximation to the proper result.

Since P_A, ΔT, and ΔM are all observable, the equation may be estimated in either a linear or nonlinear regression form and a value for the parameter b (the value of time) may thereby be derived.

[10] See p. 177 and Pearce, D. W. (ed.): *The Valuation of Social Cost*, London: Allen and Unwin, 1978.

[11] More precisely, the adjusted price should be applied only to the *addition* to output which results in response to the government purchase. To the extent that the public purchase merely displaces private purchases, units are valued properly in terms of their market price as this reflects consumer evaluation. See following note.

Taxes A further need for adjustment arises in connection with taxes. If the government purchases inputs needed in the construction of a project, the market price may include sales or excise taxes. This tax component of the price does not reflect a social cost (being merely a transfer from purchasers to the government) and should therefore be disallowed in computing the cost of the project.[12] Another major tax-related problem arises in determining the social opportunity cost of capital and, as we will see in the discussion of discounting, the appropriate treatment of taxes on capital income. Once more, shadow pricing is needed to correct for the tax.

Unemployed Resources Another aspect of shadow pricing relates to the costing of otherwise unemployed resources. The cost to be accounted for in public resource use is the lost opportunity for putting these resources to alternative uses, whether they are other public projects (in the fixed budget context) or private projects (in the open budget setting). This reasoning breaks down if the resources are otherwise unemployed and the opportunity cost is zero. Thus, it might be argued that public works are costless in a period of unemployment or may even be beneficial beyond their own value in that they create additional employment via multiplier effects.

This argument is correct as far as it goes. Using unemployed resources poorly may indeed be better than not using them at all. But it is not as good as using them for a superior purpose. Unless there are political constraints which permit only one use, cost-benefit analysis should apply the concept of opportunity cost even where resources are unemployed. Otherwise their employment in a superior alternative is impeded.

But though unemployment is no excuse for failing to evaluate the merits of alternative uses, employment effects of particular projects become relevant to benefit evaluation if alternative policies to deal with unemployment are not available. The resulting gain in employment is then an additional benefit, or the opportunity cost of labor is zero. Project A may be preferred to project B even though its intrinsic merit is less, provided that the superior effect on employment outweighs the latter shortfall. Thus, building a road in location X may be superior to doing so in location Y if X has a high unemployment rate while Y does not, even though benefit calculus in the absence of employment effects would point to Y. Such is the case provided that alternative ways of dealing with unemployment in X are not available. This may be so because unemployment is of a regional nature and not amenable to reduction by stabilization policy on a national scale. If alternative approaches, such as relocation, are available, cost-benefit analysis should compare policy packages, e.g., road construction in Y plus relocation of manpower from X, with road construction in X. To put it differently, efficient policy planning has to

---

[12] Again the shadow price should be applied only to the extent that the project purchase results in increased output but not to the extent that it reflects a diversion from private use. In the former case, the tax does not reflect a social cost. In the latter, the social opportunity cost is measured properly by the gross price (including tax) which consumers pay. More precisely, the tax should be disallowed where the government purchase results in an addition to output, while the gross price should be charged where a replacement of output is involved.

be on a comprehensive basis and cannot be limited to an isolated consideration of specific policy tools or projects.

Developing Economies The problem of shadow pricing assumes particular importance in developing economies where government investment and project evaluation frequently play major roles.[13] Consider the pricing of labor in a labor-surplus economy. Whereas labor is typically unemployed or underemployed in the traditional sector of the economy, labor costs in the developed sector may be subject to institutional forces which push them well above their competitive level. In such a situation, it becomes desirable in project evaluation to use a shadow price for labor substantially below its market price.

Another aspect of shadow pricing which is often important in developing countries relates to the exchange rate. If the local currency is overvalued, as is frequently the case, both imports and exports will be undervalued relative to that of domestic goods. One of the implications is that imported capital goods are cheap relative to domestic inputs, especially where labor is overvalued. In consequence, an excessively capital-intensive method of production is encouraged. Once more, proper project evaluation will apply a corrected or shadow price for the market rate of exchange, reflecting its value in the absence of measures to support it.

Cost Effectiveness Analysis

In some instances use of cost-benefit analysis may not be feasible simply because a precise measure of benefits cannot be obtained. This still leaves open the more limited task of cost effectiveness analysis. That is to say, a comparison may be made between the costs of achieving the same outcome by different procedures. As noted below, this technique proved of special importance in the evaluation of weapons systems.

E. ASSIGNING WEIGHTS IN PROJECT SELECTION

Projects frequently do not generate only one type of benefit or cost. Various benefits and costs may result, and it may be desirable to assign them different weights. Moreover, the benefit mix may differ depending on how the project is designed, and the design may affect the way in which similar benefits are divided among various sectors of the economy, or among income groups. All these alternatives must be considered in designing the project so as to maximize total benefits.

Multiple Objectives

Frequently, an expenditure project does not yield one single type of benefit but serves a number of objectives. For instance, a particular weapon system may have various defensive and offensive uses, expenditures on education may serve both to reduce illiteracy and to stimulate scientific progress, projects differ in their distributional implications, and so forth. In designing the project, one or the other ob-

[13] See p. 605.

jective may be emphasized. In such cases, a comparison among projects involves attributing relative weights to the various benefits which result.

Suppose, for instance, that $3 billion is to be spent on schools and to be distributed between elementary and higher education. Also suppose that for each $1 billion spent, outlays on elementary education contribute more to literacy than do outlays on secondary education, but their contribution to advancing technology is less than that of higher education. For this purpose, we may think of literacy units as measured by the number of students receiving a given test score and of technology units as the number of science majors that result. Using alternative expenditure allocations, we then have these options:

	EXPENDITURES ON		UNIT GAINS IN	
Expenditure Pattern	Elementary Education	Higher Education	Literacy	Technology
	(in Billions of Dollars)			
I	3	0	12	3
II	2	1	10	8
III	1	2	7	12
IV	0	3	3	15

The figures showing unit gains in the literacy column tell us that expenditure pattern I yields a gain four times as large as pattern IV, and so forth, without expressing absolute values of these gains in dollar terms. The same holds for the column showing gains in technology, where pattern I is one-fifth as effective as pattern IV. If a choice is to be made, a common measure of valuation for the two types of unit gains is needed. This may be in terms of resulting increase in GNP, or it may involve other considerations. For example, the gains in education may be valued on cultural grounds, quite apart from the resulting addition to GNP as measured by the official statistics, and a dollar value may be put on this gain.

When moving from pattern I toward pattern II, we find that 2½ technology units are gained for each literacy unit lost, and with a move from pattern II to III, the substitution ratio is 1⅓ technology units for each literacy unit lost. Finally, movement from pattern III to IV results in a gain of only ¾ technology unit for each literacy unit given up. If 1 literacy unit is valued at 2½ technology units or more, pattern I will be chosen; if at between 1⅓ and 2½ technology units, pattern II will be chosen. If 1 literacy unit is valued at ¾ to 1 technology unit, pattern III would be chosen, and if valued at less than ¾ technology unit, pattern IV would be the chosen education program mix. This is shown in Figure 9-3, where the dotted lines i_1, i_2, i_3, etc., are the social indifference curves pertaining to literacy and technology. The tradeoff between literacy and technology units in production gives us a convex "project transformation" frontier as illustrated by points I to IV in the figure. As shown, II is now the preferred pattern, since it places us on the highest possible social indifference curve i_4. At this point the marginal rate of substitution of technology units for literacy units as a matter of social valuation (the slope of indifference curve i_4 at the point of tangency II) equals the marginal rate of trans-

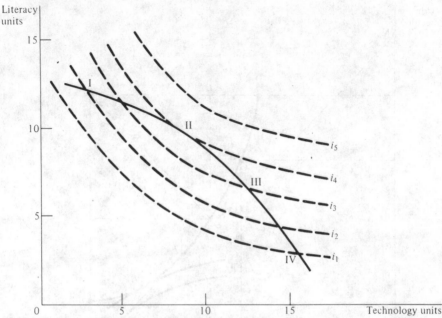

FIGURE 9-3 Multiple objectives and program selection.

formation of the educational output (the slope of the project transformation curve at the point of tangency II).

Sectoral Allocation of Police

Another illustration is given by the problem of allocating police forces among sections of a city.[14] Suppose there is an uptown precinct X and a downtown precinct Y. Population size is the same in both but the crime rate is higher in Y. Assume further that crime prevention is subject to increasing cost in both districts. The question is how a given police budget shall be allocated between X and Y. Among various targets, the following may be considered:

1. Equal number of crimes prevented in each sector
2. Equal protection, or equal number of crimes still committed in each sector
3. Maximum crime reduction for both sectors combined
4. Equality of the marginal rate of transformation between crime reduction in the two districts and the marginal rate of substitution of utilities derived from crime reduction in the two districts

Which of these goals is preferable on equity and/or efficiency grounds?

The alternative solutions to the problem are illustrated in Figure 9-4, where the crime level in sector X is measured on the vertical axis and that in Y on the horizontal axis. *AB* is a transformation schedule showing what combinations of re-

[14] See Carl S. Shoup, "Standards for Distributing a Free Government Service: Crime Prevention," *Public Finance*, 1964, pp. 393–394; and Douglas Dosser's comment, ibid., pp. 395–401.

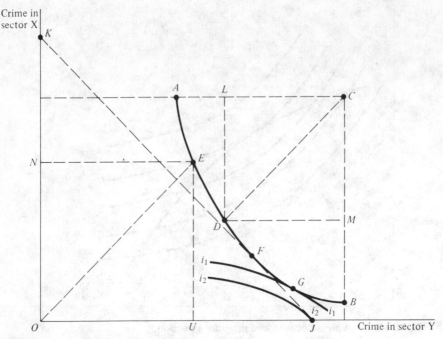

FIGURE 9-4 Police allocation among sectors of city.

maining crime levels can be obtained with a given budget.[15] If the entire police force is used in X, crime levels will be shown by B; if it is all allocated to Y, crime levels will be as shown by point A. If there is no protection for either, the location is at C.

To implement goal 1, the appropriate solution is at D, obtained by drawing a line through C at a 45° angle with the axes and taking its intersection with the transformation curve. Crime in X will fall by CM and in Y by CL, where $CL = CM$. To implement goal 2, the solution is at E, obtained by drawing a 45° line through the origin and again taking its intersection with AB. Remaining crime will equal ON in X and OU in Y with $ON = OU$. To implement goal 3, the marginal cost of crime prevention must be equal in both sectors. The solution is at F where the slope of the transformational function equals -1, it being tangent to the line JK where $OK = OJ$. Goals 1 to 3 cannot be ranked without involving some distributional judgment, which judgment is made explicit in goal 4.

Goal 4 calls for a social welfare function which values crime prevention in X and Y as expressed by indifference curves $i_1 i_1$ and $i_2 i_2$. The optimal solution is

[15] The slope of AB reflects the assumption of increasing cost of crime prevention in each sector. The function is concave from above rather than convex, since we plot "crime remaining" rather than "crime prevented." To simplify matters, we also assume equal population size for the two sectors and disregard spillover effects between them. On the latter point, see p. 452.

given at G, where AB is tangent to the highest possible indifference curve.[16] This is where the marginal rate of transformation of crime reduction in X into crime reduction in Y equals the marginal rate of substitution of the social value assigned to crime reduction in Y for that in X. The analyst thus recommends assignment in line with G, which given the indifference curves as expressed by the policy maker is the efficient solution. As drawn here, the policy maker considers crime in sector X to be more harmful than in Y, since with equal weights, the shape of the ii curves would be such that the point of tangency falls at D.

F. EFFICIENCY AND EQUITY ONCE MORE

We have argued that projects should be undertaken if their benefit to the community exceeds their cost. This implies ready aggregation of benefits and costs as experienced by individual members of the community, a matter which must now be looked at more closely.

When Are Projects Efficient?

Returning to our earlier definition of Pareto efficiency, we note that a project is efficient if it benefits at least one person while hurting no one. But there will rarely be a project which meets this condition. Consider a road project which costs $100,000. It is financed out of general revenue, so that A, B, and C pay $33,333 each. For A and B the benefits equal $50,000, whereas for C the benefit is only $30,000. Total benefits, or $130,000, exceed total cost, or $100,000, and by simple aggregation the project carries. It does so even though C loses and the strict requirement of Pareto optimality (i.e., that no one should be made worse off) is violated. To deal with such a situation, it has been suggested that the concept of efficiency be relaxed to hold a project efficient if the gainers (A and B) *could* compensate the loser (C) and remain better off than before. Under this criterion, aggregation yielding a net gain of $30,000 is validated and the project is held to be efficient. But C will derive little comfort from the fact that he *could* be compensated. This has led to the further requirement that for the project to be efficient, compensation *must* in fact be paid. Whether or not the project is efficient thus depends on how efficiency is defined.[17]

If compensation must be paid, this could take the form of transfers from A and B to C. More conveniently, the problem may be met by distributing the tax burden so as to leave no one with a net loss. A system of benefit taxation, geared to charge in line with each individual's marginal evaluation, would ensure that there are no net losers. This would render the project Pareto-efficient; but, as we saw in Chapter 4, preferences are not readily revealed and the exclusion of free riders, even if possible, may be inefficient.

---

[16] The indifference curves are convex from above because we plot remaining crime rather than absence of crime.

[17] See p. 82.

Distributional Considerations

Another problem of aggregation relates to distributional considerations.[18]

Should Weights Be Applied? A first question is whether distributional weights should be allowed for in assessing benefits and costs. Consider project I, which provides for a playground in a high-income community, and project II, which provides an identical playground to a low-income community. Suppose that the cost and the level of utilization are the same. How should the benefits from these projects be ranked? If we could determine the dollar value of the project to the users, the high-income community would set a higher value than would the low-income community. Such would be the case simply because high-income consumers can afford to pay more. This suggests that project I should be valued more highly. But social considerations might call for the opposite. A dollar spent by the poor community might be valued more highly, so that project II in this case would be preferred.

This problem would not arise in a situation where prior to introduction of the project there prevails what society considers an optimal state of distribution. In this case, the valuation of the projects based on consumer demand would also be optimal from a social point of view but would not be so if the prevailing distribution is not optimal. Social evaluation, as determined by the social welfare function, then diverges from private evaluation. As a result, project II might be preferred. This would be compatible with a broader concept of efficiency, as previously defined.[19]

A similar situation arises where two projects render an identical service but at different cost. Suppose that a naval vessel is to be built. Project I would place the construction site in a location where wages are relatively high, while project II would place it in a low-wage location. Also suppose that other (capital, material, and transportation) costs are lower in the project I location, leaving it with a lower total cost. In the absence of distributional considerations, project I wins, since it gives a higher excess of benefits over costs. But if distributional weights are allowed for, project II might rank higher, because it benefits low-wage earners. Once more, project choice is affected by distributional weights. Note also that it now becomes necessary to reconsider our earlier stricture that only real and not pecuniary benefits and costs should be considered. Since distributional weights are applied, both types of benefits and costs must be allowed for.

Given a state of distribution which diverges from what is considered optimal, the use of distributional weights in cost-benefit calculation may thus be used as a means of distributional correction. But there remains the question whether project evaluation is the best available instrument for that purpose. If distributional adjustments can be made through a general tax-transfer process, this may well be preferable. Low-income families in the case of the playground projects would then be given support in cash which they could spend as they wished rather than receive it

---

[18] See Burton Weisbrod, "Income Redistribution Effects and Benefit-Cost Analysis," in S. B. Chase (ed.): *Problems in Public Expenditure Analysis,* Washington, D.C.: Brookings, 1968; and "Collective Action and the Distribution of Income: A Conceptual Approach," in *The Analysis and Evaluation of Public Expenditures,* Joint Economic Committee, 91st Cong., 1969.

[19] See p. 84.

in playground form. Such a separation of issues would be in line with the principles laid down in Chapter 1. However, the political process may not permit this, leaving redistribution via project evaluation preferable to no redistribution at all.[20]

The appropriateness of using distributional weights in cost-benefit analysis thus depends on the circumstances of the particular case. While there is a presumption in favor of locating projects where the cost is least or the benefits are largest, situations arise where distributional weights are in order. The same holds for public purchases in general. Whereas the rule should be to buy where the cost is least, exceptions based on distributional considerations may at times be appropriate.

Objective Function If distributional weights are used they must be specified and entered into the "objective function," which defines the social welfare that is to be maximized. Stated in general form, this objective function is then given by

$$W_s = \alpha \sum_{i=l}^{m} (G_i - L_i) + \beta \sum_{j=n}^{z} (G_j - L_j)$$

where gains G and losses L of individuals 1 to m are given weight α, while those of individuals n to z are given weight β. The choice of groupings may refer to income brackets, regions, or whatever characteristics are relevant to the government's objective function.

Choice of Weights The difficulty is how to determine the proper set of weights. Short of returning to the philosophical issues discussed in Chapter 6, attempts have been made to derive such weights from the evidence provided by past behavior. Thus a clue might be obtained by comparing past project decisions with what they would have been if based purely on an efficiency analysis without distributional weights. Or weights might be derived by analyzing the income tax, based on the assumption that when setting the rates, Congress intended to distribute the income tax burden in line with a rule of equal sacrifice.[21] One may then compute the marginal income utility schedule which is implicit in the prevailing tax-liability distribution. Results such as these are of interest but assume that past policy action was in fact based on rigorous application of a social utility rule, which is hardly a realistic assumption.

But though it is difficult to derive a social income utility function, it may well be desirable for the government to state explicitly what function it proposes to use. A table such as the following might serve as an illustration:

---

[20] As noted below, redistribution via a tax-transfer process also carries an efficiency cost, and this cost *may* be larger than that which results if redistribution is implemented via an "optimal" set of selective commodity taxes and subsidies. (See p. 291.) Use of distributional weights in project evaluation is equivalent to a commodity subsidy (as applied to public projects) and may be appropriate on these grounds. However, if distributional adjustments are to be made by interfering with resource allocation, it would be arbitrary to limit this correction to *public* projects.

[21] See p. 81.

Income	Marginal Social Weights
Under $10,000	10
$10,000–$20,000	5
$20,000–$30,000	2
Over $30,000	1

Benefits and costs of the project may then be weighted accordingly, depending on the group on which they fall. This would permit consistency in the use of distributional weights in cost-benefit analysis, as well as in that of dealing with the distribution of the tax burden. Also, inclusion of such a function in the party platform might be a helpful piece of information for the voter.

G. DISCOUNTING AND THE COST OF CAPITAL

So far we have disregarded the fact that benefits and costs accrue over time and not instantaneously. This situation must now be addressed. Some expenditures, such as current salaries for firefighters, yield immediate benefits, while others, such as investments in fire trucks, river basin developments, or turnpikes, yield a benefit stream over many years. To evaluate such benefit streams, future proceeds (or costs) must be translated into present values. They must be discounted, to allow for the fact that future benefits are less valuable than present ones. The same applies to the evaluation of costs. The opportunity cost of resources withdrawn from the private sector should now be measured in terms of the present value of private consumption forgone, where future consumption losses (due to forgone investments) are similarly discounted to their present value.

Importance of Discounting

The evaluation of projects and their ranking is highly sensitive to the discount rate used. This is illustrated in Table 9-3, where the present values of benefits and benefit-cost ratios for various investments are compared.[22]

[22] The present value PV of a sum R due in n years, discounted at the rate of interest, i, is

$$PV = \frac{R}{(1+i)^n}$$

The present value of an income stream, $R_1, R_2, \ldots, R_n$ for n years equals

$$PV = \frac{R_1}{(1+i)} + \frac{R_2}{(1+i)^2} + \frac{R_3}{(1+i)^3} + \ldots + \frac{R_n}{(1+i)^n}$$

For a case where the R's are constant, the above expression reduces to

$$PV = R\frac{1-(1+i)^{-n}}{i}$$

and can conveniently be obtained from annuity tables. For the case of a perpetual constant R (annuity), the above expression becomes

$$PV = \frac{R}{i}$$

TABLE 9-3
Present Value and Discount Rates

Projects	X	Y	Z
Cost, dollars	10,380	10,380	10,380
Number of years	5	15	25
Annual benefits, dollars	2,397	1,000	736
PRESENT VALUE OF BENEFIT STREAM IN DOLLARS			
Interest rate, percentage			
3	10,978	11,938	12,816
5	10,380	10,380	10,380
8	9,571	8,559	7,857
PRESENT VALUE OF BENEFIT-COST DIFFERENTIAL ($B - C$) IN DOLLARS			
3	598	1,558	2,436
5	0	0	0
8	− 809	− 1,821	− 2,523
BENEFIT-COST RATIO (B/C)			
3	1.057	1.150	1.235
5	1.000	1.000	1.000
8	0.922	0.825	0.757

We consider three investments X, Y, and Z with equal cost and with income flows covering five, fifteen, and twenty-five years, respectively. The annual incomes are chosen such that present values of benefits are the same at a 5 percent rate of discount. As we move from a 5 percent to a 3 percent rate, Z becomes the best and X the poorest choice. Reducing the discount rate will raise present value more if the period over which income accrues is longer. Moving to an 8 percent rate has the opposite effect. Project X now becomes most attractive and Z least. Raising the rate of discount favors the relatively short investment. While the present value of all investments rises as the discount rate is reduced and falls as it is raised, the ranking of the various investments changes in the process.

Based on these present value figures, we obtain the corresponding benefit-cost differentials ($B - C$) and the corresponding benefit-cost ratios (B/C). With the initial cost of building the project assumed to be $10,380, the annual returns are chosen so that with a discount rate of 5 percent the net benefit ($B - C$) equals zero or the benefit-cost ratio (B/C) equals 1 for all investments.[23] The present value of benefits equals that of costs, and whether to invest or not is a matter of indifference. At the 3 percent rate, all three investments are profitable with net benefits positive, but Z ranks highest and X ranks lowest.[24] At the 8 percent rate, none of the three investments pays its way, but X is now best and Z has become last. As will be seen from this illustration, the ranking of various investments and their acceptability depends greatly on which discount rate is used. The lengths of the income stream

---

[23] We assume for the time being that all costs are incurred in the first year, overlooking additional considerations which arise when costs are spread out over longer periods.

[24] Since all investments involve the same cost, ranking may be in terms of net benefits ($B - C$) or, for that matter, in terms of B only.

dealt with in public projects cover a wide range, so that finding the "proper" rate is of major importance.

Choice of Discount Rate: (1) Private Rate

In choosing the discount rate, government may proceed on the premise that it is desirable to use a rate equal to the time preference of private consumers; or it may substitute a social discount rate of its own. We begin with the former view. The rationale for using the private rate of discount is that it reflects consumer choice between present and future consumption. Just as public policy accepts the valuation of oranges and apples by the prices which they fetch in the market, so should it honor the individual's valuation of future relative to present consumption. Given the condition of perfectly competitive capital markets and absence of risk, all consumers will borrow and lend at the same rate. Moreover, with perfect markets, this rate equals the marginal efficiency of investment. Thus there exists an equality between the marginal rate of substitution of present for future consumption and their marginal rate of transformation in production. The rate of interest, like other competitive prices, is at its efficient level. In practice, this seemingly simple solution is complicated by various factors, including market imperfections, uncertainty, risk, and taxes on capital income.

Imperfect Markets   The assumption of perfectly competitive capital markets is unrealistic. Due to market imperfections, such as differential access to credit and investment institutions, different individuals may be confronted with different costs and returns to their borrowing and lending. Since there no longer is a single rate which reflects the time preference of consumers, some average must be used.[25]

Uncertainty   Since the future level of interest rates is uncertain, short- and long-term rates in the capital market differ. Once more, the question arises about which rate should be used in discounting. Should it be the rate on one-, two-, or five-year deposits? Should the yield on short- or long-term bonds be used? Since the term structure of market yields may be taken to reflect the probable cost of capital in future years, a case can be made for choosing a yield on a maturity which corresponds to the period over which the benefit stream of the public investment will extend.

Risk   Since some investments are more risky than others, gross rates of return differ by the amount of risk premiums. To have the discount rate reflect "pure" time preference, one should use the yield on a "safe" investment, i.e., an investment which has little or no default risk, such as federal government bonds.[26]

Income Tax   Lenders must pay income tax on their capital income. The proper measure of their time preference, therefore, is the *net*, or after-tax, rate of return and

---

[25] It has been suggested that in choosing this average, weights should be used which reflect the position of taxpayers who contribute to the finance of the project. In this case, the correct discount rate depends on how the project is financed. See Otto Eckstein, "A Survey of the Theory of Public Expenditure Criteria," in James Buchanan (ed.): *Public Finances: Needs, Sources and Utilization*, Princeton, N.J.: Princeton University Press, 1961.

[26] For a discussion of the risk involved in the public investment itself, see p. 160.

not the gross or market rate. If the consumer lends at rate i, his or her net return, or i_n, equals $(1 - t)i$, where t is the consumer's personal tax rate. Since different consumers are in different marginal tax brackets, net rates will differ among individuals. Again, the best that can be done is to use an average rate. If the gross rate is, say, 8 percent and the marginal tax rate on the average is 30 percent, the net rate would be 5.6 percent.

Macro Policy A more general difficulty arises from the very existence of a macroeconomic system which generates unemployment and inflation. The case for application of the market rate rests on the proposition that this rate can be taken to secure an efficient allocation of consumption over time. This rationale involves a model of national income determination such that planned saving is always matched by investment, with neither unemployment nor inflation occurring. This is hardly the case in the real-world setting. Rather, conditions are typically such that stabilization measures are needed to maintain macro balance, i.e., full employment and stability of the price level. These measures may be taken in various combinations of monetary and fiscal restraint or expansion, all of which result in different levels of interest. Given the fact that stabilization policies are needed in the modern market economy, the market does not reveal a unique "correct" level of interest rate by which "true" consumer time preference is reflected.

Conclusion In the presence of these complications, it is evident that the seemingly simple idea of using "the" private rate meets with considerable practical difficulties. Instead, some average or approximate rate must be used.

Choice of Discount Rate: (2) Social Rate

So far we have proceeded on the assumption that the rate of discount used in project evaluation should equal the time preference of consumers in the private sector, provided that this may be derived from observed market rates. There are also reasons for using not the time preference rate of private consumers but for substituting a social rate in its place:

1. Individuals are said to suffer from "myopia," so that in arranging their private affairs, they underestimate the importance of saving and overestimate that of present consumption. Such may be the case especially in low-income countries where the advantage of higher income levels has not been experienced and where aspiration levels are low. Hence, the consumers' time discount is too high and government should correct this error by applying a lower rate.

2. Next come several arguments related to the welfare of future generations. One argument is that people are too greedy and do not care sufficiently about the welfare of those who follow them. If they did, they would save more so as to leave future generations with a larger capital stock and hence higher level of income. The government, as guardian of future generations, can offset this by using a lower rate of discount and investing more. Saving is viewed as a merit good. This may be a decision faced by the planning board of a developing country, which must choose between more rapid development and an early increase in the level of consumption.[27]

3. Alternatively, it is held that people do in fact care about future generations and that they would derive pleasure from contributing to their welfare. But any one

[27] See p. 585.

person acting alone cannot contribute enough to make a difference, even though he or she would be willing to save more if others contributed as well. As in all cases of benefit externality, the private market results in undersupply. Once more the government can remedy this by using a lower rate of discount, thereby increasing the range of eligible public investment.

4. The concern with future generations may not simply be one of benevolence but may reflect a broadened application of just distribution rules so as to include intergeneration equity.[28] For instance, the goal may be to equalize per capita consumption over time. Under this criterion, the requirement for current saving and capital formation (or, more precisely, for passing capital stock to the future) will depend on factors such as population growth, availability of exhaustible resources, and, above all, technical progress. With technical progress raising future productivity, the capital stock needed to sustain the consumption standard may fall, calling for a higher discount rate.

5. Another view of intergeneration equity calls for the saving rate to be set such that the equilibrium growth path of the economy produces the maximum level of consumption for all generations. Each generation should do for other generations as it would want other generations to do for itself. This ''golden rule'' requires that in equilibrium the rate of return to capital (and with it the rate of interest) should equal the growth rate of the economy which, in turn, equals the growth rate of population. This interest rate then provides the ''correct'' rate of discount to be used in project evaluation.[29]

Considerations 1 through 3 and most likely 5 suggest that the social rate should be set below the private rate so that use of the social rate calls for a higher level of investment. Using the social rate rather than the private rate in product selection will then give a higher present value of the benefit stream, passing projects which might be excluded by the use of the private rate.[30] Moreover, use of the social rate will result in the choice of longer-lived projects. Once more, this is an important instance of shadow pricing.

Opportunity Cost of Capital

The choice of discount rate is important, but it is only part of the problem. The other part is to measure the social cost involved in withdrawing resources from private use. This ''social opportunity cost'' equals the loss of consumption, current or future, which results as these resources are withdrawn.

Resource Withdrawal from Consumption Suppose that the government undertakes a project at cost C of $1 million in material, labor, and equipment. Assume further that this resource withdrawal is financed in such a way (e.g., by a consumption tax) that private consumption falls by $1 million. This is by how much consumers value the lost consumption and hence its social value. Such at

---

[28] See p. 82.

[29] See E. M. Gramlich, *Benefit-Cost Analysis of Government Programs*, Englewood Cliffs, N.J.: Prentice-Hall, 1981, pp. 101–108.

[30] This conclusion must be qualified. As we will see presently, use of a lower discount rate also increases the opportunity cost of capital. Depending on the timing involved, this may more than offset the increased present value of benefits.

least is the case unless market imperfections as discussed previously call for corrections in the form of shadow prices.

Resource Withdrawal from Investment: Without Tax   Next let the resource withdrawal be reflected in reduced private investment and capital formation. The loss now takes the form of a future consumption stream, corresponding to the income stream that is forgone. To determine the present value of this income stream, it must again be discounted at the market rate. Assuming a perfectly competitive market, we find that this discounted value equals C. Such must be the case, since in a competitive market there exists a unique rate of interest and investors will invest up to the point where their costs are covered by the present value of the return as discounted by the market rate. Thus, the social opportunity cost of capital (a term not to be confused with "social rate of discount") is properly measured by the private cost of investment. Once more, C is the proper measure of social cost.

If markets are imperfect, different investments in the private sector may yield different returns, so that the income stream which is lost by diverting resources from private investment may depend on precisely which investment is reduced. This is impossible to determine, so the analysis must proceed by choosing an average return.

Resource Withdrawal from Investment: With Tax   We now complicate matters by adding a corporation tax on capital income and a personal income tax on interest income. This is shown in Figure 9-5, where II is the investment schedule, showing the returns that may be obtained at various levels of investment, and SS is the savings schedule, showing the levels of saving forthcoming at various rates of interest or return on savings. In equilibrium E, savers save and lend OA to investors

FIGURE 9-5   Income taxes and discounting.

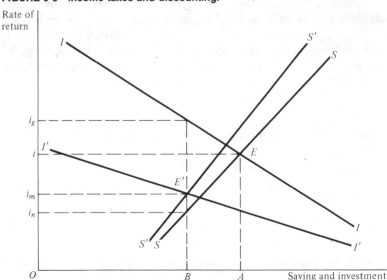

who then invest that amount. The rate of return obtained by investors on their marginal investment equals i, which is also the return which the savers receive.

Now let a corporation tax be imposed. As a result, the investment schedule will swivel down, with $I'I'$ showing the reduced levels of investment that will now be undertaken at various gross (before corporate tax) rates of return. As an individual income tax is added, the savings schedule shifts to the left, with $S'S'$ now showing the higher gross (before personal tax) rates of return which borrowers must pay the savers to generate given amounts of saving. The new equilibrium is at E', the intersection of the $I'I'$ and $S'S'$ schedules, with OB the level of saving and investment. The gross (before corporate taxes) rate of return on investment now equals i_g, while the net return to the investor (also called the market rate) equals i_m. In the equilibrium position, i_m also equals the gross rate of return before personal tax obtained by the saver. The net (after personal tax) rate of return to the saver, finally, is given by i_n, which also reflects the saver's rate of time preference.

Two conclusions follow. First, we note that under a private rate approach, i_n is now the correct rate of discount to use in determining the present value of the income stream which is derived from the public project. Second, we note that the opportunity cost of capital now exceeds the dollar value of reduced private investment, i.e., the market cost of the project, or \$1 million. To see why, note that this private investment cost C_p as recorded by the market equals the discounted values of the investment income *net* of corporation tax, with the market rate, or i_m, used as rate of discount. This reflects the behavior of the investor who will invest up to the margin where his or her cost is covered. In contrast, the income stream to be discounted in determining the social opportunity cost of capital C_s, is the rate of return *before* corporation tax, or i_g. Whereas the investor obtains only a return net of tax, or i_m, this does not matter since the tax is a transfer from investor to government and a pecuniary but not a social loss. Moreover, the rate of discount to be used in obtaining the social value of the i_g stream is not i_m but the consumer's rate of prime preference i_n. We thus discount a larger income stream at a lower rate, and for both these reasons arrive at a higher present value. Thus C_s exceeds C_p.[31]

Conclusion   Summarizing the preceding discussion and using the simplifying assumption of constant and perpetual returns, we note that the present value of the net benefit (PVNB) of a project may be defined as follows:

[31] Assuming a perpetual income stream, we find that the cost of the investment to the private investor C_p thus equals

$$C_p = \frac{(1 - t_c)\, i_g C_p}{i_m} \tag{1}$$

while the social cost equals

$$C_s = \frac{i_g C_p}{i_n} \tag{2}$$

Therefore $C_s > C_p$ for two reasons: in (2) the numerator is larger and the denominator is smaller than in (1).

$$\text{PVNB} = \frac{B}{i_n} - \left[\gamma C + \frac{(1 - \gamma)i_g C}{i_n} \right]$$

where the first term on the right measures the present value of its annual benefits B, as discounted by i_n, and the second term measures the opportunity cost of resource withdrawal.[32] With the fraction γ thereof withdrawn from private consumption, the first component shows the opportunity cost of this part of the resource withdrawal, where C is again the market price of the resource inputs. The second component shows the opportunity cost of resource withdrawal from private investment, equal to the forgone gross income stream $(1 - \gamma)i_g C$, discounted again at the net rate i_n. If a social rather than a private rate approach is taken, the above formula is simply adjusted by substituting i_s for i_n.

The value of γ will depend on how the investment is financed. In the case of income tax finance, it will equal the taxpayers' marginal propensity to consume. Some taxes, such as sales taxes, fall most heavily on consumption; others, such as estate duties, fall more heavily on saving.[33] Furthermore, loan finance will tend to have a heavier displacement effect on savings and on capital formation than will tax finance.[34] The way in which a project is financed thus affects its eligibility under cost-benefit analysis. Finance which draws on saving involves a higher opportunity cost and leaves fewer projects eligible than does finance which draws on consumption. This tends to correct for the fact that taxes on capital income leave private investment short of its efficient level.

Further Problems

Before we turn to actual practice in the use of discount rates and determination of opportunity cost, three further aspects of the discounting problem will be noted.

Internal Rate The preceding discussion was based on the assumption that project evaluation is to be carried out by discounting at a uniform rate of discount, private or social. But this is not the only possible procedure. Instead of determining the profitability of a project by measuring the present value of the net income stream, we may turn the table and ask what discount rate would be needed to

[32] These simplifying assumptions may be readily qualified to allow for the more realistic case of finite investments with uneven income streams. Further complications arise (1) because the loss of private capital income due to the reduction in investment does not fully reflect the resulting decline in national income, except for the case of the marginal investment dollar, and (2) because the outcome may be affected by the extent to which the loss of income in the private sector would have been saved and invested, as well as by the extent to which the gained public income stream is so used. See Martin Feldstein, "Net Social Benefit Calculation and the Public Investment Decision," *Oxford Economic Papers*, vol. 16, no. 1, March 1964, pp. 114–131.

[33] Note that tax aspects have threefold importance for project analysis. First, the value of γ will be determined by the way in which the project is financed, i.e., by the choice between taxation and borrowing and between various types of tax. Second, income taxation enters in determining the net rate of return which the lender can receive in the market, and hence the proper rate of discount. Third, taxation enters because the corporation tax drives a wedge between the gross and net rate of return received by the investor, and hence influences the social opportunity cost of capital.

[34] Such at least is the case in the shorter run. In the longer run, it might be argued that the difference disappears due to tax finance of debt service. See Martin Feldstein, "Financing in the Evaluation of Public Expenditures," in W. Smith and J. Culbertson (eds.): *Public Finance and Stabilization Policy: Essays in Honour of Richard A. Musgrave*, Amsterdam: North-Holland, 1974.

equate the present value of the benefit stream with the cost of the asset. Thus, by setting the present value of benefits equal to the present value of costs, we get the expression

$$\sum_{j=0}^{n} \frac{B_j - C_j}{(1 + i)^j} = 0$$

and solve for i, the internal rate of return.[35] In ranking two projects, we give preference to the one which has the higher internal rate. This approach has the advantage of bypassing the thorny question of what rate of discount to use in determining present values. However, it also has some serious shortcomings.

Closer analysis shows that if the net benefit stream fluctuates such that annual net benefits alternate between positive and negative there is more than one internal rate which will satisfy the above equation. Moreover, ranking by internal rate of return may differ from ranking by discounting with a common rate. Thus, two investments of different maturity may have the same internal rate, but their ranking will differ if benefits are discounted with a market rate. If the market rate is above the internal rate, the shorter investment now ranks first, and vice versa if the market rate is lower. For these and other reasons, the internal-rate approach is not commonly used, although it may be drawn upon to provide additional evidence on project rating. This is the case especially for very long term investments, where it is difficult to predict future levels of interest rates and hence the appropriate private rate of discount.

Outside Borrowing   The preceding discussion applied to project evaluation by a national government, drawing on resources within its own economy. Actually, project evaluation is frequently undertaken by local governments which draw on outside capital markets or by national governments of developing countries which obtain funds from New York or the World Bank.

This factor would not greatly change the problem if all capital markets were perfect, with interest rates being the same in all locations and for all transactors. But such is not the case. A local government may be able to borrow at rates in the New York market quite different from those available at local banks and to local savers. Or the government of a developing country may borrow from the World Bank at 5 percent while domestic rates are 20 percent. Given such market imperfections, it cannot be argued that benefits should be discounted at the time preference rate of local residents. Rather, project evaluation should discount benefits at the borrowing rate and undertake the project if positive net benefits are recorded. Where international borrowing is involved, allowance must be made, however, for future debt service and effects on the balance of payments.

Inflation   Since the inflation rate tends to be reflected in the nominal interest rate, the latter rises with inflation. But a higher rate of discount means a lower

[35] Returning to the second equation in footnote 22, we may substitute the asset cost C for PV, enter the income stream $R_1, \ldots, R_n$, and with the help of annuity tables, solve for i.

present value, thus affecting project eligibility. This effect of inflation may be neutralized in two ways. One is to use the nominal rate of interest (including its inflation premium) for discounting, and at the same time using the nominal (inflated) value of the benefit stream. The other is to adjust the nominal rate of interest for inflation, discounting with the real-rate component only, while measuring the benefit stream in real terms. In either case, distorting effects of inflation are avoided. It appears, however, that U.S. practice has combined the measurement of benefits and costs in real terms with the use of a nominal rate of interest. As the latter rises with inflation, this results in an unduly restrictive evaluation policy.

Current Practice

Actual practice falls considerably short of these sophisticated considerations. Current practice in the federal government is to apply a 10 percent discount rate to the benefit stream of the project and to compare this with the dollar cost of its construction.[36] No attempt is made to adjust for the social opportunity cost of capital. A special rate applies to water projects where, as legislated by Congress, a rate equal to the yield of long-term United States bonds is to be used. This yield can, however, be changed each year by one-quarter of 1 percent only and now stands at about 7 percent.[37]

No explicit rationale is given for these rules. Use of the bond rate for discounting may be rationalized by taking it to reflect consumer time preference, although as noted above, a further reduction to adjust for individual income tax would then be in order. The 10 percent rate, in turn, may be taken to reflect the bond rate grossed up by the corporation tax rate, thus approximating the gross yield on private investment. A popular, if fallacious, justification for this is that the government should recover its entire project cost, defined to include the cost of borrowing plus the loss of corporation tax revenue, because taxable income in the private sector is reduced. This line of reasoning confuses private and social profitability. The purpose of the government is to maximize social welfare and not profits as calculated by the private firm.

The grossed-up bond yield is useful, however, as an indicator of the gross income stream displaced as private investment is reduced. Following the proposition that government should undertake an investment only if it matches the social yield of the private investment forgone,[38] we properly measure the forgone income stream as income gross of corporation tax. This rule has the advantage of simplicity, but to be correct both the private and public investment streams should then be discounted by the proper rate of discount. Assuming that a private rate approach is

---

[36] See Office of Management and Budget, Circular No. A-94, Revised, Mar. 27, 1972.

[37] Water Resources Development, Public Law 93-251, 93d Cong., Mar. 7, 1974. Also see Water Resources Council, *Water and Related Land Resources, Establishment of Principles and Studies for Planning (Federal Register,* vol. 38, no. 174, part III), Sept. 10, 1973, p. 9 in final section on "Final Environmental Statement."

[38] See A. C. Harberger, "The Opportunity Cost of Public Investment Financed by Borrowing," in R. Layard (ed.): *Cost-Benefit Analysis,* Baltimore: Penguin, 1972, chap. 12. Harberger qualifies this approach by calling for a discount rate reflecting a weighted average of i_n and i_g , as defined above. The weights depend on the elasticities of the saving and investment schedules.

followed, this proper rate is given by i_n , the consumer's lending rate net of income tax and not by the gross rate of return on private investment. The latter should enter in computing the opportunity cost of capital but not in selecting the discount rate.

H. RISK AND ECONOMIC CHANGE

It remains to consider some further aspects which can be of major importance in cost-benefit analysis, including the treatment of risk and dynamic change.

Risk

Project benefits may not be readily predictable at the outset, since public project planning, no less than private investment, proceeds under uncertainty. Thus, highway planning involves forecasting population growth in the area, a weapons program involves forecasts regarding future weapons technology or strategic developments, and so forth. Such risk and uncertainty regarding future benefits reduce their present value and must be allowed for in investment planning. Whereas it may be argued that in certain situations the social risk is less than the private risk involved in particular activities, it does not follow that risk is a minor matter in public project planning.[39]

Allowance can be made for risky outcomes by weighting the various possible outcomes by their probabilities, with the sum of the probabilities equal to 1. The sum of these appropriately weighted outcomes will then be used in the analysis as the expected value of the benefits, $E(B)$. Thus,

$$E(B) = p_1 B_1 + p_2 B_2 + \ldots + p_n B_n \qquad \text{where } p_1 + p_2 + \ldots + p_n = 1$$

In cases where numerical probabilities are unknown, the analyst may resort to various techniques derived from game theory to aid in the selection process, but this takes us beyond the scope of this book.[40]

It may also be assumed that the expected value of benefits as obtained above exceeds its "certainty equivalent" because of a prevailing aversion to risk. There is considerable evidence that people would derive greater utility from receiving, for instance, the certainty of $10 than from receiving a 50 percent chance of $15 together with a 50 percent chance of $5, the expected value of which would be $10 = [.5(15) + .5(5)]. The degree of risk attached to a range of possible outcomes may be expressed as the standard deviation of the probability distribution. It has therefore been suggested that a risk premium be added to the discount rate used for public project discounting purposes, the premium designed to reflect the magnitude of this standard deviation.

---

[39] For a discussion of the pros and cons of allowance for risk in project evaluation, see Layard, ibid., pp. 53–57.

[40] See R. Dorfman, "Decision Rules under Uncertainty," in Layard, ibid., chap. 15.

Dynamic Aspects

The valuation of costs and benefits, finally, is complicated by the fact that both benefits and costs occur over time. This is evident with regard to benefits which flow from an investment project, the economic life of which may extend far into the future. But it also holds for costs. While capital costs are typically incurred at the outset, substantial operating costs may have to be undertaken in future years. One major implication of this time dimension of benefits and costs is the need for discounting, a problem discussed in an earlier section. Another aspect is that the valuation of benefits and costs may change over time. Project evaluation must therefore allow for the dynamics of economic development. This is of particular importance for developing countries. Not only may relative prices change, but so may the extent of price distortions. The case for setting a shadow price of labor much below its market price, for instance, may disappear over time as previously unemployed and underemployed labor comes to be drawn into the modern sector and wages move more nearly in line with the social opportunity cost of labor. Allowing for such structural changes will have considerable significance for projects which have a long time horizon.

Brief mention should also be made of a further problem which is presented by changes which are associated with the passage of time (as distinct from the age of the project). The profile of benefits and costs over time may be such as to suggest that postponement of the project may be in order. For instance, if future demand for the output of the project is expected to increase, while costs of production due to improved technologies will decrease, the benefit-cost analysis should be made under alternative starting times. The effects of one year's postponement will be the change in the present value (today) of future benefits minus the change in the present value of costs. The project should be delayed until this net change (if favorable) is maximized.[41]

I. SUMMARY

In developing some basic concepts of project evaluation, we have distinguished between divisible and lumpy projects.

1. Where projects are freely divisible, the best solution is reached by equating the marginal benefits from the last dollar on each project (where the budget is fixed) and on public and private projects (where the budget total is open).

2. Lumpy projects in a fixed budget should be chosen so as to maximize the sum of net benefits. In an open budget such projects should be adopted as long as total benefits exceed costs.

In measuring the social benefits and social costs of public projects, certain rules must be followed:

3. Only real costs and benefits should be included and pecuniary costs and benefits should be excluded.

---

[41] See S. Marglin, *Approaches to Dynamic Investment Planning,* Amsterdam: North-Holland, 1963.

4. Both direct and indirect costs and benefits should be included.

5. Valuation of intangible benefits and costs is more difficult than and poses problems similar to those caused by the valuation of social goods.

6. Intermediate-type benefits can be valued more readily than benefits of the final type.

7. Even if intangible benefits cannot be valued readily, cost-effectiveness analysis may be helpful.

8. Shadow pricing corrects for distortions introduced by monopoly, taxes, and unemployed resources.

9. Shadow pricing is of special importance in developing countries where labor tends to be overvalued and foreign exchange undervalued.

In selecting the particular projects to be undertaken, allowance must be made for the fact that multiple objectives may be involved.

10. Where alternative projects differ in their relative capacity to serve one or another objective, the two objectives must be valued so as to permit comparison.

Cost-benefit analysis raises some further problems of weighting and selected issues in welfare economics.

11. Project evaluation based on a simple aggregation of benefits and costs will not yield Pareto-efficient solutions where some individuals emerge as net losers.

12. Where the distributional implications of alternative projects differ, such differences may be allowed for by the introduction of distributional weights. The appropriateness of applying such weights depends on the availability of alternative means of securing distributional adjustments and on the efficiency cost of using them.

Where the benefit stream from a public project accrues over future years, present value must be determined by discounting. Care must be taken to follow proper procedures in determining the cost of resource withdrawal where such withdrawal is from private investment.

13. In choosing the discount rate, government may aim at a rate which corresponds to that used in the private sector or it may wish to apply a social rate of discount.

14. In the former case, the proper rate of return is given by the rate of return on capital net of corporation and individual income tax, because this reflects the time preference of consumers.

15. This rationale applies to competitive markets but is complicated by risk differentials, market imperfections, and taxes on capital income. The rate typically used is the long-term bond rate, grossed up by the rate of corporation tax.

16. Choice of a social rate usually rests on the proposition that the private sector tends to underestimate the social value of future consumption and capital formation, thus calling for the use of a lower rate by the public sector.

17. As distinct from the issue of discount rate, correct procedure calls for careful determination of the social opportunity cost of capital. This issue arises where resource withdrawal from the private sector is from private capital formation rather than from consumption. The social opportunity cost of capital equals the discounted value of the gross (before-tax) income stream, and this exceeds the actual dollar cost (or discounted value of the net income stream) of the private investment forgone.

18. Current federal practice is to use a 10 percent rate of discount in all cases except for water projects, where a rate equal to the long-term bond yield is used.

FURTHER READING

For systematic treatment of cost-benefit analysis, see:

Gramlich, E. M.: *Benefit-Cost Analysis of Government Programs*, Englewood Cliffs, N.J.: Prentice-Hall, 1981.

Layard, R. (ed.): *Cost-Benefit Analysis: Selected Readings*, Baltimore: Penguin, 1972. (A collection of key articles with an excellent summary in the introduction.)

Mishan, E.: *Cost-Benefit Analysis*, 3d ed., New York: Allen and Unwin, 1982.

Pearce, D. and Nash, C.: *The Social Appraisal of Projects, A Text in Cost-Benefit Analysis*, New York: Halsted, 1981.

For further discussion of various aspects of cost-benefit analysis, see:

Dasgupta, P., S. A. Marglin, and A. K. Sen: *Guidelines for Project Evaluation*, New York: United Nations Industrial Development Organization, 1972.

Haveman, R. H. and J. Margolis (eds.): *Public Expenditures and Policy Analysis*, 3d ed., Skokie, Ill.: Rand McNally, 1983.

Little, I. M. D. and J. A. Mirrlees: *Project Appraisal and Planning for Developing Countries*, New York: Basic Books, 1974.

Williams, A.: "Cost-Benefit Analysis: Bastard Science? And/or Insidious Poison in the Body Politic?" *Journal of Public Economics*, August 1972.

Chapter 10

Case Studies in Expenditure Policy: (1) Public Services*

A. National Defense: *Major Issues; Cost Effectiveness in Weapons Design; Modernizing Strategic Forces; Industrial Impact; Effects on Productivity Growth.* **B. Highways:** *Intergovernmental Cooperation; User Charge Finance; Use of Cost-Benefit Analysis; An Illustration; Estimated Returns on Maintenance of National Highway System.* **C. Outdoor Recreation:** *Measuring Benefits to Users; Other Benefits.* **D. Education:** *Policy Issues; Benefit-Cost Analysis for Higher Education.* **E. Summary.**

We will now take a closer look at a varied sample of expenditure programs and the issues which they pose. National defense, highways, environmental protection, and education will be considered in this chapter, with major transfer programs taken up in the next.

A. NATIONAL DEFENSE

The changing role of expenditures for national defense is shown in Table 10-1.

*Reader's Guide to Chapter 10: The preceding principles of project evaluation are now applied to a wide range of public services, including national defense, transportation, outdoor recreation, and education. While the information needed for a rigorous application is rarely available, cost-benefit analysis nevertheless proves useful in designing a more efficient program of public services.

TABLE 10-1
Expenditures in National Defense*

	1960	1970	1979	1987
National defense				
Current dollars	47.5	78.6	113.0	274.0
1982 dollars	129.7	198.9	132.0	239.2
As percentage of GNP	9.4	7.9	4.6	6.1
As percentage of budget	50.5	38.5	22.5	27.4
By type, current dollars				
Personnel	13.4	23.0	40.9	72.0
Operations and maintenance	12.3	21.6	44.8	76.2
Procurement	11.8	21.6	29.0	80.7
Research and development	6.2	7.2	13.1	33.6
Other	3.8	5.2	6.2	11.5
Total	47.5	78.6	133.9	274.0

*See Department of Commerce, *Survey of Current Business,* and U.S. budgets.

Total outlays, including the four services (Army, Navy, Air Force, and Marines) now account for nearly one-third of the federal budget. While the defense share declined during the 1960s and 1970s, this trend was reversed in the 1980s, reflecting the Reagan Administration's major effort to strengthen and modernize military capacity. With defense outlays nearly tripling during the 1980s and doubling in real terms, defense has been a major contributor to budget growth, although considerably outdistanced by the growth of social programs. The picture changes, however, if transfers are excluded and only purchases are considered. Defense then accounts for 75 percent of the total budget and for nearly the entire increase over the recent decade, becoming *the* major factor in the direct role of the budget as a customer of private firms and user of economic resources.

In the lower part of the table, Department of Defense outlays are broken down by major categories, including personnel, operations and maintenance, procurement, and research and development. The United States, as distinct from its continental NATO partners, does not require military service, so that personnel costs account for a substantial part of the total. Procurement and outlays for operations come next, but research and development has also become an important and perhaps the most critical component of the defense budget.

Major Issues

National defense offers a classic case of a social good, as defined in our earlier discussion. Given modern technology, the individual citizen cannot provide for his or her own security, and protection which is provided collectively cannot be withdrawn from particular users. But national defense also poses the most complex and vital issues in expenditure planning. There is no simple way in which voters as ultimate consumers can assess the costs and benefits involved. Broad issues of foreign policy are involved, as well as willingness to accept the risk of military conflict. Judgments must be made regarding the effectiveness of avoiding such conflict by strengthening retaliatory power. Policies viewed as defensive by one side may be taken as offensive by another, so that the adversary's likely responses must be taken into account, creating a gaming situation the outcome of which is difficult to predict.

The desirable balance between the four services and the selection of particular weapons systems, moreover, will depend upon the likely scope and location of potential contingencies, with quite different mixes called for in dealing with local conflicts and with involvement in a major continental confrontation. Most important, defense planning must strike a balance between provision for conventional and atomic warfare, ranging from atomic weapons for tactical use in the support of ground forces to intercontinental ballistic missiles. This balance in particular is a central problem for U.S. defense planning, with its dual responsibility towards NATO allies and home protection.

To fully comprehend the complexity of these issues, it should be noted that the growth of destructive power has not only raised the cost of major conflict to that of ultimate destruction but in doing so may also have served to forestall the occurrence of lesser (though still disastrous) conventional conflict among major powers, which might otherwise have occurred.

Cost Effectiveness in Weapons Design

Underlying these momentous policy issues, there arise a host of technical problems involving the design of particular weapons systems such as missiles, planes, vessels, and armor so as to efficiently meet their assigned tasks. It is here that cost-benefit or, more precisely, cost-effectiveness analysis can be most useful and came first to be applied on a large scale in defense planning during the 1960s.

Modernizing Strategic Forces

The central effort now under debate relates to the modernizing and build-up of U.S. strategic forces. Primarily intended to deter nuclear attack, the goal is to establish a triad of strategic systems involving delivery by land-based missiles, submarine-based missiles, and bombers, with each capable of surviving a potential attack. The budget needed to implement this plan is expected to reach $40 billion by the end of the decade. In addition to this build-up of strategic offensive forces, there has been added the Administration's Strategic Defensive Initiative, or Star Wars, with the aim of building a space-based defense system against the entry of hostile missiles. The feasibility of this project remains highly controversial among scientists, and thus involves a high-risk undertaking. It has, however, become a major bargaining chip in United States–Soviet negotiations to reduce conventional forces. Looking at the future of the defense budget, it remains to be seen whether restriction of strategic weapons will permit substantial budget cuts without being matched by an offsetting expansion of conventional forces.

Industrial Impact

As noted before, the growth in defense programs has been a major factor in budget expansion, especially in the decade of the 1980s. As such, it has also been a major contributor to the federal deficit, the economic implications of which will be noted later. Apart from this, the defense build-up also had a major impact on the structure of industry and on productivity growth. There is an important difference in this respect between the growth of defense and that of social programs. The latter in large part involve transfers and thus a redirection of private demand from taxpayers to benefit recipients. In the case of defense, the diversion is from private demand for consumer goods and housing to government purchases from defense industries. This includes the manufacturing sector in general, with aerospace, shipbuilding, and electronics being the primary beneficiaries. In all, private sector employment sustained by defense purchases during the mid-1980s accounted for about five million jobs, with their primary location being in the Western and Southern states.[1] Defense outlays thus have a major impact on the industrial and regional base and thereby also on the pattern of defense politics.

Effects on Productivity Growth

Heavy emphasis on research and development in defense spending, equal in magnitude to such outlays in private industry, may also have important bearing on technical progress and hence productivity growth.[2] On the one hand, productivity gains in defense industries may spill over into the private sector, as evidenced by the heavily defense-driven progress in computer technology. On the other hand, absorption of scientific talent in the defense effort diverts such inputs from private industry, thereby tending to lessen its technical advance. In line with this, it has been noted that countries with a low defense share in GNP, such as West Germany and Japan, have experienced faster productivity growth during recent decades than has the U.S. economy, but factors other than defense may also explain this divergence. The long-run effect on productivity growth will depend on what is done to increase the availability of scientific personnel and the budgetary contribution thereto.

B. HIGHWAYS

Next to defense, highway investment offers much the most important part of tangible public capital formation. Federal concern with highway construction is also of long standing, with federal participation dating back to the Federal Aid Road Act of 1916. Whereas highway investment in the earlier stages was directed primarily at building up a nationwide traffic net, total road mileage has not risen greatly during recent decades. Rather, emphasis has been on improving road quality, by shifting to concrete roadbeds, for example. Highway expenditures, including all levels of government, amounted to $62 billion in 1986, including $30 billion of capital outlays, $18 billion for maintenance, and the remainder for related services and interest. The system now offers a road net of nearly 4 million miles and serves 135 million vehicles. Divided into functional classes, 69 percent of the mileage is in local roads, 21 percent in collector roads, 9 percent in minor arteries, and 1 percent in interstate highways. The corresponding shares in mileage traveled,

---

[1] See R. A. Stubbing, "The Defense Budget," in B. Mills and J. Palmer (eds.): *Federal Budget Policy in the 1980s,* Washington, D.C.: Urban Institute, 1984.

[2] See Congressional Budget Office, *Modernizing U.S. Strategic Offensive Forces: Costs, Effects, and Alternatives,* Washington, D.C., November 1987.

however, are 14, 17, 40, and 20 percent, reflecting the much lower utilization of local roads.

The highway system as a case study in public finance has three unique features: It offers an example of neatly integrated federal-state-local cooperation; it is largely user-financed, thereby approximating benefit taxation; and it offers a fertile ground for cost-benefit analysis.

Intergovernmental Cooperation

The federal-state-local division of labor is shown in Table 10-2. Half the revenue drawn from the public (line 6) is contributed by the states, with the remainder divided about equally between federal and local levels. The federal government (line 8) then transfers almost its entire revenue to lower levels of governments, taking the form of matching grants, much the larger part going to the states. The bulk of highway outlays is thus made at the state level, including provision for interstate as well as major in-state roads. Local government, in turn, remains responsible for local roads.

This division of labor reflects the federal concern with nationwide roads, state concerns with intrastate roads, and local concerns with local roads. Roads comprising the federal highway system now cover 20 percent of total mileage but nearly all interstate arterial roads. Only 1 percent of principal arterial miles and 4 percent of lesser arterial miles remain outside the federal highway system. And although only 20 percent of road mileage is included, such roads cover nearly 80

TABLE 10-2
Receipts and Disbursements for Highways, 1986
(In Billions of Dollars)

	Federal	State	Local	Total
A. *From own sources*				
Current receipts from highway users				
1. Taxes	12.1	22.1	.7	34.9
2. Tolls	—	2.1	.5	2.6
3. Total	12.1	24.2	1.2	37.5
4. Other current receipts	2.8	5.3	14.2	22.3
5. Bond issues and reserves	.2	2.3	2.4	4.9
6. Total	15.1	31.8	17.8	64.7
B. *Intergovernmental grants*				
7. Received	—	13.2	7.8	21.0
8. Made	− 14.2	− 7.2	− .6	− 22.0
9. Net	− 14.2	6.0	7.2	− 1.0
C. *Funds available (6 + 9)*				
10. Available	.9	37.8	25.0	63.7
D. *Uses*				
11. Capital outlays	.5	22.1	6.4	29.0
12. Maintenance	.1	6.7	11.2	18.0
13. Other, net	.3	9.0	7.4	16.7
14. Total	.9	37.8	25.0	63.7

Source: U.S. Department of Transportation, *Highway Statistics,* 1986, p. 38. *Highway Trust Funds and other relevant trust funds are included under federal. Line 4 includes finance from general fund appropriations and other taxes and fees. Line 12 includes administration, law enforcement, and interest.*

percent of total miles traveled. Outlays on roads in the federal system are given matching grants ranging from 90 to 70 percent, depending on the class of roads. The federal matching program, as noted before, dates back to 1916. Directed initially at new investment, matching of maintenance programs has been an increasing element since the 1960s. With the interstate system now nearly completed, this redirection reflects the natural maturing of the system.

User Charge Finance

Returning to Table 10-2, we see that the cost of the highway program (lines 1–3) is sustained in large part out of imposts on highway users. At the federal level, revenue is drawn primarily from excise taxes on motor fuel, proceeds from which are transferred to the Highway Trust Fund for disbursement in matching grants. At the state level, revenue is drawn from registration and other motor vehicle fees, used in turn as the base for federal support and in part given as grants to local government. The financing of highways thus approximates a system of benefit taxation. The federal contribution to nationwide roads is financed by nationwide taxes, whereas the state contribution is sustained by assessments on state motorists via gasoline taxes. Only the local contribution is drawn from general revenue, i.e., property tax payments by local residents and by special assessments.

But although this pattern reflects a spirit of benefit taxation, it does so in a crude way only. Direct toll receipts (line 2 of the table) play only a very minor role, with the benefit relation largely based on average travel by members of certain groups (e.g., by residence, type of vehicle, etc.) rather than by frequency and cost of individual use. Frequency of individual use enters in the case of motor fuel excises and license fees which differ by type of vehicle. Such differences, however, are related only vaguely to resulting benefits or damage costs. Some sophisticated form of toll charges may become possible with respect to urban traffic as technology advances,[3] but this is not likely to replace more general sources of user finance.

Use of Cost-Benefit Analysis

In order to assess the efficient level of highway expenditures, the resulting benefits and costs must be determined. Whereas the problems involved are much simpler than those previously encountered in the design of defense planning, they are complex nevertheless.

Rationale of Project Evaluation   Our problem is that of a state highway department which must decide whether to improve highway facilities between two cities. Is such an investment worthwhile, and how extensive should the new facility be?

To answer the question, we must evaluate the benefits and costs involved. Benefits are measured in terms of reduced travel cost to the user. This approach is possible because travel is an "intermediate good," entering into the final product, which is "being at the point of destination." Reduction in travel cost is a reduction in the price at which this final product can be purchased. The better the available

---

[3] See p. 44.

facilities, the lower will be the cost per trip for any given volume of traffic. Also, the greater the volume of traffic, the higher will be the cost per trip.

This is shown in Figure 10-1. The total number of trips is measured along the horizontal axis, and dollar costs and prices per trip are measured on the vertical axis. Schedule SF_1 shows the marginal cost per trip to the road user at which various traffic volumes can be accommodated with a given level of highway facilities F_1, and SF_2 and SF_3 show the same for expanded levels of facilities F_2 and F_3. We may think of the subscripts as reflecting the number of lanes in the highway. With any given facility, the cost per trip rises with increasing traffic volume or number of trips, mainly owing to crowding and longer driving time. The SF schedules thus represent travel supply schedules to the users, where their own travel cost is the "price" which they must pay to make a trip in terms of travel time, accident cost, automotive expenses, and so on. Their demand schedules are not known, but we observe point L which shows that with existing facility F_1, the number of trips equals OA, with an average user cost per trip of OB. We estimate that if costs are reduced by expanding facilities from F_1 to F_2, users will move from L to M. The number of trips will increase to OC with a user cost of OD. This estimate may be based on observing the effects of expanding facilities in other locations. LM may

FIGURE 10-1 Highway user demand at various levels of facility.

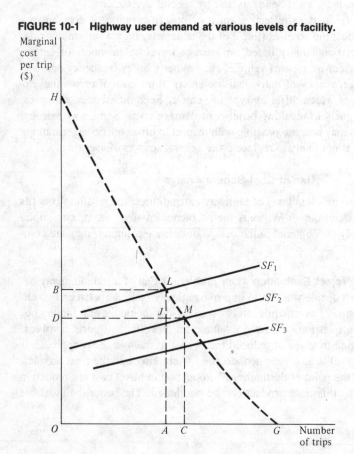

then be regarded as the estimated demand curve over the relevant range. It is extended here to G and H to develop the subsequent analysis.

The gain from increasing the facility level from F_1 to F_2 may be measured as the area DHM minus BHL, or as $DBLM$. $DBLM$ is the gain in consumer surplus which results from introduction of the new facility. Of this, $DBLJ$ reflects the cost saving on the old number of trips OA, while JLM reflects the gain on the additional trips AC. This latter gain on the new trips equals JLM, not $ALMC$, because $AJMC$ is offset by the additional user cost which results as the number of trips is expanded.

Turning now to Figure 10-2, we see that levels of highway facility (measured again in terms of lanes) are measured on the horizontal axis. The demand schedule DD reflects the marginal benefit which consumers derive from various facility levels, assuming the optimum use (as defined in Figure 10-1) for each level. Thus, at facility level F_2, the marginal benefit (obtained by moving from F_1 to F_2) equals OP, as shown in Figure 10-2, where OP equals the area $DBLM$ in Figure 10-1. These marginal benefits must then be assessed against the costs to the highway department of securing the expansion of facilities. The marginal costs of expansion are shown in Figure 10-2 by the supply schedule SS, which represents the resource costs of supplying additional lanes.[4] To allow for economies of scale in construction, the marginal costs of adding lanes is assumed to decline with the scope of expansion. Thus the marginal cost of moving from facility level F_1 to level F_2 equals OR, that of moving from F_2 to F_3 equals OV, and so forth. If facilities were divisible, facility level F^*, where marginal cost equals marginal benefit, would be

FIGURE 10-2   Highway user demand for various levels of facility.

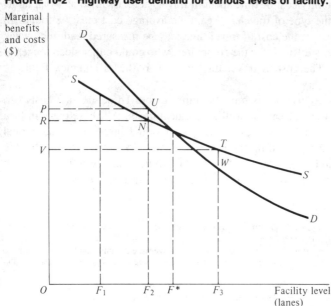

[4] See also Figure 9-2.

best. But facilities are lumpy, so that only certain points on the supply schedule, corresponding to F_1, F_2, and F_3, are possible. Choice of F^*, the intersection of DD and SS, is not feasible. The best solution is therefore to choose level F_2, because in moving from F_2 to F_3 additional benefits (or F_2UWF_3) would be outweighed by additional costs (or F_2NTF_3). Marginal user benefits of OP still exceed marginal costs OR, but expansion to the next feasible facility level F_3 would result in higher marginal costs than benefits.

An Illustration

This is the principle which underlies the typical cost-benefit calculation for highways such as is shown in Table 10-3. Column I gives the situation at facility level F_1, column II after expansion to F_2, and column III after expansion to F_3.

Calculation of Net Benefits to Users   Benefits, as noted previously, are to be measured in terms of savings in reduced travel time and other transport costs to the user. The first step, therefore, is to determine the reduction in travel cost which results from the expansion of facilities. Column I shows the computation of travel cost prior to project expansion. The first item is the cost of travel time. If we assume that the average trip takes thirty minutes (line 1) and that the average cost of travel time is $4 per hour, the money cost of travel time per trip prior to expansion is $2 (line 2, column I).

Figuring the average cost of travel time is far from simple. The required time, here assumed at thirty minutes, depends on the type of road as well as on traffic conditions. As any consumer well knows, travel time differs greatly between peak and slack hours, so that the average time requirement must be determined. Furthermore, the opportunity cost of time spent in travel, here assumed at $4 an hour, varies according to the type of traveler. Again the average cost must be found. In the case of a truck driver, the cost of travel time may be measured readily by wage rate, but the estimate is difficult for the commuter, who could either sleep longer or get to work sooner. The cost of travel time per trip is thus a complex figure to estimate.[5]

Next, certain other user costs must be allowed for. These are fuel costs (including taxes)[6] and wear of car, as well as accident costs. All these costs in turn depend on the type of road as well as on the type of vehicle used. These additional costs are shown in line 3. Setting them at an average 15 cents per mile for the preexpansion case and taking our road to be 11.7 miles long, we find that such costs equal $1.75 (line 3).[7] We thus arrive at the total variable user cost per trip of

---

[5] See A. J. Harrison and D. A. Quarmby, "The Value of Time," in R. Layard (ed.): *Cost-Benefit Analysis*, Baltimore: Penguin, 1972.

[6] The proper treatment of gasoline taxes depends on the governmental unit involved. Thus a state should not count its tax as a part of gasoline cost, whereas a locality which does not receive the revenue may include it.

[7] Cost estimates for various types of vehicles and roads are given in Marshall F. Reed, Jr., *The Economic Cost of Commuting*, Technical Study Memorandum 13, Washington, D.C.: Highway Users Foundation, 1975; also see *Road User Benefit Analysis for Highway Improvements*, Washington, D.C.: American Association for State Highway Officials, 1977.

TABLE 10-3
Profitability of Highway Construction

	Preexpansion Level F_1 (I)	After Expansion to F_2 (II)	After Expansion to F_3 (III)
Estimation of benefits to users			
1. Time per trip (minutes)	30	18	16
2. Time cost of trip ($4 per hour)	$2.00	$1.20	$1.07
3. Other cost per trip	$1.75	$1.90	$1.95
4. Total variable cost per trip	$3.75	$3.10	$3.02
5. Number of trips per year	1,000,000	1,500,000	1,600,000
6. Total variable costs per year	$3,750,000	$4,650,000	$4,832,000
7. Cost savings per trip	- - - - - -	$0.65	$0.08
8. Cost savings on previous number of trips	- - - - - -	$650,000	$120,000
9. Cost savings on additional trips	- - - - - -	$162,500	$4,000
10. Total benefits per year	- - - - - -	$812,500	$124,000
11. Present value of benefits (8 percent, 25 years)	- - - - - -	$8,673,438	$1,323,700
Estimation of project cost			
12. Capital cost	- - - - - -	$4,000,000	$2,000,000
13. Annual maintenance cost	$50,000	$60,000	$68,000
14. Increase in maintenance cost	- - - - - -	$10,000	$8,000
15. Present value of increased maintenance cost (8 percent, 25 years)	- - - - - -	$106,750	$85,400
16. Total project cost, present value	- - - - - -	$4,106,750	$2,085,400
Evaluation			
17. Benefit-cost ratio (line 11 ÷ line 16)	- - - - - -	2.11	0.63
18. Present value of net benefits (line 11 − line 16)	- - - - - -	$4,566,688	− $761,700
19. Internal rate of return (percentage)	- - - - - -	20	3

$3.75 (line 4). Assuming 1,000,000 trips to be made on the old facility, we estimate that total variable costs are $3,750,000 (line 6). Assuming our preexpansion road to correspond to facility level F_1 in Figure 10-1, we see that this level corresponds to area *OBLA*. Total benefits from the existing facility level are not shown. To determine them, the entire demand schedule for the service (i.e., area *OHLA* in Figure 10-1) would have to be known. We assume that operation of the existing facility F_1 is worthwhile, which is the case if benefits exceed user and maintenance costs. The cost of the original construction need not be considered, since it is a sunk cost.

Now an expansion is considered. The project is lumpy, so expansion must take the form of adding successive lanes. Expansion from facility level F_1 to F_2 involves addition of one lane, costing $4 million and corresponding to *OR* in Figure 10-2. Expansion from F_2 to F_3 adds a second lane and costs $2 million, corresponding to *OV* in Figure 10-2. Column II shows the situation after expansion to F_2. We note that the time per trip has gone down to eighteen minutes, while other costs per trip have increased slightly to $1.90. More gasoline is used at the higher speed and wear is increased. On balance, the total variable cost per trip has fallen by 65 cents. The number of trips has increased to 1,500,000 and total annual travel cost has gone up to $4,650,000. This corresponds to area $ODMC$ in Figure 10-1.

We are now ready to compute the net user benefits from project expansion as reflected in the net savings in user cost. As shown in line 4 of the table, expansion to facility level F_2 reduces travel cost per trip from $3.75 to $3.10, or by 65 cents. Applying this to the old number of trips, we obtain a saving of $650,000 (line 8), corresponding to area $DBLJ$ in Figure 10-1. Regarding the 500,000 additional trips, we count only one-half the saving, or 32.5 cents, thus obtaining a further gain of $162,500 (line 9), corresponding to the triangular area JLM in Figure 10-1.[8] Total benefits, corresponding to the area $DBLM$ in the figure, thus amount to the combined annual cost savings of $812,500 (line 10).

Since the benefits (cost savings) will occur in the future, the present value of the future stream of benefits must be obtained by discounting. Suppose that the planning horizon extends twenty-five years ahead and that a discount rate of 8 percent is applicable. As shown in line 11, this gives us a present value of $8,673,438 for the benefit stream generated by expanding facilities to F_2.

The same procedure is followed in column III of the table for raising facilities from F_2 to F_3. Travel time is reduced further and other costs rise slightly. The total saving in user cost is 8 cents per trip and the number of trips rises slightly to 1,600,000. Following the same procedure as before, we estimate that the present value of anticipated benefits (or costs savings to users) equals $1,323,700.

Calculation of Costs   Turning now to the costs involved in the expansion of facilities, note that the main items to be considered are construction costs, site costs, and maintenance costs.

Construction costs are measured in terms of market price and need no further explanation. Site acquisition is by eminent domain and involves evaluation of the taken property, but this may again be based on fair market value, reflecting the opportunity cost of the land in alternative uses. As shown in line 12, total construction costs are assumed to be $4 million for the F_2 expansion and $2 million for further expansion to F_3. These capital costs are undertaken at the outset, so that no discounting is needed.

Road maintenance costs are partly dependent on traffic volume and type and are partly independent thereof. The estimation of maintenance cost thus involves some of the same considerations which arise in estimating the savings in user cost. Maintenance costs are assumed to increase by $10,000 per year in raising the facility level from F_1 to F_2 and by a further $8,000 in going from F_2 to F_3. The present values of these maintenance-cost streams, accruing over a twenty-five-year period, are shown in line 15, and total costs (both construction and operating) in present-value terms are shown in line 16. These costs correspond to OR and OV for the F_2 and F_3 expansions, respectively, in the supply schedule of Figure 10-2.

---

[8] Counting half the savings, or 32.5 cents, is a rough-and-ready procedure for measuring the gain in consumer surplus which results, since it assumes a linear demand schedule between traffic volumes A and C in Figure 10-1. In the absence of better information, this is the best that can be done.

Comparison of Costs and Benefits   We are now ready to compare the present value of costs and benefits. For raising facilities from F_1 to F_2, benefits exceed costs by \$4,566,688 (line 18) and, as shown in line 17, the benefit-cost ratio is 2.11. The internal rate of return on the F_2 expansion is 20 percent. For raising facilities from F_2 to F_3, costs exceed benefits at the chosen 8 percent rate of discount by \$761,700, the benefit-cost ratio is only 0.63, and the internal rate of return falls to 3 percent. It follows that expansion to F_2 is profitable, while expansion to F_3 is not. The high return to expansion to F_2 also suggests that a modified extension beyond it, but less ambitious than F_3, would be desirable. If projects can be carried out in small units and the budget is flexible, additional expansion to F^* in Figure 10-2 would indeed be desirable until the incremental benefits and costs are the same and the benefit-cost ratio becomes 1 for the last unit of expanded facilities. But given the lumpiness of the project, expansion to F_2 is the best that can be done.

Indirect Benefits and Costs   Benefit measurement in the preceding illustration has allowed for benefits to direct highway users only. These "direct" benefits are relatively easy to measure, owing to the nature of transportation as an "intermediate" good. But in a fuller analysis, other benefits or costs must be considered as well.

Important indirect benefits may result from the repercussions of transport expansion on economic development. Thus expansion of facilities between two cities may generate economic development of the region and permit a better division of labor between the two locations. The resulting benefit will exceed the gain as measured above since factor earnings in both locations will increase. In developing countries in particular, the opening of communication brings heretofore unutilized resources into use and establishes communication with the market. The early development of canals, the growth of the United States railroad system in the middle of the nineteenth century, and today's highway construction in Latin America are cases in point. The developmental gains to the economy resulting from such growth in transport facilities are more difficult to predict and cannot be formulated simply in terms of reduced travel cost.

On the cost side, social cost may exceed the direct construction cost in a variety of ways. Dwellings may have to be destroyed and their replacement cost must be included as an indirect though tangible cost. Beyond this, a throughway may disrupt established communities and force relocation, introducing a further indirect and, this time, intangible cost. The true social cost may, in fact, greatly exceed the replacement cost of housing. Moreover, the pecuniary losses and gains which result may have important distributional implications. The destruction of low-cost housing may not hurt the landlord, who is compensated, but nevertheless places a burden on the tenants if the supply of low-cost housing is reduced in the process.

Estimated Returns on Maintenance of National Highway System

It remains to be seen how these principles of cost-benefit analysis enter into governmental estimates of highway needs. As may be expected, the underlying procedures are less refined than called for by the preceding section, but they nevertheless follow the basic rationale of cost-benefit analysis and suggest some interesting results.[9]

The first step is to estimate the cost of certain standards of road systems, including quality features such as lane width, pavement conditions and operating speed. This involves assumptions regarding future travel growth, weather conditions, resource costs, and so forth. The cost of meeting a range of standards is thus established, beginning with maintenance of present road conditions and followed by various degrees of improvement.

The second step is to find the resulting benefits for any given program. Such benefits are measured by the reduction in user cost, which are defined to include operating costs, accident costs, and time costs. Accident costs are defined so as to include the costs to society only, without allowing for loss of life and for suffering. Travel time in turn is valued at rates ranging from $7 for passenger cars up to $14 for four-axle trucks. Given the estimated costs and benefits, the rate of return on investment in highway maintenance can then be determined. Such calculations, prepared recently by the Congressional Budget Office are shown in Table 10-4, giving the rates of return on highway maintenance in 1984–1985.[10]

As shown at the bottom of the table, and taking the entire highway system (with the exception of some small rural roads), the annual user cost amounted to $878 billion, with about $250 billion thereof in time cost. Highway maintenance costs for 1984 and 1985 combined amounted to $23 billion. This investment is estimated to have resulted in an annual reduction in user cost by $10 billion or by slightly above 1 percent. These annual savings are estimated to continue over a period of ten years. To obtain the rate of return on the investment, we find the discount rate at which the present value of the two-year cost stream equals that of the ten-year benefit stream. Thus the internal rate of discount of 43 percent shown at the bottom of the table is obtained. We also note that the rates of return on different parts of the system vary widely, with those on urban roads generally above those on rural roads. Nevertheless, returns in most cases and for the system as a whole are very high, much above what can be expected on other public investments and a multiple of returns on private investment. It does not follow, however, that there should be a massive expansion of such programs. Since the quality of road maintenance obtained by the current level of outlays is fairly high, step-ups would yield rapidly declining marginal returns. Note also that we are here dealing with maintenance of an essentially completed road system and not with the creation of new roads. In the past, when the latter was of major importance, benefit estimation would have been more complex, because it would have involved external benefits accruing from the opening of new territories. This, however, has become by now a minor part of the problem, thus simplifying benefit estimation.

---

[9] See Committee on Public Works and Transportation, *The Status of the Nation's Highways, Condition and Performance*, Department of Transportation, June 1987. Also see statement by E. M. Ehrlich, Assistant Director of Natural Resources and Commerce, Committee on Environment and Public Works, U.S. Senate, February 29, 1988.

[10] See forthcoming publication by CBO. I am indebted to Jenifer Wishart of CBO for helpful comments.

TABLE 10-4
Investment and Returns on Highway Maintenance, 1984–85
(In Billions of Dollars at 1986 Prices)

Highway System (All Levels of Government)	ANNUAL AMOUNTS			Rate of Return on Investment, Percent‡
	Vehicle Miles of Travel (Billions)	Capital Maintenance Cost, 1984–1985*	User Cost of Travel, 1985†	
Rural highway systems				
Interstates	154.1	3.4	72.8	− 4
Other principal arterials	145.9	3.4	71.1	16
Minor arterials	136.9	3.3	68.1	28
Major collectors	163.2	2.3	90.5	7
Minor collectors	43.3	0.8	27.0	57
All rural	643.4	13.1	329.4	16
Urban highway systems				
Interstates	216.4	4.5	91.4	31
Other freeways and expressways	97.4	1.1	41.4	117
Other principal arterials	279.0	2.5	203.9	136
Minor arterials	201.7	1.4	149.2	50
Collectors	89.5	0.6	65.0	130
All urban	884.1	10.0	550.9	75
All systems	1,527.5	23.1	880.3	43

*Includes capital disbursements for reconstruction, major widening, bridge rehabilitation and replacement, safety construction, and other rehabilitation. Thus it includes all capital disbursements except those for new construction.
†Includes costs for vehicle operations, accidents and property damage, and estimates for the costs of time spent during travel.
‡Based on a ten-year life for the rehabilitation and reconstruction projects.
Source: Congressional Budget Office, highway study to be published in Spring 1988.

C. OUTDOOR RECREATION

As our next case, we consider the evaluation of projects for outdoor recreation, say, a public park. The benefits which accrue include (1) benefits to the users, (2) benefits to the surrounding community, and (3) certain other benefits, such as preservation of the natural beauty of the environment, which are of a more or less intangible sort. As before, we focus first on user benefits, which are considered the major component of the benefit calculation.

In contrast to highways, we now deal with a social good which is in the nature of a final or consumer good rather than of an intermediate good. The problem is to evaluate the benefits, such as reduced congestion, which are derived from the park itself or its expansion and not, as in the case of roads, from the reduced cost of obtaining other benefits, such as those of getting to a destination. The question of what a visit to the park is worth must be faced. Given the answer, we can then compare the present value of costs and benefits along much the same lines as in the preceding illustration.

Measuring Benefits to Users

Various techniques of benefit measurement have been suggested and used. They include direct pricing through user charges, estimation of willingness to pay hypothetical user chargers, use of prices paid for similar private facilities, costs in using the facilities, and the construction of indices such as merit-weighted user days.

User Charges Let us assume our park to be such that "exclusion" can be readily applied, i.e., that the administrative cost of limiting admission to those who pay the price is insignificant. We have seen that in the absence of crowding, exclusion is incompatible with efficient use of the particular park since consumption is nonrival. However, individual parks are not planned in isolation. A park agency will be confronted with providing parks in different locations, and the experience gained from A may be used for planning the location of B. A case can thus be made for testing the profitability of park construction by charging fees in one initial park, even if attendance cost is zero, so as to obtain a measuring rod for further park construction. If the present value of prospective fees from park A exceeds the project cost, similar facilities will be called for in other locations where demand conditions are expected to be similar. The inefficiency which results from underutilizing park A (or from having constructed a park which proves unprofitable) may be more than offset by the increased efficiency in planning other park construction made possible by the information gained.

Hypothetical User Charges Instead of experimenting with actual user charges, market survey techniques may be used in an attempt to obtain the same information and without suffering the cost of excluding potential users. Such users may be asked how much they would be willing to pay for various facilities or how much use they would make of given facilities at various prices. By this means, an attempt can be made to construct a simulated demand schedule and to evaluate benefits without the inefficiency of exclusion. But the difficulty is that the respondents are not likely to tell the truth: they will give too high an evaluation if they wish to encourage the construction of the facility and too low a figure if they wish to discourage it. Nevertheless, this approach has proved to be of some use and has been strongly advocated by several experts.

Prices for Private Facilities In some instances it may be possible to draw a parallel to prices paid for more or less similar private facilities. Thus, fees paid for membership in a private club providing similar facilities may be indicative of the consumption value obtained by the use of the public park. There are two weaknesses to this approach. First, it may well be that the price paid for the private facility is depressed because another public facility is available free of direct charge. Thus, use of the price paid for admission to the private facility understates the value of the additional public park. Second, a factor working in the opposite direction is that the price paid for the private facility may include a premium for "exclusiveness" generated by membership in the private facility. Thus, the value of the public park would be overstated. For the method to be reliable, it would be necessary for the two facilities to be fairly comparable, a condition that will rarely be found.

Costs Incurred Approaching the estimation of the dollar value of recreation benefits indirectly, some studies have made use of the personal costs incurred by

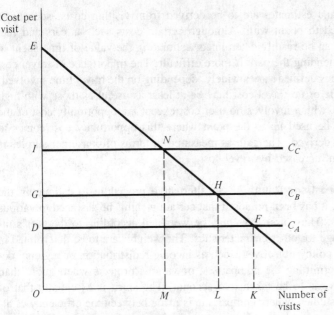

FIGURE 10-3 Outdoor recreation.

users in securing their outdoor recreation. These costs are then taken as a proxy for how the user values the benefits received.

Suppose first that there is only one visitor to the park whose cost per visit equals *OD* in Figure 10-3, with number of trips equal to *OK*. His marginal costs and benefits both equal *OD*, and given his demand schedule *EF*, his total benefits equal *OEFK*, this being the benefit total which has to be compared with investment costs in evaluating the project. Unfortunately, however, this demand schedule is not known, and all that can be observed is point *F* thereon. Whereas the *ODFK* component of his total benefit can be measured given point *F*, the demand schedule *EA* would have to be known to determine his consumer surplus, or *DEF*.

Ingenious methods have been developed to arrive at such an estimate. For this purpose, let community X, which is contemplating construction of a park, observe the experience of community Z, which has undertaken such a project. Let there be three visitors, living five, ten, and fifteen miles from the project, whose travel cost equals *OD, OG,* and *OI*, respectively. Also, suppose that their respective number of trips equals *OK, OL,* and *OM*. As plotted in Figure 10-3, we now have *F, H,* and *N* as three points on the demand curve. With more visitors and distances added, a more complete *EF* pattern may be obtained. The total benefit, derived as the sum of *OEF + OEHL + OENM,* is then compared with the investment cost of the project. In practice, matters are more complicated. There are a large number of travelers of the *A, B,* and *C* types each of whose benefits must be aggregated. Moreover, benefits which accrue in the course of time must be discounted to their present value, prior to comparison with the investment cost involved in arriving at a benefit/cost ratio. Also, allowance must be made for maintenance costs. The basic problem, however, remains of how to arrive at a demand schedule so that benefits, including consumer surplus, can be estimated.

If these demand estimates are to be derived from visiting costs, such costs must be determined to begin with. Although certain costs such as cars and fuel needed for travel can be readily determined, estimating the value of time spent in travel and while attending the park is more difficult. The importance of travel cost in total user cost thus defined varies widely, depending on the travel time involved, and parks with little or no travel cost may be at least as useful as those with high travel cost. A park which involves no user cost except the opportunity cost of the time spent should be used up to the point where this opportunity cost comes to exceed the benefit derived. The gain as measured in terms of consumer surplus is reduced rather than increased by travel cost.

Merit-Weighted User Days   As an alternative procedure to estimating the value of user days, it has been proposed that certain weights be assigned to various user characteristics. Thus, user days may be weighted according to the user's income, residence, age, or other characteristics. The weights are to be determined in terms of specified policy objectives, such as income redistribution or regional development, thus permitting the comparison of various projects where more than one policy objective is to be taken into account. The spirit is essentially that of cost-effectiveness studies, where comparison is made between the efficiency of alternative uses of given funds in achieving a desired set of objectives and where the value weights to be attributed to these objectives are given in advance.

Other Benefits

So far, only benefits accruing to and valued by users have been allowed for. In addition, other benefits may enter. Outdoor recreation projects are frequently part of broader programs aimed at multiple objectives, e.g., water resource or regional development projects. Thus, a dam may be built to generate power, to control floods, to serve irrigation, *and* to yield recreational facilities. The benefits from the various products must then be evaluated in conjunction with one another so as to obtain the best product mix.

Outdoor recreation, moreover, may be considered a merit good, so that social valuation exceeds the value attributed by private users, resulting in a writing-up of their benefit evaluation similar to a subsidy to private-type merit goods. Similar considerations arise with regard to objectives such as conservation of natural beauty or of wildlife. These objectives involve social values which cannot be measured readily by market tests and thus tend to be set aside. Possible conflicts between social- and private-time preference are also involved, relating in this instance to the interests of future versus present generations. In recreation as elsewhere, it is natural for economic analysis to focus on those aspects of the problem which permit analogy to market pricing and which are therefore more feasible to deal with. These are by no means the only, or even in some cases the most important, aspects.

D. EDUCATION

As shown in Table 10-5, public expenditures on education in 1986 amounted to

TABLE 10-5
Expenditures on Education
(In Billions of Dollars)

	1970			1986		
	Elementary and Secondary	Higher Education	Total	Elementary and Secondary	Higher Education	Total
Public						
Federal	3.4	2.4	5.8	9.9	7.0	16.9
State	15.8	6.3	22.1	70.5	29.6	100.2
Local	21.7	.8	22.5	65.1	2.0	67.1
Other	.1	6.3	6.4	.4	26.9	27.4
Total	41.0	15.8	56.8	146.0	65.6	211.6
Private	4.7	8.9	13.6	13.3	35.5	48.6
Total	45.7	24.7	70.4	159.3	100.9	260.2

Source: Statistical Abstract for the United States, 1987, p. 115.

$212 billion with 70 percent thereof going to elementary and secondary and 30 percent to higher education. Provision of the former has traditionally been a local function, relying on property tax finance. However, over the recent decades, the state contribution has become increasingly important and now pays for over one-half of school finance. Nevertheless, operating the actual school system has remained under local direction, with state funding passed on to the local level via a system of grants. Public provision for higher education, in turn, is largely a state responsibility, although it is supported by a substantial federal contribution. Education expenditures now account for nearly 30 percent of total outlays at the state-local level and thus play a very major role in that sector's public finances. Private expenditures on elementary and secondary education in turn account for less than 10 percent of the total, leaving the provision of schooling an essentially public undertaking. The contribution of the private sector is higher, however, in the case of higher education where approximately one-third is privately provided.

Policy Issues

The public debate over education policy is a continuing process, as it should be in a democratic society. It raises the broad issues of what should be taught in public schools, how teaching should proceed, and who is entitled to education. More recently, there is the further question of whether public financing should be limited to public schools or whether financial aid should be given to private institutions.

Entitlement to Education The states in general have wide freedom in designing their own fiscal structure and they in turn control local finances most directly responsible for the provision of school services. But as noted earlier, state constitutions have been interpreted as entitling the individual citizen to a level of school services which does not depend on the local property tax base, and the United States Supreme Court has recognized that availability of educational services is supported by the equal protection clause of the United States

Constitution.[11] This constitutional case against linkage of school finance to the local property tax base has been resolved in part by the recent trend toward increased reliance on state, as distinct from local, finance for education. At the same time, no constitutional arguments have as yet been advanced which might call for an entitlement to comparable education services across state lines.

Public versus Private Education   Elementary and high school education, as noted before, is very largely provided through public schools, including 90 percent of the student body. There has been a rising debate, however, over whether such a public "monopoly" is desirable. This has been associated in recent years with concern over the quality of education provided by the public schools. A more efficient output, so it is argued, would be obtained if there was competition between public and private institutions. This is to be accomplished, so the proponents argue, while continuing to depend on public financing of education. Parents would be free to choose between sending their children to public schools or to receive vouchers for payment of private school finances, vouchers which the schools would then present for payment to the government.

Proponents of public education in turn argue that education is a matter of great public interest and should therefore be provided publicly. But can the case for public schools simply be derived from the proposition that education generates externalities? Such externalities do result and tend to be disregarded by private demand which values the student's own gains only. As education thus assumes the quality of a social good, private investment therein falls short of the social optimal level.[12] This does not require, however, that education must be provided by public schools. The needed correction can also be applied by subsidizing private education, whether it is through subsidies to schools or through grants to student outlays by vouchers. A similar conclusion follows even if education is considered a "merit" good, where the individual is taken to undervalue particular benefits which society wishes him or her to obtain. Nor does the case for public as distinct from private schools follow from the proposition that the importance of education for the individual calls for equal provision, or at least effective minimum standards. This principle, reflecting a major instance of "categorical equity," can once more be implemented whether public financing goes to support public or private school organizations.

The points raised so far pertain to the level of education, not the choice between public and private institutions. More relevant to that choice is the proposition that the efficiency of schools would be raised by increased competition and that competition would best be provided by private schools. Perhaps so, but ways may also be developed to secure increased competition within the public system, including reduction in the size of school districts and increased student mobility.

The basic issue, after all is said and done, is not to be found within the above considerations. Rather, it involves the proposition that the nature of education differs in the two settings. In the case of public schools, the context of what is taught

---

[11] See p. 28.
[12] See pp. 6 and 106 above.

and the values that are to be transmitted will be set by the broader community as the outcome of a political process. In the private school setting, school programs will reflect the views of particular groups in the society, bounded by religious, cultural, national, or other characteristics. The choice then is between providing for a common core and encouraging divergency in education. This is a choice which involves basic problems of how society is to be viewed, problems which are not simply fiscal in nature but involve a much broader range of issues.[13]

Benefit-Cost Analysis of Higher Education

The principles of cost-benefit analysis may again be applied to measuring the return to investment in education. Methods of cost-effectiveness analysis may be applied to specific problems such as alternative inputs (computers, tutorials, smaller classes) in improving performance in, say, mathematics classes. Or they may be applied on a larger scale to estimate rates of return on investment in education. Some of the problems which arise are illustrated here in the context of higher education.

Estimating Benefits Beginning with the benefit side, various types of benefit may be distinguished, including (1) increased earnings by the student, (2) the satisfaction which the student may derive from a more educated life, and (3) external benefits accruing to society from the influences of a better-educated public. Of these three, only (1) permits ready measurement and will be included in the following illustration.

The first step then is to determine the increase in the student's lifetime earnings that is a result of education. This gain in earnings has been estimated by observing earnings differentials among people with various levels of education and attributing these differentials to the influence of education. The earning increment is then projected over the student's working life as shown in lines 1 to 3 of Table 10-6. Absolute amounts of earnings over a 44-year period are shown in column I, while discounted values (at 3 percent) are given in column II.

Estimating Costs The costs of higher education are shown in lines 4 to 9. Line 4 shows the four-year cost incurred by the institution in "producing" a bachelor's degree. One of the problems in estimating this item is to distinguish between costs incurred directly in producing a bachelor's degree and other costs serving graduate work and research. There is also the problem of how to handle costs incurred in the accumulation of excess academic credits and how to deal with dropouts. The amounts of line 4 do not allow for these latter items and if included might double the recorded amount of institutional costs.

Lines 5 to 7 show costs incurred by the student. The amount of tuition shown in line 5 is an average figure and varies greatly between state and private institutions. The cost of room and board as shown in line 6 somewhat overstates the proper amount because it reflects total rather than incremental costs. Line 7 shows the amount of forgone earnings, again substantially lower for female students. Line

---

[13] On the question of private versus public schools, see Henry J. Levin, "Education as a Public and a Private Good," *Journal of Policy Analysis and Management,* vol. 6, no. 4, 1987.

TABLE 10-6
Returns to Higher Education for Male Workers
(In Thousands of Dollars)

	I	II
	Zero Discount	3% Discount
Lifetime Earnings		
1. Earnings of college graduates	1,605	1,380
2. Total earnings of high school graduates	1,104	975
3. Gain (1 − 2)	501	405
College costs		
4. Incurred by institution	25	23
Incurred by student		
5. Tuition	9	8
6. Room and board	7	6
7. Forgone earnings	45	42
8. Total (4 × 6 + 7)*	77	71
9. Private (5 + 6 + 7)	61	56
Net benefits		
10. Total (3 − 8)	424	334
11. Private (3 − 9)	440	349
Benefit/cost ratios		
12. Private (3/8)	6.5	5.7
13. Total (3/9)	8.2	7.2
Internal rate of discount		
14. Private	14.4	
15. Total	18.7	

*Line 5 not included because it also appears as part of line 4.

Source: For lines 1 and 2, columns I and II, see *Statistical Abstract of the United States,* 1984, p. 470. The figures show the lifetime earnings from age twenty-five to sixty-four for college and high school graduates, men and women. The estimates are based on 1979 patterns of earnings by age groups for high school and college graduates, which patterns are assumed to continue in the future.

For lines 4 to 10, see U.S. Department of Education, *Estimating the Cost of a College Education and Institutional Cost Analysis,* 1987. The amounts shown refer to all institutions combined and thus hide substantial differences between types of institutions. The source does not differentiate between male and female students and we assume that the amounts given in lines 4, 5, and 6 are the same for both sources. The combined figure on forgone earnings in the source is given at $35,000, applicable to male and female students. It is here raised to $45,000 applicable for male students, in line with corresponding earnings of high school graduates as given in Bureau of the Census, *Money Income of Households, Families, and Persons in the United States, 1982,* Table 49.

For lines 4 to 9, column II, it is assumed that costs accrue at equal amounts over a four-year period.

For lines 14 and 15, it is assumed that the earnings of lines 1 and 2 are spread in equal amounts over a period of forty-six years, i.e., from age eighteen to sixty-four.

8 records total costs and line 9 shows private cost only. All these costs are incurred over a four-year period, and their discounted value is again shown in column II. The net of benefits minus costs (private and total) is given in lines 10 and 11, with corresponding cost-benefit ratios shown in lines 12 and 13. Lines 14 and 15, finally, give the internal rates of discount, based on the assumption that the resulting stream of income gains will accrue in equal annual amounts extending over a period of forty-four years, i.e., from high school graduation to retirement at age sixty-four. As shown in lines 12 and 13, the benefit-cost ratios (discounted values) are 6.5 and 8.2 for total and private costs, respectively, and the corresponding internal rates of discount are 14.4 and 18.7 percent. These rates are somewhat

above those usually given,[14] but Table 10-6 makes use of available data and is helpful to show the estimating procedures involved.

In interpreting the outcome, you must keep a number of points in mind: (1) the internal rate of return is overstated by assuming the gain to accrue in equal annual amounts rather than allowing the gain to rise with age; (2) the cost figures are understated because they do not allow for the cost of excess academic credits or for dropouts, allowance for which might double institutional costs; (3) the benefit data pertain to average rather than marginal values. The latter, which are relevant for investment decisions, are likely to be lower. For these and other reasons, the returns here arrived at may substantially overstate the return to education. At the same time, it should be noted that the benefits here included allow for gains in terms of private earnings only, while disregarding external benefits to society which may accrue from a better educated public. In short, the problem is more complicated than can be captured in a simple calculation such as this.

Finally, note that the above data apply to male students only. The gain for female students, based on the underlying earnings estimates, are shown to be very much lower, approximately one-third of those for male students, with a correspondingly lower rate of return. This result, however, reflects earnings patterns which prevailed in 1979. It does not therefore allow for improvements in the position of women in the labor market, and more complete labor-force participation such as may be expected to develop in the course of the working life of students now in college.

E. SUMMARY

Application of cost-benefit analysis to various types of public services raises a wide range of quite distinct issues, and different procedures have been developed to deal with them.

Beginning with national defense, decision on the scope and pattern of weapons design involves issues such as these:

1. The equipment to be provided will depend on the pursuit of foreign policy and its national goals, as these will affect the likelihood and type of military contingency that may arise. Effective assessment of cooperative or hostile responses on the part of potential adversaries is of crucial importance.

2. Given specific capability requirements, the cost effectiveness of various weapon designs can be compared, and an efficient package can be chosen.

3. With rapidly changing technology, a weighing of short and long run objectives becomes important.

4. Allowance has to be made for interaction between weapon development and the advance of technology, with both favorable and unfavorable side effects on private industry to be considered.

Turning to highway and road construction, a quite different set of considerations arise:

---

[14] See for instance R. B. Freeman, "The Decline in the Economic Rewards to College Education," *The Review of Economics and Statistics,* 1977, which estimates rates of return of around 10 percent.

5. Since the transportation system involves all levels of government, close intergovernmental cooperation in expenditure planning is called for.

6. Finance by user charges may submit highway outlays to a market test but is of limited applicability only.

7. Application of cost-benefit analysis calls for determining the optimal level of facilities to equate marginal costs and benefits.

8. Careful calculation of costs and of benefits to users is required.

9. Estimated returns on various levels of highway maintenance have been examined.

Application of cost-benefit analysis to facilities for outdoor recreation was considered.

10. User charges may be used to evaluate user benefits, but exclusion costs arise in the absence of crowding.

11. Methods have been developed to estimate benefits in an indirect fashion.

Application of cost-benefit analysis to investment in education is of special interest and once more raises a variety of issues:

12. Education has been singled out as a public service which individuals are entitled to receive.

13. While it is widely agreed that education should be paid for publicly, this leaves open the question of whether it is better provided in public or in private institutions.

14. Techniques have been developed to measure the costs and benefits, and thereby rates of return, on higher education.

FURTHER READINGS

Case studies in cost-benefit analysis may be found in:

Chase, S. B. (ed.): *Problems in Public Expenditure Analysis,* Washington, D.C.: Brookings Institution, 1968.

Dorfman, R. (ed.): *Measuring Benefits of Government Investments,* Washington, D.C.: Brookings Institution, 1965.

Harberger, A. C.: *Project Evaluation,* London: Macmillan, 1972.

Haveman, R. and Margolis, J., *Public Expenditures and Policy Analysis,* 3d ed., Boston: Houghton Mifflin Co., 1983.

Chapter 11

Case Studies in Expenditure Policy: (2) Low-Income Support and Social Insurance*

A. Low-Income Support Programs: *Medicaid; Supplementary Security Income; Food Stamps; Low-Cost Housing; Welfare.* **B. Effects on Work Incentives:** *How Serious is the Disincentive Problem?; Alternative Benefit Patterns; Negative Income Tax.* **C. Social Insurance Programs:** *Retirement and Disability Insurance; Health Insurance; Unemployment Insurance.* **D. Issues in OASI:** *1983 Reforms; The Long-Run Outlook; Public versus Private Provision; Income Redistribution; Payroll Tax Finance versus Budgetary Contributions; Effects on Capital Formation; Effects on Labor Supply.* **E. Summary.**

In this chapter, we turn to major income-maintenance and social security programs, rendered mostly through the form of transfer payments. Such programs are largely a federal responsibility, and an overview is given in Table 11-1. The programs may be divided into those directed primarily at improving the position of the poor and others providing for various kinds of social insurance available across a wider range.

*Reader's Guide to Chapter 11: Having dealt with the application of cost-benefit analysis to various types of public services, we now turn to transfer programs. Here command over resources is transferred from one sector of the private economy to another, directed in most instances at assistance to low-income groups or to provision for social insurance. Once more the task is to secure maximum benefits at minimum cost.

TABLE 11-1
Major Federal Social Programs, 1988*
(In Billions of Dollars)

Low-income support	
Medicaid	30.7
Housing assistance	10.5
Food stamps	13.5
Child nutrition	7.1
Supplementary security income (SSI)	12.6
Family-support payments (AFDC)	11.1
Subtotal	85.5
Insurance programs	
Social security (OASI, DI)	219.7
Medicare	78.8
Unemployment	15.7
Subtotal	314.2
Total	399.7

*Estimated levels, *The Budget of the Federal Government*, fiscal year 1989.

A. LOW-INCOME SUPPORT PROGRAMS[1]

As shown in the upper part of Table 11-1, there are a number of major programs aiming at low-income support. AFDC (Aid to Families with Dependent Children), also referred to as *the* welfare program, accounts for only a small part of this larger system. In the following, brief reference will be made to the major components, followed by a more careful look at AFDC and the general problem of how welfare can be best provided.

Medicaid

Medicaid, much the largest of the low-income programs, is a joint federal-state undertaking, with the federal government matching state outlays by 50 percent or more, depending on the state's per capita income and other factors. The program covers all persons receiving assistance under AFDC, as well as most persons in the SSI (Supplementary Security Income) program, as well as other eligible persons over sixty-five. In all, 22 million persons received Medicaid assistance in 1985, with dependent children the most important group. Medicaid pays the premium for Medicare and also covers certain additional benefits. Each state administers and designs its own program, subject to guidelines set at the federal level. Reflecting the rising costs of medical services, the cost of Medicaid has increased sharply, and efforts are under way to slow the upward trend.

Supplementary Security Income

Payments under the SSI system are received by over 4 million people. Eligibility is limited to the aged (over sixty-five) and to the blind and disabled. Payments are

---

[1] For a survey of major provisions under the various programs, see "Facts and Figures About Social Security" and "Social Security Programs in the United States," in *Social Security Bulletin*, April and May 1987.

received by individuals whose income falls short of $4,080, with the payment equal to the amount of shortfall. Eligibility also limits assets that may be held to $2,000 per individual and $3,000 for couples. These amounts, applicable for 1987, are indexed as are social security payments. States may supplement the federal program and may opt to have their assistance administered at the federal level.

Food Stamps

Under the food stamp program, households (now not limited to the aged) are given food stamps which are accepted in payment by grocery stores for food purchases. To be eligible, a household must have less than $2,000 in disposable assets (1987 level) and a gross income not over 130 percent of what is defined as the poverty income for that household size. About 20 million persons receive food stamps with an average annual value (1987) of around $500. The program is paid for at the federal level and operates through local welfare offices.

Low-Cost Housing

The federal government provides housing subsidies for low-income tenants through various programs, with about 20 million households receiving such assistance. The assistance is provided via low-interest mortgages for the construction of buildings which accrue largely though not entirely to low-income tenants.

Welfare

Aid to Families with Dependent Children (AFDC), the so-called welfare program, is by no means the largest item in the system of low-income support, but it has been the most controversial one and at the center of discussion over welfare reform.

The AFDC program provides for federal matching grants to support states in offering cash and certain noncash support to families with dependent children. For families to be eligible, children to be assisted must be needy and deprived of the support of at least one parent. The children must live at home and be under eighteen. The income of families to be eligible must be below 185 percent of the standard need for families of that size. Given these federal requirements, the states are then free to set the level of standard needs which in turn results in widely different supply levels across the states. In 1985, average monthly payments per family ranged from $115 in Alabama to $603 in Alaska, with an average of $348. In all, 3.7 million families were recipients of AFDC payments.

The welfare program has been subject to extensive criticism and for different reasons.

1. The program results in widely differing support levels across states, which may be unacceptable from a national point of view.

2. The program's eligibility requirements and their enforcement may be seen as demeaning. Moreover, it encourages family disintegration, since payments are generally limited to families in which the male head is absent. Also note that male heads of households are eligible for assistance in only twenty-three states.

3. The level of benefits, especially in low-benefit states, is considered inadequate for a decent minimal standard of living.

4. Single persons and childless couples are excluded from the welfare system unless they are blind or disabled.

5. The working poor are not helped, because a parent who works full time is excluded. Such is the case even though 40 percent of the poor live in families headed by a full-time worker.

6. Welfare administration would be simplified by unifying the various parts in a single system and, as some critics maintain, making all support in cash form.

7. Most important, the program is seen as discouraging work because the level of benefits falls as own earnings rise. Thus, the system in effect imposes a high marginal rate of tax on earnings. AFDC recipients are permitted a certain amount of earnings without loss of benefits, and they are permitted to hold up to $1,000 of property. However, if their earnings exceed these amounts, benefits are reduced by one-third of the excess, and if earnings rise further, by 100 percent thereof. These offsets to earnings are similar to tax rates on earnings of from 33 to 100 percent.

8. The focus of the problem has changed from providing relief in a severely depressed economy to dealing with the welfare of children in single-parent families which have come to account for nearly 50 percent of births.

As is evident from these objections, the welfare system is considered unsatisfactory on many grounds. In particular, it is widely agreed that benefits should be extended to the working poor and to poor families without children and that interstate differentials in benefit levels should be reduced. There is also a widespread feeling that the system is abused by beneficiaries who are able to work but choose not to. As just noted, work incentives are reduced by the implicit rate of tax, because a substantial increase in earnings is needed to make the net gain worthwhile. Abuse and natural response are difficult to distinguish. However, whatever the scope of the phenomenon may be, its presence interferes with the public's willingness to render support to those truly in need. The superior solution is to provide work opportunities and child-care facilities for those able to work. Having done so, abuse may then be checked by building a work requirement into the system. Proposals for welfare reform advanced over the past decade have attempted to move in this direction, and quite major work-oriented reforms are now in process. However, progress has been slow, and the design of a workable and widely acceptable work-fare system remains a difficult task. There must be determination of what type of job must be accepted, at what wage rate, and in what location. Availability of jobs in the private sector above all depends upon economic conditions, and maintenance of a high-employment economy is essential to resolve the problem. Beyond this, there is the question of how far the public sector should serve as an employer of last resort, if and when placement in the private sector is not feasible.

B. EFFECTS ON WORK INCENTIVES

The central problem in designing a satisfactory income-maintenance scheme, as all this suggests, is thus how best to serve the needs of low-income families while minimizing disincentive to work.

How Serious Is the Disincentive Problem?

Various experiments have been designed to compare the outcome under various payment schemes. Allowing for the difficulties involved in such experimentation, we must interpret the outcome with care. However, the experiments suggest that work effort is affected adversely, but less so than might be expected. Thus the estimated effects on men range around 7 percent, while those for women were estimated at 17 percent.[2]

Alternative Benefit Patterns

Given a limited amount of funds available for support, the most effective way of aiding low-income families would be to distribute it by filling in income deficiencies from the bottom, thereby ensuring as high a minimum level as the available budget permits. But this approach implicitly imposes a high marginal rate of tax over the low-income range and thus reduces work incentives. Both income and substitution effects are adverse to work effort. To dampen the latter effect, the aid must be extended higher up the income scale, a policy which in turn reduces the amount of aid which can be given where it is most needed.

A number of alternative aid patterns and their implicit marginal rate of tax are shown in Figure 11-1. In the upper part of each panel, earnings are shown on the horizontal axis and income received (after tax and transfers) is measured on the vertical axis. The 45° line OG shows income in the absence of transfer and tax. Plan I presents the crudest of all approaches, where a fixed subsidy equal to OM is given provided earnings fall short of $OB = OM$ and where the subsidy is lost once earnings exceed OB. As shown in the upper left figure, the subsidy at various levels of earnings is given by the broken line MAB, and total income received (or earnings plus subsidy) is given by the dotted line $MDAG$. As shown in the lower figure, this means that the marginal tax rate up to earnings OB is zero. But for the first dollar above OB, an exceedingly high marginal rate ($100 \times OM$ percent) applies; then the rate again drops to zero. A person earning OB would have to raise his or her earnings by BF only to stay even. Whereas such a scheme may seem absurd, it does in fact apply where eligibility for low-income services is lost once income exceeds a fixed limit, as, for example, in eligibility for Medicaid and, in some state programs, for aid to families with dependent children and an unemployed father (AFDC-UF).

Plan II, shown in the second panel of Figure 11-1, is more reasonable but still involves a heavy disincentive. This is a plan where the subsidy equals the difference between earnings and a set minimum level of income. If this level is set at OM', the subsidy at various levels of earnings now follows $M'B'$, while total income (earnings plus subsidy) follows $M'A'G$. As shown in the lower diagram, the marginal tax rate now equals 100 percent up to earnings OB' and becomes zero thereafter. Thus, subsidy recipients have no incentive to work until they can extend their earnings beyond OB'.

Plan III, shown in the third panel, is designed to reduce the disincentive. As in plan II, the subsidy declines as earnings rise but less rapidly. Whereas, in formula II, no subsidy was given to persons whose earnings reached OB' (in turn equal to the minimum OM'), benefits in plan III are now enjoyed up to earnings OB''. The subsidy line equals $M''B''$ and the total income line follows $M''A''G$. The

---

[2] For an evaluation of these programs, see Alicia H. Munnell (ed.): *Lessons from the Income Maintenance Experiment*, Federal Reserve Bank of Boston, 1986.

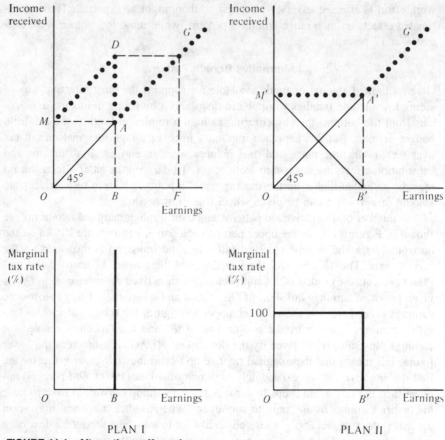

FIGURE 11-1 Alternative welfare plans.

marginal tax rate as shown in the lower part of the figure is now less than 100 percent since the subsidy is reduced by only part of the recipient's earnings. As shown here, it equals 50 percent up to earnings OB'', where OB'' is equal to twice the minimum income level OM''. The benefit structure under AFDC is of this type. A welfare mother who earns an extra $2 loses $1.34 in support (over a certain range of earnings), thus paying a tax of 62 percent. The food stamp and public housing programs have similar provisions. Plan III has the advantage of imposing a lesser disincentive, since the implicit tax rate on earnings is lower than in plan II. But it has the disadvantage of either calling for a lower basic subsidy M (as shown in the figure) or involving a higher cost.

Plan IV belongs to a quite different type of approach because the grant is not given as a lump-sum amount but as a percent of earnings up to a set level and declining thereafter. The grant thus traces the pattern shown by OCB with the grant equal to AC/AD percent of earnings up to OA. The grant then decreases by AC/AD percent of earnings in excess of OA and vanishes as an income of OB is reached. OEF shows the total income line. The tax rate, as shown in the lower part of the diagram, is negative (i.e., a subsidy) up to earnings AB, positive from OA to OB,

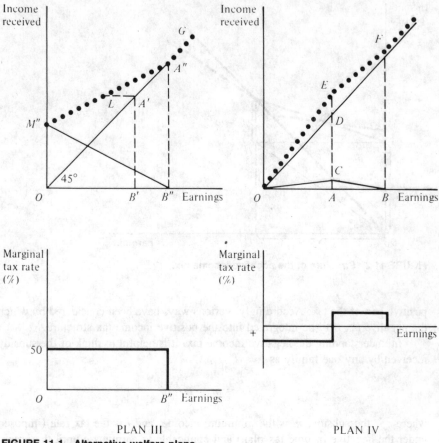

PLAN III   PLAN IV

FIGURE 11-1   Alternative welfare plans.

and zero above *AB*. This is the scheme followed by the earned income credit, with *OA* equal to $5,714, *AC/AD* equal to 14 percent, and *OB* equal to $17,000. Here the substitution effects up to *OA* are favorable as the wage rate is increased, with disincentive effects setting in only above that level. The disadvantage of the scheme, however, is that no grants are received in the absence of earnings and the grant rises with increasing earnings or declining need. Thus, redistribution toward the lower end is weaker.

Negative Income Tax

Plan III and variants thereof are also referred to as a negative income tax. The support given to people with no or low earnings may be viewed as a negative tax. As earnings rise, the negative tax falls and at some point reaches zero, after which a positive tax becomes due. The principle is simply that of extending the positive rate structure under the regular income tax downward, going beyond the zero-bracket range of the personal exemption into a negative range. As such, it is a logical extension of the principle of progressive taxation which is generally accepted for the

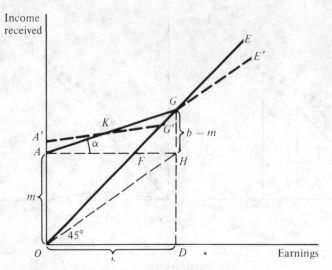

FIGURE 11-2 Structure of the negative income tax.

positive part of the tax. Accordingly, various ways have been considered by which the negative tax may be integrated into the positive income tax structure.[3]

In understanding the negative income tax, it is helpful to think of the subsidy received by any one family as

$$s = m - te$$

where s is the subsidy, m is the minimum income, and t is the tax rate (imposed under the negative income tax plan) and applicable to earnings e until the break-even point is reached. The subsidy thus becomes zero where earnings equal m/t, which is also referred to as the break-even level b. Thus, if the tax rate is 50 percent, b will be equal to $2m$. For the design of a negative income tax plan, the interesting variables are m, b, t, and the budgetary cost C. The relationship among these variables is shown in Figure 11-2. Minimum income m equals OA and the total income (earnings and subsidy) line is AGE. Break-even income b equals OD. The slope of the total income line AG or tan α equals HG/AH, or the fraction of earnings which are retained as earnings rise.[4] This fraction also equals $1 - t$ or $1 - m/b$.

The subsidy at each earnings level equals the distance between the total income line AG and the 45° line. Assuming an equal number of earners at each level,

---

[3] Integration involves such problems as family size, the definition of income (or absence thereof), the tying in of the tax rate on earnings below the break-even point with the regular income tax rates applicable above that level, and so forth. See J. Tobin, J. A. Pechman, and P. Mieszkowski, "Is a Negative Income Tax Practicable?" *Yale Law Journal*, November 1967.

[4] Thus, with earnings OD, total income received equals DG, or the sum of DH (the minimum income allowance) and HG, which is what is left of earnings OD after the tax.

total cost C may be taken to correspond to the area OGA.[5] It follows that for a given cost C, a higher m can be obtained only at the cost of a higher t and a lower b; or that a lower t can be had only at the cost of a lower m and a higher b. Suppose that m is to be raised to OA'.[6] The new total income line $A'G'E$ must then intersect the 45° line at a point below G since the additional cost reflected by the area AKA' must be offset by cost reduction equal to area $KG'G$. Raising m thus raises t by lowering the slope of the total income line and lowers the break-even point b. Since a high m and low b make for greater redistribution toward the lower end, we again see how the desire to redistribute conflicts with the desire to avoid disincentives from a high marginal rate of tax, and how this dilemma arises not only at the upper but especially at the lower end of the income scale.

C. SOCIAL INSURANCE PROGRAMS

We now turn from low-income supports to more broadly based programs of social insurance. The oldest and largest part of the social insurance system is the Old Age and Survivors Insurance (OASI). Enacted in 1935, the program was extended in 1956 to provide benefits for disabled workers or Disability Insurance (DI). A health insurance plan (HI), giving medical benefits for persons over sixty-five and referred to as "Medicare," was passed in 1965 and together with Supplementary Medical Insurance (SMI) has become an important part of the system.

As shown in Table 11-2, OASI is by far the largest component of the system, followed by HI and DI.

Retirement and Disability Insurance

When OASI was enacted in 1935, the legislation specified that the program should include all workers under age sixty-five who were engaged in commerce and industry (except railroads) in the United States. Government and railroad employees already had separate schemes. A major expansion in coverage occurred in 1950, when regularly employed farm and domestic workers were included as well as the

---

[5] *OGA* is the *net* cost left after deducting tax revenue *ODH* (obtained by applying t to earnings up to *OD*) from gross cost *ODHA*. This net cost remains to be financed by increasing tax rates applicable to income in excess of *OD*. The resulting net income line (after allowing for the necessary increase in income tax rates above *OD*) is illustrated by *AGE'*.

[6] More generally, the system is defined by two equations:

$$t = m/b \tag{1}$$

$$C = \sum_{i=o}^{i=b} s_i = \sum_{i=0}^{i=b} n_i\,(m - e_i\,t) \tag{2}$$

In equation 2, the cost C is defined as the sum of the subsidies s applicable at each level of earnings i times the number at each level of earnings. The subsidy to a family at any one level in turn equals the flat payment m minus the product of tax rate and earnings. Given C, we have two equations with three unknowns, m, b, and t. Substituting, we may write

$$C \sum_{i=0}^{i=b} n_i\,t\,(b - e_i) \tag{3}$$

TABLE 11-2
Overview of Social Security System, 1986*

	OASI	DI	HI	Total
Benefits (billions of dollars)	177	17	50	259
Beneficiaries (millions)	34	4	19	**

*Annual rate 1986; *Social Security Bulletin,* 1987.
**Total cannot be added due to overlap.

nonfarm self-employed (except certain professionals, who had entered by 1965). In 1983, federal civil service (new employees) was added to the system, with coverage elective for state and local employees. Coverage of the working population has now become virtually complete, with covered workers comprising over 90 percent of the labor force.

Financing   Old age, survivors, and disability insurance (OASDI) is financed by a payroll tax, i.e., a tax on wage and salary income. Capital income is not included in the base. Half the tax is paid by the employer and half by the employee.[7] The original legislation levied a combined rate of 2 percent on the first \$3,000 of wages. Since then the tax rate and ceiling have been raised many times, and a revised schedule was introduced in 1983.

The level of payroll tax rates (payable by employee and employer both) as provided under the 1983 legislation, and their eventual level in 2000, is as follows:

	1988	1990	2000
OASI (Old Age and Survivors Insurance)	5.53%	5.60%	5.48%
DI (Disability Insurance)	0.53	0.60	0.71
HI (Health Insurance)	1.45	1.45	1.45
Total	7.51%	7.65%	7.65%

Combining employer and employee contributions, 1988 payroll taxes now total 15.02 percent and are scheduled to rise to 15.3 percent in 1990. As of 1987, the tax applies to the first \$43,800 of wage and salary income, which amount is indexed and subject to annual adjustment. Earnings of the self-employed are subject to a slightly lower rate.

Old-Age Benefits   Workers may retire at age sixty-five and claim full benefits or at age sixty-two and claim 80 percent of benefits. Determination of OASI benefits follows a complicated procedure. Applicable to most workers, it involves two steps. Step 1 is to derive the average monthly earnings on which contributions are paid. In computing the average, past earnings are totaled and divided by the number of months. For this purpose, monthly wages received since 1950 (or after reaching age twenty-five) and up to age sixty-five are included. In obtaining the average wage base, past monthly wages are adjusted upward or indexed to allow

[7] For a discussion of the payroll tax, see p. 439.

for the rise in the general wage level since the monthly wages were received.[8] In step 2, this figure of average indexed monthly earnings (AIME) is then used as the base to which a schedule of benefit rates is applied. The schedule for a worker reaching age sixty-five in 1987 began with 90 percent on the first $310 of AIME, fell to 32 percent for the next $1,556, and to 15 percent for the remainder. For a couple with only one earning spouse, the family benefit equals 150 percent of the single benefit. Where both spouses meet the covered-earnings requirement, they both receive their benefit claims.

Maximum benefits are computed by a special formula, with the 1987 maximum of $789 for a single retiree and of 1.5 times this amount, or $1,183, for a single earner couple. The formula also favors low-income earners, resulting in an effective minimum benefit of $430 for a single person and of $510 for a couple (1987 level). The average monthly benefit for a single worker in 1987 was $487, with recent retirees receiving a larger and earlier retirees a lower benefit. At an annual rate of $5,844, the average about matched the poverty threshold for aged individuals. The system also authorizes retirees to obtain a limited amount of wage or salary earnings, which limit is dropped after age seventy is reached.

The OASI system is now thoroughly protected against inflation. On the contribution side, the wage ceiling up to which earnings are taxed has been indexed since 1981 to rise with the average wage level. On the benefit side, computation of AIME, as noted before, involves upward adjustment of past monthly wages to allow for the increase in the average wage level, thereby correcting for inflation (so as to render wages comparable in real terms) and also for the average productivity gain. Moreover, the bracket limits in the benefit formula are indexed to rise with the average wage level, and the benefit payment as determined at the time of retirement is indexed thereafter to rise with the cost of living. The replacement cost (ratio of benefit to preretirement income), estimated at 41 percent for low and at 21 percent for high earners, will thus remain unchanged over the years.

Throughout the years, OASI has been a controversial subject and continues so today. Its economic effects, solvency, and implications for equity will be noted further in Section D below.

Disability Benefits Disability benefits are paid to persons who prior to age sixty-five suffer a disability. Benefits are computed in a way similar to that of retirement benefits, and only limited earnings are permitted. The number of recipients now totals 4 million. Annual benefits in 1987 amounted to over $26 billion and have more than quadrupled over the past fifteen years. This reflects both an increased number of claimants and rising benefit levels.

Health Insurance

The Medicare program has been the most rapidly growing part of the social security system, rising from $7 billion in 1972 to close to $80 billion in 1988. The amount involved now equals nearly 40 percent of OASDI payments. Rapid further

---

[8] For this purpose a set of index numbers is provided by which to raise the retiree's monthly wage receipts.

growth may be expected due to a continued rise in the cost of medical services well ahead of the average inflation rate.

The major share in the cost of Medicare goes to finance hospital insurance, based on a payroll tax contribution of 1.45 percent on employer and employee each. Individuals who are eligible for social security retirement are eligible for Medicare at age sixty-five. The benefit provides basic protection against the cost of hospital services, post-hospital care, and certain home-health services. The benefits of Medicare, as noted before, are also available under the Medicaid program, where they are paid for out of the general budget. The lesser share of the program, providing for the cost of physicians' services and drugs, is financed in part by a matching contribution of the insured and the remainder out of the general budget. A major expansion of coverage for long term hospital care was added in 1988, together with an increase in payroll tax. The latter for the first time is related to liability under the income tax.

Beyond this, political controversy centers around whether health insurance should be extended to include not only the aged but the entire population and, if so, how this should be done. If coverage were extended to disaster insurance only, e.g., to major surgery, the amounts involved would be relatively limited. But if a broad coverage is applied, very large amounts equal to or exceeding those involved in OASDI may be called for. Instead, a divided system might be used, calling for direct-fee finance of public health insurance in line with the cost of risks, while subsidizing fees payable by low-income contributors out of general budget revenue.

In examining possible restructuring of Medicare, we have a further question about how such changes would affect the form in which medical services are supplied, the role of private insurance carriers, the freedom to choose doctors, and so forth. As has been noted at the beginning of this book, a distinction should be drawn between public provision and public production. Broadening of health insurance may involve varying degrees of public control over the supply of medical services, a question into which we cannot enter here.

Unemployment Insurance

National unemployment insurance came into existence with the Social Security Act of 1935. It now encompasses over 90 percent of the private-sector work force and has found general acceptance as an essential social institution.

As distinct from OASI, DI, and HI, the system is financed by an employer-paid payroll tax only, with the federal rate now at 6.2 percent. Additional state-imposed payroll taxes for the finance of the state systems may be credited against the federal tax, subject to certain requirements regarding the design of state systems. Combined taxes thus differ across states. All contributions, federal or state, are paid into the Federal Unemployment Trust Fund, with separate accounts kept for each state. Payments accordingly are also made through the federal system.

The benefit payments fluctuate with the level of employment and in 1985 amounted to $15 billion. Individual benefits are related to weekly wages and typically account for 50 percent thereof, with payments made for a period of twenty-six weeks.

Congress in 1970 provided for financial support from the federal government to pay benefits for an additional thirteen weeks beyond its normal benefit period of twenty-six weeks when the unemployment rate exceeds 4.5 percent and for states which show an especially sharp rise in unemployment. Extended in later years, this points to a more uniform approach to unemployment insurance on a nationwide basis. However this may be, it is generally recognized that unemployment insurance can provide only a temporary solution and cannot take care of widespread unemployment. An effective approach to such unemployment calls for appropriate measures of macro and work-force policies, as well as adjustments in market structures.

D. ISSUES IN OASI

The design of OASI involves certain basic issues which have been debated since the introduction of the system and which are now under renewed discussion. The main issues are:

1. Is the system solvent?
2. Should provision for retirement be privatized?
3. Is the system equitable across generations?
4. Should the system be redistributional?
5. Should it be paid for by payroll tax finance or budgetary contribution?
6. How does the system affect capital formation?
7. How does the system affect labor supply?

1983 Reforms

OASI is designed to be a self-supporting system. Benefit payments are meant to be financed by payroll taxes, without a contribution from other sources in the budget. For this purpose, payroll tax receipts are channeled into trust funds—with separate trust funds for the major components of the system—and payments are made out of these funds. A schedule of payroll tax rates, current and future, is set so as to plan for an adequate flow of future revenue covering the next seventy-five years for OASI and DI, and twenty-five years for HI. This requires long-term prediction of both the benefit level and receipts, involving prediction of economic variables (such as future wage levels, labor force participation, retirement age, and unemployment rate) as well as demographic factors (such as birth and death rates). Since these variables are difficult to predict, it is not surprising that tax rate schedules had to be revised frequently.

System Solvency after the 1983 Reform   This situation came to a head most recently in 1983. It then appeared that trust fund receipts would become insufficient to meet benefit obligations for the second half of the eighties. As will be explained below, a decision had been made at an early stage in the lifetime of the social security system to finance benefits on a pay-as-you-go basis rather than to rely on extensive reserve accumulation. At the same time, it was considered prudent to retain a reserve in the trust funds equal to from 20 to 30 percent of annual benefit payments. By 1982, the reserve in the OASI fund had dropped to 15 percent and it appeared that it would be exhausted by 1984 with deficits to follow.[9] A lack of receipts owing to unemployment, rising benefits as a result of inflation, and

---

[9] See "Report of the National Commission of Social Security," *Social Security Bulletin*, U.S. Department of Health and Human Services, vol. 46, no. 2, February 1983.

a faulty method of benefit calculation had contributed to this crisis. It also appeared that the system would run into difficulties in the more distant future of the next century, when the baby-boom generation would retire and claim benefits, with the birth rate declining. To deal with these problems, a presidential commission was appointed. The recommendations of the commission were adopted by Congress in an unprecedentedly prompt and bipartisan action. This legislation, so it is now estimated, will keep the system solvent for the remainder of the eighties and under reasonably optimistic assumptions, will yield substantial surpluses for the early decades of the next century.

The resulting reform legislation, based on the commission's recommendation, included the following measures:

1. The scheduled increase in tax rates up to 1990 was speeded up.

2. The automatic cost of living adjustment in benefits (COLA) was postponed for one quarter in the mid-1983 adjustment.

3. Fifty percent of benefits obtained by recipients with incomes in excess of a certain indexed amount were made taxable.

4. New federal employees and employees of nonprofit organizations were included in the system. Withdrawal of state-local workers from the system was prohibited.

5. Beginning in 1985, a fail-safe mechanism was applied. The COLA adjustments will be limited if the trust fund ratio falls below 20 percent. In that case, COLA should be based on the lower of the increase in consumer prices and money wages rather than on the former.

6. Addressing primarily the longer-run problem, Congress also provided that beginning in the year 2000, the retirement age is to be increased gradually from sixty-five to sixty-six, reaching that level in 2009. A further increase from sixty-six to sixty-seven is to be made over the years 2021 to 2027.

The Long-Run Outlook

These adjustments will ensure solvency of the system through the eighties and nineties. Over the longer run, the outlook hinges on both economic and demographic factors which are difficult to predict. Estimates by the actuary of the system therefore cover a range of assumptions.[10] As shown in Table 11-3, alternative I, which is the most optimistic, assumes a growth of real GNP at 3 percent or more, with unemployment below 3 percent and inflation at only 2 percent. The middle assumption, IIB, assumes a gradually declining growth rate from 3 percent in the 1990s to 2 percent in 2000, with unemployment of 6 percent and an inflation rate of 4 percent. Alternative III, the most pessimistic, assumes GNP to grow at less than 2 percent with unemployment of 6 percent or higher.

The outcomes thus differ substantially with the underlying assumptions. Under the most pessimistic conditions of alternative III, a large deficit develops after 2010, requiring an increase in payroll tax rates by of about 10 percentage points by 2050. Under the generally used middle assumption IIB, the system remains in surplus until about 2020, building up a substantial trust fund balance, reaching over 20 percent of GNP. Thereafter, a deficit results, with the fund exhausted around the

---

[10] See OASI Trust Funds, Board of Trustees, *1987 Annual Report*, 1983, p. 65.

TABLE 11-3
Estimated OASDI Trust Fund Surplus or Deficit as Percent of Taxable Payrolls

	ALTERNATIVE ASSUMPTIONS			
	I	*IIA*	*IIB*	*III*
1988	1.71	1.53	· 1.41	.81
2000	3.61	2.83	2.36	1.09
2015	2.96	1.16	1.09	− 0.75
2020	1.79	0.15	− 0.51	− 2.39
2050	1.89	− 1.76	− 2.69	− 10.75
2065	2.29	− 1.81	− 2.75	− 13.14

Source: 1987 Annual Report, Board of Trustees of the OASDI Trust Fund, p. 65.

middle of the century and then calling for a tax increase of up to 5 percentage points. Critics point to the more pessimistic assumption and note that payroll taxes will have to be raised eventually, but the outlook is far from alarming. The IIB set of assumptions is not overly optimistic, current tax rates are adequate for a sustained period and the eventual increase, when necessary, appears to be modest, especially if compared with payroll tax rates abroad.

Public versus Private Provision

Why should not individuals be left to decide how they wish to distribute their income over time? The answer is that although most people will provide for their old age, some will fail to do so. Assuming that society will not permit its imprudent to go hungry when they become aged, this will over time impose a further burden on the more prudent. To protect themselves against this contingency, they will impose compulsory insurance. Alternatively, the compulsory approach may be viewed as a paternalistic decision by society to protect the imprudent against starvation in old age. There is thus a clear case for requiring mandatory provision for old age. Also, there is a clear case for requiring that this be done by insurance. The advantage of taking out a retirement insurance rather than providing on one's own is that the length of life is uncertain. By pooling the risk with others, the cost of provision is reduced.

It does not follow, however, that the insurance arrangement must be public. The size of private companies is such that they can exhaust the economies of scale in spreading risk. Under a mandatory system, private insurance would have to be supervised so as to ensure competitive terms, and this itself might make some case for the public approach; but there are other considerations to be allowed for as well.

Rates of Return   Public insurance, as an ongoing process, may be able to offer a better deal. Under a private system, a reserve must be accumulated that is sufficient in amount to finance the benefits for all insured and to provide the insured with a return equal to the interest that was earned. Under the public system, a pay-as-you-go approach may be used so that no such reserve is required. Each working person can be asked to support the retired population and in turn can be supported after retirement by the next generation. Viewing this arrangement as a continuing process which never ceases, we may show that the rate of return to the participants will be higher under the public system, provided that the combined rates of population and productivity growth (i.e., the growth of the tax base) will exceed the real rate of interest.[11] Such was the outlook when the social security system was introduced, but this advantage of the public system has weakened as the rate of both population and productivity growth have declined.

Intergeneration Equity   The choice between social and private insurance thus carries distributional implications across generations. As proponents of privatization point out, the outlook for an aging population and a declining birthrate renders the public system less attractive to the younger generation. Under the social security system, those now entering the labor force will have to support a growing group of retirees whose claims have been established in the past, without there being a sufficiently strong support group when they themselves reach retirement. Thus it has been suggested that retirement insurance can be obtained by the now young at more favorable returns than are offered by OASI. The comparison depends upon assumptions regarding rates of return and risk involved, as well as on the outlook for future taxes that will be needed under the present system. As noted above, reasonable estimates suggest that the present level of rates will be adequate for many decades and that even an eventual increase in required rates is likely to be modest. Nevertheless, declining population growth may raise problems inherent in the present type of system.

The social insurance system may be viewed as a social contract across generations. The working generation of today assumes the responsibility of supporting today's retirees, under the supposition that it in turn will be supported by the subsequent generation of workers.[12] The system in this respect does not differ from the tradition of family support in which children supported their aged parents. But what should the terms of support be? Under the present approach, retirees are provided with a benefit equal to a set percentage of their prior earnings, an arrangement which poses no problem in a setting of more or less constant population and productivity. But given declining birthrates and/or death rates, the ratio of retirees to working population rises. For the system to remain in balance, the replacement rate will then have to fall or the tax rate will have to rise until a new equilibrium (population stability) is reached.[13] This difficulty would be avoided by exchanging the fixed replacement approach for a formula which would relate benefits not to past earnings of retirees but to the earnings of those currently in the labor force. Retirees would be assured a per capita benefit equal to an agreed-upon percentage of per capita earnings (*net* of their social security contribution) of the working pop-

[11] See Henry Aaron, "The Social Insurance Paradox," *Canadian Journal of Economics and Political Science,* August 1966.

[12] The social insurance system as originally conceived was designed to avoid this problem by building up a reserve fund based on the contribution of current earners and before beginning benefit payments at the time of their retirement. Benefits for each generation would then be financed out of the trust funds' earnings provided for by their preceding accumulation. However, this approach was soon abandoned with extension of benefits to the initial generation of retirees.

[13] See Richard A. Musgrave, "A Reappraisal of Social Security Financing," in Felicity Skidmore (ed.): *Social Security Financing,* Cambridge, Mass.: MIT Press, 1981.

ulation. In this way, the risks of changes in population growth and productivity would be shared between workers and retirees in a fair fashion. Having determined the desired ratio of current benefits to current earnings at, say, 60 percent, the tax rate would be set and be adjusted periodically to meet this cost, with the solvency of the system unaffected by changes in age structure or productivity.

Income Redistribution

Apart from the question of intergeneration equity, the design of the social insurance system raises the further problem of redistribution across income groups. If the system were conducted strictly as an insurance plan, each person would receive benefits which would reflect the same rate of return on his or her contribution. The pensioner in turn would have a contractual right to such benefits. As distinct from this approach, the system from its inception has been redistributive, granting a more favorable treatment to those with lower lifetime earnings.

One way of viewing the degree of redistribution inherent in the OASI system is to compare the *distribution* of payroll tax payments by *income brackets* with that of benefits. Applied to the total population, the net benefit thus defined decreases when moving up the income scale. This is not surprising, since capital income (which is not included in the tax base) rises as a share of total income when moving up the scale. But this overstates the degree of redistribution as applied to lifetime earnings. Since incomes of retirees are low relative to their lifetime income, the degree of redistribution on a lifetime basis is less pronounced.

A better picture is obtained by considering what happens to the ratio of benefits to covered earnings as earnings rise. In 1986, the ratio of benefits to prior year earnings for a worker retiring at sixty-five ranged from 69 percent for earnings of $4,805 to 23.9 percent for earnings equal to $42,000.[14]

This comparison, however, still remains unsatisfactory. To obtain a valid picture, we should estimate the *rates of return* which workers with various levels of contribution receive from their investment in social security claims. That is to say, we should estimate the expected benefit and cost streams and then compute the internal rate of return inherent in these two streams.[15] Workers who enjoy a higher wage rate will also have a higher lifetime income. Given the benefit formula which discriminates against successive slabs of earnings and sets a benefit ceiling, workers with higher incomes receive a lower rate of return. There are, however, a number of factors which work in the other direction. For one thing, some low-wage earners enter the labor force at an earlier date, which lengthens the contribution period. For another, the lifetime earnings of low-wage earners tend to peak at an earlier age. As a result, their tax contributions are made sooner, which lowers the internal rate of return. Moreover, low-wage earners have a lower life expectancy and thus on the average have a shorter retirement period over which benefits are received. These factors dampen the redistributive pattern, but a substantial differential remains. Thus it has been estimated that for a white married couple with less than seven years of schooling (and a corresponding typical level of lifetime

---

[14] Based on *Social Security Bulletin, Annual Statistical Supplement,* 1986, p. 33. See also *Social Security Bulletin,* March 1978, p. 13.
[15] See p. 156 for a discussion of this concept.

income), the internal rate of return is close to 5 percent, whereas for a white couple with over thirteen years of schooling (and a corresponding lifetime income), the rate is only 4.4 percent.[16] Since such redistribution would not occur in a private system, the latter would be to the advantage of high earners, and vice versa, for those in lower brackets.

Payroll Tax Finance versus Budgetary Contributions

Even though Congress accepted the reality of pay-as-you-go finance and recognized the redistributive nature of the system, it has held steadily to the idea that the system should be considered as providing for insurance and not old-age relief. This called for the finance of benefits from (1) a separate tax that is earmarked as social security contribution and (2) a tax related to the earnings base of the prospective retiree. In past years, this position has been attacked by economists who have argued that the contributory nature of the system is fictitious, that payroll taxes are an undesirable form of finance, and that the division between employer and employee contributions is misleading since the entire burden is likely to fall on the wage earner anyhow.[17] Given that each generation of retirees has its benefits paid for by those of working age and that there is substantial intrageneration redistribution, reliance on the contributory principle is said to make little sense. Benefits, so the critics conclude, should be financed out of the general budget, making use of superior forms of taxation. Moreover, they should be viewed as part of a general income-maintenance program, applicable to all low-income persons whether young or old.

The argument is persuasive but pays too little attention to the social role of the system and how retirees perceive it. Under a contributory approach, they may view their benefits as entitlements which have been earned rather than a support given to them on a charitable basis. This view has social merit and should be respected in the financial design of the system. Nor is some element of redistribution incompatible with the spirit of social as distinct from private insurance. As a compromise position, it has been suggested that the system be divided into two parts. One would be on a strictly contributory and nonredistributive basis, also referred to as a quid pro quo system, while the other would be financed out of the general budget and would be strictly redistributional in approach.[18] The latter would involve an expansion of the principle of low-income support underlying the Supplementary Security Income payments.

Effects on Capital Formation

We now turn to the effects of the system on the performance of the economy, beginning with its impact on the rate of savings. With old-age needs provided for by social security benefits, so it is argued, people will find it less necessary to set

[16] Based on provisions similar to those of the 1983 amendment. See Dean R. Leimer, *Projected Rates of Return to Future Social Security Retirees Under Alternative Benefit Structures*, in Social Security Administration, Policy Analysis with Social Security Research Files, Social Security Administration, Research Report 52, 1978.

[17] See p. 440.

[18] For such a proposal, see Alicia Munnell, *The Future of Social Security*, Washington, D.C.: Brookings, 1977, chap. 5.

aside private savings. They save by paying payroll tax and accumulating benefit claims. This would leave total savings unaffected if their contributions were in turn saved and invested by the trust fund. But such is not the case since the system is on a pay-as-you-go basis, so that this year's contributions are used to pay this year's benefits. The hypothesis is that saving is curtailed and as a result, less capital is accumulated and the economy grows less rapidly. This is the basic reasoning behind the proposition that the social security system as now operated reduces saving and thereby is detrimental to growth.[19] At closer consideration, it is not so obvious, however, that people will replace their private saving with their "social security saving." Various aspects may be distinguished:

1.   The availability of social security benefits may induce earlier retirement, which will increase the need to accumulate for old age.[20]

2.   Availability of a minimal retirement income may increase people's taste for security and raise their savings target.

3.   Even if private saving in anticipation of retirement is reduced, the social security system need not result in a *continuing* reduction in net saving for society as a whole. As the system is introduced, and assuming pay-as-you-go finance to begin with, the initial generation of contributors may replace private saving by its payroll tax contribution, thus causing an initial reduction in net saving. In the ongoing system, not only does the prospect of social security benefits displace private saving by the young but benefit payments also displace private dissaving by the old.

4.   Suppose that prior to the introduction of the system, each generation saved to provide for its own retirement. As the system is introduced, working people realize that their children will have to support them later on. As an adjustment thereto, the working population will increase its saving so as to raise bequests to be left to their children. Thus increased saving for bequests will take the place of saving for retirement, with no initial reduction in saving.

5.   Alternatively, suppose that prior to the social security system children supported their parents in old age. Once more, savings would not be affected, as direct support of parents by children is replaced by payroll tax support.

Given this variety of a priori expectations of what the result might be, it is not surprising that the debate over empirical evidence has also remained inconclusive. Moreover, even if it should be the case that the social security system has a depressing effect on saving, it does not follow that revision of the system is the most appropriate way of increasing saving. The most obvious way of doing so would be to raise taxes in the general budget or to reduce expenditures at large, thereby reducing public sector dissaving. As noted above, it indeed appears that the social security system for the next two decades will be a substantial contributor to national saving by building up a trust fund surplus, thereby contributing to a closing of the overall budget deficit.

[19] This case has been argued most forcefully by Martin Feldstein. See, for instance, his "Social Security, Induced Retirement and Aggregate Capital Accumulation," *Journal of Political Economy*, September–October 1975. For different views and a critique of Feldstein's position, see Selig Lesnoy and Dean R. Leimer, "Social Security and Private Saving, Theory and Historical Review," *Social Security Bulletin*, June 1985.

[20] See Alicia Munnell, *The Future of Social Security*, Washington, D.C.: Brookings, 1977, chap. 6; and Alicia Munnell, *Effect of Social Security on Personal Saving*, Cambridge, Mass.: Ballinger, 1974.

Effects on Labor Supply

As in the case of welfare payments, there has also been increasing concern over the effects of social security on labor supply. Whereas in the former case a high marginal tax rate (implicit in the benefit formula) was seen to induce substitution of leisure, here the availability of benefits after retirement reduces the cost of buying leisure by surrendering income. Obviously, the availability of retirement benefits may be expected to result in retirement earlier than would be the case without such recourse. But this is not the correct comparison. Rather the comparison must be drawn between such availability under the social security system and its availability under a private saving arrangement. Effects on labor supply are thus linked to effects on saving.

There are, however, some specific features of the system which bear directly on retirement decisions. One is the provision which permits early retirement at age sixty rather than allowing availability of benefits at age sixty-five only. This option is taken at the cost of reduced benefits but has nevertheless been an inducement to early retirement.[21] The latter may reflect the effects of rising income and work habits, as well as the availability of benefits. Another relative factor is the limited permission to obtain earnings after benefits are received. For beneficiaries aged sixty-five to seventy, the first $8,000 may now be obtained without penalty, whereas one-third of earnings in excess thereof are offset by reduced benefit payments. As noted before, no such penalty applies after age seventy.

More generally, there is the question of at what age benefits should become available. As noted above, the present level of sixty-five is to be raised somewhat after the year 2000, a measure undertaken to strengthen the solvency of the system rather than with reference to labor supply. This approach, it would seem, runs contrary to the very objective of the old-age system, which is to enrich the later years in the worker's life.

E. SUMMARY

The social welfare system may be divided into two major parts, one dealing with income maintenance for the poor and paid for by general revenue, the other providing for various forms of social insurance.

1.   Systems of low-income support include health services provided by Medicaid, Supplementary Security Income provided to the needy aged, welfare payments to families with dependent children, and support for low-cost housing.

2.   Among these programs, Medicaid is much the largest item. Provided to the needy aged, it offers services similar to those supplied by Medicare.

3.   The welfare program provides a cash income to families with dependent children. The federal government offers matching grants to the state systems and benefits vary widely across states. Various reform proposals are under consideration, trying to shift the system toward a "work-fare" basis.

4.   Disincentive effects result as the benefit formula, by reducing the benefits while income rises, in effect imposes a high marginal tax rate on earnings.

---

[21] For a summary of the discussion over retirement effects, see Henry J. Aaron, *Economic Effects of Social Security*, Washington, D.C.: Brookings, 1983, chap. 5.

5.   Various approaches have been explored to reduce the conflict between distributive effectiveness and disincentive.

6.   The negative income tax offers a generalized approach to this problem.

Turning now to the insurance systems, we find that the basis of finance shifts from general budgetary support to direct contributions, mostly via the earmarked payroll tax.

7.   Much the most important item in this category is OASDI, the old-age survivors and disability insurance. Other important components of the system are medical and unemployment insurance.

8.   OASDI is financed through payroll tax contributions, split equally between employer and employee. Benefits are available at age sixty-five and are determined by a benefit formula. Only wage and salary earnings are taxable, not capital income. Benefits and other provisions are indexed so as to protect the system against inflation.

9.   The Medicare program offers hospital insurance and, like OASDI, is financed by employer and employee contributions.

10.   Unemployment insurance is financed by employer contributions and although under federal direction is administered by and varies across the state level.

Various aspects of the social insurance system have been under lively discussion, with special emphasis on OASDI.

11.   Based on the 1983 reform provisions, the OASDI system may be expected to accumulate a substantial surplus during the next twenty years, with a deficit emerging thereafter, and accumulations in the fund exhausted by 2050.

12.   Consideration is given to the pros and cons of replacing social security with private retirement insurance.

13.   With an aging population, problems of intergeneration equity arise and may be dealt with in various ways.

14.   Attention is given to potential detrimental effects of the social security system on the rate of saving and retirement.

FURTHER READINGS

For current data on the social security system and discussion of policy developments, see *Social Security Bulletin,* Washington, D.C., U.S. Department of Health and Human Services. Also see:

Aaron, Henry: *Economic Effects of Social Security,* Washington, D.C.: Brookings, 1982.
Aaron, H. J.: *Why Is Welfare So Hard to Reform?* Washington, D.C.: Brookings, 1973.
Meyer, C.: *Social Security: A Critique of Radical Reform Proposals,*
Munnell, Alicia H.: *The Future of Social Security,* Washington, D.C.: Brookings, 1977.
Skidmore, Felicity (ed.): *Social Security Financing,* Cambridge, Mass.: MIT Press, 1981.

Part Four

Principles of Taxation

Chapter 12

Introduction to Taxation*

A. **Categories of Revenue:** *Taxes, Charges, and Borrowing; Taxes in the Circular Flow; Taxes on Holding and Transfer of Wealth; Personal versus In Rem Taxes; Direct versus Indirect Taxes; Transfers as Negative Taxes.* B. **Requirements for a "Good" Tax Structure. C. Summary.**

We now leave the expenditure side of budget policy and consider the revenue side. Although good economic analysis calls for joint consideration of both aspects, the practice is to deal with them as more or less separate issues. In this and the following chapters we examine the principles, economic and otherwise, of tax policy and the requirements for a good tax system. After this foundation has been laid, we proceed in Part Five to deal with the more specific aspects of the U.S. tax structure.

A. CATEGORIES OF REVENUE

Government receipts may take the form of taxes, charges, or borrowing. We begin with a brief look at the various forms of receipts, considering how they may be distinguished and what their characteristics are.

*Reader's Guide to Chapter 12: Taxes are grouped in line with their impact in the circular flow of income and expenditures, as well as with regard to other important kinds of characteristics. The requirements for a "good" tax structure are outlined.

Taxes, Charges, and Borrowing

Taxes and charges are withdrawn from the private sector without leaving the government with a liability to the payee. Borrowing involves a withdrawal made in return for the government's promise to repay at a future date and to pay interest in the interim. Taxes are compulsory imposts, whereas charges and borrowing involve voluntary transactions. Among these three sources, taxes provide much the larger part of receipts.[1] More will be said about the distinction between charges and taxes when discussing benefit taxation in the next chapter, and the economics of borrowing are examined in a later part of the book.

Taxes in the Circular Flow

One helpful way of distinguishing among types of taxes is to consider their point of impact in the circular flow of income and expenditures in the economy.

Impact Points Figure 12-1 presents a simplified picture of the circular flow of income and expenditures in the private sector, together with the major points at which the various taxes are inserted. The monetary flow of income and expenditures shown in the figure proceeds in a clockwise direction, while the real flow of factor inputs and product outputs (not shown) moves in a counterclockwise direction. Thus, income (1) is received by households and divided into consumer expenditures (2) and household savings (3). Consumer expenditures flow into the market for consumer goods and become receipts (4) of firms selling such goods. Savings flow through the capital market and are channeled into investment (5). They then become expenditures in the market for capital goods and turn into receipts (6) of firms producing such goods. Gross business receipts (7) then become available as outlays (8) for use by the firm. A part is set aside to cover depreciation (9), and the remainder (10) goes to purchase the services of labor as payroll (11), of capital as profit and interest (12), and of other inputs in the factor market. Together these represent the various factor shares in national income. These shares are paid out to suppliers of factors—as wages (13), and as capital income (14), such as dividends, interest, and rent. They thus become income (1) of households. Some profits, however, are withheld as retained earnings (15) rather than paid out as dividends. Retained earnings, together with depreciation allowances, comprise business savings (16) and combine with household savings (3) to finance investment or the purchase of capital goods. Thus the circular flow in income and expenditures is closed.[2]

We may now locate the impact points of various taxes as shown in Figure 12-1. Taxes may be imposed on household income at point 1, on consumer expenditures at 2, on business receipts from retail sales or value added at 4, on total gross receipts of business at 7, on business receipts net of depreciation at 10, on payrolls at 11, on profits at 12, on wage receipts at 13, on retained earnings at 15, or on capital income at 14. The major taxes in the United States system are readily iden-

---

[1] See p. 318.
[2] Since the national income accounts take an ex post view, saving and investment must be equal as a matter of accounting identity.

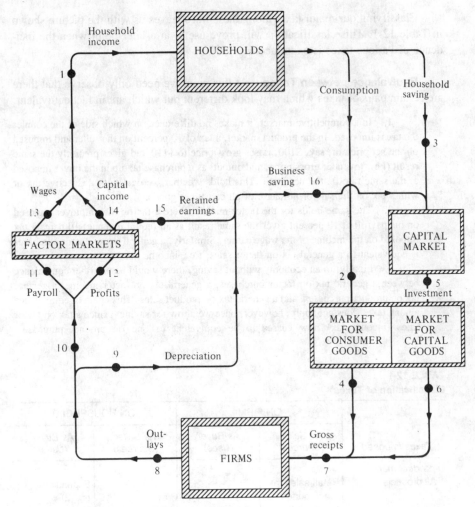

FIGURE 12-1 Points of tax impact in circular flow.

tified with these various points of impact on the private sector. The personal income tax is imposed at 1, the corporation income tax at 12, the retail sales taxes at 4, the employer contribution to the payroll tax at 11, and the employee contribution to the payroll tax at 13. Taxes imposed at 2 do not exist in our tax structure but are potential candidates for tax reform and will be discussed later under the headings of the expenditure tax (2) and value-added tax of the income type (10).

Classification of Taxes Referring again to Figure 12-1, we note that the various taxes may be classified as follows:

1. They may be imposed in the product or in the factor markets.
2. They may be imposed on the seller's or the buyer's side of the market.
3. They may be imposed on households or firms.
4. They may enter on the sources or uses side of the taxpayer's account.

Classifying our major taxes along these lines leaves us with the picture shown in Table 12-1. This classification will prove useful at a later point when the incidence of various taxes is examined.

Equivalence between Taxes   At this point we need only observe that there are certain pairs of taxes which may look different but which are in fact equivalent.

1. In a competitive market, it makes no difference on which side of the counter the tax is imposed. In the product market, a tax of 10 percent on the seller and imposed on the net price of, say, $100, raises gross price to $110 and gives precisely the same result (i.e., revenue, gross price, and output) as a purchase tax upon the buyer imposed at the same rate on the net price. This holds whether we deal with a selective tax or with a tax on the sale or purchase of all consumer goods.

2. The same holds for the factor market where a tax on the employer imposed on his payroll at 10 percent gives the same result as an (equal revenue) 10 percent tax imposed on the income of the wage earner. Similarly, a general tax on factor purchases is equivalent to a general tax on factor sales, i.e., income tax.

3. Finally, in an economy without saving, there would be a further equivalence between a general tax on factor purchases, a general tax on factor income, a general tax on product purchases, and a general tax on product sales. This chain of equivalence among taxes does not apply, however, once we allow for savings, since a tax on factor sales (income tax) now ceases to be equivalent to one on product purchases.

TABLE 12-1
Classification of Taxes*

	ON FIRM		ON HOUSEHOLD	
Taxes Imposed	As Seller (Sources)	As Buyer (Uses)	As Seller (Sources)	As Buyer (Uses)
In product market All products	Retail sales tax Value added (consumption type) (4)	- - - - - -	- - - - - -	Expenditure tax (2)
Some products	Cigarette tax Gasoline tax (4)	- - - - - -	- - - - - -	Telephone tax Gasoline tax Property tax (2)
In factor market All factors, all employments	- - - - - -	Value added (income type) (10)	Income tax (1)	- - - - - -
Some factors, all employments	- - - - - -	Employer's payroll tax (11)	Employee's payroll tax (13)	- - - - - -
Some factors; some employments	- - - - - -	Corporate profits tax Property tax (12)	- - - - - -	- - - - - -

*Numbers in parentheses refer to impact points shown in Fig. 12-1.

Keeping in mind these identities and how various taxes fit into the national income accounts will be helpful in analyzing similarities or differences among them and in tracing taxpayer responses in our later discussion of incidence and effects of taxation.

Taxes on Holding and Transfer of Wealth

Taxes may be imposed on the holding of wealth or stocks rather than on transactions or flows generated in current production. The principal example is the property tax. Interpreted as a tax on capital income (in the case of business property) or of consumption (for owner-occupied residences), it might readily be incorporated in Figure 12-1 and Table 12-1. Other wealth taxes, such as those imposed on the transfer of wealth by inheritance or gift, however, cannot be so included.

Personal versus In Rem Taxes

Cutting across the above categories, we distinguish between personal taxes and in rem taxes. Personal taxes are taxes which are adjusted to the taxpayer's personal ability to pay; in rem taxes (taxes on "things") are imposed on activities or objects as such, i.e., on purchases, sales, or the holding of property, independently of the characteristics of the transactor or the owner.

In rem taxes may be imposed on either the household or the firm side. But personal taxes, by their very nature, *must* be imposed on the household side of the transaction. Thus, if proceeds from the sale of factors of production are to be taxed in a personal fashion, the tax must be imposed on households as a personal income tax. Taxes imposed on factor payments of firms cannot distinguish the taxpaying ability of particular income recipients. All sources of income must be combined in the taxpayer's base so as to measure his or her ability to pay. Similarly, if consumption is to be taxed in a personal fashion, the tax must be placed on the household in the form of a personal expenditure tax. A sales tax imposed on firms is not responsive to the particular consumer but gives the same treatment to all households which undertake the taxed transaction. The same again holds for the taxation of wealth under the property tax, as against a net worth tax relating to the entire wealth position of the individual owner.

The distinction between person and in rem taxes is of crucial importance when it comes to the equity of the tax system. Equity must be evaluated in terms of the resulting burden distribution among people. Since the burden of all taxes, including those imposed on "things," must ultimately be borne by persons, their equity must be evaluated by the resulting burden distribution among persons. As such, in rem taxes are inferior to well-designed personal taxes imposed directly so as to allow for the particular taxpayer's ability to pay. Since personal taxes must be assessed on the household side, such taxes tend to be generally superior in equity to those imposed on the firm side.

Direct versus Indirect Taxes

Finally, brief attention should be given to the frequently used distinction between "direct" and "indirect" taxes. Although this distinction is ambiguous, most writers define direct taxes as those which are imposed initially on the individual or household that is meant to bear the burden. Indirect taxes are taxes which are imposed at some other point in the system but are meant to be shifted (a concept which will be examined presently) to whomever is supposed to be the final bearer of the burden. Personal taxes, such as the individual income tax, are thus direct; and most in rem taxes, such as sales and excise taxes, are indirect.

The term "excise," finally, refers to a subcategory of indirect taxes and is applied to certain selective sales taxes imposed at the manufacturer level. A legal rather than economic category in nature, it appears in the constitutional provision that direct taxes must be imposed on a population basis, while others, such as "duties, imposts, and excises," need not be.

Transfers as Negative Taxes

Transfer payments by government may be viewed as negative taxes. Whereas taxes take from the private sector without a direct quid pro quo, transfers render a payment without requiring a return service. Transfer payments or grants might thus be entered into Figure 12-1, but flowing in the opposite direction as the tax stream. Social security benefits might appear next to the income tax, subsidies to business might parallel business taxes, and so forth. This is a perspective which we have dealt with earlier, especially when discussing proposals for a negative income tax and when examining social security benefits.

B.   REQUIREMENTS FOR A "GOOD" TAX STRUCTURE

The U.S. tax system, like that of any other country, has developed in response to many influences—economic, political, and social. It has not been constructed by a master architect in line with the optimal requirements for a good tax structure. Yet, ideas about what constitutes a good tax system have had their influence. Economists and social philosophers, from Adam Smith on, have propounded what such requirements should be. Among them, the following are of major importance:

1. Revenue yield should be adequate.
2. The distribution of the tax burden should be equitable. Everyone should be made to pay his or her fair share, a matter to be dealt with in the following chapter.
3. What matters in this context is not only the impact point at which the tax is imposed but its final resting place. The problem of incidence, explored in Chapter 13, must thus be allowed for.
4. Taxes should be chosen so as to minimize interference with economic decisions in otherwise efficient markets. Such interference as shown in Chapter 14 imposes "excess burdens" which should be minimized.
5. The tax structure should facilitate the use of fiscal policy for stabilization and growth objectives, a topic dealt with in Chapter 30.
6. The tax system should permit fair and nonarbitrary administration and it should be understandable to the taxpayer.
7. Administration and compliance costs should be as low as is compatible with the other objectives.

These and other requirements may be used as criteria to appraise the quality of a tax structure. The various objectives are not necessarily in agreement, and where they conflict, tradeoffs between them are needed. Thus, equity may require administrative complexity and may interfere with neutrality, efficient design of tax policy may interfere with equity, and so forth. These conflicts will be considered as we proceed.

C. SUMMARY

In considering the impact of various taxes in the circular flow of income and expenditures in the economy, we noted that:

1. Taxes may be imposed in the factor or in the product markets.
2. Taxes may be imposed on the buyer's or the seller's side of the market.
3. Certain taxes, though different in appearance, are equivalent to each other.

Considering major types of taxes, a distinction was drawn between:

4. Personal and in rem taxes.
5. Direct and indirect taxes.
6. Positive and negative taxes.

Examining the requirements for a good tax system, we noted that:

7. The good tax system should be designed so as to meet the requirements of equity in burden distribution, efficiency in resource use, goals of macro policy, and ease of administration.

FURTHER READINGS

Among the most important classics on a good tax system, the following may be noted:

Smith, A.: *The Wealth of Nations,* London: Everyman's Library, 1910, book V, chap. II, part II. "On Taxes," especially the early pages dealing with his famous "canons" of good taxation.
Mill, J. S.: *Principles of Political Economy,* London: Longman's, 1921, book V, chap. II.
Pigou, A. C.: *A Study in Public Finance,* London: Macmillan, 1928, Part II.
Also see references on pp. 72 and 296.

Chapter 13

Approaches to Tax Equity*

A. Application of Benefit Principle: *A General Benefit Tax; Specific Benefit Taxes; Taxes in Lieu of Charges; A Note on Earmarking.* **B. Ability to Pay: (1) Horizontal Equity and Choice of Tax Base:** *Horizontal and Vertical Equity; Income versus Consumption as Tax Base; Wealth as Tax Base; Conclusion.* **C. Ability to Pay: (2) Vertical Equity and Rate Structure:** *Equal Sacrifice Rules; Social Welfare Approach.* **D. Summary.**

We begin the discussion of tax principles with the equity objective. Although not always controlling, it is a basic criterion for tax-structure design. Everyone agrees that the tax system should be equitable, i.e., that each taxpayer should contribute his or her fair share to the cost of government. But there is no such agreement about how the term fair share should be defined. As noted in our earlier discussion of distributive justice, a variety of approaches may be taken. In particular, two strands of thought may be distinguished.

Reader's Guide to Chapter 13: All are agreed that the tax system should be fair and equitable, but there is less agreement about how to interpret this requirement. In this chapter we examine the principles of benefit and ability-to-pay taxation. In connection with the latter we take a careful look at how ability to pay should be measured and whether income or consumption offers the superior index. Next we consider how the tax burden should be distributed among people with unequal ability to pay. The problems examined here are elusive but basic to an understanding of tax policy.

One approach rests on the so-called benefit principle. According to this theory, dating back to Adam Smith and earlier writers, an equitable tax system is one under which each taxpayer contributes in line with the benefits which he or she receives from public services. According to this principle, the truly equitable tax system will differ depending on the expenditure structure. The benefit criterion, therefore, is not one of tax policy only but of tax-expenditure policy. This is in line with our approach in Chapter 4, where we viewed the economics of the public sector as involving a simultaneous solution to both its revenue and its expenditure aspects.

The other strand, also of distinguished ancestry, rests on the ability-to-pay principle. Under this approach, the tax problem is viewed by itself, independent of expenditure determination. A given total revenue is needed and each taxpayer is asked to contribute in line with his or her ability to pay.[1] This approach leaves the expenditure side of the public sector dangling and is thus less satisfactory from the economists's point of view. Yet actual tax policy is largely determined independently of the expenditure side and an equity rule is needed to provide guidance. The ability-to-pay principle is widely accepted as this guide.

Neither approach is easy to interpret or implement. For the benefit principle to be operational, expenditure benefits for particular taxpayers must be known. For the ability-to-pay approach to be applicable, we must know just how this ability is to be measured. These are formidable difficulties and neither approach wins on practicality grounds. Moreover, neither approach can be said to deal with the entire function of tax policy.

The benefit approach will ideally allocate that part of the tax bill which defrays the cost of public services, but it cannot handle taxes needed to finance transfer payments and serve redistributional objectives. For benefit taxation to be equitable, it must be assumed that a "proper" state of distribution exists to begin with. This is a serious shortcoming since in practice, there is no separation between the taxes used to finance public services and the taxes used to redistribute income. The ability-to-pay approach better meets the redistribution problem but it leaves the provision for public services undetermined.

Notwithstanding these shortcomings, both principles have important, if limited, application in designing an equitable tax structure, one which is acceptable to most people and preferable to alternative arrangements.

A.   APPLICATION OF BENEFIT PRINCIPLE

As we have seen in our earlier discussion, the political process involves determination of both tax and expenditure policy and in a democratic framework tends to

---

[1] Historically, the benefit principle of taxation derives from the contract theory of the state as understood by the political theorists of the seventeenth century, such as Locke and Hobbes. Subsequently it was woven into the greatest-happiness principle of the utilitarians, such as Bentham. It appeared early in classical economics in Adam Smith's first canon of taxation, which in one sentence combines both the benefit and the ability-to-pay approaches: "The subjects of every state ought to contribute towards the support of the government as nearly as possible in proportion to their respective abilities; that is, in proportion to the revenue which they respectively enjoy under the protection of the state" (Adam Smith, *The Wealth of Nations*, vol. 2, edited by E. Cannan, New York: Putnam, 1904, p. 310). Benefits are here viewed in terms of protection received and are thus related to income which, in turn, is also a measure of ability to pay.

approximate application of the benefit rule. People, or some majority thereof, would not be willing to sustain a fiscal program if, on balance, they did not benefit therefrom. We have also noted that by relating particular tax to particular expenditure decisions, a more rational decision process may be achieved. Let us now see how the benefit principle may be applied as a guide to tax-structure design.

A General Benefit Tax

Under a strict regime of benefit taxation, each taxpayer would be taxed in line with his or her demand for public services. Since preferences differ, no general tax formula could be applied to all people. Each taxpayer would be taxed in line with his or her evaluation. Still, some pattern might be expected to emerge. The typical mix of private goods purchased is known to vary with the income level of the consumer household, and similar patterns may be expected to prevail for social goods. But instead of noting how quantities bought (at the same price) will vary with income, we now ask how much various consumers are willing to pay for the same amount. Unless the social good in question is what economists call an "inferior" good, consumer valuation may be expected to rise with income. To simplify, suppose that taxpayers have the same structure of tastes (i.e., pattern of indifference curves) so that persons with the same income value the same amount equally. People with incomes of $10,000 value a given level of public services at, say, $1,000. With 1,000 units of the service supplied, they would be willing to pay $1 per unit. Making the usual assumption that marginal utility of income falls with rising income, others with incomes of $20,000 would be willing to pay a higher unit price of, say, $2. In this case, a proportional rate schedule will apply. If they are not willing to pay as much as $2 but only, say, $1.50, the appropriate rate schedule will be regressive. If they will pay more, a progressive schedule will be in order.[2]

The appropriate tax formula thus depends upon the preference patterns. More specifically, it depends upon the income and price elasticity of demand for social goods. If income elasticity is high, the appropriate tax prices will rise rapidly with income; but if price elasticity is high, the increase will be dampened. This relationship may be specified as follows: With income elasticity $E_y = (\Delta Q/Q)/(\Delta Y/Y)$ and price elasticity $E_p = (\Delta Q/Q)/(\Delta P/P)$, we have $(\Delta P/P)/(\Delta Y/Y) = E_y/E_p$. The left side of this equation expresses the elasticity of the tax price with respect to income. If this elasticity equals 1, both change at the same percentage rate and the ratio of tax to income remains constant. That is to say, the tax is proportional. If E_y/E_p is larger than 1, the ratio rises and the tax is progressive, and if E_y/E_p is less than 1 the tax is regressive. Thus the required rate structure will be proportional, progressive, or regressive, depending on whether income elasticity of demand for public goods equals, exceeds, or falls short of price elasticity.

This finding is interesting, but it does not permit easy implementation. The relevant price and income elasticities are not known or readily derived from market observation as in the case of private goods. Moreover, they will differ among var-

---

[2] Returning to Figure 5-4 (p. 69), we note that the taxes paid by A and B for OH units of social goods equal KM and LN, respectively. If $KM/OM = LN/ON$, a proportional tax rate is required. Since $OM > ON$, a situation where $KM/OM > LN/ON$ calls for a progressive rate structure; and one where $KM/OM < LN/ON$ calls for regression.

ious types of public services. It is not at all obvious which elasticity (income or price) will be larger and by how much, especially if the entire budget is considered. The question of rate structure thus remains open. Nevertheless, this line of reasoning points up the fact that the rationale for or against progressive taxation may be discussed in terms of benefit taxation as well as in terms of the usual ability-to-pay context. Even if the latter points to progression, the former need not do so.

Specific Benefit Taxes

Whereas the general benefit tax is of interest mainly as a theoretical concept, practical applications of benefit taxation may be found in specific instances where particular services are provided on a benefit basis. This may be the case where direct financing is made via fees, user charges, or tolls. Or certain taxes may be applied indirectly in lieu of charges, as is done in the taxation of gasoline and other automotive products for purposes of highway finance.

Under what conditions is this technique feasible and desirable? The case for finance by direct charges to the user is clear-cut where the goods or services provided by government are in the nature of private goods, i.e., where consumption is wholly rival. Benefits can be imputed to a particular user who can be asked to pay. The issuance of licenses, the financing of municipal transportation, and the provision of airport facilities are more or less in this category. Where benefits are internalized, the government may act in a capacity similar to that of a private firm and the same principles of pricing are appropriate. As has been pointed out in recent years, a considerable range of public services might be placed on this basis, thereby easing the pressure on general revenue finance. By using a market mechanism, a more efficient determination of the appropriate level of supply becomes possible.

Taxes in Lieu of Charges

In other instances, where imposition of direct charges is desirable but too costly, a tax on a complementary product may be used in lieu of charges. Gasoline or automobile taxes may be used in lieu of tolls. The yield of automotive taxes (on gasoline and cars) in the United States, including all levels of government, roughly matches the cost of highway expenditures. In the case of the federal highway program, gasoline tax proceeds are earmarked for the Highway Trust Fund, and the income of the fund is used to defray the cost of a federal highway network. In the instance of state and local financing, such direct earmarking does not always exist, but proceeds from highway user taxes nevertheless go largely into road finance.

How effective an approach to benefit taxation does this offer? Although it may be true that such taxes place the total cost of highways on all drivers as a group, it is questionable whether the equity objective of benefit taxation for the individual driver is met. Whereas gasoline use depends on distances driven, not each mile driven results in the same variable cost, nor does it require the same capital outlay in providing new road facilities. Driver X, using road A, may be called upon to support road B, used by driver Y. Gasoline taxes, therefore, are only a rough approximation to the benefit rule in highway finance. Nor will such taxes effectively enter into the determination of demand for new highway construction. Expenditure decisions are made for specific outlays, while taxes are paid independently of particular highways used, so that there is no direct linkage between the two at a disaggregated level. Moreover, there has been increasing support in recent years for legislation which will permit diversion of Highway Trust Fund receipts into the financing of mass transportation. This is justified as a way of internalizing the external costs of highway use.

Another illustration is given by certain uses of the property tax. Special assessments may be used to charge dwellings in a certain block for the cost of improvements which service their particular location. At a more general level, the property tax has traditionally been viewed as a charge for services rendered by local government, it being assumed that the benefits which result are roughly proportional to property values. How well founded this belief is remains to be seen.[3]

Social security taxes may provide another instance of benefit taxation. Payroll tax contributions by the employee may be considered a strict benefit tax, provided that the later benefit payments stand in direct relation to the contribution and that the benefit formula is not redistributive.[4] The same cannot be said for the employer contributions unless they are passed on to the employee.

A Note on Earmarking

Finally, a word on earmarking in relation to benefit taxation. Fiscal experts have argued that earmarking is poor budgeting procedure, since it introduces rigidities and does not permit proper allocation of general revenue among competing uses. Thus, it is inefficient to freeze, say, 50 percent of sales tax revenue as the state contribution to the cost of elementary education. The appropriate allotment may be larger or smaller than this amount. Moreover, it may be desirable to use the sales tax for other purposes.

At the same time, other uses of earmarking may be appropriate and in line with the benefit approach. First, particular taxes may be linked to particular expenditures because tax payments are equivalent to (or are held to approximate) charges imposed on the consumer. As just noted, this holds to some extent for gasoline taxes. Such linkage may be both efficient (in charging for variable costs) and equitable (in distributing costs in line with benefits received). Second, linkage of voting on particular taxes with specified expenditure votes may be helpful in inducing preference revelation and thus contribute to better expenditure decisions. Such may be the case even if the tax base is not linked to benefits received. Thus, it might be decided to finance defense out of, say, a value-added tax while drawing on the income tax for nondefense purposes. This might establish a clearer link between expenditure and tax votes on these two areas of federal budgetary activity and thus improve decision making. Depending on how it is used, earmarking may thus be an arbitrary procedure leading to budgetary rigidity, or it may be a helpful device for approximating benefit taxation and more efficient expenditure selection.

---

[3] See p. 411.
[4] As noted before, these assumptions do not hold for the present U.S. system. See p. 203.

B. ABILITY TO PAY: (1) HORIZONTAL EQUITY AND CHOICE OF TAX BASE

Although the benefit principle may be applied directly to the finance of certain governmental functions, it does not solve the general problem of tax-structure design. The range of expenditures to which specific benefit taxes may be applied is relatively limited and the bulk of tax revenue is not derived (nor derivable) on a specific benefit basis. Even though tax legislation should be related to expenditure legislation in the political process, application of the benefit rule in this broader sense does not obviate tax formulas and a rule by which they are designed. Moreover, we have noted that benefit taxation, even at its best, can relate only to the financing of public services and not to the redistributive function of the tax-transfer process.

Thus an alternative principle of equitable taxation must be applied. This is the rule that people should contribute to the cost of government in line with their ability to pay.[5] Under this approach, the tax problem is viewed by itself, independent of expenditure determination. A given total revenue is needed and each taxpayer is asked to contribute in line with his or her ability to pay. This approach can encompass the redistribution function, especially if transfers are indirect as negative taxes; but it has the disadvantage that it leaves the determination of public services out of the picture.

Horizontal and Vertical Equity

Taxation according to ability to pay calls for people with equal capacity to pay the same, and for people with greater ability to pay more. The former is referred to as horizontal equity and the latter as vertical equity. The horizontal equity rule merely applies the basic principle of equality under the law. If income is used as the index of ability to pay, income taxation is the appropriate instrument and people with the same income should pay the same tax. The vertical equity rule is also in line with equal treatment but proceeds on the premise that this calls for different amounts of tax to be paid by people with different ability to pay. Person A, whose income is higher, should pay more than B. In this sense, both equity rules follow from the same principle of equal treatment and neither is more basic.

Moreover, implementation of either rule requires a quantitative measure of ability to pay. Ideally, this measure would reflect the entire welfare which a person can derive from all the options available to him or her, including consumption (present and future), holding of wealth, and the enjoyment of leisure. Unfortunately, such a comprehensive measure is not practicable. The value of leisure, in particular, cannot be measured, so that some second-best but observable measures must do. Given this constraint, what is the best index to use: is it income, consumption, or wealth?

---

[5] The origin of the ability-to-pay principle predates the benefit rule. It dates back to the sixteenth century and has found prominent supporters ever since. They include a wide range of thinkers such as Rousseau, Say, and John Stuart Mill. In the twentieth century, ability to pay has been emphasized primarily by redistribution-oriented writers.

Income versus Consumption as Tax Base

Income has been the most widely accepted measure of ability to pay, but more recently there has been growing support for consumption as the superior choice. To be sure, income has served as *the* base of personal taxation under the income tax, whereas the consumption base has been used in the impersonal or in rem form of sales and excise taxes. Thus, use of the income base has been more equitable than use of the consumption base. But it does not follow that the income base remains superior if the consumption base is used in the form of a personalized expenditure tax, with allowance made for family size and expenditure taxed at progressive rates.[6] This is the premise on which our present comparison will be based.

Comprehensiveness of Bases Both income- and consumption-base advocates agree that the respective bases should be defined comprehensively.

For the *income base* this means that income (looked at from the *sources* side of the household account) should be thought of as a person's entire accretion to his or her wealth, including all forms thereof. As we will examine in detail later on, a person's economic capacity and hence ability to pay is increased whether income accrues in the form of money income (such as wages, salaries, interest, or dividends), as imputed income (such as imputed rent from owner-occupied housing), or as an appreciation (whether realized or not) in the value of assets.[7] The same requirement of comprehensiveness can be stated if we look at income from the uses side of the household account. Income then equals increase in net worth (or saving) plus consumption during the period. The two formulations amount to the same, provided that increase in net worth and consumption are also given a comprehensive definition.

For the *consumption base,* the requirement of comprehensiveness calls for inclusion of all forms of consumption, whether this takes the form of cash purchases or whether the consumption stream is derived in imputed form. Since income equals increase in net worth (or saving) plus consumption, whereas the consumption base includes consumption only, the consumption tax differs from the income tax by excluding income which is saved.

Which Is the Better Base? Assuming that both bases are defined comprehensively, which is the better choice? Hobbes, writing over 300 years ago, argued that a person should pay tax on what is consumed but not on what is saved "and left for use by others." Vice should be taxed and virtue be rewarded. A more realistic view, however, is that saving is undertaken to postpone own-consumption, not as an altruistic act. We thus define individuals A and B as in similar position if they have the same consumption options, independent of the particular time path of consumption which they may choose. This is shown in Table 13-1, where both A and B receive a wage income of $100 in period I but A consumes at once while B saves and consumes in period II.

Consider first the income tax. We note that A pays in period I only, while B

---

[6] For examination of such a tax, see p. 224.
[7] For discussion of income definition, see p. 404.

TABLE 13-1
Comparison of Income and Consumption Taxes during Two Periods
(In Dollars)

	INCOME TAX (I)		CONSUMPTION TAX (II)		TAX ON WAGE INCOME (III)	
	A	B	A	B	A	B
Period I						
Wage income	100	100	100	100	100	100
Tax	10	10	10	—	10	10
Consumption	90	—	90	—	90	—
Saving	—	90	—	100	—	90
Period II						
Interest	—	9.00	—	10	—	9
Tax	—	0.90	—	11	—	—
Consumption	—	98.10	—	99	—	99
Saving	—	—	—	—	—	—
Total tax	10	10.90	10	11	10	10
Present value	10	10.82	10	10	10	10

pays in both periods. After paying the same tax as A in period I, B pays a further tax on interest income in period II. B's tax for both periods thus equals $10.90 as against A's tax of $10. Under the consumption tax, A pays tax in period I while B pays in period II. B's tax is again higher, but it is also payable later. Since a tax postponement is a gain to the taxpayer (after all, the money can be invested at interest in the interim), it is reasonable to compare the discounted value of the tax burdens. As shown in the last line of the table and discounting at a rate of 10 percent, this value is the same for both A and B under the consumption tax, but B pays more under the income tax. Seen in this context, the consumption-tax approach gives the fair solution since it places the same burden on people with equal potential consumption. As we will see later, a similar conclusion in favor of the consumption base is arrived at on efficiency grounds,[8] as distinct from our present concern with defining equal position in the context of horizontal equity.

Relation to Tax on Wage Income   Turning to columns IIIA and IIIB of Table 13-1, we further note that the expenditure tax may be likened not only to an income tax which excludes savings from its base but also to an income tax which excludes capital income while taxing only wages. A tax on wage income alone would tax both A and B in only the first period and would be similar to the consumption tax in that both bear the same present value burden. This way of comparing the taxes is of interest because some observers who find it reasonable to exempt saving from tax might be startled by the idea of exempting capital income. This runs counter to the traditional thought from Adam Smith on, which states that if there is to be any discrimination, it should be in favor of wage ("earned") rather than capital ("unearned") income.

[8] See p. 290.

Treatment of Bequests Returning to the consumption base, we note now that our two-period model of Table 13-1 was drawn up so as to let all income be consumed within the two-period time span. Suppose now that B does not consume in period II but leaves an estate to C. In this case, B would pay nothing. A tax would be paid only later on by C if and when C consumes. No tax would be paid if C also abstains and passes the entire estate to D and so on to future generations. This problem is avoided, however, by including B's bequest along with B's consumption in his or her tax base. Leaving a bequest, after all, is one way in which B can use his or her funds and thus should be taxed as part of that use. Putting it differently, the definition of the tax base should be changed from "*own-consumption,* independent of timing," to "*all uses,*" including not only own-consumption but also the granting of gifts and bequests. While it may be argued in response that leaving bequests will only postpone the tax to when the heir consumes, such postponement may be indefinite. Moreover, under a progressive tax, bracket rates would then apply across generations rather than to the lifetime of the individual taxpayer. More will be said about this later when the personal expenditure tax is discussed.[9]

Further Limitations Some further qualifications to the superiority of the consumption base may be noted:

1. The proposition that individuals with equal present value lifetime incomes are in equal position assumes that future income and needs are known, so that an optimal disposition can be made. In fact life is uncertain and preferences change, which makes it difficult to establish ex ante that people are in equal positions.

2. The proposition that individuals with incomes of equal present value are in the same position, independent of when the income accrues, assumes further that there are perfect capital markets allowing all taxpayers to borrow and invest at the same rate. This is an unrealistic assumption. Lower-income consumers have less ready access. They will thus find the consumption tax especially burdensome during periods of the life cycle when high outlays are needed.

3. As will be noted later, transition from the present system of income taxation to an expenditure tax would pose serious problems of equity during the transition period.

In all, it appears that the preconditions for a perfect consumption base would be difficult to realize. Its superiority, although arguable in a purist model, thus becomes less evident in practice. Moreover, any final choice among the two bases must allow for imperfections in base definition—whether they are owing to technical or political factors—which will inevitably arise.[10]

Wealth as Tax Base

Having considered income and consumption as tax bases, we must now consider the role of wealth. Viewing wealth as the capitalized value of capital income, we

---

[9] See p. 404 below. A more sophisticated case against inclusion has been made as follows: B, so the argument goes, has the choice (1) to consume now, (2) to consume later, and (3) to leave a bequest to C. All three options give utility to B. In the case of B, B's utility is derived from pleasure in C's consumption. But this pleasure is a function of C's consumption *net* of C's tax. Inclusion of the bequest in B's tax base with subsequent taxation of C's consumption would thus impose a double tax on the utility which B derives from bequeathing. See G. Brennan, "Death and Taxes: An Attack on the Orthodoxy," *Public Finance,* no. 3, 1978. See also p. 432 below.

[10] See p. 406.

may view a tax on wealth as equivalent to a tax on such income. If capital yields an income of 10 percent, a 10 percent tax on the latter would be equivalent to a 1 percent tax on the former. A tax on wealth would thus impose a tax on capital income, whereas the consumption base would in effect exclude capital income from the income tax. Viewed this way, the case for the consumption tax is also a case against an additional tax on wealth.

There is, however, another aspect to the problem which should not be overlooked. Saving to permit postponement of consumption involves accumulation of wealth, and its holding generates an additional utility. Whether it is in the form of increased security or economic power, this gain should be added to potential consumption as a further component of the base, thus calling for some taxation of wealth or of income along with a consumption-based tax.

Even though this shows the consumption tax to be defective, it also improves the rating of the income tax. However, we cannot conclude that the income tax is superior: the discrimination against the saver which it imposes may more than offset the additional tax justified by wealth-holding satisfaction. Nevertheless, wealth utility offers one more reason why the case for the consumption base is not clearcut. This is especially so if consumption never occurs and bequests are passed on from one heir to another.

Moreover, there may well be a case for the taxation of wealth involving considerations other than ability to pay. Thus society may be concerned with the effects of concentrated wealth holdings on the distribution of political power. Where this is the case, the tax base might be defined properly in terms of a person's gross wealth, as distinct from the ability-to-pay approach, where wealth would have to be defined in terms of net worth, i.e., assets minus indebtedness.[11]

Moreover, society's concern with inequality or vertical equity may be related not only to income but also to the uses to which it is put, i.e., to the distribution of consumption or of wealth. Regarding consumption, concern might be with minimum consumption standards or with the unpleasantness of conspicuous consumption. Regarding wealth, concern might be with inequalities in social and political power which result from inequalities in wealth. What is considered an acceptable degree of inequality may differ for the two cases, thus calling for more than one tax instrument.

Conclusion

In the last resort, the choice of tax base cannot be made in a theoretical vacuum. It depends on the structure of the economy in which the taxation occurs and the "tax handles" which this structure provides. In an agricultural society where most income is derived and consumed on farms, the income tax approach would be extremely difficult to apply. A tax on property or cattle, as in Colonial America, would offer a more feasible way of approximating taxable capacity. Similarly, developing countries find it difficult to reach capital income under the income tax. In such situations, a tax on real property, which can be readily detected, offers a useful supplement. Nor do these difficulties apply to developing countries only. The

----

[11] See p. 223.

individual income tax, as applied in the United States, is far from comprehensive and it is even less so in most other nations. As shown below, some forms of capital income are excluded from the tax base and others are given preferential treatment.[12] For these reasons, a supplementary tax on wealth may be called for, if only as the second-best means of approximating taxation under a comprehensive income tax.

Moreover, although choosing the proper index of economic capacity is important, it is only a first step in designing an equitable tax structure. The second step is to apply this index—be it income, consumption, or wealth—to the complexity of economic and legal institutions. In this process, a host of highly technical and difficult problems arise. How should corporations be taxed, how should capital gains be treated, how should depreciation be timed, how should the particular problems of financial institutions be dealt with and so on? Since the economy itself is complex and the tax law must be tailored thereto, no single concept of tax base can be implemented to perfection. Moreover, an equitable tax system cannot be simple. An excessively complex tax structure, on the other hand, leads to lawful tax avoidance (some taxpayers adapt their activities to minimize liabilities) as well as illegal evasion, which in turn undermines equity. Tax policy, therefore, is an art no less than a science; and equity is to be sought as a matter of degree rather than as an absolute norm.

C. ABILITY TO PAY: (2) VERTICAL EQUITY AND RATE STRUCTURE

We now leave the question of how the tax base is to be measured and take it to be in terms of income. People with equal income should then pay the same tax. The question to be considered now is how the taxes payable by people with different incomes should differ. How should the problem of vertical equity be resolved? Though applied here to differentials in income, similar reasoning also holds for differentials in consumption.

Equal Sacrifice Rules

Returning to our earlier discussion of equity in distribution, we recall two distinct approaches to this problem, one based on a postulated marginal utility of income schedule, which is taken to apply to all individuals, and the other based on a social welfare function. Vertical equity in taxation has again been viewed along both these lines. With respect to the former approach, vertical equity, since John Stuart Mill, has been viewed in terms of an equal-sacrifice prescription. Taxpayers are said to be treated equally if their tax payments involve an equal sacrifice or loss of welfare.[13] The loss of welfare in turn is related to the loss of income, as measured by the taxpayer's marginal utility of income schedule. That schedule is assumed to be known and the same for all people. Given this premise, the equal sacrifice rule calls for people with equal income (or ability to pay) to contribute equal amounts of

---

[12] See p. 335.
[13] See John Stuart Mill, *Principles of Political Economy*, edited by W. J. Ashley, London: Longmans, 1921, p. 804.

tax. Furthermore, people with different incomes should pay different amounts. The more difficult question is how these amounts should differ. To answer it, one must know the shape of the marginal utility of income schedule, and even then the answer differs, depending on how the term "equal" is interpreted. In particular, does equal sacrifice call for a progressive tax?

Alternative Rules   The answer depends on both the shape of the income utility schedule and the rule that "equality of sacrifice" is defined by. It may be interpreted to mean, equal *absolute,* equal *proportional,* or equal *marginal* (least total) sacrifice. These concepts may be explained with the help of Figure 13-1, where the left diagram pertains to low-income taxpayer L and the right to high-income taxpayer H. MU_L and MU_H are the respective marginal utility of income schedules, which are identical and assumed to decline at a decreasing rate. L's income before tax is OB and that for H is OB'. The total utilities derived by L and H are $OBDM$ and $OB'D'M'$, respectively. If a given revenue T is to be drawn from the two, how will it be allocated under the three rules?

Absolute Sacrifice   Under the equal absolute sacrifice rule, L, with income OB, pays CB, while H, with income OB', pays $C'B'$, where $CB + C'B'$ is the needed revenue T. The loss of utility or sacrifice incurred by L equals $CBDE$ while the loss to H equals $C'B'D'E'$, and T is distributed such that $CBDE = C'B'D'E'$.

If marginal utility were constant (MU parallel to the horizontal axis), equal absolute sacrifice would require tax liabilities to be the same for all incomes. Equal sacrifice would call for a head tax. But with a declining MU schedule, tax liability must rise with income. This much is clear, but it does not follow that a progressive tax will be called for. As may be shown mathematically, the required tax distribution will be progressive, proportional, or regressive, depending on whether the

FIGURE 13-1   Measures of equal sacrifice.

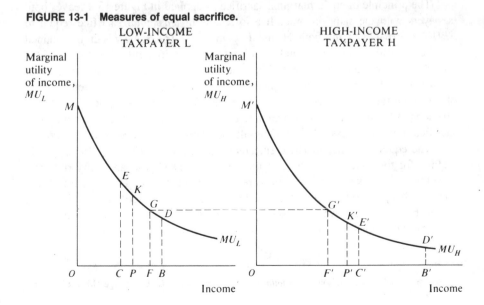

elasticity of the marginal income utility with respect to income is greater than, equal to, or less than unity.[14] Even though it seems reasonable to assume that the *MU* schedule falls, there is no intuitive answer about its rate of decline. Thus, there is no ready basis on which to conclude whether equal absolute sacrifice calls for progression, not to speak of the proper degree of progression.

Proportional Sacrifice   If the tax burden is distributed in line with equal proportional sacrifice, L will pay *PB* and H will pay *P'B'*, with *PB* + *P'B'* again equal to *T*. The tax is divided between the two so that the fraction of pretax utility lost for L (or *PBDK/OBDM*) is the same as that for H (or *P'B'D'K'/O'B'D'M'*). Under this rule, it is evident that a constant *MU* schedule will call for proportional taxation. It can also be seen that a declining but straight-line *MU* schedule calls for progression, but generalizations become difficult if the *MU* schedule falls at a decreasing rate, as is usually assumed. The result in any particular case depends on the level and slope of the *MU* schedule, as well as on the initial distribution of income and the amount of revenue that is to be raised.

Marginal Sacrifice   Under the equal marginal sacrifice rule, L pays *FB* and H pays *F'B'*, where *FB* + *F'B'* is the required revenue *T*. The marginal sacrifice is the same, since *FG* = *F'G'*. At the same time, the total sacrifice for both (or *FBDG* + *F'B'D'G'*) is minimized. After-tax incomes are equalized at *OF* = *O'F'*.

If the marginal utility of income were constant, the distribution of the tax bill under *equal marginal* sacrifice would be indeterminate. Any distribution drawing at least some small amount from all taxpayers would meet the requirement. Given a declining *MU* schedule, equal marginal sacrifice calls for "maximum progression"; i.e., the leveling down of income from the top until the required revenue is obtained. The rate of decline does not matter in this case.

The principle of equal marginal sacrifice as applied in Figure 13-1 leaves both taxpayers with the same income. It also results in *least total* sacrifice (equal to *FBDG* + *F'B'D'G'*) for both H and L combined. The same result is obtained whether we use an equal marginal, or a least total, sacrifice rule. But suppose now that the revenue requirement is less than the excess of H's over L's income. Here, equal marginal sacrifice cannot be achieved and the result must be stated in terms of least total sacrifice. To achieve least total sacrifice, the tax is applied so as to lop off incomes from the top down, leaving all those who pay tax with equal marginal sacrifice, but not necessarily including all individuals in the tax-paying group.

The equal marginal sacrifice rule may thus be viewed as an efficiency rule (calling for total sacrifice to be at a minimum) rather than as an equity rule; and once this step is taken, the argument is readily extended beyond the amount of revenue that happens to be required. Instead of saying that the sacrifice due to taxation should be minimized, we can also say that the welfare derived from what is left over should be maximized, thus leading us to the previously examined utilitarian

---

[14] See Paul A. Samuelson, *Foundations of Economic Analysis*, Cambridge, Mass.: Harvard, 1947, p. 227.

view of a just distribution.[15] After all, if maximum satisfaction from private income is called for, the adjustment should not be limited to the amount of revenue needed to finance public services.

Conclusion Comparing the results for L and H, we find that L does best under the equal marginal rule, followed by equal proportional and equal absolute sacrifice. It is also evident that H pays more than L whatever rule is chosen. This simply reflects the declining slope of the marginal utility schedule. We have also seen that the tax formula will be progressive under the equal marginal rule, with the outcome uncertain for the equal absolute and proportional sacrifice rules.

Whereas these are interesting results, their application, as we have noted, depends on two assumptions, namely (1) that the shape of the marginal utility schedule is known, and (2) that the same schedule applies to all taxpayers. Neither of these conditions are met. Psychology does not give us the answer to 1, and there is reason to believe that capacities to derive utility do in fact differ among individuals.

Social Welfare Approach

Concerns such as these have led to an alternative approach. This postulates a social welfare function, i.e., a social valuation of the marginal utility of individual incomes.[16] Also, it is postulated that income assigned to all individuals should be evaluated accordingly.

Suppose then that this schedule is as shown in Figure 13-1, with the prevailing distribution again such that L receives *OB* and H receives *OB'*. Evidently this distribution is not in line with what it would be if social utility was maximized or, which is the same, if the marginal social utility of income were equated across both H and L, dividing the income equally among them. The loss of social welfare is minimized by again following the equal marginal sacrifice rule, thereby moving the distribution of disposable income toward equality.

The fact that the prevailing degree of progression falls far short of this pattern reflects a number of considerations. Although considerations of fairness based on a social welfare function enter, they differ and do not carry exclusive weight. Society also wishes to give weight to entitlement to earnings, a compromise position noted in our earlier discussion of distributive justice.[17] Moreover, as shown in the following chapter, considerations of deadweight loss must be allowed for and this enters as a check to progression in burden distribution.

D. SUMMARY

Two traditions in the analysis of equity criteria were distinguished, including the benefit and ability-to-pay approaches.

1. The benefit principle has the advantage of linking the expenditure and tax sides of budget policy, but it is not readily implemented, since consumer evaluation of

---

[15] See p. 78.
[16] See p. 83.
[17] See p. 81.

public services is not known to tax authorities but must be revealed through the political process. However, in some instances, benefit taxation can be applied.

2.   The benefit principle as applied to the financing of public services excludes redistributional considerations and presumes them to be dealt with in another part of the budget process.

3.   The ability-to-pay principle calls for a distribution of the tax burden in line with the economic capacity of the taxpayer. It has the advantage of permitting inclusion of distribution considerations but the disadvantage of dealing with the tax problem in isolation, the provision of social goods being left out of the picture.

4.   The ability-to-pay principle calls for a distribution of the tax burden in line with horizontal and vertical equity. To obtain horizontal equity, taxpayers with equal ability to pay should contribute equally. To secure vertical equity, taxpayers with unequal capacity should contribute correspondingly different amounts.

Implementation of equitable taxation in line with ability to pay requires the definition of a specific index by which ability to pay is to be measured.

5.   Ideally, this index would encompass all forms in which economic welfare is derived, including leisure as well as present and future consumption. Unfortunately, such a comprehensive index is not feasible, the value of leisure in particular not being measurable.

6.   Income is the most widely used general measure of economic capacity. Used for this purpose, income should be defined broadly so as to include all forms of accretion, independent of the sources from which it is derived and the uses to which it is put.

7.   An alternative measure of capacity is in the form of consumption. Applied as an expenditure tax, the consumption base may be made the basis for personal and progressive taxation.

8.   Given the framework of an idealized system of lifetime taxation, the consumption base is preferable, on grounds of horizontal equity, to the income base. This advantage becomes questionable, however, once a more realistic framework is considered.

9.   Bequests and gifts should be included in the base of the consumption tax.

10.   Holding of wealth involves a utility which escapes taxation under a consumption tax, calling for a supplementary tax on the holding of wealth.

Determination of the proper distribution of the tax burden among unequals involves complex considerations of vertical equity.

11.   Based on the premise of known and equal marginal utility of income functions, the principle of vertical equity may be formulated so as to call for equality of sacrifice. This may or may not require progressive taxation, depending on how equal sacrifice is defined and on the slope of the marginal utility of income schedules.

12.   Since it is debatable whether and how such schedules can be measured and compared, implementation of the ability-to-pay principle must make use of a socially determined income utility or social welfare function.

FURTHER READINGS

For an exposition of the accretion concept of income, see:

Goode, R.: "The Economic Definition of Income," in J. Pechman (ed.): *Comprehensive Income Taxation*, Washington, D.C.: Brookings, 1977.

Simons, H.: *Personal Income Taxation*, Chicago: University of Chicago Press, 1938.

For the debate over income versus consumption as tax base, see:

Bradford, D. "The Case for a Personal Consumption Tax," in J. Pechman (ed.): *What Should be Taxed: Income or Consumption?*, Washington, D.C.: Brookings, 1980.

Kaldor, N.: *An Expenditure Tax*, London: Allen, 1955, chap. 1 and appendix to chap. 1.

For a discussion of vertical equity and progression, see:

Blum, W. J., and H. Calven, Jr.: *The Uneasy Case for Progressive Taxation*, Chicago: University of Chicago Press, 1953.

Mill, J. S.: *Principles of Political Economy*, London: Longman's, 1921, book V, chap. II.

Pigou, A. C.: *A Study in Public Finance*, London: Macmillan, 1928, part II, chaps. 1 and 2.

Chapter 14

Tax and Expenditure Incidence: An Overview*

A. Nature of Tax Burden: *Tax Burden and Resource Transfer; Magnitude of Burden.* **B. Concepts of Incidence:** *Statutory Incidence, Economic Incidence, and Tax Shifting; Alternative Concepts of Incidence.* **C. Measuring Incidence:** *Burden Distribution among Whom?; Burden Impact from Sources and Uses Side; Measuring Changes in Distribution.* **D. Incidence of the U.S. Fiscal Structure:** *Estimation of Tax-Burden Distribution; Expenditure Benefits Allowed For.* **E. Summary.**

The economic effects of taxation are manifold. They include micro effects on the distribution of income and the efficiency of resource use as well as macro effects on the level of capacity output, employment, prices, and growth. All these effects interact. Thus, the distributional effects (or incidence) of particular budget measures depend on their effects on capacity output and employment just as the latter depend on concurrent changes in distribution. Nevertheless, each type of effect

---

*Reader's Guide to Chapter 14: The determination of tax and expenditure incidence poses complex issues to be considered in subsequent chapters. In this chapter we deal with the general formulation of the problem, and derive a quantitative picture of the incidence of the U.S. fiscal structure, including tax burdens, expenditure benefits, and net positions. This chapter presents a basic introduction to the incidence problem, important for the general reader who may wish to bypass the more detailed analysis of Chapter 15.

is of interest in itself and must be considered as such in policy formulation. One policy may be superior with regard to distributional results but inferior with regard to efficiency, growth, or employment effects. Tradeoffs must then be made. Moreover, as a matter of exposition, not all aspects can be dealt with at once. Keeping in mind the general fact of interdependence, we begin with the effects of budget policy on the state of distribution. It is these effects which we have in mind when talking about the "incidence" of tax policies.

A. NATURE OF TAX BURDEN

Before considering who bears the tax burden, we must examine what the concept of burden implies. Here a distinction must be drawn between budget operations which involve a resource transfer to the public sector and others which do not.

Tax Burden and Resource Transfer

In the first case, the government imposes taxes to finance the purchase of goods and to pay public employees needed to provide social goods and services. Suppose that the government collects $1 billion and spends it on highway facilities. As a result, the resources available for private use are reduced by a like amount. This is the opportunity cost of the highway services, the gross burden which their provision imposes on the private sector as a whole. Tax incidence refers to the way in which this gross burden is shared among individual households. The burden in turn is accompanied by the benefits of highway services which must be allowed for to derive the net gain or burden (or to determine the net incidence) of the entire transaction. If the program is worthwhile, the benefits should outweigh the costs.

When budget operations do not involve resource transfers to the public, the government simply collects taxes from the private sector and returns transfers to that sector. There is no shift of resources to public use and no opportunity cost in reduced private resource availability. Some may gain while others will lose, but taxes being equal to transfers, there will be no net change in income available for private use. The problem of incidence is now merely one of tracing the redistribution of privately available income among households.

Magnitude of Burden

Implicit in the preceding argument is the simplifying assumption that the tax burden is equal to the revenue collected. On this basis, the opportunity cost of $1 billion of public resource use equals the $1 billion of revenue that is needed to pay for it. By the same token, obtaining $1 billion in taxes and spending it on transfers leaves private income unchanged and involves no resource cost. This view of tax burden oversimplifies matters and must now be reconsidered.

Excess Burden The total burden may exceed the revenue collected because an efficiency loss, or "excess burden," results. To illustrate, suppose that $1 billion revenue is collected from a tax on automobiles. The sum total of tax collections from various consumers equals $1 billion, but the burden imposed on the private sector will be larger, because the tax interferes with consumer choice. Thus, some people may forgo a car purchase because of the tax payable. They pay no tax but their budget choice is less satisfactory than it was before and they therefore suffer a burden which is not reflected in total revenue. Others may buy a cheaper car and pay a tax on the reduced amount. In both cases the consumer's expenditure pattern has been distorted by the tax and each suffers a burden which is greater than that which would have applied if he or she had paid the same amount as a flat charge. Because of this, the overall burden suffered by the private sector tends to exceed the amount of revenue obtained. An additional burden—referred to by economists as excess burden or deadweight loss—results. The nature of this burden will be examined further in Chapter 16.

Input Effects　There is another reason why tax revenue and total burden as measured by the loss of income available for private use may differ. Imposition of the tax may lead to a change in factor supply and hence in total output. We may illustrate this case by supposing that the same revenue as in the previous examples was collected under a progressive income tax. As a result, workers may work more or less because the tax is imposed. Let us suppose that they work less and as a result, their earnings fall. If this decline in earnings is counted as part of the burden, the total burden once more exceeds tax revenue; and the opposite is true if people work harder so that their earnings rise as a result of the tax. Similarly, tax policy may lead to a change in the rate of savings and investment and hence in the rate of output growth. These changes will again be reflected in the level of pre-tax income, once more causing the change in income to differ from the amount of revenue.

Employment Effects　Furthermore, changes in output may result, not because of adjustments in factor inputs in response to changes in after-tax factor rewards but because of resulting changes in the level of aggregate demand and unemployment. Introduction of a tax may reduce the level of employment, or an increase in expenditures may raise it. This once more complicates the problem of observing the effects of taxation on the distribution of income. As is evident from these considerations, the concept of tax burden is more complex than suggested by the simple formulation in which revenue and burden are set equal to each other. However, this assumption remains a useful approximation when dealing with the problem of burden distribution in an operational way. We will accept it for purposes of this chapter.

B.　CONCEPTS OF INCIDENCE

In a discussion of tax incidence, certain concepts and issues must be clarified if confusion is to be avoided. Quite apart from the difficulties of measurement, one ought to be clear on just what it is that one wishes to measure.

Statutory Incidence, Economic Incidence, and Tax Shifting

Taxes, according to Justice Holmes, are the price of civilization, but the question is, who pays? As we saw earlier, taxes are not voluntary purchase payments but mandatory impositions, payable in line with whatever tax statute has been legislated. Although these statutes in the end are a reflection (more or less imperfect) of voters' preferences, once legislated they become mandatory levies, imposing burdens which the individual taxpayer will try to avoid or to pass on to others. To determine who pays, we must thus look beyond the tax statutes and the pattern of statutory incidence, i.e., beyond those on whom the legal liability for payment rests. This involves two considerations. First, it must be recognized that in the end, the entire tax burden must be borne by individuals. Though taxes may be collected from business firms, their ultimate burden must be traced to individual households in their capacity as owners of the firms, as employees, or as consumers of their products. Second, the final burden distribution may differ from that of statutory liabilities, whether the tax is imposed on individuals or on firms. Individuals as well as firms may adjust their sales and purchases, thus affecting the position of others.

Suppose first that Jones is called upon to pay a given amount, say, $100 of tax, independently of what he does. Such a tax, referred to as a lump-sum tax, cannot be escaped. Yet, Jones will adjust himself to this loss by cutting back his purchases oʀ savings, or by increasing his work effort. Although he cannot escape payment of the tax, his adjustment thereto will affect the people with whom he transacts and thus will have further repercussions. Moreover, taxes are rarely imposed in lump-sum form. The tax law typically expresses liabilities as a function of some aspect of economic behavior, such as earning income, making sales, or making a purchase. Since such taxes are imposed on economic transactions and since transactions involve more than one party, the transactors on whom the statutory liability rests may avoid tax payments by cutting back on the taxable activity; or they may attempt to pass on the burden to others by changing the terms under which they are willing to trade. Their ability to do so will depend upon the structure of the markets in which they deal and the way in which prices are determined.

Thus, imposition of an income tax may lead to reduced hours of work, thereby driving up the gross wage rate and burdening the consumer. Or, an automobile excise levied on the sellers may cause them to raise their prices, hoping to pass the burden of tax to the buyers, who in turn will attempt to avoid it by substituting other purchases. A tax on the use of capital may lead a firm to substitute labor, and so forth. In each case, the taxpayer's ability to make such adjustments will depend on the willingness of the other transactor to go along. If the seller raises the price, the buyer will fight back by purchasing less, so that the outcome will depend on the response of the two parties. Nevertheless, the resulting chain of adjustments—the process of "*shifting* the tax burden"—may lead to a final distribution of the burden or *economic* incidence, which differs greatly from the initial distribution of liabilities or *statutory* incidence.

Legislators are quite aware of this. When imposing a manufacturer's tax on automobiles, they do not intend this burden to fall on the manufacturer. If they wished it to do so, they would impose a tax on the manufacturer's profits. Manufacturers merely serve as convenient collection points and are meant to pass the tax forward to the consumer in the form of higher automobile prices. Determining the actual distribution of the tax burden therefore requires an analysis of the economic adjustment process, or the transmission of the burden from its impact point (the place of statutory incidence) to its final resting point (the place of economic incidence). This process is generally referred to as "shifting."

As a matter of ultimate policy concern, it is obviously the distribution of the burden *after* shifting that counts. If this distribution is to be as intended, legislators must choose tax formulas which give the desired result in terms not of statutory incidence but of the economic incidence which ensues after the system has adjusted to the imposition of the tax. This, to say the least, is no simple task, even for the economist who may be called upon to advise what the final incidence of particular taxes will be. As we will see later, especially tough problems arise with regard to the corporation profits tax and the property tax.

Alternative Concepts of Incidence

Although the expenditure side of the budget should be allowed for, concern with incidence has traditionally focused on the tax side of the picture. There are three ways in which the narrower problem of tax incidence may be viewed, namely, as absolute, differential, or budget incidence.

Absolute Tax Incidence   One way is to examine the distributional effects of imposing a particular tax while holding public expenditures constant. Suppose that income taxes are increased without there being a corresponding change in expenditures or an offsetting change in other taxes. In determining the distributional consequences of such a change, one can hardly overlook the macro effects which follow from the resulting decline in aggregate demand. Depending upon the state of the economy, this decline may lead to unemployment, a decline in price level, or a reduced rate of inflation. Each result will have its distributional implications which cannot be separated from those of the tax change itself. At closer consideration, the concept of absolute incidence is not a satisfactory one.

Differential Tax Incidence   To avoid this difficulty, one might examine the distributional changes which result if one tax is substituted for another while total revenue and expenditures are held constant. Thus, the government may replace $1 billion of income tax revenue with a cigarette excise yielding an equivalent amount.[1] This policy change involves no resource transfer to public use and (disregarding the issue of excess burden for the time being) imposes no net burden on the private sector. It merely involves a redistribution among households. Households whose income tax is reduced will gain, while others with high cigarette purchases will lose. Going beyond this, tobacco growers and cigarette workers will lose, while others producing the output purchased by former income taxpayers stand to gain. The resulting total change in the state of distribution is referred to as "differential incidence."

The concept of differential incidence also applies when we compare alterna-

---

[1] As a first approximation, the "equivalent amount" may be defined as the same amount of dollars. But this may be too simple a view. Allowing for changes in relative prices and hence possible changes in the cost of goods bought by government, we find that the equivalent amount is that which permits government to make the same real purchases.

tive ways of raising or lowering revenue. This view of tax incidence is particularly useful because actual tax policy decisions usually involve such issues.

Budget Incidence   Still another way of looking at the problem is to consider the changes in household positions which result if the combined effects of tax and expenditure changes are considered. The income available to particular households for private use will now be affected not only by tax but also by expenditure measures. In the case of transfer programs, private incomes are added to, just as they are reduced by, taxes. In the case of provision for public services, the necessary purchases (whether of the services of civil servants or products) affect the distribution of private income through their effects on earnings. Thus, the expenditure side of the budget has its effects on private incomes as do taxes; and since tax and expenditure effects occur simultaneously, they cannot be separated in this case.

Considering the economy as a whole, we see that the overall effects of an increase in government purchases and taxes by $X now involves the following:

1. Earnings from production for sale to private buyers are reduced by $X.
2. Earnings from production sold or services rendered to government are increased by $X.
3. Disposable income of earners is reduced by $X.
4. Government revenue is increased by $X.
5. Benefits from public services are increased by $X.
6. Benefits from private services are reduced by $X.

When the economy is looked at as a whole, these transactions balance, but as far as individual earners or consumers are concerned, they do not wash out. Each item may have a different distributional pattern, and the overall incidence of the budget transaction should include them all. Moreover, they interact, so that it is difficult to separate tax from expenditure incidence. However, such a separation becomes more feasible if we take the differential incidence approach. In that case, items 2, 4, and 5 are held constant, while different taxes (yielding different patterns with regard to 3 and 1) are examined.

C. MEASURING INCIDENCE

Since incidence deals with how the tax burden is distributed, what are the relevant groupings and how is the burden distribution to be measured? To begin with, it must be clearly understood that the entire tax burden is in the end borne by individuals. Legal persons such as corporations are owned by individuals and taxes levied on such enterprises must be traced to their owners, customers, or employees.

Burden Distribution among Whom?

In studying the distribution of the tax burden, we are concerned therefore with its incidence among individuals or households. This differs from the approach taken by the classical economists (David Ricardo, for instance) who viewed the incidence problem in terms of the impact of tax burdens on the suppliers of capital, labor, and land. For them, incidence theory was primarily an aspect of the theory of factor shares or factor pricing. This approach was also useful from the point of view of

public policy since in their time, industry, labor, and agriculture did in fact reflect
the major social groups. Today the pattern is more mixed, and primary concern—
from the viewpoint of social policy—has moved to the size distribution of income.
A person receiving only a small amount of capital income and unable to work is
poor, whereas a person receiving a large salary is well off. This is also in line with
the global income tax approach, where our concern is with the person's level of
total income, independent of the particular source from which it is derived.

If one wishes to analyze a practical incidence problem—e.g., the distributional changes which result if the corporation tax is replaced by a value-added tax,
or if a sales tax is substituted for a property tax—it is not feasible to determine what
happens to each of the over 50 million households in the economy. To make the
task manageable, households must be grouped by categories. For this purpose, our
primary concern is with the distribution of the burden among households grouped
by *income* classes. At the same time, other groupings, such as that by age or type
of family, are also of interest.

Burden Impact from Sources and Uses Side

Substitution of one tax for another will improve the position of some households
and worsen that of others. Changes in the position of any one household may be
measured in terms of the resulting change in its real income. Real income may
change because disposable income changes or because there is a change in the price
of the products purchased. Taking a somewhat simplified view of the matter, we
note that the disposable real income (DRY) of a household may be defined as

$$\text{DRY} = \frac{E - T_y}{P + T_s} = \frac{DY}{GP}$$

where E = earnings
  T_y = income tax
  P = price (at factor cost) of products bought
  T_s = sales tax addition thereto

DY is disposable or after-tax money income, and GP is the gross (or market) price.
We can now see how DRY is subject to both direct and indirect tax effects.

Primary effects of tax changes which operate on the earnings, or *sources,* side
of the household account will change T_y , while primary effects which operate on
the expenditure or *uses* side of its account will change T_s . Thus an increase in
income tax lowers DRY via an increase in T_y and hence a fall in DY. An increase
in sales tax lowers DRY via an increase in T_s and hence in GP.

In addition, the general adjustment process may result in secondary changes
from the sources side, or in $E,$ and in secondary changes from the uses side, or in
P. Although such secondary effects may be of great importance to particular households, chances are that they will not result in a systematic offset to such changes in
the size distribution of DRY as have resulted in line with the primary effects. As
we will see later for taxes on earnings such as the individual income tax, distributional results tend to be dominated by effects from the sources side, whereas in

other cases, such as selective excise taxes, changes on the uses side are of primary importance.

Although households differ widely in their sources and uses patterns, there are generally applicable relationships between the level of income and the pattern of sources as well as the level of income and the pattern of uses. This factor will prove to be a strategic feature of our incidence analysis. Since the share of capital income rises as we move up the income scale, a tax on capital income tends to be more progressive than a general income tax, while a tax on wage income only tends to be regressive. Similarly, a tax on luxury products, such as champagne, tends to be progressive, whereas a tax on mass-consumption items—say, beer—tends to be regressive. These relationships, as we will presently see, play a key role in dealing with the incidence of various taxes.

Measuring Changes in Distribution

A comprehensive measure of incidence may be obtained by comparing the state of distribution before and after a particular tax change. Such a comparison is illustrated in Figure 14-1. Measuring the cumulative percentage of disposable income on the vertical axis and the cumulative percentage of households (ranked from the lowest to the highest) on the horizontal axis, the curve *OAB* shows the percentage of income received by the lowest 10, 20, 30, etc., percent of households. Thus the lowest 20 percent of households receives 6 percent of income and the lowest 80

FIGURE 14-1   Measure of income equality.

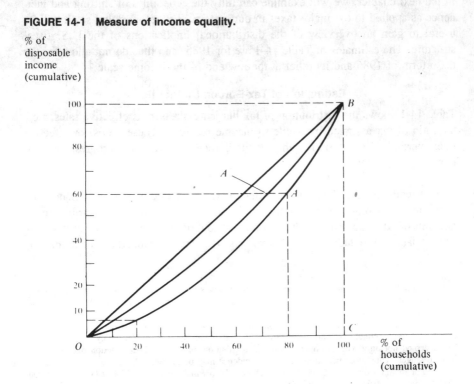

percent receives 60 percent, leaving 40 percent for the highest 20 percent.[2] If distribution were equal, curve OAB would coincide with the straight line OB. Given a state of unequal distribution, the ratio of the two areas $OABC/OBC$ may be taken as the index of equality. It will equal 1 if the distribution of income is totally equal.

Suppose now that the distributional pattern with the existing tax system is as indicated by OAB but that due to a tax change it becomes $OA'B$. This means that distribution has become more equal—since $OA'BC/OBC > OABC/OBC$—and in this sense the effect of the tax change has been progressive.[3] Note, however, that this change may have come about in two ways. Thus, the distribution of the initial tax burden might have changed, e.g., the rates of the income tax may have been made more progressive while holding total revenue constant. Alternatively, yield may have been increased without changing the progressivity of the rate structure, e.g., by raising all liabilities by the same percentage.

The total effect on distribution, therefore, depends not only on the extent of the progressive nature of particular taxes (i.e., how fast the effective rate or ratio of liability to income rises as we move up the income scale), but also on the overall level of taxation and the underlying distribution of income. A high but moderately progressive level of taxation may have a greater impact upon the distribution of income than does a low-level but sharply progressive system.

D. INCIDENCE OF THE U.S. FISCAL STRUCTURE

In the next chapter, we will examine carefully the economics of shifting and incidence as applied to the major taxes in our system. But before doing so, it will be useful to gain an overview of the distributional implications of the U.S. fiscal structure. The estimates of Table 14-1 are for 1985, and thus do not allow for the tax reform of 1986 and its relief at the low end of the income scale.[4]

Estimation of Tax-Burden Distribution

Table 14-1 shows the distribution of tax burden expressed as effective rates, i.e., the ratio of tax assigned by decile to income received. These ratios, or effective rates, permit us to determine whether the burden distribution is progressive, proportional, or regressive.

Procedure The derivation of effective rates is based on (1) an estimated distribution of income among family units and (2) an estimated distribution of amounts of tax. The former is based on a distribution of money income as given by census data and includes transfer payments. It is then expanded by including cer-

---

[2] To obtain the complete picture and allow for changes from the sources side as well, disposable income would have to be expressed in real terms, i.e., be deflated by the relevant index of consumer prices. The figures here refer to money income.

[3] $OA'B$ need not lie inside OAB throughout, but the two curves may intersect. If so, distribution may become more equal over part of the range and less so over another. Social policy, of course, must be concerned not only with the overall state of distribution but also with distribution over particular income ranges. Thus more partial measures of incidence may be devised.

[4] For detailed discussion, see J. A. Pechman, *Who Paid the Taxes, 1968–1985*, Washington, D.C.: Brookings, 1985. Also see p. 248 below.

TABLE 14-1
Tax Burden as Percentage of Family Income, 1985*
(Effective Rates of Tax)

Decile of Family Unit†	ALL LEVELS							BY LEVELS	
	Income Tax (1)	Corporation Tax (2)	Property Tax (3)	Sales and Excise Taxes (4)	Payroll Taxes (5)	Personal Property and Motor Vehicle Taxes (6)	Total (7)	Federal Total (8)	State and Local Total (9)
CASE A‡									
1	3.7	1.6	2.2	7.0	2.2	0.1	17.1	10.8	6.2
2	3.5	1.3	1.9	5.8	3.3	0.1	15.9	10.8	5.1
3	5.2	1.0	1.5	4.9	5.1	0.1	18.1	12.6	5.5
4	7.4	0.9	1.5	4.6	6.7	0.2	21.2	15.1	6.1
5	9.1	0.8	1.4	4.2	7.6	0.2	23.3	16.8	6.5
6	9.8	0.7	1.2	4.0	7.7	0.2	23.7	17.0	6.7
7	10.8	0.8	1.2	3.9	7.6	0.2	24.6	17.6	6.9
8	11.9	0.9	1.3	3.7	7.3	0.2	25.4	18.8	7.1
9	13.3	1.0	1.3	3.3	7.1	0.2	26.3	17.9	7.4
10	13.5	3.6	3.1	1.9	4.1	0.1	28.5	17.9	8.5
All	10.9	1.8	2.0	3.4	6.2	0.1	24.5	17.2	7.3
CASE B§									
1	4.0	3.6	3.9	7.2	5.1	0.1	24.0	14.1	9.9
2	3.4	2.8	3.0	5.7	5.0	0.1	20.1	12.9	7.2
3	5.1	2.4	2.5	4.8	5.8	0.2	20.7	13.9	6.8
4	7.1	2.2	2.3	4.5	6.9	0.2	23.2	15.8	7.3
5	8.7	1.9	2.1	4.2	7.4	0.2	24.4	16.9	7.5
6	9.5	1.9	2.1	4.0	7.2	0.2	25.0	17.3	7.6
7	10.4	1.8	2.1	3.8	7.1	0.2	25.5	17.6	7.8
8	11.5	1.8	2.1	3.7	6.9	0.2	26.2	18.3	7.9
9	13.0	1.7	2.0	3.2	6.6	0.2	26.7	18.7	8.0
10	14.5	2.2	2.2	1.9	4.0	0.1	25.0	17.5	7.5
All	10.9	2.1	2.1	2.3	3.4	0.2	24.9	17.2	7.7

*See J. A. Pechman, *Who Paid the Taxes, 1966–1985,* Washington, D.C.: Brookings, 1985. See also J. A. Pechman, "Pechman's Tax Initiative Study: A Response," *American Economic Review,* vol. 76, December 1986; and J. A. Pechman, *Who Paid the Taxes, 1966–1985,* Revised Tables, Washington, D.C.: Brookings, 1986. Data given in Table 14-1 are based on the latter.

†Family income is defined to include transfer payments from government.

‡Corresponds to variant 1c in Pechman study. Income tax is assumed to be borne by payer; corporation revenue tax by capital income; sales and excise tax by consumers; property tax on land by landowner; property tax on improvements by capital income; payroll tax by employees.

§Corresponds to variant 3b in Pechman study. Income and sales tax as in Case A; corporation income tax one-half on capital income, one-half on consumers; property tax on land to landowners; property tax on improvements, one-half to shelter and one-half to property income; payroll tax, one-half on employers and one-half on employees.

tain other income components. The distribution of tax burdens in turn is based on reasonable assumptions regarding the incidence of various taxes. Thus, we assume that the income tax is borne by the earner and that sales and excise taxes are shifted to the consumer. For the corporation tax, two sets of assumptions are used, with case A assigning the tax to capital income and case B dividing it between capital income and consumers. The distribution of the property tax is also shown for alternative assumptions, case A assigning the tax to capital income and case B dividing it between capital income and consumer expenditures on housing. The payroll tax, finally, is divided between wage income and consumption in case A while assigned entirely to wage income in case B. As will be seen in the next chapter, these alternative assumptions cover a range of theoretical reasoning, with those underlying case A making for a more progressive burden distribution than those used for B.

Results   The pattern of effective rates is given in Table 14-1. Column 1 shows the income tax to be progressive (the effective rate rises) throughout the income scale. This gives the income tax a unique position in the tax structure as the key engine of progression. Next comes the picture for the corporation tax as shown in column 2. Beginning with case A, incidence is regressive over the lower end of the scale, reflecting the fact that a substantial share of low-bracket income (especially by retirees) is received in the form of capital income. This contrasts with the upper end of the scale where the tax becomes progressive. Note also that the burden of the tax at the lower end is larger in case B, reflecting its now partial absorption by consumption. The property tax, as shown in column 3 is once more regressive at the bottom and progressive at the top end of the scale but largely proportional over a wide middle range. As before, the case B assumptions render the tax less progressive. Sales and excise taxes, shown in column 4, are regressive throughout, reflecting the fact that consumer expenditures as a percent of income fall when moving up the income scale. Payroll taxes, similarly, are regressive throughout, as wages as a percent of income decline when moving up the income scale. Note also that the burden at the lower end is higher for case B, where the entire incidence is taken to fall on wage income.

The overall pattern for the system as a whole is shown in column 7. For case A the effective rate rises slowly throughout the income scale, showing that the system is slightly progressive. The outcome for case B in turn records a bouncing but essentially flat pattern. The tax system, therefore, leaves the distribution of income essentially unchanged. Columns 8 and 9, finally, show the overall pattern broken down by federal and state and local taxes. Note how the progressive contribution stems from the federal tax system, with that for state and local taxes following an essentially proportional pattern. As noted before, this reflects the decisive contribution of the federal income tax, as against the weight of sales and excise taxes at the state-local level. These patterns for case A are also plotted in Figure 14-2.

Conclusion   The general conclusion which emerges is that the distribution of the tax burden is progressive over the lower-middle range of the income scale, but mostly proportional over the middle and higher ranges. The distribution of transfers is highly pro-low income. The net pattern, accordingly, begins with a high positive rate at the bottom of the scale and then declines and turns negative before the mid-decile is reached. While these results may be accepted as a clear indication of the general outcome, certain major shortcomings should nevertheless be kept in mind:

  1.   As we have seen by comparing cases A and B in Table 14-1, the result is affected significantly by the underlying incidence assumption, a topic to be examined more closely in the next chapter.
  2.   Our incidence assumptions have related to what may be called the initial, or

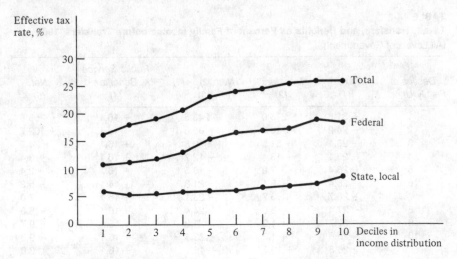

FIGURE 14-2   Effective rates of tax.

impact, incidence, without accounting for general equilibrium effects—also a matter to be explored in the next chapter.

3. No allowance has been made for deadweight losses, with the total burden being assumed to be equal to the amount of revenue collected, an aspect to be reconsidered in Chapter 16.

Expenditure Benefits Allowed For

Whereas the analysis of incidence has been related mostly to the taxation side of the fiscal process, what really matters is the net effect on distribution which results as both sides of the budget are allowed for. Such a perspective is offered in Table 14-2 and in Figure 14-3. For this purpose, households are now arranged by deciles of income excluding transfers. We then impute to each decile of income recipients losses due to taxation and gains due to transfer receipts.[5]

Taxes as percent of income now yield a pattern which is regressive at the very bottom, somewhat progressive over the middle range, and flattening out at the top. Effective rates are generally higher than in column 7 of Table 14-1, because transfer payments are now excluded from the income base. We also find the system to be more regressive at the lower end, since this is where the transfer income is received. Column 2 shows transfers as percent of income, yielding a highly regressive (meaning now pro-poor) distribution. Combining the two as shown in column 3, we arrive at the net pattern. Moving from the bottom up, we note that the effective rate again begins at a high level and declines rapidly thereafter, becoming negative before the middle of the income scale is reached. The combined tax-transfer impact on income is thus substantially redistributive, a result which comes about largely because of the pro-low income pattern of transfer payments. The resulting pattern is also shown in Figure 14-3.

---

[5] The picture given here offers a rough approximation only inasmuch as it assumes that the distribution of income before tax and transfers would be the same in the absence of the budget as it proves to be in its presence.

TABLE 14-2
Taxes, Transfers, and Benefits as Percent of Family Income before Transfers, 1985
(All Levels of Government)

Deciles of Family Units	Taxes* (1)	Transfers* (2)	Net* (2) − (1) (3)	Public Service Benefits† (4)	Net (5)
1	− 31.5	+ 275.0	+ 243.5	+ 16.1	+ 259.6
2	− 24.2	+ 110.8	+ 86.6	+ 16.1	+ 102.7
3	− 25.1	+ 31.9	+ 6.8	+ 16.1	+ 24.9
4	− 25.1	+ 13.1	− 12.7	+ 16.1	+ 3.4
5	− 26.4	+ 7.9	− 18.5	+ 16.1	− 2.4
6	− 26.4	+ 5.1	− 21.3	+ 16.1	− 5.2
7	− 26.7	+ 3.7	− 23.1	+ 16.1	− 7.0
8	− 27.4	+ 3.0	− 24.4	+ 16.1	− 8.3
9	− 27.7	+ 1.9	− 25.8	+ 16.1	− 9.7
10	− 26.6	+ 1.2	− 25.4	+ 16.1	− 9.3
Total	− 26.8	+ 10.7	− 16.1	+ 16.1	0.0

*J. A. Pechman, *Who Pays the Taxes, 1966–1985,* Washington, D.C.: Brookings, p. 53. Ratios in column 1 repeat assumptions of case A, Table 14-1. However, ratios differ since they are now based on income net of transfers.

†To simplify, we set expenditures to equal receipts, thereby overlooking a slight deficit in the combined federal-state-local budgets. With taxes equal to 27.5 percent of family income and transfers equal to 10 percent, this leaves a 17.5 percent ratio for public services.

FIGURE 14-3   Taxes, transfers, and service benefits as percent of income before transfer.

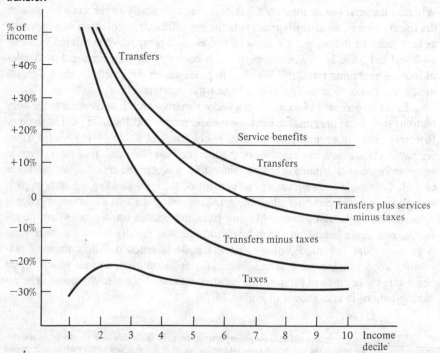

Since expenditures from public services are excluded from column 3, the group as a whole is left with a net loss. An attempt is made in columns 4 and 5 to close the picture by allowing for the benefits of public services as well. We assume for this purpose that the budget was balanced, so that such benefits as percent of income equal 26.8 minus 10.7, or 16.1 percent. In column 4, we assume such benefits to be distributed in proportion to income (before taxes and transfers), with column 5 giving the net result, now allowing for all budget components.[6] There is still a high positive return at the bottom of the scale, with the break-even point reached at about the middle of the income scale, and a net pattern which is less detrimental over the upper part of the range. An alternative allocation of service benefits on, say, a per capita basis would shift the net pattern so as to render the distribution still more favorable toward the lower end of the scale.

E. SUMMARY

Various concepts of incidence were considered and the following distinctions were drawn:

1. Statutory incidence differs from economic incidence and it is the latter that matters.

2. The opportunity cost of resource transfer to public use, associated with an increase in public services, imposes a burden on consumers as a group because resources are withdrawn from private use. This transfer is to be distinguished from redistribution among consumers which arises in the case of tax-financed transfers or tax substitutions.

3. Owing to efficiency costs, employment, and output effects, the tax burden may exceed the revenue gain.

4. Budget incidence allows for distributional effects of both tax and expenditure policies.

5. To formulate the problem of tax incidence, the differential approach is most useful.

The problem of incidence deals with the effects of fiscal operations on the distribution of real income among households:

6. Incidence thus involves taxation effects on both the sources and uses side of the household account.

7. Distributional changes which result are viewed primarily in terms of distribution among income brackets, but other groupings may also be considered.

8. An overall measure of incidence may be derived by observing the resulting change in the coefficient of inequality.

9. Taxes may be grouped as direct or indirect, and as in rem or personal. The latter distinction is most important.

A survey of the estimated distribution of tax burdens and expenditure benefits in the U.S. fiscal structure shows the following:

---

[6] Note that this assumption relates to the distribution of *benefits* from public services and not to the distribution of private *earnings* realized in their production. Such earnings should be viewed as a substitute for private earnings forgone. While the two earnings patterns may differ, this is a different issue.

10.   The income tax is the major progressive element in the tax structure, just as the payroll tax is the major regressive element. Sales taxes tend to be regressive. The roles of the corporation income tax and of the property tax greatly depend on the shifting assumption which is applied.

11.   The distribution of the federal tax burden is progressive and that of state and local taxes tends to be proportional.

12.   Burden distribution for the tax system as a whole is progressive over the lower part of the income range and then approaches a proportional pattern.

13.   The distribution of benefits is strongly pro-poor, owing to the role of transfer payments, especially at the federal level.

14.   The resulting distribution of net benefits is distinctly pro-poor, but more or less proportional over the remainder of the income range.

FURTHER READINGS

For empirical studies of tax burden distribution, see:

Brownlee, K., and W. Johnson, *The Distribution of the Tax Burden,* Washington, D.C.: American Enterprise Institute, 1979.

OECD, *The Tax/Benefit Position of Selected Income Groups in OECD Member Countries,* Paris: Organization for Economic Cooperation and Development, 1978.

Pechman, J. A., *Who Paid the Taxes, 1966–1985,* Washington, D.C.: Brookings, 1985.

Reynolds, M., and E. Smolensky: *Public Expenditures, Taxes, and the Distribution of Income,* New York: Academic, 1977.

See also Further Readings for Chapter 15.

Chapter 15

Principles of Tax Incidence*

A. Partial Equilibrium View of Product Taxes: *Responses to Unit and Ad Valorem Tax; Role of Demand and Supply Elasticities; Division of Burden; Coverage and Time Period.* **B. Partial Equilibrium View of Factor Taxes:** *Adjustments in Price and Quantity; Demand and Supply Elasticities; Burden Distribution.* **C. Incidence in General Equilibrium:** *Product Taxes; Factor Taxes; Partial Taxes on Factor Income and Capitalization; Estimation Models.* **D. Imperfect Markets:** *Product Taxes; Tax on Wage Income; Payroll Tax; Profits Tax.* **E. Macro Aspects:** *Employment Effects; Inflation Effects; Growth Effects.* **F. Summary.**

The final incidence, or burden distribution, of a tax will depend on how it is imposed initially, what rate structure is used, how the base is defined, and how general is its coverage. But this is only the beginning. In the end, economic incidence will depend on how the economy responds. This response depends on conditions of demand and supply, the structure of markets, and the time period allowed for ad-

Reader's Guide to Chapter 15: This chapter lays out the principles of tax incidence. Sections A and B give a partial equilibrium view of product and factor taxes, and section C considers incidence in a general equilibrium setting. Section D allows for imperfect markets and E considers macro effects. A further discussion of product tax incidence, not obligatory for the less technical reader, follows in the appendix.

justments to occur. Adjustments to a tax will cause factor and product prices to change, and these changes will affect households from both the sources and uses sides of their accounts, thus determining the burden distribution among them. The final outcome depends on the interaction of these changes in a general equilibrium system. The task of incidence theory, as of any economic theory, is to cut through these complex forces and to identify the strategic elements in each case. We begin with a partial equilibrium view and consider the responses of sellers and buyers in the particular market in which the tax is imposed. Thereafter we turn to a more complex general equilibrium setting where repercussions in other product and factor markets are taken into account.

Competitive markets are postulated in both cases. Market imperfections and macro aspects are allowed for in the concluding sections and in the appendix to this chapter.

A. PARTIAL EQUILIBRIUM VIEW OF PRODUCT TAXES

A product tax may be imposed per unit of product, in which case it is referred to as a "unit tax." State taxes on gasoline, cigarettes, and liquor and the federal tax of $9 per barrel of beer illustrate this type. Alternatively, the product tax may be imposed as a percentage of price, in which case it is referred to as an "ad valorem tax." The federal tax on firearms, imposed at 10 percent of manufacturer's price, illustrates this type. General product or "sales taxes" are necessarily of the ad valorem form, with a uniform rate applied to a wide range of products.

Responses to Unit and Ad Valorem Tax

Figure 15-1 shows introduction of a tax into a competitive product market. SS is the supply schedule prior to tax and DD is the demand schedule. Price equals OB and output equals OC.

FIGURE 15-1   Adjustment to unit and ad valorem product taxes.

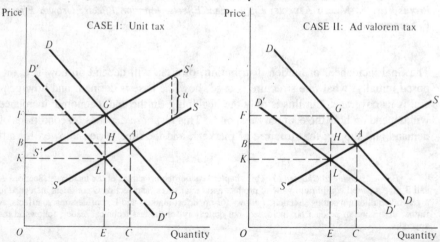

Unit Tax With respect to case I, a tax of u per unit is imposed. The tax enters as a wedge between the market price which sellers get and the net price which they keep. Since sellers are interested in the net price, they must now charge a higher market price to cover their cost. The supply schedule which confronts buyers therefore rises from SS to $S'S'$, the vertical distance between the two schedules being equal to u. Buyers purchase less and quantity falls to OE, given by the intersection of DD with $S'S'$. Market price rises to OF and the net price to sellers falls to OK. Since in this example the product is produced under conditions of increasing cost, the net price falls as quantity declines. Because of this, the market price rises by less than the tax. Thus, at the new quantity OE, the market price has risen by BF whereas the tax per unit of output equals KF.

Note that the introduction of the tax in case I of Figure 15-1 was depicted as a parallel upward shift in the *supply* schedule from SS to $S'S'$, which is in line with the usual practice of imposing the tax on the seller, who adds tax to net price and keeps only part of the gross price which he collects. The same result would be obtained, however, if the tax was imposed on the buyer, with only part of his payment going to the seller and the rest to the Treasury. In this case, the tax may be depicted by a downward shift in the net *demand* schedule to the left. With the supply schedule now unchanged, the new equilibrium is set by the intersection of SS and $D'D'$ at L. The new output again equals OE.

Ad Valorem Tax Imposition of an ad valorem tax is shown in case II of Figure 15-1. The tax again forms a wedge between the gross or market price paid by the buyer and the net price received by the seller. Since the ad valorem tax is a function of price, it *must* now be shown as a change in the demand schedule. Moreover, since the tax is determined as a percentage of price, the adjustment is reflected in a swivel rather than a shift of the schedule. The demand schedule thus swivels from DD to $D'D'$, with the amount of tax per unit falling as the quantity sold rises. The rate of ad valorem tax, commonly expressed as the ratio of tax to net price kept by the seller, equals GL/EL. The new equilibrium is at the intersection of SS and $D'D'$, the price paid by the buyer equals GE, and the net price received by the seller is LE. The amount of tax per unit is GL and revenue equals $KFGL$.

Note that the ad valorem rate in case II is chosen so as to give the same yield as a unit tax of GL. For a given unit tax u, there is always an ad valorem rate t such that both give the same revenue. The relationship between the two rates, as may be seen from the diagram, depends on the supply and demand schedules.

Role of Demand and Supply Elasticities

As a tax is imposed on a particular item, its price will rise and the quantity bought or sold will decline. The magnitude of these changes will depend on the elasticities of supply and demand. Understanding of this rule is the first step in incidence analysis. The importance of demand and supply elasticities is shown in Figure 15-2.

Beginning with case I, SS and DD are the supply and demand schedules prior to tax, with price equal to OP and quantity equal to OQ. Now a unit tax equal to u is imposed, raising the supply schedule to $S'S'$. The new equilibrium is at B, price rises to OP_1, and quantity falls to OQ_2. Now suppose that supply is less elas-

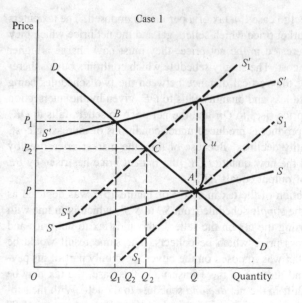

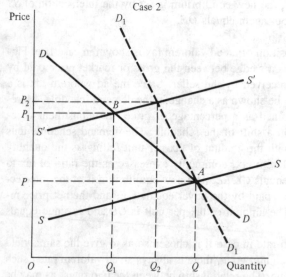

FIGURE 15-2 Role of supply and demand elasticities.

tic, as shown by S_1S_1, and post-tax supply schedule $S'_1S'_1$. The new equilibrium is at C, price rises less sharply to OP_2 and output falls by less to OQ_2. The less elastic is supply, the less will be the resulting rise in price and the less will be the fall in quantity.

Turning now to the role of demand as is given in case II, the pre-tax position A is given as before, with price at OP and quantity at OQ. As the tax is imposed, the supply schedule shifts to $S'S'$ with price increase to OP_1, with the new equilibrium at B and output reduced to OQ_1. Had the demand schedule been less

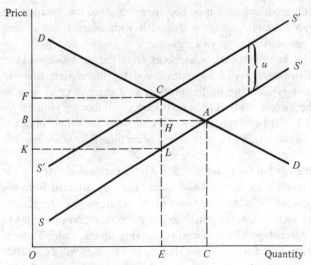

FIGURE 15-3   Burden shares.

elastic as shown by D_1D_1, the new equilibrium would have been at C, the price would have risen more sharply to OP_2 and output would have fallen to OQ_2 only. The less elastic is demand, the greater will be the rise in price and the less will be the fall in quantity.

In short, the rise in price will be the greater the more elastic is supply and the less elastic is demand. The fall in quantity will be the smaller, the less elastic are both schedules.

Division of Burden

Turning to Figure 15-3, the tax burden is given by $KFGL$. We may now think of this burden as divided between buyers and sellers, such that the buyer pays $BFGH$ and the seller contributes $KBHL$. The former reflects the additional amount which the buyers must pay for quantity OE, compared with what they would have paid at the old price. The latter, similarly, reflects the smaller amount which the sellers receive in net income for the sale of OE, compared with what they would have received before. As we will see later, this is not a wholly satisfactory way of looking at tax burden and its division, since it disregards the problems of excess burden.[1] But it nevertheless suggests an interesting rule—namely, that the burden of the tax is divided between buyer and seller as the ratio of elasticity of supply to elasticity of demand in the relevant range of the demand and supply schedules.[2]

---

[1] See p. 279.

[2] By rotating DD and SS around A in Figure 15-3, we may see that the buyer's share in the burden increases as demand becomes less and supply becomes more elastic, i.e., the demand schedule steepens and the supply schedule flattens.

It may be shown that $B_b/B_s = E_s/E_d$, where B_b and B_s are the buyer's and seller's shares of the burden, respectively, E_s is the elasticity of supply, and E_d is the elasticity of demand. Thus, E_d over the relevant range equals $(EC/OC)(OB/FB)$, while E_s equals $(EC/OC)(OB/KB)$. We thus obtain E_s/E_d equal to BF/BK, where BF is the buyer's share and BK the seller's share.

Therefore, if you bought a product which now becomes subject to tax, you will be in a better position to avoid the tax and leave the seller with a larger part if your demand is elastic while the seller's supply is inelastic.

The burden borne by buyers affects households from the uses side of their accounts. The burden distribution will be progressive if the income elasticity of demand exceeds 1, i.e., if expenditure on the product as a percentage of income rises when moving up the income scale. Taxes on luxuries will thus be progressive while those on necessities will be regressive. A general sales tax on all products will be regressive since consumption as a percentage of income falls when moving up the income scale.

To the extent that the burden falls on the seller, factor earnings derived in the production of the taxed product are reduced and households are affected from the sources side of their accounts. Whether the tax will be progressive or regressive now depends on whether factor earnings generated in the production of the taxed product rise or fall as a percentage of income when moving up the scale. Thus, if the product requires highly skilled workers, the decline in earnings will be distributed progressively, whereas the opposite holds if unskilled labor is involved.

The final effect of a product tax thus involves both aspects. Both the uses and sources sides thus enter in determining whether the tax is regressive, proportional, or progressive, but the initial impact on the uses side is likely to be the key factor. This is the case since there is no systematic relation between the distribution in consumption of any particular product and the distribution of the factor earnings which it generates. Pending specific evidence to the contrary, it may thus be concluded that the burden distribution is dominated from the uses side, so that the burden of a tax on luxuries is distributed progressively while that of a tax on necessities is distributed regressively. To a lesser degree, the latter also holds for a general tax on consumption, because the share of income consumed (rather than saved) falls when moving up the income scale.

Coverage and Time Period

We have seen that a product tax tends to fall on the consumer if demand is inelastic while supply is elastic, and on the producer when the opposite holds. What determines which set of conditions applies?

Consumer economics tells us that the price elasticity of demand for a particular product depends on consumer preferences, i.e., their willingness to give up the consumption of a particular product for that of another. If a particular product is essential and if only a small part of the budget is spent thereon, price elasticity will be low. A tax on salt is likely to be borne by the consumer. Moreover, the price elasticity for a group of products (such as cars in general) will tend to be lower than that for a particular item in that group (such as blue Pintos with air conditioning). The reason, of course, is that substitution is easier in the latter case. Selective taxes thus leave the consumer in a better position to avoid payment than do broad-based taxes.

A tax on Fords can be avoided by purchase of a Chevrolet; a tax on cars in general can be avoided, if less conveniently, by the use of buses or airplanes; but a general sales tax can be avoided only by consuming less and saving. Another important feature is that elasticity increases with the length of the response period.

Budget adjustments take time, since consumption habits do not change readily. The price elasticity of demand, therefore, will be higher and the consumer will be in a better position to avoid the tax in the long run than in the short run.

Parallel considerations apply to the elasticity of supply. Once more, supply can be changed more readily if only a minor change in product is involved. The production line can be retooled to produce Mustangs rather than Pintos, while it would be very difficult to shift to airplanes. Thus suppliers as well as buyers will find their ability to avoid tax to be greater if coverage is limited. The time factor similarly reappears on the supply side. Indeed, it is even more important here than for demand. Supply cannot readily be changed in the short run unless inventories are available, since retooling may be needed and new machinery may have to be acquired. But substantial changes can be made over time.

Since both demand and supply become more elastic as the tax base is narrowed and more adjustment time is allowed, we cannot generalize who (sellers or buyers) will gain in the process.

B. PARTIAL EQUILIBRIUM VIEW OF FACTOR TAXES

Taxes imposed in the factor market typically apply to the sale of factor services, i.e., to the income which the factor service yields. They take the form of a percentage charge against such income and thus belong to the ad valorem tax family. As distinct from the case of product taxes, the tax rate is defined typically as a percentage charge against the gross (before-tax) income of the factor. Once more the same result may be obtained by an equivalent rate tax imposed on the buyer, i.e., in the form of a factor purchase tax, such as the employer contribution to the payroll tax.

Adjustments in Price and Quantity

The analysis is quite similar to that for product taxes. As seen by factor suppliers, the factor tax appears as a downward swivel of the demand schedule for their services, and outcome again depends on the elasticities of demand and supply.

Tax on Wage Income   Figure 15-4 shows a tax on wage income in a competitive labor market. Quantity (hours worked) and price (wage rate) equal OC and OB, respectively, with equilibrium at E. As a tax at rate EF/EC is imposed on the gross (before-tax) wage, the worker's net wage rate falls, thus swiveling the net demand schedule from DD to $D'D'$. Since it is the net schedule that matters to the worker, the new equilibrium is at G, the intersection of $D'D'$ with the supply schedule SS. Hours worked fall from OC to OH, the gross wage rate rises from OB to OI, and the decline in the net wage or BK falls short of the tax per workhour, or IK.

Tax on Capital Income   Figure 15-4 may also be interpreted as applying to other factor earnings, such as a tax on capital income. For this purpose, we need merely substitute the rate of return to capital for the wage rate and capital employed for hours worked. The rest of the argument is the same.

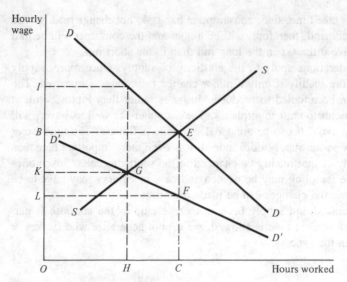

FIGURE 15-4   Adjustment to factor tax.

Tax on Rent of Land   Turning to a tax on income from land, we find the supply to be fixed. With supply totally inelastic, income derived from land depends on demand only and is thus in the nature of economic rent. The entire burden falls on land, with the gross return remaining at *OBEC* and the net return falling to *OLFC*, that is by the amount of tax, *LBEF*.

Demand and Supply Elasticities

As for the case of product taxes, the outcome again depends on the elasticities of supply and demand. Consider the tax on wage income. As noted previously for a product tax, we again find that the rise in price (the gross wage) will be greater the more elastic is supply and the less elastic is demand; and that the fall in quantity (manhours worked) will be the smaller the less elastic are both schedules.

Supply and demand elasticities will again be larger if the tax is selective rather than general. The personal income tax is a general tax, aimed at income from all employments of factors.[3] A worker cannot escape tax by moving from one employment to another, nor can investors by changing their investment. The burden, therefore, is likely to stay put with the payor of the tax. But the situation differs with the corporation tax, which applies to capital earnings in the corporate sector only. As we will see presently, investors may avoid the tax by moving into a tax-free sector.

As in the case of the factor tax, adjustments cannot be made at once but take time. This is especially important with regard to the demand for capital. After a firm has acquired a plant or has put equipment in place, nothing can be done if

---

[3] As we will see later, the actual income tax is not as general as it should be. See p. 335.

income derived therefrom is taxed. Demand is wholly inelastic. The income from a sunk investment is in the nature of a "quasi-rent" and the firm must bear the tax. But as time passes, adjustments may be made. Outworn capital may not be replaced and previously planned expansions may be canceled. The supply of investment funds likewise is more flexible over the longer run as savings habits are sticky within a short period.

Burden Distribution

The primary impact of a tax on factor earnings is from the sources side of the household account. A flat-rate tax will thus impose a progressive burden distribution if earnings from the taxed factor rise as a percentage of income when moving up the income scale; and it will be regressive if the opposite is the case. This tends to render a tax on wage income regressive, just as it tends to render a tax on capital income progressive. Such is the case because the wage share in income falls and the capital share rises when moving up the income scale. There is, however, an exception to this rule at the lower end of the scale, where capital earnings of the elderly and pensioners comprise a relatively large share of income.

Turning to the uses side, we see that a tax on factor earnings raises the prices of products which draw heavily on the taxed factor. This impact from the uses side will be progressive or regressive depending on whether these products are of the luxury or necessity variety. Such effects from the uses side may cushion or run counter to the burden impact from the sources side. A tax on capital earnings, for instance, will be progressive from the sources side; but some capital-intensive products such as housing take up a larger share of low-income budgets, which may render the tax regressive from the uses side. Such offsets may occur, but barring special evidence to the contrary, it is reasonable once more to expect that there will be no systematic relationship between the distribution of earnings from a particular factor and the distribution of expenditures on the products into which the factor enters. This being the case, we may expect the impact from the sources side to be controlling.

C. INCIDENCE IN GENERAL EQUILIBRIUM

The preceding discussion makes a good start on incidence analysis, but it does not tell the entire story, because the analysis was limited to what happens in the particular market of the taxed item and is therefore partial in nature. But the economy is an interdependent system in which all prices are related to each other. Changes in the price and quantity of one product or factor affect those of others. Households not directly involved in the taxed market may lose or gain, and those which are directly involved may become subject to further indirect effects.

Product Taxes

Returning to the case of perfectly competitive markets, we saw how imposition of a product tax leads to a rise in the price of the taxed product and to a decline in its quantity. Thus consumers of the taxed product are burdened from the uses side and suppliers from the sources side. Turning now to repercussions in other markets, we see that two further chains of adjustment result:

1. As consumers buy less of the taxed product, the demand for other products is increased. If production is subject to increasing cost, this will raise their price, while lowering that of the taxed product. Thus, the burden from the uses side will be spread to consumers of other products.

2. As the output mix changes, so does the derived demand for various factors of production. Suppose that the taxed product is highly capital-intensive while products which are substituted for it are labor-intensive. Such substitution leads to an increase in the return to labor and a decrease in the return to capital. As a result, further effects from the earnings side come about.

Indeed, as the impact of the tax works its way through the general adjustment process, a chain of effects on both the uses and sources sides of household accounts will result, and there is no a priori way of predicting the end result. Nor do we, at the present state of the art, have econometric models which are sufficiently precise to predict the outcome. Must we then conclude that nothing can be said about incidence? Hopefully not. Reasoning in the partial equilibrium setting, we concluded with a strong presumption that the uses effect of product taxes is controlling, so that substitution of a tax on luxuries for a tax on necessities will render the tax structure more progressive, and vice versa. We argued that unless there is specific evidence to the contrary, the burden pattern on the uses side will not be canceled out by indirect effects on the sources side and vice versa. Allowing for the general equilibrium setting, we must now assume further that secondary adjustments in other product and factor markets being broadly diffused, will follow a more or less neutral pattern.

Factor Taxes

Similar considerations apply to factor taxes. The initial effect in the partial equilibrium setting was to reduce the net return to the taxed factor, thus burdening its suppliers from the sources side; and to raise the price of products into which the factor enters, thus burdening the consumers of these products from the uses side. Allowing now for repercussions in other factor and product markets, we see that these further adjustments occur:

1. As the supply of the taxed factor falls off, the relative scarcity of other factors declines. As a result, their rates of return will fall. Thus, the impact on the earnings side, initially centered on the taxed factor, comes to be shared to some extent by other factors. An especially important aspect of this mechanism arises with the effects of capital taxes on capital accumulation, an aspect of tax incidence which we will consider further later on.[4]

2. As the prices of products which draw heavily upon the taxed factor rise, their consumers will be burdened. As they tend to substitute other products, the prices of such products will rise, thus spreading the burden impact from the uses side among a broader group of consumers.

[4] See p. 270.

Once more, these adjustments continue until they have worked themselves through the system and a new equilibrium is reached. As in the case of the product tax, there is no a priori way of predicting the precise outcome, but once more some hypotheses can be advanced. Reasoning in the partial equilibrium setting, we concluded that substituting a tax on capital for a tax on labor income, or steepening the schedule of income tax rates, will render the burden distribution more progressive. The initial impact from the earnings side was not likely to be offset by changes from the uses side. Expanding this hypothesis to the general equilibrium setting, it may be assumed further that subsequent adjustments in other factor or product markets will not reverse this initial pattern.

Partial Taxes on Factor Income and Capitalization

The effects of a selective tax on factor income differ, depending on whether the taxed factor is mobile or not.

Immobile Factors Consider first the case of an immobile factor, such as land. Let the rental income from land be taxed in location A but not in B. The tax in A will then be "capitalized" and come to be reflected in a reduced value of the taxed asset.

To see why, note that the value of a capital asset equals the capitalized (present) value of its income stream. Thus, if an asset yields a permanent income stream of $20 per year, and if the interest rate (as represented by, say, a U.S. bond) is 10 percent, an investor will pay $200 for that asset. This is the price at which he will obtain the same return as he would if he purchased a bond. We thus have $PV = R/i$, where PV is the present value, R is the annual income, and i is the market rate of interest. Suppose that there are two assets A and B, both of which provide an annual income of R, so that $PV_A = PV_B = R/i$. Now a tax at rate t is imposed, but on the income from A only. We then have $PV'_A = [(1 - t)R]/i$ and $PV_A = R/i$, so that $PV'_A = (1 - t)PV'_B$. The tax on A has been capitalized and has reduced its value. This loss of value is suffered by the person who owns the asset when the tax is imposed. If he or she wishes to sell the asset later on, the buyer will pay only the reduced price. The buyer will not pay more, since he or she must obtain the same yield as from investment in a tax-free asset. The tax thus comes to be stuck with the initial owner. If the tax should be repealed later on, the value of the asset will rise and a gain will accrue to whoever owns the asset at that time.[5]

There are various instances in which tax capitalization is of particular importance. Most evident is the case of the property tax on land. Imposed at different rates in different jurisdictions, these rate differentials come to be reflected in land values. High property tax rates (other things being equal) should go with low land values. Another instance is given by the corporation tax. Since the tax applies to capital income in the corporate sector only, it reduces the net return from corporate capital relative to that in other sectors. Accordingly, the price of shares, which reflects the value of that net return, will fall. Such at least will be the case in the short

---

[5] See p. 369 for the bearing of this on corporate tax reform.

run, where previously invested capital is locked into the corporate sector. A further case of capitalization arises in the context of tax exempts, i.e., securities issued by state and local governments, interest from which is exempt from federal income tax. Here the process of capitalization works in the opposite direction. Tax exemption is equivalent to a subsidy, and the subsidy is reflected in an increased value of the bond.[6]

Mobile Factors Turning now to the case of mobile factors, we find that selective taxation of factor incomes or of assets in particular uses induces movement of factors into tax-free uses until net returns are equalized.

Beginning with the *corporation tax,* we see that the flow of capital to and from the corporate sector is elastic in the longer run. Since the tax applies to the corporate sector only, capital will move from the corporate to other sectors where the tax does not apply. As a result, output in the corporate sector will fall, and the *gross* rate of return on the remaining capital in the corporate sector will increase. The opposite development will take place in the tax-free sectors, with output increased and the rate of return to capital decreased. If there are perfect capital markets with no obstruction to the movement of capital, this capital flow will continue until the net (after-tax) rate of return in the corporate sector equals the untaxed rate of return in the other sectors. The tax burden on corporate profits is thus spread to capital invested in the untaxed sectors. In the longer run, the burden is thereby shifted in part to capital invested in the untaxed sectors.

This situation is shown in Figure 15-5, where the two panels depict the two sectors respectively. Before the tax is imposed, schedule *CD* on the left-hand panel represents the marginal efficiency of capital in the corporate sector. It shows the various rates of return attached to different sizes of the capital stock invested in that sector. A similar schedule, *FG,* is shown on the right-hand panel for the other sector. Before tax, total capital is divided between the two sectors, with *OH* invested in X (the corporate sector) and *OM* invested in Y (the unincorporated sector), where *OH* plus *OM* equals the total capital stock. In this way, the return to capital in both sectors is equated at the margin and equals *OI.*

Now a tax on capital income originating in the corporate sector is imposed. The net return per unit of capital to investors in this sector now equals $(1 - t)r,$ where r is the gross rate of return and t the rate of tax. This schedule of net returns is represented by *ED* in the left panel. As a result, capital will move out of the taxed and into the tax-free sector where the rate of return to the investor is higher. This reallocation of capital continues until investment in the corporate sector falls to *OK,* where the net rate of return is *OP.* At the same time, investment in the unincorporated sector rises to *OL* and the rate of return falls to *OP.* Thus the *net* rates of return to the investor are equalized in both sectors. It is therefore evident that the tax burden on capital in the long run will be shared by investors in both the taxed and untaxed sectors. After an initial period during which the burden on capital falls on the owner of capital in the taxed sector only, this burden will eventually come to be shared by the owners of capital in both sectors. The tax on the corporate

[6] See p. 335.

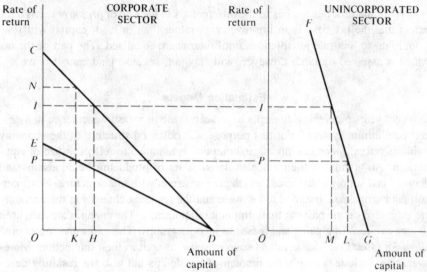

FIGURE 15-5 Tax on capital income from one sector.

sector continues to be capitalized, but gross returns rise as capital moves out of the corporate sector. Thus part of the initial decline in net return is recouped.

Beyond this, the adjustment process may involve further changes from both the uses and sources sides. On the sources side, the shift in output from the corporate to the unincorporated sector may affect returns to labor as well as to capital. Thus, if the output of the unincorporated sector is more labor-intensive, the return to labor will rise in the process and the burden on capital will be increased further.[7] On the uses side, consumers of products produced in the corporate sector will be burdened, since prices rise with falling supply. At the same time, consumers of products produced in the unincorporated sector will benefit, since such products will experience a relative decline in price. These subsequent effects, however, are not likely to overrule the progressive nature of the tax as reflected in its initial impact on the net return to capital.

---

[7] See Arnold C. Harberger, "The Incidence of the Corporation Income Tax," *Journal of Political Economy*, June 1962; reprinted in Arnold C. Harberger, *Taxation and Welfare*, Boston: Little, Brown, 1974, pp. 135–162.

The problem is straightforward if production relationships in both sectors are such that substitution between capital and labor leaves factor shares unchanged, i.e., that the elasticity of substitution is unitary throughout. This is the widely used assumption made in the so-called Cobb-Douglas production function. The flow of capital from the taxed to the tax-free sector then leaves factor shares unchanged. Labor's net income is unaffected and the entire tax falls on capital. Harberger considers this to come fairly close to the actual situation.

Matters are more complex if the elasticities of substitution are other than unity. The burden on capital will then tend to be the greater (and that on labor the smaller), the lower the elasticity of substitution between labor and capital in X as compared with that in Y. The burden on capital will also tend to be the larger, the lower the elasticity of substitution in consumption of the two goods. However, these are tendencies only. The various relationships are interwoven in a complex fashion and no simple conclusion emerges. Moreover, Harberger's analysis holds total factor supplies constant and, as noted in the text, the outcome changes further if factor supplies to the economy as a whole change.

A similar analysis applies to the differentials in the rate of *property tax*. To the extent that the tax base is in improvements rather than in land, capital will flow from high- to low-rate jurisdictions until returns are equalized. The part of the tax which is assessed on land, however, will stay put, because land cannot move.

Estimation Models

In recent years pioneering attempts have been made to measure incidence in a general equilibrium system.[8] For this purpose, the observed structure of the economy (with its prices, incomes, inputs, and outputs) is assumed to reflect a state of equilibrium. An attempt is then made to derive a set of production relationships and demand and supply elasticities, which are consistent with this structure. Next, certain tax changes are assumed to be made and the resulting changes in the economy are estimated on the basis of these implicit relationships. The changes are then used to measure resulting gains and losses to income groups. The gains and losses now allow for effects on both uses and sources sides, as well as their interaction. Moreover, they include not only the amount of tax dollars but also the resulting deadweight loss, a topic to be examined presently.

Whereas the outcome does not differ greatly from that of the partial analysis,[9] the comprehensive approach promises to give a more complete picture, allowing for the manifold interactions that result in response to a tax. However, such models also reflect a set of simplifying assumptions about how the economy functions, including that of perfectly competitive markets. The insights gained by a more partial analysis permits alternative market assumptions to be introduced and thus remains a useful part of the analysis.

D.   IMPERFECT MARKETS

As noted before, the preceding analysis was based on the assumption of perfect markets. But markets are not perfect, so imperfections must now be allowed for.

Product Taxes

In Figure 15-1, we observed the adjustment to a unit tax in a competitive market. The case of a unit tax under conditions of monopoly is given in Figure 15-6. *AR* and *MR* are the average and marginal revenue schedules before tax, respectively, and *MC* is the marginal cost schedule. Output is at the intersection of *MC* and *MR* and equals *OA,* while price equals *OB*. As the unit tax of amount *u* is imposed, the *MC* schedule shifts up to *MC'*. Output falls to *OC* and the price rise *BD* falls short of the unit tax *EH*. Tax revenue equals *EHGF*. As in the competitive case, the resulting changes in output, price, and revenue depend on the elasticities of demand and supply.

---

[8] See J. B. Shoven and J. Whalley, ''Applied General Equilibrium Models of Taxation and International Trade,'' *Journal of Economic Literature,* vol. 22, no. 3, September 1984.
[9] See also the reference to Devarajan, Fullerton, and Musgrave, p. 272 below.

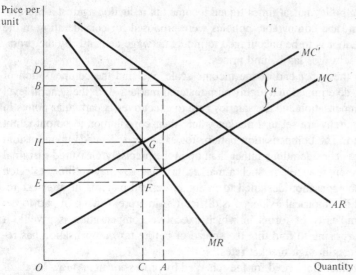

FIGURE 15-6   Unit tax under monopoly.

Tax on Wage Income

In a competitive labor market, wage rates are set by the intersection of the demand schedule (recording the value of the marginal product of labor) and the supply schedule (showing the minimum price at which various quantities of labor are forthcoming). With labor supply rather inelastic, a tax on wage income tends to be absorbed by labor. But matters become more complex if a realistic view is taken.

Wages in the modern economy are not determined in highly competitive markets. Factors other than productivity enter and a large part of the wage structure is set by collective bargaining. Even wages in nonunionized sectors are influenced by wage rates in the unionized sectors. The question then arises whether the income tax on wage income may not enter into the bargaining decision. Will not the union be able to shift an increase in income tax by demanding higher pay, and will not the employer be able to pass on the cost of higher wages to the consumer?

Much as unions would like to react this way, the question is whether they can do so. The answer is no if all parties to the bargain behaved as maximizers prior to tax. Under these rules, unions and employers have already struck the best bargain which they are able to obtain, and imposition of the tax does not change this position. To alter the conclusion, one would have to assume that prior to tax unions had asked for less than they were able to obtain. If they had done so, union leaders under pressure to protect take-home pay might demand greater wage increases if tax and withholding rates were to rise. This does not seem to have been a major factor in the United States, where unions traditionally respond to changes in the cost of living but not to tax-induced changes in take-home pay. Yet, such a response is not impossible. This is shown by countries such as Sweden, which engage in highly centralized collective bargaining and set wage rates as part of a general incomes policy. With income levels viewed in terms of after-tax wages, the income tax comes to be part of the overall wage settlement. Similarly, in the

United Kingdom policy has at times traded income tax reduction against a promise of wage restraint, and comparable policies were proposed for consideration in the United States. Labor is to be encouraged to moderate wage demands by the promise of tax relief if wages lag behind prices.

Turning to the upper end of the income scale, we find the compensation of executives to be determined in a highly administered market. Both the general level of executive compensation and the salaries paid to executives at particular points in the business hierarchy are set in a market where their contribution to output is not readily measured. The compensation pattern for executives depends upon custom and general status considerations rather than upon the precisely measured marginal productivity of their services. In such a market, tax changes may well be reflected in changes in compensation designed to maintain desired patterns of after-tax remuneration. While empirical evidence is difficult to interpret (owing in part to the tax-induced complexity of forms in which executive compensation is given), it would not be surprising to find that the spread of before-tax compensation has responded to changes in high bracket rates.

Similar considerations hold for fees charged by professionals. At low levels of taxation, lawyers or surgeons may find it prudent to charge less than what the market will bear. But as tax rates are raised, they may compensate by making upward adjustments to their fees.

Payroll Tax

Given perfect markets, we saw that it is a matter of indifference whether a tax is imposed on the buyer's or seller's side of the counter. This rule holds for taxes in the factor as well as in the product market. Given a perfectly competitive labor market, the division of the payroll tax between employer and employee contributions is thus a fiction, the outcome being precisely the same on whichever side of the market the tax is applied. Yet, as a matter of legislative intent, this sharing provision was introduced to "divide" the burden. While this leaves open the question of whether the employer's half was "meant" to fall on profits or on consumers, the intention was clearly to saddle employees with only one-half the contribution. Was this statutory division of rates mere stupidity or, as is frequently the fact when there are differences between theory and practice, are there other aspects to the problem which the preceding argument overlooks?

Raising the question is to point to the answer: Markets need not operate in a competitive fashion and real-world responses may differ from the above model. If payroll taxes are increased, unions may accept an increase in the employer contribution without demanding a wage increase, but they will hardly agree to a reduction in their wage rate in order to offset an increase in the employer contribution. Firms, in turn, will not absorb the increase in *their* contribution in reduced profits but will make it an occasion to raise prices. As a result, the employer contribution may be translated into a product tax with the burden falling on the consumer.[10]

Profits Tax

Finally, consider the case of a tax on capital income. In a competitive market, incidence will depend on the elasticities of demand and supply for capital services.

[10] See p. 440.

How is the outcome changed if the services of capital are priced in an imperfectly competitive market?

Monopoly At first sight, one would expect a firm which occupies a monopoly position in the product market to be better able to shift a tax on profit income than a firm which operates under competitive conditions. The competitor, after all, is a price taker, while the monopolist is a price setter. But closer consideration shows that the monopolist must absorb the tax. The reason is that the pure monopolist will have maximized profits prior to tax and hence can do no better after the tax is imposed. Since the tax is imposed so as to equal x percent of profits, the firm will remain best off by having the largest possible gross profits. With a tax rate of 34 percent, 66 percent of $100 million is better than 66% of below $100 million. Therefore, the output and price which give maximum profits without tax will still be the best position after the tax is imposed. In other words, the monopolist finds the corporation's profits reduced by the tax and cannot pass it on to the consumer via higher prices and still remain a profit maximizer.[11]

This situation is illustrated in Figure 15-7, which gives the familiar diagram for profit maximization of the monopolist. Before tax, profits are maximized at output *OA*, where marginal revenue (*MR*) equals marginal cost (*MC*). Price equals *OB* and profits are *CDEB*. As a tax of one-third is imposed, the *MR* and *MC* curves remain unchanged but net profits are cut to *CDFG*.

In the short run at least, the tax is again absorbed by profits in the taxed sector. Moreover, such may remain true even in the longer run. If firms in the taxed sector enjoy monopoly profits, it may be to their advantage, even after their profits are reduced by the tax, to remain where they are rather than to shift to the untaxed sector where they would enjoy a less sheltered position. The earlier conclusion that the tax is shared equally by capital in all sectors must then be qualified.

In practice, a potential monopoly may choose not to exploit potential market power to the fullest. That is to say, it will operate at a larger output and sell at a lower price than it would if profit maximization were its only goal. It may be satisfied with obtaining a target rate of return, say 15 percent, on invested capital. A higher rate of return may be considered "gouging" and socially improper; management may feel that a prudent profit target may help to maintain profits in the long run; or it may fear that excessive returns would invite antitrust action.

As a tax is imposed, the firm finds that its net rate of return has fallen below

---

[11] If *TR* is total revenue and *TC* is total cost, then profits, *P*, equal $TR - TC$. Profits are maximized at a level of output where $dP/DQ = 0$, that is, where

$$\frac{d(TR)}{dQ} - \frac{d(TC)}{dQ} = 0 \quad \text{or} \quad MR = MC$$

After imposition of a profits tax at rate *t*, the monopolist seeks to maximize $(1 - t)(TR - TC)$. Differentiating this with respect to Q and setting equal to zero gives us

$$(1 - t)\frac{d(TR)}{dQ} - (1 - t)\frac{d(TC)}{dQ} = 0$$

Dividing by $(1 - t)$ again leaves us with MR = MC.

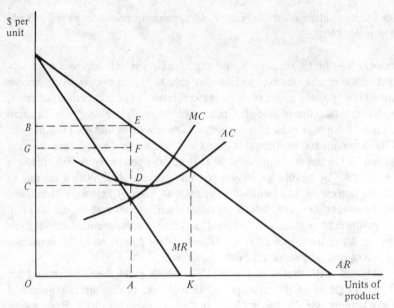

FIGURE 15-7   Profits tax under monopoly.

the target level. It will then be driven to exploit its monopolistic position, to restrict output and raise price in order to restore its net profit position. As it does so, it moves closer to the maximum profit position at output OA in Figure 15-7. In this way the burden will be passed to the consumer. Whether the entire burden can be passed on in this fashion will depend on the rate of tax relative to the pre-tax profit slack. The basic point is that the tax may induce the firm to make fuller use of its monopoly power; and to the extent that it does so, the burden is passed on.

Oligopoly Behavior   Another possibility of price adjustment arises in an oligopoly situation. Here prices and output are not set in the traditional profit-maximizing manner. The price tends to be established by the price leader in the industry and no one firm will wish to depart from it for fear of losing its sales if it raises price or of having its competitors follow suit if it tries to undercut the price. In such a situation, an increase in the tax rate may act as a signal to firms to raise price in concert. Since each firm has reason to expect that the others will act similarly, it can raise price without concern for its competitive position.

Sales Maximization   Over the years, various writers have criticized the classical assumption of profit maximization. While granting that firms will maximize something, they hold that profits may not be the only, or even the primary, objective of maximization. Rather, a firm may wish to maximize its sales or market share.

Since the profits tax does not change total sales as a function of price, simple sales maximization would again lead to the conclusion that the tax does not change output and price. The impact would therefore still be on profits. But a firm is not likely to maximize sales while disregarding profits altogether. Sales maximization

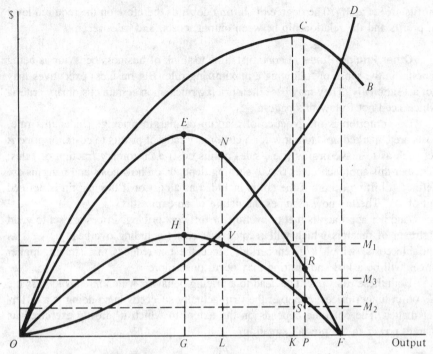

FIGURE 15-8 Profits tax under sales maximization.

may well be an objective, but it must be tempered by a minimum profit constraint. Defining the latter as net profits, we then have a behavior pattern which may well lead to shifting.

This situation is shown in Figure 15-8, where the curve OCB gives total sales receipts at various levels of output, while curve OD shows total cost.[12] The corresponding levels of profits or receipts minus costs are given by OEF. Under profit maximization, output is at OG with profits at GE. As a 50 percent tax is imposed, the level of net profits is given by OHF. Net profits are still maximized at OG but fall to GH. No shifting occurs. Under sales maximization, the output prior to tax depends on the profit constraint. With required minimum profits given by M_1, the firm prior to tax will produce at OK, or somewhat short of the point of maximum sales OP. As the tax is imposed, output is cut to OL. Net profits remain at their original level and the tax is fully shifted, with gross profits rising from LV to LN or by the amount of tax. Next, suppose that the profit minimum is set much lower, say, at M_2. Output before tax will now be at OP, since sales maximization leaves profits PR above the desired minimum. Moreover, sales continue to be maximized even after tax, since net profits PS will still meet the minimum requirement. Output remains unchanged at OP, the tax is absorbed in reduced profits, and there will be no shifting. A situation of partial shifting, finally, is indicated where minimum

[12] See W. Baumol, *Economic Theory and Operational Analysis,* 3d ed., Englewood Cliffs, N.J.: Prentice-Hall, 1973, p. 326.

profits are set at M_3. The degree of shifting depends therefore on the required level of profits and the relationship between output, costs, and sales receipts.

Other Pricing Rules Economists like to think of business behavior as being rational in the sense of following a maximizing rule. But business executives may not act rationally. They may base their pricing rules upon certain customary criteria which need not follow this pattern.

One criterion is the practice of markup or margin pricing. Under this rule, costs are "marked up" to allow for a customary ratio of profits to costs, or price is set such as to leave profits (i.e., sales minus cost) a customary fraction of sales. Whether this approach gives rise to shifting depends on how costs and margins are defined. Shifting occurs if the tax is included as a cost or if the margin is defined net of tax. The tax now assumes the nature of an excise tax.

Another approach is that of average or full-cost pricing. Prices are set to yield a stream of receipts which will recover full cost (including overhead as well as variable costs) within a given period. Since the tax reduces this stream, higher prices will be asked and shifting may occur once more.

Both these rules may thus lead to a pricing behavior which *intends* to pass the tax on in higher prices. Whether the firm actually succeeds in so doing is a different matter. The outcome depends on the extent to which it already exercised its market power in the pre-tax situation.

Imperfections in Labor Market So far, we have considered the possibility that firms operating under various forms of administered pricing may attempt to raise product price to recoup profits. As a result, the burden is passed "forward" to consumers. Another possibility is that the burden will be passed "backward" to the wage earner through reduction in the wage rate.

Once more, such adjustments cannot occur in a competitive labor market where the wage earner is paid the value of his or her marginal product and is paid the same return by firms which are profitable as by others which are not. If labor markets are imperfect, the situation may differ. If labor is weak and employers are in a monopsonistic position, the wage rate may be set below the value of labor's marginal product. The situation may then be similar to that of restrained monopoly pricing in the product market. Employers in the pre-tax setting may not fully exploit their position, but the tax may lead them to utilize their market powers more fully, with the result that part of the tax burden is passed to labor.

A similar outcome may result in a quite different setting where labor is in a strong position. Wage rates are set under collective bargaining, but unions in making wage demands may (and frequently do) allow for the profitability of the firm. They may aim to divert a share of monopoly profits to the wage earner while leaving the firm in what they consider an adequate profit position. Since this position depends on corporate profits *after* tax, an increase in the profits rate may reduce wage demands. In this way, part of the increase in tax may again be passed backward to the wage earner.

Faulty Definition of Tax Base A final factor which may account for forward shifting into higher prices is based on imperfections in the definition of the tax base. The profits tax base may diverge from profits as defined in economic theoɩ and include items which in fact are part of a firm's cost. Thus, profits as defined under the tax law do not allow for deduction of imputed interest on equity-financed working capital. Since such interest is a cost of doing business, the tax base is overstated. Part of the tax becomes an addition to cost and may be reflected in output and price. This possibility, however, is not likely to be very important, since most deductions from taxable profits are liberally defined.

Who Pays?   We have noted a variety of situations where the corporation may be able to recoup part of the tax by raising prices or reducing wages, thus passing on the burden to its consumers or its employees. The nature of the corporation tax then becomes more like that of an excise or wages tax. As was shown in Table 14-1, the resulting burden pattern may vary substantially, depending on what adjustment process applies.

E. MACRO ASPECTS

Following the conventional approach, we have viewed the problem of incidence in terms of changes in supply and demand and in relative product and factor prices. The adjustments to tax were taken to operate in a full-employment economy, without allowance for taxation effects on the level of employment. Similarly, no consideration was given to taxation effects on the rate of inflation or on capital formation and productivity growth. All these may have further distributional effects and bearing on tax incidence. A more careful consideration of these issues will follow later on, but they must be noted once more briefly here to round out the picture.

Employment Effects

Changes in the level of taxation will affect the level of aggregate demand and thereby the level of employment. If tax reduction increases employment, those previously unemployed will obtain earnings. Income available for private use will increase not only because the tax bite is reduced but also because employment rises. Inversely, if the level of employment falls, the loss of income will exceed the additional tax take. Thus it is no longer possible to equate changes in the tax burden with changes in the amount of tax collected. This difficulty may be avoided in part by viewing the problem in terms of differential incidence,[13] but even here taxes of equal yield may differ in their employment effects.

Inflation Effects

An increase in taxes by reducing aggregate demand may check inflation and thereby affect the state of distribution. Debtors will lose as their liabilities rise in real terms while creditors gain. Moreover, not all product prices and incomes move together, so that real incomes are affected. Thus changes in relative position may

[13] See p. 238.

result even though the tax increase itself was neutral, i.e., in the form of a proportional income tax.

Growth Effects

Finally, tax policy may affect the rate of growth. Different taxes will have different effects on the rate of saving and investment and thereby on capital formation. As the rate of capital formation is increased or reduced, factor earnings and hence incomes before tax will be affected. Thus, substitution of a tax on wage income for a tax on capital income will be regressive in the short run, but the final outcome cannot be assessed without also considering its effects on factor earnings.[14] All these aspects must be allowed for in assessing the full implications of a particular tax policy.

F. SUMMARY

The task of incidence theory is to trace the final burden distribution of a tax. Beginning with the point of statutory impact, we first consider the responses of buyers and sellers in the particular market in which the tax is imposed and then trace its repercussions in other markets until the entire economy has adjusted itself. This is a complex process, but certain general rules and conclusions can be reached.

Beginning with a partial equilibrium perspective and considering product taxes imposed in a competitive market, we concluded as follows:

1.   Imposition of the tax raises price and lowers quantity.

2.   A unit tax enters through a parallel upward shift in the supply schedule. An ad valorem tax enters through a downward swivel of the demand schedule.

3.   The magnitudes of price and quantity changes depend on the elasticities of demand and supply.

4.   The burden will be distributed between sellers and buyers in the ratio of elasticity of demand to that of supply.

5.   Both schedules are more elastic for a selective than for a general tax, and both become more elastic if a longer period of adjustment is allowed for.

6.   Given a pair of equivalent rates, it does not matter on which side of the market the tax is imposed.

7.   The distributional impact of a product tax (i.e., whether it is progressive or regressive) involves both the uses and sources sides of the household account. The former is likely to be decisive, leaving a tax on luxuries progressive and a tax on necessities regressive.

8.   The resulting price increase will be dampened if the tax is imposed in a monopolistic market.

Turning to a similar view of factor taxes, we find that the tax typically applies to the sale of factor services and takes the form of an ad valorem tax.

9.   The tax raises the gross rate of return to the factor, while reducing factor supply and lowering the net rate of return.

10.   The magnitude of adjustment and distribution of the burden between sellers and buyers again depends on the elasticities of demand and supply.

[14] See p. 312.

11. Once more, households are affected from both the uses and the sources sides of their accounts, but the sources side now tends to be decisive.

12. A tax on capital income tends to be progressive, whereas a tax on wage income tends to be regressive.

13. The outcome may differ depending upon the structure of the market in which the tax applies. Incidence of a tax on wage income may be affected by collective bargaining. A tax on executive or professional incomes may be shifted to consumers due to administered pricing. While a profit-maximizing monopolist cannot shift a profits tax, shifting may occur under other forms of market behavior.

Allowing for broader repercussions in a general equilibrium setting, we reach the following conclusions:

14. As product X is taxed, its price rises and consumers tend to substitute purchases of product Y. As a result, the return to factors strategic to the production of X will fall while that of other factors strategic to Y will rise. Thus effects from the earnings side are broadened into other markets. Similarly, increased demand for Y will tend to raise the price of Y, thus broadening the impact on the uses side to consumers of Y.

15. Similar considerations apply to a factor tax. A tax on factor X will tend to reduce its supply, which in turn will lower the returns obtained by factor Y, thus broadening effects from the earnings side.

16. Where a factor tax is limited to earnings in certain uses only, and the taxed factor is immobile, the tax will be capitalized and reflected in a reduced asset value. Where the taxed factor is mobile, its employment will move to tax-free sectors until net rates of return are equalized. Thus the burden of the corporation profits tax is spread to capital employed outside the corporate sector. Similar considerations apply to local property tax differentials.

Next, allowance has been made for market imperfections and their impact on tax incidence:

17. Product taxes will raise prices less under monopoly than under competition.
18. A profit-maximizing monopolist cannot shift a tax from profits.
19. Other situations suggest that the corporation tax may be shifted.

Finally, allowance was made for the fact that changes in tax policy may generate macro effects which also bear on burden incidence, including:

20. Employment effects.
21. Inflation effects.
22. Growth effects.

FURTHER READINGS

For general presentation of the theory of tax incidence, see:

Break, G. F.: "The Incidence and Effects of Taxation," in A. A. Blinder and R. M. Solow (eds.): *The Economics of Public Finance,* Washington, D.C.: Brookings, 1976, pp. 112–129.

McLure, C. E., Jr., and W. B. Thirsk: "A Simplified Exposition of the Harberger Model," *National Tax Journal,* March 1975.

Mieszkowski, P. M.: "Tax Incidence Theory: The Effects of Taxes on the Distribution of Income," *Journal of Economic Literature,* December 1969, pp. 1105–1124.

For empirical estimation of general equilibrium incidence, see:

Ballard, L., D. Fullerton, J. B. Shoven, J. Whalley: "A General Equilibrium Model for Tax Policy Evaluation," *National Bureau of Economic Research,* Chicago: University of Chicago Press, 1985.
Devarajan, S., D. Fullerton, and R. Musgrave: "Estimating the Distribution of Tax Burdens: A Comparison of Different Approaches," *Journal of Public Economics,* vol. 13, April 1980, pp. 155–182.
Shoven, J. B.: "Applied General Equilibrium Models of Taxation and International Trade," *Journal of Economic Literature,* vol. 22, no. 3, 1984.

APPENDIX: INCIDENCE OF UNIT AND AD VALOREM TAXES

I. PRICE AND OUTPUT EFFECTS OF A UNIT AND AN AD VALOREM TAX UNDER COMPETITION

Given a linear demand schedule for product X relating average revenue (AR) or price to quantity sold (Q),

$$AR = a - bQ$$

and a linear market supply schedule relating average unit cost (AC) to Q,

$$AC = c + dQ$$

the industry is in equilibrium where demand and supply intersect at a quantity Q_0 such that $AR = AC$ or $a - bQ_0 = c + dQ_0$ and

$$Q_0 = \frac{a - c}{b + d} \quad \text{with} \quad P_0 = a - b\left(\frac{a - c}{b + d}\right)$$

Unit Tax

After a unit tax u is imposed, the average net revenue schedule AR_n becomes

$$AR_n = a - bQ - u$$

and the industry is in equilibrium where $AR_n = AC$ or

$$a - bQ - u = c + dQ_1$$

with the new (post-tax) equilibrium quantity Q_t given by

$$Q_t = \frac{a - c - u}{d + b}$$

The post-tax (gross) price P_t then becomes

$$P_t = a - b \left(\frac{a - c - u}{b + d} \right)$$

The change in the gross price $(P_t - P_0)$ is then

$$\Delta P = \frac{bu}{b + d}$$

Under conditions of constant cost, $d = 0$ and the change in price reduces to $\Delta P = u$.

Ad Valorem Tax

For the case of an ad valorem tax, it is convenient to define the tax rate t_g as applying to gross or market price, such that tax per unit $T = t_g P_g$ rather than as t_n where $T = t_n P_n$. While the t_n version is used in the tax statutes, use of the t_g version simplifies the algebraic statement. Since $t_g = t_n/(1 + t_n)$, the results may be adapted by substituting t_n thus defined for the t_g in our equations. For the case of an ad valorem tax imposed at rate $t = t_g$, the average net revenue schedule then becomes

$$AR_n = (1 - t)(a - bQ)$$

and the gross price becomes

$$P_t = a - b \left(\frac{a - ta - c}{b - tb + d} \right)$$

The change in price is therefore given by

$$\Delta P = bt \left[\frac{ad + bc}{(b + d)^2 - tb(b + d)} \right]$$

For the case of constant cost, this reduces to

$$\Delta P = \frac{ct}{1 - t}$$

We note that for the case of the unit tax, the change in price is a function of the slopes of the demand and supply schedules only, while for the ad valorem tax the intercepts of the two functions also enter as determinants of the price change. Given the value of u or of t, the resulting change in gross price from either tax will be the greater the larger is b (the slope of the demand function) and the smaller is d (the slope of the supply function).

II.   PRICE AND OUTPUT EFFECTS OF UNIT AND AD VALOREM TAXES UNDER MONOPOLY

In the case of a linear demand and supply schedule, it may be shown that the increase in price under conditions of monopoly is one-half that of the competitive case. The average revenue schedule AR again is

$$AR = a - bQ$$

while the total revenue schedule TR is

$$TR = AR \cdot Q = aQ - bQ^2$$

Marginal revenue MR is thus

$$MR = \frac{dTR}{dQ} = a - 2bQ$$

The average cost schedule is again

$$AC = c + dQ$$

with total cost TC equal to

$$TC = cQ + dQ^2$$

and marginal cost MC equal to

$$MC = \frac{dTC}{dQ} = c + 2dQ$$

Setting MR equal to MC, we obtain

$$a - 2bQ_0 = c + 2dQ_0$$

or

$$Q_0 = \frac{a - c}{2(b + d)}$$

and the pre-tax price is

$$P_0 = a - b\left(\frac{a - c}{2(b + d)}\right)$$

Unit Tax

After imposition of a unit tax u, the net marginal revenue schedule becomes

$$MR_n = a - 2bQ - u$$

and the new quantity Q_t is obtained by setting $MR_n = MC$, so that

$$Q_t = \frac{a - c - u}{2(b + d)}$$

Thus, the gross price after tax (P_t) equals

$$P_t = a - b \left(\frac{a - c - u}{2(b + d)} \right)$$

and the change in price becomes

$$\Delta P = \frac{bu}{2(b + d)}$$

which equals one-half the change in the competitive price. For the constant cost case, where $d = 0$,

$$\Delta P = \frac{1}{2} u$$

Ad Valorem Tax

With imposition of an ad valorem tax at rate t, the net marginal revenue schedule now becomes

$$MR_n = (1 - t)(a - 2bQ)$$

and the new quantity where $MR_n = MC$ equals

$$Q_t = \frac{(1 - t) a - c}{2[(1 - t) b + d]}$$

and the gross post-tax price then becomes

$$P_t = a - \frac{b}{2} \left(\frac{(1 - t) a - c}{(1 - t) b + d} \right)$$

Thus, the change in price resulting from the tax equals

$$\Delta P = \frac{bt}{2} \left(\frac{ad + bc}{(b + d)^2 - tb(b + d)} \right)$$

again one-half that for the competitive case.

III.   MAXIMIZATION OF REVENUE UNDER A UNIT TAX

For a competitive industry and using linear schedules, let the demand schedule be defined by

$$P_D = a - bQ$$

and the supply schedule by

$$P_s = c + dQ$$

After imposition of a unit tax (u), the gross supply becomes

$$P_{sg} = c + dQ + u$$

Equating P_D with P_{sg} , we get

$$Q_t = \frac{a - c - u}{b + d}$$

Tax revenue then equals

$$R = uQ_t = u\frac{(a - c - u)}{b + d}$$

Chapter 16

Excess Burden and
Efficient Tax Design*

A. **Administration and Compliance Cost:** *Administration Cost; Compliance Cost.* B. **Tax Distortions in Partial Equilibrium:** *Choice among Products; Choice between Goods and Leisure; Choice between Present and Future Consumption; Tax on Rent; Choice between Investments; Tax Rate, Revenue, and Excess Burden.* C. **Tax Distortions in General Equilibrium:** *Conditions for Economic Efficiency; Choice among Products; Choice between Goods and Leisure; Choice between Present and Future Consumption; Multiple Choices; Optimal Taxation;* D. **Magnitude of Excess Burden.** E. **Further Considerations:** *Market Imperfections; Social Welfare Weights; Expenditure Analysis.* F. **Summary.**

Having examined tax equity, incidence, and the distribution of the tax burden we now turn to our second requirement for a good tax structure, namely, that the taxing process should be efficient. Tax administration should not be wasteful and

*Reader's Guide to Chapter 16: This chapter deals with the unpleasant proposition that the taxing process is costly. The burden placed on the economy exceeds what the government gets in revenue. In Section A, we consider administration and compliance costs. In Section B, we take a first look at the problem of excess burden or efficiency cost. Tax interference with various economic decisions is examined in a simplified partial equilibrium setting. Section C restates this analysis in general equilibrium terms as applied to single choices; and Section D allows for multiple choices and the interrelation between consumption, saving, and work. The less theoretically inclined reader may wish to pass over Sections C and D.

compliance cost for the taxpayer should not be unnecessarily large. Moreover—and this is a more subtle point—the "excess burden" of taxation or its "dead-weight loss" should be minimized. These two aspects will be considered in turn.

A. ADMINISTRATION AND COMPLIANCE COST

Economists have given little attention to the problem of administration and com-pliance costs, but it is an important issue in the operation of the fiscal system.

Administration Cost

Assessment and collection of taxes require personnel and equipment. This activity provides an important public service and, like all public services, it should be pro-vided efficiently. The desired quality of service should be offered at minimum cost. The cost of federal tax administration as reflected in the budget of the Internal Rev-enue Service (IRS) for the fiscal year 1989 was $11 billion, a substantial sum but only about 1 cent per dollar of federal tax revenue. This cost is obviously subject to large economies of scale. Overhead costs can be spread among taxpayers and higher rates yield higher revenue without greatly adding to costs. At the same time, the cost of administration per dollar of revenue rises with the complexity of the tax law. Thus, income tax administration is more costly than is that of the payroll tax. A head tax would be cheapest. Here, as elsewhere, quality is expensive. In setting criteria for efficient administration, these issues arise:

1. First there is the choice of appropriate technologies and administrative pro-cedures. In recent years, the IRS has been increasingly computerized, which reduces cost and provides more detailed information. Nevertheless, it is impossible to check all returns in detail. Only a limited number of returns are audited carefully (in fact, less than 10 percent) and they have to be chosen so as to make enforcement most effective.

2. The question therefore is how far auditing and enforcement should be car-ried. Should it be carried to the point where at the margin an additional dollar of cost brings in less than a dollar of revenue? Hardly so, since the cost of administration is a resource cost, whereas the revenue gain is only a transfer. The marginal dollar of ad-ministration cost, therefore, has to be balanced against the value of more equitable ad-ministration.

3. As in all matters of legal rules, better compliance can be secured either by threatening a higher penalty if the offender is caught or by spending more on enforce-ment so as to increase the probability of being caught. The former is cheaper than the latter but is less acceptable on equity grounds.

4. Next, there is the question of how complex the tax structure should be. A head tax is cheaper to administer than a sales tax, and a sales tax is cheaper than an income tax. A tax on gross income is cheaper than one which attempts to determine net income, and so forth. As will become apparent in Part Five, an equitable tax system for a highly complex economy is itself inevitably complex. Yet such complexity in-creases administration and compliance costs. Once more a tradeoff is needed.

5. Finally, it is evident that tax administration in a federal system is more costly than it is in a highly centralized system, since much of the administrative apparatus may come to be duplicated many times.

As this brief discussion suggests, tax administration and enforcement offer interesting problems in policy design and tradeoffs, not only for the administrator but also for the economist.

Compliance Cost

Depending on the particular tax, compliance cost may be much larger than administration cost. In a recent survey of compliance cost under the personal income tax, it was estimated that taxpayers on the average spent 21.7 hours on tax compliance, including both account keeping during the year and the actual process of filing returns.[1] Valuing this time at its average and after-tax hourly wage, we estimate that the average own-cost was $231. Adding to this the average cost of professional advice of $44, we calculate that the average cost per taxpayer was $275. While rising up to an income of $50,000, the survey showed compliance cost to remain a fairly steady percent of income thereafter. Applying the average to 97 million taxpaying units, we arrive at a total of $26 billion, equal to 7 percent of total income tax revenue of $380 billion.

Income tax compliance cost of 7 percent is thus a major factor, which reflects the nature of the income tax as a personal tax. The corresponding ratio is much lower for in rem taxes, such as the sales or payroll tax. The existence of compliance cost must thus be evaluated in terms of what it buys. Our income tax system, as noted below, is based on declarations submitted by the taxpayer, in the hope that this will lead to more complete recording and a fairer base on which to determine tax liability. This procedure is costly for the taxpayer but socially worthwhile if justified by a more equitable outcome. Policy once more must choose between equity considerations which may call for a more complex law and the saving in compliance cost which goes with simplification.

B. TAX DISTORTIONS IN PARTIAL EQUILIBRIUM

We now examine a second and more sophisticated aspect of tax efficiency. If you pay $1,000 in tax, the burden which this imposes on you may well be in excess of this amount. Unless imposed in the form of a lump-sum tax (i.e., a tax, such as a head tax, which is unrelated to economic activity), a tax interferes with economic decisions and distorts efficient choice. This distortion is burdensome to you, while being of no help to the Treasury. Efficient policy should therefore minimize this burden, referred to variously as excess burden, deadweight loss, or efficiency cost.

The most obvious way of avoiding this cost, of course, would be to obtain all revenue from a head tax, with everyone paying the same amount. This would avoid all excess burdens, but it would clearly be unacceptable on equity grounds. As shown above, if taxes are to be related to ability to pay, they must be based on economic indices such as income, consumption, or wealth.[2] Equitable taxation must therefore be based on economic activity and as such inevitably interferes with economic

---

[1] See J. Slemrod and N. Sorum, "The Compliance Cost of the U.S. Individual Income Tax System," *National Tax Journal,* vol. 37, no. 4, 1984.

[2] See p. 223 for a discussion of such bases.

choices, thereby causing an excess burden. The task of tax policy, as we will see shortly, is to reach a compromise solution which allows for both criteria. Among equally equitable taxes, the more efficient one should clearly be used; but a less efficient one may be preferable if the tradeoff between equity and efficiency so indicates.

Choice among Products

We begin with the effects of a tax on consumer good X and see how the consumer responds. To begin with the simplest setting, we consider the impact of the tax in the market for X only, leaving a general equilibrium view of the problem for later on. We return for this purpose to the concept of consumer surplus as applied in our earlier discussion of cost-benefit analysis.[3]

Figure 16-1 is a partial-equilibrium market demand and supply diagram for products X and Z. The demand schedule for X is shown as DK, while SV is the supply schedule. To simplify, we assume constant costs.[4] Beginning with case I in Figure 16-1, we find that the pre-tax equilibrium is at A, the price being OS and the quantity OC. Now a unit tax, $u = SS'$, is imposed. As the tax is added to cost, the supply schedule rises to $S'V'$ and the new equilibrium is at G. The gross price (inclusive of tax) rises to OS' while output falls to OL and tax revenue equals $SS'GF$. Since we are dealing with a case of constant cost, consumers (in line with our earlier argument) bear the entire burden, defined as $SS'GF$ and equal to revenue. Whereas, prior to tax, they would have paid $OSFL$ for the amount OL, they must now pay $OS'GL$, the additional amount being $SS'GF$, or tax revenue.

This, however, is not a complete description of the consumer burden. Prior to tax, consumers paid $OSAC$ for amount OC but would have been willing to pay $ODAC$.[5] Since all units under competitive pricing are priced at their marginal value, consumers received a "consumer surplus" equal to the difference between actual and potential payment, or SDA. Under the tax, their consumer surplus has been reduced to $S'DG$. They have thus suffered a loss of surplus equal to $SS'GA$. Of this, $SS'GF$ is offset by the government's revenue gain, but the triangle FGA remains as a deadweight loss or "excess burden" to the economy.

What determines the magnitude of the excess burden? As may be seen by rotating DK around point A as the pivot, the triangle FGA becomes smaller as demand becomes less elastic (the DK schedule becomes steeper). If demand is wholly inelastic, consumers do not adjust their purchase to price, and the tax cannot interfere with consumer choice. The tax becomes equivalent to a lump-sum tax. There will be no excess burden.

We may now compare the excess burden if an equal revenue is obtained from product X (case I), the demand for which is moderately inelastic in the initial equilibrium, and from product Z (case II), the demand schedule for which is highly inelastic. Pre-tax quantity and price are the same in both cases, but the unit tax FG

---

[3] See p. 135.

[4] See p. 272 where variable costs are allowed for.

[5] Under certain assumptions regarding the utility function, the demand schedule may be taken to measure the marginal value of consumption applicable to successive quantities. Adding the vertical blocks under the demand curve from O to C, we obtain the total utility derived from the consumption of OC or $ODAC$. The necessary assumption is that the marginal utility of income remains constant.

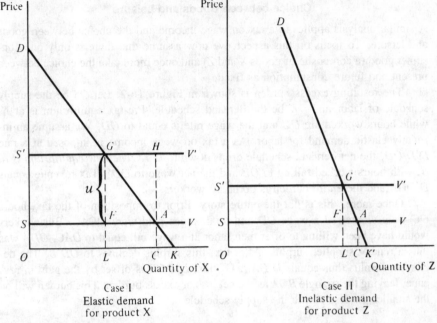

FIGURE 16-1 Excess burden of an excise tax.

needed for yield $SS'GF$ is less for Z than for X. We note that for Z, where demand is highly inelastic, the excess burden FGA is smaller.

Assuming constant cost, we observe that the excess burden for the case of a linear demand schedule is given by the triangle FGA, which in turn is equal to $\frac{1}{2}(\Delta P \cdot \Delta Q)$.[6] With ΔP equal to the unit tax u and price elasticity of demand $E = (\Delta Q/Q)(P/\Delta P)$, this triangle by substitution equals $\frac{1}{2}[(u^2E)(Q/P)]$. If demand is wholly inelastic so that E is zero, excess burden also equals zero and then rises with E. Note also that excess burden rises as the square of u, a point to which we will return shortly. For the case of an ad valorem tax at rate t, we have $t = \Delta P/P$ and by similar substitution obtain $FGA = \frac{1}{2}(Et^2PQ)$ where in equilibrium $u = tP$. Note that the triangle FGA, for the case of a nonlinear demand schedule does not measure the exact efficiency cost but becomes an approximation only.

The argument may be extended to measure the quality of the tax by viewing excess burden as a surcharge or percent of revenue. Returning to Figure 16-1, we see that this ratio equals $FAG/SS'GF$.[7] Its surcharge becomes zero when E is zero and reaches infinity as E rises to infinity.

---

[6] Allowing for the fact that real world demand curves are not linear, triangle FGA is an approximation only.

[7] Substituting, we obtain

$$FGA/SS'GF = \left[\frac{1}{2}\,u\,\frac{E}{P}\right]\left[1 - u\frac{E}{P}\right]$$

The surcharge is zero when E is zero and becomes infinity as E rises to infinity. See Arnold Harberger, *Taxation and Welfare*, Boston: Little, Brown, 1974, p. 35.

Choice between Goods and Leisure

A similar analysis applies to a tax on wage income and the choice between goods and leisure. To focus on this aspect, we now assume that there is only one consumer good (a composite of goods X and Z) and once more take the choice between present and future consumption as fixed.

The resulting excess burden is shown in Figure 16-2. Let OS be the supply schedule of labor and DK be the demand schedule. Pre-tax equilibrium is at A, while hours worked are OC and the wage rate is equal to OD. We assume an infinitely elastic demand for labor. As a tax on wage income is imposed at a rate $D'D/OD$, the net demand schedule drops down to $D'K'$. *The new equilibrium is at B*, with hours worked falling to OE and the net wage to OD'. Tax revenue equals $D'DGB$ and the entire burden is borne by workers.

Once more, this is not the entire story. Prior to imposition of the tax, hours OC were worked at a wage OD and total wages paid were $ODAC$. But workers would have been willing to offer their labor at a wage bill equal to OAC. ODA was thus a rent or supplier surplus. After tax, this surplus declines to $OD'B$. The decline in surplus thus equals $D'DAB$. Of this, $D'DGB$ is offset by the gain in revenue, leaving the triangle BGA as the net loss or excess burden. This burden will be the smaller the less elastic the supply schedule.

Choice between Present and Future Consumption

The argument may be repeated once more for a tax on interest and its effect on the supply of saving. Returning to Figure 16-2, we now measure the rate of interest on the vertical axis and saving on the horizontal axis. Prior to tax, borrowers are willing to pay interest rate OD and saving equals OC. As a tax at rate $D'D/OD$ is imposed the net demand schedule drops to $D'K'$ and saving falls to OE. Revenue equals $D'DGB$, the saver's loss of surplus equals $D'DAB$, and the excess burden equals BGA. A further view of distortion in the consumption-saving decision is given below, where a comparison is drawn between a general income tax and a consumption tax.[8]

Tax on Rent

A tax on the rent of land is of particular interest in this context because land, as a factor of production, is inelastic in supply, so that taxation of land rent involves no excess burden. Returning to Figure 16-2, let us suppose that acreage is measured horizontally and land rent is measured vertically. Suppose further that the supply schedule is given by EG. Imposition of the tax now leaves supply unchanged and revenue equals $D'DGB$, and there is no deadweight loss. This is one of the reasons why economists have for long considered land rent a favored base of taxation and why the case for land taxation was dramatized in the United States by Henry George and his single-tax movement.[9]

The underlying idea, however, goes beyond the case of land. Excess burden is absent wherever surplus can be isolated out as a base of taxation. Thus, in Figure

[8] See p. 290.
[9] See Henry George, *Progress and Poverty*, 1879, R. Schalkenbach Foundation, 1954.

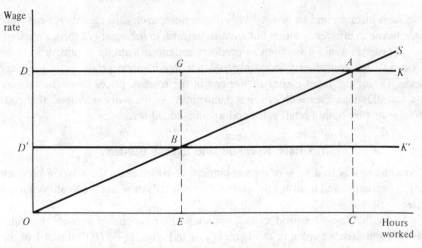

FIGURE 16-2 Excess burden of tax on wage income.

16-1 above, the consumer of X, prior to tax, derives a surplus equal to *SDA*. Or, in Figure 16-2, the worker derives a surplus of *ODA*. If it were possible to tap this surplus without imposing a tax at the margin, no distortion would result. In principle, the idea of taxing rents of all kinds has great merit, but unfortunately it is difficult in practice to determine the amount of surplus involved.[10]

Choice between Investments

Distortions in investment choices arise where capital income in various industries is taxed at differential rates. As noted in our previous discussion of incidence, this is of particular importance in the context of the corporation tax. As shown there, the tax causes capital to move from the corporate to the unincorporated sector, thereby equating net returns and spreading the tax burden among all capital income. Ms. Jones, who invests in the corporate sector after the tax has been imposed, is not discriminated against. At the same time, the efficiency cost of partial taxation remains in place as the capital stock in the corporate sector is less, relative to that in tax-free sectors, than it would be under a general tax. Thus output is distorted from its efficient mix. Similar considerations also arise within the corporate sector when tax provisions, such as depreciation rules, are more favorable to one industry than to another. A further instance of differential taxation of capital arises in the context of a federal system such as ours where various states tax corporate income at different rates, thus affecting the location of capital and causing a further efficiency cost.[11]

The individual income tax also gives rise to distortions in capital flows. The preferential treatment of home ownership diverts capital into owner-occupied residences, the preferential treatment of capital gains favors investments which gen-

---

[10] See Abba P. Lerner, *The Economics of Control*, p. 232, 1944, Macmillan, New York.
[11] See p. 391.

erate such income, and so on. As we will see later, such differentials are not only burdensome in efficiency terms but are also harmful to the equity of the tax system.

In order to avoid distortions in production there is a strong argument in favor of taxing final consumer goods only and not intermediate products or producer goods. Taxing the latter causes distortions in the relative prices of production inputs and thus interferes with efficient factor use. As we will see below, this condition is met by both a retail sales and a value-added tax.

Tax Rate, Revenue, and Excess Burden

In concluding this first view of excess burden, consider again the relation between tax rate, revenue, and deadweight loss and what it tells us about the quality of a tax system.

Using the case of a product tax, we show the relationship between tax rate, revenue, and excess burden or deadweight loss in Figure 16-3. DD' in part 1 of the figure is the demand schedule and BS is the supply schedule. Prior to imposition of a tax, output equals OA, price equals OB, and consumer surplus is given by the triangle BDC. Now a tax at rate EB/OB is imposed. The supply schedule rises to EF and consumer surplus drops to EDF. The decline equals $BEFC$, of which $BEFH$ is recouped in tax. The excess burden or deadweight loss incurred in the process equals $BEFC - BEFH$, or HFC. As the tax rate is raised to IB/BO, output falls to OJ, revenue rises to $BIKL$, and consumer surplus falls to IDK. The loss in consumer surplus now equals $BIKC$. With $BIKL$ recouped in tax, the excess burden rises to LKC. A still further increase in tax rate to UB/BO drops output to OM and revenue to $BUNR$ and raises deadweight loss to RNC.

The resulting levels of revenue and excess burden, corresponding to the various tax rates are plotted in part II of the figure. Two important findings emerge: (1) We see how revenue first rises and then falls after the tax rate is increased beyond the ZB/BO level, a relationship popularized in recent years by Professor Laffer.[12] (2) We also note that the deadweight loss rises at an increasing rate as the tax rate is increased, with an increase in rate above ZB/BO clearly counterproductive. (3) We note that the deadweight loss rises at an increasing rate as the tax rate goes up.[13] The quality of the tax, defined as the ratio of revenue to deadweight loss thus falls with a rising rate of tax. Similar observations may be applied to other taxes, so that the tax structure should be designed so as to equate deadweight losses at the margin, thereby minimizing its total weight. As noted below, this formula for tax design must be qualified, however, by allowing for welfare weights to be attached to tax burdens (revenue received and deadweight loss) at different points in the income scale. Minimizing total deadweight loss, therefore, is not the only relevant consideration.

---

[12] For a linear demand schedule, revenue is maximized at rate ZB/OB such that $DZ' = Z'C$. For further discussion, see D. Fullerton, "On the Possibility of an Inverse Relationship between Tax Rates and Government Revenues," *Journal of Public Economics*, vol. 19, no. 1, 1982.

[13] As noted before, the deadweight loss rises at the square of the tax rate. See p. 281.

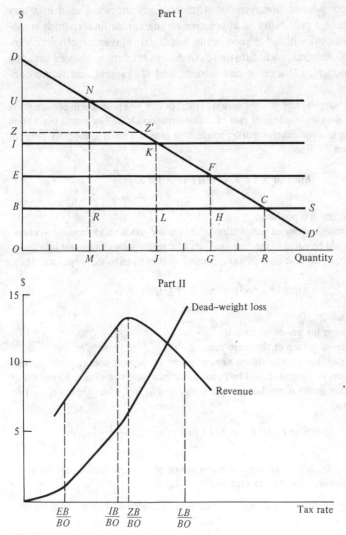

FIGURE 16-3 Revenue and excess burden.

C. TAX DISTORTIONS IN GENERAL EQUILIBRIUM

In the preceding discussion, the measure of excess burden was viewed in terms of loss of surplus, whether by consumers, workers, or savers. This is a helpful way of looking at the problem, since the triangle which represents the excess burden lends itself to measurement. We will return to this later. But the preceding exposition suffers from being a partial equilibrium approach and may invite misleading conclusions.

Conditions for Economic Efficiency

To understand how excess burdens arise, we return briefly to the conditions which must be met if resource allocation is to be efficient.[14]

Economists consider an arrangement efficient if resources are used in a way which does not leave a possibility of alternative arrangements under which somebody could be better off without anyone being worse off. Economic efficiency involves various requirements, including these conditions relating to choices between (1) alternative products, (2) income and leisure, and (3) present and future consumption:

1. The marginal rate of substitution (MRS) of any two products in consumption should be equal to their marginal rate of transformation (MRT) in production. Such will be the case in a competitive market where both rates are equal to the price ratio for the two products.[15] Thus,

$$\text{MRS of X for Z} = \text{MRT of X for Z} = \frac{P_x}{P_z}$$

where X and Z are two products.

2. The marginal rate of substitution of leisure for goods (as expressing workers' preference) should be equal to the marginal rate of transformation of leisure into goods (via work effort), with both rates in a competitive system equal to the wage rate. Thus,

$$\text{MRS of } L \text{ for } Y = \text{MRT of } L \text{ for } Y = w$$

where L = leisure
Y = income (or goods in general)
w = price of leisure or the wage rate

3. The marginal rate of substitution of future for present consumption (as valued by consumers or savers) should be equal to the marginal rate of transformation of present into future goods in production with both equal to $1/(1 + i)$, where i is the rate of interest. Thus,

$$\text{MRS of } C_f \text{ for } C_p = \text{MRT of } C_f \text{ for } C_p = \frac{1}{1 + i}$$

where C_f and C_p are future and present consumption and i is the return paid for postponing consumption or the rate of interest.

Whenever any of these conditions is not met, economic welfare can be improved by rearrangement designed to meet it.[16]

---

[14] Less theoretically inclined readers may wish to skip this section.

[15] The MRS of X for Z is defined as the amount of Z which the consumer is willing to surrender for an additional amount of X. The MRT of X for Z is the amount by which the output of Z must be cut to produce an additional unit of X.

[16] This may be illustrated with regard to divergence from condition 1 as follows: Consumers will adjust their budget mix so that their marginal rate of substitution in consumption equals the price ratio. Let the price of good X equal $6 while that of good Z equals $3. The rate at which consumers are willing to substitute good X for good Z is therefore 2 (i.e., two units of Z for each unit of X), being equal to the ratio of the price of X to that of Z. Suppose, however, that the rate of transformation of X for Z in production is 3 (i.e., three units of Z must be given up to produce one additional unit of X). In this case, it will be efficient to produce and consume more of good Z and less of good X. This will be so because one additional unit of Z (worth ½ of X to the consumer) may be gained by giving up only ⅓ unit of X in production. The satisfaction derived from the additional units of Z exceeds that lost through the reduction in X. Hence, there will be a welfare gain. As more Z and less X are consumed, the marginal utility of Z falls while that of X increases, thus raising the marginal rate of substitution of X for Z in consumption. However, as production shifts toward Z, the marginal rate of transformation of

The cause of excess burden may now be viewed in terms of interference with the cited efficiency conditions. Selective excises interfere with condition 1, a general consumption tax with condition 2, and a general income tax with both conditions 2 and 3.

Choice among Products

Distortions in product choice arising from a selective product tax are now shown in Figure 16-4, applicable to a particular consumer. The horizontal axis measures units of product X and the vertical axis measures units of product Z. To simplify matters, we assume that there are only these two goods and that the choice between income and leisure (the level of income) and that between present and future consumption are fixed. With a constant cost production function, the price line AB may be drawn as a straight line and the ratio of prices P_x/P_z equals OB/OA. Consider a consumer with income fixed at a level sufficient to purchase OB of good Z. As we view a particular consumer, the price ratio may be assumed to remain constant over the relevant range. The consumer can then allocate consumption between X and Z along the price line AB which is the opportunity locus. Given the consumer's preference pattern as expressed by indifference curves i_1, i_2, i_3, the choice will be combination E' since this places the consumer on the highest possible indifference curve i_1. At this point, the marginal rate of transformation in production, as given by the slope of the price line, equals the marginal rate of substitution in consumption, as given by the slope of the indifference curve.[17]

Now let a tax be imposed. Suppose first that the government uses a *head* or *lump-sum* tax such that the liability is the same whatever the consumer's economic characteristics and response. As a result, the price line will shift to the left parallel to AB. Since relative prices are not affected, the slope of the price line remains unchanged. If the tax equals AA' in terms of X or BB' in terms of Z, the consumer's new price line (opportunity locus) will be $A'B'$ and the new equilibrium will be at E''. The consumer now retains OC of Z, and CE'' of X. $E''D = A'A$ is the government's revenue in terms of product X. As before, the equality of the marginal rate of substitution, the marginal rate of transformation, and the price ratio is maintained. Resources are allocated efficiently and there is no excess burden.

Next suppose that the government obtains revenue $E''D$ by imposing a *general* tax on consumption. Applied at the same rate to X and Z, the tax inserts the same wedge between the gross and net prices of both. The price line again moves to $A'B'$, being parallel to AB, with the tax rate equal to AA'/OA' or BB'/OB'. Equilibrium is once more at E''. The producer remains in equilibrium with the ratio of net prices equal to the marginal rate of transformation while the consumer's marginal rate of substitution equals the ratio of gross prices. Since the tax applies equally to both X and Z, the net and gross price ratios are the same and MRS = MRT. With total outlay on X and Z held fixed, a uniform rate tax on both products is in fact equivalent to a lump-sum tax.

X for Z in production tends to fall, thus contributing to the equalization process. The final result will yield a MRS, MRT, and price ratio all equal to somewhere between 2 and 3. This is the best possible position.

[17] For an explanation of indifference curves, see Jack Hirshleifer, *Price Theory and Applications,* Englewood Cliffs, N.J.: Prentice-Hall, 1976, chap. 3.

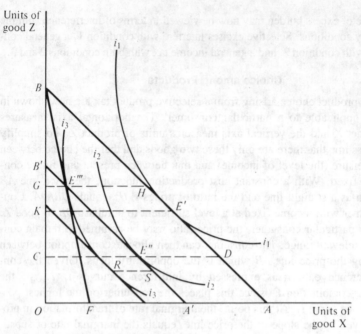

FIGURE 16-4   Adjustment to selective and general taxes.

The situation differs, however, with a *selective* tax, imposed on one product, say, X only. The tax now enters as a wedge between the net and the gross price of X, with no such wedge for Z. To be efficient, the ratio of the *net* price of X to the price of Z available to the producer must equal the MRT of X for Z in production, while the ratio of the *gross* prices of Z and X to the consumer must equal the MRS of X for Z in consumption. The two ratios are now rendered unequal. Condition 1 is not met and inefficient allocation results.

Returning to Figure 16-4, we note that the government, in order to obtain the same revenue $E''D$ from a tax on X only, must apply a rate equal to FA/OA.[18] The consumer now finds that P_x has risen relative to P_z so that $P_x/P_z = OB/OF$. The price line or opportunity locus swivels from BA to BF and the consumer now purchases less of X than he or she did under the general tax. The new equilibrium is at E'''. It will be seen that at E''' the slope of BF, or the MRS, exceeds that of $B'A'$, or the MRT. The consumer now surrenders BG of Z to purchase GE''' of X, while retaining OG of Z. Whereas E'' falls on i_2, E''' falls on the lower curve i_3.[19] The burden imposed on the taxpayer by a selective consumption tax is thus greater than that which would have resulted under a lump-sum tax providing equal revenue. It is the movement from i_2 to i_3 that reflects the excess burden.

---

[18] We know that the new equilibrium must fall on $B'A'$ since the government is to obtain the same revenue of $A'A$. To find the new price line BF, we therefore draw a line through B such that it is tangent to an indifference curve at its point of intersection with $B'A'$.

[19] This follows because (1) E''' lies northwest of E'', and (2) indifference curves cannot intersect. Point 1 holds because E''', the marginal rate of substitution of X for Z in consumption must exceed the marginal rate of transformation in production, due to the tax wedge.

To put the matter differently, the general tax has an "income effect" only, involving reduced purchases of both X and Z and a shift from E' to E''. The selective tax has in addition a "substitution effect," or replacement of X by Z because of the relative price change resulting in a shift from E'' to E'''. The burden reflected in the move from i_1 to i_2, as caused by the shift from E' to E'', is inevitable if revenue $A'A$ is to be raised. This further burden (reflected in the move from i_2 to i_3) occurs with the selective tax only.

Choice between Goods and Leisure

A similar argument applies to a tax on wage income. To simplify, we now hold fixed the choice among products as well as that between present and future consumption. Leisure is measured on the horizontal and goods on the vertical axis of Figure 16-5. We consider an individual with leisure OA which may be traded for OB of goods. With wage rate OA/OB and the preference pattern given by the indifference curves, the pre-tax equilibrium will be at E, work effort equals HA, and the individual is on indifference curve i.

FIGURE 16-5   Burden of Income Tax.

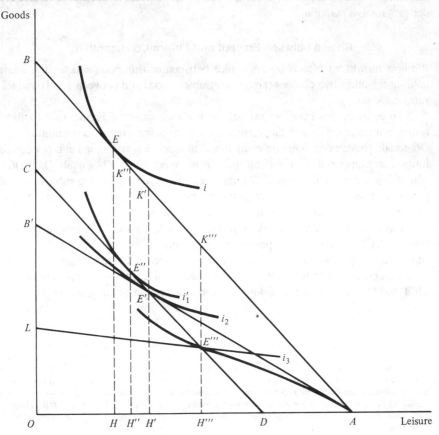

Proportional Tax   Now a flat rate or proportional income tax is imposed at rate $B'B/OB$. The opportunity locus switches to AB' with the new equilibrium at E' and work reduced from HA to $H'A$. Revenue equals $E'K'$ and the taxpayer has dropped from i to i_2. This reduction welfare would have been less had it been possible to obtain the same revenue while including leisure in the tax base. In that case, the opportunity locus would have shifted parallel from BA to CD; the new equilibrium would be at E'' with revenue unchanged at $E''K'' = E'K'$. The taxpayer would now be on i_1, which though below i is above i_2. The reduction in work effort, now given by HH'', is less as the substitution effect of a reduced wage rate is avoided. The tax would in effect be a lump-sum tax, without deadweight loss. Unfortunately, it is difficult to measure the value of   isure, so that in practice such a tax cannot be imposed.

Progressive Tax   Suppose now that the same amount of revenue is to be obtained by a progressive tax. In that case, the opportunity locus is moved to a curve such as AL. The flattening slope of this curve when moving to the left reflects the fact that with progressive rates the marginal rate of tax rises with income. The new equilibrium is now at E''', with revenue unchanged at $E'''K''' = E'K'$, but hours are reduced further by HH'''. The taxpayer now is dropped from i_2 to i_3, reflecting the additional excess burden due to the increased substitution effect under progressive taxation.[20]

Choice between Present and Future Consumption

We now turn to tax effects on the choice between consumption and saving, while holding the other two choices (among consumer goods and between goods and leisure) constant.

To consider this case, we relabel the horizontal axis of Figure 16-4 to show future consumption C_f and the vertical axis to measure present consumption C_p. OB equals present consumption available if all income is consumed and OA equals future consumption available if all income is saved. Thus, OA equals $(1 + i)OB$ where i is the rate of interest. BA thus represents all possible combinations of present and future consumption available to the individual, given his or her current income. Pre-tax equilibrium is at E' located on indifference curve i_1.

If a general consumption tax, applicable alike to C_p and C_f and yielding a revenue of AA', is imposed, the price line once more shifts, paralleling BA to $B'A'$, and the new equilibrium is at E'' located on the lower indifference curve i_2. Since both C_p and C_f are reduced at the same rate, relative prices are unchanged, the MRT and MRS of present for future consumption remain equal, and no excess bur-

---

[20] Such at least is the case if we compare the excess burden of obtaining the same revenue from a particular taxpayer under the two types of rate schedules. But the problem is more complicated if we consider what happens as the same revenue is drawn from a group of taxpayers under a proportional and a progressive tax. As a progressive tax is substituted for the proportional tax, the marginal rates applicable to high-income taxpayers will rise and their excess burden will increase. But there will also be a decline in the marginal rates applicable to lower incomes, and their excess burden will fall. The outcome thus depends on the elasticity of supply (and hence sensitivity to excess burden) at various income ranges.

den results. The general consumption tax is now neutral and equivalent in its excess-burden aspects to a lump-sum tax.

An income tax, however, reduces the ratio C_f / C_p, since the net interest rate is reduced by the tax and less is gained by postponing consumption.[21] As noted already in our discussion of tax equity, it discriminates against the saver and is in favor of the consumer. The price line swivels to BF and equilibrium moves to E'''. An excess burden (equal to the loss of welfare in moving from i_2 to i_3) results, because the tax now destroys the equality between the MRT of present into future consumption as seen by the producer (equal to $1 + i_g$, where i_g is the gross rate of return to capital) and the MRS as seen by the consumer (equal to $1 + i_n$, where i_n is the net after-tax return). The consumption tax is thus superior in efficiency terms to the income tax. Such at least is the case in the present context, although certain previously noted qualifications must again be allowed for.[22]

Multiple Choices

Our discussion so far has related to a taxpayer confronted with a single choice, be it between products, consumption or saving, leisure or income. Before proceeding to multiple choices, these conclusions may be drawn:

    1. With income and saving fixed, a general consumption tax imposes no deadweight loss and is superior to a selective consumption tax which distorts the choice between consumer goods.

    2. With income and the choice between consumer goods fixed, a consumption tax is preferable to an income tax which by taxing capital income distorts the choice between present and future consumption.

    3. With saving and the choice between consumer goods constant, both income and consumption taxes distort the choice between income (or consumption) and leisure.

Only a lump-sum tax or a hypothetical tax on potential income would be free of deadweight loss. These are interesting conclusions but their significance is lessened by the restrictive nature of the underlying assumptions which permitted us to allow for only one set of choices at a time.

To arrive at a more realistic view, we must allow for various choices to be open concurrently. Consider a situation where there is a choice between both (1) products X and Z and (2) income (or combinations of X and Z) and leisure L. Can it still be argued that an equal-rate tax on X and Z is preferable to a tax on X or Z only, or for that matter, to some combination of unequal rates on both?

The answer is no. The threat of potential distortion now becomes triangular: The tax may distort the choice between X and Z, X and L, and Z and L. Let the initial tax apply at the same rate to both X and Z. Thus there is no distortion be-

---

[21] Prior to tax, consumers may enjoy their entire income Y in the form of current consumption C, or they may save it, earn an income equal to iY, and enjoy a future consumption of $(1 + i)C$. The ratio between present and future consumption is thus: $C/[(1 + i)C]$. With a general consumption tax, present consumption equals $(1 - t)C$ and future consumption equals $(1 - t)(1 + i)C$, with the ratio of the two remaining unchanged at $C/(1 + i)C$.

    With an income tax, present consumption is $(1 - t)C$, but future consumption equals $(1 - t)C + (1 - t)(1 - t)iC$, so that the ratio becomes $C/[1 + i(1 - t)]C$.

[22] See p. 283.

tween X and Z, but the choices between X and L and Z and L are both biased in favor of L. Suppose now that the rate on Z is reduced while that on X is raised. This introduces a distortion between X and Z and increases that between X and L. But it reduces the distortion between Z and L. If X is a boat the enjoyment of which is complementary to leisure, and Z is work clothing the consumption of which is rival to leisure, a higher rate of tax on X and a lower rate of tax on Z may be desirable so as to correct for the defect which arises because leisure cannot be taxed. Thus the presumption in favor of a general equal-rate tax on X and Z breaks down once flexibility in the leisure-income choice is introduced.

Similar reasoning shows that there is no longer a necessary presumption for ranking a general consumption tax ahead of the income tax. The consumption tax, to be sure, is neutral as between C_p and C_f, whereas the income tax discriminates against C_f, but both discriminate between C_p and L as well as between C_f and L. The outcome now depends on the relative substitutabilities between C_p and L, and C_f and L. Since the tax base is smaller under the consumption tax, a higher rate is needed to obtain the same revenue as under the income tax. Thus, discrimination in favor of leisure is increased, and this may have a further bearing on the outcome.

Optimal Taxation

We conclude that no longer can a hard and fast rule be drawn. The "optimal mix" of taxes, defined as that which minimizes excess burden, may comprise a complex set of taxes and rates, and even then the outcome would be second best to a hypothetical tax under which leisure could be included in the base. Nevertheless, economists have addressed the problem of how to design such a solution, composed of a set of commodity taxes. Now familiar under the heading of "optimal taxation," this analysis has been applied to both commodity and income taxes.[23]

Returning to the simple partial equilibrium view of Figure 16-1, we have seen that the excess burden involved in obtaining a given amount of revenue from commodity X would be larger than that obtained from commodity Z. We have also seen that as the tax rate for each commodity is increased the excess burden rises in proportion to the square of the tax rate. In order to minimize the total excess burden, we should therefore collect the revenue from the two taxes so as to equate the excess burden imposed by the last dollar of tax on each product.

Allowing now for the fact that leisure is not fixed and that the demand among products and for products and leisure is interdependent, economists have developed a set of rules, depending on the circumstances of the case. Thus, a distinction may be drawn between three situations: Case 1, where there is substitutability in consumption among products, but not between products and leisure; case 2, where there is substitutability between products and leisure but not among products; and case 3, where both substitutions may occur.

If a given revenue is obtained, the set of optimal tax rates for case 1 should be

---

[23] The question was raised initially by A. C. Pigou (*A Study in Public Finance*, London: Macmillan, 1928) and dealt with by Ramsey (*Economic Journal*, 1927). For more recent references see Further Readings at the end of this chapter and W. J. Baumol and David E. Bradford, "Optimal Departures from Marginal Cost Pricing," *American Economic Review*, June 1970, pp. 165–283; and David F. Bradford and Harvey S. Rosen, "The Optimal Taxation of Commodities and Income," *Compilation of OTA Papers*, vol. 1, U.S. Department of the Treasury, 1978.

such as to equalize the resulting percentage change in price for all products, i.e., an across-the-board equal-rate ad valorem tax is called for. This in fact is the previously considered setting of Figure 16-4. Moreover, it has been demonstrated that the set of tax rates for case 2 should be such that the resulting percentage changes in prices will be inversely proportional to the elasticity of demand for the various products. This is not surprising, because it is the failure of demand to be wholly inelastic which causes excess burden to arise. The solution for case 3 involves both types of elasticities of substitution (between products and between products and leisure) and is of a more complex form. In all, the optimal pattern will be such as to tax more heavily products which are inelastic to price but complementary to (are consumed in conjunction with) leisure, such as recreational goods. Taxing goods the demand for which is complementary to leisure may be viewed as an indirect way of taxing leisure.

As the preceding analysis demonstrates, determining the optimal system of raising a given revenue (i.e., so as to minimize aggregate deadweight loss) is a fascinating challenge to the economic theorist. But as is usually the case, this ideal cannot be accomplished in practice. The necessary information regarding demand and cost elasticities is hardly available and the complexities of a large set of differential rates imposed on a wide range of commodities would be intolerable. It is thus not surprising that there continues to be a practical case in favor of a uniform rate product tax, even though an optimal approach would call for differentiation among products. One of the reasons for this is that more harm might be done by misguided differentiation than would be gained from attempting at efficiency by a differential pattern.

D. MAGNITUDE OF EXCESS BURDEN

Much effort has been directed in recent years to measuring the quantitative significance of excess burden. This is important for two reasons. For one thing, the deadweight loss inherent in alternative taxes should be considered in constructing a good tax system. For another, the deadweight loss of the marginal tax dollar in such a system must be known to determine the proper size of the budget, because it sets the cost (tax dollar plus deadweight loss) which need be measured against the benefits derived from the marginal expenditure dollar. Applied to the budget in general, the principles of cost-benefit analysis previously considered in the context of particular projects may thus be repeated on a broader scale.

Estimates of excess burden have focused largely on the income tax and resulting changes in labor supply. That is to say, they have been in line with the perspective of Figure 16-2. The results have ranged widely and so far should be viewed as controversial. Methodological issues remain to be resolved and empirical estimation of labor supply is as yet in an early stage. At one end of the scale it is estimated that the deadweight loss of the average tax dollar on labor income ranges from 7 to 28 percent, with 15 percent a likely middle figure. As may be expected, the deadweight loss imposed by the marginal tax dollar is substantially larger and may be a multiple of the average figure.[24] The loss ratio also differs for particular

---

[24] See the references to E. K. Browning and J. A. Hausman at end of chapter.

workers. The ratio is higher for female than for male workers since the former have a higher elasticity of labor supply. Also, it is higher for upper income workers since they pay at a higher marginal rate.

At the other end of the scale, the validity of these high estimates has been questioned.[25] Workers in many settings are not flexible in their choice of hours. Transfer recipients at the lower end of the income scale may be out of work and cannot reduce their working time, and so forth. A more realistic appraisal of progressive taxation may call for comparison with a proportional rate rather than with a lump-sum tax. More recent trends toward earlier retirement may be a reflection of shifting patterns which began long before the move toward higher tax rates. For these and other reasons, estimates at the lower end of the scale suggest a level of excess burden substantially below that of the high range. Also, it must be recalled once more that the overall burden of taxation or tax-transfer processes cannot be determined without subsequent allowance for distributional weights.

E. FURTHER CONSIDERATIONS

It remains to note certain further considerations which qualify the deadweight loss analysis as usually applied.

Market Imperfections

The preceding analysis, dealing with tax-induced distortions and resulting efficiency costs, by its very nature assumed that the market itself operates in an efficient fashion. Where this is not the case, tax instruments (or regulation) may be used to offset and correct for such inefficiencies. Thus a tax which discriminates against monopoly profits or a tax which counters external costs may serve as a corrective device and thus pose efficiency gains rather than losses. This is not a major issue in the overall design of the tax structure but is nevertheless a consideration that should be noted in the context of this chapter.

Social Welfare Weights

Moreover, here as in other connections, distributional considerations must also be allowed for. The problem is not simply one of minimizing aggregate tax burden in absolute dollar terms. It must also be considered who would bear the burden, i.e., a social welfare function must again be introduced.[26] A dollar of revenue obtained from a tax on bread may cause a smaller deadweight loss than one obtained from a tax on caviar, but the two are likely to come to rest at different points on the income scale. After allowing for social welfare weights (or, to use more recent terminology, for the community's "equality aversion"), we may find that the latter burden is the lesser of the two. This further complicates the problem and qualifies the result obtained by efficiency analysis alone. Such is the case especially since it may well be that items of low-income consumption tend to be less elastic in demand and hence preferable in the context of minimizing deadweight loss.

---

[25] See reference to G. Buttless and R. Haveman at end of chapter.
[26] See p. 231.

Expenditure Analysis

Considerations similar to those here directed at taxation may also be applied to the expenditure side of the budget. Transfer payments or subsidies may be viewed as negative taxes and may be dealt with in a similar fashion. Transfers unrelated to income carry a negative income effect (recipients tend to work less) but no substitution effect and thus remain free of deadweight loss. Transfers relating negatively to income are opposite to the income tax in their income effect but like the income tax impose a substitution effect. As we noted in our earlier discussion of welfare programs, this effect is detrimental to work effort and imposes a deadweight loss.

Integration of public services into efficiency analysis is more difficult. To the extent that the tax-expenditure process succeeds in improving the choice of goods, including choice not only among private but also among social goods, it contributes to the efficiency of the economic process. Indeed, provision of certain public services is a precondition to the very functioning of society, including its ability to produce private goods. Deadweight losses result as a by-product of providing public services, since taxes are needed to pay for them and to solicit preference revelation. Deadweight losses thus raise the cost of public services and curtail their efficient level of provision; at the same time, efficient resource use requires that that level of provision should be forthcoming.

F. SUMMARY

Operation of the tax system is costly in that the burden exceeds what the government gets in revenue. This involves costs of tax administration and compliance as well as an excess burden which arises as conditions of efficient resource use are interfered with:

   1.   The cost of tax administration is small relative to the revenue obtained. Nevertheless, interesting problems arise with regard to how intensively tax administration should be conducted.
   2.   Compliance costs by taxpayers are substantially larger than are administration costs.

A more subtle problem of tax cost arises because taxes other than a lump-sum tax carry substitution effects which involve an excess burden. Taking a partial equilibrium approach, we compared various taxes and reached the following conclusions:

   3.   A selective consumption tax interferes with the choice between products, whereas a general consumption tax does not.
   4.   An income tax interferes with the choice between present and future consumption, whereas a general consumption tax does not.
   5.   An income tax and a general consumption tax both interfere with the choice between goods and leisure.
   6.   The excess burden imposed by a progressive income tax exceeds that of a proportional tax, because the excess burden depends upon the marginal or bracket rate.
   7.   A partial tax on capital income distorts investment choices.
   8.   Taking a general equilibrium with all choices flexible, we can no longer conclude that a general sales tax must be superior on efficiency grounds to a selective

product tax or that a general consumption (sales) tax must be superior to an income tax. Only a head tax imposes no excess burden.

9. An optimal set of product tax rates which minimize excess burden would stress the taxation of products that are price-inelastic and complementary to leisure.

10. Empirical measurements of the magnitude of efficiency costs is difficult, with estimates varying widely for different taxes and suggesting an overall burden equal to perhaps 15 percent of revenue for the average tax dollar and substantially higher for the marginal dollar.

11. The efficiency cost of transfers may be viewed in much the same way as that of an income tax if, as is the case under welfare programs, transfers fall as income rises.

12. In order to evaluate deadweight loss, social welfare weights should be applied to the dollar amounts.

13. Taxes used to correct for market imperfections may generate an efficiency gain.

14. With taxation needed for securing preference revelation for public services, deadweight loss may be viewed as a cost thereof.

FURTHER READINGS

On the concept of excess burden, see:

Harberger, A.: *Taxation and Welfare,* Boston: Little, Brown, 1974, chaps. 1–3, 8.

On the measurement of excess burden, see:

Browning, E. K.: "On the Marginal Welfare Cost of Taxation," *The American Economic Review,* March 1987.

Buttless, G., and R. Haveman, "Taxes and Transfers: How Much Economic Loss?," *Challenge,* March/April 1987.

Hausman, J. A., in H. Aaron and J. Pechman (eds.): *How Taxes Affect Economic Behavior,* Washington, D.C.: Brookings, 1981.

On the theory of optimal taxation, see:

Atkinson, A. B.: "How Progressive Should Income Tax Be?" in E. S. Phelps (ed.): *Economic Justice,* Baltimore: Penguin, 1973.

Atkinson, A., and J. E. Stiglitz: *Lectures on Public Economics,* Maidenhead: McGraw-Hill, 1980, chaps. 11–14.

Baumol, W. J., and D. F. Bradford, "Optimal Departure from Marginal Cost Pricing," *American Economic Review,* June 1970, pp. 265–283.

Bradford, D., and H. Rosen, "The Optimal Taxation of Commodities and Income," *American Economic Review,* Papers and Proceedings, May 1976.

Sandmo, A.: "Optimal Taxation—An Introduction to the Literature," *Journal of Public Economics,* July–August 1976.

For a broad-based evaluation of the tradeoff between equity and efficiency, see:

Okun, A. N.: *Equality and Efficiency: The Big Trade-Off,* Washington, D.C.: Brookings, 1975.

Tobin, J.: "On Limiting the Domain of Inequality," *Journal of Law and Economics,* October 1970.

Chapter 17

Taxation Effects
on Capacity Output:
A Supply-Side Perspective*

A. Effects on Work Effort: *Tax Effects; Expenditure Effects; Magnitude of Effects; Why Do Effects on Work Effort Matter?* **B. Effects on Private-Sector Saving:** *Composition of Private-Sector Saving; Household Saving; Business Saving; Conclusion.* **C. Effects on Private Investment:** *Nature of Investment Function; Profitability Effects; Loss Offset and the Return to Risk; Research and Development.* **D. Growth Effects and Tax Incidence. E. Summary.**

The preceding analysis dealt with taxation effects on the efficiency of resource use in the private sector. Now we turn to the effects on the *supply* of resource and the level of *capacity* output, i.e., the level of output or GNP which may be reached under conditions of full employment of labor and full utilization of capital stock. Whereas such supply-side effects are of minor importance in the short run, they may well be a major factor in determining economic growth over the longer pull. We assume for this purpose that the level of full-employment output is maintained

*Reader's Guide to Chapter 17: The effects of taxation on the functioning of the economy operate from both the demand and supply side. Leaving the former to Chapter 30, we here focus on the latter. This includes effects on work effort, saving, and investment and thereby on the level of output at full employment and on the growth rate of the economy. Although by no means a new problem, it thus fits into what in the 1980s has come to be referred to as "supply-side economics."

automatically, i.e., that aggregate demand neither falls short of nor exceeds the value of this output as measured at prevailing prices. By the same token it is assumed further that demand expands in line with capacity-output. Problems which arise if demand is deficient or excessive (thus creating unemployment or inflation) will be noted in a later chapter,[1] as will be the public sector's own contribution to capital formation.

The level of capacity output, or the size of total GNP, is of some interest in itself, but what matters for economic welfare is the level of output or income per person. With any given population size, total capacity output determines the feasible level of per capita income, so that output must grow if the standard of living is to rise. Over the years, per capita output has increased greatly, growing at an annual rate (corrected for price change) of about 2.5 percent during this century. Reflecting the powers of compound interest, output per head (again corrected for price change) is now about five times what it was in 1900. In addition, hours of work are substantially shorter, so that the total welfare gain has been even larger. Whereas the merits of economic growth came under critical scrutiny in the debate of the 1960s,[2] the pendulum thereafter again swung toward emphasis on growth. Whatever the urgency of continuing growth for high-income countries may be, it is evident that economic growth remains the only hope for escape from misery for the majority of the world's population in the less developed countries; and if adequate aid from high-income countries is to be forthcoming (as it should be and under the pressure of events will have to be), so must economic growth in the developed countries be maintained.

The major determinants of capacity output are the level of factor inputs—including natural resources, labor, and capital—and the state of technology or productivity with which resources are used. Since the supply of natural resources is more or less given by nature, the major determinants of GNP growth are the rates of growth of labor input and of the capital stock, and the speed of technical improvement. We begin with the effects of fiscal policy upon these variables in the private sector.

A.   EFFECTS ON WORK EFFORT

The effects of labor supply on economic growth are twofold. An increase in population results in an increase in output; but unless output rises at the same percent-

---

[1] See p. 499.

[2] This criticism involved a number of propositions which are frequently confused and must be separated to appraise the case for or against growth:

    1.   A first proposition is that an affluent society should spend more time on creative use of leisure than on increased output of goods. This may well be true but is not an argument against growth properly defined. A proper measure of growth should include both increased leisure time and increased goods.

    2.   A second proposition is that growth generates cost externalities such as pollution. This again is an argument not against growth but for a proper measure of growth in which external costs and benefits are accounted for. If growth is to occur, output must rise net of external costs.

    3.   A third and more difficult proposition is that mankind is not up to living comfortably but needs the discipline of poverty to keep out of trouble, i.e., paradise lost cannot be regained. Judge for yourself.

age rate as population, per capita income will fall. Population growth, therefore, may depress rather than increase per capita output. This outcome, of course, was the dismal fate which Thomas Malthus predicted some 175 years ago. Even though economic development in the industrial countries has managed to combine rising per capita income with rising population, the Malthusian specter still darkens the prospects of economic development in the less developed countries.

However this may be, fiscal instruments are not a major factor in population policy. Personal exemptions under the income tax, although related to family size, are hardly sufficient to enter into family planning, and expenditure programs for birth control are hardly within the realm of fiscal economics. Fiscal policy, however, enters the picture via effects on labor input with a given population. Changes in labor input—whether in hours worked or labor force participation—are positively related to the level of both total and per capita output.

Tax Effects

We begin with the effects of taxation on labor supply.

Income Tax The effects of the income tax on work effort are by no means obvious. The tax generates an "income effect" which is favorable to working more, so as to recoup lost income. But it also generates a substitution effect which works in the opposite direction. Since the reward for surrendering leisure is reduced, people will tend to work less. The net result depends on which of these two effects is stronger.

As shown in Figure 17-1, the wage rate prior to tax equals OA/OB and the worker may choose positions on the opportunity locus AB. He or she selects C, the point of tangency, with indifference curve i' and hours worked equal to DB. As a tax at wage rate AE/AO is imposed, the opportunity locus swivels down to EB and the taxpayer moves to F on indifference curve i''. Leisure is increased and work has fallen by DG. Suppose, however, that the slope of the lower indifference curve is as shown by $i''*$. In that case, the worker moves to H, with work rising and leisure falling by ID.[3] The former case reflects an upward slope in the labor supply schedule, whereas the latter reflects a backward-sloping schedule.

If the labor supply schedule is upward-sloping, as most textbooks draw it, the negative substitution effect outweighs the positive income effect and work effort is reduced. Yet seen in the historical perspective, it is evident that rising wage rates have been accompanied by reduced hours of work, i.e., a substantial part of the gains from productivity growth has been directed into increased leisure. Although this does not prove that the short-run supply schedule of labor is backward-sloping (in which case taxation would raise rather than lower the amount of labor supplied), it should not be readily assumed that an income tax must reduce effort. Even though we all seem to know someone who has been discouraged by taxation and has worked less, most of us seem to respond by working more.

---

[3] Both i'' and $i''*$ satisfy the condition that when moving vertically from i'' to i', the slope of i' must be constant or steeper, and when moving horizontally to the right, the slope of i' must be constant or less steep. This reflects the condition that the marginal rate of substitution of leisure for income falls as income rises relative to leisure.

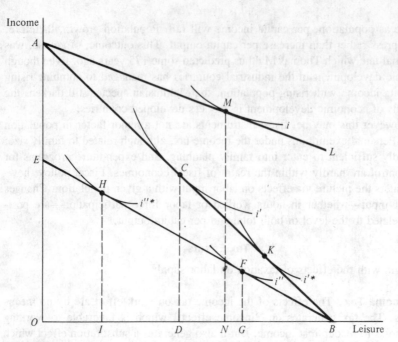

FIGURE 17-1   Taxation effect on work-leisure choice.

As noted before, much depends on the marginal rate of tax.[4] Any one person will work less under a progressive than under a proportional rate schedule if the same amount of tax is paid in both cases. Yet work effort for taxpayers as a group need not be lower under a progressive schedule. The net effect depends on how wage earners at various points on the income scale respond. Earners at the upper end (where rates will be higher than under a proportional tax of equal yield) have more flexibility in hours worked but may also be less responsive to changes in the net wage rate, since other forms of motivation (prestige, interest in work, etc.) may dominate. Employees at the lower end of the scale have less flexibility in their work effort responses and also face lower marginal rates of income tax.

The tax treatment of working wives also has an important bearing on labor force participation. In the absence of free child care centers and with inadequate allowance for deduction of child care expenses under the income tax, the net wage rate obtained by the working wife may be exceedingly low or negative so that there is little incentive (other than psychic income or a need to get out of the house) for entering the labor force. However, this impediment is reduced by allowance for a substantial child care credit.[5] A special deduction for two-earner couples, also favorable to work effort, was discontinued in 1986.

Sales Taxes   Effects on work effort are generated not only by the income tax but also by commodity or sales taxes which raise prices and thereby reduce the real wage rate. Such at least will be the case unless wage earners operate under a

---

[4] See p. 289.
[5] See p. 347.

"money illusion" and consider their money wage rate only. But will not the disincentive effects be less severe than under an income tax? After all, the worker may escape the consumption tax by saving, thereby avoiding such detrimental effects on work effort as may result from an income tax. Note, however, that the comparison must be between taxes of equal yield. Since the consumption base is smaller, the rate of consumption tax must be higher, and there is no ready way of predicting which will be more favorable to work effort. The question is whether leisure is traded more readily for present or for future consumption.

Turning to selective consumption taxes, we note that the work-leisure choice will be affected differently, depending on which types of commodities are taxed. If the tax rests on goods which are complementary to work (such as work clothing), effort will be retarded more than if the tax is on items (such as food) which are relatively neutral to the work-leisure choice. A tax on "leisure products" such as motorboats or vacation trips, on the other hand, will reduce the value of leisure, thereby reducing the opportunity cost of increased hours of work. With rising standards of living, an increasing share of income goes into the purchase of goods the consumption of which involves leisure time, so that taxation of leisure (through the taxation of leisure goods) becomes more feasible. The nature of leisure use thus becomes an important factor in tax analysis.

Expenditure Effects

Work incentives are affected not only from the tax but also from the expenditure side of the budget.

Transfer Payments Transfer payments may be treated as negative taxes. The income effect accordingly is now negative and goes to reduce effort. The direction of the substitution effect depends on whether transfers rise or fall with income. If they are related positively to income, as would be the case with a wage subsidy or the earned income credit, the wage rate in effect rises, yielding a positive substitution effect. Two opposing effects enter so that as in the tax case, the outcome is uncertain. Returning to Figure 17-1, we may now view EB as the pretransfer opportunity locus, with the worker at F. Introduction of the income subsidy swivels the locus to BA, and the response may involve a move to positions such as C or K.

The situation differs, however, if the transfer, as in the case of welfare payments, falls as income rises. A still negative income effect is then combined with a now negative substitution effect and hours fall. Defining now AB as a pretransfer locus, the transfer may be depicted as a swivel in the opportunity locus to AL, with the worker moving from C to M. Leisure also rises from OD to ON and work falls to NB.[6] This is the problem of detrimental work effort effects encountered in the context of welfare programs.[7]

Public Services Similar considerations also apply to the provision of public services. A general public service, such as the judicial system, has no particular bearing on the work-leisure choice, thus leaving a neutral substitution effect. This

[6] A shift to the left from C would contradict the condition of note 3 above.
[7] See p. 190.

effect may be negative, however, if the service is in support of leisure activity, such as improved road facilities to vacation sites; or it may be work-inducing if the service is in support of work activities, such as improved access to work locations. As per capita income rises, the latter type of service tends to increase, reflecting the community's rising preference for leisure.

Magnitude of Effects

As tax and expenditure effects are combined, the difficulty of predicting the net result further increases. In recent years studies have been undertaken, however, to measure the magnitude of the taxation effect upon labor supply.[8] These estimates differ by type of worker but, on the whole, are modest in magnitude. Thus it has been estimated that the income tax reduces average hours worked by married men by 8 percent and that most of this reduction would be eliminated by transition to a proportional rate with equal revenue.[9] At the same time, estimates show that the modest effect on labor supply hides a larger effect in terms of deadweight loss, because a substantial substitution effect (which causes the latter) is offset in part by the income effect. Estimates also show that the labor supply effect on women is larger, even though their labor force participation has increased substantially over the past two decades.[10] Finally, the studies suggest that the largest part of the problem does not arise in the context of the income tax but as a by-product of high marginal rates of tax which are implicit in the welfare system. As noted before, this is a major concern in the debate over welfare reform.[11]

Why Do Effects on Work Effort Matter?

Before leaving the timely issue of taxation effects on work effort, let us consider once more why these effects matter. The following four reasons may be put forth.

1. Substitution of leisure for goods in response to a progressive tax-transfer system may set an effective limit to redistribution.
2. Differences in leisure responses greatly complicate the analysis of just distribution.
3. Tax and expenditure policies which distort the choice between income and leisure impose an efficiency cost.
4. A tax-induced reduction in work effort reduces output and GNP.

Points 1 and 2 stand by themselves, but points 3 and 4 are easily confused. To distinguish between them, we note that the substitution of a wage subsidy which raises effort and output is no less burdensome in terms of efficiency cost than is that of an income tax which lowers them. Whereas in the tax case a larger reduction in work effort is associated with a higher efficiency cost, the efficiency cost of

[8] See p. 283.
[9] See Jerry A. Hausman, "Labor Supply," in Henry J. Aaron and Joseph A. Pechman (eds.): *How Taxes Affect Economic Behavior,* Washington, D.C.: Brookings, 1981; Sheldon Danziger, Robert Haveman, and Robert Plotnick, "How Income Transfer Affects Work, Saving, and Income Distribution," *Journal of Economic Literature,* vol. 19, no. 3, September, 1981; and J. Hausman and J. Poterba, "Household Behavior and the Tax Reform Act of 1986," *Economic Perspectives,* vol. 1, no. 1, 1987.
[10] See p. 292.
[11] See p. 190.

the subsidy will be the larger the more work is *increased*. High work effort, therefore, cannot be identified with low efficiency cost. Concern with point 4 in particular tends to be biased by the conventional definition of output which excludes leisure. Once leisure is included and properly valued, the distinction between 3 and 4 disappears.

B.   EFFECTS ON PRIVATE-SECTOR SAVING

Perhaps the major impact of fiscal policy upon capacity output is through its effect on saving and on capital formation. Since labor is more productive if it is combined with a larger capital stock, capital formation raises productivity. The larger the share of income which is saved and invested, the higher will the future level of income be. Thus, by influencing this share, fiscal policy has an important impact upon economic growth, i.e., the future level of per capita income. But economic growth has its costs. If the share of income which is currently used for capital formation is increased, that available for current consumption will be reduced. The policy problem is therefore one of choosing between present and future consumption. The terms on which this choice can be made have been the subject of much analysis during the past decade, and a brief review of the problem is given later on in this chapter. Here our concern is with the more immediate question of how saving and investment in the private sector are affected by fiscal measures.

Effects of tax policy upon saving in the private sector matter because (1) they bear on the division of resource use between consumption and capital formation and hence upon the growth of capacity output, and (2) they enter into the effects of fiscal policy upon the level of aggregate demand. Our present concern is with aspect 1 only, aspect 2 having been dealt with in earlier chapters.

Composition of Private-Sector Saving

Gross saving in the private sector, as shown in Table 17-1 for 1987, amounted to $672 billion, or 16 percent of GNP. A large part thereof, however, goes into capital consumption allowance or depreciation and is thus needed to maintain the existing capital stock.[12] Net savings available for addition thereto amounted to $193 billion, or 5 percent of GNP only. Nearly two-thirds of net savings in turn are household savings with corporate savings (in the form of undistributed profits) providing for only one-third thereof.

Household Saving

The division of household income into consumption and saving has received much attention by economists. At the heart of Keynesian economics and the genesis of modern macro theory was the proposition that consumption is a function of disposable income (i.e., income after tax). Since then, this relationship (referred to as the "consumption function") has proved more complex than had been thought ini-

---

[12] Since capital consumption allowances are entered as a financial charge against investment cost, they only approximate the decline in the value of capital assets. Note also that funds for replacement investment permit the use of new techniques, so that productive capacity may increase even though no net investment occurs.

TABLE 17-1
Sources of Private-Sector Saving, 1987
(In Billions of Dollars)

	Corporations	Personal*	Total
Gross saving	370	302	672
− Capital consumption allowances	296	183	479
Net	74	119	193

*Includes households and unincorporated enterprise.
Source: Survey of Current Business, March 1988, p. 10.

tially. Current consumption has been shown to depend not only on the level of current income but also of past and expected income. Moreover, not only is consumption a function of income, but other factors, such as the rate of interest and consumer wealth, also enter.

Household Saving as a Function of Income   Personal saving as a percentage of disposable income (i.e., personal income after personal taxes have been deducted) has ranged between 7 and 8 percent in the 1960s and 1970s but dropped to below 4 percent in the late 1980s. If all households saved at this same rate, the effect on personal saving of an income tax would be the same no matter how the tax bill was distributed among them. But in fact the fraction saved (the *average* propensity to save) rises as we move up the income scale. Thus, taxes collected from higher incomes may be expected to fall more heavily on saving than do those collected from lower incomes. The difference in the savings impact of more and of less progressive taxes, however, is less than one might think. The reason is that the difference in the consumption-savings impact of a dollar of tax paid by households at the $20,000 and the $100,000 levels of income depends on the differences in their respective *marginal,* and not their average, rates of saving; and though the average propensities to save differ sharply, the respective marginal propensities differ much less. Replacement of the present progressive income tax rate structure with a proportional rate tax (leaving exemptions unchanged) might be estimated to raise household saving no more than 10 percent. Based on differentials in the propensity to save, feasible tax structure changes are not likely to have a major effect on the savings rate of the economy.

Household Saving as a Function of the Rate of Return   Taxation effects on saving may result not only because the taxpayer's income is reduced but also because an income tax reduces the net rate of return on saving, thus lowering the rate at which the household can substitute future for present consumption. As a result, one may expect the savings rate to be reduced. The magnitude of the substitution effect is difficult to assess. However, as we will note presently, economists still debate about whether saving is highly elastic to the rate of interest. Indeed, not all households may budget their lifetime consumption so as to save more when the rate of return rises. If their saving is geared to reaching a set level of retirement income, they may, in fact, save less when the rate of return increases.

Consumption versus Income Tax A consumption tax tends to be more favorable to saving than an income tax, for various reasons:

1. Consumption taxes tend to be distributed regressively, whereas an income tax tends to be progressive in its distribution. With the marginal propensity to consume falling as income rises, the consumption tax (being paid more largely by lower-income households) thus has a heavier impact on consumption and a lighter impact on saving than does the income tax.

2. A consumption tax does not reduce the rate of return on saving and therefore avoids the substitution effect of the income tax, which is adverse to saving.

3. The superiority of the consumption tax in favoring saving is increased greatly under an expenditure tax, where the use of progressive rates would increase a tax penalty on the marginal dollar of consumption.

For these reasons, the use of consumption taxes has been especially advocated in developing countries where a higher rate of saving is necessary to expedite economic growth, but a similar case can be made for the U.S. economy.

Tax Incentives The income tax, as noted below, offers various savings incentives, including IRAs, Keogh, and 401K plans.[13] About half of personal savings flows through these channels that in large part may be expected to have been forthcoming even without such tax advantages. Incentives such as these may secure an addition to saving but primarily serve to divert savings from other forms, without raising net savings. Indeed, tax-deductible saving may be financed out of borrowing or be offset by consumer credit and mortgage finance. An expenditure tax with progressive rates, as we will see below, proves a more effective savings incentive than does preferential treatment under the income tax.

Business Saving

Depreciation Charges As noted in Table 17-1, much the larger part of business saving is in the form of capital consumption allowances or depreciation charges. Since the profits tax is imposed after the deduction of depreciation, depreciation reserves are not reduced by the profits tax. But their timing may be affected. If the law permits depreciation to be taken at an accelerated pace, tax payments are moved to a later date and depreciation reserves will be accumulated more rapidly. If the stream of depreciation is generated by a one-shot investment, this will be followed by reduced saving later on. But if a continuing stream of investment is considered, the tax, as we have noted earlier, may be postponed permanently and corporate saving may be raised on a continuing basis.[14]

Retained Earnings Provided that the profits tax is not shifted, after-tax profits are reduced by the tax. This reduction may in turn reduce corporate saving by lowering retained earnings, or it may be reflected in reduced dividends.

Over the past decade, dividends have been below 20 percent of corporate cash

---

[13] See p. 340.
[14] See p. 385.

flow (depreciation plus profits after tax) and around 30 percent of net profits after tax. Empirical studies of dividend behavior show dividends to be a function of current cash flow and past dividend levels. They suggest that the short-run impact of the corporate tax dollar on corporate saving might be as high as 75 percent, and the long-run impact might be of the order of 50 percent. The savings impact of the corporate tax dollar is thus substantially above that of most other taxes. A policy designed to foster saving, therefore, calls for restraint in the taxation of business profits.

Conclusion

Even though the magnitude of taxation effects on saving remains a matter of controversy, certain conclusions may be drawn. Suppose that the rate of net saving in the household sector were to be raised from, say, 4 to 6 percent of GNP, still much below that found to prevail in most other countries. Even drastic tax changes, including transition to an expenditure tax, could hardly meet this goal. Indeed, the decline in the savings rate of U.S. households from 7 percent in the 1950s, 1960s, and 1970s to below 4 percent in the 1980s occurred during falling levels of taxation and unusually high interest rates. The poor savings performance of U.S. households, compared with rates of over 20 percent in Japan and over 10 percent in most European countries, thus reflects structural factors in the economy, including consumer behavior and the ready availability of consumer credit rather than taxation effects.

C. EFFECTS ON PRIVATE INVESTMENT

Saving is a necessary condition for capital formation but it is not a sufficient one. Investors must also be willing to invest, and taxes once more enter into this decision.

Nature of Investment Function

The response of investors to taxation depends on the nature of the investment function. Even though theory tells us how investors should behave if they seek to maximize profits, it does not follow that this describes how real-life investors do in fact behave. They may wish to maximize sales or market shares rather than profits, or they may apply rules of thumb which do not conform closely with maximizing rules. Not only is the theoretical framework controversial, but empirical testing is difficult. Statistical dependence of investment on changes in sales, for instance, may be taken to suggest that investment responds to capacity needs, or that sales serve as a proxy for profit expectations. Empirical findings support both views, but the distinction is crucial for assessing tax effects.

To assess the investment effects of taxation, a model of investment behavior must be specified. Three major approaches may be noted:

    1.   Investment is expressed as a function of the expected net rate of return.
    2.   Investment is considered a function of past changes in sales and of existing capacity in relation to sales.
    3.   Investment is taken to be a function of the availability of internal funds, including after-tax profits and depreciation charges.

All approaches seem reasonable on a priori grounds and actual behavior may be determined as a combination of the three. According to approach 1, which reflects the hypothesis of profit-maximizing behavior, investors will invest up to a point where the present value of the expected income stream equals cost. The profits tax here enters by reducing the expected net rate of return. According to approach 2, investment responds to the need for increased capacity generated by past increases in sales, the so-called accelerator effect. Here the major impact of taxation is through its effects on sales, including sales to consumers and to government. According to approach 3, where the willingness to invest is conditioned on the availability of internal funds, taxation enters via its effects on the flow of such funds, whether it is in the form of depreciation reserves or retained earnings.

Profitability Effects

Since economic analysis is typically based on approach 1, we must take a closer look at tax effects on the profitability of investment or the net (after-tax) rate of return. Given an economy where full employment is maintained automatically, the levels of investment and saving are determined by the intersection of the investment and saving schedules, with investment determined as a function of the rate of interest and saving dependent on both income and the rate of interest. The model is illustrated in Figure 17-2, where II is the investment schedule showing the available rates of return as investment proceeds at various levels (annual rates) and SS shows the supply of saving (out of full-employment income) at various rates of interest. Before tax, the two are equated at an interest rate OB and investment and saving equal OA.

Required Return with Tax   Now a profit tax at rate DE/DO is imposed. As a result, the investment schedule expressed in terms of net rates of return swivels downward as shown by $I'I'$. In the new equilibrium, the gross rate of interest rises to OD, the net rate falls to OE, and investment and saving shrink to OC. As may

FIGURE 17-2   Tax effects on investment.

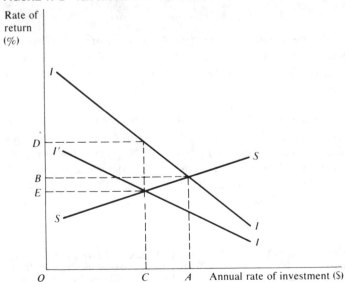

be seen from the figure, the decline in investment will be the larger the more elastic are both the *SS* and *II* schedules.

In line with our later discussion, we note that the tax rate *DE/DO* is a function not simply of the statutory rate of tax, but also of the speed with which depreciation may be taken.[15] Both enter into the effective rate of tax and the resulting reduction in the net rate of return.

The same story may be told algebraically as follows. In the absence of tax, investors will carry investment to the point where

$$r_g = i + d \tag{1}$$

where r_g = gross rate of return
$\quad i$ = cost of borrowing
$\quad d$ = stream of depreciation needed to recover capital

The rate of return must be sufficient to match the market rate of interest plus depreciation, with the right side of the equation also referred to as the rental cost of capital. After a tax is introduced, this becomes

$$r_g - (tr_g - t_d) = i + d - c \tag{2}$$

where the left side now expresses the after-tax or net rate of return. The tax, shown in parentheses, includes two terms, with tr_g showing what the tax would be if no depreciation were allowed and t_d deducting the tax saving which results because depreciation allowable at rate $_d$ can be taken. The value of t_d depends upon the rate at which depreciation is allowed as given by $_d$. Moreover, the required rate of return is reduced by the rate of investment credit c. Equation (2) may also be written as

$$r_g = \frac{i + d - t_d - c}{1 - t} \tag{3}$$

with the right side being the rental cost of capital in the presence of tax.[16] Whereas it has become customary to show the tax as increasing rental cost in line with equation (3), it may also be viewed, and more simply so, as a reduction in the rate of return in line with equation (2).

Comparison of Incentives   For additional investments to become eligible, the Treasury must reduce the rental cost of capital. As will be seen from equation (3), this may be accomplished by reducing t or by raising $_d$ and c. For any given investment, there will be values of t, $_d$ and c which are equivalent in giving the same reduction in the required level of r_g. They will thus give the same investment incentive. Since the Treasury loses (in terms of present value of revenue forgone)

---

[15] See p. 381.
[16] For further discussion, see Dale W. Jorgenson, "Capital Theory and Investment Behavior," *American Economic Review*, May 1963. Also see Dale W. Jorgenson, "Econometric Studies of Investment Behavior: A Survey," *Journal of Economic Literature*, December 1971; and Gary Fromm (ed.), *Tax Incentives and Capital Spending*, Washington, D.C.: Brookings, 1971.

what the taxpayer gains, it would seem a matter of indifference which of the approaches is chosen. In a realistic setting, this is, however, not the case:

1. The change in $_d$ and c can readily be limited to new investment and that in t cannot. Since tax relief for old investment has no pay-off in incentive terms, a greater incentive can be given (for an equal revenue loss) by adjusting $_d$ or c.

2. An increase in c involves a larger immediate revenue loss to the Treasury than does an equivalent increase in $_d$. Whereas the present value of the revenue loss to Treasury and investor are identical if both use the same discount rate, the Treasury may use a lower rate so that raising $_d$ is less costly. However, given imperfect credit markets and preference for internal finance, some investors may prefer an increase in c.

3. Most important, the various adjustments have different effects on different types of investment. As we have seen earlier, the speeding up of depreciation favors long investments while the investment credit favors short investments, with only the combination of initial allowance and economic depreciation yielding a neutral result. Lest the gain of increased investment be offset by the inefficiencies of investment distortions,the latter approach is clearly superior.

Loss Offset and the Return to Risk

The investment response, as given in Figure 17-2, is straightforward but it oversimplifies matters. Investment is not a safe bet with a guaranteed return but rather a risky venture which may or may not pay off. The rate of return as shown on the *II* schedule is thus based upon a range of probable returns and may be taken to reflect the expected value of this probability distribution.[17]

An investor in search of income who surrenders his liquidity and purchases

---

[17] If $q_1, q_2, \ldots, q_n$ are expected rates of return (positive and negative) and $p_1, p_2, \ldots, p_n$ the respective probabilities of their occurrence, so that $\sum_{i=1}^{n} p_i = 1$, we have

$$y = \sum_{i=1}^{n} q_i \, p_i$$

where y is the mathematical expectation of the percentage yield. This may be divided into a positive part and a negative part, such that

$$y = g - r$$

where g is the expected value of the positive part of the distribution and r is the absolute expected value of the negative part.

If we think of the return on investment α as a return on risk taking, we may write this as

$$\alpha = \frac{g - r}{r}$$

A tax without loss offset reduces this to

$$\alpha = \frac{(1 - t)(g - r)}{r}$$

whereas under a tax with loss offset, it becomes

$$\alpha = \frac{(1 - t)(g - r)}{(1 - t)r} = \frac{g - r}{r}$$

thus leaving the return on risk taking unchanged.

real assets (or equity therein by buying shares) undertakes a risk. He may get his money back with a substantial return or he may lose all or part of it. To make an investment means to gamble, and the investor should be interested in the gamble only if the value of probable gains outweighs that of probable losses. Since the investor's marginal utility of income may be expected to decline, an even-money (fifty-fifty) bet is not acceptable. If the tax worsens the odds by reducing the expected return, investment will fall. However, it is not at all obvious that the tax really reduces the odds. A tax will reduce the investor's return if he wins, but provided that loss offset is allowed for, it will also reduce his loss if he loses. Given a proportional tax, both probable gains and probable losses will be reduced at the same rate. Depending on the circumstances of the case, the tax may induce him either to increase or to reduce his risk taking.[18]

The possibility of increased risk taking is shown in Figure 17-3 where the rate of return is measured on the vertical axis and risk is shown on the horizontal axis.[19] To simplify, suppose that the investor chooses between holding cash (which we assume to be completely safe) and a single alternative, say a corporate bond, of given risk.[20] The opportunity line OA shows the combinations of risk and return available to him by choosing different mixes of cash and bonds. With 100 percent cash holding, he will be located at O where he incurs zero risk and receives a zero return. If all his funds are invested in bonds, he will be located at B, with risk OC and return OD. Each indifference curve shows combinations of risk and return which are equally satisfactory to him, with i_2 superior to i_1 and i_3 superior to i_2.[21] Before tax, the investor places himself at E_1, the point of tangency of the opportunity line OA with the highest available indifference curve i_2. His risk equals OF and his return equals OG.

Now a 50 percent tax is imposed and we assume that full loss offset is assured. If the investor does not change his portfolio mix, he will now find himself with half the risk and half the return that he had before, i.e., in a position similar to that provided by portfolio mix H prior to tax. Since prior to tax, he would have improved his position by moving from H to tangency point E_1, he will now choose to move from E_1 to K. At K his gross risk and return have doubled but his net risk and return are what they were at E_1 before imposition of the tax. Although his private risk taking has remained unchanged, total risk taking, as seen from the point of view of the economy as a whole, has increased. The government has become a partner, because it takes half the return and assumes half the risk. This sequence

---

[18] The significance of changes in the level of risk taking may be interpreted in two ways. If reduced risk taking involves the choice of less risky industries while holding total investment constant, the rate of growth may decline, since more risky investments may have a higher potential for raising productivity. If reduced risk taking means the choice of a portfolio with a larger cash component, the effect may be to reduce the level of aggregate demand, thereby stepping outside the "classical" system and causing unemployment.

[19] Figure 17-3 follows James Tobin, "Liquidity Preference as Behavior toward Risk," *Review of Economic Studies,* February 1958.

[20] A convenient measure of risk is the standard deviation of probable gains and losses, but certain other measures of dispersion will do as well.

[21] The indifference curves are drawn so as to show increasing risk aversion. Successive increases in risk call for rising additions to the rate of return if the investor is to remain equally well off. This follows from the assumption that the utility of income schedule rises at a decreasing rate as income increases.

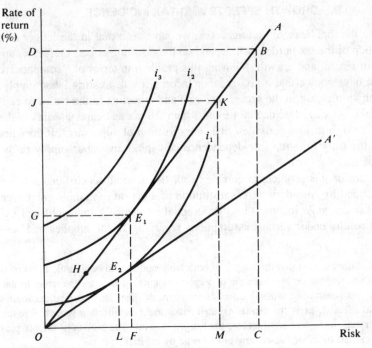

FIGURE 17-3 Taxation and risk taking.

comes about because loss offset is permitted. Without loss offset, the tax would swivel the opportunity line from *OA* to *OA'* and the new equilibrium would be at a tangency point E_2, with risk taking decreased to *OL*.

This illustration shows that under certain conditions, a tax with loss offset will *increase* risk taking. This somewhat startling result is here obtained on the basis of rather simplifying assumptions, but it continues to hold under a more sophisticated approach. The investment choice is not simply one between cash (assumed to be riskless) and one risky asset. Inflation renders cash holdings risky, and choices among alternative risky assets must be allowed for. The outcome then depends on the precise nature of the investor's preferences or the shape of his indifference curves. The net result may be either to increase or to reduce risk taking, and no simple generalization regarding the outcome is possible.[22]

Research and Development

Since the advance of productivity depends upon technological progress as well as the growth of capital stock, the tax treatment of research and development expenditure is of special importance. Such outlays may be expensed, i.e., they may be deducted in the initial year even though they are largely in the nature of investment outlays.

---

[22] For further discussion, see Martin S. Feldstein, "The Effects of Taxation on Risk Taking," *Journal of Political Economy*, September–October 1969; and J. E. Stiglitz, "The Effects of Income, Wealth and Capital Gains Taxation on Risk Taking," *Quarterly Journal of Economics*, May 1969.

D.   GROWTH EFFECTS AND TAX INCIDENCE

In discussing the incidence of various taxes, we have seen that in the longer run, the distribution of the tax burden will depend on the resulting effects on factor supplies, rates of return, and growth. Viewing this problem in terms of "comparative statics," we have shown that a tax on labor income, by depressing labor supply, may result in an increase in the gross wage rate and a decline in the return to capital, so that the net wage rate declines by less than the tax and capital shares in the burden.[23] Although this properly describes the direction of adjustment, it does not account for the truly long-run interdependence of capital and labor supply in the context of balanced growth.

The nature of this problem is complex, but the general conclusions reached may be described by considering the substitution of a tax on capital income for an equal-yield tax on wage income (the "differential incidence" approach) and examining the results under various assumptions regarding factor supplies and savings rates.

1.   Suppose first that the supply of both labor and capital is inelastic to the rate of return and that the savings rates out of wage and capital income are the same. In this case, our tax substitution will not affect factor supplies. The rate of capital accumulation is unaffected, as is the capital-to-labor ratio under equilibrium growth. Pre-tax rates of return to factors are therefore unchanged as well. The burden of the tax previously carried by labor comes now to be borne by capital.

2.   Next suppose that the supply of labor is elastic, while retaining the other assumptions. As the tax on capital income is substituted for the tax on wage income, labor supply increases. Our earlier discussion, based on a comparative-static approach, suggested that the tax substitution, by increasing the net wage rate, would result in an increase in hours worked. This in turn would reduce the gross wage rate and increase the return to capital, so that part of the burden would continue to be shared by labor. But this will not occur in the context of a balanced-growth model, where there will again be a full transfer of the burden to capital. The increase in hours worked will not affect the long-run growth rate of labor supply, which will still be determined by population growth; and, as may be seen from the determinants of economic growth, it is the rate of population growth which determines the equilibrium rate of income growth. Since we assume that the propensity to save is the same for capital and labor income, there will also be no change in the growth of the capital stock. With the capital-to-labor ratio in equilibrium growth unchanged, the pre-tax rates of return to capital and labor will also be unaffected. With the tax on labor income replaced by a tax on capital income, the burden is thus transferred from labor to capital.

3.   The situation differs, however, if the supply of capital is elastic to the rate of return. As a result, the substitution of a tax on capital income reduces capital accumulation. While the growth rate of income remains unaffected (as it is still determined by the growth of population), the equilibrium capital-to-labor ratio will now be lower. Because of this, the pre-tax rate of return to capital will be increased while that to labor

---

[23] See Martin Feldstein, "Tax Incidence in a Growth Economy with Variable Factor Supply," *Quarterly Journal of Economics,* November 1974; and Martin Feldstein, "Incidence of a Capital Income Tax in a Growth Economy with Variable Savings Rates," *Review of Economic Studies,* 1974; and Marian Krzyzaniak, "The Long-Run Burden of a General Tax on Profits in a Neo-Classical World," *Public Finance,* no. 4, 1967.

will be reduced. Only part of the tax burden is transferred and labor shares part of the profits tax burden.

4. Finally, consider a situation where both factor supplies are inelastic to the rate of return but where the savings rate out of capital income is higher than that out of labor income. Replacement of a tax on wage income by a tax on capital income now results in a reduced rate of capital formation and changes similar to those under situation 3 result. Once more, labor bears part of the burden of a tax on capital income. Putting situations 3 and 4 together, we conclude that the remaining share of the tax burden borne by labor will be the larger (*a*) the more elastic the supply of capital relative to that of labor and (*b*) the higher the savings rate out of capital income relative to that out of labor income.

Although the tax effects involved in these relationships are complex and depend on the underlying structure of the growth model, it is not unreasonable to assume that, say, one-third of the burden of a tax on capital income comes to be borne by labor. This reasoning, it must be noted, pertains to the very long-run result after the return to balanced growth has taken place. Given the very long time period involved,[24] the more limited approach of the comparative-static type of analysis may be more relevant for policy purposes. In this setting, elasticity of labor supply does matter, and the slower process of changes in capital accumulation due to different savings rates will be of less importance.

E. SUMMARY

In this chapter, various effects of fiscal measures on the level of capacity output were considered. They may operate through effects on work effort, saving, and investment. Beginning with effects on work effort, we concluded:

1. An income tax may reduce or increase work effort, depending on whether the substitution effect outweighs the income effect, or vice versa.

2. There is no ready way of telling whether the level of work effort will be higher under an income tax or under a consumption tax.

3. Transfer payments which are related positively to income generate conflicting income and substitution effects but opposite to those of an income tax, with the net outcome again in doubt.

4. Transfer payments which are related negatively to income will reduce effort.

5. The same negative result tends to hold for free provision of social goods.

6. A distinction must be drawn between resulting excess burden and resulting changes in work effort.

In considering effects on the level of saving, we drew a distinction between household savings and savings by businesses:

7. Household saving as a percentage of income (the average propensity to save) rises with income, but the marginal propensity to save rises less. Since differences in the savings impact of more or less progressive taxes depend on differences in the marginal propensities, they are less important than one might expect.

---

[24] See Ryuzo Sato, "Fiscal Policy in a Neo-Classical Growth Model: An Analysis of Time Required for an Equilibrium Adjustment," *Review of Economic Studies*, February 1963.

8. Income taxes may also affect saving because they reduce the net rate of return.

9. A consumption tax tends to fall less heavily on saving than does an income tax.

10. A large part of the corporation tax tends to be reflected in reduced corporate saving.

The effects of taxation on investment may operate in a number of ways, including their impact on profitability and the availability of internal funds:

11. A profits tax tends to reduce the level of investment by reducing the net rate of return.

12. Investment may be stimulated by reducing the rate of tax, speeding up depreciation, or granting an investment credit. To avoid distortion, the stimulus is best given by an initial allowance combined with economic depreciation for the remainder.

13. If that full-loss offset is assured, the tax may raise or reduce the return to risk taking.

14. Tax policy encourages technological progress by permitting research and development expenditures to be expensed.

FURTHER READINGS

Aaron, Henry J., and Joseph A. Pechman (eds.): *How Taxes Affect Economic Behavior*, Washington, D.C.: Brookings, 1981.

Feldstein, Martin: *Capital Taxation*, Cambridge, Mass.: Harvard University Press, 1983.

Jorgenson, Dale W.: "Capital Theory and Investment Behaviour," *American Economic Review*, May 1963.

Part Five

Tax Structure

Chapter 18

Development and Composition of United States Tax Structure*

A. Development of U.S. Tax Structure: *Federal Level; State Level; Local Level; All Levels*. **B. Comparison with Other Countries. C. Summary.**

Economic analysis has much to contribute to our understanding of how taxation works and how it affects the economy. As we have seen in the preceding chapters, some important conclusions may be drawn regarding the incidence or burden of various major types of taxes. But much depends on how particular taxes are designed in detail and on how the tax structure is fitted into the highly complex set of economic institutions in which it must operate. Concern with this question is the subject matter of Part Five of our study.

A. DEVELOPMENT OF U.S. TAX STRUCTURE

Paralleling the growth in public expenditures, the overall level of taxation as shown in Table 18-1 has risen substantially in recent decades. The picture (see line 4 of

---

*Reader's Guide to Chapter 18: A brief survey of how the U.S. tax structure has developed since the beginning of the century.

TABLE 18-1
Development of United States Tax Structure*

	1902	1913	1922	1927	1940	1950	1960	1970	1986
I. TAX REVENUE AS PERCENT OF GNP									
1. Federal	2.3	1.7	4.6	3.6	5.7	13.6	18.2	19.8	19.7
2. State	0.7	0.8	1.4	1.8	4.4	3.4	4.5	6.0	6.5
3. Local	3.2	3.3	4.2	4.7	4.5	2.9	3.8	4.2	4.1
4. Total	6.2	5.8	10.2	10.1	14.5	19.9	26.5	30.0	30.3
II. PERCENTAGE COMPOSITION OF TAX REVENUE									
Federal									
5. Individual income tax	—	—	56.8	25.6	16.9	40.7	45.4	48.1	42.6
6. Corporation income tax		5.3	(56.8)	36.6	19.8	27.1	24.0	17.5	6.8
7. Sales and excises	47.6	45.6	24.4	14.6	31.6	19.2	12.8	8.4	4.8
8. Customs duties	47.4	46.8	9.3	17.0	5.8	1.1	1.2	1.3	1.7
9. Death and gift	1.0	—	4.1	2.6	6.3	1.8	1.8	1.9	0.8
10. Payroll	—	—	1.2	2.1	14.2	9.0	14.2	22.3	40.0
11. Other	4.1	2.3	4.2	1.4	5.5	1.1	0.7	0.5	0.7
12. Total	100.0	100.0	100.0	100.0	100.0	100.0	100.0	100.0	100.0
State									
13. Individual income tax	—	—	4.1	4.0	4.7	7.4	9.9	16.0	24.9
14. Corporation income tax	—	—	5.5	5.3	3.5	6.0	5.3	6.5	6.8
15. Sales and excises	17.9	19.9	27.2	42.8	51.0	55.6	54.0	52.2	48.7
16. Property tax	52.6	46.5	33.0	21.2	5.9	3.1	2.7	1.9	2.2
17. Payroll	—	—	10.1	7.9	24.5	18.8	19.4	16.4	14.4
18. Death and gift	29.5	33.6	20.1	18.9	10.3	9.1	1.9	1.7	3.2
19. Other	—	—	—	—	—	—	6.9	5.2	—
20. Total	100.0	100.0	100.0	100.0	100.0	100.0	100.0	100.0	100.0
Local									
21. Individual income tax	—	—	—	—	—	0.8	1.3	1.4	4.0
22. Corporation income tax	—	—	—	—	—	0.1	(1.3)	(1.4)	1.1
23. Sales and excises	—	0.2	0.6	0.6	2.8	5.9	7.7	8.1	26.9
24. Property	—	91.0	96.4	96.8	91.3	86.2	85.0	82.1	62.3
25. Payroll	—	0.2	0.5	0.6	1.5	2.3	2.9	3.2	2.8
26. Other	11.4	8.6	2.5	2.1	3.9	4.7	3.0	2.5	2.9
27. Total	100.0	100.0	100.0	100.0	100.0	100.0	100.0	100.0	100.0
All Levels									
28. Individual income tax	—	1.5	27.0	9.8	8.1	29.3	33.0	35.4	33.5
29. Corporation income tax	—	(1.5)	(27.0)	13.9	8.7	19.6	17.3	12.8	8.2
30. Sales and excises	19.8	16.1	15.1	13.2	28.5	23.6	19.1	17.2	17.0
31. Customs duties	17.7	13.6	4.2	6.0	2.3	0.7	0.8	0.9	1.1
32. Property	51.4	58.6	44.0	48.8	30.3	13.0	12.7	11.9	8.9
33. Payroll	—	0.1	2.1	2.4	13.3	9.7	13.4	18.5	29.2
34. Death and gift	11.1	10.1	7.5	5.8	8.9	4.2	1.5	1.6	0.8
35. Other	—	—	—	—	—	—	2.1	1.7	0.1
36. Total	100.0	100.0	100.0	100.0	100.0	100.0	100.0	100.0	100.0

TABLE 18-1 *(Continued)*
Development of United States Tax Structure*

	1902	1913	1922	1927	1940	1950	1960	1970	1986
				III. LEVELS AS PERCENT OF TOTAL					
37. Federal	37.4	29.1	45.2	35.5	38.8	68.3	68.5	65.8	64.8
38. State	11.4	13.2	13.9	18.0	30.0	17.3	17.1	20.1	21.5
39. Local	51.3	57.6	40.9	46.5	31.2	14.4	14.5	14.1	13.7
40. Total	100.0	100.0	100.0	100.0	100.0	100.0	100.0	100.0	100.0

*Calendar years through 1950, fiscal years 1960 on. Detail may not add to total due to rounding. Local motor vehicle and operator's licenses included in "other" to 1950 and in sales taxes thereafter.
Sources: 1902–1950: U.S. Bureau of the Census, *Historical Statistics for the United States: Colonial Times to 1957*, pp. 724, 727, 729. 1960, 1970, and 1975: U.S. Bureau of the Census, *Governmental Finances*, 1959–60, 1969–70, and 1974–75. 1986: See *Survey of Current Business*, July 1987. State-Local breakdown estimated.

the table) is similar to that of Table 8-2, where expenditure growth was shown. As with expenditures, the growth of tax revenue must be seen in relation to that of GNP and not in absolute terms. Omitting the temporary wartime peaks, we note that tax revenue as percent of GNP hovered around 6 percent in the first two decades of the century and around 10 percent during the twenties. By 1940, the level had risen to nearly 15 percent. In each of the following three decades the ratio was to rise by about five percentage points, reaching 20 percent in 1950, 26 percent in 1960, 30 percent by 1970, 34 percent by the end of the decade and falling off somewhat thereafter. The causes of increase are similar to those underlying the development of the expenditure side and need not be restated. Instead, we now focus on the major changes in the composition of the tax structure which accompanied this overall growth. For this purpose, it is useful to begin with a separate view of the various levels of government before proceeding to the overall picture.

Federal Level

Throughout the nineteenth century, much the larger part of federal revenue was drawn from customs duties. Even in this century, we find an almost exclusive reliance on indirect taxes up to World War I, with revenue divided about equally between customs duties and domestic excises (see lines 5 through 12 of Table 18-1). The introduction of the Sixteenth Amendment in 1913 opened the way for income taxation, and by the early twenties income taxes had come to supply nearly 60 percent of federal revenue. Excises had declined in relative importance, and customs duties had become only a minor item. The increase in the ratio of total federal revenue to GNP (line 1) was met largely by the introduction of federal income taxes, with the corporation tax leading the individual income tax.

The relative importance of the income taxes continued to rise slowly during the twenties while the excise tax share declined. This trend was reversed in the Depression years of the thirties, when excise rates were raised in a futile attempt to balance the budget, and revenue from the income taxes suffered from the decline in national income. The late thirties also brought the advent of payroll taxes associated with the creation of the social security system.

World War II finance brought the second major expansion of income taxation and of the individual income tax in particular. Over the decade of the 1940s, the individual income tax share rose from 17 to 41 percent of federal revenue while the corporation income tax share increased from 20 to 27 percent. The ratio of federal tax revenue to GNP doubled in this period, and the ratio of individual income tax to GNP rose from 1 to 6 percent. In the process, this tax was transformed from a tax on the rich, paid by a small fraction of high-income recipients, to a mass tax paid by almost all income earners. The number of income taxpayers rose from 7 million in 1939 to 50 million in 1945 and came to include 98 percent of all those employed.

The fifties brought a further sharp rise in the ratio of federal tax to GNP. Accounted for largely by increased payroll taxation, it resulted in a declining share of revenue from other taxes, with only the individual income tax showing further gain. During the sixties, the growth in the overall federal tax-to-GNP ratio had slowed down. While the payroll tax ratio continued to rise, making it the second most important tax in the system, the shares of the corporation income tax and of excises declined sharply. Notwithstanding these changes, the individual income tax has remained the largest component, contributing 43 percent of the 1986 total. Payroll taxes are next with nearly 40 percent, followed by the corporation income tax with 7 percent. Indirect taxes provided only 4 percent. This highly income- and payroll-tax-intensive revenue structure stands in sharp contrast to the earlier federal tax system with its heavy reliance on customs duties and indirect taxes. While the transformation of the income tax into a mass tax and subsequent developments in rate structure and tax base have rendered it less progressive, it is still *the* major progressive component of the tax system.[1] It is not surprising, then, that the predominance of the individual income tax continues to render income tax reform one of the most lively aspects of federal tax policy. The corporation profits tax, on the other hand, has been in steady decline over the last three decades and now contributes little over 10 percent of federal revenue.

Since the 1950s, the most striking development has been the increase in the payroll tax share, reaching 40 percent of the total by 1986. Taken by itself, this tax is regressive, so that its rise has tended to offset the progressive impact of the income tax. It should be noted, however, that the rise of the payroll tax has been paralleled by an increase in social security benefits. As we will see later, this raises the question of whether the burden of this tax should be considered by itself or in conjunction with the benefits which it finances.

State Level

At the state level, the major development over the first half of the century (see lines 13 to 20 of Table 18-1) was the dwindling of the property tax share from 53 to 1 percent, and a rise in the importance of sales and gross receipts taxes, particularly retail sales and gasoline taxes. Owing to the preponderance of these taxes, state taxation, as was noted earlier, is less progressive and may even be regressive in its distributional impact. This traditional pattern has, however, been subject to

---

[1] A tax is said to be regressive, proportional, or progressive depending on whether the ratio of tax revenue to income falls, remains constant, or rises as we move up the income scale. See p. 536.

change. Line 13 shows a substantial rise in the share of the individual income tax over the past two decades, as well as a decline in the general sales and excise tax share. These developments have not been sufficient, however, to reverse the highly sales-tax-intensive nature of state taxation.

Local Level

The ratio of local tax revenue to GNP, as shown in line 3 of Table 18-1, has remained fairly stable over the decades, as has its ratio to GNP. Local taxation has traditionally been almost entirely a property-tax system. As shown in lines 21 to 27, the property tax provided up to 90 percent of local tax revenue up to World War II with a sharp drop in recent years. This reflects an increase in the use of sales and income taxes in recent decades, especially in urban jurisdictions, but it still remains a relatively minor factor in the overall picture. As we will see later, the distributional impact of the property tax is not easily assessed, leaving it a matter of contention whether the local tax structure is progressive or regressive.[2]

All Levels

The changing composition of the combined tax structure—which is what matters for overall tax policy—reflects both changes at each level and their changing weights in the total picture. As shown in lines 37 to 40 of Table 18-1, the federal share was relatively stable at 30 to 40 percent of the total from 1900 to 1940 but rose sharply during the forties, reaching 68 percent in 1950 and settling at about two-thirds thereafter. The state share, at 17 percent by 1950, since then rose to 23 percent, while the local share continued to decline. Whereas state and local taxation accounted for over two-thirds of the total prior to World War II, by 1960 it had dropped to little more than 30 percent. The overall picture has thus been one of increasing centralization, with the federal share rising primarily at the cost of the local.

The historic trend toward revenue centralization made for heavier reliance on income and payroll taxation in the overall tax structure (lines 28 to 36). Whereas income taxes (individual and corporate) provided only 17 percent of total revenue in 1940, they now furnish 42 percent. Over the same period, the share of sales taxation fell from 28 to 17 percent, that of payroll taxes rose from 13 to 30 percent, and that of property taxes tumbled from 30 to 9 percent. These changes have left the United States with an overall tax structure which is highly income- and payroll-tax-intensive.

B. COMPARISON WITH OTHER COUNTRIES

As shown in Table 18-2, the U.S. tax structure is in line with the general pattern present in other advanced industrial countries. The overall level of U.S. taxation as viewed by the ratio of revenue to gross domestic product (GDP) is distinctly at the lower end of the scale (line 3).[3] This continues to be the case, although to a lesser

---

[2] See p. 419.
[3] The denominator in these ratios is GDP rather than GNP, as used in Table 18-1. GDP includes domestic output only, while excluding earnings from abroad.

TABLE 18-2
International Comparison of Tax Structure, 1978*
(All Levels of Government)

As Percentage of Total	Netherlands	Sweden	Norway	France	United Kingdom	Germany	Canada	United States	Australia	Japan
TAXES AS PERCENTAGE OF GDP										
1. Excluding payroll tax	28.6	35.4	40.1	24.2	30.6	24.6	29.5	22.6	30.9	18.5
2. Payroll tax	17.6	14.2	7.2	18.1	6.8	11.5	3.4	8.1	—	7.6
3. Total	46.2	49.6	47.3	42.3	37.4	36.1	32.9	30.7	30.9	26.1
INCOME TAXES AS PERCENTAGE OF GDP										
4. Personal income tax	12.2	20.3	16.1	5.5	10.9	11.2	11.2	11.3	13.5	6.3
5. Corporate income tax	3.0	1.2	6.3	2.1	2.3	2.0	3.4	3.1	3.4	4.5
6. Total income taxes	15.2	21.5	22.4	7.6	13.2	13.2	14.6	14.4	16.9	10.8
AS PERCENTAGE OF TOTAL TAX REVENUE										
7. Personal income tax	26.3	41.0	34.0	12.9	30.0	29.9	35.2	36.7	24.2	43.7
8. Corporation income tax	6.6	2.5	13.2	5.0	7.7	5.5	11.3	10.1	11.2	17.3
9. Property tax	3.4	0.9	1.7	3.6	12.1	2.6	9.2	10.0	8.3	8.2
10. Payroll tax	38.1	28.6	15.2	43.2	16.9	34.1	10.4	26.4	31.4	29.6
11. Product taxes	24.8	24.3	35.4	30.0	28.8	27.0	32.8	16.6	31.2	16.3
12. Total†	100.0	100.0	100.0	100.0	100.0	100.0	100.0	100.0	100.0	100.0

*Revenue Statistics of OECD Number Countries, 1965–1981, tables 4, 3, 10, 12, 11, 13, 23, 15, 16. Organization for Economic Cooperation and Development, Paris 1982.
†Includes items not specified.

degree, if payroll taxes are excluded (line 1). The pattern remains similar for the personal income tax (line 4), although prior to 1981 legislation the United States ranked with the higher countries with regard to the corporate tax (line 5).

The composition of tax structures, shown in lines 7 to 12, shows the U.S. system with a relatively high income tax share (lines 7 plus 8) and a low share of sales and excise (product) taxes (line 11). These differences reflect the structure of the various economies, e.g., the importance of the corporate sector in the United States, differences in the degree of fiscal centralization, and varying tax policies and attitudes.

C. SUMMARY

The U.S. structure has undergone major changes over the years, especially at the federal level:

    1. Before World War I, the federal tax system relied entirely on indirect taxes, with heavy emphasis on tariffs. Now the latter contribute only a very minor share of total revenue.

2. With World World II, the income tax became the major federal revenue source.

3. More recently, the payroll tax has come to contribute an important and increasing share of federal revenue.

4. State revenue, prior to the thirties, relied heavily on the property tax, but this tax then came to be reserved almost entirely for local use. Primary reliance of the states came to be on sales taxation, both general and selective. Since the sixties, income taxation also has come to play a major role.

5. Local taxation always has relied and still does rely very largely on the property tax.

6. The increase in the federal share in total tax revenue has been a major factor increasing the importance of income taxation in the overall revenue system.

A comparison of the U.S. tax system with that of other major countries shows that:

7. The overall level of taxation in the United States is comparatively low.

8. The U.S. system relies more on income and less on indirect taxes.

Chapter 19

Individual Income Tax: Defining Taxable Income*

A. Major Provisions: *Determining Taxable Income; Application of Bracket Rates; Payment Procedure.* **B. Structure of the Tax Base:** *Size Distribution of Tax Base; Distribution of Tax Base by Income Source.* **C. Principles of Income Definition:** *Gross Income versus Net Income; Capital Income versus Labor Income; Real Income versus Nominal Income; Accrued Income versus Realized Income; Imputed Income; Earnings versus Transfers; Bequests and Gifts; Regular versus Irregular Income.* **D. Practice of Income Definition: (1) Exclusions:** *Tax-Exempt Interest; Capital Gains; Savings and Pension Plans; Transfer Receipts.* **E. Practice of Income Definition: (2) Deductions:** *Rationale for Itemizing Deductions; Evaluation of Major Deductions.* **F. Practice of Income Definition: (3) Credits.** **G. Summary.**

The individual income tax is by far the most important single tax and the kingpin of the federal if not the entire U.S. tax structure. It is therefore the first tax to be considered and one to be dealt with at greater length. This is called for especially

Reader's Guide to Chapter 19: This is the first in a series of chapters dealing with the particulars of various taxes. The practically inclined reader will find these chapters of particular interest. The theorist in turn is urged to take them seriously, since little good can come of theorizing about the principles of taxation and its economic effects unless one knows the statutes and how they work. While studying the structure of the income tax, students are urged to examine the Individual Income Tax Return, Form 1040, and its major subschedules, and practice filling one out.

since the federal income tax underwent a major reform in 1986, perhaps the most significant overhaul since the early 1940s when it became the primary revenue source of World War II.

A.   MAJOR PROVISIONS

The basic principle of the U.S. individual income tax is that the taxpayer's income from all sources should be combined into a single or "global" measure of income. Total income is then reduced by certain exemptions and deductions to arrive at income subject to tax. This is the base to which tax rates are applied when computing tax.

Determining Taxable Income

The key concepts in the derivation of taxable income are thus adjusted gross income (AGI) and taxable income. The provisions given below are those which apply beginning in 1989, when the transition phase of the 1986 reform is completed.

Adjusted Gross Income   Income from all sources except those specifically excluded (see below) is combined to determine "total income." This includes wages, interest, dividends, rent, royalties, profits from unincorporated business operations, and so forth. From this certain "adjustments to income" are deducted to arrive at AGI. Although the resulting amount is referred to as adjusted *gross* income, such nomenclature is misleading since in the economist's language AGI reflects a *net* income concept, i.e., income net of costs incurred in earning that income. Unincorporated business income is included in AGI on a net basis, and adjustments are made for certain personal costs incurred in earning income (such as moving expenses and certain employee business expenses) before arriving at AGI. Even though AGI is meant to give a comprehensive measure of the taxpayer's income position, we will find that it falls far short of being as comprehensive as it should be. Noncash income (such as imputed rent and unrealized capital gains) is omitted and certain forms of cash income (such as most pension benefits) are specifically excluded.

Personal Exemptions   AGI thus determined is then reduced by the allowable amount of personal exemptions. These allow for $2,000 per taxpayer, spouse, and each dependent, or twice their pre-1986 level. The exemption for a single person thus equals $2,000; for spouses filing joint returns, $4,000; for a family of four, $8,000; and so forth, rising with the number of dependents. Beginning in 1989, these amounts are to be adjusted annually for inflation.

Deductions   The remainder is then given the benefit of a further amount of tax-free income, referred to as standard deduction. This amount equals $3,000 for single and $5,000 for joint returns, subject again to inflation adjustment. Instead of claiming this amount, taxpayers may choose to itemize their deductions. Among allowed itemized deductions, the most important are interest paid on mortgages, certain state and local taxes, and charitable contributions. Other deductible items

TABLE 19-1
Pattern of Bracket Rates*

Rate, Percent	Single Returns, $	Joint Returns, $
15	0 – 17,850	0 – 29,750
28	17,850 – 43,150	29,750 – 71,900
33	43,150 – 100,480	71,900 – 171,090
28	100,480 +	171,090 +

*Returns without dependents.

include unusually high medical expenses and casualty losses. However, usually only higher-income taxpayers choose to itemize, since for most taxpayers the standard deduction exceeds what could be claimed by itemizing. In all, nearly two-thirds of returns choose the standard deduction, whereas only one-third itemize.

Tax-free income thus equals exemptions and standard or itemized deductions. If the two are combined, the tax-free amount for single returns equals at least $5,000 and for joint returns $9,000. If two dependents are added to the latter, the tax-free amount is $13,000. These amounts are about in line with the definition of poverty income.

Application of Bracket Rates

Next the tax is computed by application of the rate schedule. This schedule is legislated in the form of marginal or bracket rates, applicable to successive slabs of income. Whereas prior to 1986 the law provided for fourteen bracket rates ranging from 11 to 50 percent, there are now only two basic rates of 15 and 28 percent. However, a 5 percent rate is added over a certain income range so that, as shown in Table 19-1, bracket rates first rise with successive slabs of income but then decline for the top slab. This arrangement is designed to "phase out" the benefits derived from the personal exemption and from the lower 15 percent rate applied to the first income bracket. Higher incomes are thus left with a flat rate of tax of 28 percent on AGI minus deductions. The rates shown in Table 19-1 apply for 1988 and, as noted below, will be adjusted for inflation thereafter.

As the above rules regarding exemptions, deductions, and bracket rates are applied, the picture given in Table 19-2 emerges. Lines 1 to 5 show AGI, exemptions, deductions, taxable income, and tax for a joint return without dependents.

TABLE 19-2
Pattern of Effective Rates
(Joint Return, No Dependents)

1. AGI	10,000	25,000	50,000	100,000	1,000,000
2. Exemptions	4,000	4,000	4,000	4,000	4,000
3. Deductions*	5,000	5,000	5,000	20,000	200,000
4. Taxable income	1,000	16,000	41,000	76,000	796,000
5. Tax	150	2,400	7,612	17,618	223,972
6. Tax as percentage of AGI	1.5	9.6	15.2	17.6	22.4

*Below $50,000 set at standard rate level, then assumed at 20 percent of AGI.

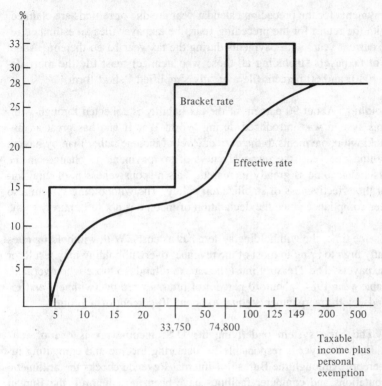

FIGURE 19-1   Bracket rates and effective rates (joint return, no dependents).

Line 6 shows the tax as percent of AGI, a ratio referred to as the effective rate. This rate rises sharply from a zero base over the lower to the middle income range, then flattens out moving toward the top bracket rate now at 28 percent. The main factor behind this pattern is the heavy weight of the personal exemption at the lower end of the income scale, which declines when moving up the income range. With the greatly flattened pattern of bracket rates under the tax reform of 1986, the rate graduation plays a much lesser role in driving up the effective rate.

A similar picture is given in Figure 19-1, which shows the step-up in bracket rates and the gradually rising effective rate moving toward and flattening out at 28 percent.[1]

Payment Procedure

It remains to note certain major procedural aspects of the income tax.

Filing Requirement   A filing requirement applies to all incomes in excess of $4,400 for single and $7,560 for joint returns. The filing date is April 15, at which

---

[1] The effective rate as shown in Figure 19-1 equals the ratio of tax to taxable income plus exemption or, which is the same, AGI minus deduction. This is the ratio which becomes a flat 28 percent, reached after use of a 33 percent bracket rate over a certain income range has removed the earlier gain from the exemption and from the initial 15 percent bracket rate. Note also that the slope of the effective rate schedule as shown in Figure 19-1 is a function of the scale used on the horizontal axis.

time final payments for the preceding calendar year are due or refunds are claimed. Together with the return for the preceding year, the taxpayer files an estimated return for the current year, with payments during the tax year based thereon. About 40 percent of taxpayers (including all those who itemize) must file the more detailed form 1040, and 60 percent file a greatly simplified "short form."

Withholding   About 90 percent of the tax liability is collected through withholding. This system was introduced during World War II and has great advantages. By linking tax payments to the current level of income rather than by having them lag behind one year, the responsiveness of tax payments to changes in the level of personal income is greatly increased. This responsiveness is of vital importance for the effectiveness of stabilization policy. The withholding system also ensures fuller compliance since the declaration of income is not left entirely to the recipient.

At the same time, the withholding system has its costs. With withholding rates set sufficiently high to bring in most of the revenue, overwithholding may result for particular taxpayers. The Treasury must then make refunds to those who overpaid. For the taxable year 1984, about 70 percent of returns were overwithheld and received refunds, with overpayments equal to about 30 percent of liabilities.

Audit   The basic system underlying the U.S. income tax is one of self-assessment. Each taxpayer is responsible for declaring income and computing income tax thereon. Although the Bureau of Internal Revenue checks the arithmetic of tax computations and computer facilities have been most helpful, the Bureau cannot carefully audit 100 million returns a year. The cost of doing so would be excessive. However, spot checks are made to keep taxpayers on their toes. Returns with unusual features (e.g., very high deductions or unusual sources of income) may be audited, and at various times particular groups of taxpayers, such as doctors or cattle ranchers, may be singled out for special attention. Nevertheless, the extent of auditing is relatively limited. This should change in time, when increasingly sophisticated use of computer facilities (involving not-as-yet-feasible cross-checking between returns) should greatly facilitate the task of a more comprehensive audit.

B. STRUCTURE OF THE TAX BASE

Having surveyed the major provisions of the income tax, we now turn to the size, composition, and distribution of the tax base.

Size Distribution of Tax Base

The distribution of the tax base by adjusted gross income brackets, shown in Table 19-3, is of great importance for tax policy because it shows where the money comes from.[2] The data, based on 1984 returns, are not readily summarized, but they suggest these conclusions:

---

[2] Note that the figures given in Table 19-3 are for 1984, the latest available year, but the general pattern does not change significantly for later years. For a rough adjustment to 1989 levels, you may raise the dollar levels as given in the table by about one-third.

TABLE 19-3
Distribution of Income Tax Base, 1984*
(Taxable Returns Only)

Adjusted Gross Income (Dollars)	Number of Returns (Millions)	AGI (Billions of Dollars)	Taxable Income (Billions of Dollars)	Tax (Billions of Dollars)
Under 5,000	4.6	16.5	14.4	0.9
5,000– 10,000	12.5	95.5	75.1	5.4
10,000– 15,000	13.4	166.2	132.4	12.8
15,000– 20,000	11.3	196.2	159.6	18.5
20,000– 30,000	16.2	402.3	326.7	44.8
30,000– 50,000	17.0	646.1	514.2	87.3
50,000–100,000	5.6	362.7	283.4	66.0
100,000–200,000	0.8	99.8	77.5	25.8
200,000–500,000	0.2	57.4	44.2	18.8
Over 500,000	0.04	54.3	43.7	21.6
Total	81.6	2,097.0	1,671.2	301.9

AS PERCENTAGE OF TOTAL				
Under 5,000	5.6	0.7	0.9	0.3
5,000– 10,000	15.3	4.6	4.5	1.8
10,000– 15,000	16.4	7.9	7.9	4.2
15,000– 20,000	13.8	9.4	9.6	6.1
20,000– 30,000	19.9	19.2	19.5	14.9
30,000– 50,000	20.8	30.8	30.8	28.9
50,000–100,000	6.9	17.3	17.0	21.9
100,000–200,000	0.8	4.8	4.6	8.5
200,000–500,000	0.2	2.7	2.6	6.2
Over 500,000	0.05	2.6	2.6	7.2
Total	100.0	100.0	100.0	100.0

*Details may not add owing to rounding.
Source: *Individual Income Tax Returns 1984*, Statistics of Income Division, Internal Revenue Service, 1986, p. 16.

1. The lowest 52 percent of returns (with AGI below $20,000) received 22 percent of AGI and contributed 12 percent of revenue. The share of the tax base received by this lower half of returns is relatively small, and its contribution to total revenue is minor.

2. The next 40 percent (with AGI between $20,000 and $50,000), which we may think of as including the lower-middle-income range, received 50 percent of AGI and contributed 43 percent of revenue. Thus this range covers a substantial part of the total and is a major contributor to revenue.

3. The next 7 percent, which we might consider the middle-upper range (with AGI from $50,000 to $100,000), received 17 percent of AGI and contributed 22 percent of the revenue. Once more, this range covers a major part of the tax base and revenue source.

4. Finally, the top 1 percent (with AGI in excess of $100,000) received 10 percent of AGI and contributed 21 percent revenue. Although the ratio of contribution to base is high for this group, its base is a relatively small part of the total. Since the number of rich people is relatively small, the tax base provided by this group is limited.

In all, we conclude that the bulk of the revenue must be drawn from the broad middle-income ranges. The revenue potential of the bottom 25 percent is quite small, and the revenue share obtained from the top of the income scale can also contribute only a quite limited part of total revenue. Whereas income levels at the top of the income scale are very high, the number of correspondingly rich people is also small.

The distribution of the tax base in turn determines the addition to total yield obtained from successive bracket rates. The initial rate of 15 percent applies to the entire base and contributes over two-thirds of the total revenue, with less than one-third added by the rate increments of 13 and 5 percent.

In evaluating this result, one must keep in mind that the tax base itself reflects the statutory definition of taxable income with all its imperfections. A more comprehensive definition of taxable income would raise the revenue potential of the higher brackets and thus increase their liabilities. But even if all high-income preferences were eliminated, AGI in the brackets above, say, $100,000 would still be only a minor part of the tax base and the additional revenue obtained from high bracket rates would be limited. Moreover, as we will see in the next chapter, adoption of a comprehensive base would also raise taxable income over the lower and middle ranges of the income scale. After all the adjustments were made, the middle range would still remain the primary source of revenue, this being the range over which most of the income is received.

Distribution of Tax Base by Income Source

If the income tax were a truly global tax, the distribution of income by source would not affect the burden distribution. But even though our income tax is meant to be global rather than schedular, elements of differential treatment among income sources remain. The distribution by income source is thus of considerable interest.

As shown in the upper half of Table 19-4, the composition of AGI by source changes greatly as we move up the income scale. As shown in column I, the share of wage income in total income forms an inverted U-shaped pattern, rising first and then falling sharply. The importance of capital income shows the reverse pattern, with such income at the bottom of the scale reflecting mainly pension receipts of retirees. High-bracket income is largely in the form of capital income. Of special importance for our subsequent discussion is the sharp rise in the capital gains share (column V) at the high-income levels. But, although capital income is much more important as a share of total income in the high-income brackets than in the lower-income brackets, it does not follow that the bulk of capital income accrues to the very rich. As shown in the lower part of the table, this is not so. About 40 percent of dividend, interest, rent, and royalty income goes to returns below $50,000. In all, capital income weighs much more heavily in the upper-income groups, but a substantial share of total capital income also goes to the middle- and lower-income ranges. The importance of this distribution for income tax policy will become apparent as we move along.

C.   PRINCIPLES OF INCOME DEFINITION

The basic income concept upon which the determination of income tax liability in practice rests is AGI. How satisfactory a concept is AGI? Or, more precisely, how

TABLE 19-4
Distribution of Tax Base by Type of Income, 1984
(Taxable Returns Only)

Adjusted Gross Income (Dollars)	Wages and Salaries (I)	Business, Professions (II)	Partnerships (III)	Dividends, Interest (IV)	Sale of Capital Assets (V)	Pensions and Other (VI)	All Sources (VII)
		PERCENTAGE OF AGI DERIVED FROM EACH SOURCE					
Under 10,000	79.8	2.1	– 1.3	14.6	1.9	2.9	100.0
10,000– 20,000	82.1	2.5	0.1	10.8	0.6	3.9	100.0
20,000– 30,000	87.9	2.9	0.1	7.6	0.4	1.1	100.0
30,000– 50,000	90.4	2.6	—	6.9	0.7	– 0.6	100.0
50,000– 100,000	81.8	5.3	0.4	11.3	2.3	– 1.1	100.0
100,000– 500,000	64.5	6.3	– 0.3	17.6	9.0	2.9	100.0
500,000–1,000,000	43.2	3.5	– 1.7	20.2	24.3	10.5	100.0
Over 1,000,000	22.6	3.0	0.1	20.6	36.5	17.2	100.0
Total	82.9	3.3	—	10.0	2.4	1.4	100.0
		PERCENTAGE OF EACH SOURCE GOING TO VARIOUS BRACKETS OF AGI					
Under 10,000	5.1	3.4	– 347.4	7.7	4.3	12.2	5.3
10,000– 20,000	17.1	12.8	117.9	18.7	4.1	53.2	17.3
20,000– 30,000	20.3	16.4	52.9	14.5	3.6	16.7	19.2
30,000– 50,000	33.6	23.7	60.5	21.2	8.4	– 14.6	30.8
50,000– 100,000	17.1	27.3	328.1	18.5	16.6	– 15.0	17.3
100,000– 500,000	5.8	14.0	– 96.8	13.1	28.3	17.2	7.5
500,000–1,000,000	0.5	0.9	– 83.8	1.9	9.5	7.8	0.9
Over 1,000,000	0.5	1.5	68.6	3.4	25.2	22.5	1.7
Total	100.0	100.0	100.0	100.0	100.0	100.0	100.0

Source: Individual Income Tax Returns 1984, Statistics of Income Division, Internal Revenue Service, 1986, p. 18.

good a measure of taxable capacity does it furnish? In our earlier discussion of tax bases we concluded that income and consumption are the prime candidates for a broadly based personal tax, and we need not here review their comparative merits.[3] Given the choice of income as tax base, it is evident that income, as an index of taxpaying capacity, should be defined broadly as total accretion to a person's wealth. All accretion should be included, whether it is regular or fluctuating, expected or unexpected, realized or unrealized. No consideration should be given to how the income is used, i.e., whether it is saved or consumed.

 Moreover, income from all sources thus defined should be treated uniformly and be combined in a global income total to which tax rates are applied. Without globality, the application of a progressive rate schedule cannot serve its purpose of adapting the tax to the taxpayer's ability to pay. This view of the income tax, as expounded by Henry Simons, has been widely accepted by students of taxation.[4] Appealing and clear enough in principle, the accretion concept must now be considered more closely for what it implies in practice and how well it is satisfied by the AGI definition.

Gross Income versus Net Income

Income under the accretion approach should be measured in terms of net income, i.e., income after the costs of earning it are deducted. As noted before, the tax law attempts to define adjusted gross income as a net income concept, since costs incurred in earning income are usually, though not always, deducted. Thus, income from business activity is taxed on a net basis, i.e., after deducting costs incurred. The law also permits deduction of certain work-related expenses, such as membership fees in professional associations. Tax-free recovery of costs of investment in education, on the other hand, is not allowed. In other instances, items which are more nearly income are treated as costs, e.g., entertainment expenses charged on expense accounts. As shown below, there is also a question of what interest deduction should be allowed. But these are exceptions rather than the rule; AGI, as defined by the statute, is generally in line with the principle of *net* income.

Another principle in defining net income is that losses should be allowed for fully. Since accretion is designed to measure consumption plus increase in *net* worth, operating losses should be deducted in arriving at the net income of a business. Losses reduce net worth just as gains increase it, and the government should be a partner in both cases. Although the law does not go so far as to grant a refund in case of net losses, it does make substantial provision for the spreading of losses over past and future years. As was noted earlier, adequate allowance for losses is of key importance for the investment effects of an income tax.[5]

Capital Income versus Labor Income

According to the accretion concept it does not matter from what source income has been derived. Yet writers on taxation have traditionally distinguished between "earned" (or wage) and "unearned" (or capital) income, implying that the former

---

[3] See p. 224.
[4] See Henry Simons, *Personal Income Taxation*, Chicago: University of Chicago Press, 1950.
[5] See p. 309.

should be taxed less heavily. As noted below, the earned income credit makes a substantial allowance of this kind at the lower end of the income scale. This may be rationalized as allowing for disutility of work, or as a convenient device to grant low-income relief. Neither argument is convincing. If disutility of work had to be allowed for, it would surely be necessary to distinguish among types of jobs; and if relief is to be granted to low incomes, it should be made available also to low-income families with capital (e.g., retirement) income.

Notwithstanding these considerations, the income tax differentiates among sources of income in various ways. Thus, wage income at the lower end of the scale is favored by the earned income credit. Capital income is favored by tax exemption of interest on state and local securities and by larger evasion due to incomplete coverage under withholding. Prior to 1986, it also benefited from the partial exclusion of long-term gains from taxable income.

Real Income versus Nominal Income

If income is to serve as a measure of ability to pay, it should be defined in real terms. An increase in money income which is matched by a rise in prices does not constitute a gain in real income. Hence tax liability in real terms should not be affected. This consideration became of major importance during the inflationary climate of the late 1970s and early 1980s. As is noted later, steps have been taken since then which go far to protect this structure of the income tax against inflation.[6]

Accrued Income versus Realized Income

Given our definition of income as based on accretion to wealth, it should be a matter of indifference whether gains (1) have been realized in terms of cash, as is the case with wages or the sale of assets which have appreciated in value, or (2) have been permitted to accrue by way of raising the value of assets which continue to be held. Whether or not a realization occurs is a matter of portfolio choice for the investor and should not affect income as measured for purposes of taxation. As we will see presently, this has important bearing on the controversial topic of capital gains taxation.

Imputed Income

Some people hold earning assets that bring cash income; others hold durable consumer goods that earn imputed income. The most important example is the owner-occupied residence. The resident obtains an "imputed rent" equal to the return he or she could obtain by letting the house. Since accretion is defined as increase in net worth plus consumption, such imputed consumption values should be included in the tax base. AGI, by adhering to a cash income concept, does not include imputed income. This omission, as we will find out later on, causes inequities in the tax treatment of houseowners and renters.

Income received in kind, such as food grown on farms, the services of company cars, or gains from fringe benefits, are similarly omitted in AGI but should be in the income concept. This is especially important where payments in kind, in the form of various fringe benefits such as company cars, may be substituted for cash payments to avoid income tax. At the same time, the inclusion of imputed income becomes unworkable if carried too far. Thus, a good case could be made conceptually for imputing earnings to housepersons for domestic services and child care. If this were done, AGI might be raised substantially. This, however, would pose serious problems of measurement and other issues which will be considered when we examine the tax treatment of the family.[7]

An even more puzzling problem is posed by leisure. If a person chooses leisure, this is evidence (so economic logic would tell us) that he or she values it by the income equivalent lost in not working. The logic of accretion would suggest that income in kind, received in the form of leisure, be included in the tax base, but implementation of such a rule, as noted earlier in our discussion of distributive justice, is impracticable.[8]

Earnings versus Transfers

From the economist's point of view, national income is the sum of factor earnings during the period, reflecting in turn the value of output which the factors have produced. Transfers received from government or private sources (such as gifts or bequests) are not components of income in the national income sense. But it does not follow that they should be excluded for taxable income as is largely the case. Choosing a suitable definition of taxable income is an issue in tax equity not in national income accounting. A person's taxable income need not be the same as his or her share in national income; nor need total taxable income equal total national income.

Bequests and Gifts

Private transfers, such as bequests and gifts, also remain outside the income tax. Such transfers are neither deducted by the donor nor included by the donee. In terms of the accretion concept, the receipt of bequests or gifts constitutes an addition to the economic capacity of the recipient, just as does accretion from other sources. Although such transfers are taxed separately under the estate and gift taxes, a good argument can be made for including them in the income tax base of the recipient as well.

If this were done, would it follow that such transfers should be deducted from the tax base of the transferor? Not necessarily. The income concept is based on accretion, not use, and there is no reason why the aggregate tax base should have to equal total earnings as defined in national income. Once more we will return to this when considering the taxation of bequests and gifts.

Regular versus Irregular Income

The argument is sometimes made that irregular and unexpected income should not be included for tax purposes. But there is little justification for this position. Although there is an advantage to certainty, even uncertain accretion adds to the re-

[7] See p. 362.
[8] See p. 223.

cipient's wealth. After all, why should wages be taxed but gambling gains be exempted? A problem arises, however, in that progressive rates tend to discriminate against fluctuating income. Prior to 1986, this was met by an averaging provision, but with the narrowing of rate differentials, the averaging provision became less necessary and has been repealed.

D. PRACTICE OF INCOME DEFINITION: (1) EXCLUSIONS

Examination of the tax law shows considerable departures from these principles. Some forms of accretion, such as imputed income, simply do not appear, while others are specifically excluded from AGI. We now consider some of the key items in the latter group.

Tax-Exempt Interest

Interest on state and local securities, issued for use by such governmental units is excluded from taxable income under the federal income tax. Although this exclusion was originally based on the constitutional provision that any one level of government should not tax the instrumentalities of another, a 1988 ruling of the U.S. Supreme Court held that federal taxation of such interest is permissible under the Sixteenth Amendment.[9] But though inclusion can no longer be ruled out on constitutional grounds, an early policy reversal is unlikely.

On its merits, exclusion is undesirable because it undermines the equity of the income tax. Moreover, tax exemption is an inefficient means of supporting state and local government borrowing. Beginning with equity aspects, exclusion gives the greatest advantage to high-income taxpayers with capital income. The gains from exemption rise with the investor's tax bracket. While this advantage has been reduced over the years by the cutback in upper bracket rates, it is still significant. For an investor whose marginal rate is 15 percent, a tax-exempt security yielding 5 percent is equivalent in net yield to a taxable issue yielding 5.88 percent. For an investor whose marginal rate is 33 percent, the equivalent yield on a taxable issue is 7.46 percent. This explains why the great bulk of tax-exempts held outside banks are held by wealthy individuals. Of the $12 billion of estimated revenue loss from interest exemption (fiscal year 1989), over $8 billion involve individual returns, with most of the benefits going to taxpayers with AGI above $100,000. The remainder, accruing to trust accounts and financial intermediaries, also largely benefits upper-income groups. Moreover, they are another major cause of horizontal inequity among upper-bracket taxpayers.

Apart from being inequitable, the exemption is an *inefficient* way of subsidizing state and local governments. More aid could be given at the same cost if the federal government were to subsidize state and local interest payments directly. Because interest on state and local securities is tax-exempt, such securities are worth more to investors. Therefore they will pay a higher price or, what amounts to the same, accept a lower before-tax yield. Because of this, the governments can issue

---

[9] State of South Carolina vs. J. A. Baker, Secretary of the Treasury; Supreme Court of the United States, 1988 U.S. Lexis 1873; 56 USLW 4311, April 20, 1988.

securities at a lower interest cost. However, less than the entire revenue loss is passed on to state and local governments in the form of lower borrowing costs.

Consider the following situation: Mr. H, who pays at a marginal tax rate of 33 percent, has $800 to invest, whereas Ms. L, who pays at a rate of only 15 percent, has $200. Both can invest in federal securities at 10 percent, giving them a net yield of 6.7 and 8.5 percent, respectively. They will not purchase state and local securities yielding below this level. If $1,000 of such securities are to be placed, the yield must be at least 8.5 percent so that both will participate. State and local governments then save $15 in interest cost, since they now lend at 8.5 rather than 10 percent. The federal government, however, loses income tax revenue of $26.40 + $3.00 = $29.40, which it would have obtained had H and L invested in taxable 10 percent issues. The net cost of governments is $29.40 − $15 = $14.40. This amount accrues to Mr. H, whose earnings are $68 as against after-tax earnings (in the absence of the exclusion provision) of $53.60. Ms. L, the marginal investor, has $17 in tax-free income, the same as that from investing in taxable 10 percent issues.

In practice, matters are more complicated, but our illustration shows why the device is inefficient: the subsidy must be set sufficiently high to attract the marginal investor, while investors with higher-bracket rates could have been attracted for less. The same aid could be given to state and local governments through a direct subsidy of $15, leaving them with the same net interest cost of $85. Or, by giving a direct subsidy of $29.40, that gain could be multiplied and damage to tax equity would be avoided. Moreover, by raising the yield, the market for state and local securities would be broadened as investment by savings institutions would be attracted.

Proposals to provide for a direct subsidy for tax exemption on new issues have been advanced over the years, but have been rejected by Congress. State and local governments, like other groups, prefer their subsidies in hidden form, and they fear that a direct subsidy would be less permanent in nature. For these reasons, the combined opposition of governors, mayors, and high-bracket taxpayers has, to date, been too strong to permit a sensible reform. On the contrary, the range of tax-exempt issues has been widened in recent years by the inclusion of special issues, such as industrial development bonds (sponsored by state or municipal governments and public agencies), with the proceeds available for certain uses such as rental housing, emergency facilities, and airports.

Capital Gains

Turning now to the treatment of capital gains, we arrive at what has been one of the most important and controversial issues in income definition. The debate involves two major aspects: (1) whether realized gains should be treated as ordinary income, and (2) whether unrealized gains should be taxable as well.

Treatment of Realized Gains Prior to the recent tax reform of 1986, realized capital gains were included fully if the asset was held for one year or less, but only at 40 percent if the asset was held for a longer period. This provided a strong incentive to receive capital income in the form of capital gains rather than as operating profits, dividends, or interest. This incentive rose with the taxpayer's bracket rate. It is not surprising, therefore, that the share of capital gains in AGI rises sharply as we move up the income scale. As was shown in Table 19-4, capital gains in 1984 rose from around 2 percent of AGI at the $50,000 level to 36 percent at the top of the scale.

The damage to tax equity was evident. Horizontal equity was damaged because of resulting differentials in tax liabilities at given levels of income; and vertical equity was interfered with because the capital gains preference went far in offsetting the bite of progressive taxation on capital income. As will be seen in the next chapter, the capital gains benefit became a major source of tax preference for high incomes.

No valid case can be made on equity grounds for giving such preferential treatment to realized gains as compared with, say, operating profits. Income is received in both cases and there is no basis on which to distinguish the two. Whereas a special problem arises in that capital gains are discontinuous and volatile, so that they would pay more under progressive rates than would an equal amount of income received in a steady flow, this difficulty can be met through adequate averaging provisions. Nor can it be argued convincingly that capital gains should be given special treatment because they frequently are not expected as is "regular" income but are windfalls which happen to accrue without intention. This may be the case for some gains though not for others; and even where gains are unexpected, they nevertheless add to the recipient's taxable capacity.

This debate was resolved by the tax reform of 1986, which provided for full inclusion of all realized gains in taxable income. The reform thereby took a major step toward improving the income tax base as a measure of accretion, but it remains to be seen whether this gain can survive the course of future legislation.

Treatment of Unrealized Gains But what about the treatment of unrealized gains? Since AGI is defined in cash terms and includes cash income only, unrealized gains are not taxed. This is clearly in contravention of the accretion principle. According to this principle, income as an index of taxpaying ability should be measured as accretion to wealth. All increments should be included, whether realized (turned into cash) or not. If Mr. Jones holds corporate shares which have appreciated in value by $100,000, this is the amount by which his net worth has risen and which he would have been able to turn into cash if he had so chosen. The fact that he has retained this particular asset shows that he preferred continued holding over the available alternatives, e.g., sale with consumption or reinvestment in some other asset. Whether the gain is realized or not is irrelevant to whether or not there has been an increase in economic capacity. Provided that realization is possible, the decision whether or not to realize is a problem in portfolio (asset) management and not in the accretion of income. Postponement of the tax until realization gives an unfair advantage to such income. The Treasury in effect grants an interest-free loan on the amount of the postponed liability. If no realization occurs, this gain will in fact last forever, because no tax becomes due.

Nevertheless, these conclusions have been subject to continuous debate, as shown by the following arguments:

1. "Unrealized gains should not be taxed because the owner has refrained from consumption." Although there has been no consumption, this is not relevant in defining the base of an *income* tax. Here the principle is that all income should be taxed, independently of how it is used; and even under a consumption tax, the distinction between realized and unrealized gains is not the decisive issue.[10]

2. "Unrealized gains should not be taxed because in the absence of realization we do not know whether they really exist." Thus, in the early origins of bookkeeping the Venetian merchant was well advised not to count his proceeds until his captain had returned to home port and delivered the treasure chest. Prudent accounting would call for "realization" in cash (or gold) before income was said to exist. But institutions change and the analogy is quite inappropriate for, say, a holder of AT&T shares which can be sold at once. As is noted later, measurement of some unrealized gains may be difficult, but this is not an insuperable obstacle.

3. "Taxation of unrealized gains requires the owner to pay a tax even though he or she has not obtained cash with which to pay it." The observation is correct, but does it matter? As would be necessary with other debts that may come due, it is not unreasonable to ask the taxpayer to liquidate part of his or her assets to make the tax payment if needed. For situations in which partial liquidation is not possible (e.g., a family business), adequate time must be granted.

4. Finally, the following argument is occasionally made: For income to be received, it must be "separated" from the asset. This view, which had much legal support in the earlier stages of the income tax discussion, is hard to fathom from the economist's point of view. Separation is a matter of investment choice, whereas income accrues when the asset value is increased.

Following the accretion approach to a comprehensive tax base, unrealized as well as realized gains should be considered taxable and included with income from all other sources. At the same time, full taxation of gains would also have to be matched by full allowance for losses. Moreover, as is discussed later on, full taxation of capital gains also calls for an inflation adjustment.[11]

Implementation Problems   Although the case for inclusion is clear in principle, is there a feasible way of reaching unrealized gains? Full taxation of realized gains can be implemented without technical difficulties, but the situation is more difficult for unrealized gains. Taxation of unrealized gains on a current basis is not feasible owing to the impracticality of annual valuation of all assets. Some assets, such as traded securities, could be valued and taxed periodically, say, every five years, but other assets (e.g., paintings or farms) may be more difficult to value. It has therefore been proposed that accrued gains be taxed at death or transfer (by gift) as if realized at that time. Referred to as "constructive realization," this would reduce the need for valuation to a single time, thus reducing this task to manageable proportions. By permitting averaging and the spreading of payments over a period of time, inequities which would arise from forced liquidation of assets may be avoided. Under such a procedure, all gains would be eventually taxed,

---

[10] Under a consumption tax, unrealized gains would be excluded and realized gains would be included *only if consumed*. Realized gains which are not consumed but are reinvested or held as cash would be excluded. On the other hand, consumption financed by drawing down balances would be subject to tax.

[11] See p. 361.

thus reducing the lock-in effect. A constructive realization provision has been proposed at various times, but has not been accepted by the Congress.

Although constructive realization would move unrealized gains into the tax base, it would still leave capital gains with some advantage. Whereas other income is taxed on a current basis, the tax on unrealized gains would be delayed until death, thus leaving the taxpayer with the possibility of earning income thereon in the meantime. Tax delay is equivalent to receiving an interest-free loan, the value of which may be substantial, especially for young investors who can anticipate a long holding period.

Savings and Pension Plans

Saving involves the setting aside of current income for future use, with contributions to pension plans equivalent to other forms of saving. Since a global income tax should include all income, independent of how it is used, pension contributions and other forms of saving should not be deductible when made; and when benefits are received later on, only the component which reflects interest should be taxed. An alternative, allowing for deduction of contributions when made with full taxation of subsequent benefits, would be less satisfactory since it would leave the taxpayer with two advantages not enjoyed by other savers. Since tax payments are postponed, the taxpayer would receive an interest gain on the deferred tax. Moreover, as his or her future income is likely to be smaller, a lower bracket rate would apply. As shown in Table 19-5, the actual treatment of pension and insurance plans varies and usually falls short of the proper solution.

OASI Beginning with Old Age and Survivor's Insurance (OASI), we note that employee contributions may not be deducted and are thus included in the tax base. Employer contributions, however, are not. Viewing OASI as a contributory system, we see that the correct procedure would thus be to tax that half of benefits which reflects employer contributions but only the interest component of that half which reflects the employee contribution. The law does not provide accordingly. Instead, all benefits are tax-free at low-income levels, whereas one-half of benefits are taxable where the recipient's AGI (expanded to include tax-exempt interest and

TABLE 19-5
Tax Treatment of Pension Plans

	TYPE OF PLAN		
	OASI	Company Plan	Self-employed
Inclusion of contribution in employee's taxable income when made			
Employee contribution	Yes	Yes	No
Employer contribution	No	No	*
Taxation of benefits when received			
Recoupment of employee contribution	No	No	Yes
Recoupment of employer contribution	No	Yes	*
Interest	No	Yes	Yes

*Not applicable.

one-half of benefits) exceeds $32,000 (joint return). This eliminates preferential treatment for that group, while continuing it for the larger group of retirees who receive lower incomes.

The case for inclusion of benefits in the tax base becomes the stronger if OASI is viewed as a redistribution scheme rather than as insurance. The proper solution then becomes to treat benefits like other forms of accretion and to tax them accordingly. Benefits would remain tax-free only where the recipient's income falls below the tax-free limit applicable to all other sources of income. Payroll taxes, similarly, would not be deductible. They would become part of general revenue and be treated like all other federal taxes.

Unemployment Insurance The contribution to unemployment insurance is made entirely by the employer, and thus does not enter the employee's tax base. Although benefits were excluded as well prior to 1986, they are now included as taxable income to the recipient.

Company Retirement Plans The treatment of company retirement plans comes closer to the full inclusion of the base. The correct procedure is applied with regard to the *employee* contribution. The contribution is not deductible from taxable income when made and only the interest component of the benefits is taxed later on. The *employer* contribution is not included in the employee's tax base when made, but the entire benefits are taxed later on. Thus only the postponement gain remains. In addition to the interest gain, postponement gives the advantage of spreading income to a time when earnings will be lower. This is of special importance for highly paid executives and causes extensive use of deferred-payment arrangements.

Life Insurance Treatment of the savings component of life insurance, finally, is similar to that of the employee contribution under OASI. Premiums remain part of taxable income when made and benefits are not taxed, thus permitting interest to escape. Forms of insurance which carry no savings component (such as term insurance) yield no interest earnings. Benefits are properly exempt, without allowing deduction of premiums when paid.

Private Plans In recent years and especially under the revenue legislation of 1981, savings incentives through tax postponement have been broadened in various ways. The upper limit for exclusion of employee contributions to retirement plans is now set at $2,000. Self-employed individuals may exclude contributions up to 25 percent of their first $30,000 of earnings to an individual (KEOGH) plan. By postponing tax, the saver can obtain a higher return and is thus expected to save more. The very feature which would be considered inequitable in the context of a broad-based income tax is thus introduced as a savings incentive. The effectiveness of such incentives was considered in an earlier context.[12]

---

[12] See p. 303.

Transfer Receipts

Welfare Transfer receipts from government, such as welfare and veterans' benefits, are excluded from AGI, but there is no good reason for this exclusion; $1,000 received in benefits adds no less to a person's economic capacity than does $1,000 received in wages. Although the transfer recipient's income will frequently be too low to justify its taxation, this situation should be taken care of by devices such as exemptions and the low-income allowance, devices which apply equally to all sources of low earnings.

Scholarships The law excludes from taxable income scholarship grants to individuals who are candidates for degrees at an educational institution. The amount excluded is limited to that required for tuition and course-related expenses.

E. PRACTICE OF INCOME DEFINITION: (2) DEDUCTIONS

As noted at the outset of this chapter, the taxpayer is given a choice between (1) claiming the standard deduction, and (2) itemizing deductions. With the former equal to $3,000 for single and $5,000 for joint returns, the option to itemize will be chosen only by taxpayers whose itemized deductions exceed these amounts. It is not surprising, therefore, that itemizing occurs largely in higher-income returns.

The standard deduction was introduced initially to facilitate compliance and administration. It was to serve as a substitute for deductions otherwise available by itemizing, thus relieving low-income returns of that chore. But since then it has been increased to rise substantially above that amount. It has thus become a hybrid between presumptive itemizing and the granting of an additional exemption now unrelated to family size.

As shown in Table 19-6 low-bracket returns typically do not itemize, but the percentage of itemizers rises sharply when we move up the income scale. Thus the percentage of itemizers rises from 7.6 percent at the bottom of the scale to practically 100 percent at the top.

TABLE 19-6
Type of Deduction by AGI Brackets, 1984
(Taxable Returns)

AGI	Number of Returns (Millions)	Number Itemizing (Millions)	Percent Itemizing
Under 10,000	17.1	1.3	7.6
10,000– 20,000	24.7	5.7	23.1
20,000– 30,000	16.2	8.8	54.3
30,000– 50,000	16.9	14.1	83.4
50,000–100,000	5.7	5.4	94.7
Over 100,000	1.0	1.0	100.0
All	81.6	36.3	44.5

Individual Income Tax Returns 1984, Statistics of Income Division, Internal Revenue Service, 1986, p. 13.

Table 19-7, which includes itemized returns only, shows various itemized deductions as a percentage of AGI for such returns. As shown in column VI, the ratio of total itemized deductions to AGI of itemizers is highest at the bottom, reflecting the fact that such returns will use itemizing only in unusual cases, such as heavy medical expenses. The ratio then falls and settles at around 23 percent.

Particular items vary in importance by income levels. Medical deductions are most important for the lower end of the income scale. Interest deductions (reflecting mainly mortgage interest) dominate in the low-middle range. Charitable contributions weigh heavily at both ends of the scale, with deduction of state and local taxes declining in importance when moving up.

Rationale for Itemizing Deductions

The principle of income taxation calls for a comprehensive tax base, including all forms of accretion. This approach establishes a prima facie case against deductions, yet some deductions may be justified.

Equity Aspects   Equal income may not imply equal ability to pay if taxpayers are in otherwise different positions. This is recognized with regard to family size but may apply also in other respects. Taxpayers with heavy emergency expenses, such as large medical bills, may be said to have less taxable capacity than others with equal income but no such emergencies. It is also reasonable to suggest that such situations will be of special importance for low-income taxpayers. This principle is reflected in the allowance for medical expenses which may be deducted if in excess of 7.5 percent of AGI. A similar argument can be made regarding casualty losses and losses from theft, such losses now being allowed above 10 percent of AGI. If designed properly, emergency deductions are not objectionable and may indeed be helpful in securing a more equitable tax base. Similar considerations arise in connection with extra exemptions for the blind. To the extent that being

TABLE 19-7
Itemized Deductions as Percentage of AGI in Itemized Returns, 1984

AGI Class (Dollars)	Taxes (I)	Interest (II)	Contributions (III)	Medical Expenses (IV)	Other (V)	All (VI)
Under 5,000	16.1	53.0	5.7	31.6	15.8	122.2
5,000– 10,000	12.1	23.1	6.8	24.9	3.4	70.3
10,000– 15,000	9.7	17.0	5.1	10.1	1.9	43.8
15,000– 20,000	8.5	13.6	3.8	4.7	1.8	32.4
20,000– 30,000	8.0	12.3	2.8	1.8	1.7	26.6
30,000– 50,000	7.7	10.7	2.3	0.8	1.5	23.0
50,000– 100,000	8.0	10.4	2.6	0.6	1.4	23.0
100,000– 500,000	8.3	9.3	3.8	0.3	1.5	23.2
500,000–1,000,000	7.5	7.0	4.6	0.1	1.2	20.4
Over 1,000,000	6.8	5.8	5.9	*	1.2	19.7
All	7.9	10.5	2.9	1.1	1.5	23.9

Source: Individual Income Tax Returns 1984, Statistics of Income Division, Internal Revenue Service, 1986, Table 2.1, pp. 57–59.

blind calls for extra expenses, the equal treatment principle justifies an extra allowance. The same case cannot be made, however, with regard to the extra exemption for the aged. The objective, after all, is not to maximize the tax base but to secure a fair measure of taxable capacity.

Incentive Aspects Deductions may be viewed as a way of providing an incentive to use income in a "meritorious" form such as charitable contributions or to encourage expenditures on items which generate external benefits. The deduction here acts as a matching grant by which the government reduces the cost of certain activities for the taxpayer, thereby inducing the individual to spend more on this activity. If the particular activity merits support and if tax deduction is the best technique of giving it, the resulting gain may outweigh the damage to tax equity. There is no law of nature which says that taxation must not be used for purposes other than revenue collection. Rather, the question is whether the supported activity merits a subsidy, and if so, whether the subsidy should be given in this form. More will be said about this when we consider charitable contributions.

Evaluation of Major Deductions

Total itemized deductions for 1984 amounted to $359 billion, or 27 percent of otherwise taxable income for itemizers.

Mortgage Interest and Housing First in importance are deductions for interest payments. Such deductions in 1984 accounted for 28 percent of total itemized deductions, with mortgage interest accounting for the larger part thereof. As with taxes, a distinction must be drawn between interest paid as a cost of doing business and interest paid on consumer debt. Deductibility of business interest is clearly appropriate for the simple reason that taxable income should be defined as net income. But deductibility of interest on consumer debt, such as mortgages, is a different matter. Whereas both types of interest are cost payments or negative income streams, the treatment of the corresponding benefit streams differs. In the case of business borrowing, the benefit stream is normally included as taxable business income, whereas in the instance of mortgage or consumer debt, the benefit stream (in the form of imputed rent or other services) is not treated as part of the resident's taxable income.

Consider three people, each with $100,000 to invest and wishing to live in a $100,000 house. Also assume that the return on all capital is 5 percent. Mr. R decides to rent and invest his funds in shares. As shown below, he receives $5,000 in dividends. Assuming the 28 percent rate to apply, he pays a tax of $1,400. Mr. O decides to own his house outright and pays $100,000 in cash. He buys no shares and receives no dividend income but benefits from imputed rent of $5,000. Since this is not counted as taxable income, he pays no tax. Ms. M purchases a $100,000 residence by taking up a mortgage, while using her $100,000 to purchase shares. She derives $5,000 in dividends but pays $5,000 interest. Since the latter can be deducted, she is again left without taxable income. Now compare the three as in line 5. They all have the same net worth and live in similar houses, but R pays $1,400 in tax while O and M are tax-free.

	Renter R	Equity Owner O	Mortgage Owner M
1. Owner's imputed rent	0	$5,000	$5,000
2. Interest paid	0	0	$5,000
3. Dividends	$5,000	0	$5,000
4. Taxable, present law	$5,000	0	0
5. Tax, present law	$1,400	0	0
6. Variant 1 tax	$1,400	0	$1,400
7. Variant 2 tax	$1,400	$1,400	$1,400
8. Variant 3 tax	0	0	0

How can the three be placed in an equal position? Removal of the interest deduction (variant 1) will not do. While M would lose her advantage and be placed in the same position as R, O would remain free of tax. In order to treat all alike, we must either make imputed rent taxable while continuing to allow deduction of interest (variant 2) or disregard imputed rent and deduct interest but make rent payments deductible as well (variant 3). With variant 2, O and M must both pay the same tax as R; with variant 3, R's liability is removed and no one pays. Both solutions are neutral as between the various types of housing arrangements, but variant 2 shows no preference for housing whereas 3 makes all housing expenditures tax-exempt. From the point of view of a global income tax, variant 2 is clearly the preferred solution. Equal treatment should apply not only among people who consume housing in different forms, but also among those who consume housing and others who consume different items.[13]

The case for preferential treatment would thus have to be made on incentive grounds. The question then is whether the incentive should be given to ownership in particular or to housing expenditure in general. The present procedure, which gives preferential treatment to ownership, is difficult to defend, especially since low-income housing is more largely in rental form. But even generalized tax relief for housing (ownership or rental) is of dubious validity. Support for low-cost housing in particular may be desirable, calling for limitation of the tax preference to rental payments and interest deduction on such housing. But for this purpose, tax preferences are hardly the appropriate solution. Taxes paid by truly low-income families are too low (if the family is taxable at all) to make a substantial difference. Rental subsidies and direct provision for low-cost housing offer superior approaches.

However strong the case for inclusion of imputed rent may be in principle, it is politically unacceptable and not in the cards. Given this situation, would removal of the interest deduction (variant 1) be desirable as a second-best solution? As noted before, this would equalize the position between R and M, but leave O in a preferred position. Moreover, it would differentiate the treatment of O and M, who

[13] The question may be raised whether—from the point of view of the tax structure as a whole—preferential treatment of housing under the income tax might be considered an offset to the extra burden imposed on housing under the property tax, provided that its proceeds are used to finance general (rather than housing-oriented) expenditures. See p. 410.

are now in similar positions. Nevertheless, there would be an equity gain in such a change. The Rs and Ms are more numerous than the Os, so that horizontal equity would be improved by equalizing their treatment. No such correction was made by the 1986 reform. As a reflection of the political power of homeowners, even a limited proposal to disallow deduction of mortgage interest on second homes was rejected.

Consumer Credit   Prior to the 1986 reform, interest on consumer credit was deductible, along with mortgage interest. Deduction of interest on consumer credit was discontinued by the reform. Interest costs incurred in the conduct of a business continue to be deductible as they should be, but deduction of personal interest is no longer allowed.

State and Local Taxes   Deduction of taxes is clearly appropriate where they enter as a cost of doing business, and such deduction is permitted for both federal and lower-level taxes. In addition, the law permits deduction of income and of property taxes imposed by state and local governments even where they are nonbusiness taxes paid by households and consumers. Deductibility of sales taxes, however, was discontinued by the 1986 reform.

The case for tax deductibility hinges on whether such tax payments are to be viewed as uses of income for the purchase of public services or whether they should be considered as a loss of income to the taxpayer. In the first case, deduction is inappropriate; in the second it would be in order. Even if public services are recognized as useful, the fact remains that tax payments need not reflect the valuation placed thereon by individual taxpayers. Taxpayers must pay the tax, and though they have a vote, they do not have a veto. The case for deductibility of state and local taxes is thus not without merit. At the same time, this case is less valid for a tax such as the property tax which is used to render specific local services than for the sales tax which is used more broadly. Viewed in this way, the 1986 reform (which discontinued sales while retaining property tax deduction) made the incorrect choice.

There is also the further question of whether allowance should be in the form of deduction from taxable income, as now provided, or as a credit against federal tax. In the former case, the benefit from the allowance rises with the taxpayer's income and marginal rate, whereas in the latter case, the benefit per dollar of state-local tax is the same throughout the income range.

At closer consideration, we find that the problem of tax deductibility or neutral treatment of taxation at the various levels of government opens broad questions of how fiscal federalism should be structured and indeed how tax systems should be integrated at the international level. To this we will return at a later point.

Charitable Contributions   Charitable contributions in 1984 accounted for 10 percent of itemized deductions. Taxpayers may deduct contributions to a wide range of nonprofit institutions up to 50 percent of AGI. Property which has appreciated may be donated and deducted at market value, without payment of capital gains tax, but such donations are limited to 30 percent of AGI.

With a revenue cost of deductions for charitable contributions of over $10 billion, Congress, in effect, treats this amount as a public contribution to charitable institutions. These contributions, however, are made as matching grants to private donors, leaving it to them to select the recipient. The matching rate equals the donor's marginal tax rate. A high-income donor with a bracket rate of 33 percent must sacrifice only 67 cents to make a gift of $1, while a low-income donor who uses the standard deduction or who is not subject to tax must put up $1. A philosopher-economist might observe that the opportunity cost of virtue falls as one moves up the income scale. It remains to be seen how the recent reduction in the top bracket rate from 50 to 28 or 33 percent will affect the level of giving, especially for institutions which depend on high-income patrons.

The merit of charitable deductions is not easy to judge. On the pro side it is evident that without the pincer effect of high marginal rates and deductibility, charitable contributions would be considerably less. Taking charitable giving as a whole, it has been estimated that charities gain about what the Treasury loses in revenue. The incentive is no bargain, but neither is there a significant leakage. It is argued that without such deductions, charities would suffer a severe loss and some might not survive. Congress would hardly be willing to spend corresponding amounts for such purposes. Moreover, there may be an advantage in decentralizing the choice of supported projects. On the con side, it is argued that some of the functions now supported by charity should be the responsibility of the state and that allocations made from public funds (whether as a direct appropriation or via special tax provision) should be subject to public direction and scrutiny. The issue carries broad social and cultural implications which go much beyond the purely fiscal aspects of tax policy.

Once more, there is the further question of how the benefits should be given, i.e., whether in the form of a deduction or a credit. The former is to the advantage of high-bracket donors, and the latter benefits those in low brackets. Thus deductibility saves the high-bracket donor 28 (or 33) cents per dollar of giving; the low-bracket donor saves 15 cents only. A uniform credit of, say, 23 percent might involve the same revenue loss, while raising the attractiveness of giving for the latter and lowering it for the former group. Empirical work suggests that there would be little change in total giving, but that there would be a substantial change in its composition.[14] Contributions to churches, which figure heavily in low-income giving, would increase, while there would be a sharp drop in giving to educational institutions and other charities which are preferred by high-income donors. It appears that in designing the incentive, public policy can hardly be neutral regarding the way in which charitable donations come to be distributed among types of charities.

Costs of Education We have observed instances where the law permits deductions which are inappropriate or questionable, but there are other instances where a further allowance may be appropriate. This applies in particular to the case

---

[14] The conclusion that *total* giving would be unaffected is based on the finding that the price elasticity of giving (including giving to all charities) is close to unity and varies little with income. See M. Feldstein, "Income Tax Charitable Contributions, Parts I and II," *National Tax Journal*, March and June 1975. This conclusion is based on the finding that the price elasticity of giving for educational institutions and other high-income charities is considerably above unity and that for churches and other low-income charities is substantially below unity.

of investment in education. Although scholarship proceeds are largely excluded from the base, no allowance is made for own-financed student costs. Many proposals have been made to grant such relief, including a deduction from AGI and a credit against tax. The distributional results differ and the previously noted issues in the choice between credit and deduction again arise. Against such tax incentives, it is argued that assistance to education can be granted more equitably and efficiently through subsidies.

Yet there is one form of tax relief for education which would have particular merit as a tax device. Expenditures on education may, at least in substantial part, be considered as a form of investment in human resources and undertaken to increase earnings in later life. These earnings will be taxed, although they constitute a net income only to the extent that they exceed the capital cost. Therefore, the taxpayer should be allowed to recover his or her cost in computing net income; in other words, depreciation should be permitted against human as well as against physical investment. The appropriate solution—in line with charging depreciation over asset life—would be to allow such charges against the student's income after the investment is made, rather than as a current deduction from parents' income while education costs are incurred.[15]

F. PRACTICE OF INCOME DEFINITION: (3) CREDITS

In addition to exemptions, exclusions, and deductions (all of which go to reduce taxable income), the law also permits certain credits against (deductions from) tax. These include the child care credit, credit for the elderly, and earned-income credit.[16] The difference between the credit and the former devices is that the credit gives the same benefit independent of the taxpayer's rate bracket, whereas a dollar of reduction in taxable income gives greater relief to the higher-rate brackets.

G. SUMMARY

The principle of accretion may be stated without too much difficulty, but implementation is troublesome and the actual definitions of AGI and taxable income fall far short of full implementation. In some instances, this reflects the technical difficulties which permit only approximation to the correct solution. In others, however, the deficiencies reflect policy intent of granting preferential treatment. But although implementation is imperfect, a crucial fact is that the specific issues of income definition, as they arise in practice, must be measured against the yardstick of an income concept which provides a meaningful and consistent criterion of equity. In the absence of such a norm, technical issues of taxable income definition applicable to particular cases cannot be settled in a consistent and equitable fashion and the ever-present pressures for loophole snatching cannot be resisted.

Among the basic features of the income tax law by which liabilities are determined, we have noted the following:

[15] For such a proposal, see Richard Goode, *The Individual Income Tax*, rev. ed., Washington: Brookings, 1975, chap. 5.
[16] See p. 355.

1. Tax computation begins with adjusted gross income. Although referred to as "gross" income, reference is to a net income concept, i.e., income after deducting the costs of doing business.

2. Taxable income is defined as AGI minus personal exemptions and minus deductions.

3. Deductions may be itemized or a flat standard deduction may be used.

4. The tax is computed by applying bracket or marginal rates, now ranging from 15 to 28 percent, with a midrange hump of 33 percent.

5. A distinction is drawn between bracket and effective rates, defined as the ratio of tax to AGI.

6. The effect rate rises gradually from zero and approaches a top bracket rate of 28 percent.

7. The personal exemption may be viewed as a zero-rate bracket, and together with the standard deduction it is a major force in income tax progression over the lower- and middle-income range.

Regarding the size and structure of the tax base, our findings were these:

8. The bulk of income tax revenue comes from the middle range of the income scale.

9. Wage income is most important for low-income brackets, and capital income for high-income brackets.

The ideal definition of AGI is given by a broad-based or accretion concept of income. However, numerous difficulties arise in implementing it.

10. Costs of doing business are appropriately excluded in arriving at net income, but they are not always easily defined.

11. The appropriate treatment of capital gains has for a long time been a controversial issue. Realized gains are now fully included in the tax base, but unrealized gains are excluded.

12. Exclusion of interest from state and local securities is inequitable and an inefficient form of assistance to these governments.

13. Various forms of nonmoney income, such as the value of services rendered by housepersons, are not included.

After AGI is determined, certain deductions are made in moving to taxable income.

14. The standard deduction is used mainly by lower incomes, while higher-income returns choose to itemize.

15. The extent to which various itemizable deductions may be justified differs. Among the most important items are state and local taxes, mortgage interest, and charitable contributions.

16. State and local income and property taxes are deductible, but deduction of the sales tax has been disallowed.

17. Mortgage interest is deductible and results in preferential treatment of homeowners.

18. Equitable treatment of homeowners would call for inclusion of imputed rent with deduction of mortgage interest.

19. Special problems arise in the treatment of social security and private pensions.

FURTHER READINGS

Details on the income tax statute may be found most conveniently in the *Federal Income Tax Forms and Instructions*, provided each year together with the 1040 return. A more detailed presentation may be found in such publications as the *U.S. Master Tax Guide*, published annually by the Commerce Clearing House. For further reading on the income tax, see p. 368 below.

Chapter 20

Individual Income Tax: Further Problems*

A. Tax Base in Relation to GNP and Personal Income. B. Tax Preferences. C. High-Income Problems: *Tax Shelters; Minimum Tax.* **D. Treatment of Low Incomes:** *Level of Tax-Free Minimum; Earned-Income Tax Credit; Child Care Credit.* **E. Patterns of Progression:** *The Meaning of Progression; Changing Patterns; Measuring Progression.* **F. Inflation Adjustment:** *Exemptions and Bracket Limits; Capital Income.* **G. Choice of Taxable Unit:** *Family-Unit Approach; Earner-Unit Approach; Dependents and Stay-at-Home Spouses.* **H. State and Local Income Taxes:** *State Income Taxes; Local Income Taxes.* **I. Summary.**

In this chapter, the broad outline of the income tax given above is followed up by further considerations of certain strategic problems.

A. TAX BASE IN RELATION TO GNP AND PERSONAL INCOME

*Reader's Guide to Chapter 20: This chapter presents more on the structure and workings of the individual income tax, including the implications of tax preferences and tax expenditures, rate structure, and definition of the taxable unit, as well as the effects of inflation. Except for section E on measuring progression, all this material is needed for an understanding of how our income tax works.

Table 20-1 shows the relationship between GNP and tax base for 1984. Comparing line 19 with line 1, we see that income actually subject to tax was only 46 percent of GNP. For a tax which is meant to offer the most comprehensive measure of ability to pay, this seems a poor performance. Closer consideration, however, shows that perhaps half of the difference may be explained by appropriate adjustments.

Consider first lines 1 to 7, which show the movement from GNP to personal income. Deduction of capital consumption allowances is clearly in order as the income concept underlying the income tax is to be on a net basis. Inclusion of transfer payments and government interest is also correct since these add to the taxpayer's capacity to pay. The deduction of taxes, however, is questionable, as we have noted in the preceding chapter.

Lines 8 to 12 show the adjustment of personal income as defined in the national income accounts to the concept of AGI as defined by the tax law. National income data are used in making the adjustment. We deduct transfer payments which are in personal income but mistakenly not in AGI. We then add employee contributions to social security, because these are included in AGI but not in personal income. We thus obtain a value of AGI as estimated from Department of

TABLE 20-1
From GNP to Income Actually Subject to Tax, 1984
(Billions of Dollars)

1.	GNP	3,663
2.	− Capital consumption allowance	681
3.	− Taxes*	700
4.	+ Government transfer payments	399
5.	+ Government interest	418
6.	− Other, net	67
7.	Personal income	3,012
8.	− Transfer payments	417
9.	− Imputed income†	195
10.	+ Personal contribution to social insurance	132
11.	+ Capital gains	54
12.	AGI, Department of Commerce base	2,586
13.	− Unexplained gap	496
14.	AGI reported	2,140
15.	− Exemption	131
16.	− Standard deduction	116
17.	− Itemized deduction	242
18.	+ Other	150
19.	Taxable income	1,701

*Includes excise and sales taxes, property taxes, corporation profits tax, employer and employee social security contributions.

†Includes imputed income such as imputed rent and "other labor income" (such as fringe benefits and employer contributions to pension plans) covered by the Department of Commerce concept of personal income but not counted as part of taxable wages.

Sources: For lines 1 to 10, see Department of Commerce, *Survey of Current Business,* June 1985, pp. 6–9. For lines 10 to 18, see U.S. Treasury Department, *Individual Tax Returns,* Statistics of Income, 1984, p. 13 ff. We list as standard deduction what in 1984 was referred to as the zero-bracket amount.

Commerce data. Comparing this estimate of AGI (line 12) with the value of AGI as actually reported (line 14), we find a gap of about 5 percent of reported AGI. This seems to suggest that tax administration is 95 percent effective; but as shown below, this is a questionable conclusion.

Lines 14 to 18 show the further adjustments made in moving from reported AGI to the amount actually subject to tax. To arrive at what the Treasury calls taxable income, we reduce AGI by the amount of exemptions. Next, deductions from taxable income, examined in the preceding chapter, are taken out. These involve the standard deduction taken by taxpayers who do not itemize as well as itemized deductions claimed by others.

The amount of taxable income actually reported may thus be reconciled fairly well with the GNP accounts of the Department of Commerce. However, a full-income concept with a more prudent definition of the tax base and reduced evasion might well yield a base of taxable income from one-third to one-half above that now obtained.

B. TAX PREFERENCES

We have seen that the statutory definition of taxable income, after allowing for exclusions and deductions, is by no means identical with the theoretical concept of accretion. Substantial differences exist and in most cases result in a taxable income below that called for by the accretion concept. Whereas it remains debatable in particular instances how a base loss should be defined, it is evident that the loss and the resulting diminution in revenue or "tax expenditures" is large. The latter term is used because failure to collect the revenue owing to gaps in the base of taxable income is in fact the same as collecting the revenue and then making an expenditure to leave the taxpayer in the same position. Thus failure to include mortgage interest in the tax base is equivalent to taxing homeowners fully and then paying them a corresponding subsidy. The resulting level of tax expenditures or revenue loss from 1988 is estimated at $281 billion. With an estimated actual revenue from the income tax of $400 billion, this equals over 40 percent of a potential revenue total of $681 billion.

As shown in Table 20-2, the largest loss results from the treatment of insurance and pension plans, owing to failure to include employer contributions to health insurance and to pension plans, exclusion of social security benefits, and exclusion of pension contributions to individual plans. Next come benefits from failure to fully tax realized capital gains, followed by homeowner benefits and deductibility of state-local taxes. Other major items are the deduction of charitable contributions and exclusion of interest on state and local securities.

The existence of these preferences would be of little concern if base reductions due to tax preferences were a fixed proportion of the "full" base for all taxpayers. In this event, they could be readily neutralized by correspondingly higher rates. But, in fact, the incidence of preferences varies considerably, both with regard to average taxpayers in various income brackets and with regard to particular taxpayers within a bracket. Thus vertical and horizontal inequities result.

Beginning with the former, we find that the benefits from tax expenditures—

TABLE 20-2
Tax Expenditures*
(Fiscal Year 1988 in Millions of Dollars)

Exclusion of employer contributions to health insurance	30,205	
Exclusion of pension contributions, employer plans	58,185	
Exclusion of pension contributions, individual plans	13,350	
Exclusion of social security benefits	16,610	
Exclusion of certain Medicare benefits	6,000	
Total		124,350
Incomplete taxation of realized capital gains	26,380	
Deductibility of mortgage interest on owner-occupied homes	19,855	
Deductibility of property tax on owner-occupied homes	7,205	
Deductibility of state and local taxes	14,845	
Exclusion of interest on state-local debt	8,040	
Deductibility of charitable contributions	9,475	
Total		85,800
Other		71,095
Grand total		281,245

*The amounts reflect the cost of providing taxpayers with the benefits now derived from incomplete coverage. These amounts are more or less equivalent to the resulting revenue loss.
Source: See *Special Analyses, Budget of the United States Government, Fiscal Year 1988.* Also see J. Pechman, *Federal Tax Policy,* 5th ed., Appendix C, 1987, The Brookings Institution, Washington, D.C.

as can be seen readily from the table—are by no means limited to high-income groups. Indeed, a large part of the revenue loss reflects insurance and pension arrangements the benefits of which are widely spread. Other items, such as housing preferences, focus primarily on the middle-income range and still others, such as capital gain loopholes and tax-exempt interest, are of primary benefit to higher incomes. It should be noted, however, that even though the larger part of the revenue loss occurs over the lower and middle range into which most taxpayers fall, the benefit as percent of full liabilities is larger at the upper end.

Horizontal inequities result because individual taxpayers with equal incomes do not share equally in the resulting benefits. Thus, homeowners benefit relative to renters, recipients of tax-exempt income benefit relative to salary earners, and so forth. Prior to the 1986 reform, major loopholes to investors in real estate and partnerships resulted in large tax differentials at the higher-income level. Most of these tax loopholes have been closed by the reform, but tax expenditures remain a major problem. As noted before, the resulting revenue loss still reaches 40 percent of what present rates could yield with a truly comprehensive base.

C. HIGH-INCOME PROBLEMS

Special problems of tax avoidance arise in connection with various types of capital income.

Tax Shelters

As noted before, losses may be offset against income and interest may be deducted when computing taxable income. Both provisions are in line with a sound concept of net income as tax base. In combination, they have, however, led to substantial abuses and to the opening of tax shelters. To illustrate, a partnership could have been established to engage in housing investment. On the basis of a small equity contribution, this could have permitted the partners to incur large mortgage debts. Interest payments thereon resulted in heavy losses over an initial period before adequate returns were obtained. By investing in partnerships, the investor was thus enabled to write off such losses against other income, thereby reducing tax thereon. Subsequently, when the property was sold, the capital gain would be taxed at preferential rates only. The Tax Reform Act of 1986 has set certain limitations on such ventures:

1. Realized capital gains are now taxed at regular rates.
2. Interest (in excess of $10,000) on funds borrowed to finance investment may be deducted against investment income only.
3. Losses resulting from passive investment activities such as investment in partnerships may not be offset against general income from all other sources.
4. Losses from investment in which the investor is an active participant can be offset against his or her other income, but subject only to an at-risk limitation, such that offsets are limited to the investor's own equity funds.

These limitations are designed to rule out the previous widespread practices undertaken by investment activities which generate losses and thereby result in reduction of tax liabilities.

Minimum Tax

The embarrassing occurrence of minimal tax liabilities at high levels of income, brought about by compounding of exclusions, deductions, and various tax-shelter devices, has led to the introduction of a so-called minimum tax. First enacted in 1969, this provision has been strengthened much since, most recently by the tax reform of 1986. It now calls for a tax of 21 percent imposed on the "alternative minimum taxable income." To obtain the latter, taxable income is increased by disallowing certain "preference items" in its computation. These include provisions relating to accelerated depreciation and use of the installment method of accounting.

D. TREATMENT OF LOW INCOMES

The problem of vertical equity in the income tax is not only a matter of how heavily high-income taxpayers should be taxed. It is also and perhaps more importantly a question of how little those with low incomes should pay.

Level of Tax-Free Minimum

There is fairly general agreement that an initial slice of income should not be taxed. Taxable income should be defined as AGI minus this basic allowance. In defining this allowance, we might use the level below which the taxpayer is considered to be "in poverty." Since the poverty level differs with size of family, the level at which the tax begins differs accordingly.

The starting point for tax liability depends on various factors. First, there is the personal exemption of $2,000 per taxpayer, spouse, and each child. Family size is allowed for, the implicit assumption being that additional dependents do not generate economies of scale. Next, there is the standard deduction, equal to $3,000 per single and $5,000 per joint return, with no allowance for dependents made in this connection. Allowing for these amounts, the tax-free limit rises from $5,000 for single to $9,000 for joint returns and to $13,000 for joint returns with two dependents. Substantial allowance is thus made for family size, with the resulting tax-free amounts corresponding roughly to the poverty-line levels of income as estimated by the Department of Agriculture.

The tax-free limit, as noted before, not only is important in setting the floor for tax liability but also dominates the rise of the effective rate or pattern of progression over the lower-middle-income scale. The effective rate of tax (defined as ratio of tax to AGI) at low levels of AGI is very low, simply because the tax-free amount is a very large fraction of AGI. As AGI rises, the tax-free amount falls relative to AGI, so that the effective rate rises as would have been the case even if only one bracket rate applied. Putting it differently, we can say that the tax-free amount may be viewed as a zero-rate bracket and thus as an integral part of the rate structure. The major significance of granting a tax-free amount thus rests with its bearing on the pattern of effective rates over the lower-middle-income range. This benefit is maintained, even though the tax reform of 1986 has provided for a vanishing of the resulting benefits over the higher-income range.

Earned-Income Tax Credit

The pattern of tax liabilities and effective rates as shown in Table 19-2 of the preceding chapter is modified further by the earned-income credit. For earned income only, taxpayers with dependents are permitted a credit against tax (deduction from tax) equal to 14 percent of earned income up to $5,714 with a maximum credit of $800. The credit is then reduced by 10 percent of earnings in excess of $9,000 and thus disappears when earnings reach $17,000. An inflation adjustment for these amounts is provided for. The credit applies only to returns with dependents and, most important, is refundable in situations where the credit is in excess of previously determined tax.

As shown in Table 20-3, application of the earned-income credit raises the tax-free limit from $7,000 to $11,000 for a single return and from $11,000 to

TABLE 20-3
Tax Liability with Earned Income Credit

SINGLE, ONE DEPENDENT				JOINT, ONE DEPENDENT			
AGI	Tax	Credit	Net	AGI	Tax	Credit	Net
1,000	- - -	140	− 140	1,000	- - -	140	− 140
7,000.	- - -	800	− 800	8,000	- - -	800	− 800
7,100	15	800	− 785	9,100	- - -	790	− 790
9,000	300	800	− 500	11,000	- - -	600	− 600
9,100	315	790	− 475	11,100	15	590	− 575
11,000	600	600	- - -	13,400	360	360	
17,000	1,500		1,500	17,000	900	- - -	900

$13,400 for a joint return, assuming one dependent in each case. Below these levels, a negative tax (refund) is received, with the amount of negative tax first rising and then falling to zero. Application of the earned income credit may be viewed as a first step toward a negative income tax, that is to say, an income tax which encompasses both a falling negative rate (transfer) as income rises toward a break-even point and a rising positive rate as income increases above that point. If principles of progressive taxation call for the former, they may well also suggest the latter. Such proposals were under active discussion two decades ago, as was noted in our earlier examination of welfare reform.[1] For now it should be noted only that the earned-income credit falls short of a full negative income tax approach because it is limited to earners and to returns with dependents only. As a result, the tax liability for returns with dependents is substantially lower at the bottom of the scale than for returns without dependents. Similarly, low-income recipients whose income comes from other sources, such as pensions, do not benefit.

Child Care Credit

In line with general concern for women's rights and a fair treatment of family income, the law provides further for a child care credit. The allowance is given in the form of a credit against tax equal to 30 percent of employment-related child care expenses for returns with AGI below $10,000 and falling to 20 percent for returns above $28,000. Eligible expenses are limited to $2,400 per child for the first two children. The credit can be claimed by working singles or by spouses if both are employed.

E. PATTERNS OF PROGRESSION

The income tax has traditionally been viewed as an instrument of progressive taxation. Just how progressive is it and what changes have there been in the pattern of progression?

The Meaning of Progression

Returning to Table 19-2 and Figure 19-1, we note the rising level of effective rates (tax as percent of AGI) when moving up the AGI scale. The tax is said to be progressive over an income range for which this ratio rises, proportional for a range over which the ratio is constant and regressive over a range for which it falls. For the tax to be progressive, it is not enough therefore for the liability to rise with income. An increase at a rate below that of the rise in AGI leaves the tax regressive. Also, the tax is more progressive the more rapidly the ratio of the tax to GNP increases. In Figure 19-1, this was indicated by the slope of the effective rate curve. We thus note that the income tax is most progressive over the lower-middle range and then flattens out and becomes essentially proportional over the higher ranges. As noted before, the decisive factor over the lower-middle-income range is the declining weight of the personal exemption and standard deduction rather than

[1] See p. 191.

rising bracket rates. A further discussion of how effective progression may be measured follows at the end of this section.

Changing Patterns

The pattern of bracket rates has changed greatly over time and offers a fascinating insight into the course of tax policy.

Past Trends   As shown in Table 20-4, the spread of bracket rates has been reduced sharply in recent decades. With a spread of 23 to 94 percent during World War II, the postwar adjustment initially provided for a 17 to 84 percent spread. Thereafter, the bottom rate showed little change while the top rate dropped from 91 to 70 percent in the 1960s and 1970s. Since then there were two sharp reductions, to 50 percent in 1981 and 28 percent in 1986. Rates in the middle range also declined but less sharply so.

Reviewing this historical pattern, we find a continuing trend toward reduced progressivity of bracket rates, especially at the upper end of the income scale and most distinctly so under the recent tax reform of 1986. This picture, however, is somewhat misleading. What matters in the end is the pattern of effective rates (ratio of tax to income) and not simply that of bracket rates. Effective rates also depend on the level of exemptions and deductions and (most important for the upper-income range) on the comprehensiveness or lack thereof with which taxable income is defined. Due to base omissions, past patterns of effective rates have been less progressive than suggested by that of bracket rates, leaving the shrinkage in effective rate progression less pronounced than the table might indicate.

Tax Reform of 1986   How does the tax reform of 1986 fit this pattern? At the lower end of the scale, the reform provided for a reduction in effective rates by raising exemptions while leaving bracket rates generally unchanged. Over the middle-upper range, the base was broadened with the resulting increase in liabilities offset by rate reduction so as to leave effective rates unchanged. The reform thus was neutral regarding revenue and vertical equity over the middle-upper range. At the same time, the closing of loopholes improved horizontal equity and

TABLE 20-4
Development of Rate Structure
Applicable Bracket Rates (Percent) at Selected Levels of Taxable Income, Joint Returns

Taxable Income	1944	1950	1963	1978	1981	1986
$ 2,000	23	17	20	14	11	15
10,000	42	24	26	21	16	15
20,000	59	35	38	28	22	15
50,000	78	54	59	49	38	28
100,000	92	68	75	59	45	33
200,000	94	81	89	68	50	28
400,000 +	94	84	91	70	50	28

Source: J. Pechman, *Federal Tax Policy*, Washington, D.C.: Brookings, 1987 5th ed., p. 315.

the efficiency of the system. These were clear-cut gains. But the reform, in the process, also chose to maintain the pre-reform pattern of effective rates intact rather than to implement that pattern which would have prevailed had pre-reform bracket rates been made effective by a full base definition.

This consideration is illustrated in Table 20-5. Column 1 of the table gives the pre-reform pattern of effective rates while column 2 gives the post-reform pattern. As will be seen, the two are quite similar over the middle and upper range. Column 3, in turn, shows the pattern of effective rates which would have resulted had the 1986 reform combined its base-broadening with a proportional (say, 9 percent) cut in pre-reform bracket rates. Revenue would have again been maintained unchanged, but the resulting pattern of effective rates would have been more progressive than that shown in columns 1 and 2. Failure to consider such a move, it might be argued, ratified the previously hidden retreat from the principle of progressive taxation. With the lowering of the top rate to 28 percent, a major step was taken in the direction of a flat-rate income tax. A flat-rate tax, to be sure, would still retain effective rate progression over the lower range, because the personal exemption would continue to provide a zero-rate bracket. But effective rate progression would largely disappear from the middle up. Seen in this broader perspective, the significance of the 1986 reform much transcends its accomplishments as a cleaning-up operation.

Measuring Progression

The distinction between progressive, proportional, and regressive taxes is readily drawn. A tax is progressive if the ratio of tax to income rises when moving up the

TABLE 20-5
Effective Rates for 1988
(Joint Return, One Dependent)

AGI (Pre-reform Law)	Pre-reform Law* 1	Reform Law 2	Alternative Patterns† 3
0– 10,000	0%	0%	0%
10,000– 20,000	5.2	4.3	1.6
20,000– 30,000	8.8	8.3	5.6
30,000– 50,000	12.3	11.0	9.6
50,000– 100,000	16.5	16.0	15.5
100,000– 200,000	23.8	21.8	26.2
200,000– 500,000	29.6	25.0	34.8
500,000–1,000,000	29.8	26.8	37.6
1,000,000 +	27.9	26.6	41.6
Total	14.5	13.4	13.4

*1986 law applicable to 1988 levels of income. Bracket limits and exemptions are applied as estimated for 1988 levels.

†1986 rates (including zero bracket amount) are applied to broadened base, increased exemptions, and standard deductions under the reform. To avoid double counting, the reform standard deduction is reduced by zero bracket amount. Effective rates thus arrived at are then reduced by 9.0 percent so as to equalize total revenue with that of column 2.

Source: Brookings Tax Simulation File. Effective rates are tax liability divided by the appropriate definition of AGI. I am indebted to Chuck Byce for providing the calculation. For further discussion, see R. A. Musgrave, "Short of Euphoria," The Journal of Economic Perspectives, vol. 1, no. 1, 1987.

income scale, proportional if the ratio is constant, and regressive if the ratio declines. This distinction is obvious, but the situation is more complex if we wish to measure the *degree* of progression or regression.

As was shown in Table 19-2, the average-rate curve (ratio of tax to taxable income or AGI) rises and is therefore progressive throughout the income scale, but the *degree* of progression varies between points in the scale. There is no single "correct" way to measure the degree of progression.

Various measures may be applied, including:[2]

1. The ratio of change in effective rate to change in income
2. The ratio of percentage change in liability to percentage change in income
3. The ratio of percentage change in after-tax income to percentage change in before-tax income

Measure 1, which may be referred to as *average-rate progression*, gives the slope of the curve obtained by plotting the effective rate against income. The value of the coefficient is zero for a proportional tax and positive for progression. The effective-rate curve tends to flatten out and progression tends to decline as we move up the income scale. Measure 2, which may be referred to as *liability progression*, records the elasticity of the tax liability with respect to income. The coefficient measures the slope of the curve obtained by plotting tax liability against income on a double-log chart. Proportionality is now reflected in a coefficient of 1 and progression in a coefficient above 1. Measure 3 or *residual income progression* records the elasticity of after-tax income with respect to income. It gives the slope of a curve obtained by plotting before- and after-tax income on a log chart. The coefficient again equals 1 for a proportional tax but progression is now indicated by a coefficient of less than 1. Progression under all indicators tends to decline as we move up the income scale but may rise over particular income spans.

Coefficients for measures of progression are shown in Table 20-6 as they apply to various income spans. The degree of progression as measured by the various coefficients differs considerably, as does the change in the level of progression over various income spans. Not even the direction of change must be the same. As

---

[2] Applied to discrete income intervals, the corresponding formulas are:

1. $\dfrac{T_1/Y_1 - T_0/Y_0}{Y_1 - Y_0}$

2. $\dfrac{T_1 - T_0}{T_0} \cdot \dfrac{Y_0}{Y_1 - Y_0}$

3. $\dfrac{(Y_1 - T_1) - (Y_0 - T_0)}{(Y_0 - T_0)} \cdot \dfrac{Y_0}{Y_1 - Y_0}$

where Y_0 and Y_1 are the lower and higher levels of income and T_0 and T_1 are the corresponding tax liabilities.

These measures, as here written, relate to discrete income *spans*. Alternatively, one might consider the slope of the various curves at particular income *points*. In this case expression 2 becomes $(dT/T)(dY/Y) = (dT/dY)/(T/Y)$ or the ratio of marginal to average rate of tax.

See Richard A. Musgrave and Tun Thin, "Income Tax Progression, 1928–48," *Journal of Political Economy*, December 1948.

TABLE 20-6
Measures of Progression
(Joint Return without Dependents)

AGI (Dollars)	TAX Liability (Dollars) (I)	TAX Average Rate (II)	DEGREES OF PROGRESSION* Average-Rate Progression (III)	DEGREES OF PROGRESSION* Liability Progression (IV)	DEGREES OF PROGRESSION* Residual Income Progression (V)
10,000	105	1.1			
			0.71	14.7	0.85
20,000	1,650	8.2			
			0.24	4.8	0.56
50,000	7,692	15.4			
			0.12	1.75	0.65
100,000	21,616	21.6			
			0.04	1.33	0.46
200,000	50,800	25.4			
Coefficient for proportional tax			0	1	1
Coefficient for progressive tax			>0	>1	<1
Coefficient for regressive tax			<0	<1	>1

*Values computed from formulas in footnote 2, p. 359, reflect progression over specified AGI ranges.

we move up the income scale, the coefficient for average-rate progression falls, indicating declining progressivity. The coefficient of liability progression also decreases throughout as we move up the scale, once more indicating falling progressivity. But for residual income progression the trend is reversed, i.e., progressivity rises, this being reflected now in a declining coefficient. Although all these measures describe the same set of liabilities, that of residual income progression is perhaps the most interesting. Concern with the progressivity of the tax structure, after all, is not only with the way in which the tax burden is distributed but also, and perhaps primarily, with the way in which the distribution of after-tax income is affected. The latter is reflected in residual income progression. Thus, if a new piece of legislation brings an increase in residual income progression (reduction in our coefficient), this signals that the distribution of residual income has become more equal.[3]

To avoid confusion in comparing progression over different income ranges or for different tax structures, it is necessary to specify exactly what measure is used. This is of special importance with respect to what happens to progression when tax rates are changed. When rates are to be increased or reduced, Congress may consider it desirable to do so in a neutral fashion, calling for an across-the-board change. But what is meant by neutrality?

[3] Note that the degree of residual income progression depends upon the level as well as the slope of the effective-rate curve, whereas the other measures depend on its slope only. Residual income progression is thus similar in nature to our earlier and more comprehensive approach of "effective progression," where changes in the equality of the entire residual income distribution were measured. See p. 335. For further discussion, see Ulf Jacobson, "On the Measurement of the Degree of Progression," *Journal of Public Economics*, January–February 1976, pp. 161–168.

Suppose that taxes are to be increased. If average-rate progression is held constant, all liabilities are increased by an equal percentage. Bracket rates are increased by a rising number of percentage points as we move up the scale. If liability progression is held constant, all bracket rates are increased by the same number of percentage points. If residual income progression is held constant, bracket rates are increased by a falling number of percentage points as we move up the scale. Representatives of low-income groups will thus be inclined to interpret neutrality in the sense of average-rate progression, with liability progression next and residual income progression last. Representatives of high-income groups will be inclined to take the opposite view. Amusingly, the orders of preference are reversed when it comes to a tax reduction. Thus, theoretical concepts may carry their political implications.

F. INFLATION ADJUSTMENT

After the inflationary experience of the late 1970s and 1980s, much attention has been paid to the impact of inflation upon the structure of the income tax. This problem arises not only regarding the nominal level of exemptions, standard deductions, and bracket rates, but also and in a more complex way, regarding the treatment of capital income.

Exemptions and Bracket Limits

As prices rise, the real value of exemptions and standard deduction declines. As a result, the level of real income at which the tax begins to apply falls. Moreover, as prices rise, the real value of bracket limits declines, so that the level of bracket rates applicable to a given level of real income rises. For both these reasons, income tax liability increases more rapidly than do prices, i.e., they increase in real terms.

While repeated consideration was given to adjustment in bracket limits, the real value of exemptions was permitted to decline sharply during the inflation of the late 1970s and early 1980s. The tax reform of 1986 corrected for this, and restored the real value of exemptions to approximately their 1978 level. This legislation also provided for an extensive system of indexing, including exemptions, standard deductions, limit of bracket rates, and cut-offs relating to the earned-income credit. The income tax, insofar as wage and salary income is concerned, has thus been largely inflation-proofed.

Capital Income

Some further problems arise, however, regarding the treatment of capital income.[4] As noted before, realized capital gains are now subject to regular tax, as is appropriate. However, the tax applies whether the increase in value has occured in merely nominal or real terms. Equal treatment of capital gain would call for taxation of real gains only, and hence for an inflation adjustment therein.

---

[4] The reader may wonder whether similar problems of neutrality do not also apply with regard to wage income. The answer is no, provided that exemptions and bracket rates are indexed.

A similar problem arises also with regard to creditor losses in the real value of nominal debt as well as debtor gains. An accretion system based on income defined in real terms should allow a loss to the creditor as well as impute a gain to the debtor. As was suggested in 1986, such a solution might be approached by reducing taxable interest income by the rate of inflation, but Congress did not accept this proposal. A further inflation issue arises in the treatment of depreciation. As prices rise, the recovery of capital cost loses in real value and an inflation adjustment is again in order. As noted below, this has not been provided for by the reform of 1986, with reliance on accelerated depreciation being the preferred though less adequate solution.[5]

G.   CHOICE OF TAXABLE UNIT

Proper treatment of the taxpaying unit under a progressive income tax is a controversial matter to which there may be no fully satisfactory solution. It is also a problem which has been affected by two recent socioeconomic trends, one being the increased participation of women in the labor force and the other being the increasing frequency of cohabitation without marriage.

Family-Unit Approach

We begin with the hypothesis which traditionally has applied to most income tax discussion, that the tax-paying unit and the measurement of ability to pay should refer to the family unit. We will then consider an alternative which defines the taxpaying unit in terms of the individual earner.

Principles   Looking at the matter from the point of view of taxation by ability to pay, equity calls for compliance with these three rules:

  1.   Units with the same income and the same numbers should pay the same tax.
  2.   Among units with the same income, the unit with the smaller number should pay more and that with the larger number should pay less.
  3.   Given a progressive rate schedule, the tax (as a percentage of income) for equal-number units should rise with income.

Rule 1 requires no explanation because it simply represents the requirement that equals should be treated equally. It need be noted only that it is a matter of indifference for gauging ability to pay in the family-unit context whether the given income is contributed by a single earner or by multiple earners. Rule 2 reflects the proposition that a single person living at, say, $30,000 is better off than a couple with the same amount. Although certain consumption items (e.g., the light in the living room) serve two persons as well as one, others (e.g., chairs to sit on) are more costly for two. Thus, it is only fair for the tax on singles to be somewhat higher than the tax on marrieds with the same income, so that such a differential (if at the appropriate level) should not be viewed as a discriminatory "singles" tax. Rule 3, finally, follows directly from the principle of progression, and no further explanation is needed. A system complying with these equity rules will not affect the marriage decision, be it for a single earner or for two earners.

[5] See p. 386.

Joint and Single Returns The instruments by which such an outcome can be reached include the personal exemption and the use of differentiated rate structures for various types of returns. As noted above, the exemption is set at $2,000 per person (single, spouse, and dependent) permitting the combined exemptions to rise with the size of the unit. The standard deduction and bracket limits also differ for single and joint returns. As a result, liabilities rise more slowly for the joint return. Although past systems tended to discriminate against singles, the present law succeeds in achieving a high degree of neutrality. This is shown in Table 20-7. The single earner (lines 1 to 4) experiences a tax reduction upon marriage which may be taken to reflect his or her increased costs.

For the case of two earners, the combined liability is essentially unchanged upon marriage. This is the case where earnings are unequal (lines 5 to 12) as well as where they are at equal levels (lines 13 to 20). To the extent that marriage reduces joint costs, this tends to favor marriage.

Cohabitation without Marriage The tax law so far makes no allowance for cohabitation in the absence of marriage, with each partner remaining subject to a single return.

TABLE 20-7
Income Tax Liabilities for Single and Joint Returns, 1988*

	COMBINED AGI			
	$10,000	*$25,000*	*$50,000*	*$100,000*
Single earner				
1. Tax, single	750	3,280	9,720	24,562
2. Tax, joint	150	2,400	7,613	20,918
3. Difference (2 − 1)	− 600	− 880	− 2,107	− 3,644
4. (3 ÷ 1)	− 0.8	− 0.3	− 0.2	− 0.1
Two earners: ¾ to ¼				
5. AGI of A	7,500	18,750	37,500	75,000
6. AGI of B	2,500	6,250	12,500	25,000
7. Single tax on A	375	2,063	6,570	17,137
8. Single tax on B		188	1,125	3,280
9. (7 + 8)	375	2,251	7,695	20,417
10. Joint tax	150	2,400	7,613	20,918
11. (10 − 9)	− 225	149	− 82	501
12. (11 ÷ 9)	− 0.6	0.1		
Two earners: ½ to ½				
13. AGI of A	5,000	12,500	25,000	50,000
14. AGI of B	5,000	12,500	25,000	50,000
15. Single tax on A	0	1,125	3,280	9,720
16. Single tax on B	0	1,125	3,280	9,720
17. (15 + 16)	0	2,250	7,560	19,440
18. Joint tax	150	2,400	7,613	20,918
19. (18 − 17)	150	150	53	1,478
20. (19 ÷ 17)	—	0.1	—	0.1

*Tax computation uses standard deduction or 10 percent of AGI, whichever is higher.

Earner-Unit Approach

An alternative view of the problem followed by some European countries is to disregard the family setting and to consider the individual earner as a basic unit. In this case, the combined liability of the couple will depend on how earnings are distributed. There would be no difference with a proportional rate, but the difference may be substantial under progressive rates. As compared with the joint return, this European approach grants a more favorable treatment to the lower earner and has thus received the support of women's rights groups. However, the narrowing of bracket rates under the recent legislation has reduced the importance of the distinction.

Dependents and Stay-at-Home Spouses

Returning to the family-unit approach, two further issues are to be noted.

Allowance for Dependents   In the process of measuring the ability to pay of a family unit, the number of dependents should obviously be allowed for. A large family with a given AGI has a lower ability to pay than does a small family with the same AGI. The question is only who should be considered a dependent and how the allowance should be made. One question involves issues such as the treatment of children living away from home and earning some income. Another involves the question of whether the allowance should be given as a deduction from AGI, as is now the case, or as a credit. If the cost of an additional child is to be measured in terms of a standard (say, average) expenditure per child, the credit approach is appropriate; but if the cost is to be measured in terms of what the particular taxpayer undertakes, the deduction approach becomes preferable. Since a taxpayer with a higher income spends more per child, it would then be appropriate to give a larger tax benefit. If the former interpretation were chosen, a substitution of a credit for the additional exemption now granted would be in order.

Another aspect of the tax treatment of dependents involves the standard deduction. Whereas this allowance is larger for joint than single returns, it is independent of the number of dependents. As the allowance has increasingly taken on the nature of an additional exemption (rather than an approximation of what otherwise would be itemized deductions), a good case can be made for permitting it to rise not only with a move from a single to a joint return but also with the number of dependents.

Stay-at-Home Spouses   Finally, there is the question of how to deal with spouses who do not earn outside income but stay at home, whether to keep house, to tend children, or to enjoy leisure. Consider a family of two spouses A_1 and A_2 where A_1 earns outside income while A_2 does not; and compare them with another family of two spouses B_1 and B_2 both of whom have outside jobs. Assume that the wages of A_1 and B_1 are the same and that A_2 has the same earnings potential as B_2. Under present law the B family pays more than the A's. Yet our equal option rule tells us that both should pay the same, as does our earlier conclusion that imputed income should be considered part of accretion.[6]

---

[6] See p. 333.

In principle imputed earnings (in terms of wages forgone) of stay-at-home spouses should be included in the tax base. Moreover, in principle, the same procedure would have to be applied to stay-at-home singles or, for that matter, to earners who work part-time. This would in fact call for a tax on potential income, which would be the ideal (if impracticable) solution on both efficiency and equity grounds.[7]

A less ambitious solution might be to impute to the nonearning spouse A_2 an income equal to the standard cost of housework and child care (the cost which would be incurred if this work were done by outside help) without attempting to estimate the potential wages of A_2. Such an approach would be more practicable and the imputation would be increased with the number of children. In the absence of such an arrangement, the child care credit now given to the earner helps to even the score.

H.   STATE AND LOCAL INCOME TAXES

As noted before, the income tax is primarily a federal tax. In 1986, 82 percent of individual income tax revenue went to the federal government, 14 percent to the states, and 4 percent to local governments. As a percent of their tax revenue, the three levels of government derived 42, 20, and 3 percent from this source, respectively. Nevertheless, the income tax is used by forty-two states and in recent years has also become increasingly important at the local level.

State Income Taxes

Structure of State Taxes   Of the forty-two states (including Washington, D.C.) which use a general income tax (applicable to both earned and unearned income), most make use of AGI as defined under the federal income tax. Where the federal base is used, certain adjustments are made, with interest on federal securities and frequently capital gains excluded.[8] Most states permit a 10 percent standard deduction. Personal exemptions have been typically around the federal level or somewhat higher, with a few states using a credit in lieu of an exemption. Rates in all but four states are progressive, ranging typically from 2 to about 8 percent but reaching as high as 13.75 percent in New York. Even though rate progression is moderate, the effective rate (even in states using a flat rate schedule) is strongly progressive, over the lower-income ranges, owing to generally high exemptions. Three states (Vermont, Nebraska, and Rhode Island) determine liability under the state tax as a percentage of federal tax. Some states tax capital income at a higher rate while others exempt wage income. Most states permit income tax paid to other states as a credit against their tax and short of one-half permit deduction of the federal tax. We thus find considerable variety among the state income taxes, but the typical pattern is one of approximating federal AGI and exemptions and of progressive rates from 2 to 8 percent.

---

[7] See p. 223.
[8] For these and other relevant facts, see Tax Foundation, *Facts and Figures on Government Finance,* 1986.

Deductibility   State income taxes are deducted in computing taxable income under the federal income tax, and the federal income tax is deducted by a minority of states in computing taxable income for purposes of the state tax. The deductibility provisions are important because they determine the *net* addition to the tax burden which results from the state tax.

Suppose first that only the federal government permits deductibility and that a 10 percent state tax is imposed. The net cost (increase in combined state and local tax) per dollar of state tax depends on the taxpayer's federal rate bracket. If this bracket is 28 percent, the net cost of each dollar of state tax equals 72 cents, with 28 cents recouped through the reduction in federal tax. If the bracket rate is 15 percent, the net cost equals 85 cents, since only 15 cents is recaptured in reduced federal tax. The incremental tax caused by a flat-rate state tax is thus regressive. Matters are complicated further if the state also allows deductibility of the federal tax.[9] This deduction further reduces the net liability imposed by an increase in the state tax and adds to its regressivity in net terms. Moreover, closer consideration shows that the net gain to the taxpayer from deduction of the federal tax is slight, whereas the revenue loss to the state is substantial.[10] It is inadvisable, therefore, for states to permit deduction of the federal tax.

Now it might be argued that this is not relevant since the state should consider the liability that *it* imposes, without considering repercussions on the federal tax. Yet to overlook these repercussions is unrealistic since, in fact, a substantial part of state taxes is financed by recoupment of federal tax. By the same token, the recent reduction in federal tax rates has made the state income tax more costly. All this raises questions of how the tax system should be designed in a federal state, a matter to which we will turn to later on.[11]

Limitations   It is not a matter of accident that state income tax rates are relatively modest as compared with federal rates. This reflects the fact that at higher rate levels, interstate rate differentials would come to have significant effects on economic location. Unless all jurisdictions were to use the same rate structure, the role of distributional adjustments through progressive taxation at the state and local level is quite limited; but with uniform rates, policy would in fact be a national one. The function of redistribution, as we will see later on, must be largely centralized.[12]

---

[9] To apply mutual deductibility on a current basis, the taxpayer would have to be adept in solving simultaneous equations; and the process would be difficult because the appropriate rate brackets would be unknown. In practice, the problem is solved, however, by deducting last year's tax.

[10] Let the federal and state statutory tax rates be f and s. With federal deductibility, the effective federal rate becomes $f(1 - s)$ and the combined rate is $f(1 - s) + s$. With mutual deductibility, the effective federal rate is $f(1 - s)/(1 - fs)$ and the net state rate is $s(1 - f)/(1 - fs)$, the combined rate being $[f(1 - s) + s(1 - f)]/(1 - fs)$.

Assuming $s = 0.10$ and $f = 0.28$, we find that the combined rate prior to deduction of the federal tax at the state level is 35.2. With mutual deductibility, it becomes 0.33 giving a reduction in the net tax of 1.9 cents per dollar of income. At the same time, state revenue falls from 10 to 7.4 cents per dollar of income.

[11] See p. 469.

[12] See p. 459.

Local Income Taxes

Even though income taxes at the local level are relatively unimportant in overall magnitude, they are of considerable importance in some of the larger cities. New York City, for instance, derives over 20 percent of its tax revenue from this source. Some form of income tax is now imposed by about 4,000 local governments, including cities, counties, and over 1,000 school districts. The rate is typically 1 to 2 percent and in most cases no exemptions are granted. Local earnings by nonresidents are included in the tax base, which in some cases is limited to wage and salary income.

I. SUMMARY

Taxable income amounts to less than 50 percent of GNP. Tax preferences or tax expenditures result in a deficient definition of taxable income and thereby weaken the equity of the income tax in both its horizontal and vertical aspects.

1. Of the difference, about one-third is accounted for by the gap between GNP and personal income, one-half by that between personal income and AGI, and the remainder arises when moving from AGI to taxable income.

2. Only a small fraction of the gap is unexplained.

3. Preferences result in a loss of over one-third of the revenue which would be obtained under a full tax base.

4. Preferences are important throughout the income scale, with pension contributions weighing heavily at the lower end, homeowner benefits most significant in the middle, and capital gains preferences and exclusion of tax-exempt interest most important at the top.

5. Horizontal inequities result because the benefit of tax preferences is distributed unequally among taxpayers with the same income broadly defined.

High-income taxpayers have benefited from certain tax shelters which in recent years assumed major proportions.

6. To deal with the growth of tax shelters, carryover of losses and interest deductions have been limited by 1986 legislation.

7. There has also been a substantial tightening of the minimum tax.

Special relief is given to low-income taxpayers via certain tax credits.

8. The earned-income credit offers substantial relief to earned-income recipients with dependents, limited to the lower end of the income scale.

9. The child care credit is designed to provide relief to low-income taxpayers with dependents, applicable to single returns or two joint returns where both spouses are employed.

The progressivity of the income tax is examined.

10. Progressive taxation is defined as measured by the slope of the effective rate schedule.

11. The spread of bracket rates has been reduced repeatedly over the past twenty years.

12. The Revenue Act of 1986 reduced the top rate from 40 to 28 percent. However, the impact upon the effective degree of progression has been offset largely by base-broadening over the upper-income ranges.

13. Debate over the appropriate degree of progression continues, involving a variety of considerations.

14. Various ways of measuring the degree of progression are examined.

The importance of inflation adjustments is noted.

15. Exemptions, standard deductions, and bracket limits have been indexed, thereby making the wage earner's income tax inflation proof.

16. Making capital income inflation proof remains to be completed, including indexing of capital gains, interest, and depreciation.

The appropriate choice of the taxable unit has been a matter of controversy over the years.

17. Within the family-unit approach, the tax is now essentially neutral regarding marriage choice.

18. An alternative approach is offered by defining the taxable unit as the individual earner.

19. Tax treatment of imputed income of stay-at-home individuals remains to be resolved.

The role of income taxation is primarily at the federal level, although the income tax is used as well by many states.

20. State income tax rates typically range from 2 to 8 percent.

21. Whereas state income taxes are deductible under the federal tax, only a minority of states permit deduction of federal tax.

FURTHER READINGS

A concise compilation of income tax provisions may be found in the Treasury's *Form 1040 General Instructions,* which accompanies the annual return form.

For a sample of the voluminous literature on income tax see:

Bradford, D.: *Blueprints for Basic Tax Reform,* 2d ed., Arlington, Va.: Tax Analyses, 1984.

McLure, C., and Treasury staff: *Tax Reform for Fairness, Simplicity, and Economic Growth,* Department of the Treasury, November 1984.

Pechman, J. A.: *Federal Tax Policy,* 5th ed., Washington, D.C.: Brookings, 1987.

Simons, H.: *Federal Tax Reform,* Chicago: University of Chicago Press, 1938.

Surrey, S.: *Pathways to Tax Reform,* Cambridge, Mass.: Harvard University Press, 1973.

Symposium on Tax Reform, *Economic Perspectives,* vol. 1, no. 1, 1987.

Chapter 21

Corporation Income Tax: Structure and Integration*

A. **Structure of Federal Corporation Income Tax:** *Determination of Taxable Income; Derivation of Tax Base; Structure of Tax Base.* B. **Should There Be a Corporation Tax?** *The Integrationist View; The Absolutist View; Other Reasons for Corporation Tax.* C. **Integration:** *Full Integration; Partial Integration;* D. **Further Aspects of Base Definition:** *Debt versus Equity Finance; Inventory Accounting; Expense Accounts; Tax Shelters and Minimum Tax.* E. **Summary.**

The corporation income tax, like the individual income tax, is primarily a federal tax, with over 90 percent of corporation tax revenue accruing at the federal level. However, the corporation income tax is also used by most states, although at much lower rates. Special problems posed by state corporation taxes will be considered later on, our initial concern here being with the federal tax. Even though this tax has furnished a rapidly declining share of federal revenue—now about 10 percent as against nearly 30 percent three decades ago—it has remained at the center of the tax debate.

---

*Reader's Guide to Chapter 21: The purpose of this chapter is to appraise the role of the federal corporation tax. The central question is whether there should be an "absolute" corporation tax or whether it should be integrated with the individual income tax. If so, how should such integration be accomplished?

A.   STRUCTURE OF FEDERAL CORPORATION INCOME TAX

The federal corporation tax is now imposed at rates of 15 percent on the first $50,000 of net income, 25 percent on the next $25,000, and 34 percent in excess thereof. The latter compares with a top rate of 40 percent prior to 1986 and 50 percent in earlier years. Whereas nearly 90 percent of all corporations are taxed at the lower rates only, over 90 percent of all profits are subject to the top rate. As shown below, this reflects the fact that large corporations furnish the bulk of the tax base, the size distribution of corporate profits being much more unequal than that of individual income by individual income tax brackets.

Determination of Taxable Income

The basic principle in determining taxable income is simple enough. Gross income of the corporation is reduced by costs incurred in doing business, and the rest is net income subject to tax. Certain problems posed by exclusions and deductions under the individual income tax again arise, such as capital gains, tax-exempt securities, and charitable contributions. Other issues are added, further complicating the design of an equitable and efficient corporation tax. This involves determining just what items should be deductible as business costs and what the timing of such charges should be. Different industries present different problems and it is difficult to design a uniform tax treatment for such divergent industries as, for instance, manufacturing and banking. Given the legal complexities of corporations and their interrelationships, it is evident that a fair corporation tax cannot be a simple tax.

Derivation of Tax Base

Whereas the individual income tax is a general tax (or at least aims at being so), the profits tax applies to capital income only. Moreover, it is limited to capital income which (1) accrues in the form of profits, and (2) originates in the corporate sector. Corporate profits as reported in the national income accounts contribute about half of total profit income and one-third of total capital income.[1] Thus the corporate tax covers only part of the base if viewed as a tax on profits and only a fraction thereof if viewed as a tax on capital income.

Taxable corporate profits differ from profits as defined in the national income accounts in that inventory valuation gains (or losses), repatriated foreign income and realized capital gains are included. Certain other items such as depletion al-

[1] Based on the following figures for 1986:

	In Billions of Dollars
1. Corporation profits	253.2
2. Profits of unincorporated enterprise	261.9
3. Rental income of persons	16.7
4. Net interest	251.1
Total	783.7

See U.S. Department of Commerce, Survey of Current Business, July 1987. Note that item 2 includes profits as well as salary equivalents of owner-operators.

lowances and state income taxes are deducted. There is no counterpart to personal exemptions, but a substantial loss of revenue results from accelerated depreciation.

Structure of Tax Base

The structure of the corporation tax base, as shown in Table 21-1, differs strikingly from that of the individual income tax. The total number of returns is much smaller and there is a much heavier concentration of returns at the lower end of the scale. In 1983, 46 percent of the returns were from corporations with assets of less than $100,000, and 80 percent had assets of less than $500,000. Yet these returns contribute only 8 percent of net income and 2.5 percent of tax. Turning to the other end of the scale, we note that corporations with assets of over $250 million comprise less than one-tenth of 1 percent of returns but contribute 57 percent of total net income and 67 percent of tax paid. This reflects the predominating importance of large enterprises in the corporate sector. From the revenue point of view, then, only the large and giant corporations matter.

B.   SHOULD THERE BE A CORPORATION TAX?

The role of the corporation tax in a good tax system is by no means obvious. If the appropriate tax base is viewed in terms of consumption, there is clearly no case for a corporation tax. Corporate source income should then become taxable only if and when it is distributed and spent by the recipient. But the case for a corporation tax may be questioned even in the context of an income-based approach. Here taxation at the corporate level may be viewed as a mere device for integrating corporate source income into the individual income tax, or it may be viewed as an additional

TABLE 21-1
Corporation Tax Returns by Size Group, 1983

Size of Total Assets (Thousands of Dollars)	RETURNS		NET INCOME		TAX*	
	Number (Thousands)	As Percentage of Total	In Billions of Dollars	As Percentage of Total	In Billions of Dollars	As Percentage of Total
Under 100	1,774	55.9	1.0	0.4	2.4	2.2
100– 500	904	28.5	6.2	2.7	2.5	2.3
500– 1,000	215	6.8	4.4	1.9	1.9	1.8
1,000– 5,000	205	6.5	14.0	6.0	6.8	6.3
5,000– 10,000	28	0.9	6.4	2.8	3.6	3.3
10,000– 50,000	31	1.0	17.5	7.5	9.5	8.8
50,000–100,000	6	0.2	7.4	3.2	3.9	3.6
100,000–250,000	4	0.1	12.4	5.3	6.2	5.8
250,000 and over	4	0.1	163.6	70.2	71.2	65.9
Total	3,171	100.0	232.9	100.0	109.0	100.0

*Tax net of foreign tax credit and investment credit.
   Source: Commissioner of Internal Revenue, *Statistics of Income, 1984, Corporate Income Tax Returns,* Washington, D.C., 1987, p. 48, table 6.

"absolute" tax on corporate source income, to be imposed before net income is allocated to the shareholder. Under U.S. law, the latter view continues to apply. The federal corporation tax of 34 percent is taken out first and cannot be credited against the shareholder's personal income tax on dividend income. Proposals to integrate corporate income into the individual income tax were rejected in the tax reform of 1986.

The Integrationist View

Those who take the integrationist position view the problem of taxation at the corporate level merely as a way of including all corporate-source income in the individual income tax base. Their basic proposition is that in the end, all taxes must be borne by people and that the concept of equitable taxation can be applied to people only. Moreover, they hold that income should be taxed as a whole under a global income concept, independently of its source. Proceeding on the assumption that the corporation income tax falls on profits, they criticize such a tax because profits when distributed are taxed twice—first at the corporation level under the corporation tax and then at the personal level as dividends under the individual income tax.

Consider taxpayer A who pays personal income tax at the 28 percent rate. Her share in the profits of corporation X is $100 on which the corporation pays a tax of $34. The remainder, or $66, is distributed in dividends to A, who then pays an income tax of $18.48. The combined tax equals $52.48. In the absence of a corporation tax, the income tax paid on $100 of dividends would have been $28, thus leaving an "excess tax" of $24.48. Next consider shareholder B, who pays personal income tax at a rate of 15 percent. For him, the combined tax equals $34 plus $9.90, or $43.90. The income tax under an integrated system would have been $15, thus leaving an excess tax of $28.90, somewhat above that of A. Failure to integrate imposes an additional burden and that burden per dollar of corporate source income is larger for the smaller shareholder whose individual income tax is lower. At the same time, note that dividends are likely to comprise a larger share of A's than of B's income. This being the case, the extra tax as a percent of total income may be larger for A than for B. However this may be, the extra tax is unjustified from the integrationist's point of view, because all income (including that derived from corporate source) should be taxed at the same rate. In place of the corporation tax, there should be source withholding of individual income tax on corporate source income.

The preceding illustration has assumed that profits after tax are in fact distributed as dividends. In reality such is not the case, because at least half of profits after corporation tax tend to be retained. In the absence of imputing retained earnings to the shareholder (as would be the case under the integrated system) the corporation tax thus serves the purpose of reaching retained earnings. With the new sets of rates introduced in 1986, the corporate rate of 34 percent now exceeds the individual income tax rate applicable on distribution, but (except for the low-income shareholder) the margin has become slight.

The Absolutist View

Those who take an opposing position believe that the integrationist approach rests on an unrealistic view of the corporation. The large widely held corporation—

which accounts for the great bulk of corporation tax revenue—is not a mere conduit for personal income. It is a legal entity with an existence of its own, a powerful factor in economic and social decision making, operated by a professional management subject to little control by the individual shareholder. From this it is concluded that being a separate entity, the corporation also has a separate taxable capacity which is properly subject to a separate and absolute tax. Whether profits after tax are distributed or retained is irrelevant in this context.

This "absolute" or "classical" view of the tax is hardly tenable. Corporations do indeed act as distinct decision-making units, only more or less vaguely related to the wishes of the shareholders, thus calling for a regulatory policy at the corporate rather than the shareholder level. Moreover, tax devices may be useful under certain circumstances for such regulatory purposes. However, this is quite a different matter from proposing that a corporation has an ability to pay of its own and should be subject to a distinct tax.[2] Obviously, all taxes must in the end fall on somebody, i.e., on natural persons. Corporate profits are part of the income of the shareholders and, in the spirit of the accretion approach to the income tax, should be taxed as part of their income. There is no reason why they should either bear an extra tax or be given preferred treatment.

Once more, note that this view of the corporation tax rests on the assumption that the tax falls on profits and is not passed on to consumers or wage earners. To the extent that such shifting occurs, the intent of the absolutists to impose an extra tax on corporate source income is thwarted. The tax, in this case, becomes an inferior and arbitrary sales or wages tax, without a rational place in an equitable tax structure.[3]

Other Reasons for Corporation Tax

Even though there is no valid argument for an absolute corporation tax on individual ability-to-pay grounds, a number of other considerations might justify such a tax. However, it would hardly be of the same order of magnitude or structure as the federal profits tax.

Benefit Consideration   Corporations may be called upon to pay a benefit tax. Government renders many services which benefit business operations by reducing costs, broadening markets, facilitating financial transactions, and so forth. Most of these services, however, do not accrue solely to corporations but to other forms of business organization as well. The rationale would therefore be for a general tax on business operations rather than for a tax on corporations only. Although there are certain governmental costs incurred in connection with corporations in particular, these costs are a minor factor and hardly justify a tax. The privilege of operation under limited liability is, of course, of tremendous value to corporations,

---

[2] One may, of course, speak of the ability of a corporation to pay a certain tax without going bankrupt or without curtailing its operations. The concept of capacity to pay as used in this sense, however, relates to the economic effects of the tax rather than to ability to pay as used in the context of equity considerations.

[3] It is inferior because the implicit rates of sales or payroll taxation will vary arbitrarily with the profit-sales ratio (margin) or the profits-wage bill ratio of particular corporations.

but the institution of limited liability as such is practically costless to society and hence does not justify imposition of a benefit tax. The purpose of benefit taxes is to allocate the cost of public services rendered, not to charge for costless benefits.

To the extent that a benefit tax is appropriate, two further questions arise. One relates to the level at which such a tax should be imposed. Since most public services which accrue as benefits to business are rendered at the state and local levels, it is evident that such a tax would not be primarily a federal matter. The other relates to the appropriate tax base. This will differ with the service rendered, but in most cases it will not be profits. Thus, real property would best reflect the value of fire protection; employment would reflect the input of school expenditures; transportation would reflect road services; and so forth. If a general proxy is to be used, total costs incurred in the state or locality might be the best overall measure, with value added (which includes profits as well as other factor costs) being a second possibility.

Regulatory Objectives   A different case for an absolute corporation tax may be made if the tax is viewed as an instrument of control over corporate behavior. The appropriate form of corporation tax then depends on the particular policy objective that is to be accomplished.

1.   The control of monopoly has been traditionally undertaken through regulatory devices, but a tax approach might be used. This, however, would not call for a general tax on profits, which would not be effective in correcting monopolistic behavior. Rather, it would call for a more complex tax, related to the degree of monopolistic restriction.

2.   If it were desired to restrict the absolute size of firms or bigness (which is not the same as restricting monopoly or market shares), a tax might again be used for this purpose. Here, a progressive business tax would be called for. The reason for progression, however, would not be ability to pay, as in the individual income tax. Large firms might be owned by small investors and small firms might be owned by wealthy investors. Rather, progression would be used to discriminate against the large firm and curtail what are considered to be undesirable social effects of bigness. The question then arises about whether such a tax should not be on asset size or sales rather than on profits. Even if bigness is held undesirable, it is not a reason for penalizing the profitable big firm in particular.

Although we have no full-fledged experience with such an approach (a progressive corporation tax was recommended by the Roosevelt administration in 1936 but rejected), a limited application is found in the three-rate schedule which applies various lower rates to small firms. This is a subject to which we will return later on.[4]

3.   An excess profits tax may be imposed in periods of emergency (such as wars) when direct controls over wages and prices are needed. Wage constraints under such conditions cannot be applied effectively without corresponding profit constraints, and a tax on excess profits is a helpful tool in this connection. The United States imposed such a tax in both world wars as well as during the Korean war. Although sound in principle, the excess profits tax is difficult to administer since excess profits are not readily defined. Such profits may be measured by comparison with a base period, but inequities may result from differences in initial position; or, a standard rate of return may be used, in which case risk differentials can hardly be overlooked, thus posing the difficult problem of what rates are appropriate for what industries.

[4] See p. 396.

A different type of situation in which a selective excess profits tax may be called for was created by the recent oil crisis and the removal of price controls on oil, leading to the imposition of a windfall profits tax.

4.   As a stimulus to capital formation and growth, it may be desirable to encourage corporate saving and to discourage dividend distribution. This objective may be accomplished by imposing a tax on dividends paid out while exempting earnings retained. Alternatively, it may be held desirable to encourage corporate distributions and to discourage retentions in order to improve the functioning of the capital market or to increase consumption expenditures. This goal may be achieved by imposing a tax on undistributed profits while exempting profits which are paid out as dividends. Such a tax was imposed in the late thirties with the intention of stimulating consumer spending.

5.   Finally, the corporation tax may be used to provide incentives or disincentives to investment, as distinct from corporate savings. Devices like accelerated depreciation and, prior to 1986, the investment tax credit may be used for this purpose, and they may be applied on a cyclical or a secular basis. The effectiveness of such measures will be considered in more detail later on, but it should be noted here that such incentives may also be given directly—i.e., in the form of investment subsidies or grants—rather than as relief under the profits tax.

In all, these considerations suggest that tax instruments may be helpful devices in controlling corporate behavior but in most cases, a form of taxation would be required which differs from the profits tax.

C.   INTEGRATION

As noted before, there is much to be said for viewing the corporation as a conduit of income accruing to the individual shareholder and for integrating corporate-source income with the individual income tax. What adjustments in the tax structure would be called for to accomplish this objective?

Full Integration

To secure complete integration, the adjustment must integrate the tax treatment for both retained earnings and dividend distributions. This may be accomplished either via the partnership method or through full taxation of capital gains.

Partnership Method   This solution is to impute total profits to the shareholders and to tax them under the individual income tax. Where earnings are retained, the corporation would inform its shareholders that a specified amount has been retained on their behalf and added to their equity; the shareholders would then include this amount when computing their taxable income.

At the same time, it would still be highly desirable to apply source withholding to profit income. Just as the corporation acts as a withholding agent for the individual income tax on the wage income of its employees, so it will act as withholding agent for the profit income of shareholders. Suppose that a certain shareholder receives a profit share of $1,000 and is notified accordingly. The corporation pays a withholding tax of, say, 20 percent, leaving the shareholder with a net profit of $800. Whatever part thereof is distributed in dividends, the shareholder will gross up and include the entire $1,000 in his taxable income. If his marginal rate is 28 percent, the tax thereon equals $280. Against this he will credit the $200 paid at the source, thus paying an additional $80. A shareholder whose marginal rate is 15 percent owes a tax of $150. Inasmuch as $200 has been withheld, she will receive a refund of $50. By using this grossing-up procedure, the taxpayer will pay at her proper marginal rate. If the withholding rate exceeds her personal rate, a refund will be due to her.

In other words, shareholders are treated for tax purposes as if they were partners in an unincorporated business. Since their tax is paid when the profits accrue, capital gains which reflect an increase in share value caused by retention of profits must then be excluded from subsequent capital gains taxation. This is done by permitting shareholders to write up the base (add to the purchase cost of their shares) by an amount equal to their share in retentions.

This procedure seems eminently fair, and it has been among the standard proposals made by tax reformers for a long time. However, certain difficulties with the method have been pointed out. It has been argued that the taxpayer should not be required to pay a tax on income which has not been "received." Hence, it is "unfair" to impute retained earnings to the person's taxable income. This objection is essentially the same as that raised against the taxation of unrealized gains but it is not convincing. For one thing, a substantial part of the tax will be paid by source withholding, thus imposing no liquidity problem on the shareholder. The remainder, payable where the individual's marginal rate exceeds the withholding rate, may be financed by a sale of shares. This approach may not be feasible in the case of closely held corporations which are not traded, but here shareholders may obtain the necessary cash by raising their payout ratios.

It is also argued that the partnership approach, although feasible for small and closely held corporations, would not be practicable for large and widely held firms. Since shareholders move in and out of the securities market, it might be difficult to allocate profit shares among them. Moreover, difficulties arise in connection with incentive measures, such as the investment credit. Management, which typically makes the investment decision, might not respond to a credit the benefits of which are passed through to the shareholder, and the pass-through process itself invites technical difficulties. Nevertheless, these problems should not prove to be beyond solution if a serious effort at integration was made.

However this may be, it should be noted that integration by the partnership method does not in any way bypass the problems involved in determining taxable income of corporations. This determination remains as important as it is under the absolute corporation tax. Integration by the partnership method does not simplify tax administration but places new demands upon it.

Capital Gains Method   Alternatively, full integration might be secured through full taxation of all (including unrealized) capital gains, combined with a repeal of the profits tax. The distributed part would then appear in the shareholder's income as dividends, while the retained part would appear as capital gains. No determination of taxable profits would be needed. Under this approach, periodic (say quintennial) taxation of unrealized gains on traded shares might be combined with taxation at death or transfer of other assets. However, in the absence of taxation at the corporate level, investment incentives such as the investment credit would now have to be granted at the shareholder level or be given as a direct subsidy to the corporation.

Partial Integration

Whereas full integration has been discussed over the years, it has never been considered a realistic move. However, at times the practice has been to provide some degree of partial integration. Thus prior to 1986, the first $200 of dividend income (joint returns) was excluded from taxable income. Note that the relief was given via an exclusion rather than as a credit against income tax. As a result the benefit to the dividend recipient was permitted to rise in line with his or her marginal rate of tax, thus favoring high-income shareholders. However, dividend exclusion was discontinued in 1986, along with the reduction in the corporate rate to 34 percent. With the corporate rate now fairly close to most shareholders' personal rate, the present setting may be viewed as approaching an integrated treatment for retained earnings. But "double taxation" continues to apply to dividends paid.

D. FURTHER ASPECTS OF BASE DEFINITION

Issues in corporate finance, not surprisingly, are more complex than are those of the individual household, and so are the problems of corporate tax design. Only a few samples will be noted here.

Debt versus Equity Finance

Interest which corporations pay on borrowed funds is deducted when taxable income under the corporation tax is determined. Interest is treated as a cost of doing business just as are wage payments. In the absence of integration, this leaves the provider of funds with an incentive to lend rather than to undertake equity investment. In the former case, only the personal income tax need be paid on interest received. In the latter, dividend distribution suffers double taxation. A similar distortion in favor of debt finance arises from the management perspective. If funds are secured via debt finance, interest paid may be deducted from taxable profits, whereas no deduction is permitted from earnings on equity capital. Introduction of full integration would restore neutrality. In its absence, neutrality might be restored (1) by disallowing the deduction of interest under the corporation tax, but only at the cost of broadening the scope of double taxation. Or, neutrality might be restored (2) by permitting deduction of imputed interest on equity capital under the corporation tax, thereby reducing the scope of double taxation. However this may be, heavy reliance on internal sources of finance has caused the equity share to rise rather than to fall, with little evidence that adverse tax treatment has had a major effect.

Inventory Accounting

Increases in the value of inventories (i.e., stock in trade held as a normal part of conducting business over the taxable year) are included in the firm's operating profits. These changes may be measured on either a LIFO (last-in, first-out) or a

FIFO (first-in, first-out) basis. Once selected, the procedure must continue to be used by the firm.[5] LIFO gives smaller profits in periods of rising prices and smaller losses when prices fall. It thus makes for a more stable tax base over the business cycle than does FIFO. Being used by most corporations, LIFO also makes for a continuously smaller tax base under conditions of sustained inflation, automatically excluding inflation gains from the tax.

Expense Accounts

Expenses accounts and "expense-account living" have been a much discussed topic. When entertainment expenses are treated as deductible business costs, the net cost of such outlays is reduced by nearly one-third and activities which hardly deserve public subsidy are encouraged. Moreover, by making payments in kind rather than in cash, the corporation may help its employees to reduce their personal income tax. Thus, if a $10,000 car is furnished to the executive, the cost to the corporation is the same as if his or her salary were raised by this amount. But a salary gain would increase the individual's tax liability, whereas the car services may not.

This avenue of individual income tax avoidance may be closed either by including income in kind in the individual's taxable income or by disallowing deduction of such costs at the corporation level. A modest effort was made in the Revenue Act of 1964 and again in that of 1978 to limit deductibility and to reduce expense-account allowances. But even though the "three-martini lunch" has remained a feature in the tax reform debate, efforts to limit expense accounts have met with heavy opposition and have not been very successful. After much discussion, deduction was limited to 80 percent under the Revenue Act of 1986. Since making detailed distinctions between deductible and nondeductible items would cause serious administrative difficulties, the British practice of disallowing almost all entertainment expenses is perhaps the only feasible alternative, but hardly one which the Congress will entertain.

Tax Shelters and Minimum Tax

As in the case of the income tax, the 1986 reform provided for a substantial tightening of tax shelters and of the minimum tax. The corporate minimum tax is now imposed as an addition (rather than an alternative) to the regular tax. To determine its base, certain preference items (still allowed in reducing taxable income for the regular tax) are aggregated and subject to a tax of 20 percent. These items include a range of provisions, including accelerated depreciation allowance, bad-debt deductions and other practices which have resulted in a questionable shrinkage of the tax base. As in the case of the income tax, the minimum tax serves to prevent compounding of benefits derived from questionable provisions in the regular tax. This is helpful, but hardly a substitute for a more appropriate definition of the regular tax base.

---

[5] Suppose that at the end of 1987 an automobile dealer had a stock of ten cars, acquired at $5,000 each. In 1988 twenty additional cars are acquired at $6,000, while five cars are sold at $7,000 each. Stock at the end of 1988 is twenty-five cars. Under the LIFO method, profits are $5 \times (\$7,000 - \$6,000)$, or $5,000. Under the FIFO method, profits equal $5 \times (\$7,000 - \$5,000)$, or $10,000. Since prices have risen, FIFO profits are larger.

E. SUMMARY

1. The 1986 legislation has reduced the rate of corporation tax from 46 to 34 percent, repealed the investment credit, and tightened the definition of taxable income, including in particular a reform of depreciation rules.

An analysis of the corporation income tax points to three key features:

2. The corporation tax has been of declining importance as a source of revenue.

3. The corporation tax covers only part (say, one-third) of all capital income, but unlike the personal income tax base, the bulk of taxable profits is received by a small number of very large corporations.

In assessing the role of the corporation tax in the good tax structure, we have distinguished between a view of this tax as an absolute tax on corporations as such and its role in integrating the taxation of corporate-source income under the individual income tax. As a basis for an absolute corporation tax, it might be argued that:

4. Corporations should be charged for benefits received from public services. Such a tax, however, would be smaller in amount than the traditional corporation tax and also different in form.

5. Various regulatory uses of taxation with regard to controlling size or monopoly power might be made but would also call for different forms of taxes.

The case for corporate taxation as a major revenue source must be based on its role as an ability-to-pay tax. Here we have drawn these conclusions:

6. The equity of the corporation tax must be assessed in terms of the impact of its burden among individuals, not firms. Provided that the corporation tax will not be passed on to consumers or wage earners, its burden must be attributed to shareholders or recipients of capital income at large.

7. Since all sources of income should be treated equally, this calls for integration of corporate-source income into the personal income tax.

8. Failure to integrate discriminates against lower-income shareholders.

Various techniques of integration were examined, including both full and partial integration:

9. Full integration may be obtained by the partnership or the capital gains method.

10. Implementation of either approach involves administrative difficulties, but these should not prove insoluble.

11. Partial integration may be obtained by excluding dividends from corporation tax or by granting a dividend credit at the shareholder level.

12. Integration was disregarded by the 1986 tax reform.

FURTHER READINGS

Pechman, Joseph A.: *Federal Tax Policy,* 5th ed., Washington, D.C.: Brookings, 1987, chap. 5.

McLure, Charles, Jr. (ed.): *Must Corporation Income Be Taxed Twice?* Washington, D.C.: Brookings, 1979.

Also see references to preceding chapter.

Chapter 22

Corporation Income Tax: Further Issues*

A. Depreciation Rules: *Timing of Depreciation; Economic versus Accelerated Depreciation; Expensing and Initial Allowance; Inflation Adjustment.* **B. Investment Tax Credit. C. Who Bears the Tax? D. Small Business:** *Should Rates Be Progressive?; Aid to Small Business.* **E. State Corporation Taxes. F. Foreign Investment Income. G. Summary.**

The debate over the corporation tax and its design, more than that for any other tax, has centered around its potential effects on the health of the economy and in particular upon investment. Here some of the major issues to be noted in this context are examined.

A. DEPRECIATION RULES

Whether one thinks in terms of an absolute corporation tax or of partnership-type integration, taxable income must be defined and the countless difficulties which

*Reader's Guide to Chapter 22: Economists' key concern in the definition of the corporation tax base has been with accounting for capital costs, including the design of a neutral arrangement as well as that of incentive provisions. The problems raised in this chapter are thus among the most interesting issues in the economics of tax analysis.

this definition poses must be faced. Here the treatment of depreciation presents one of the most difficult and important problems.

Timing of Depreciation

Since the corporation tax is a tax on *net* income, all costs of doing business must be deducted in arriving at taxable income. In the case of wage payments or the purchase of materials, deductions are made when payments occur. In the case of capital investment, such deductions are made over time. The law must determine the rate at which the investor is permitted to recover the cost of the investment. The timing of the recovery of capital cost is important because the present value of tax liability is reduced when depreciation is charged. Deduction of capital costs gives rise to tax savings to the investor, and these are greater the earlier the capital costs are deducted. Thus the present value of the tax and hence the resulting reduction in earnings depend not only on the tax rate but also on the timing of depreciation deductions. These factors involve both the time span over which depreciation is charged and the speed at which it proceeds within this interval.

Length of Recovery Period   The length of the period over which capital is recovered or depreciation is charged has traditionally been set in line with the "useful service life" of the asset. The Internal Revenue Service thus set "guideline lives," in line with "good business practice," ranging from three years for automobiles, over ten or more years for machinery, and forty to sixty years for structures. About eighty fairly broadly defined classes of assets were distinguished. The Revenue Act of 1971 introduced the so-called asset depreciation range (ADR) system, permitting the taxpayer to raise or lower these service lives by 20 percent. This traditional system was changed drastically by the Economic Recovery Tax Act of 1981, when recovery periods were reduced sharply, allowing for depreciation periods of three, five, ten, and fifteen years. This ARS system was designed to offset the impact of inflation and to provide an investment incentive; but it also resulted in a widely differing burden of taxation by type of investment. Further changes in depreciation rules were made in 1982 and the 1986 tax reform greatly modified the 1981 legislation. The new MACRS (Modified Accelerated Cost Recovery System) distinguishes eight asset classes. Most equipment falls into a 7-year class, with residential structures in a 27.5-year class and other structures in a 31.5-year class. These new asset lives continue to fall short of economic lives but less so than under the preceding system. Also, they are differentiated more nearly in line with economic lives and are thus less distorting.

Rate of Depreciation within Recovery Period   The rate of depreciation within the time span of the recovery period depends on which of several write-off methods are applied. Structures are required to use the *straight-line* method, where the same amount C/n is written off each year, with C being the asset cost and n the asset life. Thus, for a $100,000 asset with a life of ten years, $10,000 is deducted each year. Equipment is depreciated under the *declining balance method,* with twice the straight-line percentage deducted the first year and this same percentage then applied to the as-yet undepreciated amount in each successive year. Thus, $20,000 is deducted the first year, $16,000 the second year, and so forth. Still another method not allowed for under present law is the *sum-of-years-digits method*; the fraction deducted each year equals the ratio of remaining years to the sum of the years over the service life. Thus, for a $100,000 asset with a 10 year useful life, the sum of the years is $10 + 9 + 8 + \ldots + 1 = 55$. The charge for the first year is $^{10}\!/_{55}$ of $100,000 = $18,111; for the second year the charge is $^9\!/_{55}$ of $100,000 = $16,374; and so forth.

As shown in Table 22-1, the present value of depreciation is higher under the double-declining balance than under the straight-line method, and the difference increases with the length of service life. The same holds if we compare the sum-of-years-digits method with the straight-line method. As between declining balance and sum-of-years digits, we note that the former is preferable for short, and the latter for long, investments.

Economic versus Accelerated Depreciation

The effective rate of tax depends on both the nominal rate (now 34 percent for the larger corporations) and the rate at which depreciation is permitted. The faster the depreciation rate, the lower the effective rate of tax. When considering an investment, the investor weighs the present value of its net income stream against the cost of the asset. This present value equals the present value of the income stream before tax minus the present value of tax payments thereon. The latter in turn may be viewed as equal to the present value of the gross tax (as it would be if no depreciation were allowed) minus the present value of the tax savings due to depreciation. This negative component will be the larger and as shown in Table 22-1, the net tax will lower, the more rapidly depreciation may be taken. This result comes about because the present value of the tax savings will be the higher the sooner they are realized. Speeding up depreciation (whether by shortening the depreciation pe-

TABLE 22-1
Present Value of Depreciation
(In Dollars, Asset Cost $100,000)

Service Life (Years) (I)	Straight Line (II)	Double-Declining Balance (III)	Sum-of-Years Digits (IV)
	6 PERCENT DISCOUNT		
5	86,750	87,811	87,515
10	75,787	78,716	79,997
20	59,055	64,661	67,680
50	32,460	40,935	44,756
	10 PERCENT DISCOUNT		
5	79,534	81,100	80,614
10	64,469	68,528	70,099
20	44,663	51,539	54,697
50	20,806	28,829	31,439

Source: Harold Bierman, Jr., and Seymour Smidt, *The Capital Budgeting Decision,* 2d ed., New York: Macmillan, 1966.

riod or permitting faster recoupment within the period) thus reduces the effective rate of tax by postponing the due date of the tax liability. From the investor's point of view, acceleration is equivalent to an interest-free loan, with the present value of interest savings thereon equal to the present value of the resulting tax saving.[1]

Neutrality of Economic Depreciation It is evident, therefore, that rapid depreciation is helpful to the investor and especially to the investor in long-lived assets. The gain from early deduction (or the length of tax postponement gained) is the greater the longer the waiting period that otherwise would have applied. What then is the "correct" rate of depreciation which treats all investments in an impartial or neutral fashion?

Looking at any one investment in isolation, this poses no great problem. The Treasury loses from more rapid depreciation what the taxpayer gains, so that the same burden—defined as present value of tax—may be imposed by various combinations of tax rate and depreciation rate. A lower tax rate and slower depreciation rate will give the same present value of tax as a higher tax rate and a more rapid depreciation rate. If all investments were the same, it would make little difference which combination were chosen to provide the Treasury with a given revenue stream. The difficulty arises because investments differ in length and profitability and thus fare differently under the various policies. Yet they should be treated equally, as a matter of both equity (investors with the same income should pay the same tax) and neutrality (taxation should not distort the pattern of investment). What depreciation pattern is required to secure an equitable and neutral income definition?

The depreciable asset, as noted before, may be looked upon as generating two income streams. One is a positive income stream of earnings, arising from the use of the asset. The other is the negative income stream, or diminution of capital, which results as the asset is worn out and declines in value because of obsoles-

---

[1] Consider an investment giving a constant annual income stream R for n years. Prior to tax, the investor equates the cost of the investment with the present value of its income stream so that

$$C = R_n A_n$$

where C is the cost of the investment and A_n is the present value of an annuity of \$1 for n years, discounted at the market rate of interest.

After tax, we have

$$C = R_n A_n - t(R_n A_n) + t\frac{C}{d}A_d$$

where t is the tax rate and d (assuming straight-line depreciation) is the number of years over which depreciation is spread. A_d is the present value of an annuity of \$1 over d years. The second term on the right-hand side of the equation is the present value of gross tax, and the third term is the present value of the tax saving due to the depreciation allowance.

The present value of the net tax equals

$$t\left(R_n A_n - \frac{C}{d}A_d\right)$$

cence. Netting out, the asset gives rise to a net income stream, the present value of which is the value of the asset. Assets with equal present value of net income streams should carry an equal burden as defined by the present value of the tax.

Such will be the case where depreciation is charged in line with the actual diminution in asset value, thus taxing the true net income stream as it is received each year. The current value of the asset at any one time equals the capitalized value of the future income stream which it generates. The decline in the current value therefore equals the capitalized value of the reduction in the income stream which, in turn, is the capital cost or economic depreciation which should be charged along with costs in computing net income.

With tax depreciation equal to economic depreciation, imposition of the tax will reduce the value of the net income stream by the statutory rate of tax. The effective rate will thus equal the statutory or nominal rate and this will be the case independent of the length of asset lives. Thus, imposition of a tax will not alter the ranking among investments of different length and hence will not distort the investor's choice among them. If depreciation is permitted to be taken at a more rapid rate, the longer investment will gain most and benefit from a lower effective rate. Thus investment choices will be distorted and more capital will flow in that direction. The opposite holds if the permitted rate of depreciation falls short of the economic rate.

There is thus a strong case for the use of economic depreciation, but although the principle is clear, it is not easily applied. Modern capital equipment does not wear out evenly and it frequently becomes obsolete before it has been "used up." Obsolescence rates will differ and cannot be predicted. Thus, the best that can be done is to gear service lives to actual business practice while relying on the assumption that the latter will tend to reflect the "true" service life and time path of the income stream. With that practice as the standard, more rapid rates of depreciation may be referred to as "accelerated" depreciation.

Effective Rate of Tax   It should be evident from the preceding discussion that the level of nominal rate and changes therein is a very inadequate indicator of the level of effective rate. The effective rate is given by $(r_b - r_a)/r_b$, where r_b is the rate of return before tax and r_a is the net or after-tax rate of return. The effective rate thus equals the percentage reduction in return due to tax. It depends on both the statutory rate and the rate of depreciation.

The 1986 legislation resulted in a slight increase in the average effective rate, because the reduction in the nominal rate was outweighed by the repeal of the investment credit and by a modest lengthening of depreciation periods.[2] At the same time, some types of assets, such as equipment and in particular those with relatively short asset lives such as automobiles, experienced a sharp increase while others, such as industrial buildings, enjoyed a shortening. As shown in Table 22-2, the effective rates under the new regime are more nearly uniform, reflecting a pattern of depreciation more in line with economic depreciation, as well as the repeal of the investment credit, which itself tended to favor short-lived investments.

---

[2] For discussion of the investment credit, see p. 386.

TABLE 22-2
Effective Rates of Tax

	Prior to 1986 Reform*	1986 Reform
Trucks, buses, and trailers	0.2	29.9
General industrial machinery	− 3.3	38.0
Industrial buildings	45.6	37.0

*Allows for effects of investment credit.
Source: A. Auerbach, "Tax Reform: Cost of Capital," The Journal of Economic Perspectives, vol. 1, no. 1, Summer 1987, p. 77.

Single versus Continuing Investment In the preceding discussion we viewed the impact of accelerated depreciation on the net return of a single investment. For such an investment, which is made once and then withdrawn, accelerated depreciation does not reduce the total amount of tax that will be paid. The liability is reduced in the earlier years and increased in the later years. The gain (equivalent to an interest-free loan) results from a once-and-for-all tax postponement, with the Treasury losing revenue in the earlier years and recouping it thereafter. But not so for the case of a continuing investment. Suppose that the asset is replaced as it wears out so as to keep the depreciable base unchanged. The taxpayer's gain from postponement (and the Treasury's loss) then rises over the early years and thereafter levels off. After a while, the Treasury's loss of revenue ceases but there is no recoupment of the initial loss so long as continuous reinvestment takes place. Recoupment takes place only after reinvestment ceases. Finally, there is the case of a firm with continuing expansion of depreciable assets. If depreciation is sufficiently fast and expansion sufficiently sharp, such a firm may be able to postpone tax payment indefinitely. All payment is avoided and no ultimate recoupment occurs.

Expensing and Initial Allowance

The cost of wage payments or of materials purchased is deducted when made. Such costs are "expensed." What would happen if the same were done with regard to capital write-offs, that is, if acceleration were carried to the extreme and the cost of investment were made deductible when incurred? An investor who is engaged in a single investment may not be able to take advantage of such an immediate write-off. It may not be possible to realize the tax savings until enough income has accrued against which the entire depreciation can be charged. But suppose that the corporation has income from other investments against which the write-off can be charged at once. In this case, the investor bears no tax and the Treasury obtains no revenue.

To see how this works, suppose that you invest $100,000 in asset A and immediately charge $100,000 as depreciation. Since you have not as yet received any income from A, you suffer a loss of $100,000. You then charge this loss against income from asset B, thereby reducing your tax liability on income from B. With a tax rate of 34 percent, the tax savings equal $34,000. You next add this amount to your investment in A, charge another $34,000 as depreciation, make another tax saving on B of $11,560, and so forth. Repeating the series, you end up with an investment in A of $100,000 + 0.34 × $100,000 + 0.34² × $100,000... = $151,500. You will have to pay a 34 percent tax on your earnings from $151,500 invested in A, leaving you in the same position as having invested $100,000 without tax. Instantaneous depreciation with continuous reinvestment of the tax saving thus annuls the tax.

Policy may not go this far, however. The law may permit only some part, say one-third, of the investment cost to be recovered by instantaneous depreciation. In this case, only one-third of the tax will be wiped out. Such will be the case for both short and long investments. This approach, also referred to as initial allowance, offers a neutral way of granting an investment incentive. A system which permits part of the tax to be expensed while depreciating the remainder in line with economic depreciation will be neutral as between short and long investments.[3]

Inflation Adjustment

Throughout this discussion we have taken it for granted that the amount of capital recovery is set by the initial investment cost, the problem being only over what period and how rapidly the write-off should occur. An additional difficulty is posed by inflation. With prices rising, recovery based on original cost will not provide tax savings sufficient to keep the firm's capital intact in real terms. As a result, taxable income is exaggerated, resulting in a hidden increase in the effective rate of tax, as measured in relation to real income. This became of increasing importance during the seventies and tended to offset the tax relief granted by the investment credit.

To correct this defect and to deal with the inflation problem correctly, two solutions are available: (1) the depreciation base may be indexed so as to rise with replacement cost; or (2) the entire depreciation may be taken in the first year, so as to eliminate the impact of inflation. However, this depreciation would be taken from a reduced base so as to allow for the fact that tax savings from depreciation are obtained sooner (and hence carry a larger present value) than if spread over the economic life of the asset. Instead of neutralizing the impact of inflation, the 1981 legislation chose to shorten asset lives and to accelerate depreciation. By 1986, inflation had abated with no further inflation adjustment considered necessary. Facing up to this basic problem, however, will undoubtedly have to be met sooner or later if inflationary conditions return.

To make matters worse, the impact on depreciation allowances is only part of the inflation story. The broader question is whether the adjustment should be limited to depreciation, or whether the entire balance sheet should not be adjusted. For companies with net indebtedness, this would call for an addition to income as the real value of indebtedness falls with rising prices. For the corporate sector as a whole, the resulting addition to net income would on balance offset or outweigh the reduction in net income due to increase in the depreciation base. Some sectors, such as public utilities, would actually experience an increase in tax liability.

B. INVESTMENT TAX CREDIT

For two decades prior to the 1986 reform, the investment tax credit provided the major incentive device. Introduced in 1964, the credit permitted a fraction (10 per-

---

[3] See Arnold C. Harberger, "Tax Neutrality in Investment Incentives," in H. J. Aaron and M. Boskin, eds.: *The Economics of Taxation,* Washington, D.C.: Brookings, 1980.

cent in 1985) of the cost of qualified investments to be credited against tax. Thus an investor who purchased an asset costing $100,000 could obtain it at a net cost of $90,000. Qualified investments on which the credit was allowed included all depreciable assets other than buildings, thus permitting a 10 percent return to be obtained tax free.

How do the two devices, investment credit and accelerated depreciation, compare? The investment credit is similar to accelerated depreciation in that it reduces the tax, but its mechanism differs. As distinct from accelerated depreciation, the investment credit involves not merely a tax postponement but an outright tax reduction. For any particular investment with a specified length of useful life, it is possible to devise a pair of accelerated depreciation and credit provisions which will yield the same present value to the investor. But the two approaches differ among investments. Whereas accelerated depreciation favors the long investment, the credit works to the advantage of the short-lived asset. The shorter asset can be replaced more frequently, thus permitting more frequent use of the credit. For this reason, the pre-1986 law reduced the investment credit if the useful life of the asset fell short of seven years and granted no credit for assets with lives of below three years.

If the credit approach is properly designed, there is much to be said for it. The credit device makes it explicit that an incentive benefit is being granted and permits depreciation to be set in line with economic asset lives. Introduction of greatly accelerated depreciation in 1981, granted on top of the investment credit, however, resulted in negative rates of tax over a wide range of investments and repeal of the credit followed in 1986.

C. WHO BEARS THE TAX?

As was shown in the earlier discussion of tax incidence, most economists view the burden of the corporation tax as falling on capital, in line with the competitive model.[4] Businesspeople frequently differ and view the tax as a cost which is passed on. The former view is correct if one assumes that all markets operate in profit-maximizing fashion. But if firms operate as restrained monopolists, if sales rather than profits are maximized, or if other pricing rules apply, firms may well attempt to pass on the tax in higher prices. Moreover, if labor markets are imperfect, higher taxes may be reflected in more limited demands in collective bargaining and thus be passed on to labor.

The outcome, therefore, depends on existing market structures and behavior. The structure of American industry—and especially the larger manufacturing corporations from which the bulk of the corporation tax is derived—is such that administered pricing is likely to occur. Shifting due to administered price adjustments (as distinct from shifting due to factor movements and changing factor supplies in the competitive market) cannot be ruled out on a priori grounds. The same holds for the highly organized labor markets in which these firms operate. Theoretical analysis is inconclusive in such a setting and further empirical investigation is needed to settle the debate.

[4] See p. 260.

There have been repeated attempts in recent years to provide such evidence. To begin with, there is the question of what one should look for. If corporate tax rates differed between industries, the problem would be fairly simple. Insights might be gained from examining resulting price changes and comparing the relative positions of various sectors before and after the tax change. This cannot be done, however, since the tax applies to all incorporated firms at more or less the same effective rate. Nor is a comparison of rates of return on investment in incorporated and unincorporated firms feasible, since no adequate data are available for the latter. The remaining possibility is to examine the experience of the corporate sector without the benefit of comparison with tax-free sectors and to explore how various elements of the corporate sector responded to the tax, including such features as rates of return on corporate equity, the share of corporate profits in value added by (i.e., income originating in) the corporate sector, and corporate profit margins. Even this approach is not too instructive, because major changes in the rate of corporation tax have been infrequent.

We begin by taking a bird's-eye view of the relevant historical statistics. Some of the key variables are given in Table 22-3. Since the major increases in tax rates occurred during World War II, and since both the thirties and forties were highly unusual periods—one being dominated by the Great Depression and the other by a major war—the best that can be done is to compare the twenties and the decades following World War II.

TABLE 22-3
Corporate Tax Rates and Profits Share*
(In Percentages)

Years	Statutory Corporation Income Tax Rate (I)	MANUFACTURING CORPORATIONS		ALL CORPORATIONS
		After-Tax Rate of Return (II)	After-Tax Profit Margin (III)	Profit Share in Income Originating in Corporate Sector (Before Tax) (IV)
1927–1929	11–13.5	8.0	5.9	21.8
1936–1939	15–19	6.3	4.6	14.8
1955–1959	52	10.9	4.9	22.4
1960–1963	52	9.5	4.5	20.6
1964	50	11.6	5.2	21.9
1965–1967	48	12.7	5.4	22.1
1968–1969	52.8	11.7	4.9	19.8
1974–1977	48	13.6	4.9	17.5
1978–1986	46	12.7	4.0	12.3

*Column I: 1968–1969 and 1970 statutory rates include surcharge. Column II: Profits after tax (excluding inventory valuation adjustment) of manufacturing corporations as percentage of stockholder's equity. Column III: Profits after tax (as in column II) as percentage of net sales by manufacturing corporations. Column IV: Profits before tax (excluding inventory valuation adjustment) of all corporations as percentage of all income originating in the corporate sector.

Sources: Columns I to IV, 1927–1929 and 1936–1939: M. Krzyzaniak and R. A. Musgrave, *The Shifting of the Corporation Income Tax*, Baltimore: Johns Hopkins, 1963, pp. 15, 17. Columns I to III, 1955–1959: *Economic Report of the President*, January 1978 and January 1986. Column IV, 1955–1959 to 1969: U.S. Department of Commerce, *Survey of Current Business and National Income and Products Accounts*, table 1.14; 1974–1977: *Survey of Current Business*, July 1978 and July 1982.

Comparison of the statutory tax rates and *after-tax* rates of return (columns I and II) for the earlier period with those for the later period at first sight supports the shifting hypothesis. In the absence of shifting and assuming no other influences, the 8 percent return of the late twenties should have fallen to below 5 percent as the tax rose from 12 to 52 percent in the fifties. Actually, no such decline occurred. Instead, the net rate of return rose by nearly 40 percent. To put it differently, the gross rate of return rose by more than was needed to secure full shifting. Similar support for the shifting hypothesis is presented by the more or less constant *after-tax* profit margin, shown in column III. With after-tax margins constant, gross margins rose to reflect the tax. Column IV, however, gives a different picture. Gross profits or profits *before* tax as a share in total income originating in the corporate sector did not rise but were much the same in post-World War II decades as in the twenties. This runs counter to the shifting hypothesis. If the tax had been passed on to consumers or wage earners to recoup profits, the share of gross profits in national income should have risen accordingly.

The evidence derived from a comparison of the twenties with the postwar decades is thus conflicting and is consistent with both the shifting and the no-shifting hypotheses. Nor can a simple answer be found in the pattern of more recent years. The decline in the corporate tax rate was not reflected in a significant gain in the after-tax profit margin or profit share, thus suggesting that the tax had not been shifted. But the after-tax rate of return also showed little gain, which is in line with a shifting hypothesis. The result is confusing, but this should not be surprising. Many nontax factors changed during this period and proved more important than tax factors, especially for the years following 1978 when adverse business conditions reduced returns before tax while rates showed little change. The impact of nontax and tax factors must be separated if taxation effects and incidence behavior are to be determined.

An empirical measure of shifting thus calls for an econometric approach, designed to isolate the effects of the corporation tax. Various studies of this sort have appeared over the years, but the issue remains controversial. One type of study has expressed the corporate rate of return as a function of various predetermined variables, such as the level of consumer demand, capacity utilization, government expenditures, and corporation tax rates. By including corporate tax rates, analysts hoped to use the regression coefficient pertaining to this variable to measure the effects of rate changes on the rate of return. Some of these studies have indicated a high degree of shifting, lending more support to a full-shifting rather than to a zero-shifting hypothesis. Other studies, however, have pointed to opposite results. Econometric analysis has not been able in a conclusive way to separate tax effects from those of concurring changes in public expenditures, economic conditions, and other factors. And as noted before, the key variable in the analysis, i.e., the rate of tax, is itself a complex concept. Yet it is the effective rather than the nominal rate which matters. As we have seen in the preceding section, the effective rate depends on depreciation rules, the investment credit, the rate of inflation, and other factors which are not easily assessed. Improved econometric techniques combined with the use of less aggregative data may in time produce better results, but the difficulties involved are substantial.

D. SMALL BUSINESS

As noted at the outset of the preceding chapter, the bulk of corporation tax revenue is derived from large corporations, but smaller corporations form the bulk of corporate taxpayers. Whereas large corporations pay at a rate of 34 percent, that applicable to smaller corporations is only 15 and 25 percent. Should the corporation tax differentiate by business size, and if so, for what reasons?

Should Rates Be Progressive?

The rationale underlying progressive rates for the individual income tax cannot be applied to the corporate sector. The corporation does not have a taxpaying ability of its own in the sense in which individuals do, and all tax burdens are ultimately borne by individuals. Nor can it be said that progressive taxation of firms is a means to progressive taxation of shareholders. There is no positive relationship between the size of the corporation and the net income of its owners. Many small corporations are owned by high-income individuals and a substantial share of dividends (the bulk of which are paid by large corporations) are received by middle-income individuals.

If a case is to be made for a progressive rate structure, it must be based on other grounds, such as a desire to restrain "bigness" and to support small firms. As noted before, restraining bigness differs from restraining monopoly. The latter is a matter of market shares, the former of absolute size. If bigness is to be restrained, a progressive tax may be called for, but such a tax would be related more appropriately to asset size than to profits. If it is bigness that is held undesirable, there is no reason to favor big firms that are unprofitable. The economic case for restraining bigness is, however, of questionable value. Middle-sized and large firms tend to be more efficient than small firms, although there is little evidence that giant size is needed to achieve efficiency. The Jeffersonian ideal is not a viable alternative for modern society, and chances are that balance between large units is the more reasonable solution.

Nevertheless, tax relief for small firms has always been and continues to be a popular political cause. This position may partly be justified to offset the superior ability of large firms to operate in imperfect capital markets and to benefit from restrictive practices. More important, however, is the persistent view that the maintenance of a small-business class is socially desirable even though it may be inefficient.

Aid to Small Business

For these and other reasons, preferential treatment of small business is an ever-present topic of tax reform. Assuming that such aid is to be given, we are left with the question of how it may be done most efficiently.

Partnership Option   The law permits corporations with no more than ten shareholders to elect taxation on a partnership basis. Under this option, given in Subchapter S of the Internal Revenue Code, no corporation tax is paid. Instead, current profits are imputed to the shareholders whether distributed or not. The corporation is thus viewed as a pass-through mechanism only, and perfect integration applies. Putting it differently, the shareholder is given the tax advantage of a partnership, but without losing the protection of limited liability. This option has been especially advantageous to shareholders of modest income whose individual income tax rate is low, and who wish to receive their investment returns in current income.

Low Initial Rate   The benefits of lower rates of corporation tax on initial amounts of income primarily accrue to small corporations. The effect of these lower rates on the liability of large corporations is not very significant. The trouble with the low initial rate is that it can readily serve as a shelter from individual income tax. With a corporate rate of only 15 percent and a shareholder individual income tax rate of 28 percent, incorporation gives a current tax advantage provided that the payout ratio is below 55 percent. A further difficulty arises because larger corporations are induced to split into multiple units (to spin off) so as to benefit from the application of lower rates. The law attempts to avoid such abuses by imposing a penalty tax on personal holding companies with large retention ratios, but it is difficult to ensure that relief to small business is not converted into relief to high-income owners.

E. STATE CORPORATION TAXES

The role of the corporation tax, like that of the individual income tax, is of primary importance at the federal level. Even though a corporation tax is imposed by forty-eight states, it provided only 8.2 percent of state tax revenue in 1984. Its contribution to local tax revenue is below 1 percent. State corporation tax rates range from 3 to 11.5 percent, with most states applying lower rates to small corporations. Allowing for deductibility from profits taxable under the federal tax, net rates range from 1.9 to 4.9 percent.

The rates of state corporation taxes are low compared with federal rates because capital is mobile and sharp rate differentials might cause capital to flow from high- to low-rate states. Even though slight rate differentials may be relatively unimportant as compared with other factors in location decisions, states tend to consider them a major factor and therefore engage in low-rate competition to attract capital. All these considerations produce a built-in tendency toward modest rates and a fair degree of uniformity.

Interesting problems arise in determining how the tax base of corporations engaging in interstate trade should be divided among the different states. Any one state may tax a corporation doing business within its jurisdiction, and various state laws use different formulas to determine what share of profits they should tax. Typically, this involves an apportionment formula, including property, payrolls, and sales within the state, with equal weight to the three factors under the so-called Massachusetts formula. It is now widely believed that a uniform set of rules should be adopted, subject to the supervision of the Treasury, and that sales should be eliminated from the formula.

Choice of the appropriate formula depends on the philosophy of base allocation. If benefit considerations are controlling, the ideal solution would be to charge in accordance with the cost of public services rendered to the firm in its various locations. As a first approximation, it might be argued that all costs are reduced equally by the provision of public services, in which case an allocation by costs incurred would be appropriate. At the same time, it would not be very meaningful to allocate profits on this basis. The benefit approach, as noted before, calls not for a profits tax but for an ad valorem charge on costs incurred.

If the philosophy of an absolute profits tax is applied, the appropriate method of apportionment should be according to the source of profits.[5] If we assume that the firm's return on capital is the same in all locations, profits should be allocated in line with the location of capital use. Sales would enter the formula, but only to the extent of capital invested in sales operations and not in the form of gross sales. The payroll factor would enter in line with the average capital requirement for payroll finance, but not total wages paid. Under such an approach, the sales and payroll factors would be weighted less heavily than in the conventional three-factor formula, while immovable capital would be included at its full value.

Until recently, it was felt that the inclusion of sales in the profits apportionment formula would be strongly in the interest of low-income states, while that of capital and payroll would be in the interest of high-income, manufacturing states. The Report of the Judiciary Committee, however, showed that the role of the sales factor had been misjudged.[6] The states which do most of the producing also offer the biggest markets and do most of the buying. Inclusion of the sales factor will affect the states to which a particular firm must pay its revenue, but the effect on overall revenue allocation is minor.

F.   FOREIGN INVESTMENT INCOME

With the rising importance of foreign investment, the tax treatment of income from such investment has become a major issue in tax policy. A U.S. corporation with a branch abroad will be taxed on the branch profits but may credit the foreign tax thereon against its U.S. tax. The same holds for profits of U.S.-owned subsidiaries, but such profits enter into the tax base only if and when they are repatriated as dividends to the U.S. parent. Until then U.S. tax is deferred. These and related issues, including the treatment of oil companies, will be considered in a later chapter.[7]

G.   SUMMARY

Depreciation rules and investment incentives have been a major and ongoing concern in defining taxable income under the corporation tax:

---

[5] See p. 372.

[6] See *State Taxation of Interstate Commerce, Report of the Special Subcommittee on State Taxation of the Committee on the Judiciary*, 88th Cong., 2d Sess., House Report No. 1480, 1964. See also C. Lowell Harriss, "State-Local Taxation of Interstate Commerce: Progress and Problems," *Innovations in Tax Policy*, Hartford: John C. Lincoln Institute, 1972.

[7] See p. 570.

1. Capital costs must be recovered to arrive at net income. Faster recovery postpones the tax payment and hence reduces its present value.

2. Assets are now divided into eight groups, in line with economic lives, ranging from seven to thirty-one years.

3. Economic depreciation equates the effective rate of tax with the nominal rate.

4. By adding to its depreciation base, a growing firm may continue to postpone paying its taxes.

5. The investment credit, previously the major incentive device, was repealed in 1986.

6. Alternative approaches not used in the United States include expensing and the initial allowance.

7. Small corporations are given preferential treatment with reduced rates of tax on an initial amount of income.

Corporation profits taxes are also imposed at the state level:

8. Such taxes provide 7 percent of state tax revenue with rates ranging from 3 to 12 percent.

9. An allocation formula is used to distribute the tax base among states.

10. Similar problems arising in the international context are examined in Chapter 26.

FURTHER READINGS

Auerbach, A. J., and D. Jorgenson: "Inflation-Proof Depreciation of Assets," *Harvard Business Review*, September–October 1980.

Auerbach, Alan: "The Tax Reform Act of 1986 and the Cost of Capital," *Economic Prospects*, vol. 1, no. 1, 1987.

Harberger, A. C.: "Tax Neutrality in Investment Incentives," in H. Aaron and M. Boskin (eds.): *The Economics of Taxation,* Washington, D.C.: Brookings, 1979.

Steuerle, E.: *Taxes, Loans and Inflation,* Washington, D.C.: Brookings, 1985.

Chapter 23

Consumption Taxes*

A. Sales Taxes in the U.S. Tax Structure: *Federal Taxes; State Taxes; Local Taxes.* **B. Issues in Sales Taxation:** *Unit versus Ad Valorem Taxes; Scope of Coverage for General Tax; Stage of Imposition.* **C. Value-Added Tax:** *Final Value as Aggregate of Value Added; Types of Value-Added Taxes; An Illustration; Collection Method; Conclusion.* **D. Burden Distribution:** *Selective Taxes; General Sales Tax.* **E. Personal Expenditure Tax:** *Determining Taxable Consumption; Treatment of Bequests; Evaluation.* **F. Summary.**

Sales taxes are like income taxes in that they are imposed on flows generated in the production of current output. But income taxes are imposed on the sellers' side of *factor* transactions (i.e., on the net income received by households) or point 1 in Figure 12-1, whereas sales taxes are imposed on the sellers' side of *product* transactions (i.e., on the sales of business firms) or point 7, with sales measured in terms of product units or of gross receipts. Sales taxes on consumer goods (point 4) may be considered equivalent to taxes imposed on household purchases, i.e., to

---

*Reader's Guide to Chapter 23: In this chapter we discuss the conventional forms of sales taxation as well as some novel approaches to the taxation of consumption, including the value-added tax, which has received much attention in recent years, and a personalized approach referred to as the expenditure tax. Consumption taxation in these various forms promises to be an active area of tax reform discussion in the future.

taxes imposed at point 2.[1] While income taxes are based on the sources side of the household account, sales taxes are based on the uses side. For a general tax on consumer goods, all uses except saving are included.

Finally, and most important, sales taxes differ from the income tax in that they are *in rem* rather than *personal* taxes. As such, they do not allow for the personal circumstances of consumers as does the individual income tax with its exemptions, deductions, and progressive rates. Sales taxes are thus inferior on both horizontal and vertical equity grounds. But even though consumption taxes usually take this form, it is not a necessary feature of consumption taxation. As we will see presently, a personal consumption or expenditure tax may be constructed which is not open to this objection.

A. SALES TAXES IN THE U.S. TAX STRUCTURE

We begin with a brief look at the role of sales taxes in the U.S. tax structure. As shown in Table 18-1, sales taxes are of only limited importance at the federal level where they produce only 4 percent of total revenue, more important at the local level with 14 percent, but become the major source of revenue at the state level, where nearly 50 percent of the total is derived from this source.[2] Charges and special assessments, although related to sales taxes in nature, are dealt with at a later point. It will be seen that they are of special and growing importance at the local level.

Federal Taxes

Federal sales taxes, once a major factor in the federal tax structure, have steadily declined in importance, giving way to the rising share of income and later payroll taxes. Also referred to as excises, federal sales taxes are all of the selective type, being imposed on specific products.[3] As may be seen in Table 23-1, the bulk of the revenue comes from a small group of products, including motor fuel, alcohol, and tobacco. Custom duties which were once very important are now a negligible factor in the overall revenue picture. Federal sales taxes are imposed largely at the manufacturer level, the major exceptions being telephone services and air transportation, which are, in effect, charged at retail. Most federal sales taxes (including those on alcohol, tobacco, gasoline, and tires) are levied on a unit basis, while others (including telephone taxes) are of the ad valorem type.[4]

State Taxes

At the state level, sales and excise taxes provide nearly one-half of tax revenue, with the general sales tax being the central item. Being more or less general, a tax on retail sales corresponds to a similar tax on consumer expenditures. Such a tax is

---

[1] See p. 213.
[2] See p. 318.
[3] The term "excise," as used in the U.S. Constitution (Art. 1, sec. 8), was to distinguish such levies from "capitation and other direct taxes" dealt with in section 9. General as well as selective sales taxes would be "excises" in this sense. See p. 26.
[4] See p. 250 for the distinction between unit and ad valorem taxes.

TABLE 23-1
Sales Taxes in the U.S. Tax System
(Fiscal Year 1983, in Billions of Dollars)

	Federal	State	Local	Total
General sales tax	- - -	53.6	11.2	64.8
Other, domestic				
Motor fuel	5.8	10.8	0.2	16.8
Motor vehicle and operator license	- - -	6.3	0.5	6.8
Alcoholic beverages	5.6	2.7	0.2	8.5
Liquor stores		2.8	0.5	3.3
Tobacco products	4.1	4.0	0.2	8.3
Other	17.3	7.1	1.3	25.7
Customs	8.7	- - -	- - -	8.7
Total	41.5	87.3	14.1	142.9

Source: Tax Foundation, *Facts and Figures on Government Finance*, Washington, D.C., 1986, p. A13.

now imposed by all but five states. Rates range from 2 to 7 percent, and the comprehensiveness of base varies. Moreover, the states also make substantial use of selective taxes. As shown in Table 23-1, the primary objects of selective taxation are again gasoline, liquor, and tobacco. These and most other selective sales taxes are imposed on a unit basis, although ad valorem taxes are also used. The general sales tax is imposed at the retail level, as are most selective taxes. However, manufacturers' taxes are used as well. As will be noted later, the choice between taxation at the retail level (involving taxation at destination of the product) and taxation at the manufacturer level (involving taxation at the origin) has important bearing on the size of the tax base available to any jurisdiction as well as the distribution of the tax burden between jurisdictions.[5]

Local Taxes

Sales and excise taxes in 1983 provided 14 percent of local tax revenue. Two-thirds came from general sales taxes, now imposed by thousands of municipalities, usually as a surcharge to the state tax and at rates ranging up to over 4 percent. Selective sales taxes are of minor importance at this level.

B.   ISSUES IN SALES TAXATION

Sales taxation, as seen by the preceding survey, may take different forms, including definition of base, coverage, and point of collection.

Unit versus Ad Valorem Taxes

A further distinction is between taxes which are imposed by unit of product and others which are assessed on their value. Most excise or sales taxes on particular products take the former approach, which includes taxes on fuel, tobacco, and liquor. Others, such as taxes on airline tickets, are imposed on an ad valorem basis.

[5] See p. 469.

Also, and more important, the general sales tax takes the latter form. Of the two bases, the ad valorem form is clearly the more meaningful one. In the case of the general sales tax, it also has the advantage that relative prices remain unchanged and thus it interferes less with consumer choice.[6] Further differences between the unit and ad valorem approach which arise in the context of incidence analysis were considered previously and need not be reexamined here.[7]

Scope of Coverage for General Tax

Sales taxes of a more or less general type (as distinct from taxes on particular products) may differ with regard to scope of coverage. In particular, should such a tax cover all transactions as in the case of the turnover tax, should the base be set equal to GNP, or should only consumption be included?

Inferiority of Total Transaction Base To begin with, the turnover tax which applies to the total of all transactions may be eliminated because it is least desirable. Under this tax, a product is taxed repeatedly as it moves through the stages of production. Thus, the sale of iron ore is taxed when it moves from mine to steel mill; the sale of steel is taxed when it moves from the mill to a rolling plant; sheet metal is taxed when it is sold to an automobile body plant, and so on until the final tax is imposed on the retail sale of the car. As a result, the tax base is a multiple of GNP and high yields can be obtained at very low rates. With a GNP of $4,000 billion, a comprehensive 1 percent turnover tax could yield $156 billion, or about half the yield of the income tax. Such a procedure has political appeal and in the past has been advocated at various stages of the fiscal debate. Inclusion of total transactions would do no harm if each product went through the same number of transactions, so that the combined turnover tax liabilities as a percentage of value at final sale would be the same. But they are not. A turnover tax, therefore, imposes arbitrary discrimination against products which involve many stages of production and distribution. Moreover, in order to avoid the tax, firms will attempt to join with their suppliers, thus encouraging vertical integration and reducing competition. Further inequities are introduced as the tax is "pyramided" from stage to stage, by entering into the base of each successive stage. For these reasons, the turnover tax is considered an inferior form of taxation, and the recent replacement of the turnover tax by the value-added tax in European countries reflects a belated recognition of this fact. The United States, fortunately, has never suffered from a turnover tax.

GNP Base versus Income or Consumption Base Granted that such double-counting should be avoided, there remains a choice about whether to base the tax on gross national product, national income, or consumption. Most general sales taxes are, or at least aim to be, of the consumption type.

The GNP type would impose a sales tax on both consumer and capital goods. Thus, its base would be equivalent to that of a tax on gross income, i.e., an income

---

[6] Note that the ad valorem base remains relevant even if concern is with minimizing dead weight loss. See p. 292.

[7] See p. 213.

tax which does not allow for depreciation. Such a tax would be objectionable on both equity and efficiency grounds. With regard to equity, it would offend the basic dictum of income taxation which says that income from all sources should be taxed fully, but on a net basis. With regard to efficiency, it would compound the discrimination against saving which even a tax on net income involves.

These objections do not apply if the tax is limited to a base which in fact equals national income or GNP minus indirect taxes and depreciation. Such a tax would be similar in base to a general income tax and (as will be noted later) may be implemented via an income-type value-added tax. Since the income base is already drawn upon in the form of personal taxation under the income tax, the consumption base is left as the most likely candidate for taxation. This base is thus the one most generally used and must thus be considered more closely.

Comprehensive versus Narrow-Based Consumption Tax   The so-called general or retail sales tax aims at a comprehensive coverage of consumption. With consumption expenditures of $3 trillion (1987), a truly comprehensive 10 percent tax might thus yield $300 billion, as compared with about $400 billion for the federal income tax. The consumption base thus offers a very major revenue potential. However, the amount of the base is reduced because certain consumption items are typically excluded by state sales taxes, with most of the slippage accounted for by omission of housing (rent payments and imputed rent of owner-occupiers), home-consumed food, utilities, and medical services. Consequently, the revenue from state retail taxes typically includes only one-half of the full-base amount.[8]

Stage of Imposition

We now turn to the stage at which the tax is to be imposed. This decision involves the choice of the best stage for single-stage taxes, as well as the choice between a single- and a multiple-stage approach. Whereas setting the scope of coverage is a substantive issue in determining what kind of tax is to be applied, choosing the stage or stages of collection is essentially a matter of administrative efficiency in implementing a tax on the chosen base.

Manufacturing versus Retail Level   In dealing with single-stage taxes, we must ask whether the tax should be imposed at the manufacturing, the wholesaler, or the retail level.

If the tax is to be general, the retail base is preferable because it permits the imposition of a uniform ad valorem rate. Equal-rate ad valorem taxes imposed on various products at the manufacturing level result in dissimilar equivalent rates at the retail level, because the ratio of retail to manufacturer's prices differs among products. Imposition of differential rates to allow for this diversity would be a dif-

---

[8] State revenue from retail sales taxes in 1984, imposed on an average of 5 percent, amounted to $62 billion. With total consumption of $2.4 trillion, the full yield would have been $120 billion. See also Charles E. McLure, Jr., *The Value Added Tax, Key to Deficit Reduction*: Washington, D.C., American Enterprise Institute, 1987.

ficult and clumsy way to approximate what can be done better with a uniform tax at the retail level.

If the tax is to be selective, the answer to our question is less evident. If the product is identified at the manufacturing stage, e.g., low- or high-priced cars or television sets, it will be advantageous to tax at that level, since selective retail taxation may be more difficult. In other situations (e.g., fabrics which may be made into low- or high-priced garments), selection may not be possible. Differentiation here may have to be related to the nature of the final product at retail. Nevertheless, the general presumption in favor of retail, applicable to the case of the general tax, is weakened for the selective case.

In developing countries in particular, a good argument can be made for taxation at the manufacturing level, because it reduces the number of taxpayers from whom the tax must be collected and thus facilitates administration. Moreover, manufacturing establishments as opposed to retail establishments tend to be larger, more permanent, and conducted on a more sophisticated basis, with better bookkeeping methods. These characteristics improve their quality for assessment purposes. Developing countries may do better with a set of manufacturers' taxes, where the number of collection points is smaller, even though this may result in differentials in the implicit retail rates.

Retail Level versus Valued Added   The further question is whether the tax should be collected in one swoop and at the final point of sale only or whether it should be collected in slabs as under the value-added procedure. With the latter approach, the value of the product is divided into slices or slabs (the value added at each stage) to which the tax is applied at successive stages in the production process. Notwithstanding the difference in technique, the base of a value-added tax of the consumption type is the same as that of a retail sales tax; only the method of collection differs. A choice between the two, therefore, must be made in terms of administrative convenience.

Use of the multiple-stage approach in the value-added context must be distinguished sharply from its previously noted use in connection with the turnover tax. Since the value-added tax has come to be the basic instrument of tax coordination among Common Market countries, where it has replaced widespread use of turnover taxes, it has also received increasing attention in the United States. The old debate over whether there should be a federal retail sales tax has been revised in this form. A more detailed examination of the value-added approach is therefore in order.

C.   VALUE-ADDED TAX

From the economists' point of view, a properly implemented value-added tax is equivalent to a corresponding single-stage tax. Unlike the expenditure tax, the value-added tax is not a genuinely new form of taxation but merely a sales tax administered in a different form. Yet the value-added tax has come to be generally adopted by European countries and is also advocated for U.S. use. It thus deserves closer consideration.

Final Value as Aggregate of Value Added

Consider a finished product, such as shoes. Tracing it through the various stages of production, we begin with the rancher selling the hides to the tanner, the tanner selling the leather to the shoe manufacturer, the manufacturer selling the shoes to the wholesaler, the wholesaler selling them to the retailer, who finally sells to the customer. At each stage the value of the product is increased and the sales price rises accordingly. Each increment in price reflects the value added at that stage, with the value or price of the final product equal to the sum of the increments or values added at the various stages. A tax imposed on the increments is thus identical in its base to a tax imposed on the final value of the product.

Types of Value-Added Taxes

Three major types of value-added taxes (corresponding to the gross national product, net national product, and consumption bases) may be distinguished, although only the consumption type is up for practical consideration.

GNP Type Suppose now that *all* final goods and services produced and sold during a given period, i.e., the entire gross national product, were subject to a general sales tax. The tax would be applicable to both consumer and capital goods. It would be paid by the seller when the product was sold to its last purchaser, whether a consumer, a firm which adds to its inventory, or a firm which purchases capital goods. With a GNP of $4 trillion, an all-inclusive 5 percent tax would yield $200 billion. The same would be accomplished by using the value-added approach, taxing each seller at a rate of 5 percent on value added, i.e., gross receipts minus the cost of purchasing intermediate goods from prior producers in the production line. The tax base at each stage would thus equal depreciation, wages, interest, profits, and rent. It would be the most comprehensive form of value-added tax, and may be referred to as a value-added tax of the GNP type. As noted before, it is equivalent to a sales tax applicable to both consumer and capital goods, with its impact point (in terms of Figure 12-1) at 7 or, which is the same, at 8.[9]

Income Type This value-added approach, as previously noted, may also be used to implement a sales tax on *net* product. Suppose that the intent is to tax net national product, equal to GNP minus capital consumption allowances or depreciation. Such a tax may be imposed in multiple-stage form by taxing the *net* value added by each firm, with net value added defined as gross receipts minus purchases of intermediate goods and depreciation.[10] The same result may also be accomplished by a general income tax, since the bases of a net product and an income tax are in fact the same. The value-added tax of the income type thus differs from that of the consumption type in that the former permits the firm to deduct depreciation

---

[9] See p. 213.

[10] Such a tax could not be imposed as a tax on the total *net* value of the product when the last sale is made, since this procedure would require the recording of depreciation costs incurred by all producers further down the line. Thus, only the value-added approach is feasible if a sales tax is to be imposed on net product.

while the latter permits it to deduct gross investment, i.e., purchase of capital goods.[11]

Consumption Type   Next consider a tax which is to be imposed on consumption only, in any of three ways, namely, a flat-rate consumer expenditure tax inserted at point 2 in Figure 12-1; a retail sales tax inserted at point 4; or a tax on the incremental value added in the production of consumer goods. The last method is referred to as the consumption type of value-added tax.

The base of the value-added tax is now defined as the firm's gross receipts minus the value of all its purchases of intermediate products (materials and goods in process) as well as its capital expenditures on plant and equipment. By permitting each firm to deduct its capital expenditures, we are left with the value of consumer goods output only. Such a tax is therefore equivalent to a general retail sales tax on consumer goods, the two differing in administrative procedure only.

An Illustration

An illustrative computation of the various types of value-added tax is given in Table 23-2.

The consumption base, shown in line 10, is computed for each firm by taking total sales receipts (line 4) and deducting the purchase of intermediate and capital goods (lines 6 and 9).[12] The income base, shown in line 11, is computed for each firm as sales (line 4) minus the cost of intermediate goods and depreciation (lines 6 and 7). The GNP base, shown in line 12, finally equals total sales (line 4) minus the purchase of intermediate goods (line 6). Adding the bases for the three firms, we obtain the base for the entire economy, as shown in the last column. The total

---

[11] The base of the income-type tax therefore exceeds that of the consumption-type tax by the difference between gross investment I_g and depreciation D, i.e., by net investment I_n. Disregarding governmental purchases, indirect business taxes, and net exports, we find that this relationship is brought out by the following identities:

$$GNP = I_g + C$$
$$I_g = D + I_n$$
$$NNP = I_n + C$$
$$NY = NNP$$

where NNP = net national product
 NY = national income
 I_g = gross investment
 I_n = net investment
 D = depreciation
 C = consumption

Note that GNP − D, equal to NNP or NY, is the base of the income-type value-added tax; and that GNP − I_g, or GNP − $(I_n + D) = C$, is the base of the consumption-type value-added tax.

[12] The table shows derivation of the three bases in line with the so-called deduction method. Alternatively, an "addition method" may be used. For the income base, this simply involves the addition of various factor payments included in line 5. The GNP base is determined by adding factor payments and depreciation (lines 5 and 7). The consumption base is determined by adding factor payments and depreciation (lines 5 and 7) while deducting the purchase of capital goods (line 9). Thus, the addition method is readily applicable to the income type but clumsy for the consumption type of value-added tax.

TABLE 23-2
Illustration of Value-Added Tax Bases

| | FIRMS | | | |
	A	B	C	Economy
Current receipts				
1. Sale of consumer goods	- - -	70	151	221
2. Sale of intermediate goods	120	45	- - -	165
3. Sale of capital goods	- - -	100	- - -	100
4. Total	120	215	151	
Current costs				
5. Wages, interest, profits, etc.	100	80	90	270
6. Purchase of intermediate goods	- - -	120	45	165
7. Depreciation	20	15	16	51
8. Total	120	215	151	
Capital costs				
9. Purchase of capital goods	- - -	- - -	100	100
Tax bases				
10. Consumption base (line 4 minus line 6 minus line 9)	120	95	6	221
11. Income base (line 4 minus line 6 minus line 7)	100	80	90	270
12. GNP base	120	95	106	321
National accounts				
13. Consumption	- - -	- - -	- - -	221
14. Plus investment	- - -	- - -	- - -	100
15. GNP	- - -	- - -	- - -	321
16. Minus depreciation	- - -	- - -	- - -	51
17. National net product (NNP) or national income (NY)	- - -	- - -	- - -	270

bases in turn equal the values of consumption, national income, and GNP as defined in the national income accounts.

Collection Method

Taking the consumption type of value-added tax, we have seen that each firm computes its tax base as sales minus purchases of intermediate and capital goods. When it has done so, there are two possibilities for collecting the tax. One, the so-called accounts method, is to ask each firm to pay its tax on the base thus determined. Another, the so-called invoice method, is to have the firm compute its gross tax by applying the tax rate to total sales and then to credit against this tax an amount equal to the tax already paid by the suppliers from which the firm has purchased intermediate and capital goods. By making the tax credit for each firm contingent on presentation of the tax receipt made out to the preceding supplier, the invoice method includes a self-enforcing element because each buyer will demand copy of such a receipt. The invoice method is used generally in European countries and constitutes an advantage of the value-added approach, especially in countries where tax compliance is otherwise poor.

Conclusion

We have seen that the value-added tax of the consumption type has the same base as a retail sales tax with corresponding coverage. Such being the case, why should there be such a strong difference of opinion regarding which of the two taxes is preferable?

One difference relates to the politics of the matter. Proponents of the value-added tax feel that it "looks" different and thus may not share the traditional disrepute of a retail sales tax, which may or may not be the case. If the retailer's gross tax is shown as a separate part of the consumer's price, the consumer should be equally aware of his or her tax under either approach. Beyond this political consideration, there are some technical differences in implementation which are of importance.

Under the retail tax, the number of taxpayers is less than that under the value-added tax, thereby facilitating administration provided that retailers can be reached effectively. In the U.S. setting, this procedure is quite feasible, but in other countries (especially in developing countries where retail establishments are small), it might not be. Under the value-added tax, on the other hand, exclusion of capital goods may be accomplished more effectively than under the retail sales tax, where it is difficult to trace the use of items purchased from the retailer. Furthermore, under the invoice method of collection, the value-added tax has an element of self-enforcement which the retail sales tax lacks.

These and other points may be cited in favor of one or the other approach, but most important is the question of how a federal consumption tax, if it were to be introduced, would relate to the existing consumption taxes at the state level. Since these taxes are in retail form, their integration with a federal consumption tax would be much easier if the latter were also imposed at the retail level. In this case, state taxes could be levied as supplements to the federal tax and the duplicative administrative costs of a federal value-added tax could be avoided. Just as in the income tax field, we are now in the process of using the federal income tax as a base for state income tax collection, so an integrated system of consumption taxation would be preferable to a set of separate tax administrations. Since it would be exceedingly difficult to integrate a federal value-added tax with retail taxes at the state level, the conclusion is that a federal consumption tax, if it were to be imposed, should also take the retail form.

D. BURDEN DISTRIBUTION

Imposed as a personal tax, seeking to meet the taxpayer's ability to pay, the income tax was ranked highly in equity terms. The same cannot be said for sales and excise taxes. Imposed in an impersonal fashion, it makes no such allowance for ability to pay.

Selective Taxes

In our earlier discussion of sales tax incidence, we concluded that the burden distribution by income groups is dominated from the uses side, i.e., by the pattern of consumer expenditures on the taxed product. The incidence of a tax on necessities will thus tend to be regressive, whereas that of a tax on luxuries tends to be progressive. With the bulk of selective sales taxes being derived from items of mass consumption, such as liquor, tobacco, and gasoline, incidence tends to be highly regressive. Moreover, such taxes discriminate among consumers of equal income but with different preferences. They thus rank poorly on grounds of both horizontal and vertical equity. Moreover, by falling on selected items of consumption, such taxes tend to involve a higher efficiency cost than a more general tax.

Given these disadvantages, why are selective sales or excise taxes in continuing use? The question is answered by considering the kinds of products that are taxed. As shown in Table 23-1, a substantial part of the revenue comes from motor fuel or other automotive taxes, levies which may be considered as in lieu of highway-user charges and (more recently) as part of an energy conservation policy. Another substantial part comes from liquor and tobacco taxes, items of mass consumption viewed widely as "demerit goods." A choice of selective excises may also be aimed at minimizing dead weight loss, but this has not as yet become a matter of applied policy.[13]

General Sales Tax

The general sales tax in the form of a retail sales tax on consumer goods is similar to a more or less general flat-rate tax on consumer expenditures.

Seen from the point of view of *horizontal* equity, a general sales tax is equitable if the index of equality is defined in terms of consumption but inequitable if the index is defined in terms of income. Families with similar incomes may have differing consumption (or saving) rates due to age or other factors. Such families will pay different amounts of tax, thus violating horizontal equity in terms of income. But given a consumption-based approach to tax equity, it is the ratio of tax to consumption base that matters.

Viewed in terms of *vertical* equity, a general sales tax is proportional as related to consumption but regressive as related to income, because consumption as a percentage of income declines (savings as a percentage of income rises) as we move up the income scale. As was shown in column 4 of Table 14-1, the sales tax is thus the major regressive element in the tax structure.[14] Looking at any given year, such is the case because the ratio of consumption to income falls when moving up the income scale. The pattern may prove less regressive, however, if considered in lifetime rather than annual terms. In that case, escape from the sales tax is provided only via the leaving of bequests.

Note also that the regressive nature of the sales tax is modified by exclusion of certain items of mass consumption from the base, such as housing and (in most states) also home-consumed food and utilities. Moreover, low-end relief may be given by permitting the consumer a credit to offset an initial amount of tax. Such a credit is now granted by six states but does not offer a very effective instrument. Although readily feasible for taxpayers subject to income tax (who may charge their credit against the latter), implementation is difficult for lower-income households where a direct payment would be needed.

E. PERSONAL EXPENDITURE TAX

Notwithstanding the usual exclusion of housing and food, the traditional approach to the taxation of consumption as implemented by selective or more general sales

---

[13] See p. 243.
[14] See p. 292.

taxes has thus remained regressive, simply because consumption outlays as a percentage of income tend to fall as we move up the income scale. Hence in the historical development, income taxation has been identified with progressive taxation and sales taxes with regressive taxation. Accordingly, the political support for income taxation has tended to come from proponents of progression, whereas that for consumption taxation has tended to come from its opponents. But there is nothing in the logic of the two tax bases which makes this necessarily so. The situation has arisen because the income tax has developed in the framework of *personal* taxation, whereas consumption taxes have been locked into the vise of the impersonal or in rem approach of sales taxation. Use of a personal type of expenditure tax would break this bondage and permit the taxation of consumption to be based on a personal and progressive basis. Such a tax was proposed by the U.S. Treasury during World War II but was given little consideration. Although it has been tried briefly in Sri Lanka and India, actual experience with such a tax under modern conditions has been absent to date. It is still a new and exciting idea and one which in recent years has gained growing support among students of taxation.[15] We will not reconsider here the basic question of whether ability to pay is measured better in income or in consumption terms, because this was examined in detail at an earlier point. However, some of the technical problems involved in applying an expenditure tax remain to be explored.

Determining Taxable Consumption

When consumption is taken as the index of taxpaying ability, all that has been said previously about the desirability of a global definition of the income tax base again applies.[16] All consumption should be included in the base and people's tax liabilities should be independent of the particular pattern of their consumption outlays. In analogy to the income tax, the taxpayer would determine his or her consumption for the year, subtract whatever personal exemptions or deductions were allowed, and apply a progressive rate schedule to the remaining amount of taxable consumption.

The idea sounds simple, but it remains to be seen how taxable consumption is to be determined. Addition of individual consumption dollars would not be feasible. One possibility would be to begin with income and deduct savings. To arrive at consumption, savings would have to be defined as *net* savings (saving minus dissaving) or increase in net worth. This would be a formidable task. The best and most feasible procedure would be to determine the taxpayer's annual consumption in line with the following schedule:

1. Bank balance at the beginning of the year
2. + receipts

---

[15] Like most new ideas, it also has a long history behind it. A personalized expenditure tax was put forth as an ideal by Alfred Marshall and proposed in detail by Irving Fisher (*Constructive Income Taxation,* New York: Harper, 1942), who felt (going back to John Stuart Mill) that income taxation is unfair because it discriminates against the saver. In modern form, the case for a personal expenditure tax has been made by N. Kaldor, *An Expenditure Tax,* London: G. Allen, 1955. Kaldor recommends such a tax as a supplement to an imperfectly functioning income tax, especially because of ineffective progression at high-income levels.

[16] See p. 332.

3.   + net borrowing (borrowing minus debt repayment or lending)
4.   − net investment (cost of assets purchased minus proceeds from assets sold)
5.   − bank balance at end of year
6.   = consumption during the year

Consumption in this way would be derived from the change in bank balances and the flow of receipts and nonconsumption payments during the year. The tax return would call upon the taxpayer to declare the listed items (broken down in more detail) just as income is shown under the income tax.

The concept of receipts as used in the above schedule equals income as defined under the income tax, adjusted to exclude capital gains but to include imputed rent of owner-occupied housing as well as all bequests and gifts received. Net investment would be defined to include net purchases of all assets, including owner-occupied residences, but excluding other durable consumer goods. Although housing consumption would be included via the imputed rent component of income, purchases of durable consumer goods, such as cars, would be treated as current consumption, with averaging permitted to avoid inequities.

In some respects, the approach would be simpler than under the income tax. The dilemma of how to deal with unrealized capital gains would disappear. If assets were sold, the proceeds would enter into the tax base unless offset by purchases of other assets or an increase in balances. Unrealized changes in the value of capital assets would be irrelevant. Also, there would be no need to determine corporate profits. Dividends would appear as receipts, and unrealized capital gains, obtained through retention of profits or otherwise, would be irrelevant until realization occurred and the proceeds were channeled into consumption. The difficult problem of depreciation accounting, similarly, would disappear. Adjustment to inflation would call only for indexing of rate brackets, because the more troublesome problem of adjusting for changes in nominal values would not arise.[17]

But an expenditure tax would also create new difficulties. For administrative and other reasons, it is essential that source withholding be applied, but this would be much more difficult under the expenditure than under the income tax. Since withholding would have to be on income, a presumptive income-to-consumption ratio would have to be applied. Moreover, withholding under a graduated rate system would be much more difficult, since the appropriate rate would depend on whether the receipts were spent or reinvested, an especially troublesome factor in the case of capital income.

Nor is this the only problem. Thus it would be crucial that there be a complete recording of cash balances at the outset. Otherwise, tax-free consumption might be financed later by withdrawing such balances. To ensure that borrowing is accounted for, lenders would have to be required to file information returns on loans made. More cross-checking would be needed. Similarly, it must be ensured that all sales of assets would in fact be declared. For this purpose it might well be neces-

---

[17] For a discussion of expenditure-tax implementation, including the transition problem, see U.S. Treasury Department, *Blueprints for Basic Tax Reform*, 1976, and John J. Minarik (ed.): *What to Tax: Income or Expenditure?*, Washington, D.C.: Brookings, 1979. For a critical appraisal, see Michael J. Graetz, ''Expenditure Tax Design,'' in the latter volume.

sary to require a balance sheet statement or at least a full listing of asset holdings in the tax return.

Other problems would arise in dealing with long-lived consumer goods such as housing. These might be taxed either as imputed consumption over their useful lives or at the time of initial outlay with appropriate averaging permitted. A further difficulty would arise in drawing a line between consumption and investment. Certain investments (such as purchase of shares in a country club or a pleasure farm) carry consumption benefits and would be difficult to classify. Outlays on education would pose a similar problem, because they again involve both consumption and investment aspects. Inclusion of imputed consumption—e.g., housing and home-grown food—would be needed to obtain a meaningful tax base, especially at the lower end of the scale. In-kind fringe benefits, difficult enough under the income tax, would assume larger proportions. Finally, the proper definition of the taxable unit would pose new problems. Unless a strict definition applied, high-consumption taxpayers might commission low-consumption taxpayers (under the guise of a gift or otherwise) to make purchases for them. Extensive provision for averaging would be called for, new international aspects of taxation would have to be dealt with, and the role of bequests would have to be considered.[18]

It would also be naive to believe that the same pressures for tax preferences and loopholes which have so plagued the income tax would not also reappear under an expenditure tax. The previously noted experience with shortfalls in the sales tax base clearly points in this direction. A realistic comparison between the two taxes, therefore, must not match an actual and defective income tax with a hypothetical and perfect expenditure tax.

In addition to these continuing considerations, serious problems would arise in the transition stage from an income to an expenditure tax. Taxpayers who have saved in the past when the income tax regime applied and are now about to dissave would be hurt by the change, as compared with others who are at an earlier stage in their cycle and will do their saving in the future. Transition provisions would be needed to avoid such hardship. On balance it is hard to say whether the administrative difficulties of an expenditure tax would be less than those now encountered with the income tax. Only practical experience would give an answer to this question.

Treatment of Bequests

As noted in our earlier discussion of concepts of tax base, a special problem arises because income may not be consumed but be left as bequests.[19] Under the income tax philosophy of accretion, the receipt of a bequest would appropriately be included in the heir's tax base, a perfect application of the accretion concept which has never been considered. But as previously noted, the accretion-based income concept discriminates against future consumption. A consumption-based tax, in turn, places equal burdens on individuals with equal present values of consump-

---

[18] See p. 431.
[19] See p. 226.

tion, rendering the tax burden independent of consumption timing. This, however, leaves open the question of how to treat bequests.

Unless bequests are included in the expenditure tax base, taxpayer X who chooses to leave a bequest escapes tax on that part of his or her income use. If the heirs continue to save, such use of income will never be taxed. To escape this difficulty, there is a good case for including bequests in the base of the expenditure tax. Definition of what constitutes a "fair tax base" is changed thereby from consumption only to include all income uses, be they for consumption or for the leaving of bequests. This view of the expenditure tax base differs from the Hobbesian rule that only consumption be taxed, with saving excluded on a permanent basis. These two interpretations of the expenditure tax base differ in their distributive implications and also in their economic effects. The choice between them will thus be a major point of controversy should adoption of such a tax come up for consideration.

Evaluation

Use of a personal expenditure tax would greatly raise the quality of consumption taxation, because it would permit adaptation to ability to pay and overcome the inherently regressive nature of a general sales tax. But even though the expenditure tax approach renders consumption-based taxation respectable, it still leaves open the questions of which base (income or consumption) is more suitable and of how bequests should be treated. However, to the extent that saving *is* meant to be favored by the tax system, the expenditure tax approach is clearly preferable to piecemeal exclusion of saved income from the income tax.

Substitution of an expenditure tax for the income tax would simplify matters in important respects, especially in an inflationary setting. But it would also create new difficulties, especially with regard to withholding. Moreover, the same pressures for preferential treatment and loophole creation which now arise under the income tax would also reappear under an expenditure tax regime.

F.   SUMMARY

The role of sales taxation in the U.S. tax structure is characterized as follows:

1.   Two-thirds of sales tax revenue accrues to the states and most of the remainder to the federal government.
2.   About one-third of the total comes from general retail sales taxes imposed at the state level. The remainder comes from selective taxes, with nearly one-half thereof drawn from the taxation of tobacco, liquor, and gasoline.

There are various ways in which sales taxes may be imposed and administered. These are the major differences:

3.   General sales taxes may be based on GNP or consumption.
4.   Consumption-based taxes may be comprehensive or more narrowly defined.
5.   Selective taxes may be designed to serve as benefit taxes, to discriminate against demerit goods, or simply to be imposed on readily available transactions.
6.   Sales taxes may be single- or multiple-stage.

7. Single-stage taxes may be imposed at the manufacturing, wholesale, or retail level.

8. Multiple-stage taxes may be of the turnover or value-added variety. Whereas the former is undesirable, the latter may serve as a helpful way of administering what in its final result is similar to a single-stage tax at the retail level.

9. Value-added taxes may be of the consumption or income type.

10. A consumption-type value-added tax is equivalent to a retail sales tax on consumer goods.

11. The value-added approach offers administrative advantages as well as disadvantages.

Sales taxes have generally been considered as regressive and have thus been contrasted with the progressive income tax:

12. The regressive nature of the sales tax arises because it falls on consumption, and consumption as a percentage of income declines when moving up the income scale.

13. Regressivity may be reduced by exemption of food and progressivity at the lower end of the scale may be introduced by the granting of a credit against income tax.

Whereas the value-added tax is simply a sales tax administered in a multistage form, a personalized and progressive expenditure tax would be a genuinely new form of taxation:

14. Such a tax could move consumption taxation from its traditional regressive form into the progressive range.

15. While removing some of the major difficulties of the income tax, the expenditure tax would also give rise to new ones.

FURTHER READINGS

For a general review of sales taxation, see:

Due, John F.: *State and Local Sales Taxation,* Chicago: Public Administration Service, 1971.

For a discussion of the value-added tax, see:

McLure, C.: *The Value-Added Tax, Key to Deficit Reduction,* Washington, D.C., American Enterprise Institute, 1987.

For discussions of the expenditure tax, see:

Aaron, H., H. Galper, J. Pechman, (eds.): *Uneasy Compromise, Problems of a Hybrid Income-Consumption Tax,* Washington, D.C.: Brookings, 1988.

Kaldor, N.: *An Expenditure Tax,* London: G. Allen, 1955.

Minarik, John J. (ed.): *What to Tax: Income or Expenditure?* Washington, D.C.: Brookings, 1979.

U.S. Treasury Department, *Blueprints for Basic Tax Reform,* Washington, D.C.: 1977, chap. 4.

Chapter 24

Property and Wealth Taxes*

A. Rationale for Wealth Taxation: *Benefit Considerations; Ability-to-Pay Considerations; Social Control; Taxation of Land; Conclusions.* **B. Composition and Distribution of Wealth:** *Stock of Wealth; Distribution of Wealth Holdings.* **C. Structure and Base of the Local Property Tax:** *History; Composition of Tax Base; Nominal Rates, Assessment Ratios, and Effective Rates; Market Value versus Income as Assessment Base; Land versus Improvement Components of Base; Circuit Breaker.* **D. Burden Distribution of Property Tax:** *Property Tax as Tax on Capital Income; Alternative Patterns.* **E. Appraisal and Outlook for Property Tax. F. Net Worth Tax:** *Foreign Experience; Structure and Base; Role of Intangibles; Rates and Exemptions.* **G. Capital Levy. H. Summary.**

Having considered the taxation of income and expenditure *flows*, we now turn to that of *stocks*, i.e., of wealth. Such taxes may be imposed on pieces of property (payable by the owner) and thus be of the impersonal in rem type; or they may be imposed on the combined property holdings of a person, or on his net worth, thus being in the nature of a personal tax. In the United States, property taxation has

---

Reader's Guide to Chapter 24: This chapter examines the role of property and wealth taxation in the tax system. The property tax, although the oldest tax in the U.S. tax structure, has been and remains *the* major local source of taxation, but its history has been controversial and in the late 1970s it became a major item of debate. Its design and incidence prove yet another important aspect of tax analysis.

been almost entirely in the form of the local property tax, imposed as an in rem tax, mostly on land and real estate. More general forms of wealth taxation, however, are applied in various other countries.

A. RATIONALE FOR WEALTH TAXATION

Some argument for wealth taxation may be made on both benefit and ability-to-pay grounds, but neither suggests a tax such as the existing property tax, imposed more or less uniformly on real property only. Benefit considerations point to a set of in rem-type property taxes on real assets while ability-to-pay considerations point to a personal tax on net worth.

Benefit Considerations

The benefit rationale for wealth taxation is that public services increase the value of real properties and should therefore be paid for by the owners. In its most general form, the supporting argument may be derived from Locke's theory of the state as a protector of property, expounded toward the close of the seventeenth century. One of the basic functions of the state, as seen by the natural-law theorists, is the protection of property; and property owners should therefore pay for the state's expenses. Whatever the merits of the premise as a theory of state, its logic points to a comprehensive tax, including a person's entire property (intangible as well as real property) in the base. Better still, the base would be defined in terms of *net* worth, i.e., the taxpayer's property minus his or her liabilities. Also, in the spirit of this approach, revenue from this tax would be limited to cover the cost incurred in rendering protection services, such as the cost of law enforcement, legislation, and judicial administration. Although the range of includable costs is debatable, certainly not all governmental functions would be covered. Use of the property tax for education finance, which takes up a large part of the revenue, cannot be rationalized in this way.

A more specific application of the benefit rule, pertinent especially at the local level, suggests that property owners should pay for particular services which go to raise property values. Building a sidewalk, for instance, increases the values of adjoining homes, as does the rendering of police protection in the precinct. In some cases, the specific benefit share derived by any one property may be measured by indices such as the length of its road frontage or its location. In others, benefit shares may have to be approximated by relative property values. This line of reasoning, however, does not point to a general tax on real property. Rather it indicates special charges or assessments, imposed to finance particular services. Such assessments, which are a special form of user charge or of public pricing, are especially made use of in local finance but so far remain of only minor importance in the overall picture. A good case can be made for wider use of such charges.

A more subtle benefit argument in support of a local property tax on real estate arises from differential service levels among communities. If the level of public services is higher in community A than in community B, this difference will be reflected in higher house values in A. Such will be the case provided that residence in A is prerequisite to the enjoyment of this higher service level. Thus, homeowners in A may be said to benefit, even though the services are not directly housing-related. A benefit link is established, via the capitalization of service benefits, between ownership and the service level. However, this link is a tenuous one and applies only to the extent that service levels in A exceed those in B. The argument does not give benefit-taxation status to a property tax on the total value but only to the differential. Moreover, if pursued carefully the analysis points to a tax on ground rent rather than a tax on total property values. The reason is that capital will move, thus equalizing net (after-tax) returns, whereas land cannot move between jurisdictions.

Ability-to-Pay Considerations

Consider now the case for wealth taxation from the point of view of ability to pay. Here the origin of the property tax must be seen in its historical context. In the Colonial period, real estate and personal property (such as cattle) were the most convenient index of "faculty," or ability to pay. A significant share of income was received in kind, so that money income as it is now defined would have been a misleading index. But under modern conditions, income is received largely in money form and wealth is more difficult to measure than income. Under these circumstances, can property taxation still be justified on ability-to-pay grounds?

In our earlier discussion of horizontal equity, two conclusions were reached. Taking income as the index of equality, we concluded that there was no case for supplementary wealth taxation, provided only that income was defined comprehensively so as to include all accretion. But in practice not all capital income is thus reached, which may leave a case for a wealth tax. Also, we noted that under a regime of a consumption tax, some additional tax on wealth might be justified to allow for benefits from wealth-holding. However, if wealth is to be taxed on ability-to-pay grounds, what is called for is not an impersonal tax on real property but a personal tax on net worth.[1] Such a tax will be considered further below.

Social Control

Alternatively, the taxation of wealth may be approached not as a matter of charging for benefits received or of ability to pay but as a form of social control. The social consequences of inequality in the distribution of wealth, as is easily seen, differ from those in the distribution of consumption, so that society may wish to deal with them separately. For this purpose, a progressive tax on wealth rather than on income would be the proper instrument. As under the ability-to-pay approach, the indication is again for a personal tax and a global wealth definition. But it might now be argued that the base should be defined in terms of gross rather than net wealth, since it is the former which determines the scope of economic control which the owner derives.

Taxation of Land

The singling out of land (as distinct from taxable property in general) has been advocated on both efficiency and equity grounds. Since the return to land is in the

---

[1] For a development of this view and a plea for a net worth tax, see Lester C. Thurow, "Net Worth Taxes," *National Tax Journal*, September 1972; and Thurow, *The Impact of Taxes on the American Economy*, New York: Praeger, 1971, chap. 7.

nature of economic rent (being a return to a factor of production in inelastic supply), it may be taxed without giving rise to an "excess burden." Indeed, land taxation may be used, especially in developing countries, to encourage more intensive utilization. Moreover, gains derived from increases in land values may be considered unjust enrichment, as initially argued by Henry George.[2]

Conclusions

Wealth taxation may be advocated on various grounds, each calling for a different type of tax. Whereas the benefit view points to differentiated taxes or charges on particular items of real property, the ability-to-pay approach points to a global and personal tax on net worth. The rationale for a uniform property tax based largely upon realty, as reflected in the existing property tax, is more difficult to establish. However, it has proved a convenient means of local taxation and one which is not likely to be dispensed with in the foreseeable future.

B. COMPOSITION AND DISTRIBUTION OF WEALTH

Although ample data on the distribution of income are available, statistics on the composition and distribution of wealth are very imperfect. Nevertheless, some picture of the scope and nature of the tax base may be derived and is needed to assess the potential of wealth taxation.

Stock of Wealth

The composition of privately held wealth in the United States for 1985 is given in Table 24-1. Privately held reproducible wealth is estimated at about $7 trillion. With a GNP of $4 trillion in that year, such wealth holdings are about 1.8 times GNP. The major categories of reproducible real wealth are housing, business plant and equipment, and consumer durables. When land is added in, the total rises to $10 trillion or 2.5 times GNP. Financial assets held by the private sector (including public debt and outside money) add over another $1.8 trillion.[3] The resulting total of $8.7 trillion equals the combined net worth of the private sector. It falls short of national wealth because wealth owned by government is excluded. As shown below, the total of $8.7 trillion is a multiple of assessed value under the property tax.

Distribution of Wealth Holdings

Although there are many data on the distribution of income, corresponding information on the distribution of wealth is not available. However, it is evident that the distribution of wealth among wealth holders is more unequal than that of income among income recipients. As we have seen in our earlier analysis of the income tax base by source, the distribution of capital income is less equal than that of wage

---

[2] Henry George, *Progress and Poverty,* New York: Appleton, 1882.

[3] Private debt is excluded because it enters both as an asset into the balance sheet of the creditor and as a liability into that of the debtor. The same holds for deposits or inside money which although an asset to the holder is canceled by debt owed to banks. Outside money (Federal Reserve credit and currency in circulation) is not offset by private debt and hence is included.

TABLE 24-1
Composition of Privately-Held Wealth, 1985

	Billions of Dollars
Reproducible wealth	
1. Residential structures	2,269
2. Commercial and industrial structures	1,987
3. Equipment	1,812
4. Household durables	1,395
5. Total	7,463
Land	
6. Farms	596
7. Nonfarm	2,000
8. Total	2,596
Financial assets, net	
9. Public debt, privately held	1,417
10. Money (M3)	437
Total	1,854
11. All forms, total	11,913

Sources: Lines 1 to 5: See U.S. Bureau of the Census, *Statistical Abstract of the United States,* 1987, p. 446. Line 6: *Ibid.,* p. 626. Line 7: Estimated. Line 9: See *Economic Report of the President,* Washington, D.C., 1987, p. 343. Line 10: See *ibid.,* p. 319.

and salary income.[4] Except for the lower end of the scale, capital income as a share in total income rises rapidly with rising income. With the distribution of capital income a proxy for the distribution of income-earning capital, the same might be concluded for the distribution of wealth. Indeed, over 20 percent of personal wealth is estimated to be held by the top 1 percent of wealth holders.[5]

C. STRUCTURE AND BASE OF THE LOCAL PROPERTY TAX

We now take a closer look at the local property tax, which is *the* major representative of wealth taxation in our tax system. As previously noted, it is still the third most important tax in the United States and continues to dominate local taxation.

History

The American property tax has its origins in early American history. Initially, it was assessed on selected items of property such as land and cattle, with different rates imposed on various categories. This "classified" property tax was the main source of revenue to the Colonies. During the eighteenth and nineteenth centuries, a greater variety of property emerged, making it difficult to maintain such differ-

[4] This, however, is a rough proxy only, because it does not allow for nonincome-earning wealth. Since the latter (mainly in the form of houses) is likely to be distributed more evenly, the distribution of total (including imputed) capital income may be less unequal. A further qualification arises with regard to "social security wealth." It has been estimated that inclusion of such wealth would reduce the share received by the top 1 percent from 26 to 19 percent. (See Martin Feldstein, "Social Security and the Distribution of Wealth," *Journal of the American Statistical Association,* December 1976.) The question arises about whether such inclusion should not be matched by allowing for negative wealth corresponding to the capitalized value of future payroll contributions.

[5] See *Statistical Abstract of the United States,* 1986, p. 122.

entiation. Thus, the tax developed into a general and uniform-tax rate. This uniform tax was applied to property independent of form, with total property viewed as a general measure of taxable capacity. This approach subsequently gave way under the increasing complexity of property forms. The growing importance of intangible property, in particular, made it increasingly difficult to apply a general tax on a comprehensive base. By the end of the century, the general property tax had been supplanted by a much narrower approach. It became a selective tax on real estate and business personalty (i.e., equipment and inventory) and has remained so ever since. Tangible property, other than real estate, held by persons now largely escapes tax, and no attempt is made to reach intangible property. Whereas the share of the property tax in total tax revenue (including all levels) has declined from over 50 percent at the beginning of the century to below 15 percent at present, this decline reflects the rising level of other taxes and increased importance of the federal sector rather than a fall in the level of property taxation.

The property tax in the United States originated as a local tax and has continued as such. It accounts for 75 percent of local tax revenue, with school districts and townships drawing their entire revenue from this source.[6] Not only does property tax revenue accrue almost entirely to local government but the tax is imposed locally. It thus differs greatly between localities in both rates and administrative procedure. Although some guidance is provided by state legislation and certain types of property (such as railroads and utilities) are assessed by the state, assessment is still far from equalized. The U.S. property tax differs sharply in this respect from that of other countries, such as the United Kingdom, where the system of "rates" is administered as a national tax although revenue goes to local governments. Among the larger countries, only Canada has a decentralized property tax of the U.S. type.

Composition of Tax Base

The distribution of the property tax base by type of assessed property is shown in Table 24-2. Of the total assessed value of $2.8 trillion in 1981, over 50 percent was in the form of residential structures and 20 percent in the form of commercial and industrial structures. Acreage and farms contributed 9 percent and personal property accounted for only 10 percent. The U.S. property tax, as noted before, is largely a tax on real estate.

The amounts shown in Table 24-2 are assessed values. Since assessment is typically below market value, the true value of assets reached by the property tax is substantially larger. Assuming an average assessment ratio of 33 percent of market value, we may estimate the 1981 value of property covered by the property tax as being $8.4 trillion. To permit comparison with the potential 1985 total of $10 trillion (items 5 and 8 in Table 24-1) the actual base may be raised by, say, 10 percent, so that a large share of real property is in fact reached in the assessment process.

Nominal Rates, Assessment Ratios, and Effective Rates

With over 75,000 assessing jurisdictions in the country, we find a bewildering variety of practices and tax rates. Comparing the level of property taxation among

---

[6] See Tax Foundation, *Facts and Figures on Government Finance,* 1986, p. 122.

TABLE 24-2
Assessed Value by Type of Real Property, 1981

	Billions of Dollars	Percentage of Total
Real estate		
Acreage and farms	247	8.9
Vacant lots	109	3.9
Residential, nonfarm		
Single-family houses	1,328	47.7
Other	191	6.9
Commercial and industrial		
Commercial	354	12.7
Industrial	196	7.0
Other	88	3.2
Personal property		
All forms	271	9.7
Total	2,784	100.0

Source: U.S. Bureau of the Census, *1982 Census of Governments*, vol. 7, 1985, p. 26.

jurisdictions is thus a delicate task. A sharp distinction must be drawn between nominal and effective rates. The latter equals the product of nominal rate and assessment ratio.[7] With assessment ratios varying widely, ranking of jurisdictions by nominal rate tells us little about their ranking by effective rates. Out of a sample of fifty large cities, nominal rates ranged from $1 to $32 per $100 of assessed value, while effective rates ranged from $0.60 to $5 of market value. The difference reflects a variance in assessment ratios of from 4 to 100 percent.[8]

Since it is the effective rate that matters, it would seem to make little difference whether properties are assessed at full market value or less. Depending on the required revenue, a lower assessment ratio simply means that the nominal rate must be correspondingly higher. Such indeed would be the case if all properties were subject to the same assessment ratio. Actually, assessment ratios differ between jurisdictions and within any one jurisdiction among types of property, conditions that cause inequities to arise.

Differentials between Jurisdictions Failure to apply a uniform assessment ratio across jurisdictions becomes exceedingly important when assessed values are used as a measure of fiscal capacity and considered in allocating state aid among

[7] We have

$$T = t_n AV \quad \text{and} \quad AV = rMV$$

where T = tax
   t_n = nominal rate
   AV = assessed value
   r = assessment ratio
   MV = market value

Also, we have $t_e = T/MV$ where t_e is the effective rate. Thus we obtain $t_e = t_n r$.

[8] See *Statistical Abstract of the United States*, 1987, p. 279.

local jurisdictions. To avoid this difficulty, an increasing number of states have introduced measures to secure uniform statement assessment practices. Short of transferring the assessment function to the state level, full uniformity is difficult to bring about. But even if assessment ratios were equalized, jurisdictions would choose their nominal rates and hence effective rates would still differ among jurisdictions. As a result, location decisions, whether by business or residents, may be affected by tax differentials, leading to inefficient location choices. This influence will be modified where higher rates of property taxation are indicative of higher service levels (rather than higher costs), so that tax differentials are offset by benefit differentials. However, such is not always the case. Resulting inefficiencies are a cost of fiscal decentralization which can be eliminated only by equalizing effective rates, at least across neighboring jurisdictions, such as units within a metropolitan area. This equalization, however, involves moving toward a more centralized revenue system, with the likely result of reduced variety on the expenditure side. This cost reflects one of the dilemmas of fiscal federalism which will be considered later on.[9]

Differentials within Jurisdictions   Although the same nominal rate applies to different types of property in any one jurisdiction, assessment ratios may differ by type of property. Thus it is estimated that the average assessment ratio in 1981 for the United States as a whole was 44 percent for residential real estate, 34 percent for commercial and industrial real estate, 29 percent for vacant lots, and 24 percent for acreage.[10] In some jurisdictions, these differentials are substantially larger. There is a tendency, in large cities in particular, for business property to be assessed at a higher rate than residential housing, and for multiunit houses to be assessed at a higher rate than single-unit residences. These differentials are not accidental but reflect a desire to impose the property tax at differential rates. Under most state constitutions such a practice is not permitted, but in six states, with Massachusetts the most recent addition, the constitution permits classification, with different assessment ratios applied to different groups of property. This ranges from over 20 separate classes in Minnesota to the more customary scheme of distinguishing between residential, commercial, and industrial properties only.

As distinct from differentiating between types of property, which may meet a legitimate policy objective, actual practice also results in substantial and unjustifiable differentiation between specific properties within the same general category. For all these reasons, sound property tax administration calls for a uniform assessment at full market value. Unless this is done, it is unlikely that uniform effective rates can be obtained. If there is to be deliberate differentiation between classes of property, i.e., if the property tax is to be classified, it should be provided for explicitly by varying nominal rates and not assessment ratios.

Market Value versus Income as Assessment Base

In addition to the need for equalized assessment, there is the more basic question of how property values should be measured. Should property be assessed on sales or

---

[9] See p. 453.
[10] See U.S. Bureau of the Census, *Census of Governments,* vol. 7, 1982, p. 29.

rental income values and should use be made of actual or potential values? The U.S. approach has been in terms of sales or market value, while the British tradition has been to assess on the basis of actual rental income derived from the asset. If there are perfect markets and optimal utilization, this difference disappears since the sales value of property equals the capitalized value of actual income and the latter is equal to its income-earning potential. But under realistic conditions, this equality does not hold.

If property is underutilized, assessment on the income base understates the value, a factor which is of special importance for developing countries.[11] Another difference between the market value and income approaches stems from differences in risk. One property with an annual income of $100,000 may have a market value of $500,000, while another property with the same income may have twice that market value. Incomes are capitalized at different rates of interest, or, to put it differently, at gross rates which add different risk premiums to the market rate on safe investment. Such is the case with regard to properties in urban slums which have high yields of income relative to market values. Such properties do better under the market value approach than under the income base of assessment. Where such differences exist, the market value offers the better base since the income base should be corrected to allow for differences in risk.

But although assessment on the basis of sales value may be preferable, sufficient frequency of sales of similar houses may not occur to provide a ready basis for evaluation. Presumptive valuation, based on type of house and location, must take its place. In some jurisdictions sophisticated procedures have been developed to carry out such valuations based on regression equations with a substantial number of variables, relating house values to a variety of characteristics. Such a procedure has the further advantage of permitting more frequent adjustments in past valuations, a feature of particular importance during an inflationary period. Ironically, it was this efficient and current assessment mechanism in California which contributed to taxpayer complaints and dissatisfaction with the property tax.

Land versus Improvement Components of Base

The property tax is imposed on the market value of a given piece of real estate without a distinction being drawn between its land and improvement components. Yet from an economic point of view, this is an important distinction; it will be examined when we deal with the incidence of this tax.

Since the supply of land is given, taxing the rent of land or imposing a tax on the value of land (reflecting the capitalized value of its rent) has long been recognized as a form of taxation which is least likely to deter incentives to invest in improvements. Moreover, the windfalls which arise from rising land values due to population and income growth might be considered as socially unwarranted gains, which was the main theme of Henry George's *Progress and Poverty,* which swept the United States in the 1890s and gave rise to the single-tax movement, calling for exclusive reliance on land taxation. Unfortunately, the exaggerated claims on behalf of the single tax have interfered with a continuing and strong case for taxing site values at a higher rate.

[11] See p. 597.

In fact, actual practice frequently does the very opposite. As will be noted later, urban property tax, by placing a tax burden on improvements, has discouraged such investment, especially in low-income housing. A heavier tax on land value combined with a lighter tax on improvement would have slowed rather than accelerated urban decay.[12]

Circuit Breaker

The property tax on residential housing is considered especially burdensome for the aged. A large number of low-income homeowners are elderly, so that the problem does pertain especially to this group. Consequently, measures have been developed to provide property tax relief for the aged and low-income families. Given mostly in the form of a credit against state income tax, some such relief provisions, referred to as "circuit breakers," are now applied by practically all states. Various techniques are used to limit the credit to low-income families. Most, but not all, states limit the relief to the aged, and all states extend it to renters by stipulating a presumptive property tax. Since vanishing or otherwise limited credits go primarily to low-income families and since exemptions under state income taxes are relatively high, most claimants are without income tax liabilities and the credits must consequently be paid as cash refunds. As in the case of sales tax credits, this provision raises the question of whether such refunds will in fact be claimed by low-income taxpayers.

D.   BURDEN DISTRIBUTION OF PROPERTY TAX

The incidence of the property tax is controversial. One view takes it to be a tax on capital income, imposed in competitive markets; another differentiates by type of assessed base and places more weight on the consequences of market imperfections.

Property Tax as Tax on Capital Income

We begin with the former view, which has gained increasing acceptance among economists in recent years.

National Tax   Suppose first that there existed a truly national tax on all capital assets. As noted in our earlier discussion of incidence, a tax on capital assets may then be viewed as a tax on capital income. Given perfect capital markets and assessment procedures, a 5 percent tax imposed on the value of an asset may readily be translated into an income tax on the income derived from the asset. Suppose that an asset worth $1,000 yields an annual income of $100, in line with a 10 percent market rate of interest. The liability under a 5 percent tax on the asset value is $50. Expressed as a percentage of the asset's income, it equals 50 percent. The 5 percent tax on the asset value (or property tax) is thus equivalent to a 50 percent tax on the property income (or income tax). Putting it more generally, the value of an asset in a perfect capital market is given by $Y = iV$, so that $V = Y/i$, where V is its value, Y is its annual income, and i is the market rate of interest obtainable on

---

[12] See Dick Netzer, "The Local Property Tax," in G. E. Peterson (ed.): *Property Tax Reform,* Washington, D.C.: Urban Institute, 1973, p. 23 and p. 571.

other investments.[13] If the same yield is to be obtained from a property tax at rate t_p and a tax on income therefrom at rate t_y, we must have $t_p\,Y/i = t_y\,Y$ or $t_p = it_y$.

In a market where capital yields a 10 percent return, the incidence of a general tax on the value of capital assets imposed at a rate of $5 per $100 of asset value is thus the same as that of a 50 percent tax on capital income. This being so, all that has been said above about the incidence of a general tax on capital income again applies. With incidence determined primarily from the sources side, such a tax reduces the net return to capital and is absorbed by the recipients of capital income. With the exception of the bottom end, such income rises as a share of total income when we move up the income scale, so that incidence is progressive. In the longer run, the reduction in the net return to capital may depress the capital stock, thereby reducing future productivity of labor, so that it may come to share the burden. While this may qualify the outcome, the pattern of burden incidence set by the short-run effect is likely to be dominant. The resulting pattern of incidence, as was shown in line 14 of Table 14-1, is regressive at the lower end of the income scale, proportional in the middle range, and progressive at the top.[14]

Local Tax   These conclusions are qualified by the fact that our property tax is not imposed at a uniform national rate but at widely varying local rates. If all local jurisdictions were to impose a tax at the same rate, the result would be similar to that of a national tax. But we have seen that they do not. Effective rates vary widely, whether the variation is due to differences in statutory rates or in assessment ratios. To understand how this affects incidence, suppose that a single jurisdiction raises its rate above the national level. What will happen?

In the *short run*, capital invested in the high-rate jurisdiction is immobile and its owners must bear whatever higher rates are imposed. As noted before for the corporation tax, the burden of partial taxes on capital income is capitalized and reduces the value of the property. This goes for improvements and sites alike. Short-run incidence is on the owners of the local property subject to the higher tax. Moreover, the burden is on the owners who held the property at the time the tax was raised. They cannot shake off the burden by selling the taxed asset.

To illustrate this fact, we assume again that the rate of return on capital before tax is 10 percent, so that an asset yielding $100 per year is worth $1,000. Now let a particular jurisdiction impose a property tax of $50 per $1,000 of property value. As noted before, such a tax is equivalent to a 50 percent income tax. Net income is reduced to $50, which capitalized at 10 percent lowers the property value to $500. If the initial owner of the asset wishes to sell it, he or she must absorb the tax loss, since the buyer will want to obtain a net return of 10 percent, similar to that

---

[13] This capitalization formula holds for a perpetual income stream. The value of a finite annuity is given by

$$V = Y\frac{1 - (1 + i)^{-n}}{i}$$

where n is the number of years over which the annual payments extend.

[14] See p. 243.

available from an investment elsewhere. The burden of the tax thus falls on the initial property owner, i.e., the owner of the property prior to the imposition of tax. Subsequent owners who purchase the old asset will do so at a lower price only and are not burdened by the tax. The loss has been capitalized and stays with the initial owner.

In the *long run,* that part of the tax which reflects land or site values remains fixed. Land cannot move, so that the original owners of land in the high-tax jurisdiction will thus suffer a permanent loss equal to their share in the tax. There is no difference in this case between the short-run and the long-run adjustment. Since income from the ownership of land is more important to high-income than to low-income groups, incidence is progressive.

The situation differs with regard to capital. Capital invested in improvements is not caught permanently. In the longer run, it will flee the high-tax jurisdiction and move to a jurisdiction where rates are lower. Maintenance expenditures on old assets will be reduced, and new investment in the high-rate jurisdiction will decline. As the capital stock in the higher-rate jurisdiction falls while that in the low-rate jurisdiction rises, the gross rate of return on capital in the former goes up while the rate of return in the latter declines. This movement continues until the *net* rate of return from investment in the high-tax jurisdiction equals the rate of return outside. The process ceases when net returns in various jurisdictions are equalized. As was the situation with the corporation tax, a tax imposed upon capital in one sector of the economy comes to be shared by the owners of capital at large.

The extent of capital outflow from the high-rate jurisdiction will depend on the outward mobility of labor. If labor can leave readily, it must be paid what it receives elsewhere and the capital outflow will have to be larger. If labor is locked in, the tax may be reflected in wage reduction, thus maintaining the earnings of capital without forcing it to leave. Since unskilled labor is less mobile than skilled labor, such a situation introduces a regressive effect. But whereas labor in high-tax jurisdictions stands to lose, labor in low-tax jurisdictions (which as a result of the adjustment comes to have a more ample capital stock) will tend to gain. Similarly, landlords and owners in the high-tax jurisdiction stand to lose from capital outflow. These effects may be of major importance if viewed from the perspective of a particular jurisdiction, although they may not greatly affect the overall or national burden distribution.

Inside versus Outside Burden The national and local tax differ in that the local jurisdiction will be concerned only with that part of the burden which is borne by its residents and not with that part which is borne by others.

Thus, suppose that real property located in jurisdiction A is owned by residents of jurisdiction B. As a result, the short-run burden will be borne by outside individuals while local residents may enjoy a free ride. But they may not fare as well in the longer run when capital can move out. Now local residents find their rents increased and wages reduced while outsiders have gained. The greater the outflow of capital, the less will be the revenue obtained and the greater will be the rise in rents and reduction in income suffered by the residents of the high-tax jurisdiction. Not only are local residents unable to export the burden of such taxes as are collected, but they lose to the outside because less capital is available to them. It is not surprising, therefore, if a particular community is hesitant to raise its tax rate much beyond that imposed by rival jurisdictions. Indeed, a community might be tempted to derive net benefits from lowering its tax below that applicable in rival jurisdictions.

Local tax policy thus involves a difficult choice between (1) the gain to be derived by shifting tax burdens to the outside through the taxation of capital owned by "foreigners," and (2) the danger of loss to the local economy from the flight of "foreign" capital. This condition, moreover, does not apply to local finance only. We will meet it again and on an enlarged scale when examining the coordination of tax policy at the international level.

Benefit Differentials   The preceding discussion has considered the tax side of the picture only, without allowance for the benefits from public services which the revenue may provide. Yet they must be taken into account when examining the overall effects of an increase in a local property tax.

Just as an increase in property tax rates may reduce property values and induce capital outflows, so may the provision of additional public services raise values and attract capital inflow. Better schools or municipal services may render the town a more attractive place in which to reside or to operate a business. The improvement raises the demand for housing and structures, leading to higher property values, and thus counteracts the effects of increased property tax rates. Thus, expenditure benefits may be capitalized no less than tax burdens, so that the combined tax and expenditure effects may leave housing values reduced, increased, or unaffected, depending on how the revenue is obtained and what it is used for.

If all property taxes were imposed in strict conformity with the benefit principle, the two effects should wash out with property values independent of tax rates. Actually, such is not the case. The property tax is used as a general revenue source and goes to finance expenditure benefits not always in close alignment with tax contributions. Nevertheless, empirical investigations show that property values respond to expenditure as well as tax differentials, thus pointing to the importance of considering both aspects.[15]

Allowance for Income Tax   Since the major complaint over the property tax came from homeowners, let us compare their position as investors in housing services with that of investors in corporate shares, allowing in both cases not only for the property tax but also for the personal income and corporation tax. Although the investor in housing services is likely to pay more in property tax, the overall tax burden remains substantially less if all three taxes are combined.[16] This outcome

---

[15] See W. Oates, "The Effects of Property Taxes and Local Public Spending on Property Values: An Empirical Study of Tax Capitalization and the Tiebout Hypothesis," *Journal of Political Economy,* vol. 77, November–December 1969.

[16] Consider individual X who invests $150,000 in her residence. With an average tax rate of 1.8 percent of market value, her property tax is $2,700 and no income tax is due. Next consider investor Y who purchases a similar property for rental purposes, yielding a rental income of $12,000. In addition

reflects the additional burden borne by the shareholder under the corporation income tax as well as the favorable treatment of the homeowner under the personal income tax.'

Alternative Patterns

We now turn to some alternative views of property tax incidence. For this purpose, we distinguish between the parts of the tax which are assessed on land and those which are assessed on improvements, with the latter divided further between commercial and residential structures.

The share of the tax assessed on land may be assigned readily to the owners of the land. Because land is inelastic in supply and immobile, there is no escaping the tax. Burden distribution will tend to be progressive. Lacking data regarding the distribution of land holdings as compared with other wealth, we may suppose that burden distribution is similar to that of a tax on capital income.

The share of the tax assessed on commercial structures may be viewed similarly to that of the corporation tax. As in that case, we may allow for imperfect markets and postulate that part of the tax, say, one-half, is passed on to consumers. This part of the burden distribution then becomes regressive.

There remains the share of the tax assessed on residential housing. As the public sees this tax, it is generally viewed as a levy on the consumer of housing services. With housing expenditures perceived as a declining share of income when moving up the income scale, the tax is taken to be regressive. How can this view of the tax, as being a tax on housing expenditures, be reconciled with the earlier interpretation which considers it a tax on capital income? The key to the puzzle lies in the fact that housing may be viewed as an investment item, but (in the case of owner-occupied housing) also as a durable consumer good. Because of this, the owner-occupier may be willing to accept a lower imputed rent on housing than on other investments. Part of the tax will be absorbed in this ownership-rent and thereby be distributed in line with consumption rather than be shared with all capital income.

This reasoning does not hold for rental property, where owners are concerned only with an investment choice. If markets are competitive, capital invested in rental housing will command the same net return as other capital, with the burden distribution in line with capital income. But the outcome may differ if, as is frequently the case, rental markets are imperfect. The tax may then lead to an increase in rent ceilings or to relaxation of previously constrained monopoly pricing. Moreover, not all property is taxed at the same rates. Effective property tax rates tend to be especially high in low-income neighborhoods, partly because property tax rates in central cities are high in general and partly because residential properties in low-income neighborhoods are often assessed at a higher rate than are higher-income

---

to the property tax, Y pays an income tax of 28 percent on rental income net of property tax, or $2,604, raising his total tax bill to $5,304. Finally, take investor Z who places $150,000 in corporate shares, and assume the corporation to acquire the same rental property. The tax bill now includes the property tax of $2,700 and a corporation tax of 33 percent on rental income net of property tax or $3,069. Also suppose that profits net of taxes are paid out as dividends, with an income tax at 28 percent, or $1,745, raising Z's total tax bill to $7,514. Comparison of the three tax bills shows the advantageous position of home owner X as compared to investors Y and Z.

surroundings.[17] The resulting additional tax on rental property may well be borne by the tenant.

Allowing for the possibilities just discussed, we find that the pattern of burden incidence under the property tax may encompass capital income, general consumption, and housing expenditures. As shown in Table 14-1, division of the burden between consumption and housing outlays renders it regressive throughout, whereas assigning one-half to capital income, one-quarter to general consumption, and one-quarter to housing outlays yields a more or less proportional pattern.

E. APPRAISAL AND OUTLOOK FOR PROPERTY TAX

The property tax, as a percentage of local tax revenue, has declined over recent decades, falling from 87 percent in 1960 to 75 percent in the 1980s. The property tax, nevertheless, has remained the predominant source of local tax revenue. The easy visibility and relative immobility of real property renders it a ready object of local taxation, and the benefits which such property derives from local public services justify its taxation. However, the property tax has come in for increasing criticism. Indeed, it ranks as the least popular type of tax, and complaints over it have been at the core of the recent tax revolt.

The problem is not that the property tax has risen much more rapidly over the years than have other taxes. On the contrary, the share of property tax revenue in total state and local taxes, as well as in local revenue only, declined during the 1970s. Indeed, the average effective rate on single-family homes declined from 1.98 percent in 1971 to 1.23 percent in 1984. In California, the very cradle of the tax revolt, the effective rate fell from 2.48 to 1.02 percent.[18]

A major factor explaining the unpopularity of the property tax is that among all major taxes, it is the only one subject to direct annual or semiannual payments. The property tax comes due in large chunks and is highly visible to the taxpayer. It thus differs sharply from the other major taxes, including the income tax which for most taxpayers is taken care of by withholding, and the sales tax, which is largely invisible and paid in small installments. Next there is the fact that taxpayers may compare their own assessed values with those of their neighbors and finding them to differ become irritated by the inequities, real or imagined, in the assessment process.

During the late 1970s, such irritations were compounded by the impact of inflation. As prices rose, so did house values, which was sooner or later reflected in higher assessed values. Even though tax rates were unchanged, taxes still rose in dollar terms and the taxpayers were angered because they felt that "the same old house" was taxed "more," while overlooking the fact that the nominal value of the house had risen and that the tax in real terms had not changed.

---

[17] See George E. Peterson, "The Property Tax in Low-Income Housing Markets," in Peterson, op. cit., p. 110. Peterson also notes that owing to higher risk, the ratio of market value to rent is lower in low-income neighborhoods, so that the tax per dollar of rent is less, thereby providing an offset to the higher assessment ratio.

[18] See Advisory Commission on Intergovernmental Relations, *Significant Features of Fiscal Federalism, 1985–86,* Washington, D.C., 1986, p. 107.

But the problem was not one of money illusion only. The value of houses during the inflationary years of the later seventies and early eighties rose more rapidly than did the average money income of homeowners. As a result, the ratio of property tax payment to income tended to rise, especially in states where, ironically, good tax administration served to secure prompt adjustment of assessed values to rising house prices. Rising housing costs relative to income were compounded, moreover, by the rising cost of mortgages. The resulting pressures came to be felt most severely by people on fixed income, especially the aged who could not afford to maintain their customary residence. All this contributed to dissatisfaction with the property tax and, during the late seventies, led to constitutional or statutory property tax restrictions in many states.[19] In most cases these restrictions took the form of rate limitations, but in some instances—such as California's Proposition 13—legislation also involved a freezing of assessed values on old property, thereby severely injuring the equity of the tax. More will be said about this and the future of the property tax when considering state-local revenue needs.[20]

F. NET WORTH TAX

In discussing the rationale for property and wealth taxation, we have distinguished between a benefit argument pointing toward differential user charges on real property imposed on an *in rem* basis and an ability-to-pay argument pointing toward a tax on net wealth, imposed on a *personal* basis. The existing property tax—which applies more or less uniformly as an in rem tax to all real property within the jurisdiction—follows neither pattern. We now turn to a brief consideration of its theoretically more attractive though less widely used cousin, the net worth tax.

Foreign Experience

A net worth tax is used in about seventeen countries, including the Netherlands, West Germany, the Scandinavian countries, and Switzerland. India and various Latin American countries also make use of this tax. In most countries the tax is imposed on natural persons only, although in some (including West Germany and India), corporations are also taxable. The definition of taxable assets usually includes intangibles as well as tangibles, and in most cases, all debt obligations are deductible. However, some countries disallow obligations not related to the acquisition of taxable assets. Natural persons are granted exemptions and rates are either proportional (typically 1 percent or less) or progressive (ranging up to 2.5 percent).

The net worth tax, except in the Swiss cantons, is imposed at the central level. Countries making use of this tax usually impose it in addition to the ordinary property tax, with net worth tax revenue typically only a small fraction (below 5 percent) of total revenue. Nevertheless, as noted at the outset of this chapter, a net worth tax is a potentially important component of the tax structure. For one thing, it may serve as a supplement to ineffective coverage of capital income under the

---

[19] See *Significant Features of Fiscal Federalism, 1987,* op. cit., p. 116.
[20] See p. 475.

income tax. As we will see later, this aspect is of particular importance in developing countries, where it is especially difficult to reach capital income. For another, the net worth tax may serve as a supplement to an expenditure tax. It might thus become a serious candidate for federal attention if an extensive shift from income- to consumption-based taxation should occur. It remains to be seen, however, whether imposition of a federal wealth tax would be permissible under the Sixteenth Amendment.

Structure and Base

Some of the problems and difficulties posed by the implementation of a net worth tax may be noted briefly.

Tax Base   The net worth tax relates to ability to pay. Hence it should be imposed on individuals and not on corporations. Corresponding to the partnership view of the corporation profits tax, the net worth of the corporation should be imputed to the owners. As is the case with the income tax, the base should be defined globally, so as to give equal treatment to all components of net worth. Moreover, the principle of uniformity should be applied to both the asset and the liability side of the balance sheet. Intangible as well as tangible and nonearning as well as earning assets should be included. Similarly, all debt obligations should be deductible.

Measuring Net Worth   Administration of the net worth tax calls for identification of the taxable assets and for verification of debts claimed. In short, it calls for tax returns which include an annual balance sheet in which the taxpayer's assets and liabilities are listed.

With regard to accounting for assets, authorities must be assured that all assets have in fact been declared. Moreover, there is a problem of asset valuation. Difficulties inherent in current valuation of all assets have already been discussed in connection with capital gains taxation. Here, as there, approximations must be used. Thus, assets subject to property tax (especially if assessment is equalized) may be valued on that basis, while others, such as traded securities, may be valued by market quotation. For the remainder, rough approximations (such as cost of acquisition minus depreciation) must be used. Similar difficulties arise with deductible debts. The difficulties of administering a bona fide net worth tax are considerable. It is not surprising, therefore, that the net worth tax easily degenerates into a tax on real estate only. But the difficulties are not insurmountable. Linkage with the administration of the income tax, and particularly with the administration of an expenditure tax, might in fact introduce a valuable element of self-enforcement. Asset acquisitions must be declared to minimize the expenditure tax, but this declaration also adds to the base of the net worth tax.

Role of Intangibles

A net worth tax by its very nature must include intangibles, both assets and liabilities, in its base. How does this affect the overall size of the base and its distribution among wealth holders?

Private Claims Consider first a setting in which there is no public debt or government-issued money. All debt instruments are between private persons. Suppose that there are two individuals, A and B, whose wealth positions are as follows:

	A	B	A + B
Real property	$ 100	$ 50	$ 150
Debt owed	10	⎫	
Debt claims	—	10 ⎬	
Net worth	90	60	150

As shown in the illustration, the total base for a tax on real property and a net worth tax is the same at $150. But they differ otherwise. If we collect $15 from a 10 percent tax on all real property, A pays $10 while B pays $5. If we collect a similar amount from a tax on net worth—i.e., a tax which includes debts claimed and deducts debts owed—A pays $9 while B pays $6. At first sight this suggests that A prefers the net worth tax and B the property tax. But the market will adjust accordingly. As the tax on real property is imposed, borrowers will not be willing to pay the same rate of interest as they did before, since the net earnings from their investment in real property is reduced. Lenders will have to be satisfied with a lower rate of interest, so that part of the burden is passed from A to B. In the end, the burden distribution will be the same as it would have been under a net worth tax, i.e., in line with distribution of net worth. If a proportional rate is applied, the choice between the two taxes is thus a matter of indifference.

But they differ if the tax is imposed at progressive rates. Returning to our illustration, we see that the burden distribution of a progressive rate tax on real property (where A's base is twice B's) will obviously differ from that assessed on the net worth base (where A's base exceeds B's by only 50 percent). Since a personal tax calls for assessment in line with ability to pay, the net worth tax is the superior form of wealth taxation.

Claims against Government A further difference arises if we allow for claims against government, whether such claims are in the form of public debt or money backed by Federal Reserve credit and the Treasury. Such claims add to the wealth of one private holder without reducing that of another. Unlike private debt, they are thus an addition to the net worth base for the group as a whole, so that the base of the net worth tax exceeds that of the tax on real property. Suppose that the above illustration is expanded as follows:

	A	B	A + B
Net worth from above	$ 90	$ 60	$ 150
Claims against government	70	20	90
Net worth, total	160	80	240

In this case, collection of $15 under a flat-rate net worth tax will call for a rate of 6.2 percent, drawing $9.88 from A and $5.12 from B. To obtain the same revenue from a tax on real property, a 10 percent rate is needed, with payments of $10 and $5, respectively. The market once more will compensate for the reduced net return on real property, but A's burden will remain higher under the net worth tax than under that on real property.[21]

Rates and Exemptions

A net worth tax, being a personal tax in nature, could be imposed with progressive rates. With privately held wealth for 1985 of about $12 trillion (see Table 24-1), a 1 percent rate would yield $120 billion, or about 35 percent of the yield then provided by the income tax. Owing to the more unequal distribution of wealth holdings, the revenue gain from rising bracket rates would be more substantial. Note, however, that a rate of 1 percent imposed on wealth, with a 10 percent return on wealth holding, would be equivalent to a 10 percent tax on capital income. Thus, the nominal level of rates would be very much lower than that under the income tax.

As in the case of the income tax, allowance could be made also for a personal exemption, so as to provide relief at the lower end of the scale.

G.   CAPITAL LEVY

Still another type of wealth taxation takes the form of a capital levy. Imposed on a once-and-for-all basis, such levies have been used by various countries in emergency situations such as monetary reforms to terminate postwar inflations, but there is no record of such levies in U.S. fiscal history. If truly in the nature of a once-and-for-all tax, which is neither anticipated nor expected to be repeated, such a levy differs from other forms of wealth taxation because it has no disturbing effects on economic behavior. This feature adds to its attraction as an instrument of redistributional taxation, but the underlying assumption of unique application and nonanticipation disqualifies it as part of the normal tax structure.

H.   SUMMARY

The role of wealth taxation in the tax structure may be based on either benefit or ability-to-pay considerations, but neither points to the present type of real property tax:

    1.   Wealth may be taxed on an in rem basis as under the property tax or on a personal basis as under the net worth tax. The latter is superior on ability-to-pay grounds.

    2.   The net worth tax may be used as a corrective to imperfect taxation of capital income under the income tax or as a supplement to a consumption tax.

    3.   The local property tax serves as a rough approximation to ability-to-pay taxation, but other and superior indices of benefits received could be devised.

---

[21] As we will note later (see p. 553), it may be argued that since public debt must be serviced, taxpayers will capitalize the increased tax liabilities which they must bear in the future, in which case a liability would be added, canceling entry of public debt into aggregate net worth. But even if this liability were allowed for in the net worth base, public debt would not simply drop out of the picture, because the distribution of debt holding would most likely differ from that of increased tax liabilities.

Regarding the composition and structure of wealth holdings in the United States, we have observed that:

4. The value of privately held wealth in 1985 was about $12 trillion.

5. Residential housing accounts for about 20 percent of privately held real property.

6. The distribution of wealth is more unequal than that of income.

The major form of wealth taxation in the United States is the local property tax. As the major source of local tax finance, it remains one of the crucial concerns of tax policy:

7. The U.S. property tax is largely a tax on real estate.

8. About one-half of property tax revenue is derived from residential property.

9. A large part of real property is covered by the property tax. However, the property tax base or assessed value is typically below half of market value.

10. A distinction must be drawn between nominal and effective rates.

11. Effective rates vary widely among jurisdictions within a state, partly because of wide variations in assessment ratios.

12. Equalizing assessments within a state is important for the distribution of state aid.

13. A circuit-breaker provision is used to reduce the tax burden on elderly property owners with low incomes.

In considering the incidence of the property tax, we find it helpful to begin with the hypothetical case of a uniform national tax on all real property:

14. Under competitive conditions, such a tax is equivalent to a tax on all capital income. As such its burden distribution is progressive, except for the lower end of the income scale.

15. If the supply of capital is elastic, the longer-run adjustment to the tax may involve sharing of the burden by wage earners and consumers of capital-intensive products such as housing.

16. The part of the tax which is imposed on residential property may be viewed as a tax on housing consumption, which suggests a regressive burden distribution.

17. For owner-occupied residences, part of the tax is absorbed in imputed rent. For rental housing, imperfect markets may place part of the burden on tenants.

The pattern is complicated further if local differentials in the U.S. property tax are allowed for:

18. If one jurisdiction raises its effective rate above the average, short-run incidence of the differential will be on the owners of property in the high-tax jurisdiction.

19. In the longer run, the burden of the tax on mobile capital (but not land) comes to be shared by all capital, including that located outside the taxing jurisdiction. In addition, two-way shifts may occur between various groups of workers and consumers inside and outside the taxing jurisdiction.

20. From the point of view of the taxing jurisdiction, an important distinction arises between those parts of the burden which are borne inside and others which are borne outside.

21. To the extent that the tax-burden differentials between jurisdictions are matched by benefit differentials from public services, house values will remain unaffected and capital will not move.

22. Firms selling in local markets are in a better position to shift the tax to consumers than are the firms selling outside the taxing jurisdiction.

As an alternative form of wealth taxation, the tax may be imposed in personal form and be applied to net worth only:

23.   Such a tax may be applied on a person's global net worth with exemptions and progressive rates similar in spirit to the income tax.

24.   As distinct from the property tax, the base would include all assets, intangible as well as tangible, but liabilities would be deducted.

25.   Equity in corporations would be treated on an integrated basis.

26.   To be effectively implemented, such a tax would have to be national rather than local in scope.

FURTHER READINGS

Aaron, Henry J.: *Who Pays the Property Tax?* Washington, D.C.: Brookings, 1975.

Advisory Commission on Intergovernmental Relations: *The Property Tax in a Changing Environment,* Washington, D.C., 1974.

McLure, Charles E.: "The 'New View' of the Property Tax: A Caveat," *National Tax Journal,* March 1977.

Netzer, Dick: *Economics of the Property Tax,* Washington, D.C.: Brookings, 1966.

Peterson, George E. (ed.): *Property Tax Reform,* Washington, D.C.: John C. Lincoln Institute and Urban Institute, 1973.

Chapter 25

Death Duties*

A. Rationale for Death Duties: *Objectives and Types of Tax.* **B. The Federal Estate Tax:** *Structure; Actual and Potential Base; Further Issues.* **C. The Federal Gift Tax. D. State Inheritance Taxes. E. Summary.**

We turn now to the taxation of wealth, not on an annual basis but at the time of transfer by bequest or gift. Taxation of bequests is much the more important item. It may be in the form of taxes imposed on the estate under the federal type of estate tax or of inheritance taxes imposed on the heir by the states. As was shown in Table 18-1, these taxes are of only minor and declining revenue importance. Even if expanded substantially, death duties could not become a major revenue source such as income or sales taxation, for the simple reason that the total base is very much smaller. Nevertheless, death duties are of considerable interest as a matter of social philosophy and as a policy instrument in adjusting the distribution of wealth. For this reason they are a potentially important element of the tax structure.

---

*Reader's Guide to Chapter 25: Death duties, although of minor revenue significance, are of potentially great importance as an instrument of distribution policy, applied in this case to wealth and its transfer. Difficult technical problems arise in implementing death duties and in making them effective.

A.   RATIONALE FOR DEATH DUTIES

Death duties may be imposed in various forms and for various reasons. Disregarding gifts for the time being, let us suppose that all transfers are made at death. The tax may be imposed either on the estate as a whole (as in the case of the federal estate tax) or on the bequest received by a particular heir (as in the case of state inheritance taxes).

At first sight, it might appear that it is a matter of indifference whether the tax is imposed on the donor as an estate tax or on the heir as an inheritance tax. As noted before, it does not matter on which side of the "counter" the tax is imposed. But applied to wealth transfer at death this equivalence holds only if we consider the case of a proportional rate tax. The two approaches differ when progressive rates are considered. Progression under the estate tax relates to the total size of the estate and the wealth of the testator, whereas that under the inheritance tax relates to the share received by the particular heir, thereby creating an important difference between the two taxes and their objectives.

Objectives and Types of Tax

Depending on what society wishes to accomplish, various situations may be distinguished:

1.   Society may wish to limit a person's right to dispose of his or her property at death. Individuals may use their property during their lifetime but their title ceases or is curtailed at death. In that case, an estate tax of the federal type is the appropriate approach. If society wishes to allow free bequests up to a certain amount, an exemption is in order. If it wishes to confiscate estates in excess of a certain limit, a 100 percent rate above that limit would apply.

2.   Society may wish to place increasing limitations on a person's right to pass on wealth as subsequent generations are reached, in which case, the level of applicable estate tax rates may rise as the property passes through successive bequests, an approach initially suggested by the Italian economist Eugenio Rignano.[1]

3.   Society may wish to limit a person's right to acquire wealth by way of bequests, i.e., without "own effort." Rugged individualism may be taken to call for this solution, with equal positions on the "starting gate" and open to inequalities that follow.[2] In that case, the tax is properly imposed on the heir, as is done by the inheritance taxes which apply at the state level. If it is desired to permit some acquisition by bequest but to differentiate between small and large acquisitions, progressive rates are called for. Given this objective, it would be sensible to combine such accessions from all sources, i.e., to relate progression to total accessions from bequests over lifetime rather than to each specific inheritance. The former is referred to as an "accessions tax."

4.   Society may have the more general objective of achieving a more equal distribution of wealth. The institution of inheritance is one of the major factors making for concentration of wealth, with inherited wealth accounting for half or more of the net worth of wealthy men and for most of the net worth of equally wealthy women.[3] Death

---

[1] See Eugenio Rignano, *The Significance of Death Duties,* London: Douglas, 1928.

[2] See p. 76.

[3] See John A. Brittain, *Inheritance and the Inequality of Material Wealth,* Washington, D.C.: Brookings, 1978.

duties, especially in the form of inheritance taxation, may thus be used to moderate inequality in the distribution of wealth.

   5.   Taxation at death may be viewed as a supplement to income taxation rather than as an additional tax on transfer. Under the accretion approach to the income tax, receipt of an inheritance is properly included in the heir's income.[4] In the absence of such inclusion, an inheritance tax (with rates related to the heir's income) might be viewed as correction for a defective income definition. The same might be said for the role of an estate tax (with rates related to the testator's consumption) as a correction for effective base definition in the case of an expenditure tax which does not include bequests in its base.

   6.   The estate tax may be viewed as an alternative to the taxation of capital income during the recipient's lifetime. The view may then be taken that substitution of an estate tax for highly progressive taxation of capital income will reduce resulting disincentive effects on saving and investment, considerations noted earlier.[5]

Consequently, the choice between an estate and inheritance tax approach to the imposition of death duties will depend on the objectives which such taxation is designed to accomplish. Only if rates are proportional is it a matter of indifference which approach is chosen. And although the objectives differ, they need not be mutually exclusive. Pursuing both objectives 1 and 3, society may wish to impose both an estate tax, thereby limiting the testator's right to dispose, and an inheritance tax designed to limit the heir's right to receive and/or to compensate for noninclusion of bequests into taxable income. Choice among these objectives and selection of the appropriate tax, it should be noted, are issues which should be distinguished from the previously considered question of how transactions at death (the receipt of an inheritance or the leaving of bequests) should be treated under an income or expenditure tax.[6]

B.   THE FEDERAL ESTATE TAX

We now turn to the federal estate tax and some of its problems. From a technical point of view, this tax and the closely related problem of gift taxation have been among the most complex areas of the tax law. Death duties are applied at both the

---

   [4] Liberal averaging provisions would be needed so as not to penalize the heir through bunching of income under a progressive rate schedule.
   •   A more complicated question is whether in the income tax framework, the testator should be permitted to deduct the tax from his own income. If not, would there not be double taxation of such income, first at the donor's and then at the donee's level? Following Henry Simons' accretion concept, such "double taxation" is not objectionable. (See Henry Simons, *Personal Income Taxation*, Chicago: University of Chicago Press, 1938, p. 56.) The donor makes such use of his income as he chooses and the recipient experiences a new accretion. But the leaving of bequests *is* discriminated against if we note that the donor derives utility from the heir's gain, a utility which relates to the heir's gain net of tax. Mr. A who wishes to leave a bequest is thus discriminated against as compared with Mrs. B who consumes her assets before death. (See G. Brennan, "Death and Taxes: An Attack on the Orthodoxy," *Public Finance, Finances Publiques,* no. 3, 1978.) The rationale for imposing a supplementary death duty must then be based on society's wish to limit property entitlement at death.
   [5] See p. 303.
   [6] See p. 334 and p. 407.

federal and the state level, with the former in the form of an estate and the latter largely in the form of an inheritance tax.

Structure

As shown in Table 25-1, the federal estate tax applies at rates ranging from 18 to 50 percent. These rates apply to the entire estate without allowing for a personal exemption. The law then permits a credit of $192,800 to be deducted from tax. This, in effect, leaves estates up to nearly $600,000 tax free.

The resulting pattern of liabilities as shown in Table 25-1 involves effective rates of 15 percent at the $1 million and 37 percent at the $2.5 million level. These rates are substantially below those applicable prior to 1981, when bracket rates ranged up to 70 percent and the credit was limited to $50,000. As a further relief, the 1981 legislation also extended the marital exemption (i.e., exemption of estates left to the spouse) from 50 to 100 percent thereof.

The composition of taxable returns for 1983 is shown in Table 25-2. We find a total of 35,000 returns and an average rate of tax (tax as percent of gross estate) of 16 percent. As in the case of the income tax, most estates fall at the lower end of the scale, but a substantial part of the tax base now appears in the upper range. As is evident from the table, the tax reaches a small fraction of total estates out of the potential base that might be reached.

Actual and Potential Base

With the number of taxable estates at 35,000 and the annual number of deaths at about 2 million, it is evident that only a minute fraction of estates is reached. Although in many cases the size of the estate will be so small as not to justify inclusion in the base, there nevertheless remains a substantial shortfall of potential coverage. Whereas precise data are not available, the following calculations provide a perspective on the problem. The volume of privately held wealth (1986) may be estimated at, say, $10 trillion.[7] Assuming 3 percent of total wealth to pass through

TABLE 25-1
Unified Transfer Tax Rate Schedule (1988)

Size of Taxable Estate	Bracket Rate, Percentage	Tentative Tax (Low End of Bracket)	Tax after Credit	Tax as Percentage of Taxable Estate (Lower Bracket Limit)
0– 10,000	18	—	—	0
10,000– 20,000	20	1,800	—	0
100,000– 150,000	30	23,800	—	0
500,000– 600,000	37	155,800	—	0
1,000,000–1,250,000	43	345,800	192,800	15.3
2,500,000 and over	50	1,025,800	933,000	37.3

[7] See p. 414.

TABLE 25-2
Taxable Estates, Federal Estate Tax, 1983

	Number of Returns	Gross Estate (Billions of Dollars)	Tax after Credit (Billions of Dollars)	Tax as Percentage of Gross Estate
300,000– 500,000	17,105	6.6	0.6	9.0
500,000–1,000,000	11,678	8.0	1.2	15.0
1,000,000–2,500,000	4,589	6.7	1.3	19.4
2,500,000–5,000,000	1,223	4.2	0.8	19.0
5,000,000 and over	552	7.0	1.3	18.6
Total	35,148	32.7	5.2	15.9

Source: Statistics of Income Bulletin, vol. 4, no. 2, fall 1984. Estates under $300,000 not required to file.

estates each year,[8] we are left with a potential base of about $300 billion. Suppose further that the first $50,000 is to be exempted and that half of the estates exceed this amount This would leave $300 billion minus $50 billion, or $250 billion, as the potential base, an amount seven times that shown in Table 25-2.

If society so wished, a substantial expansion in the base could thus be obtained by reducing the tax-free limit of bequests. Nevertheless, even drastic efforts in this direction would hardly render the estate tax a major revenue producer relative to other sources, such as the income, property, or sales tax, because death is too infrequent an event. The major role of death duties in the tax structure is not so much one of revenue raising as that of an instrument by which to moderate the distribution of inherited wealth. The drastic estate tax reduction of 1981, although not of great importance in revenue terms, was thus of major significance as a matter of social policy.

Further Issues

Estate tax design raises a host of technical issues, only some of which are noted here.

Capital Gains   Assets for purposes of estate tax are valued by their market value at the time of the owner's death rather than at the cost of original acquisition. The stepped-up basis is then used again for purposes of capital gains taxation at the time of sale of such assets by the heir. Thus only appreciation from the time of death is counted, leaving appreciation prior to death untaxed. Under 1976 legislation, the heir was to carry over the original base of the testator so as to apply the heir's capital gains tax to the full appreciation of the assets when the gain is realized. Application of this provision, however, was postponed and then dropped in subsequent legislation, leaving a substantial loophole in the taxation of capital gains.

Marital Deduction   Problems of how to treat the family unit, encountered already in the income tax context, reappear under the estate tax. As just noted, the

[8] See John C. Brown, "Transfer Tax Yield," National Tax Journal, March 1969.

limitation on marital deduction was removed in 1982 so that any amount may now be left tax-free to the surviving spouse. This is in line with the family unit approach to income taxation. Property left to the spouse is treated as if it had been joint property, even though prior to death separate titles were held. No such provision is made, however, with regard to children or other family members. Bequests left to children are taxable just as are those left to heirs outside the family unit. As noted below, such is not the case under inheritance taxes at the state level, where preferential treatment is extended to relatives other than spouses. What constitutes the proper solution depends upon how society views the role of the family in relation to the entitlement to dispose over property at death.

Generation Skipping and Trusts   Next there is the further problem of implementing the intent of the law as established. Here the use of trusts enters as an instrument of tax avoidance. Trusts may take many forms, the most usual of which runs as follows: Mr. Jones with an estate of $1.5 million wishes to leave his property to his spouse, after whose death it is to go to his children. If the property is passed to his spouse directly, no tax is due under the marital deduction, but a tax must be paid later on if the bequest made by his spouse exceeds her exemption allowance. To avoid this later tax, Mr. Jones will leave $600,000 to a trust with his spouse as life tenant, charging this against the exemption equivalent (1988 level) of the credit; and he will leave the remaining $900,000 to her directly, this amount being exempt under the marital deduction. Suppose that she uses $200,000 thereof prior to her death. At the death of the spouse, the trust passes tax-free to the children as life tenants, with a further $600,000 passed on to them tax-free under the will of the spouse, who now claims a second exemption. Only $100,000 becomes subject to tax. In addition, the original trust may be drawn so as to provide for tax-free passage of the property to a third generation at the death of the children.[9] Thus the funds are passed through two generations without tax.

Given these tax benefits, trust arrangements are advantageous to wealthy decedents and wide use is made of them. Although there is nothing wrong with trust arrangements as a way of designing bequests, the tax implications of such arrangements should be neutralized. Even though the revenue loss due to generation skipping is not very large, the equity implications are unfortunate. This factor was recognized in 1976 by legislation which limited such trusts to $250,000 for each child. Under a more drastic correction, the trust would be made taxable as received by the successive tenants.[10]

Charitable Contributions   Charitable contributions are of no less importance under the estate than under the income tax. Generally speaking, there is no limit to the deduction of charitable contributions under the estate tax. Such contributions

---

[9] The permissible chain of life tenants is not unlimited, such limitations as apply being a matter of state law. According to the law of most states, the trust must terminate (the property must accrue to the remainderman) not later than twenty-one years after the death of the last life tenant living when the trust is established. This effectively limits the trust arrangement to a hundred years or so.

[10] Under British law, the trust is included in the estate of the first life tenant and the estate tax is allocated between the property and the trust. Several objections have been raised to this procedure, but it would seem to be the most feasible.

have gone to establish the Rockefeller, Carnegie, and Ford foundations, and bequests are a major source of support for private universities. For large estates the resulting tax saving pays up to one-half of the contribution and thus encourages testators to use their funds in this fashion.

The role of charitable contributions under the estate tax, as under the income tax, poses cultural, social, and political issues which go much beyond the realm of tax policy and which cannot be pursued here. Organizations supported by tax-deductible contributions serve many useful purposes which would not be forthcoming from the public budget, but tax deductibility also permits a high degree of private control in the use of what are essentially public funds. The law thus places certain restrictions on the use of such funds, especially for political purposes.

In addition, it is necessary to ensure that the setting up of tax-free foundations is not used to accomplish essentially private purposes. Thus, a foundation may be set up to maintain family control over a particular business. If the estate tax had to be paid, the business would have to be sold and control would go to the public. If a foundation is established which owns the business, continued control may be maintained via control over the foundation. Legislation has tried to deal with this problem by requiring the broadening of control over time. It also imposed certain restrictions, including a requirement to file tax returns, to pay a 4 percent tax on investment earnings and to dispose of all earnings.

Family Business   Critics of the federal estate tax argue that it threatens the institution of family-owned businesses and farms. One concern is that the heir may be forced to liquidate under unfavorable terms in order to pay the tax. This concern is hardly decisive because it may be met by liberal provision for installment or delayed payment. Nevertheless, payment of the tax may require eventual liquidation, which need not involve breaking up the business unit. The unit may be sold as a whole or part of the equity may be transferred outside. But the extent of family control will be disturbed, an inevitable consequence of imposing a death duty, where the estate takes the form of a family holding. It is a consequence that has to be accepted if by imposing a death duty, society wishes to limit entitlement to property at death.

C.   THE FEDERAL GIFT TAX

The federal estate and gift taxes are integrated into a transfer tax covering both components. At the time of death, the taxable base is determined as the sum of estate plus gifts made prior to death with the rates shown in Table 25-1 applicable to this total. Previous payments of gift tax in turn are then credited against the total tax. The credit of $192,800 is thus a unified credit, applicable against the tax liability on both these bases.

D.   STATE INHERITANCE TAXES

Death duties at the state level take various forms. They are applied most commonly in the form of inheritance taxes, imposed on the heir. In 1985, such taxes were used in twenty-two states. Exemption levels and rate schedules typically differ, depending on the heir's family relationship to the deceased. This approach is illustrated by the pattern used under the Minnesota law, as follows:[11]

	Rates, Percentage	Exemption
Spouse	5	All
Child and parent	5	50,000
Brother and sister	5–12.5	1,000
Other	10–31	500

Twenty-eight states use not inheritance taxes but estate taxes, with bracket rates from 1 to 21 percent and exemptions substantially below those at the federal level. Since state estate taxes may be credited in part against the federal estate tax, states may gain free tax revenue for at least this amount. Accordingly, all states, including those which impose inheritance taxes, have a minimal estate tax to pick up this credit.

Just as is the case with the federal trend, state reliance on death duties is declining. Some states, including California, have recently abandoned their inheritance tax. Since retirees are relatively mobile, death duties imposed at the state level are especially open to interstate tax competition, thus limiting their potential use below the federal level.

E. SUMMARY

The structure of death duties in the U.S. tax system includes an estate tax at the federal and inheritance taxes at the state level. Neither type of tax plays a major role as a revenue producer. In part this reflects the simple fact that death is an infrequent event, but beyond this only a small part of the potential tax base is reached. Liberal exemptions and deductions reduce the base of the federal estate tax to a small fraction of the potential; and various tax avoidance devices, mainly in the form of trust arrangements, further add to the revenue loss.

But although limited in revenue importance, death duties are a significant instrument of social policy. Since passage of wealth through bequests is one of the major factors in the concentration of wealth holding, death duties are a suitable instrument by which to modify the distribution of wealth. Also, they are an effective instrument by which to implement society's attitude toward the passage of property rights at death. Different types of death duties will serve different objectives and the choice among them poses an important policy problem.

FURTHER READINGS

Brittain, John A.: *Inheritance and the Inequality of Wealth,* Washington, D.C.: Brookings, 1978.
Shoup, Carl S.: *Federal Estate and Gift Taxes,* Washington, D.C.: Brookings, 1967.

[11] Tax Foundation, *Facts and Figures on Government Finance,* 1986, pp. E47, 48.

Chapter 26

Payroll Tax*

A. Level of Tax Rates and Administration. B. Incidence: *Competitive Markets; Imperfect Markets.* **C. Relation to Benefits.**

It remains to consider the payroll tax which, as noted before, provides *the* source of revenue for the social security system. Its role should be seen in relation to benefit payments, an approach taken in an earlier discussion.[1] Here we will view the payroll tax simply as part of the tax system, thus neglecting the broader context. The share of payroll tax revenue in the federal tax system has risen sharply over recent decades, increasing from 9 percent in 1950 to 22 percent in 1970, and to 40 percent in 1986.[2] The tax applies to personal earnings only, but not to capital income. Since the share of capital income rises when moving up the income scale, it carries a largely regressive burden distribution and remains such even though only the first $40,000 of earnings (1988 level) are included in the tax base.[3]

Reader's Guide to Chapter 26: This chapter should be read in connection with Chapter 11, Sections C and D.

[1] See p. 195.
[2] See p. 196.
[3] See p. 243.

A. LEVEL OF TAX RATES AND ADMINISTRATION

As noted earlier, the payroll tax for social security is imposed at a rate of 7.51 percent, applicable to employer and employee each, thus adding to a total of 15.02 percent. In addition, there is typically a 5 percent tax used to finance unemployment insurance and imposed on the employer only. As a matter of administration, the payroll tax is collected from the employer, including the contributions of both employer and employee, the latter's being withheld at the source. Since the tax is on gross earnings and no allowance is made for exemptions, the employee need not be required to file a return. The self-employed, of course, must file a return since there can be no source withholding.

As an in rem tax, imposed on wage income and readily subject to withholding, the payroll tax is an ideal tax from the administrative point of view. It brings in a large amount of revenue while involving a minimum of complexity and compliance cost. Even in the case of the self-employed, compliance can be relied upon since it is in the taxpayer's interest to contribute in order to obtain the resulting benefit claims. No serious difficulty arises where covered income is received from more than one source. Whereas both are subject to withholding, the upper limit of taxable wages remains set on a global basis because overwithholding may be credited against individual income tax. Moreover, if more than one member of a family is in covered employment and subject to tax, the secondary earner may choose between his or her separate claim and the benefits due him or her under the spouse's claim.

B. INCIDENCE

By dividing the payroll tax into two parts, with half payable by the employer and half payable by the employee, Congress evidently intended the two parts to be borne by different sectors of the economy. Whether or not this is indeed the case depends on market structures.

Competitive Markets

Congress, by imposing separate taxes on employers and employees evidently intended to spread the burden, but it is readily seen that given perfectly competitive markets, the burden pattern is the same, on whichever side of the market the tax is collected.

This pattern is shown in Figure 26-1, with DD the demand schedule for labor and SS its supply schedule. Initial equilibrium is at E, with supply of OA and a wage rate of OB. Introduction of the employee tax at rate CF/OF raises the supply schedule facing the employer from SS to $S'S'$, the difference between SS and $S'S'$ being the employee's tax.[4] At the same time, introduction of the employer tax at rate FG/OF, set so as to equal CF/OF, reduces the net demand schedule facing the workers from DD to $D'D'$. With both taxes in place, equilibrium shifts to E', the gross wage rate rises to OG, the net (after both taxes) wage falls to OC, and labor

---

[4] Note that both contributions are made at the same rate and applied to the same base, equal to OF, which is net of tax for the employer and gross of tax for the employee.

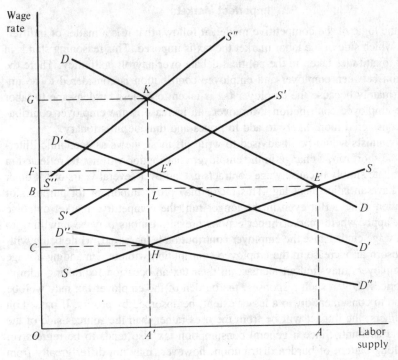

FIGURE 26-1 Incidence of payroll tax.

supply is reduced to OA'. The total tax equals $CGKH$, with $CFE'H$ collected from the employee and $FGKE'$ from the employer.[5] Exactly the same result would have been obtained had the entire revenue been collected as an employee tax at rate CG/OC thereby raising SS to $S''S''$, or by an employer tax also at rate CG/OC thereby dropping DD to $D''D''$. Gross price, net wage, and revenue remain the same in all three cases. Given a competitive market, the differentiation between employer and employee contribution is therefore a fiction.

At the same time, it does not follow that labor bears the entire burden. As shown earlier, such will be the case only if the supply of labor is entirely inelastic.[6] Since this is hardly so, we may expect some decline in hours worked, with a corresponding increase in the wage rate before tax. This in turn will be reflected in a sharing of the burden by other factors of production, the marginal product of which is reduced as labor hours become more scarce; and it will also be shared by the consumers of labor-intensive products the relative price of which will rise. Even though all this will affect the final outcome, it is nevertheless useful as a first approximation to assume that the burden falls on labor.

---

[5] The fact that $GKE'F$ is collected from the employer and $CFE'H$ from the employee must not be confused with the division of the burden between the demand and supply side of the labor market where (see p. 253) it might be argued that $BGKL$ is borne by the former and $CBLH$ by the latter. This division would remain the same if the entire tax were collected from either side.

[6] See p. 255.

Imperfect Markets

Within the logic of the competitive model, it follows that it is a matter of indifference on which side of the labor market the tax is imposed. This reasoning stands in contrast to attitudes taken in the political debate over payroll tax policy. There the distinction between employer and employee contribution is considered to be important, mainly because the employer tax is taken to be less burdensome to labor than the employee contribution. Moreover, an increase in the employer contribution is considered more likely to add to prices and thus be inflationary.

Economists would be ill-advised to write off these views as economic illiteracy. In the short run, a change in the employer contribution will not be reflected in the wage rate simply because wage contracts extend over several years or for other reasons have an adjustment lag. This factor may prove important for purposes of stabilization policy. But even in the longer run, the competitive market outcome may not apply where market imperfections prevail. Unions may be unwilling to accept a wage cut because the employer contribution is increased, while being willing to absorb an increase in the employee contribution without demanding a wage hike. Employers may find an increase in their tax an occasion for raising administered prices. Given such responses, the burden of the employer tax may well be passed on to consumers or, to a lesser extent, be absorbed by profits. If passed on to consumers, the impact will be from the uses rather than the sources side of the household account. Since a general consumption tax also tends to be regressive, the resulting pattern of burden distribution, however, may not differ greatly from that of the competitive case.

C. RELATION TO BENEFITS

Viewed as part of the tax structure (rather than as a component of the social security system), the payroll tax has a low ranking on equity grounds. It imposes an additional tax on wage income only while excluding capital income entirely. Moreover, the ceiling renders the tax proportional up to a certain point and regressive thereafter. On all accounts it hardly seems a tax which is worthy of so major a role in the tax system. To obtain a complete picture, it is necessary however to view the role of the payroll tax in relation to the transfers which it finances and the net benefits of burdens that result. This view reflects the spirit of a contributory system and, as noted earlier, there is much to be said for such an approach. This remains the case even though the system, as we have seen, involves a redistributive component and does not follow a strict principle of quid pro quo.[7]

FURTHER READINGS

Aaron, Henry: *Economic Effects of Social Security,* Washington, D.C.: Brookings, 1982.
Brittain, John A.: *The Payroll Tax for Social Security,* Washington, D.C.: Brookings, 1972.
Also see Readings for Chapter 11.

[7] See p. 203.

Part Six

Fiscal Federalism

Chapter 27

Principles of
Multiunit Finance*

A. Spatial Dimension of Allocation Function: *Benefit Regions; Optimal Fiscal Community; Extensions of Model; Voting by Feet.* **B. Tax-Structure Design. C. Spatial Aspects of Distribution Function. D. Spatial Aspects of Stabilization Function. E. Summary.**

So far, our discussion has been largely in terms of a fiscal system with a single level of government only. We must now allow for the fact that fiscal operations are typically carried out by many units of government or jurisdictions. In the United States, this multiple unit system includes the federal government, fifty state governments, the District of Columbia, and some 80,000 local jurisdictions. Canada, Australia, and West Germany are further illustrations of a three-tier arrangement, whereas the United Kingdom, Switzerland, and Holland operate with two tiers only—central and local. This multiunit fiscal structure, as it prevails in any particular country, reflects the historical forces of nation-making, wars, and geography.

*Reader's Guide to Chapter 27: The principles of multiunit finance which are considered in this chapter may be viewed as an extension of our discussion of social goods in Chapter 4. The problem is first dealt with in a setting where the spatial location of fiscal functions is determined by considerations of economic efficiency only. Based on the feature of spatial benefit limitation, this leads to important findings regarding the structure of the allocation function.

Typically, modern nations have not been formed as a free association of individuals but have emerged by a combination of preexisting sovereign jurisdictions which then join into national units. In so doing, member jurisdictions (such as the colonies and then states in the United States) may retain certain fiscal prerogatives while surrendering others, thereby joining in a compact which determines the fiscal aspects of the federation.

Political history thus tells much in explaining the structure of fiscal arrangements in any one country, but not all. There are also good economic reasons why certain fiscal functions should be operated on a more centralized level while others should be decentralized. Historical influences aside, we may consider what spatial fiscal structuring would be desirable if the arrangement could be determined on the grounds of economic considerations only. Taking each of the three major functions—allocation, distribution, and stabilization—we will begin with this efficient setting as our basic model. In the following chapter we consider how the nature of fiscal arrangements changes in the context of a federation, thereby permitting us to place the current discussion of a "new federalism" into focus.

A.   SPATIAL DIMENSION OF ALLOCATION FUNCTION

To focus on economic efficiency in the provision for public services, we assume that a group of people, having landed on a new planet, consider what spatial fiscal arrangements should be made. We also suppose that individuals will permit their location choices to be determined by fiscal considerations. The question is whether social goods and services should be provided on a centralized or a decentralized basis. If the latter, what spatial arrangement of fiscal organization is most efficient in rendering such public services? To begin with and to link up with our earlier discussion of the theory of social goods,[1] we will assume that all publicly provided goods and services are pure social goods, i.e., they conform with the characteristic of nonrival consumption. Let us then ask why the efficient provision of such goods might call for a multiunit system of government.

Benefit Regions

The crucial feature which was noted already in our discussion of social goods is that of spatial limitation of benefit incidence.[2] Some social goods are such that the incidence of their benefits is nationwide (e.g., national defense, space exploration, cancer research, the Supreme Court) while others are geographically limited (e.g., a local fire engine or streetlight). Therefore, the members of the "group" who share in the benefits are limited to the residents of a particular geographic region.

Allocation theory as applied to the public sector has led us to the conclusion that public services should be provided and their costs shared in line with the preferences of the residents of the relevant benefit region. Moreover, given the fact that a political process is needed to secure preference revelation, it follows that particular services should be voted on and paid for by the residents of this region. In other words, ser-

---

[1] See p. 45.
[2] See p. 54.

vices which are nationwide in their benefit incidence (such as national defense) should be provided for nationally, services with local benefits (e.g., streetlights) should be provided for by local units, still others (such as highways) should be provided for on a regional basis. Given the spatial characteristics of social goods, there is thus an a priori case for multiple jurisdictions. Each jurisdiction should provide services the benefits of which accrue within its boundaries, and it should use only such sources of finance as will internalize the costs. The spatially limited nature of benefit incidence thus calls for a fiscal structure composed of multiple service units, each covering a different-sized region within which the supply of a particular service is determined and financed. Even though some services call for nationwide, others for statewide, and still others for metropolitan-area-wide or local units, the argument so far does not call for an ordering of "higher-level" and "lower-level" governments. Rather, we are faced with coordinate units covering regions of different sizes.

Optimal Fiscal Community

The theory of multiunit finance must provide an answer to the question of what constitutes the optimum number of fiscal communities and the number of people within each community. To deal with this complex problem, we begin with a simple model which allows for one public service only, the benefit incidence of which is limited to all within a given geographical area but vanishes beyond it.[3] To simplify, we also assume that consumers have identical tastes and incomes, so that they agree on the desirability of social-goods provision. The crux of the problem is that the cost to each consumer will be less the larger the number of consumers who partake of the benefits. Since we postulate a pure social good so that the quality of service received per person is not affected by the number of participants, it follows that the efficient solution calls for all consumers to congregate in the same benefit area. The presence of savings from cost sharing due to large numbers leads to a single benefit area and, in fact, to a unitary structure of fiscal provision. There are, however, other considerations which may pull in an opposite direction, toward a multiunit solution. One must allow for the fact that people may dislike crowding. Even the number of angels that can dance on the head of a pin is limited. Thus the design of optimal community size must strike a balance between the advantage of sharing in the cost of a given level of public services and the disadvantages of crowding. To bring out the nature of the problem, we begin with two simplifying assumptions, i.e., that people are similar in their preferences and income and that public services are pure social goods, subject only to spatial limitation of benefits.[4]

Optimal Community Size   The first step, involving the choice of *optimum size for a given service level,* is shown in Figure 27-1. We assume that a given level of social goods is provided, the total cost of which (the cost to the group as

---

[3] Instead of assuming that benefits are uniformly distributed within a specific area, it may also be postulated that the intensity of benefits tapers off as one moves away from the location of the service facility. Such would be the situation, for instance, with the quality of television reception. Residents would have a tendency to move toward the center, a tendency which would be restrained only by dislike of crowding.

[4] The less technically inclined reader may wish to bypass this section, based on James M. Buchanan, "An Economic Theory of Clubs," *Economica,* February 1965.

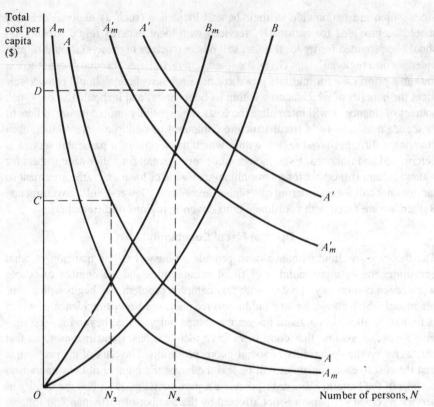

FIGURE 27-1 Choice of optimum size for given service level. (*AA* curve: per capita service cost or *Z/N*; $A_m A_m$ curve: marginal savings in per capita service cost; *OB* curve: per capita crowding cost; OB_m curve: marginal per capita crowding cost.)

a whole) equals *Z* dollars. Let us suppose further that each member pays a price equal to the marginal benefit received, which (given equal tastes and incomes) means that the cost is split equally among them. The *AA* curve then shows the per capita service cost (measured on the vertical axis) for various community sizes (measured on the horizontal axis). This cost decreases as numbers *N* increase. Since the total cost remains equal to *Z* throughout, the curve *AA* is a rectangular hyperbola with per capita cost equal to *Z/N*. It reflects a form of "decreasing per capita cost" with increasing numbers of consumers in the group.[5] The $A_m A_m$ curve, which is derived from the *AA* curve, shows the marginal saving of (or reduction in) per capita service cost that results as the group number is increased.[6] If this were all there was to be considered, the optimal group size would be such as to include

---

[5] The curve is similar in form to that of decreasing average fixed cost with increasing output as drawn in the usual cost-curve diagram for the individual firm.

[6] Mathematically, $A_m A_m$, the marginal saving in per capita service cost, is equal to

$$\frac{d(Z/N)}{dN} = \frac{Z}{N^2}$$

i.e., the negative of the slope of the *AA* curve.

the entire community. The community would be expanded so long as $A_m A_m$ were positive (i.e., AA were downward-sloping), no matter how large the group became.

The situation changes if the cost of crowding is allowed for. Let OB trace the per capita cost or disutility of crowding for various sizes of the group while OB_m shows the marginal per capita crowding cost. The optimal size of the community will then be given by ON_2, where OB_m is equated with $A_m A_m$, calling for N_2 members in this case. The community will be expanded in numbers so long as the extra per capita savings from cost sharing with a larger group exceeds the incremental per capita costs of crowding. Beyond this point, further expansion of the group would reduce total welfare and is therefore not undertaken. Various governmental units of size ON_2 will thus be established with per capita costs for each unit set at OC. With a total population P and given total service cost Z in each community, there will be P/N_2 jurisdictions with per capita costs of Z/N_2.

Such is the solution for a service level with total cost Z, but we can readily see from Figure 27-1 what happens if the service level increases. The AA and $A_m A_m$ curves shift up and the optimum size of the group increases. Thus, for a higher service level involving cost Z', the per capita service cost curve rises to $A'A'$ and the marginal curve to $A'_m A'_m$, with the optimal group size increasing to ON_4 at a per capita service cost of OD and with the group enlarged to N_4 members.[7]

Optimal Service Level   We now turn to the second step, which is to determine the optimal service level for any given group size. This is shown in Figure 27-2, where various service levels are measured along the horizontal axis and per capita unit service cost on the vertical. DD is an individual's demand schedule for the service, and since tastes and income levels are identical for all, it is representative for all members of the community. $S_1 S_1$ is the cost schedule for the service showing cost to the community as a whole. The unit cost of the facility is here shown to rise with the service level, the slope of $S_1 S_1$, depending on the nature of the facility and its production function.[8] $S_2 S_2$ is the supply schedule which presents itself to the individual if the community contains N_2 members, $S_4 S_4$ reflects the supply schedule in an N_4-member community, and so forth. The vertical level of $S_2 S_2$ is one-half of $S_1 S_1$, that of $S_4 S_4$ is one-quarter of $S_1 S_1$, and so on. Given a tax structure which divides total cost equally, all face the same SS schedule. Since the same quantity is available to each member of the community, the service level purchased by various sizes of community will be determined at the intersection of the DD curve with the supply curve pertaining to the particular community size. Thus, the service level purchased with N_1 members will be that corresponding to the intersection of $S_1 S_1$ with DD, namely, OQ_1; the level purchased by N_2 members will

---

[7] Two features of this presentation should be noted: (1) Up to a certain community size, crowding costs may be negative, i.e., additional numbers may be considered a gain (e.g., from increased social contacts) rather than a disutility; (2) since we are here dealing with a pure social good, we assume the OB curve to be independent of the service level. If the "congestion phenomenon" is allowed for (i.e., a decline in service quality with rising numbers), the OB curve will swivel down to the right as service levels are increased. In this case, the increase in group size when moving from level Z to level Z' will be greater than that shown in Figure 27-1.

[8] See the section on economies of scale, p. 452.

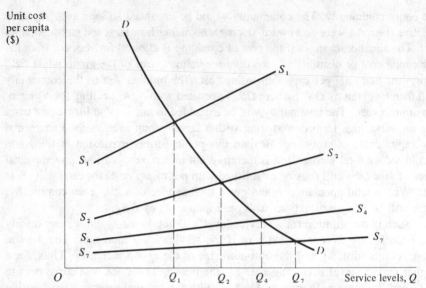

FIGURE 27-2   Choice of optimum service level for given community size.

be OQ_2 and the level desired by an N_4-member community will be OQ_4, as shown on the diagram.[9]

Optimal Structure   In the final step, the two considerations are combined in Figure 27-3, with community size N measured on the horizontal axis and service levels Q on the vertical axis. Returning to Figure 27-1, we find that a service level involving a total cost Z calls for a community size N_2, that a higher level involving cost Z' calls for size N_4, and so forth. This relationship is traced in line NN of Figure 27-3, which shows the optimal community size at each service level (measured in quantity terms), that corresponds to the various cost levels (Z, Z', etc.) of Figure 27-1. Turning to Figure 27-2, we find that community size N_1 calls for service level Q_1; size N_2 calls for Q_2, and so forth. This relationship is traced in line QQ of Figure 27-3, showing the optimum service levels for various community sizes. The overall optimal solution is at E, where the two lines intersect, the optimal service level being Q_7 and the optimal group size N_7.

Extensions of Model

The model of efficient design thus calls for multiple fiscal units differing in size and regional scope. Some will be nationwide (such as the provision for defense) while others will be quite local (such as the provision for streetlights). Now a number of complications must be allowed for.

---

[9] Alternatively, the same solution might be obtained by taking S_1S_1 to reflect the supply schedule for the group and by picking its intersection with successive vertical additions of demand schedules as the size of the group is increased.

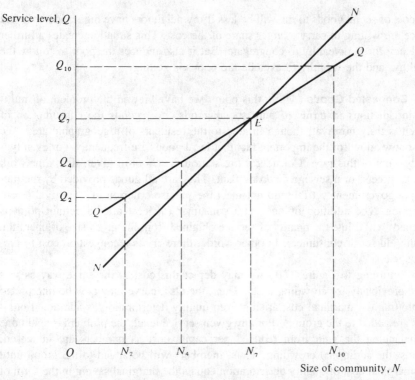

FIGURE 27-3 Combination of optimum size and service level. (*NN* line: optimal community size at various service levels; *QQ* line: optimal service level at various community sizes.)

Difference in Taste If we assume all tastes to be the same, local fiscal units will be similar; but tastes differ. Since people differ in their preferences for public services, the efficient solution will call for people with similar tastes to be grouped together. Thus, the system will contain multiple units, some similar and some different with regard to both size and composition of the public sector. At the same time, splitting up into smaller units will be at a cost. As the number of people in any one jurisdiction is reduced, some of the advantage from larger numbers (in terms of reduced per capita cost) is lost. Nevertheless, provision for local goods through a multiple system of differentiated fiscal units will remain more efficient than a uniform pattern of central provision.

Differences in Income The resulting structures of fiscal units will differ also because people have different incomes. Preferences with regard to social goods will differ by income groups. Demand will be more income-elastic for some services than for others. As a result, residents are more likely to be satisfied with the budget vote if their income varies little from the average for the community. Because of this, people with equal income will want to join in the same community.

But note also that the price (or taxes) which people are willing to pay for a given supply of social goods will be higher if their incomes are larger. As a result, the cost of social goods to me will be less if my neighbors have higher incomes and hence are willing to carry a larger share of the cost. This situation creates a further tendency for the wealthy to congregate. But it also induces the poor to follow the wealthy, and the wealthy to exclude the poor via zoning.

Congested Goods Up to this point, we have viewed the problem of multiple jurisdictions in terms of pure social goods, i.e., goods the consumption of which is truly nonrival, though limited to the residents of a geographic area. We must now allow for the important fact that local goods are frequently—or even typically—not of this type. Consider a fire station, a school of given size, a network of city streets, or a sewage disposal plant. They are all goods provided by the municipal government yet they do not meet the precise criterion of "nonrival" consumption. The addition of one extra consumer (at least after a certain point is reached) will dilute the quality of service obtained from the given size of operation by the old set of consumers. In other words, there arises a congestion cost to previous users.[10]

Returning to Figure 27-1, we may depict this cost in the same way as was done previously for crowding costs. Thus, the OB_m curve may now be interpreted as plotting the marginal cost arising from quality deterioration as additional numbers are added to the group.[11] For any given service level, the problem is again one of balancing the gain from reduced per capita cost as numbers are increased, against the additional crowding. Thus, members will be added to the group until the marginal cost of quality deterioration equals the marginal saving in the form of reduced tax cost (per capita).

Economies of Scale With a given facility size, adding to the number of users may reduce the quality of service per user, which is the just-examined problem of congestion. But provision of public services may also be subject to technical economies of scale. Provision of a given service quality (and degree of congestion) for a community of 100,000 may cost, say, $1,000,000, while similar provision for a community of 200,000 may cost $1,800,000. Per capita cost in the smaller community is then $100 while for the larger community it is only $90. Sewer construction, fire protection, sanitary facilities, and many other services may be analyzed in these terms, so that technical economies of scale (as distinct from spreading a given cost over more people) must also be considered in determining optimal community size.

Benefit Overlap and Arbitration So far we have assumed that the benefit of a particular public service is confined to just the specified space over which the providing jurisdiction extends. Actually, benefits may not be uniformly distributed within any one space, and benefits from services provided by one particular jurisdiction may spill over into another jurisdiction. For the providing jurisdiction, this

---

[10] See p. 54.

[11] As noted before, an increase in service level now not only raises the AA or per capita service cost curve in Figure 27-1, it swings the OB or congestion cost curve to the right. See footnote 7. A composite OB curve may be constructed which allows for both crowding and congestion costs.

constitutes an externality which it will not take into account. Like all externalities, this results in inefficient provision and calls for correction. Such correction may result from cooperation on a bilateral basis. Thus, two jurisdictions adjoining the same lake may agree to maintain water quality. Or the spillover may involve many jurisdictions, e.g., educational services in a particular school district may generate general benefits via migration. It may then be necessary to internalize such externalities through a central system of grants designed to affect the action of particular jurisdictions. This will call for matching grants attached to those particular outlays which generate benefits outside the jurisdiction, with the matching rate depending on the fraction of benefits which are external.[12]

Voting by Feet

The preceding discussion has shown what the efficient solution would be like. As with our earlier discussion of social goods, defining the solution is only half the battle. The other is to consider how the solution may be reached. In Chapters 4 and 5 we concluded that a process of majority voting is needed to gain preference revelation, even though this can only yield a second-best solution. We now find that there may be another way, namely, "voting by feet." If we stipulate that each community is to defray its own cost of public services, individuals will find it in their interest to choose such communities as will suit their particular preferences.[13] Those who like sports will want to reside with others who are willing to contribute to playgrounds. Those who like music will join with others who will participate in building a concert hall, and so forth. Each community will do its own thing and preferences will be satisfied.[14] Of course, this mechanism will function only to the extent that fiscal considerations are a decisive factor in location choice, as distinct from job opportunities and housing, which makes the voting by feet hypothesis somewhat unrealistic, except in a setting where people work in the inner city and may choose among suburbs for residence. It is less applicable where location is determined by job and other considerations.

B. TAX-STRUCTURE DESIGN

As shown in section A, the logic of arranging fiscal structures in line with benefit regions is to enable people to "buy" and enjoy such levels and mixes of public services as suit their preferences. It is thus an inherent feature of the basic system— and especially its contribution to preference revelation via "voting by feet"—that the members of each benefit region or jurisdiction should pay for the services which that jurisdiction provides. This logic calls for an area-wide ("national," if

---

[12] See p. 461.

[13] It is interesting to observe that this is another respect in which the social-goods and private-goods cases differ. With regard to social goods, since costs are shared, it is in a person's interest to associate with others whose tastes are similar. The opposite tends to hold for private goods, where a person with unusual tastes (provided that production is subject to increasing costs) will benefit from lower (relative) prices.

[14] The proposition that optimal local budget patterns will result from location choices of individuals was first developed in Charles M. Tiebout, "A Pure Theory of Local Government Expenditures," *Journal of Political Economy*, October 1956.

you wish) tax for the finance of area-wide services and local (regionally limited) taxes for the finance of services provided by local jurisdictions. We may thus conclude what taxes are appropriate for what fiscal units or "levels" of government.

The central or national jurisdiction may conveniently use a broad-based income tax since all people (independent of location) benefit and hence should contribute. The choice of tax instruments to be used by local jurisdictions in turn should conform to the rule that each jurisdiction pay for its own benefits. Thus, jurisdiction A should charge members of jurisdiction B only to the extent that services provided by A are enjoyed by members of B. Such a rule becomes a problem because the various jurisdictions do not exist in isolation but trade with each other. Implementation of the rule is automatic if we assume that the entire revenue structure of jurisdiction A consists of strictly benefit charges. To the extent that jurisdiction A taxes income (including income earned by members of B) such taxation will merely recoup the input of A's public services into the earnings process; and to the extent that products are taxed at the point of origin (including those exported to B) such taxes will only charge for the input of intermediate public services rendered by A. Both income and products are thus taxed appropriately by the jurisdiction where production occurs. In addition, taxation of residents in A (including visiting members of B) is appropriate as a charge for public consumer goods which the jurisdiction provides.

Application of the benefit rule on an interjurisdictional basis has the further advantage that decentralized finance will not interfere with trade or the location of production within the national region. This follows since benefit taxation—requiring as it does a balance of tax burdens and benefit gains—neutralizes the impact of fiscal operations on location choice. If levels of taxation differ by jurisdiction, so will the level of services and benefits. The model of benefit taxation therefore bypasses the problem of distortion in location, a problem which arises once taxes are imposed on a nonbenefit basis across jurisdictions.

The assumption of universal benefit taxation takes care of the problem neatly. If each individual pays in line with his or her benefits received, it follows that the benefit rule applies across jurisdictions as well. The latter still holds if each jurisdiction taxes its residents on an ability-to-pay basis, provided that the burden stops within the jurisdiction and is not exported. This may, however, prove to be an unrealistic assumption. Such is the case especially for small benefit regions, but also applies at the international level, an aspect to be considered further later on.[15]

C.   SPATIAL ASPECTS OF DISTRIBUTION FUNCTION

We now turn to the distribution function. As before, we begin with its implementation in a setting unencumbered by the prerogatives which member jurisdictions in a federation may retain. Economic analysis suggests that provision for social goods proceed through a multijurisdictional setting, with national goods provided centrally and local goods provided on a decentralized basis. Can a similar multiunit case be made for the distribution function? At first this would seem to be the case.

[15] See p. 568.

Just as the allocation model pointed to a decentralized system to permit variety in the provision for spatially limited social goods, so decentralization might serve to accommodate different tastes regarding income equality or inequality.[16] Those favoring a high degree of redistribution might favor locating in jurisdiction A, while those opposing it might locate in B. Jurisdiction A might then impose a progressive income tax and transfer system, while B would only use benefit or even head taxes for the finance of public services.

The analogy is tempting but it breaks down in an important respect. As long as there exists ready mobility between jurisdictions, the following population shifts would result. High-income people who oppose redistribution would move to B, while high-income people favoring redistribution and low-income people would flock to A. High-income proponents now find that the entire burden is placed upon them. Moreover, the achievable degree of equalization would be small, because most low-income people would flock to A. The redistribution process thus breaks down unless the scheme covers individuals across A and B, i.e., the distribution function is carried out at the national or central level.[17]

Such at least is the case unless mobility is checked by nonfiscal factors such as job location, or unless A's border controls prohibit (or zoning devices deter) the immigration of low- and the out-migration of high-income people. But as such restrictions are introduced we leave the spirit of the unitary model and move to the other extreme of noncooperating sovereign jurisdictions.

D.   SPATIAL ASPECTS OF STABILIZATION FUNCTION

It remains to note that responsibility for stabilization policy cannot be left to local or regional fiscal units but must be conducted in a central fashion. Local fiscal units will be ineffective in dealing with unemployment or inflation, because markets are interrelated so that leakages result. Such will clearly be the case within the national unit where subunits share in an open market and resources and capital can flow freely. However, it also becomes increasingly the case across nations, thus calling for international coordination of macro policies.

In all, we find that economic analysis points to a clear-cut case for decentralized provision of many public services, but for national or central policy with regard to problems of distribution and with regard to the conduct of stabilization policy.

E.   SUMMARY

In this chapter we have inquired how the allocation, distribution, and stabilization functions of budget policy should be divided among units of government. Beginning with the allocation function in the basic model, we concluded the following:

---

[16] See Mark V. Pauly, "Income Redistribution as a Local Public Good," *Journal of Public Economics,* February 1973.

[17] Note that these considerations causing the rich to flee the poor and the poor to chase the rich are in addition to that noted previously in connection with the provision for social goods. See p. 54.

1. Since the benefit incidence of various social goods is subject to spatial limitation, each service should be decided upon and paid for within the confines of the jurisdiction in which the benefits accrue.

2. This principle of benefit region leads to the concept of optimal community size.

3. With pure social goods, it would be desirable to have the number of residents as large as possible, thus reducing per capita cost. However, the cost of crowding enters to limit the optimal community size.

4. The roles of congestion and of economies of scale also enter into the determination of optimal community size.

5. Allowing for differences in tastes, we concluded that people with similar tastes for social goods will join the same jurisdiction.

6. This mechanism, via voting by feet, becomes a mechanism of preference revelation.

7. The impact of differences in income on location choice was considered.

8. Benefit spillovers involve externalities which call for correction.

9. The case for decentralization in the provision of local services is linked to the proposition that the cost should be borne in the jurisdiction in which the benefits are reaped.

10. Item 9 calls for the use of nationwide taxes in the finance of national services, and for the finance of local services through taxes the burden of which accrues within the benefiting jurisdiction.

Turning to the assignment of the distribution function, we concluded that:

11. Although preferences regarding distribution differ, the distribution function must be performed largely at the central level.

Regarding the placement of the stabilization function, we concluded that:

12. The stabilization function must be central because of leakages at the local level.

FURTHER READINGS

Buchanan, James M.: "An Economic Theory of Clubs," *Economica,* February 1965.
Elazar, Daniel J.: "Federalism," *International Encyclopedia of Social Sciences*, New York: Macmillan, 1968, vol. 5, p. 360.
Tiebout, Charles M.: "A Pure Theory of Local Expenditures," *Journal of Political Economy,* October 1956.

Chapter 28

Principles of
Federal Finance*

A. Patterns of Federalism. B. Functions by Level of Government: *Allocation; Distribution of Income among Individuals; Distribution of Fiscal Capacity; Equal Levels of Provision; Conclusion.* **C. Principles of Grant Design:** *Matching versus Nonmatching Grants; General versus Earmarked Grants; Evaluation.* **D. Taxation in the Federation:** *Tax Rules; Assignment by Levels.* **E. Summary.**

In the preceding chapter we saw how certain conclusions about the regional structure of federal finances may be derived from the logic of fiscal arrangements, set in a unitary national state. This logic pointed to central provision of region-wide and local provision of local social goods; but the actual structure of jurisdictions was not derived from fiscal logic. It was shaped, as noted before, by many factors (political, geographic, and economic) setting up governmental arrangements into which the fiscal structure must be fitted. Most modern states came about through unification of separate jurisdictions, combining in the form of a federation. Such was the case for the United States, Canada, and Australia, all of which fit into this

---

Reader's Guide to Chapter 28: This chapter continues the analysis of key issues in fiscal design, now applied to the setting of a federation, leaving a review of the U.S. system and its changing pattern to the following chapter.

pattern. But the cohesiveness of federations may differ and so will their fiscal structure.

A. PATTERNS OF FEDERALISM

On the one extreme stands a concept of the federation as a means of uniting a people previously separated into sovereign political units but already linked by common bonds of nationality. While the constituent units continue within the federation, they become unalterably parts of the national whole, with much of their sovereignty surrendered when joining the federation. The federation itself derives its legitimacy directly from its citizens, whose primary allegiance is to the federation, independent of the member jurisdiction to which they also belong. At the other extreme stands the view of federalism (referred to also as confederation) as a link between diverse peoples, formed to serve specific and limited purposes, such as the conduct of foreign policy and defense or the formation of a common market. Citizens in this framework retain their primary allegiance to their respective member jurisdictions. As we will see below, both these roots are to be found in the U.S. tradition from pre-Constitution days on, and Washington versus states' rights has been debated ever since, especially in the 1980s.

The fiscal structure of federations differs, and this is not surprising. Economic analysis does not tell us what degree of closeness the member units of a federation *should* feel toward each other. Whether you hold that residents of Alaska should feel concern for the residents of Mississippi (any more than for those of, say, Bangladesh) depends on how you feel about the nature of the American Union; and even where mutual responsibility is recognized, this responsibility may take many forms and degrees. To choose among them again involves views of the polity which transcend economic concerns. Nevertheless, economic analysis can be helpful in explaining the consequences of various arrangements and in choosing the instruments by which various federal objectives may be met.

B. FUNCTIONS BY LEVEL OF GOVERNMENT

Within the context of the federation, the issue of assigning fiscal functions now becomes one of distributing them by levels of government.

Allocation

We begin again with the provision for social goods and the fact that the spatial benefit incidence of various goods and services differs. With regard to national goods, i.e., goods the benefits of which are federation-wide, the theory of federation obviously calls for central provision. By their very nature, the benefits of national goods are available throughout the nation, so that the problem of differentiated provision does not arise. All *must* share in whatever is provided, so that independent provision by the member jurisdictions would be wasteful.

By the same token, provision of goods and services the benefits of which are regionally limited is rendered more efficiently by lower-level jurisdictions. In the United States, with her three tiers of government, national defense is paid for appropriately at the federal level, highways are paid for largely at the state level, and city streets are paid for at the local level. The provision of public goods and services thus generally follows the principles set forth in the preceding chapter.

Distribution of Income among Individuals

Members of the federation may feel a stronger sense of distributive justice regarding members of their own constituent unit than regarding members of the federation at large. The stronger the sense of cohesion within the federation, the more will the problem of distribution be viewed in national federation-wide terms; and the less it is, the more will distribution be viewed within the context of the member jurisdiction only.

Once more, the prevailing degree of cohesion is a datum for economic analysis rather than something dictated by it. But as noted before, local distribution policy cannot be effective in a setting which permits ready mobility between jurisdictions.[1] Since such mobility is typically available within a federation, we further conclude that for redistribution policy to be feasible within a federation, the sense of national cohesion must be such as to view the "group" in federation or nation-wide terms. It follows that if policies aimed at adjusting the distribution of income among *people* are to be effective, they must be conducted primarily at the central or national level. By the same token, decentralization reduces the capacity to undertake redistributional policies. Implications for such policies are therefore a strategic factor in the centralization-versus-decentralization issue.

Distribution of Fiscal Capacity

The national or central government in a federation may be concerned with equity not only across individuals but also across member jurisdictions. The various states in the United States, as we will see later, differ greatly in per capita income and hence in fiscal capacity. The federal government may consider this unfortunate because of resulting differences in the terms at which public services can be provided. Whereas differences in preferences are respected—the residents of some states may wish to spend a larger share of their resources on public services—federal philosophy may call for their being able to do so on the same terms. This may be achieved through grant policies, with the appropriate grant formula depending on how "same terms" is defined:

1.   The concept of "same terms" may be taken to mean that the same *tax price* (dollars of tax per resident) should buy the same service level, in which case, the grant will be of the form

$$G_j = t_j B_j \left(\frac{C_j}{C_a} - 1 \right) \tag{1}$$

where G_j is the grant received by jurisdiction J, B_j is its tax base and t_j is the tax rate which J chooses to impose. The term in the parentheses is the matching rate, with C_j the cost of accomplishing a given service level in J and C_a the cost of doing so in the average jurisdiction. C_j may differ from C_a either because the required resources are

[1] See p. 455.

more or less costly (teacher salaries differ) or because the need is greater (there are more students relative to population).

    2. Alternatively, "same terms" may be defined as calling for the same *tax effort* (or rate of tax) to produce the same yield. The grant will then become

$$G_j = t_j B_j \left(\frac{B_j}{B_a} - 1 \right) \tag{2}$$

where B_j is the per capita tax base in jurisdiction J and B_a that in the average jurisdiction. As before, the term in parentheses gives the required matching rate.

    3. Finally, the two corrections may be combined so as to let the same tax effort or $t_j B_j$ yield the same service level. The grant then equals

$$G_j = t_j B_j \left(\frac{B_j}{B_a} - 1 \right) + t_j B_j \left(\frac{B_j}{B_a} - 1 \right) \left(\frac{C_j}{C_a} - 1 \right) \tag{3}$$

where the first term equalizes the revenue to be achieved from a given tax rate and the second equalizes the service level to be achieved with a given outlay. The matching rate now includes two components, with the first also entering into the second.[2]

These rules may be applied with regard to all local goods or with regard to selected items only. Some items may be selected because, from a national point of view, they are considered in the nature of merit goods. Programs in support of child care, for instance, might be of that type. Or certain items may be chosen because the needs which they meet are a reflection of national policies. Thus, the federal government may be held responsible for low-income support programs necessitated by the local impact of national immigration policies.

    All these grants belong to the same family, because all affect the terms at which local jurisdictions can supply public services, while leaving it to local decision to determine how much should be supplied. By the nature of this objective, they are all given in matching form, even though the grant formula will differ with the particular objective of grant policy.

Equal Levels of Provision

Alternatively, national concern may call for ensuring that specified absolute levels of provision are forthcoming in all jurisdictions. Certain services provided for by the lower-level government may be seen as merit goods by the higher level. Thus state governments may feel that children should have the availability of given levels of education, even though education is provided for locally and local residents may not wish to pay for them. Such policies may again take various forms:

    1. Typically the objective is to ensure certain *minimum* service levels. Again, the services in question may be selected because they are considered national merit goods, or because majority rule may deprive individual citizens of minimal provision. Various policy instruments are available to secure this objective. Where higher-level

---

[2] From the way in which the grant formulas are here written, it follows that the grant may be positive or negative, depending on the balance between fiscal capacity and the need for the particular jurisdiction. (See. p. 486.) This is to say, the grant is "self-financing." In reality, grants are typically made when positive only and financed out of general revenue. For further discussion of grants see p. 483.

government has the power to interfere with fiscal affairs at lower levels, it may require or mandate that a minimum service level be met, and it may do so without financial incentive. Such is the case in the United States where states can control the operation of local government. Or the result may be achieved via matching grants, with matching rates set sufficiently high to accomplish the desired level.

2. Moreover, national concern may take the form of requiring *uniform* service levels across member jurisdictions, neither higher nor lower than the specified level. Thus, a uniform level of school services may be held desirable, so as to obtain "equality of opportunity at the starting line" for all children throughout the union. This approach would suspend the principle of federalism in certain areas and apply those applicable to a centralized system.

The various objectives, finally, may be combined in many ways. Thus, grants designed to equalize the terms of provision may be "capped" and grants aimed at securing particular service levels may be more or less selective.

Conclusion

As will be seen from this brief survey, the sense of cohesion within the federation may call for various forms of concern with the provision of local social goods in member jurisdictions. The intensity and type of concern that prevails depends upon the nature of the union, but economic analysis can point to the appropriate instruments by which to implement the various objectives.

C. PRINCIPLES OF GRANT DESIGN

One major issue in grant design is whether the grants should or should not require matching by the grant recipient. Another issue is whether use of the grant proceeds should be left to the recipient's discretion or whether use should be prescribed by the grantor. Any of these grants, moreover, may or may not be related to the financial capacity and/or need of the recipient. The purpose of this section is to examine the analytical implications of the various grant instruments.

Matching versus Nonmatching Grants

Our purpose is to examine why some types of grants are more effective than others, i.e., accomplish the desired policy objective at a lower cost to the government. We begin with grants which are general in the sense that they do not distinguish among types of public services but which may be matching or nonmatching.

Nonmatching Grants   The case of a nonmatching grant is shown in Figure 28-1. Social goods are measured on the horizontal axis and private goods on the vertical axis. AB is the community budget line, showing various combinations of private and social goods which are available to it. The curves i_1i_1, i_2i_2, and so forth, are indifference curves recording the community's preferences between the two. The initial equilibrium is at E, where the budget line is tangent to the highest possible indifference line. Consumption of private goods equals OC, and the consumption of social goods equals OD. To obtain OD of social goods, CA of private goods must be surrendered so that the tax rate equals CA/OA, where OA is income measured in terms of private goods.

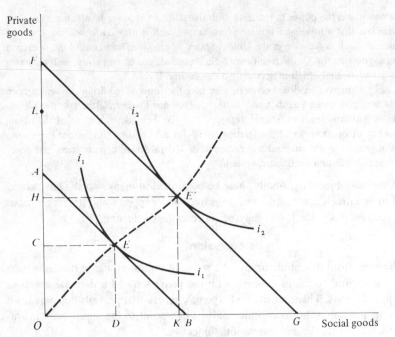

FIGURE 28-1   Response to a nonmatching grant.

Now a nonmatching grant equal to AF (measured again in private goods) is given to the community's treasury. As a result, the budget line shifts to FG and the new equilibrium is at E'. The community now obtains OH of private goods and OK of social goods. Private-good consumption has risen by CH and social-good consumption has increased by DK. Part of the grant has leaked into increased consumption of private goods rather than into increased provision of social goods, as may be expected. Since use of the grant is not tied in any way, it is equivalent to a general income subsidy. Hence, there is only an income effect which normally may be assumed to be positive and to increase outlays on both social and private goods.

But how can it be said that the grant is equivalent to an increase in income, since it is given to the government rather than to consumers and the government buys social goods only? The answer, of course, is that part of the grant may be made available for private consumption through tax reduction.[3] Consider what happens in Figure 28-1. Since the consumption of private goods rises from OC to OH, the amount paid in tax falls from CA to HA. The tax rate, therefore, declines from CA/OA to HA/OA. Tax reduction equals HC. With the cost of the grant to the gov-

---

[3] Indeed, the text argument implies that it makes no difference whether the money is given to the government or to the consumers directly. If given to the government, part is used for private goods via tax reduction. If given to consumers, part of it is used for public expenditures via increased taxes. The outcome is the same in both cases. In a realistic setting, the two procedures may well lead to different results, i.e., voting a tax reduction and not voting an expenditure increase may not be symmetrical procedures. See Wallace E. Oates, *Fiscal Federalism,* New York: Harcourt Brace, 1972, chap. 3, app. A.

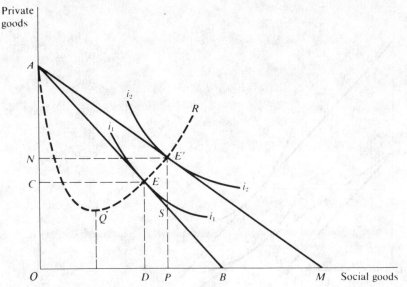

FIGURE 28-2 Response to a matching grant.

ernment equal to AF (all measured in terms of private goods), $LF = HC$ passes into tax reduction and only AL is added to expenditures on social goods.

The dotted curve OEE' finally shows an income consumption path along which the equilibrium position of the jurisdiction moves as the grant is increased, with the leakage into private goods increasing and decreasing with the slope of this line.

Matching Grants The case of a matching grant is shown in Figure 28-2. The initial equilibrium is again at E, with private-good consumption equal to OC and social-good consumption equal to OD. Introduction of a matching grant now swivels the budget line to AM, because the net price of social goods to the community has fallen relative to that of private goods. Equilibrium moves to E', with the consumption of private goods increased to ON and that of social goods increased to OP. The cost to the grantor government equals $E'S$, but not all of this is spent on social goods.[4] Instead, there is a tax reduction equal to CN, with the tax rate reduced from CA/OA to NA/OA, CN being the part of the subsidy cost which leaks into private consumption.

Although the position of E' in Figure 28-2 shows that in this instance consumption of both private and social goods has increased, this is not necessarily the case. As distinct from the nonmatching grant where only an income effect was present, we now have a substitution effect as well. Since the price of social goods has fallen relative to that of private goods, the consumption of private goods might decline. The negative substitution effect might outweigh the positive income effect.

---

[4] To find the permissible increase in social goods in the absence of a leakage, deduct SE' from DE, draw a horizontal line and find its intersection with AB.

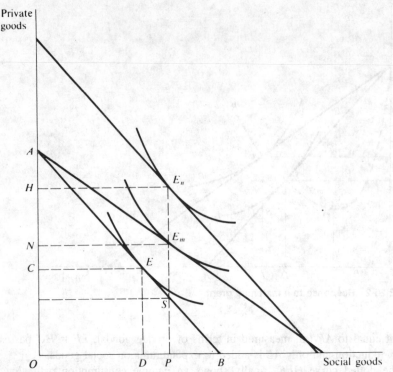

FIGURE 28-3 Comparison of matching and nonmatching grants.

In Figure 28-2, the dotted curve AQR shows the path along which E will travel as the price of social goods declines, with the movement from A to R being caused by increasing matching rates. Up to Q, this results in a decline in the purchase of private goods, and beyond Q in an increase, with the purchase of social goods rising throughout. In a situation where both E and E' lie to the left of Q, there would be no leakage of grant money, but voters would in fact support the government's effort by voting a tax increase.

Comparison of Grants The two types of grants are compared in Figure 28-3. E is again the initial equilibrium, and E_m is the new equilibrium with a matching grant. E_n is the new equilibrium with a nonmatching grant designed so that both grants secure the same provision for social goods, or OP. As before, the cost to the government under the matching grant equals E_mS and that under the nonmatching grant equals E_nS. The same objective of securing a social-goods supply of OP can thus be secured at a lower cost with the matching grant, the difference being E_mE_n.[5] This is not surprising, since a matching grant is in fact a selective grant which supports provision of social goods only, whereas the nonmatching grant is

---

[5] E_n must lie above E_m because the slope of successive indifference curves rises when moving up a vertical line, i.e., the marginal rate of substitution of private for social goods must increase.

general, since it may be used to support the purchase of additional private goods by way of tax reduction.

General versus Earmarked Grants

We now turn to grants earmarked for specific public outlays. If the government wishes to increase expenditures on a particular social good X, a selective grant earmarked for the use of X will be at least as effective in securing increased expenditures on X as will be an equal-cost general grant, and it may well be more efficient.

This principle is shown in Figure 28-4 for the nonmatching case. Measuring now social good Y on the vertical axis and social good X on the horizontal axis, let

FIGURE 28-4 Comparison of general and selective grants.

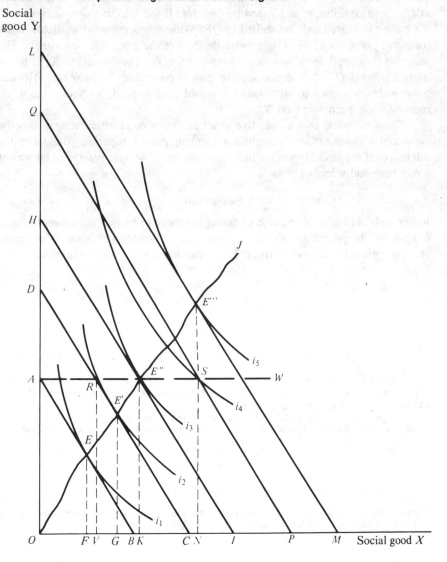

AB be the community's opportunity line prior to the grant with equilibrium at *E*. Now a general grant is given, moving the budget line to *DC*. Equilibrium shifts to *E'*, provision of X increases to *OG*, and the cost to government is *BC*.[6] If the government gives a grant of equal amount but earmarked for the use of X, only section *RC* of the new budget line will be available to the recipient, but equilibrium is again at *E'*.[7] Both types of grants secure the same increase in the provision of X. This conclusion still holds if the government wishes to raise the provision of X to *OK*. Raising X to *OK* now calls for a general grant so as to shift the budget line to *HI*, the new equilibrium is at *E"*, and the cost equals *BI*. If use of the grant is limited to X, only the *E"I* section of the raised budget line is available to the recipient, but equilibrium remains at *E"*. The situation changes, however, if the government wishes to go further, raising the provision of X to, say, *ON*. Now the general grant calls for the budget line to be shifted to *LM*, with equilibrium at *E'''* and cost of *BM*. If the selective approach is used, the budget line need only be shifted to *QP*. With only section *SP* available to the recipient, point *S* will be chosen, with the cost of the grant reduced to *BP*.[8] The selective-grant approach becomes cheaper once the provision for X is to be pushed beyond *OK*, where the income-consumption line *OJ* intersects *AW* and provision of Y comes to equal what it would have been if, without a grant, all resources had been spent on Y.

The conclusion that a selective grant becomes more efficient may now be combined with our earlier finding that a matching grant is superior.[9] Budget cost is minimized if the desired increase in a particular public service is secured by way of a matching and selective grant.

Evaluation

In line with our earlier discussion of grants as related to various objectives of fiscal federalism, the preceding analysis suggests certain conclusions about what grants are appropriate for what objectives. These conclusions may be summarized as follows:

---

[6] Note that cost is measured here in terms of X. Alternatively, it may be measured in terms of Y and then equals *AD*.

[7] A selective grant earmarked for provision of X and costing *BC* may be pictured as moving the origin to the right from *O* to *V*, where *OV* = *BC*. *VR* then becomes the new vertical axis, and the effective opportunity budget line is given by *RC*.

The presentation of Figure 28-4 oversimplifies matters because it shows a choice between two social goods only. We may visualize a third axis showing private goods, in which case a selective grant on one social good is subject to a double leakage.

[8] While *S* does as well as *E'''* in raising the provision of X to *ON*, the receiving jurisdiction will be better off at *E'''* since *S* lies on a lower indifference curve.

[9] When saying that the selective approach is more efficient, the term is used in the sense of permitting the government to achieve its objective of raising the provision of X to *ON* at a lesser cost. Using the term in the usual sense of Pareto optimality, we note that *E'''* is a tangency point and hence efficient, whereas *S* is not. This consideration, however, does not apply in this context since by promoting X the government wishes to interfere with the recipient's choice.

Grant Objective	Matching	Earmarking	Redistributive
1. To make revenue from central tax sources available to state and local government	No	No	No
2. To reduce inequality in per capita income across states	No	No	Yes
3. To increase the overall level of state-local public services	Yes	No	Optional
4. To equalize the terms at which state and local governments may provide all public services	Yes	Yes	Optional
5. To increase the level of provision for particular public services	Yes	No	Optional
6. To equalize the terms of provision for particular public services	Yes	Yes	Optional
7. To correct for benefit spillovers	Yes	Yes	No

Objective 1 is simply to enable lower-level governments to draw on revenue sources better administered at the central level. Thus, in many federations centrally collected income tax revenue is returned in part to lower-level governments in line with origin of collection. This use of "shared taxes," by its nature, is more an instrument of tax administration than of grant policy. It becomes a matter of grant policy when, in line with objective 2, centrally derived revenue is paid out to lower-level governments in line with need, as measured by an index such as the inverse of per capita income. Such a grant calls for neither matching nor earmarking and, as noted before, is second-best to interindividual redistribution at the central level. All the other objectives listed in the table call for matching grants, since matching permits the grant purpose to be achieved at a lesser cost to the grantor. But, as noted before, considerations underlying determination of the matching rate differ, depending on whether the policy is directed at absolute service levels, at the terms at which services can be provided, or at spillover adjustments.

The issue of general versus selective grants, in the context of policies 3 to 6, finally depends on whether grant policy is designed to support general or selective public services. Although the distinction between matching and nonmatching is clear-cut, that between general and selective grants is a matter of degree only. The traditional approach to the U.S. grant system was in terms of objectives 4 to 7; but as we will see below, the current trend is toward nonmatching, general, and nonredistributive grants, falling somewhere between objectives 1 and 2.

Leakages   Except for objectives 1 and 2 above, grants are designed to support particular activities, whether they are public services in general, as distinct from private uses, or selective public services only. In either case, the use of funds for other than intended purposes may be considered a "leakage," and the efficiency of various grant forms may be measured by the absence of leakage. Thus a general nonmatching grant is more likely to be directed into tax reduction than a general matching grant. The matching grant with its lower leakage is thus more efficient in raising the recipient's level of public services, because a given increase will be obtained at a lesser cost to the grantor. Similarly, if the desired objective is to increase the provision of a particular public service, the selective grant tends to be more efficient than a general grant, because leakages (including diversion into other public services or tax reduction) will be less. At the same time, even selective and matching grants are subject to a substantial degree of leakage.[10]

Note that the concept of efficiency as here used relates to the policy objective of supporting a particular use of the grant funds, whether for public services in general or for particular public services. Either policy objective involves an interference by the grantor with the recipient's freedom of choice. The situation might thus be linked to our earlier concepts of merit goods and of categorical equity, here translated to an interjurisdictional level.[11] If such interference is rejected, i.e., if grant policy is in line with objective 1, this criteria for efficiency does not apply. All restriction then becomes inefficient, whether in regard to public and private uses of funds in general (via matching grants) or with regard to the choice among public services (via selective grants).

Flypaper Effect   This reasoning just set forth also explains the role of the so-called flypaper effect, that is, the proposition that grants, since they are given to government, tend to stick with budgetary use and thus result in a higher level of services than would be the case if they were made directly to individuals.[12] Let jurisdiction A be given a grant of $1,000,000, unrestricted and without matching requirement, and suppose that (in line with Figure 28-1) this results in additional public outlays of $800,000 and a tax reduction of $200,000. If the grant had been made directly to individual taxpayers in A, the outcome might have been an increase in public services of $300,000 and a tax reduction of $700,000. For the case of matching grants, the comparison has to be between the level of public services which results if the matching rate is applied to the budget with that which would come about if matching rates were applied to individual taxpayers. In either case, the chain of events from increase in budget to tax reduction and increase in services may not yield the same outcome as a corresponding chain from increase in individual incomes to tax reduction and public service expansion.

Empirical estimates of the flypaper effect have shown it to be of significant magnitude, which is not surprising. The assumption that the indifference curves in Figures 28-1 to 28-3 are a direct reflection of community preferences is unrealistic. It may well be that political pressures for tax reduction (following a grant to the budget) are weaker than pressures against tax increase (when the grant is made to individuals). Moreover, the choice among public services may differ when financed by retention of an unrestricted grant than when financed by increased taxation.

[10] For a survey of empirical work on responses to grants, see Advisory Commission on Intergovernmental Relations, *Federal Grants: Their Effects on State-Local Expenditures, Employment Levels, and Wage Rates*, Washington, D.C.: February 1977. Also see E. Gramlich, "Intergovernmental Grants: A Review of the Empirical Literature," in W. Oates (ed.): *The Political Economy of Fiscal Federalism*, Lexington, Mass.: Lexington Books, 1977.

[11] See p. 55.

[12] This distribution in turn would be equal to such pattern of tax reduction as would result from a grant to the budget, assuming that there are no flypaper effects.

Conclusion   We conclude that evaluation of a particular grant outcome depends on the premise from which it is made. What appears as a regrettable leakage, if the grantor's wish is to be respected, may become a desirable avoidance of fly-paper effects if the preferences of local residents are to be accepted.

D. TAXATION IN THE FEDERATION

As follows from the preceding chapter, federation-wide (national) services should be financed by the federal government with federation-wide taxes and the services of member jurisdictions should be financed by taxes in their region. The interjurisdictional design of taxation in this way should follow the benefit rule.

Tax Rules

The general principle is clear but certain complications arise which are avoided in the unitary state.

Approaches to Central Finance   Whereas federation-wide services will be financed centrally, the financing may be done in different ways, depending on the nature of the federation. Two views may be taken. One is to finance by way of a central or national tax, with standards of interindividual equity applied across member jurisdictions, an approach taken by most nation-type federations, such as the United States, Canada, or Australia. The other is to assess member jurisdictions in line with their respective capacities to pay, while leaving it to them to decide how to raise the funds from their residents. Such an approach is appropriate to the finance of specific-purpose federations such as NATO or the United Nations.

Interjurisdictional Assignment of Tax Base   The principle that outlays should be paid for where the benefits accrue must be defined more specifically. If benefits accrue in A they should be paid for by the residents of A. But what if A residents own property in B? Members of jurisdiction A may then feel entitled to share in the tax base created by A-owned factors in B, and do so even though the resulting earnings do not reflect an input of public services rendered by A. In fact, member jurisdictions of federations typically tax personal earnings of "foreigners" within their borders, and the same argument may be extended to earnings from capital investment. There is no simple basis on which to determine the proper level at which foreigners should be taxed, but good manners in a federation would suggest that the various jurisdictions agree on a principle of reciprocity in treating overlapping sources of income and of residents. More will be said about this subject later when we deal with international issues of taxation.[13]

Efficiency Aspects   One key objective in forming a federation is to establish a common market in which goods and factors of production may move freely. Special attention must thus be given to the effects of differential taxation on the effi-

---

[13] See p. 573.

ciency of the federation-wide economy. Otherwise, inefficiencies may result in both factor and commodity flows, and public-sector decisions may be disturbed by low-tax competition to attract resources into the jurisdictions. The simplest answer, of course, would be to require adherence to benefit taxation or else to demand uniform taxation across jurisdictions; but either step taken would destroy most of the advantages of fiscal decentralization. However, inefficiencies may be reduced by coordination, as will be seen later, when problems of international taxation are discussed.[14]

Assignment by Levels

Actual tax systems are not likely to comply with the principles just discussed, but approximate conclusions regarding appropriate tax assignments by level of government may be drawn:

Central Level	Middle Level	Local Level
1. Progressive income tax	1. Income tax on residents	1. Real property tax
2. Death duties	2. Income tax on income to factors owned by residents and on income accruing to nonresidents but originating within jurisdiction	2. Payroll tax
3. Natural resource taxes	3. Retail sales tax	3. Benefit charges
	4. Origin-type product tax as benefit charge	

Principle Users   Use of a broad-based progressive income tax (or, for that matter, expenditure tax) is most suitable at the central level. Since the benefits to be financed are nationwide or national distribution policies are to be implemented, this approach is in line with coverage of income from all sources (independent of origin) under a global-base income tax. In the normative system, such a tax includes all corporate source income in its base and thus renders a separate corporation tax unnecessary. Similar considerations apply to central taxation of transfers by bequest or gift, especially since differential taxation invites ready movement of testatable capital. The case for national taxation of natural resources has already been noted.

At the middle level, i.e., states in the United States or provinces in Canada, a personal income tax on residents remains appropriate, but with slight progressivity only. Taxation of income (personal and corporate) originating within the jurisdiction but flowing to nonresident owners is appropriate on an entitlement basis. Sales taxation, i.e., a destination-type product tax, is appropriate at the middle level, especially where areas are sufficiently large to exclude avoidance by shopping abroad. An origin-type production tax, which includes exports, is appropriate only as a benefit charge for public services entering into production.

Turning to the local level, we find a case to be made for taxes on bases which are immobile, such as land and (to a lesser degree) improvement and structures

---

[14] See p. 574.

thereon. If income is taxed, payroll is the part of the base which can be reached most easily and which is least likely to be lost through out-migration. Charges, finally, are of special importance in the local setting, where the benefits of public services more frequently accrue to particular groups of beneficiaries, e.g., the finance of sidewalk improvements by special assessments placed on adjoining houses.

Shared Taxes Even though various taxes thus differ in their suitability for use at various levels of government, it does not follow that one and the same tax may not be used at various levels. Thus an income tax may be (and is) used by the federal government as well as by most states, which poses problems of coordination that have been noted earlier and raises the question of whether it would not be simpler to have a federal income tax only, with jurisdictions permitted to impose surcharges thereon. Alternatively, the central government might return part of the revenue to the jurisdiction of origin. Such use of "shared taxes" may be found in many federations, including Canada and the Federal Republic of Germany.

E. SUMMARY

The general issues of multiunit finance, considered in the preceding chapter, were reexamined in the more specific context of a federation:

1. Patterns of federalism may range from loose associations among independent states to subdivisions of a unified nation whose freedom of action is severely limited.

2. The degree of cohesion, in turn, will affect the assignment of fiscal functions by level of government.

3. Accordingly, public services with nationwide benefits are to be assigned to the central government while those with regionally limited benefits are to be provided for by lower-level governments.

4. Correction for policies aimed at distribution among individuals must be vested largely at the central level.

A further aspect of distributional equity within the federation relates to the relative positions of member jurisdictions:

5. The federation may be concerned with the terms at which member jurisdictions are capable of providing public services.

6. The federation may be concerned with the absolute level of such services enjoyed by residents within the various jurisdictions.

The major tool by which the central government may affect the fiscal performance of subdivisions is through a system of grants:

7. Grants may be in matching or in nonmatching form.

8. Grants may be general-purpose grants or ones that are earmarked for particular purposes.

9. Selection of the appropriate grant design depends on the objectives of central government policy.

The design of the tax system in a federation has been considered as follows:

10.   An agreement must be reached on how the tax bases are to be divided among member jurisdictions.

11.   Major taxes may then be assigned by levels, so as to minimize leakages across jurisdictions.

FURTHER READINGS

Grewal, Bhajan, Geoffrey Brennan, and Russell L. Matthew: *The Economics of Fiscal Federalism,* Canberra: Australian National University Press, 1980. This volume contains a selection of principal papers in the field.

Musgrave, Richard A.: "Approaches to a Fiscal Theory of Political Federalism," with discussion, in National Bureau of Economic Research, *Public Finances, Needs, Sources, and Utilization,* Princeton, N.J.: Princeton, 1981.

Oates, Wallace E.: *Fiscal Federalism,* New York: Harcourt-Brace, 1972. This volume offers an analysis of the principles of fiscal federalism.

Chapter 29

The Structure of
Fiscal Federalism
in the United States*

A. Origins. B. The Federal-State and Local Balance. C. State-Local Patterns: *Local Government; State Share in State and Local Finances; Differences in Tax Structure.* D. Determinants of Fiscal Position: *Defining Fiscal Position; Differentials in Capacity and Effort; Differentials in Performance and Need.* E. The Grant System: *Growth of Grant Systems; Types of Grants; Categorical Aid; Consolidation into Block Grants.* F. Federal Grants and Equalization. G. School Finance: *Constitutional Entitlements; Types of State Aid.* H. The New Federalism. I. Summary.

Having examined the general principles of multiunit and of federal finance, we now turn to the development of fiscal federalism in the United States and the current debate over reform of the system.

A. ORIGINS

The United States is a federation consisting of a central (federal) government, fifty states, and the District of Columbia. Each state in turn shares its fiscal tasks with

Reader's Guide to Chapter 29: Beginning with a brief sketch of the history and current status of fiscal federalism in the United States, this chapter examines the patterns of fiscal centralization and decentralization between levels of government and within states. This is followed by an analysis of fiscal capacity and needs. Next, the structure of the grant system is examined, and recent trends in American fiscal federalism are appraised.

local governments of various types, including cities, townships, counties, school districts, and other special service districts, 80,000 in all. Compared with that of most other countries, the fiscal structure of the United States has developed along relatively decentralized lines. At the same time, it has shown flexibility toward changing needs and attitudes, as evidenced by the expanding role of intergovernmental transfers and the reassignment of fiscal responsibilities over the past fifty years, and by today's critique of this expansion.

A look back at the development of fiscal federalism in the United States is needed to understand its current position and trends. The fiscal structure of the original confederation was designed to protect the position of the states and to ensure the fiscal weakness of the federal government, with the financing of national expenditures left to contributions by the states. But this structure was short-lived, because the Constitution of 1788 strengthened the fiscal position of the federal government and a viable system of federal finances based on customs duties and excises was established. At the same time, the Constitution set the framework for a decentralized system, without, however, determining specifically what the division of fiscal responsibilities was to be.[1] Nothing was said about the assignment of expenditure functions; and although federal taxing powers were limited by the uniformity and apportionment rules, these rules did not impose severe restrictions and eventually were relaxed further by the Sixteenth Amendment. The taxing powers of the states were similarly limited only by the strictures against the imposition of import duties and export taxes. Finally, nothing was said in the federal Constitution about the fiscal role of local governments, leaving its determination for the states to control.

The structure of fiscal federalism was thus left to develop in a flexible constitutional framework, and the relative strengths of the various levels of government have changed over the years.[2] The nineteenth century opened with a great debate between the Jeffersonian view that the function of central government should be minimized and the Federalist position which assigned it a stronger role. The divergent views of federalism in the American tradition are highlighted by the contrasting positions of Calhoun and Webster in their debate of the 1830s. "The very idea of an *American people* as constituting a single community," so Calhoun argued, "is a mere chimera. Such a community never for a single moment existed—neither before nor since the Declaration of Independence." Webster, in turn, saw the Constitution as established not through a compact between the states, "but by the people of the United States in the aggregate." Popular government was to depend upon nationhood, with "liberty and union, inseparable, now and forever."[3]

Supported by judicial interpretation, the national view of the Constitution gained over the first decades of the Union, only to give way to reemergence of

---

[1] See p. 24.

[2] For a vivid description of the changing course of fiscal federalism in the United States, see Advisory Commission on Intergovernmental Relations, *The Condition of Contemporary Federalism: Conflicting Theories and Collapsing Constraints,* Washington, D.C., 1981.

[3] Quoted from Samuel H. Beer, "Federalism: Lessons of the Past, Chances for the Future," in *Federalism: Making the System Work,* Center for National Policy, Alternatives for the 1980s, no. 6, Washington, D.C., 1982, p. 18.

states' rights in the 1830s to 1850s. The big change toward the concept of nation-hood came with the Civil War and the Fourteenth Amendment which followed it. There then came years of dual federalism, with increasingly liberal interpretation of federal powers to regulate commerce, leading up to the crucial fiscal move toward centralization through the Sixteenth Amendment, enabling the federal government to impose an income tax. The major and most important shift away from states' rights and to a national view of federalist responsibility, however, was not to come until the Depression years of the 1930s. It was then that massive legislation in many areas of social and economic life greatly expanded the role of the federal government and its responsibilities. Once more, the contingencies of World War II added to the federal role, as did the subsequent emergence of the welfare state, culminating in the Great Society programs of the Johnson administration in the late 1960s.

It now appears that the pendulum may once more have swung toward greater reliance on states and localities and a narrowed federal responsibility. As we have seen, this is combined with a more critical view of the public sector in general and its redistributive function in particular, a function which is located largely at the federal level.

B.   THE FEDERAL-STATE AND LOCAL BALANCE

These developments may be traced as we examine the changing shares in public expenditures by level of government.

Total Expenditures   As shown in Table 29-1, lines 1 to 5, local government was much the most important sector during the earlier part of the century. Its weight dropped sharply in the depression decade of the 1930s, when the federal share assumed major importance, based on the emergency of the New Deal domestic programs. The increase in the federal share continued during the 1950s, again at the cost of the local share, with little further change during the 1960s and 1970s. In all, we thus find a move toward centralization over the 1930–1960 period, with a flattening of the trend thereafter. Also, the 1987 federal share falls slightly below that for 1980, suggesting a first reversal of the trend toward centralization.

Civilian Expenditures   Lines 6 to 10 of the table focus on the changing pattern of civilian expenditures only, while excluding defense. Since defense outlays are made at the federal level, this exclusion reduces the federal and raises the state-local share. The pattern up to 1960 remains much the same. During the 1970s, the federal share now rises more sharply, reflecting the Great Society programs of the Johnson administration. Also, the decline in the federal share during the 1980s is now more marked, reflecting the effort of the Reagan administration to curtail nondefense spending.

Grants   The shares recorded in lines 1 to 10 of Table 29-1 include inter-governmental grants at the grantor level. Alternatively, the changing pattern might be shown so as to include grants at the recipient level, i.e., in terms of expenditure

TABLE 29-1
Expenditures by Level of Government
(As Percentage of Total)

	1927	1940	1960	1970	1980	1987
I. GRANTS INCLUDED AT LEVEL OF GRANTOR						
Total Expenditures						
1. Federal	33.0	53.0	68.4	65.0	69.1	67.9
2. State and local	67.0	47.0	31.6	35.0	30.9	32.1
3. State	17.7	22.5	14.8	18.0	17.9	18.6
4. Local	49.3	24.5	16.8	17.0	13.0	13.5
5. Total	100.0	100.0	100.0	100.0	100.0	100.0
Expenditures excluding defense						
6. Federal	24.7	47.3	53.2	54.2	63.6	60.5
7. State and local	75.3	52.7	46.8	45.8	36.4	39.5
8. State	19.8	25.2	21.9	24.3	21.1	21.9
9. Local	55.4	27.5	24.9	21.5	15.3	17.6
10. Total	100.0	100.0	100.0	100.0	100.0	100.0
II. GRANTS INCLUDED AT LEVEL OF RECIPIENT						
Total Expenditures						
11. Federal			63.2	57.3	59.0	61.5
12. State and local			36.8	42.7	41.0	38.5
Expenditures excluding defense						
13. Federal			30.9	33.7	44.0	46.2
14. State and local			69.1	66.3	56.0	53.8

Source: 1902, 1940: U.S. Bureau of the Census, *History and Statistics of the United States, 1980,* pp. 725, 728, 730. 1960–1987: Lines 1, 2, 6, 7: *Survey of Current Business,* various years. Lines 3, 4, 8, 9: Percentage share of states is obtained by applying to line 2 ratios as given in Advisory Commission on Intergovernment Relations, *Significant Features of Fiscal Federalism,* 1987 ed., p. 28.

to the public, as can be seen in lines 11 to 14 of the table. Since grants largely originate at the federal level, the federal share is now lower; and since grants have grown, inclusion at the recipient level also dampens the trend toward centralization, which becomes especially apparent in line 13, where civilian expenditures only are included. However, the overall pattern is not greatly affected.

Purchases and Transfers   The data given in Table 29-1 include purchases for goods and services expenditures as well as transfers. If purchases only are considered, especially with respect to nondefense purchases, the federal share becomes much smaller. Thus in 1987 the federal share in government purchases was 41 percent and that in nondefense purchases only was 13 percent. As the latter ratio shows, federal participation in the provision of public services other than defense has remained quite minimal, which is in line with the limited regional benefit incidence of most public services.

C. STATE-LOCAL PATTERNS

Although public debate has focused on the distinction between the federal government on the one side and the combined state-local level on the other, the problem of fiscal federalism in the broader sense does not end here. Even though local government is technically a creature of the states—with local prerogatives set by state constitutions and legislation—the fiscal relationships between state and local governments are of vital importance in the fiscal design of the public sector.

Local Government

The structure of local government differs in various parts of the country and so does the degree of fiscal decentralization. An overview of the huge number of local jurisdictions and their fiscal weight is given in Table 29-2.

Townships, school districts, and municipalities are about equal in number, with special districts more numerous and countries much less numerous. There is a great deal of variety in the pattern of local government among the different states. Thus, counties are of major importance in the South; school districts abound in South Dakota, Texas, and Nebraska; and townships are of special importance in the Northeastern states. Municipalities (i.e., cities) rank much ahead of the other units in fiscal importance, with school districts and counties next in line. Special districts and townships, although more numerous, are less significant in terms of the amounts of revenue or expenditures involved.

The total number of local units has shown a steady decline, from 155,000 in 1942 to 102,000 in 1957 and 82,000 in 1977, largely owing to a decline in the number of school districts, reflecting economies of scale in larger schools. At the same time, increased use has been made of special districts for particular functions, such as mass transit, parks, police, and environmental expenditures. Moreover, the larger cities have gained in independence and in some cases vie in importance with the role of their host state.

State Share in State and Local Finances

The diversity of state fiscal systems is apparent in Table 29-3, where the states' share in financing state and local expenditures (excluding federal grants) is given. As shown, the state share in total financing ranges from nearly 80 percent for the

TABLE 29-2
Units of Local Government

	Number (Data for 1982) (I)	Expenditures in Billions of Dollars (Data for 1986) (II)
Counties	3,041	77.0
Municipalities	19,076	102.2
School districts	14,851	116.2
Townships	16,734	11.1
Special districts	28,588	22.1
Total	82,290	328.6

Sources: For column I, see Tax Foundation, *Facts and Figures in Government Finance,* 21st ed., Washington, D.C., 1986, p. 114. For column II, see Advisory Commission on Intergovernmental Relations, *Significant Features of Fiscal Federalism,* 1987 ed., Washington, D.C., 1987, p. 20.

TABLE 29-3
Percentage of State Share in State-Local Expenditures from Own Resources, 1985*

	All	Welfare	Highways	Health and Hospitals	Elementary and Secondary Education
Highest	77	100	87	98	87
Average	57	82	63	54	53
Lowest	44	41	43	28	5

*The percentages shown equal (state expenditures to the public plus state outlays on local grants minus federal transfers to states) divided by (state expenditures to public plus local expenditures to public minus federal transfers to state and local governments).
Source: See Significant Features of Fiscal Federalism, 1987, p. 29.

most centralized quartile of states to below 50 percent for the least centralized. We also observe that the degree of centralization differs greatly among functions, with welfare and highway expenditures the most centralized and school expenditures the least.

Differences in Tax Structure

As shown in Table 29-4, the composition of state revenue structures also varies widely. The 1985 share of total state-local revenue which is derived from federal aid ranged from 8 to 25 percent. That derived from property taxes ranged from 36 percent in the highest state (New Hampshire) to 5 percent in the lowest (New Mexico), while the share derived from income taxes varies from 23 percent (Maryland) to 0 percent (Washington, Nevada, Texas, and Wyoming). That derived from the general sales tax ranges from 27 percent (Washington) to 0 percent (New Hampshire, Montana, and Oregon).

The share of the property tax, as may be expected, is related negatively to the degree of centralization, while that of the sales tax is related positively thereto. Highly decentralized states, such as New Hampshire, tend to derive a large share of their revenue from the property tax, whereas centralized states, such as Alaska, Louisiana, and Delaware, derive a relatively small share from this source. However, this pattern is not uniform. Colorado and New York, for instance, are below the average in centralization but nevertheless have a relatively low property tax share. The reason for New York is that New York City places substantial reliance on city sales and income taxes.

TABLE 29-4
Composition of State and Local General Revenue, 1985, in Percentages

	FederalAid	Property Tax	Income Tax	General Sales Tax
Highest state	24.6	36.0	22.9	27.0
Average	17.8	17.4	11.7	14.1
Lowest state	7.8	5.3		

Source: Advisory Commission on Intergovernmental Relations, Significant Features of Fiscal Federalism, 1987, p. 48.

D. DETERMINANTS OF FISCAL POSITION

Another aspect of fiscal diversity is reflected in the differentials in fiscal position of various jurisdictions, i.e., in their ability to meet the needs of their respective communities.

Defining Fiscal Position

We begin by defining some of the concepts related to fiscal position. The ability of a jurisdiction to carry out its fiscal tasks (its fiscal position) depends on its tax base (its capacity) relative to the outlay required for rendering public services (its need). When jurisdictions with relatively high capacity are faced with low needs, their fiscal position is strong. A standard level of services can be provided with a low ratio of tax revenue to tax base (a low-tax effort); or, putting it alternatively, a standard level of tax effort will generate a high service level relative to need (high fiscal performance). Where the opposite holds, a high effort may be needed to provide only a substandard performance level. More precisely, the various concepts are related to each other as follows:

We define the *fiscal capacity* of jurisdictions j or C_j as

$$C_j = t_s B_j \tag{1}$$

where B_j is the tax base in j and t_s is a standard tax rate.[4] C_j thus measures the revenue which j would obtain by applying that rate to its base.

We also define the *fiscal need* of jurisdiction j or N_j as

$$N_j = n_s Z_j \tag{2}$$

where Z_j is the target population, such as number of school-age children, while n_s is the cost of providing a standard service level per unit of Z, such as instruction per child.[5] N_j thus measures the outlay in j required to secure a standard level of performance or service.

We can now measure the *fiscal position* of j or P_j as

$$P_j = \frac{C_j}{N_j} = \frac{t_s B_j}{n_s Z_j} \tag{3}$$

Fiscal position thus equals the ratio of capacity to need. Setting P for jurisdictions on the average equal to 1, a value of $P_j > 1$ implies a strong fiscal position and a value of $P_j < 1$ a weak fiscal position. The value of P, properly defined, is the index to which distributional weights in grant formulas should be linked. Next, we may define jurisdiction j's *tax effort* E_j as

---

[4] To simplify, we assume that there is one tax rate and one tax base only. Actually, there are different bases, such as sales, property, and income, calling for application of a standard tax structure rather than a single rate.
[5] Our presentation again oversimplifies because it allows for one service Z only rather than for a mix of services, the importance of which will vary among jurisdictions. Moreover, a more detailed analysis would have to allow for variations in n, such as schoolteachers' salaries.

$$E_j = \frac{t_j B_j}{t_s B_j} = \frac{t_j}{t_s} \tag{4}$$

or the ratio of actual revenue in j obtained by applying j's tax rate t_j to what would be raised by applying t_s. Finally we define the *performance level M* as

$$M_j = \frac{n_j Z_j}{n_s Z_j} = \frac{n_j}{n_s} \tag{5}$$

or the ratio of actual outlay obtained by applying j's outlay rate n_j to that required to meet the standard level at rate n_s.

Assuming a balanced budget, we have

$$t_j B_j = n_j Z_j \tag{6}$$

By substituting from (6) into (3) we obtain an alternative definition of fiscal position:

$$P_j = \frac{n_j / n_s}{t_j / t_s} \tag{7}$$

Fiscal position may thus be defined as the ratio of capacity to need as in (3) or as the ratio of performance to tax effort as in (7). These concepts and problems—which arise in comparing fiscal positions both among states and among jurisdictions within states—pose one of the principal issues in fiscal reform. They are of concern both to the federal government, called upon to reduce excessive differentials among states, and to state governments, called upon to deal with excessive differentials among local jurisdictions. Moreover, the federal government has in recent years become directly involved in the fiscal position of the cities.

Differentials in Capacity and Effort

Comparison across states shows substantial differences in fiscal capacity and effort.

Capacity A first approximation to fiscal capacity is given by per capita income. This figure provides a comprehensive measure of ability to pay but does not allow for the fact that the income tax plays only a minor role in state tax structures and as yet hardly any at the local level. Retail sales and assessed property value might be preferable indicators in this respect, or capacity might be measured by combining the various bases with appropriate weights. The latter is done by applying a "standard tax structure." This involves (1) determination of the average tax rate which states as a whole apply to the major tax bases, and (2) application of this average rate to the tax bases of a particular state. Capacity is then measured in terms of the per capita yield of that tax structure.

Table 29-5 shows the range of differentials in fiscal capacity and effort among selected states. Column I shows per capita income as a percentage of average income, while column II shows fiscal capacity. Capacity is measured by the per cap-

TABLE 29-5
Fiscal Capacity and Effort

I Per Capita Income		*II* Index of Taxable Capacity		*III* Index of Tax Effort	
Average	100		100		100
High					
Alaska	131	Alaska	250	New York	158
Connecticut	130	Wyoming	181	Alaska	141
Massachusetts	118	Nevada	146	Michigan	129
New York	116	Connecticut	124	Rhode Island	123
Middle					
Florida	94	New Mexico	103	Maine	100
Washington	100	Louisiana	102	Ohio	103
Delaware	103	New York	98	Oregon	103
Nevada	104	Illinois	97	Washington	104
Low					
Mississippi	60	Mississippi	70	Nevada	65
West Virginia	74	Alabama	73	New Hampshire	69
South Carolina	76	Kentucky	77	Delaware	77
Utah	76	Tennessee	81	Tennessee	81

Source: Advisory Commission on Intergovernmental Relations, *Significant Features of Fiscal Federalism,* 1987, pp. 104, 110.

ita yield of an average tax structure in any one state, relative to the yield of that structure imposed in a hypothetical average-base state. Both state and local revenue is included. Using the per capita income measure, we find that the range is from 130 percent of the average at the high end of the scale to 60 percent at the bottom. Using the capacity index as defined by the revenue from the standard tax system, we find that the range is even wider. The capacity index ranges from 70 in the South to 180 and 200 in the wealthier states. The capacity of urban areas is typically somewhat below the average. As one would expect, the industrialized and urban states show up better with the income index, and the natural resource states (especially Alaska!) do better under the standard yield measure which includes the property base.

Effort   The simplest measure of tax effort is given by the ratio of revenue to some broad index of tax base such as personal income. A more sophisticated measure is given in column III, which shows the ratio of actual yield to that obtained by the standard tax system. We find that effort measures vary somewhat more widely than do capacity measures. The low-income states exhibit a below-average effort ratio, while high-income states rose above the average. Urban states, especially New York, although below average capacity, show a well-above-average effort ratio.[6]

---

[6] For further explanation of how the indices in Table 29-5 are derived, see A.C.I.R., *Measuring State Fiscal Capacity: Alternative Measures and Their Uses,* M-150, September 1986.

Differentials in Performance and Need

Given sharp differentials in fiscal capacities and revenue effort among states, it is not surprising to find equally sharp differentials in performance levels. As shown in Table 29-6, total per capita expenditures vary from 80 to over 400 percent of the average. The differentials are even wider with regard to certain categories such as local schools. Although there is some positive relationship between per capita income and expenditures as measured across states, especially with regard to schools and welfare, there are also frequent exceptions to this rule.

Comparison of average expenditure levels is instructive, but the levels reflect differentials in real service levels (relative to an average standard) only to the extent that per capita needs (or costs of standard service levels as measured in dollar terms) are the same in each state. As we have seen, such is not the case. Taking school expenditures as an illustration, correction should be made for cost differentials, differentials in the ratio of total to school-age population, and the share of enrollment in parochial schools. With regard to highways, comparison of per capita expenditures fails to reflect cost differentials of highway services due to density and climate. Welfare expenditures must be translated into outlay per eligible recipient, and so forth. Capacity can be measured without too much difficulty, but mea-

TABLE 29-6

Per Capita State and Local Expenditures as Percentage of Average, Fiscal Year 1983

Selected States Grouped by Per Capita Income	Education	Highways	Public Welfare	Health and Hospitals	Police and Fire	Total
United States	100	100	100	100	100	100
High						
Alaska	294	555	149	156	322	435
Connecticut	96	83	111	71	110	100
New Jersey	102	87	101	66	122	105
California	103	65	141	107	134	112
New York	118	103	175	148	143	140
Middle						
Colorado	118	117	74	50	103	102
Minnesota	116	154	141	110	86	121
Indiana	94	73	69	92	69	80
Wisconsin	117	127	139	109	109	113
Low						
West Virginia	93	129	60	82	49	87
Alabama	93	103	55	126	67	84
Arkansas	76	92	67	76	48	69
Mississippi	79	124	68	132	53	78
Selected Urban States						
New York	118	103	175	148	143	140
Massachusetts	87	74	145	104	122	106
Pennsylvania	85	92	116	67	73	90
Maryland	109	126	92	99	110	111
New Jersey	102	87	101	66	122	105

Source: Tax Foundation, *Facts and Figures on Government Finance*, 23d ed., Washington, D.C., 1986.

TABLE 29-7
Growth of Grant System

	1954	1969	1985
1. Federal aid to state and local governments (billions of dollars)	2.9	19.4	107.2
2. As percentage of state-local general revenue from own sources	11.4	20.4	21.8
3. State aid to local government (billions of dollars)	5.7	24.8	119.6
4. As percentage of local general revenue from own sources	41.7	54.0	55.3

Source: Advisory Commission on Intergovernmental Relations, *Significant Features of Fiscal Federalism*, 1987, pp. 58, 59.

suring aggregate need levels poses a more complex and as yet unresolved task.[7] Nevertheless, the per capita data of Table 29-6, although a crude index only, point to the existence of substantial differentials.

E. THE GRANT SYSTEM

In recent decades, the growth of the grant system has been among the most dynamic factors in the development of fiscal federalism in the United States.

Growth of Grant Systems

The growth of the grant system since the 1960s and some of its pertinent features are shown in Table 29-7.

Level of Grants Federal grants have grown sharply both in absolute terms and as a percentage of the own revenue of the receiving levels of government. However, the "dependency ratio" or grants as percent of own revenue has remained stable over the last two decades. Note that the data shown in lines 1 and 2 of Table 29-7 combine the state and local level, because the needed breakdown is unavailable. However, the bulk of the federal grants—say 75 percent—goes to the states. Some of this comes to be passed through to local government, but their share in direct federal grants is small.

Turning to state aid to local governments, we find a similar pattern of earlier growth, with recent stability in the dependency ratio. What also follows from the table is that local government is dependent heavily on grant receipts, now accounting for over 40 percent of its general (own plus aid) revenue.

---

[7] To obtain a comprehensive measure of need, it is necessary to postulate a set of service levels— involving such items as education, roads, welfare, health, and municipal services—and to determine what it would cost to provide them in various jurisdictions. To do this, it is necessary to define service levels in "objective terms" and to allow for cost differentials. The definition of service levels in particular is a difficult task. Should service levels be measured in terms of inputs (e.g., teacher hours per grade school child) or in terms of output (e.g., reading proficiency requirements)? How can a meaningful comparison be drawn between the service levels provided by rural and city roads? After these difficulties are met, there is the further problem of costing any particular service, with allowance for the interdependence of costs and service levels.

TABLE 29-8
Uses of Grant Funds

	FEDERAL AID TO STATE AND LOCAL GOVERNMENTS		STATE AID TO LOCAL GOVERNMENTS	
	1954	1985	1954	1985
Education	16.0	13.7	10.6	10.3
Highways	17.9	11.6	51.6	62.7
Welfare	48.5	40.2	15.3	5.0
Housing and urban revenue	13.0	10.1	17.7	10.6
Other	4.6	24.3	4.8	11.4
Total	100.0	100.0	100.0	100.0

Source: Advisory Commission on Intergovernmental Relations, *Significant Features of Fiscal Federalism,* 1987, pp. 58, 59.

Uses of Grants   With the disappearance of general revenue sharing,[8] all grants are tied to certain uses, restricted more or less narrowly depending on the particular grant in question. The composition by program of both federal and state grants is shown in Table 29-8. Much the most important among federal grants are those related to social programs of various sorts, including the federal share in income security and health. Most important among state grants to local governments are those for highways, followed by education, housing, and urban renewal. As shown in the table, this program pattern has remained fairly stable for both federal and state aid.

Types of Grants

As noted earlier, the appropriate grant design depends on how the grant objective is seen by the grantor. The resulting structure of federal grants is summarized in Table 29-9.

Following presentation in the U.S. budget, grants are now classified as general, broad-based, and "other," or categorical grants. The first group, which consists almost entirely of general revenue sharing, involves hardly any restriction with respect to use. The last group, classified as other, includes a large number of fairly narrowly defined grant programs, programs which until recently were listed as categorical aid. The middle group of broad-based aid includes aid the use of which is restricted but within fairly broad program ranges.

As shown in Table 29-9, the grant system until the early seventies was almost entirely in the form of categorical grants, but in the 1970s increased use came to be made of broad-based or block grants. This development has reflected dissatisfaction with a large number of highly specified categorical programs and a desire to leave more discretion to the recipient governments, thereby decentralizing the de-

[8] Introduced in 1972, the program of general revenue sharing provided for unrestricted and nonmatching grants to be distributed among the states on the basis of a formula reflecting elements of capacity, need, and own effort. Initially heralded as the "pathway to a new federalism," the program was terminated in 1985.

TABLE 29-9
Federal Grants by Type
(In Billions of Dollars)

	1964	1972	1982	1988
1. General purpose aid				
2. General revenue sharing	- - -	- - -	4.6	- - -
3. Other	- - -	0.5	1.9	2.1
4. Total	- - -	0.5	6.5	2.1
5. Broad-based aid	- - -	2.8	11.5	12.6
6. Categorical grants	10.0	31.0	70.2	104.4
7. Total	10.0	34.4	88.2	119.0

Sources: For 1960 see notes to Table 29-8. For other years, see *Special Analyses of the Budget of the United States Government, Fiscal Years 1984 and 1989,* Washington, D.C., OMB.

cision process. However, the trend slowed down and by 1989 nearly 90 percent of total grant funds were still dispensed in categorical form.

Categorical Aid

Categorical grants are designed to support rather closely specified programs, ranging from programs such as Medicaid ($33 billion for 1989) and Aid to Families with Dependent Children ($10.9 billion) to quite small grants such as that to the National Endowment for the Arts ($34 million). In all there are approximately 340 different grant programs, but 85 percent of the spending is concentrated in the larger 25 percent of grants.

Types Categorical grants may be "formula-based" or they may be "project" grants. Formula grants, which account for about 70 percent of the categorical grant funds, become available automatically to eligible recipients, with distribution among jurisdictions determined by the applicable formula. Project grants are made upon application by the grantee and their distribution is not based on such a formula. Since there are also in-between types of grants, neat classification is not always possible.

The formulas used differ widely among grants. Some grants begin with a flat per capita amount for each state; others set a cap on the total. The factors used in the formulas typically include population and per capita income as measures of need, but in some cases more specific indices are added. Thus, the distribution formula for the state boating-safety program allocates one-third of the funds in line with the number of registered vessels. In most cases, the resulting formulas may be viewed as a compromise between the principles (1) that each state is entitled to its "fair" share, (2) that the allocation should reflect "need" for the particular service, and (3) that "capacity" or ability to meet such needs from own-resources should be allowed for.

Another important feature of categorical grants is the matching requirement. This applies to both formula and project grants. About 60 percent of categorical grants require matching, with matching rates from 5 to 50 percent or more. However, most matching requirements are well below 50 percent. Matching rates may be uniform for the entire grant or they may vary by amount and by characteristics of the receiving jurisdiction, such as the level of per capita income. Some grants are capped, while others are open-ended. They thus reflect in varying degrees the different types of national concern discussed in the preceding chapter.

A typical nonmatching grant formula may take the form

$$A_i = a_0 + a_1\frac{P_i}{P_t}$$

with A_i the allotment to the ith state, P_i the size of the "target" population group in the ith state (such as elementary school pupils or welfare recipients), and P_t the total target population for the nation as a whole. The constant a_0 is introduced to allow for overhead administrative costs but is of minor weight. The distribution is thus essentially on a population basis. Although used in the majority of health and welfare grants, this formula makes no allowance for differentials in capacity and implies a very crude measure of need since it fails to allow for cost differentials and other factors. In other instances, further allowance for need is introduced by relating the grant to average expenditures in the area, but once more, existing expenditure levels may be a misleading indicator of actual needs. Allowance for capacity may be introduced by letting the size of the allotment vary with target population and also inversely with capacity. Or it may be linked to the matching rate.

Consolidation into Block Grants

Gaining in force during the seventies and eighties has been a drive toward consolidation of specific categorical aid programs into block grants. Such grants, also referred to as "broad-based aid," involve less central control and are easier to administer. In 1971, the Nixon administration first introduced plans for "special revenue sharing," designed to consolidate the proliferation of categorical grants into a smaller number of grant packages, and the drive for increased local discretion was resumed by the Reagan administration as one of the major planks of its New Federalism.

Although congressional response to consolidation was slow initially, there are now nine major block grants, with social services, community development, and highways being among the most important. As a consequence, the total number of grant programs has been reduced somewhat from 428 in 1980 to 340 in 1986. While the share of broad-based grants by 1982 was still only 12 percent of the total, further consolidation has been proposed. As noted below, this consolidation also involves removal of matching provisions and thereby constitutes a drastic change in the very nature of the grant system.[9]

F. FEDERAL GRANTS AND EQUALIZATION

We now turn to the effectiveness of the federal grant system in fiscal equalization. As a first approximation, we focus on redistribution of fiscal resources among

[9] For a presentation of the administration's grant program, see *Special Analyses, Budget of the United States Government, Fiscal Year 1988*, Office of Management and Budget, 1987, p. H.1.

states with high and low per capita income. Table 29-10 shows the distribution of aid among high- and low-income states. In column I, states are ranked according to per capita income, with 1 given to the lowest and 50 to the highest state. Column II shows corresponding per capita grants. An equalizing pattern would call for a negative relation. With a correlation coefficient of 0.15, there is no such relation. The same is also shown if the amount of per capita grant is regressed on per capita income.[10] Absence of an equalizing pattern across states does not mean, however, that there is no such effect across individuals in all states. Some high-income states such as New York also contain large sectors of the population which draw on low-income programs and hence on the grants by which such programs are supported.

The further question might be raised whether the grant pattern is redistributive across states if considered on a net basis. For this purpose we assume grants to be financed by federal income tax. Column III shows the corresponding amount of per capita federal income tax contributed. With a correlation coefficient of 0.91, there is a high positive relation.[11] Column IV shows per capita net receipts, equal to grants minus income tax paid for their finance. Regressing net grant receipts on per capita income, a negative relationship with a correlation coefficient of −0.44 remains.[12] Whereas we find that the redistributive effect of the federal budget across individuals was generated largely from its expenditure side, we now note that the corresponding effect across states is generated largely from the revenue side.

G.   SCHOOL FINANCE

Another critical area in the development of aid policy—this time involving the relationship between states and local jurisdictions—is that of school finance. Expenditures for elementary and secondary schools are made almost entirely at the local level, with only Hawaii as a notable exception. However, the financing of these expenditures has become increasingly a matter of state concern. Through the mechanism of state aid, state governments now provide nearly 50 percent of total education finance, and in over half the states the share is well over 50 percent. This reflects the weakness of the property tax and tax limitations, as well as the fact that fiscal capacities among local units differ widely. Since local finance is very largely derived from the property tax, equal tax efforts would result in widely differing expenditures per student; or (which is the same), widely differing degrees of tax effort would be needed to finance similar expenditure levels. The need for equalizing state aid thus arose from the desire to avoid both excessive differentials in educational opportunities and excessive differentials in tax efforts needed to provide them.

[10] The regression equation shows

$$\text{per capita grants} = 339 + 0.012 \text{ per capita income}$$
$$(2.34) \qquad\quad (1.067)$$

[11] The regression equation shows

$$\text{per capita tax} = -215 + 0.05 \text{ per capita income}$$
$$(-5.24) \qquad (15.29)$$

[12] The regression equation shows

$$\text{per capita net grant} = 551 - 0.03 \text{ per capita income}$$
$$(3.96) \qquad (-3.39)$$

TABLE 29-10
Federal Grants and Equalization, 1985

State	I Per Capita Income Rank	II Per Capita Income (1982 dollars)	III Per Capita Grants (dollars)	IV Per Capita Federal Income Tax (dollars)	V Per Capita Net Grant (dollars)
Mississippi	50	9,187	512	239	273
West Virginia	49	10,193	554	280	274
Arkansas	48	10,467	473	263	210
Utah	47	10,493	485	284	201
South Carolina	46	10,586	391	296	95
Alabama	45	10,673	434	296	138
Kentucky	44	10,824	479	297	182
New Mexico	43	10,914	579	324	255
Montana	42	10,974	723	315	408
Idaho	41	11,120	434	273	161
South Dakota	40	11,161	645	275	370
Tennessee	39	11,243	443	341	102
Louisiana	38	11,274	453	363	90
North Carolina	37	11,617	360	338	22
Maine	36	11,887	572	534	38
North Dakota	35	12,052	638	334	304
Vermont	34	12,117	617	335	282
Oklahoma	33	12,232	424	383	41
Indiana	32	12,446	363	382	− 19
Georgia	31	12,432	447	375	72
Iowa	30	12,594	406	330	76
Oregon	29	12,622	497	340	157
Arizona	28	12,795	364	386	− 22
Wisconsin	27	13,154	483	354	129
Wyoming	26	13,223	925	422	503
Ohio	25	13,226	443	394	49
Missouri	24	13,244	391	401	− 10
Nebraska	23	13,281	414	350	64
Pennsylvania	22	13,437	480	411	69
Texas	21	13,483	312	493	− 181
Michigan	20	13,608	476	421	55
Florida	19	13,742	278	477	− 199
Kansas	18	13,775	359	414	− 55
Hawaii	17	13,814	445	389	56
Washington	16	13,867	427	443	− 16
Rhode Island	15	13,906	585	399	186
Minnesota	14	14,087	501	387	114
Delaware	13	14,272	496	478	18
Nevada	12	14,488	434	512	− 78
Virginia	11	14,542	344	453	− 109
Illinois	10	14,738	434	447	− 13
Colorado	9	14,812	379	466	− 87
New Hampshire	8	14,964	393	506	− 113
Maryland	7	15,864	438	565	− 127
New York	6	16,050	696	495	201
California	5	16,065	418	485	− 67
Massachusetts	4	16,380	528	534	− 6
New Jersey	3	17,211	440	613	− 173

TABLE 29-10 (continued)
Federal Grants and Equalization, 1985

State	I Per Capita Income Rank	II Per Capita Income (1982 dollars)	III Per Capita Grants (dollars)	IV Per Capita Federal Income Tax (dollars)	V Per Capita Net Grant (dollars)
Connecticut	2	18,089	471	678	− 207
Alaska	1	18,187	1,243	752	491
Average		13,876	452	435	17

*With total grants equal to $102 billion and total income tax receipts of $314 billion, the amount of income tax paid to finance grants equals 32.4 percent of total income tax revenue. The amounts shown in column III therefore equal 32.4 percent of per capita income tax payments received from the various states.
Source: Columns I and III: *Statistical Abstract of the United States.* Column II: Tax Foundation, *Facts and Figures on Government Finance,* 1987.

Constitutional Entitlements

Interest in the state role in educational finance was heightened in the early seventies by rulings of state supreme courts that local finance of education is unconstitutional under the equal protection clause, since it deprives children in low-tax-base communities of an adequate education. Even though the U.S. Supreme Court failed to endorse this position, these decisions mirror and reinforce prevailing tendencies toward increased state concern with school finance. But given the principle of equal right to educational opportunity, it still remains to be seen how its fiscal implications are to be interpreted. The courts have been hesitant to set down the rules and the legislative search for an answer continues.[13]

Types of State Aid

State aid to equalize expenditures per pupil has taken various forms, with some approaches more equalizing than others. *Flat grants,* involving fixed payments per pupil, were widely used at the outset; but since they were small, they provided only a modest degree of equalization. Subsequently, the so-called *foundation grants* became popular and are still most widely used today. But the desire to achieve equal educational opportunity led to the promotion of further grant forms, including percentage equalization grants and what has come to be known as "district power equalization grants."

Foundation Grants The purpose of foundation grants is to equalize the tax rate which is required for providing a set minimum level of school services among jurisdictions. Thus, the grant S_i received by the ith unit equals

$$S_i = E^*P_i - t^*B_i$$

where E^* is the stipulated minimum level of per pupil expenditures, P_i is the number of pupils, B_i is the equalized assessed property tax base, and t^* is the tax rate which the state expects the jurisdiction to apply for purposes of education. The state will make up for the amount by which the cost of providing the minimum

[13] See p. 29.

expenditure per pupil exceeds the revenue obtained from the required tax rate. The formula may be modified by introducing weights which allow for wage rate differentials, grade-level compositions, and other factors determining the cost of providing a set minimum level of services; and to this may be added a more complex measure of fiscal capacity in which per capita income and property values are allowed for. In addition, requirements for public services other than education might be taken into account.

But even with these adjustments, the foundation approach has become subject to an increasing amount of criticism. The support level is frequently set very low, so that substantial differentials in tax effort remain necessary to support what the communities consider to be adequate standards, and no incentive is given for communities to provide higher service levels.

Percentage Equalization   Percentage grants were designed to overcome this defect and also to avoid the necessity of having to determine the cost of providing services at the foundation level. Under this approach, no minimum level is set and the state participates by way of a matching grant in whatever level of educational services the jurisdiction wishes to engage. To provide equalization, the matching rate declines as the jurisdiction's assessed value per student rises. As a result, the own-cost of public services is lower for poor than for high jurisdictions, thereby increasing the relative level of services which poor jurisdictions provide. As distinct from the foundation grant, this offers special support to the education minded but low-capacity unit to raise its level of educational services.

District Power Equalization   District power equalization is similar in principle but goes farther. The purpose now is to equalize the per student revenue which various jurisdictions obtain from imposing a given tax rate, even though their tax base per student may differ. We then have

$$S_i = t_i(B_a - B_i)$$

where S_i is the subsidy to jurisdiction i, B_a and B_i are the average equalized values per student in the average and ith jurisdiction respectively, and t_i is i's tax rate. Strictly applied, this formula calls for a negative subsidy (tax) if B_i is larger than B_a.

We can also express the subsidy as

$$S_i = mt_iB_i$$

where m is the subsidy rate, equal to $t_i(B_a - B_i)/t_iB_i$. Further, by setting $B_i = \alpha B_a$ and combining the two expressions, we get

$$m = \frac{1 - \alpha}{\alpha}$$

so that as α rises from 0.25 to 0.5, 0.75, and 1.0, m falls from 3 to 1, 0.33, and

0. In practice, the matching rate is typically set not at the full value of m but at a fraction thereof, so that equalization is only at a partial level.

Evaluation   As in all matters of grant analysis, choice of the appropriate grant design depends on the policy objective. If the objective is to ensure that all students receive a set minimum level of services, the foundation grant approach is appropriate.[14] If the intent is to give an incentive to own-expenditures, the matching approach is in order, while leaving it to the receiving jurisdiction to decide on the desired service level. If it is desired that a given tax effort—as measured by the tax rate which the jurisdiction imposes—should provide the same service level for all jurisdictions, independent of their tax base per student, then district power equalization will serve the purpose.

Other criteria might be established, but it is of special interest to consider the proposition that the level of school services should not depend on the level of assessed value per student. This is what the California Supreme Court had in mind when in *Serrano* vs. *Priest* it ruled that educational spending should not be a function of local wealth. Whereas the authors of district power equalization thought that such would be the result of their proposal, later analysis showed this not to be the case.[15] Power equalization merely affects the cost or tax price at which education can be purchased in terms of own-resources. Thus, if the full cost per unit of the service equals C, matching at rate m reduces it to $(1 - m)C$. Low-property jurisdictions are thus enabled to buy school services more cheaply and are encouraged to spend more. But what will be spent depends on the relationship between the price and wealth elasticities of demand for education. With m defined as $(1 - \alpha)/\alpha$, the net price in community X is half that in Y if the per capita base in X is half that in Y. Therefore, power equalization, which uses this definition of m, will eliminate all correlation between assessed value and per student expenditure only if the wealth and price elasticities of demand for education happen to be the same in absolute value. If the price elasticity is higher, a matching rate schedule which falls short of equalizing yield per tax rate would be in order.[16]

Another complication arises because jurisdictions with low assessed value per student are not necessarily jurisdictions with low per capita income. This being the case, the question arises whether equalization should be related to income or to property as the base. Given the administrative and political difficulties of legislating a grant system which would achieve a high degree of equalization (not only in tax effort but also in actual levels of education), the Advisory Commission on Intergovernmental Relations has suggested that the states assume the entire cost of education, excepting only the federal share. This approach is clearly the best one if

---

[14] With respect to the problem of school finance, a distinction might be drawn among the social interest, the freedom of parents to choose how much they wish to spend on schooling, and children's right to adequate education. The foundation approach may be taken to emphasize children's rights by ensuring a minimum level of education, whereas the district power equalization adds emphasis to parental choice by the matching grant approach.

[15] See Martin S. Feldstein, "Wealth Neutrality and Local Choice in Public Education," *American Economic Review*, March 1975.

[16] Feldstein, ibid., finds the price elasticity to be substantially higher than the wealth elasticity. Matching based on the "equal revenue for equal tax effort" rule would thus give too high a matching rate to poor jurisdictions, with the level of service related negatively to per student assessed value.

total equalization of education within the state is desired. But it is unsatisfactory to those who favor adequate minimum levels while leaving local communities the option of going further.

Which objective is to be preferred poses a major issue in social and educational philosophy. However, it is evident that the problems of grant design will remain even in the case of total state finance. If local autonomy over the expenditure side of school finance is to be maintained, as seems to be generally agreed upon it will still be necessary to decide how state funds are to be allocated among communities, i.e., how relative levels of need are to be measured.

Proposition 13 and subsequent developments have greatly limited the potentials of property tax revenue; and given the dependency of elementary and secondary education on this revenue source, the resulting revenue shortage has had a particularly forceful impact on school finance. With increased reliance on state aid, the differentials in service levels which traditionally have resulted from differentials in property tax base will give way to a more uniform pattern serviced by increased centralized (state) finance.

H. THE NEW FEDERALISM

The philosophy of the "New Federalism" as advanced by the Reagan administration has been to stress decentralization, including increased reliance on state-local outlays as well as increased discretion in the recipient's use of federal grants.[17]

A bird's-eye view of the changing federal share was given in Table 29-1. The federal share (including grants to state and local governments) in total public expenditures showed little change over the past 30 years, but focus on the global share is misleading. If defense is excluded, the federal share rose sharply from 1970 to 1980, reflecting the Johnson administration's social programs, but then turned down during the 1980s. With interest payments excluded as well, that decrease becomes more pronounced. The stable overall share in the 1980s thus hides a rise in defense and interest costs, offset in turn by a declining share in other programs. As shown earlier in Table 29-5, introduction of broad-based grants also increased the recipient's discretion, but only at a modest rate.

Whether these trends will continue in the future or whether they will be halted or reversed is difficult to predict. Much will depend on the extent to which the federal budget continues to be burdened by defense and debt service. More generally, the future course of fiscal federalism in the United States will depend on its political climate and attitudes toward public programs. Some implications of a continuing shift toward decentralization may however be noted:

  1. Cutbacks in federal participation reduce the overall tax base, a loss not likely to be offset by more intensive use of limited state-local fiscal resources. A smaller public sector is the likely result.
  2. With a federal revenue system that relies primarily on the income tax and

---

[17] For a review of this changing setting, see Robert Gleason, "Federalism 1986–87: Signals of a New Era," and John Shanan, "The Faces of Fiscal Federalism," in *Intergovernmental Perspective*, vol. 14, no. 1, Winter 1988.

state systems that rely primarily on sales and excise taxes, decentralization makes for a less progressive or more regressive burden distribution.

3. Decentralization permits differentiation in line with local preferences and thus closer adaptation of the service mix to what consumers want. Such is the case especially with regard to public services whose benefit incidence is limited to the particular jurisdiction.

4. A decentralized fiscal system is less suited to dealing with income mainte-nance and welfare programs as higher support levels offered in one jurisdiction invite influx of claimants from other jurisdictions.

5. Restriction of federal support to nonearmarked grants interferes with focus on program areas which are of special concern from a nationwide perspective and which might be seen as national merit goods,[18] such as basic activities in education and health services.

Other perspectives might be added but these will suffice to show how current trends in fiscal federalism might be appraised. As we see it, there is much to be said for leaving the responsibility for distribution-oriented programs at the federal level, with need related to individual recipient rather than to averages by jurisdic-tion. This calls for federal assumption of responsibility for income maintenance and welfare programs. Also there is much to be said for placing responsibility for the finance of elementary and secondary education at the state level, while retain-ing substantially local discretion over school administration. Turning to the design of federal grants, the categorical approach (with selectivity held within reasonable limits) has the advantage of permitting emphasis on programs which are of impor-tance from the federal perspective. Matching requirements further serve to protect the federal budget and to place a degree of own-responsibility on the recipient. Be-yond this, there may be a case for general (nonearmarked) support given to juris-dictions with quite low capacity to need ratios, an approach along the lines of the revenue sharing programs of the 1970s but on a more selective basis.

In all it is evident that a variety of approaches are required to meet the fiscal needs of a federal system, combining an appropriate degree of self-determination for subjurisdictions with an underlying sense of national cohesion.

I. SUMMARY

The U.S. fiscal structure involves three major layers—federal, state, and local—with a great variety of patterns between states and among state-local relationships within states.

1. The federal share in total expenditures which was one-third at the beginning of the century, is now nearly 70 percent. Over the same period the state share rose from 11 to over 18 percent while the local share declined from 52 to about 13 percent. The overall trend has thus been toward expenditure centralization.

2. The 1980s have brought a decline in the federal share, especially so if de-fense and interest are excluded.

3. Expenditure concentration is reduced if intergovernmental grants are in-cluded at the level of recipient rather than of origin.

[18] See p. 55.

4. The number of local units has declined but still exceeds 82,000.

5. The state share in state-local finance varies widely across states.

6. Highly centralized states derive a larger share of state-local revenue from the sales tax and a smaller share from the property tax.

Jurisdictions differ in their fiscal position and a measure of that position is helpful in grant design:

7. Fiscal position was shown to depend on the jurisdiction's capacity and need.

8. Differentials in capacity and effort among states were examined and were found to differ substantially.

9. The same was found to hold regarding differences in performance and need.

The growth of the federal grant system has been the most dynamic feature of fiscal federalism in recent decades.

10. Federal grants have grown from $19 billion in 1969 to $107 billion in 1985.

11. State aid to local governments has grown from $25 billion to $120 billion.

12. Local governments now receive over 40 percent of their total revenue from grants, largely from the states.

13. The largest program areas covered by federal grants are social service, income security, and health.

14. The most important use of state grants is for education.

Turning to the structure of federal grants, we can draw the following conclusions:

15. The weight of general-purpose grants has increased in recent years, but selective (categorical) grants still account for 90 percent of total aid.

16. Medicaid is the most important categorical grant.

17. Categorical grants are typically matching in form but differ in their allowance for capacity and need.

18. Recent trends have been toward grant simplification, applicable to broader program areas and in nonmatching form.

19. General revenue sharing, introduced in 1972, was discontinued in 1986.

Consideration has been given to the extent to which the prevailing patterns of federal grants provide for fiscal equalization:

20. Per capita grants show no inverse relation to per capita income.

21. If grants are considered on a net basis, some degree of equalization occurs.

Problems in school finance were examined, including the issue of constitutional entitlement and forms of state aid:

22. State supreme courts have held local finance of schools unconstitutional under the due process clause.

23. Various school-aid formulas were considered.

24. The trend, especially after Proposition 13, is toward increased reliance on state finance.

Recent trends pointing toward a new fiscal federalism were noted and examined:

25.   The new perspective points toward a reduced role of federal finance, with increased self-reliance at the state-local level.

26.   In the course of the 1980s, this trend has resulted in a distinct decline in the federal fiscal share, especially if expenditures excluding defense and interest are considered.

27.   A beginning has been made toward shifting emphasis from categorical toward block grants, but the larger share of federal grants still remains in categorical form.

28.   Major considerations enter into evaluating these trends just enumerated, depending upon how the nature of the American federation is to be viewed.

FURTHER READINGS

Advisory Commission on Intergovernmental Relations, *The Federal Role in the Federal System: The Dynamics of Growth*, 1981.

Advisory Commission on Intergovernmental Relations, *Significant Features of Fiscal Federalism*, 1981–82 ed., 1982. Also see other publications by the ACIR which provide an invaluable source of information on current developments in this area.

Break, G. F.: *Intergovernmental Fiscal Relations in the United States*, rev. ed., Washington, D.C.: Brookings, 1980.

Hirsch, W. Z.: *The Economics of State and Local Government*, New York: McGraw-Hill, 1970.

Rubinfeld, D. L.: The Economics of the Local Public Sector, in A. Auerbach and M. Feldstein (eds.), *Handbook of Public Economics*, Amsterdam: North Holland, forthcoming. This essay also contains extensive literature references to local fiscal economics.

Office of State and Local Finance, Department of the Treasury, *Federal State-Local Fiscal Relations*, Report to the President and the Congress, September 1985.

Part Seven

Fiscal Policy and Stabilization

Chapter 30

Principles of
Stabilization Policy*

A. Multiplier Models with Investment Fixed: *Income Determination without Budget; Income Determination with Budget.* **B. Multiplier Models with Investment Variable:** *Diagrammatic Presentation; Algebraic Presentation; Money Multiplier with Fiscal Sector; Effectiveness; Policy Mix and Crowding Out.* **C. Stabilization in the Open Economy:** *Multiplier Leakage; Capital Flows and the Fiscal-Monetary Mix.* **D. Inflation:** *Types of Inflation; Demand-Pull Inflation; Cost-Push Inflation; Fiscal versus Monetary Restriction.* **E. Rational Expectations:** *Do People Know Better?; The Policy-Ineffectiveness Theorem; The Ricardian Equivalence.* **F. Summary.**

We now turn to the third major function of budget policy which, as was noted in Chapter 1, involves its role in economic stabilization. Budget operations affect the level of aggregate demand, and changes in the level of aggregate demand affect the level of employment and of prices. Like it or not, the budget thus has important repercussions on the macro behavior of the economy and, in turn, becomes an important tool by which to affect that behavior. Moreover, budget policy affects the division of total output between consumption and capital formation and thereby the rate of economic growth. This chapter explores this set of interrelations.

Reader's Guide to Chapter 30: The principles of stabilization policy examined in this chapter follow from the models of macro theory to be found in introductory or intermediate texts. Students familiar with this material may wish to proceed directly to the following chapter.

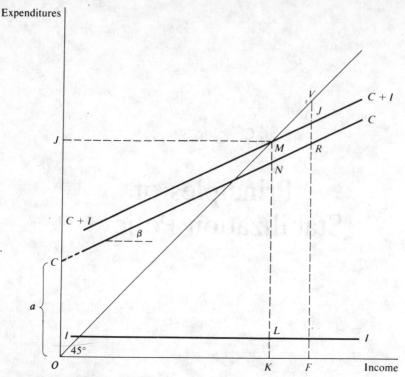

FIGURE 30-1 Income determination without government sector.

A.   MULTIPLIER MODELS WITH INVESTMENT FIXED

We begin with the simplest possible setting, in which consumption is a function of income while investment is given at a fixed level. Investment will be made an endogenous part of the system in section B.

Income Determination without Budget

We now consider how the equilibrium level of income is determined, first without and then with a budget. Income determination, in its simplest form, is shown in Figure 30-1, where income is measured on the horizontal axis and expenditures are measured on the vertical axis.[1] CC is the consumption function, showing consumption expenditures to be a rising function of the level of income. Investment expenditures, shown as II, are assumed to be constant and independent of the level of income. By adding II to CC vertically, we obtain the total expenditure line $C + I$. Equilibrium income is determined where the income received in any one period gives rise to expenditures of an equal amount which, in turn, become the income of the following period. Thus equilibrium income is shown on the diagram where the total expenditure line $C + I$ intersects the 45° line along which expenditures equal income. This point of intersection is at M, the equilibrium income level being OK,

---

[1] To simplify, we assume a closed economy so that trade effects can be disregarded. For an open economy multiplier, see p. 511.

with expenditures equal to *OJ* and *OK* = *OJ*. At equilibrium income *OK,* consumption equals *KN* and saving (or income minus consumption) equals *NM.* The latter in turn equals investment *KL.*

In equilibrium, expenditures must equal income so that saving (or income less consumption) must be offset or matched by investment spending. If the level of output (and thus of income) should exceed the level *OK,* total expenditures will be insufficient to purchase that level of output (i.e., the line *C + I* lies *below* the 45° line), and output and income will accordingly be reduced to *OK.* If, on the other hand, the level of output or income should be below *OK,* total expenditures will exceed the level of current output (that is, *C + I* lies *above* the 45° line), with the result that the level of output and income will be increased to *OK.*

The same story is told in Table 30-1. Equation (1) shows total income to equal the sum of consumption and investment, while equation (2) defines the consumption function. The constant term *a* is the intercept of the *CC* line in Figure 30-1 with the vertical axis, while the marginal propensity to consume *c* gives its slope, or tan β. The system is summarized in equation (3) where equilibrium income is obtained by substituting equation (2) into equation (1). The fraction $1/(1 - c)$ is the so-called multiplier, and the sum of the constants $(a + I)$ is the multiplicand. If $c = 0.8$, the multiplier is 5, and with *a* equal to $50 billion and *I* equal to $100 billion, income *Y* would be equal to $750 billion.

Returning to Figure 30-1, we see that the resulting equilibrium income *OK* may be such that at prevailing prices a full-employment output is produced, but this need not be the case. Suppose instead that full-employment income equals *OF.* If the amount of saving *RV* which people wish to undertake at this level of income exceeds the given level of planned investment *RJ,* income must fall until saving is reduced to *RJ.* Income thus returns to its equilibrium level *OK.* There is no automatic mechanism in this system which ensures that full-employment income is reached and maintained.

Income Determination with Budget

We now introduce government into this system to see how the level of income is affected by various budget policies.

Allowing for Government Expenditures We first add government purchases *G* to our system. As shown in Figure 30-2, these are added to the consumption function along with investment to obtain the total expenditure line *C + I + G.* Introduction of government expenditures thus raises output from *OA* to *OB.* An increase in government expenditures, by raising the total expenditure line, may thus be used to raise income. If income is below the level required for full employment, government expenditures may be used to move it there, which is also shown in equations (4) to (7) of Table 30-1. Equations (4) and (5) restate the basic equations, and (6) gives the new income level. Government purchases *G* become part of the multiplicand. Equation (7), obtained by putting equation (6) in difference form, shows the resulting increase in income. With *c* equal to 0.8, an increase in *G* of $1 billion raises equilibrium income by $5 billion. This increase will be the larger, the greater the multiplier. The same holds but with reversed signs for a decrease in government purchases.

TABLE 30-1
Income Determination and Fiscal Multipliers
(With Investment Fixed)

	Equation No.

System without government

$$Y = C + I \tag{1}$$

$$C = a + cY \tag{2}$$

$$Y = \frac{1}{1-c}(a+I) \tag{3}$$

System with government purchases

$$Y = C + I + G \tag{4}$$

$$C = a + cY \tag{5}$$

$$Y = \frac{1}{1-c}(a+I+G) \tag{6}$$

$$\Delta Y = \frac{1}{1-c}\Delta G \tag{7}$$

System with lump-sum tax

$$Y = C + I \tag{8}$$

$$C = a + c(Y-T) \tag{9}$$

$$Y = \frac{1}{1-c}(a+I-cT) \tag{10}$$

$$\Delta Y = -\frac{c}{1-c}\Delta T \tag{11}$$

System with income tax

$$Y = C + I \tag{12}$$

$$C = a + c(1-t)Y \tag{13}$$

$$Y = \frac{1}{1-c(1-t)}(a+I) \tag{14}$$

System with government purchases and income tax

$$Y = C + I + G \tag{15}$$

$$C = a + c(1-t)Y \tag{16}$$

$$Y = \frac{1}{1-c(1-t)}(a+I+G) \tag{17}$$

$$\Delta Y = \frac{1}{1-c(1-t)}\Delta G \tag{18}$$

Allowing for Lump-Sum Taxes   Next consider the role of taxes. As shown in Figure 30-3, taxation is first introduced in the form of a lump-sum tax, i.e.; a tax of fixed amount, independent of income. Adding *II* and *CC*, we obtain *C + I* and income level *OA*. Now a tax of revenue *DE* is introduced. As a result, the consumption function drops from *CC* to *C'C'*, with the horizontal distance between them equal to *DE*.[2] Consumption out of pre-tax income falls by the vertical

[2] A consumer receiving income *OE*, after paying *DE* in tax, has a disposable income equal to *OD*. Consumption thus equals *DF*, not *DH*. The consumption function *C'C'* is given by $C' = a + c(Y - T)$. Whereas it shows consumption out of before-tax income, it allows for the fact that disposable income is reduced because of tax.

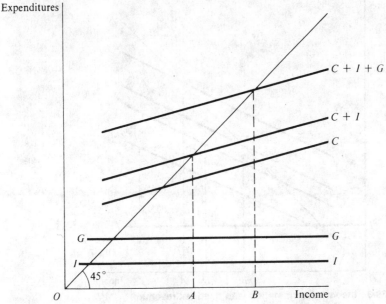

FIGURE 30-2   Income determination with government expenditures.

distance between the two. The intersection of the new expenditure line C' + I with the 45° line moves down and income falls from OA to OB. By shifting the $C'C'$ line up to the left, a subsequent tax reduction raises the total expenditure line and increases income. Thus taxation as well as expenditure changes may be used to adjust the total level of expenditures and thereby the income and employment levels as well.

The same is also shown in equations (8) to (11) of Table 30-1. In equation (9), the tax is introduced into the consumption function with the marginal propensity to consume c pertaining to disposable income, or income after tax. In equation (10), we see how the tax reduces the multiplicand. In equation (11), obtained by putting equation (10) in difference form and solving for ΔT, we see how the tax relates to income. Note, however, that the income gain due to a tax cut is less per dollar of tax than was that from an increase in government purchases. The lump-sum tax does not affect the multiplier, but it reduces the multiplicand. Since the initial change in consumption equals $c\Delta T$ only, part of the tax reduction is neutralized by its reflection in increased saving rather than in increased consumption. The same argument holds for the effects of a tax increase, which now reduces the level of expenditures less than a corresponding reduction in purchases.

Role of Transfers   Transfer payments, as distinct from government purchases G, may be viewed as negative taxes for purposes of this analysis. Thus, transfer payments R may be substituted for T in equation (11) but with the sign reversed, showing an increase in R to be expansionary. However, the resulting change in income is again less than that for an increase in G. The reason once more is that part of the increase in disposable income due to the transfer payment will be reflected in increased saving rather than in increased consumption expenditures.

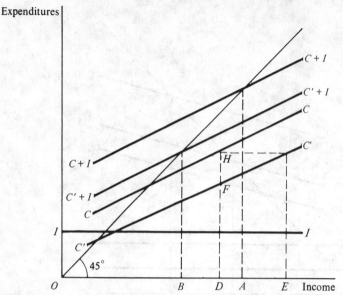

FIGURE 30-3 Income determination with fixed tax revenue.

System with Income Tax   We must now turn to the more realistic case where revenue is obtained from an income tax rather than a lump-sum tax. Introduction of such a tax does not shift the consumption function in a parallel fashion, as occurred with the lump-sum tax, but causes it to swivel downward around its point of intercept, because the tax, equal to the horizontal distance between CC and $C'C'$, increases with income. As a result, the slope of the consumption function rather than its intercept is reduced. Expansionary action now calls for a reduction in t,[3] which is shown in Figure 30-4, where CC' is the consumption function before, and CC'' that after tax reduction, with income rising from OP to OF.

This process is shown in equations (12) through (18) of Table 30-1. Note that the way in which the tax enters into the consumption function in equation (13) differs from the case of the lump-sum tax in equation (9), with the result that introduction of the tax now reduces the marginal propensity to consume out of income before tax, and thereby also the multiplier.[4] This result is as one would expect, since tax revenue T now equals tY and is a function of Y. As income rises, so does tax revenue, thus depressing disposable income and C and hence checking the

[3] The formula for a change in t corresponding to equation (11) is

$$\Delta Y = -\frac{cY_0}{1 - c(1 - t_1)}\Delta t$$

where Y_0 is the initial level of income and t_1 is the new tax rate.

[4] The relationship between consumption and income as expressed in the consumption function relates to disposable income. With an income tax, disposable income rises by less than before-tax income. As a result, the ratio of incremental consumption to incremental before-tax income is reduced— i.e., the marginal propensity to consume out of income before tax declines.

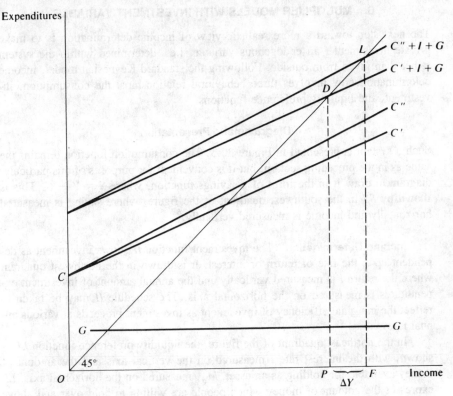

FIGURE 30-4 Tax reduction with income tax.

overall expansionary effect of an increase in G. Consequently, with $c = 0.8$, a tax rate of $t = 0.3$ reduces the multiplier from 5 to 2.27. As shown in equation (18), increasing G by $1 billion now raises Y by only $2.27 billion. The built-in response of tax yield thus dampens the effectiveness of an expenditure increase.

Balanced-Budget Increase Having noted that an increase in expenditures is expansionary while a tax increase is restrictive, we must now consider a balanced budget change such that $\Delta G = \Delta T$. In this case, the gain in income equals $[1/(1-c)]\Delta G$, the expansionary effect of increased government purchases, while the decline in income equals $-[c/(1-c)]\Delta T$, the restrictive effect of ΔT. The combined effect is $[1/(1-c)]\Delta G - [c/(1-c)]\Delta G = \Delta G$. The level of income thus rises by just the increase in government purchases and the so-called balanced-budget multiplier may be said to equal 1.0. A balanced increase in the level of the budget operation has an expansionary effect, but on a one-to-one basis only. The enlarging effect of the multiplier is absent in this case.[5]

---

[5] More detailed analysis will show that this proposition holds only under simplifying assumptions. For instance, the balanced-budget multiplier will be above 1 if the marginal propensity to consume of taxpayers is below that of other income recipients.

B. MULTIPLIER MODELS WITH INVESTMENT VARIABLE

The next step toward a more realistic view of income determination is to make private investment I an endogenous variable, i.e., determined within the system rather than given from outside. Following the standard Keynesian model, income determination now involves three behavioral relationships: the consumption, investment, and liquidity preference functions.

Diagrammatic Presentation

Such a system is presented in Figure 30-5. The consumption function remains the same as in the preceding section, but it is convenient for purposes of this particular diagram to draw it in the form of a savings function, where $S = Y - C$. This is shown by SS in the southwest quadrant of the figure, where saving is measured horizontally and income is measured vertically.[6]

Income Determination   The investment function II shows investment as dependent upon the rate of return or interest. It is drawn in the northwest quadrant where the return i is measured vertically and the annual amount of investment expenditures is measured on the horizontal axis. The schedule II may be taken to reflect the marginal efficiency of investment as investment proceeds at various annual rates.

In the northeast quadrant of the figure, the liquidity preference function LL is shown, with the interest rate i measured on the vertical axis and the amount of money available for holding as an asset, M_a, measured on the horizontal axis. LL expresses the amount of money which people are willing to hold over and above transaction needs as an alternative to other assets, such as equity and bonds at various levels of interest. The higher the rate of interest or return from investment, the greater the opportunity cost of holding money balances and the less people will wish to hold. The schedule $M_a M_a$ in the southeast quadrant, finally, shows the amount of money which is available for such purposes at various levels of income and a given money supply M. This total M may be divided between M_t, or money needed for transaction purposes, and M_a, or money held as an asset to maintain liquidity in the portfolio. Since the need for transactions money M_t rises with the level of money income, the amount left over for M_a declines.

Given these relationships, the equilibrium level of income (here equal to OA) is such that the amount of saving forthcoming from that income, or OB, just equals the level of investment which is made at an interest rate OC. This interest rate, in turn, is such that people wish to hold an amount of asset money OD which just equals the amount available at income level OA and a given money supply M. As before, equilibrium income OA may fall short of what is needed to purchase the full-employment output at prevailing prices.[7] If this out-

---

[6] With the consumption function written as $C = a + cY$ and since $S = Y - C$, we have $S = (1 - c)Y - a$.

[7] Failure of the system to adjust to a full-employment level of income may be due to various reasons, including (1) an inelastic investment function, (2) a highly elastic liquidity preference function, or (3) failure of the II and SS schedules to intersect at a positive rate of interest. Another reason fre-

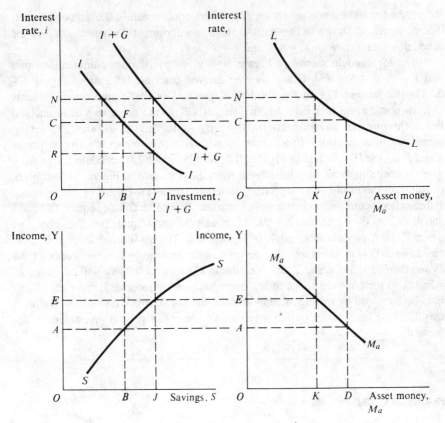

FIGURE 30-5   Income determination with investment endogenous.

put equals, for instance, OE, fiscal measures to raise output and income by an amount AE are called for.

We again introduce fiscal variables into the system to see how this can be done. Introduction of government purchases G equal to VJ, when added horizontally to the II schedule, gives us $I + G$ and permits a higher level of income. Savings rise to OJ and income to OE, while M_a falls to OK and the rate of interest rises to ON. The expansion in income in response to government purchases will now be less than it was in the absence of monetary variables. The reason is that the increased need for transactions funds M_t (due to a higher Y) reduces M_a, thus raising the interest rate i and depressing I. The transaction drain acts as a brake on expansion, as VB of private investment is "crowded out."

The IS-LM Version   The presentation of Figure 30-5 may be translated readily into the familiar *IS-LM* version, where points on *IS* reflect equilibrium in

quently cited is (4) downward rigidity of costs and prices which keep the price level from falling, thereby forestalling a possible upward shift in the consumption function which (provided a wealth term is added to the consumption function) might otherwise result as the real value of money balances rises.

the product market while points on *LM* reflect equilibrium in the money market. The economy, as shown in Figure 30-6, is in equilibrium at *Z* where the *IS* and *LM* schedules intersect, with $Y = OA$ and $i = OC$.

The *IS* schedule shown in Figure 30-6 gives equilibrium combinations of *i* and *Y* such that $S = I + G$ and may be derived from the left side of Figure 30-5. Thus at income *OA* in the southwest quadrant of that figure, saving equals *OB*. In equilibrium this calls for investment *OB* in the northwest quadrant and hence (leaving out government) for $i = OC$. At the higher income *OE*, saving equals *OJ*, thus requiring investment *OJ* with $I = ON$. We thus arrive at points *Z* and *H* on the *IS* schedule in Figure 30-6. Similarly, the *LM* schedule drawn for a given money supply $\overline{M}$ may be derived from the right side of Figure 30-5. It gives equilibrium values of *i* and *Y* such that the demand for and supply of M_a are equated. It thus reflects equilibrium in the money market. At income *OA*, M_a equals *OD* and *i* equals *OC*. At the higher income *OE*, M_a equals *OK* and *i* equals *ON*, thus giving us points *Z* and *K* on the *LM* schedule of Figure 30-6. The equilibrium level of income again equals *OA*, as in Figure 30-5, and is now determined by the intersection of the *IS* and the *LM* schedules at *Z*. An increase in *G* or *c* or a fall in *t* will cause the *IS* schedule to shift upward to the right, thereby increasing income. Income may similarly be increased by raising *M*, thus shifting the *LM* schedule down to the right. *Y* may likewise be reduced by the inverse adjustments as private investment is depressed.

FIGURE 30-6   *IS-LM* equilibrium.

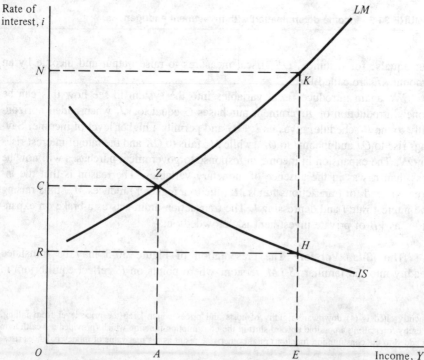

Algebraic Presentation

The matter may again be stated in algebraic form. Once more using linear functions and expanding the earlier model of Table 30-1, we now have:

$$Y = C + I + G \tag{19}$$

$$C = a + c(1 - t)Y \tag{20}$$

$$I = d - ei \tag{21}$$

$$M_a = f - hi \tag{22}$$

$$M_a = M - M_t \tag{23}$$

$$M_t = kY \tag{24}$$

Equations (19) and (20) are familiar from Table 30-1. Equation (21) is the investment function, showing I as a function of the rate of interest i. Equation (22) is the liquidity preference function, showing the demand for asset money M_a as a function of i. Equation (23) shows the total money supply M to be divided into transactions funds M_t and asset money M_a, while equation (24) defines M_t as a fraction of income. Together, equations (23) and (24) give the relationship between M_a and Y shown in the southeast quadrant of Figure 30-5. Given M, G, t and the parameters a, c, d, e, h, and k, the system determines the values of Y, C, I, i, M_a, and M_t.

By substitution, the system may again be reduced to multiplier formulas with income defined by

$$Y = \frac{1}{1 - c(1 - t) + ek/h}\left(a + d - \frac{ef}{h} + \frac{eM}{h} + G\right) \tag{25}$$

The change in income due to a change in government purchases G is then given by

$$\Delta Y = \frac{1}{1 - c(1 - t) + ek/h}\Delta G \tag{26}$$

We note that the multiplier in equation (26) is smaller than that in equation (18) of Table 30-1. A large k reduces the multiplier because it makes for a heavy transaction drain as income rises, leading to a fall in M_a, a rise in the interest rate, and hence a "crowding out" of private investment.

Money Multiplier with Fiscal Sector

By allowing for the role of money, the revised system also offers a further instrument of stabilization policy, i.e., changes in money supply, or ΔM. Returning to Figure 30-5, we see that an increase in M will shift the M_a schedule in the southeast quadrant to the right. At any given level of Y and transactions demand for money, there will now be more money available for asset holding. At income level OA, more M_a becomes available, so that the interest rate declines in line with the liquidity preference schedule LL. This in turn increases investment and hence the sustainable level of income, i.e., that level at which a correspondingly higher amount of saving is forthcoming.

Returning to equation (25), we may derive a "money multiplier" showing the increase in income with a given increase in money supply. We thus obtain

$$\Delta Y = \frac{e/h}{1 - c(1 - t) + ek/h}\Delta M \tag{27}$$

along with the expenditure multiplier given in equation (26). Monetary and fiscal measures thus offer alternative approaches to aggregate demand control.

As we will see in the next chapter, the role of money is, in fact, considerably broader than this model allows for. Changes in money supply not only enter via their effect on the rate of interest and investment but also affect consumption expenditures. Moreover, the role of money cannot be appreciated fully until changes in price level and expectations are allowed for.

Effectiveness

As follows from Figure 30-5, monetary policy is highly effective if the *LL* schedule in the northeast quadrant is inelastic. A small increase in money supply and upward shift of the m_a schedule then results in a sharp fall in the rate of interest. Moreover it is highly effective if the *I* schedule in the northwest quadrant is elastic, so that a small change in *i* results in a big change in *I*. On the other hand monetary policy is relatively ineffective if the *L* schedule is elastic while the *I* schedule is inelastic. This hypothesis, which was advanced in the Great Depression of the thirties, was a characteristic feature of early Keynesian economics. It is more likely to hold in a depressed than a buoyant economy. With regard to fiscal policy, the reverse conditions hold. A change in *G* is most effective if the transaction drain is small, the *LL* schedule is elastic, and the *I* schedule is inelastic, so that "crowding out" of private investment is of minor importance. These considerations again explain why the Keynesian approach to full-employment policy during the 1930s emphasized the fiscal instrument, because that period was characterized by an inelastic *I* and elastic *LL* schedule, while the 1960s and 1970s brought increased emphasis on monetary policy.

The same story may be told by reference to the *IS-LM* schedule of Figure 30-6. Expansionary monetary policy causes the *LM* schedule to shift to the right; and for any given increase in money supply, the gain in output (moving along the *IS* schedule) will be larger, the more elastic the *IS* schedule. Including *G* along with *I*, we may think of fiscal expansion as reflected in an upward shift of the *IS* schedule. The output gain will now be larger, the more elastic the *LM* schedule.

Finally, the argument may be put in terms of equations (26) and (27), where a high value of *e* and a low value of *h* (indicating an elastic *I* and an inelastic *L* schedule) are favorable to monetary policy, just as a high value of *h* and a low value of *e* are favorable to fiscal policy.

Policy Mix and Crowding Out

In practice, both policies may be used in combination, and the same level of aggregate demand may be secured by various mixes of fiscal and monetary expansion. But even though substitutes in the short run, the choice of mix is important in the longer-run context. Here the choice matters because it affects the division of output between C and I and hence the rate of capital formation and economic growth. Fiscal expansion is less favorable to investment than is monetary ease and is said to crowd out private investment.

The crowding-out effect of deficit finance has been in the forefront of discussion during recent years and thus deserves a further look. We have seen that a policy to increase government purchases G while holding tax revenue T constant will divert saving from private investment into the purchase of government bonds, bonds which must be issued to finance the deficit. But the resulting increase in income Y will also cause saving S to rise. With M constant, the *net* diversion thus equals $\Delta G - \Delta S$, as given by $VJ - BJ = VB$ in Figure 30-5. This result might be avoided if fiscal expansion were supported by an accommodating monetary policy so as to keep i from rising, thereby producing a mix of policy which holds I constant. However, even if crowding out occurs, this does not mean that there will be no rise in Y. It only means that the resulting increase in C will be offset in part by the decline in I.

C. STABILIZATION IN THE OPEN ECONOMY

So far we discussed various aspects of stabilization policy and the relation between fiscal and monetary approaches as seen in the context of a closed economy. But in fact most economies are intimately linked to the rest of the world, through both product and capital flows. This linkage has important implications for the conduct of stabilization policy, which must now be considered.

Multiplier Leakage

In an open economy, the effectiveness of fiscal policy is reduced substantially by the existence of trade "leakages." This is of particular importance for highly open economies such as Canada or the Netherlands and for developing countries which greatly depend upon trade. As recent years have painfully shown, trade repercussions also matter for less open systems such as that of the United States.

Fixed Exchange Rates   Under a system of fixed exchange rates, expansionary measures, by raising income, lead to increased imports. These increased imports divert purchases from domestic to foreign products, thus adding another leakage from the income-spending stream to that provided by domestic saving and thereby reducing the expansionary effect. With E for exports, M for imports, and m for expenditures on imported consumer goods as a fraction of consumption expenditures, c is again the marginal propensity to consume. Letting consumption C include expenditures on imports as well as on domestically produced goods and services, we may restate the model underlying equations (15) to (18) in Table 30-1 as follows:

$$Y = C + I + G + (E-M) \tag{28}$$
$$C = a + c(1 - t)Y \tag{29}$$
$$M = mC \tag{30}$$

$$Y = \frac{1}{1 - c(1 - t)(1 - m)}[a(1 - m) + I + G + E] \tag{31}$$

$$\Delta Y = \frac{1}{1 - c(1 - t)(1 - m)}\Delta G \tag{32}$$

Comparison of equation (32) with our earlier equation (18) shows that the multiplier has been reduced by import leakage. Thus it is more difficult for a country with large trade involvement to engage in a stabilization policy. The size of the multiplier is reduced and fiscal policy becomes less effective. Moreover, country A's expansionary policy, by raising imports, also increases the exports of its trading partner B. As a result, demand for B's output is increased and A's expansionary policy is transmitted to B. Similarly, restrictive action by A, by reducing its imports and hence B's exports, will have a restrictive effect in B. These effects may not suit B's policy intent, leading B to take countermeasures which in turn will weaken the domestic effectiveness of A's policy. Because of this interaction, it is difficult for countries with heavy trade involvement to single-handedly engage in effective stabilization policy.

Flexible Exchange Rates   In a world of fixed exchange rates, expansionary policy thus results in rising imports and a deficit in the balance of payments. If exchange rates are flexible, such an outcome need not occur. As U.S. imports rise, the supply of dollars in the foreign exchange markets rises and the value of the dollar in terms of foreign currencies falls. As a result, the prices of imported goods rise relative to those of domestic goods and will thus check the rise of imports. Moreover, exports will become cheaper to foreign buyers and will thus rise. The net effect depends on the elasticities involved, but exchange rate adjustments are not instantaneous, and the trade repercussions of fiscal policy remain a significant factor.

Capital Flows and the Fiscal-Monetary Mix

It remains to allow for the effects of stabilization policy on capital flows. International capital flows respond to interest-rate differentials and thus to the mix of fiscal and monetary policy.

An expansionary fiscal policy, unless combined with monetary expansion, will raise interest rates. By curtailing investment, the power of fiscal expansion is weakened. But rising interest rates will attract foreign capital, thereby easing rates and relieving pressure on investment. Such will be the case under a regime of fixed exchange rates. With rates variable, there will be a further sequence of effects. Increased capital inflow will raise the value of the dollar, thereby raising imports while cutting exports. By adding to the trade leakage, capital inflow now dampens the effectiveness of expansionary fiscal policy.

An expansionary monetary policy, in turn, will generate an opposite set of repercussions. A decline in interest rates will reduce capital inflow, interest rates will fall less, and the power of monetary expansion is weakened. With a system of flexible exchange rates, reduced capital inflow will lower the value of the dollar, thereby strengthening the effectiveness of monetary expansion. The international repercussions of stabilization policy thus have an important bearing on choosing the appropriate policy mix.[8]

D. INFLATION

The model of Figure 30-5, with its interacting mix of fiscal and monetary forces, was widely accepted in the 1960s and hailed as the neoclassical synthesis, incorporating both the monetarist and the Keynesian traditions. Both policies were accepted as offering effective tools. By choosing the proper mix between the two, the short-run objectives of stabilization could then be reconciled with the longer-run goals of economic growth. Beyond this, balance-of-payment considerations could be accommodated as well. Since then, the stagflation experience of the 1970s and the combination of large budget and trade deficits in the 1980s has tarnished this image and macro economics is in a process of reconsideration.

Types of Inflation

So far we have assumed that the price level remains constant, so that the impact of budgetary policy upon the level of aggregate demand was reflected in a corresponding change in output and employment. But such may not be the case. An increase in aggregate expenditures may come to be reflected in rising prices rather than in rising output. As the economy moves from a position of substantial unemployment and underutilization of capacity to one of "full employment," a further increase in the level of expenditures tends to be reflected more largely in rising prices, especially if the increase in demand is so rapid as to outrun the economy's ability to expand output. Stabilization policy must then seek to pursue a careful path so as to avoid inflation while overcoming unemployment. By the same token, a mistaken policy may become a cause of inflation. On the other hand, inflationary pressures may arise from sources other than those of stabilization policy. Stabilization policy is then called upon to curtail such inflation. These two aspects will be considered in turn.

Demand-Pull Inflation

Inflation based on demand pull may originate from either the budgetary or the private sector of the economy.

Budget Inflation   Consider first a setting in which budget policy may become a cause of inflation. Suppose that the economy is at a high level of employment and expenditures are to be increased. The government decides to absorb an increased share in output but does so without raising taxes. Aggregate demand is increased and inflation results.

To show how the inflation process proceeds, we return to our simplest model of income determination, which allows for consumption and government expenditures only, and which takes consumption to equal disposable income.[9] We now

---

[8] See also p. 540.
[9] See p. 502, equations (12) to (14).

restate the model in dynamic terms and identify the time periods in which expenditures are made or income is received. We begin with a situation of full-employment equilibrium, where the budget is balanced. We then assume that the government raises expenditures to increase its *share* in output and does so without raising its tax rate, with the additional outlays deficit-financed. We assume that the economy is in full employment to begin with, so that the entire increase in expenditures is reflected in rising prices. Rising prices in turn are reflected in rising wages, and the resulting inflation process is shown in Table 30-2.

The two policy variables are given in lines 1 and 2. They include the tax rate r and the government's share g in total expenditures. The reaction model is described in lines 3 to 7. For the two initial periods (columns I and II) the economy is in equilibrium. As shown in line 3, wage earnings available in period t or WA_t equal expenditures made and hence wages received in period $t - 1$ or WR_{t-1}. Monday's wages are paid out in the evening and become available for consumption Tuesday morning. As shown in line 4, they are reduced by the tax rate r so that consumption C_t equals $(1 - r)WA_t$. Line 5 shows the level of government spending, defined as g percent of total expenditures E_t. In line 6 we add up the two types of expenditures to obtain total expenditures E_t. These are received by business and (line 7) paid out as wages received, or WR_t. Substituting lines 3 to 5 into line 6, we have

$$WR_t = (1 - r)WR_{t-1} + gWR_t$$

so that $WR_t = WR_{t-1}$ or $g = r$. The government takes out of the income stream what it puts in; and with a private sector propensity to spend of 1, so do households. Total expenditures and income remain stable. In line 8 we measure the inflation rate or percentage change in the price level, $\dot{P}$. With constant output, $\dot{P}$ equals the percentage change in expenditures. Since E remains constant in periods I and II, $\dot{P} = 0$.

The disturbance arises in period III when g is raised to 30 percent. Period III expenditures exceed those of Period II (line 6) by 14.3 percent. Prices rise accord-

TABLE 30-2
Budget Inflation

ITEMS	TIME PERIODS							
	I	*II*	*III*	*IV*	*V*	*VI*	*VII*	*VIII*
Policy variables								
1. r, percentage	20	20	20	20	20	20	20	20
2. g, percentage	20	20	30	30	30	30	30	30
Model, in dollars								
3. $WA_t = WR_{t-1}$	100	100	100	114.3	130.6	149.3	170.6	195.6
4. $C_t = (1 - r)WA_t$	80	80	80	91.4	104.5	119.4	136.5	155.9
5. $G_t = gE_t$	20	20	34.3	39.4	44.8	51.2	58.5	66.8
6. $E_t = C_t + G_t$	100	100	114.3	130.6	149.3	170.6	195.6	222.8
7. $WR_t = E_t$	100	100	114.3	130.6	149.3	170.6	195.6	222.8
8. $\dot{P} = \dfrac{E_t - E_{t-1}}{E_{t-1}}$	0	0	0.143	0.143	0.143	0.143	0.143	0.143

ingly (line 8). C is unchanged in dollar terms but falls in real terms. WR rises since the increase in prices is translated at once into higher wage demands. WA in period IV is increased accordingly (line 3) with a similar rise in C. This offsets the increase in prices, thus preventing a further fall in the real value of C. Government, to maintain its share, must further raise G, and a further increase in E results. As shown in the numerical illustration, expenditures, incomes, and prices continue to rise at the same rate in each successive period.[10] The government imposes a continuing "inflation tax" of 14 percent, a tax which offsets the nominal rise in wages, with real wages constant from period IV on. To stop this inflation process, the government would have to reduce g to its original level of 20 percent, or raise r to 30 percent, thus shifting from an inflation tax to an outright tax. Given a progressive income tax, this development may come about automatically, thus making inflation self-terminating without further legislative action.[11]

Variation of Model   This particular outcome depends on the way in which our model was specified. Different specifications may yield different results:

1. We may change our assumptions regarding the underlying lag structure. While the model of Table 30-2 generates a constant rate of inflation, alternative and no less reasonable lag assumptions might be made which yield explosive, rising or falling rates of inflation.[12] Government expenditures may respond less rapidly to rising prices, as may wage adjustments. Wage lags depend on the length of union contracts. Shorter contracts may cause more rapid acceleration but also allow more rapid deceleration in the declining phase of inflation. Moreover, the relation of wage-rate adjustment to rising prices may take various forms. Our model has assumed such adjustments to be instantaneous, but they may lag. Adjustments may also relate to wage-price–level expectations, and these may not simply be a function of the past or of current rates of inflation. Anticipation of a rising rate of inflation may speed up the escalation process,

---

[10] Solving equations (3) to (6) of Table 30-2 for E_t we get

$$E_t = (1 - r)E_{t-1} + gE_t \qquad or \qquad E_t = \frac{1 - r}{1 - g}E_{t-1}$$

Hence

$$P_t = \frac{E_t - E_{t-1}}{E_{t-1}} = \frac{g - r}{1 - g}$$

With $t = 0.2$ and $g = 0.3$, we have $\dot{P}_t = 0.143$. As g rises or r falls, $\dot{P}$ increases.

[11] See p. 361.

[12] Suppose that consumer expenditures lag two periods, so that

$$E_t + (1 - t)E_{t-2} + gE_t$$

We then have

$$E_t = \frac{1 - r}{1 - g}E_{t-2}$$

With $g = r$ we again have a constant level of E. But as g rises to g', there now results an inflation cycle with the inflation rate fluctuating between 0 and $(g' - g)/(1 - g')$. Other assumptions regarding lags may be made which lead to a rising rate of inflation.

and so forth. Since the applicable lag structure for the various variables and the formation of expectations are empirical questions, pure theorizing about the dynamics of inflation becomes unproductive.

2. Table 30-2 shows only one among many possible budget changes. Instead of assuming that the government will raise its *share* or *g*, we might have assumed that it raised the absolute *level* of *G* from $20 to $40 and then held it at that absolute level. In that case, rising prices will squeeze out the initial gain as the value of *G* in real terms declines beginning in period IV. The inflation rate recedes from its initial level of 14.3 percent and drops to zero when *E* has reached $200 and prices have doubled. With *C* = $160 and *G* = $40, both have returned to their initial levels in real terms.[13]

3. It need hardly be added that the above illustration has been based on a minimal model of income determination. To obtain a fuller picture, a model such as that given in equations (1) to (8) earlier in this chapter would have to be put into dynamic terms. As expenditures rise ahead of tax revenues, the deficit widens and must be financed. This finance may be through borrowing from the banks, so that the money supply will rise along with the deficit. Indeed, such expansion is necessary if the inflation process is to be sustained. Unless the money supply increases at the rate of prices, money supply in real terms will decline, and this will act as a break on the level of expenditures. As the full system of income determination is allowed for, additional lags are introduced, involving the response of changes in *i* to changes in *M*, of changes in *I* to changes in *i*, of changes in *C* to changes in *Y*, and so forth. All this will affect the actual path of the inflation process, and it becomes even more difficult to generalize about the outcome.

Private Sector Inflation   The story of demand-pull inflation, as recounted here, began with a change in the expenditure share claimed by *government* outlays. Precisely the same development might occur with a shift in *private* sector demand, such as an increase in investment or an upward shift in the consumption function. Inflationary processes similar to those shown in Table 30-2 may result. Policy once more must choose between sustaining or restraining the resulting rise in prices.

Cost-Push Inflation

So far we have considered a situation where the disturbance begins with an increase in demand, public or private. The increase leads to a rise in prices, followed by an escalation of costs (wage rates) so as to keep up with rising prices. This case reflects the process of budget inflation set in motion by the excessive reliance on deficit finance during the Vietnam war of the late 1960s.

We now turn to a situation where the initial disturbance takes the form of an exogenous cost shock, such as that provided by rising oil prices in 1974 and 1980. This initial cost shock, if sustained by demand expansion, again leads to price rise and subsequent escalation into higher wages (needed to keep up with prices), generating once more a continuing inflation.

---

[13] As a further variant, we may assume that government raises *g* but postulate that wage rates remain fixed. We then experience a one-step inflation in period III with no further inflation thereafter. Period IV then shows *WA* = $100, *C* = 80, *G* = 34.3, *E* = 114.3, and *P* = 0. However, the price level has increased from 100 to 114.3 and real wages have declined accordingly. The same result follows if we combine an absolute increase in *G* with the fixed wage assumption, leaving the outcome similar to that of the preceding case.

TABLE 30-3
Cost-Push Inflation

				TIME PERIODS					
	EQUILIBRIUM		**DISTURBANCE**	**ADJUSTMENT TO SINGLE COST-PUSH**			**ADJUSTMENT TO ESCALATED COST-PUSH**		
	I	*II*	*III*	*IV*	*V*	∞	*IV*	*V*	∞
Earnings (in dollars)									
1. Wages	100	100	100	116.7	130.7	200	116.7	136.2	*
2. Oil	20	20	40	40	40	40	46.8	59.6	*
3. Total	120	120	140	156.7	170.7	240	163.5	190.8	*
Expenditures (in dollars)									
4. From previous earnings	120	120	120	140	156.7	240	140	163.5	*
5. Additional	—	—	20	16.7	14.0	—	23.4	26.3	*
6. Total	120	120	140	156.7	170.7	240	163.5	190.8	*
Price level									
7. Price index	100	100	116.7	130.6	142.2	200	136.3	159.0	*
8. Inflation rate	—	—	16.7	11.2	10.9	—	16.7	16.7	16.7

*Approaches infinity.

Such a process is shown in Table 30-3. Periods I and II again show the economy in an equilibrium position. Earnings are paid out in the form of wages (line 1) and royalties (line 2) to the owners of oil wells. Now suppose that in period III the suppliers of oil are able to raise their royalties from $20 to $40.[14] Expenditures out of period II earnings are still $120, but to buy the total output (costing $140) an additional $20 of expenditures are needed.

We assume that these are provided by government (line 5) in support of its full-employment policy. Total expenditures thus rise to $140 as shown in line 6. Assuming that full employment prevailed to begin with, we find this reflected in higher prices. As shown in line 7, the price index rises to 140/120 = 116.7 and the inflation rate (line 8) is 16.7 percent. With respect to the subsequent development, two patterns are distinguished.

We first show subsequent periods under the assumption that the increase in oil prices was a once and for all increase, with the new level held at $40 thereafter. As before, wages in period IV are increased in line with the inflation rate in period III, and so on. Inflation continues but, as shown in line 8, at a declining rate and eventually falls to zero. The initial gain in royalties is lost in the course of inflation until finally both wages and royalties have returned to their old levels in real terms. Inflation is thus a declining and finite process, but it takes time for the system to overcome the built-in "core inflation." This outcome corresponds to the preceding

[14] To simplify, we here disregard the fact that the increase in oil prices did occur abroad, thus adding the complications of foreign trade.

case of budget inflation, with government expenditures rising by a fixed amount rather than a share of GNP.

We next assume that the initial increase in royalties does not remain fixed in absolute terms but rises with inflation. As shown in the table, the system now generates a continuing inflation rate of 16.7 percent. This outcome is similar to that of the case of budget inflation given in Table 30-2, with government increasing its *share* in total expenditures. Once more the illustration might be varied by using different lag assumptions, but the above analysis will suffice to illustrate the nature of the cost-push inflation process.

Wage Cost Shock   In the preceding illustration we dealt with an initial cost shock which occurred independent of wage behavior. Wage behavior entered only through wage escalation in response to this initial shock. Such a wage response has an important role in our inflation process, but it is not the initial cause. Another situation might be considered in which the initial increase in cost takes the form of higher wage demands. Such was the case in 1971, when a round of wage increases stimulated inflation; but it was not the case with respect to the larger part of the inflationary seventies, when wage adjustments followed rather than led the inflation. Once the inflation process gets under way it is difficult to distinguish between these two roles of wage increase; yet the distinction is necessary to analyze the basic causes of the inflation process.

As is evident from these illustrations, stabilization policy conducted in the dynamic setting of the real world is more difficult than is suggested by a comparative statics view. An increase in taxes or reduction in spending may still serve to check the inflation process, but the resulting cost in terms of forgone output and unemployment will depend on how long a period is needed to subdue inflation. Moreover, policy effects now depend on the various response lags. Policy changes may become effective too late and when they are no longer needed, at which time they may be counterproductive.

Fiscal versus Monetary Restriction

Earlier in the chapter we examined how fiscal and monetary measures may be combined in generating economic expansion; a similar problem arises with regard to restrictive measures. Raising taxes and cutting current services of government comes to be reflected primarily in reduced private consumption, but monetary restriction will bear primarily upon private investment. Once more both tools may be traded off against each other and both are effective in curtailing demand. But an important aspect of the long-run outcome is reversed. With expansion, reliance on monetary measures was more favorable to capital formation and growth, whereas in the case of restriction, this goal calls for reliance on the fiscal approach.

E.   RATIONAL EXPECTATIONS

There are many reasons why the conduct of stabilization policy is a difficult task; more will be said about this later on. Nevertheless, macro analysis until recently has tended toward a fair degree of consensus concerning how policy should be conducted under these difficult conditions. The debate between the relative effectiveness of fiscal and of monetary policy in particular had led to a recognition that both tools can be effective and must be combined in proper proportions.

Do People Know Better?

More recently, an alternative model based on the assumption of "rational expectations" has been advanced. Offered as a challenge to the neoclassical, neo-Keynesian model of the fifties and sixties, this new approach arrives at a much more skeptical appraisal of what might be accomplished by stabilization policy.

To be sure, allowance for expectations is nothing new. They have always played a critical role in explaining the macro behavior of the economy. Expectations regarding changes in the rate of interest determine liquidity preference; expectations regarding changes in GNP enter into the accelerator theory of investment behavior; expectations regarding changes in the cost of living affect consumer behavior, wage demands, the escalation of inflation; and so forth. Indeed, in years past whole business cycle theories have been used on swings in optimism and pessimism of the business outlook. Concern with expectations is not new, but recent thought has stressed their role and placed it in a new perspective.[15]

Closer consideration is to be given to how expectations are formed. Changing expectations do not simply reflect business moods and "animal spirits," nor need they be based on linear extrapolation of past change. People know better, and expectations (like other economic behavior) are taken to be formed on a rational basis. This need not imply perfect foresight, but it means that all available information should be taken into account, including changes in government policy. Such changes are an important piece of information and a source of expectations. In assessing the effects of a policy change, one must allow for changes in expectations to which it gives rise and which will affect its outcome.

All this is eminently sensible. Systematic analysis of how expectations are formed is needed and the expectation effects of policy change should be allowed for. But the "rational expectation" model does not end here.[16] A combination of the role of rational expectations with a further assumption of wholly flexible prices produces a model that arrives at startling policy conclusions. One suggests that effective policy is impossible and another that certain differences among policies which seemed important do not in fact exist.

The Policy-Ineffectiveness Theorem

An economy with wholly flexible prices and wages tends to move toward a full-employment equilibrium. Unemployment will be at its "natural" level, consisting of people who are on job search or between jobs only. No policy will be needed to maintain full employment. If government announces its intent to increase money

---

[15] See Robert E. Lucas, Jr., "Expectations and the Neutrality of Money," *Journal of Economic Theory,* vol. 4–5, no. 2, 1972, pp. 103–124; and "Rules, Discretion and the Role of the Economic Advisor," in Stanley Fisher (ed.): *Rational Expectations and Economic Policy,* Chicago: University of Chicago Press and National Bureau of Economic Research, 1980, pp. 678–711.

[16] For a survey of the literature, see Robert J. Gordon, "Recent Developments in the Theory of Inflation and Unemployment," *Journal of Monetary Economics,* vol. 2, 1976.

supply at a certain rate, all economic agents will expect prices to rise at that rate. Prices and wages will move together, leaving the system unchanged in real terms— an instance of the previously noted case of an equilibrium rate of inflation at full employment.

In such an economy, all expected changes are promptly adjusted to and the system cannot move from its full-employment equilibrium unless an unexpected or "random" shock occurs. Suppose that money wages are pushed up for some reason by union demands. Producers have not anticipated this increase in cost and have not as yet raised prices. Labor costs rise in real terms and unemployment results. Can this be counteracted by expansionary policy? The answer depends on what happens to expectations. Suppose that all economic agents expect the government to take expansionary action, e.g., to increase money supply so as to sustain rising prices. They will then expect all prices and wages to rise. Labor costs in real terms will not change and the real variables of the system, including the level of employment, will not be affected by the policy action. Policy is ineffective. It is only if the policy action is not expected, and hence not anticipated by economic behavior, that policy can affect the system in real terms. But appropriate policy measures tend to be predictable measures, while random policies are not likely to be the correct ones. Hence the conclusion that appropriate policies cannot be effective.

This reasoning rests on the assumption (1) that policy changes are anticipated and (2) that such anticipations lead to immediate adjustments which occur without lags in the system. If anticipations are imperfect or if such lags occur, expansionary action may lead demand to rise ahead of costs, thereby raising employment. The impossibility theorem thus depends on the empirical validity of 1 and 2. Since perfect foresight does not exist and since stickiness and rigidities do in fact prevail[17] the theorem at best overstates its case. Although of interest in defining a model in which policy would be ineffective, the theorem is hardly a realistic appraisal of policy potentials. Given the real-world setting, stabilization policy, although difficult, can be effective. Indeed, anticipation of policy change together with credibility of policy announcement may well speed up policy results and strengthen policy effectiveness.

The "Ricardian Equivalence"

A second proposition of the rational expectations approach bears on the choice between tax and loan finance. In our earlier discussion, we have found that the two policies differ. A given increase in the level of government expenditures was shown to be more expansionary if loan-financed than if tax-financed. This was clearly the case in the initial model of Section A, where the level of investment was held fixed, but it remained so even in the subsequent model where investment was determined as an endogenous part of the system. The crowding-out effect on investment (assuming a constant money supply) was shown to reduce the expansionary effect of deficit finance, but still left it larger than that of tax finance.

[17] See Arthur Okun, *Prices and Quantities: A Macro Economic Analysis,* Washington, D.C.: Brookings, 1981.

The rational expectations approach questions this outcome. A rational individual, confronted with a deficit-financed increase in the budget, is aware that future taxes will have to be increased to finance interest charges on the additional debt. He or she will compute the present value of this increase in future taxes. After duly discounting this tax stream, he or she will find its present value to equal what he or she would have had to pay in the case of tax finance. Net worth is reduced equally in both cases. Therefore, tax and loan finance are equivalent in their economic effects—the rational consumer, being left in the same position in both cases, will react in the same way whichever method of finance is chosen.[18] There is no need, therefore, to agonize over this choice. Crowding out becomes a nonproblem, as does the issue of choosing the proper policy mix.

This proposition, referred to after the great classical economist David Ricardo as the "Ricardian Equivalence," once more appears to rest on rather unrealistic assumptions.[19] Consumers can hardly be expected to anticipate the future consequences of current loan finance. Lenders and taxpayers will not be the same people, future tax laws and their burden distribution are uncertain, and initial additions to interest service may also be loan-financed. Moreover, future debt may be devalued by inflation. All these factors make it very unlikely that individuals will respond equally to tax and loan finance, leaving no difference in policy effects on the level of aggregate demand or the division of output between consumption and investment. A case in point, the large deficits of the 1980s have been accompanied by a record low in the rate of personal saving rather than by a high rate as the rational expectation hypothesis would suggest.

F. SUMMARY

In order to examine the effects of fiscal policy upon the level of aggregate demand, we begin with a situation of substantial unemployment, where changes in overall expenditures are reflected in changes in real output rather than in prices.

1. Considering first a system in which the level of investment is given and in which there is no government, equilibrium income is determined at a level such that savings which people wish to undertake out of that income equal the given level of investment.

2. Introducing government expenditures and taxes into the system, various multiplier formulas were developed, showing that an increase in expenditures is expansionary, whereas a tax increase is restrictive.

3. Taxes (and in particular, the income tax), the revenue of which moves with income, generate automatic changes in revenue which reduce the multiplier and the expansionary effects of an increase in expenditures.

4. If allowance is made for differences in the marginal propensities to con-

[18] See Robert J. Barro, "Are Government Bonds Net Worth?" *Journal of Political Economy,* vol. 82, November–December 1974.

[19] The label may well be misplaced. While Ricardo concluded that the withdrawal of resources from the private sector reduces resources available to sustain the laboring population and that this would be the case under either tax or loan finance, he did not conclude that consumers would react equally to both types of finance. In fact, he argued that they would not consider future taxes a present burden. See Carl Shoup, *Ricardo on Taxation,* New York: Columbia University Press, 1960, p. 149 ff.

sume of various taxpayers, the expansionary effect of various tax changes will differ, depending on which taxes are adjusted.

The role of fiscal policy was then reconsidered in a setting where the level of investment is itself determined within the system.

    5. Fiscal multipliers were shown to be reduced by the monetary transaction drain, as private investment is "crowded out" by the resulting rise in interest rates.
    6. Changes in money supply were shown to offer a further instrument of stabilization policy.
    7. Monetary policy, by accommodating fiscal policy, may forestall the "crowding-out" effect.
    8. The effectiveness of monetary policy is enhanced by an elastic investment and inelastic liquidity preference schedule, whereas the opposite holds for the effectiveness of fiscal policy.

For the case of an open economy, the impact of stabilization policy on trade and capital movement has to be allowed for.

    9. The multiplier is reduced as rising imports result in a leakage.
    10. The consequences of fiscal expansion differ depending on whether exchange rates are fixed or variable.
    11. Additional considerations relating to capital movement are allowed for.

Departing from the assumption of price level stability, we next allow for inflation.

    12. A distinction is drawn between demand-pull and cost-push inflation.
    13. An excessively expansionary budget policy may result in demand-pull inflation, with the outcome depending on budget behavior and on the lag structure of the system.
    14. A similar analysis was applied to cost-push inflation.
    15. The fiscal-monetary mix was reconsidered for an inflationary setting.

As an alternative approach to the neoclassical synthesis, the rational expectation model is noted.

    16. The key role of the assumption of rational expectations is examined.
    17. The resulting theorem of policy ineffectiveness is noted.
    18. Consideration is given to the Ricardian Equivalence proposition.

FURTHER READINGS

For a more detailed analysis of the underlying models of macro theory, see middle-level texts such as R. Dornbusch and S. Fisher, *Macro Economics,* 4d ed., New York: McGraw-Hill, 1987.

Chapter 31

Further Issues in Fiscal Policy*

A. Built-in Flexibility: *Parameter Change versus Built-in Response; Measuring Changes in Fiscal Leverage; Flexibility of Major Taxes; Is Built-in Flexibility Desirable?* **B. Timing of Fiscal Effects:** *Multiplier Time Path; Accelerator; Timing of Multiplier Effects in Econometric Models; Rules versus Discretionary Policy.* **C. Tax versus Expenditure Changes. D. Capital Formation in the Public Sector:** *Public Saving and the Concept of Budget Balance; Capital and Current Budget; Investment Propensities of Public and Private Sectors; Spillover Effects.* **E. Fiscal Policy Experience:** *The Early Years; The Seventies; The Eighties; Conclusion.* **F. Summary.**

In the preceding chapter, the effect of fiscal policy was viewed in a setting of comparative statics, where the equilibrium position of the economy prior to the policy change was compared with its equilibrium position after the change. This comparison helps to bring out the major factors involved but it also oversimplifies matters. Economic change involves a dynamic process, and so do the effects of fiscal policy.

*Reader's Guide to Chapter 31: This chapter proceeds beyond the general role of the public sector in the macro economic setting and turns to certain issues particular to the fiscal role. These relate especially to its dynamic setting, including the built-in flexibility of the fiscal system and the time path of general policy effects. In addition, consideration is given to the role of the public sector in capital formation, including that of a dual current and capital budget system.

A. BUILT-IN FLEXIBILITY

A first aspect to be noted is the role of built-in flexibility. When observing changes in fiscal variables, we must make an important distinction between (1) changes in G and T which reflect changes in expenditure programs or tax rates, i.e., changes in "fiscal parameters," and (2) changes in G and T which are due to built-in flexibility, i.e., automatic responses to changes in the private sector. Changes in the level of income Y, resulting from a private sector change such as a change in investment I, will depend on these responses in G and T. As we will presently see, the distinction between parameter changes and built-in changes is important in interpreting changes in the budget picture during any given period.

Parameter Change versus Built-in Response

On the expenditure side, an expansionary *parameter* change, also referred to as a "discretionary" change, is illustrated by the introduction of a new expenditure program or the expansion of an old program. Thus, a new public works program may be instituted or the weekly benefit level of unemployment insurance may be raised. On the revenue side, a parameter change may involve the removal of an old tax or a reduction in tax rates. Corresponding illustrations of restrictive parameter changes include discontinuation of expenditure programs or increases in tax rates. As distinct from these adjustments, a *built-in* change on the expenditure side is illustrated by a change in the level of benefit payments due to a rise in the number of unemployed or a change in farm prices.

When built-in expenditure changes occur, such responses are of primary importance on the revenue side where tax yield changes automatically with changes in the tax base. Thus, income tax revenue rises or falls (at given levels of tax rates) with changes in personal income; profits tax revenue rises or falls with changes in corporation profits, and so forth.

Another way of putting the matter is that parameter changes are "exogenous" to the system of income determination, since they change the fiscal variables such as the level of purchases G or tax rates t in the system of expenditure equations by which income is determined. They are thus an initiating source of change in the overall level of expenditures or demand. Built-in changes on the other hand are "endogenous." They do not initiate changes in the economy, but because of their existence the system will respond differently to a change in, say, the level of investment than it would in their absence. Fiscal parameters are not part of the automatic response. They are exogenous and call forth a response by the system.

Measuring Changes in Fiscal Leverage

The level of deficit may change because of changes in fiscal parameters or changed responses to existing parameters. In order to determine in which direction fiscal policy has moved, it is thus necessary to separate the former from the latter. The effects of parameter changes in G or t are measured with reference to the resulting change in deficit or surplus at a *given level* of income. Thus leverage would be unaffected by fiscal responses to other changes in the economy. The reference level of income, moreover, is taken to be that which corresponds to "full" or "high"

employment. In short, changes in leverage are measured by changes in full employment surplus or deficit.

Automatic versus Discretionary Change The distinction between automatic and discretionary change is illustrated in Figure 31-1. Consider a situation
where government purchases, or G, as measured on the vertical axis, equal OM.
As shown by line MM', purchases are independent of the level of Y, as measured
on the horizontal axis. TT shows tax revenue T as a function of income, reflecting
a given tax rate t. As Y rises, so does T. Let the initial level of income be at Y_1 so
that both G and T equal OM and the budget is in balance. Now suppose that investment declines because expectations drop. As a result, income falls to, say, Y_2.
Revenue drops and the budget now runs a deficit of AB. This has come about without any change in fiscal parameters G and t. It merely reflects the decline in income
as caused by the drop in investment. Since fiscal parameters have not been
changed, it may be said that fiscal policy has been passive. But this does not mean
that the fiscal system has played no role. Had the initial level of $T = OM$ been
drawn from a lump-sum tax, the decline in income would have left the budget in
balance. But the decline would have been larger. The built-in fall in revenue has
acted as a cushion, retarding the decline in income by permitting the deficit to occur. This is the typical pattern when the economy goes into a recession and the
budget shows an increasing deficit or declining surplus.

Consider now a different story. Beginning again with income Y_1, expenditures
OM, and a balanced budget, we now assume that there are no changes in the private sector but that G is increased to ON. As a result, income rises from Y_1 to, say,
Y_3. T also rises, but by less than G. The budget again shows a deficit now equal to
RD. With $RD = AB$, we have the same budgetary outcome as in the previous case,
but the underlying circumstances are very different. In the first case, the observed
change from balance to deficit emerged as a consequence of the downturn, while in
the second it came about as a consequence of expansionary fiscal action. With Y_f
depicting the full-employment level of income, and $G = OM$, our starting position

FIGURE 31-1 Automatic versus discretionary budget change.

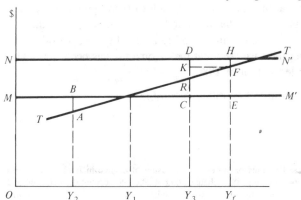

involved a full-employment surplus of EF. The first experiment, with income falling from Y_1 to Y_2, did not change this situation, with the full-employment surplus remaining at EF. But the second experiment, with income rising to Y_3, changed the full-employment surplus into a deficit of HF.[1]

Structural versus Cyclical Deficit In line with Figure 31-1, two concepts of deficit may be distinguished. One refers to the deficit which would prevail if income were at full employment, with a corresponding level of full-employment revenue being obtained. The other refers to the excess of the actual over the full-employment deficit and reflects current economic conditions. The former might be referred to as structural and the latter as cyclical. Thus, if Y_3 is the actual level of income and G equals ON, the actual deficit will be RD, the structural deficit will be $FH = KD$, and the cyclical deficit will be RK. Similar considerations apply when comparing an actual with a full-employment surplus.

Flexibility of Major Taxes

The automatic flexibility of proportional rate taxes is determined simply by the responsiveness of the tax base to changes in GNP. The built-in elasticity of revenue equals the elasticity of the tax base. For taxes with progressive rates, an additional factor enters—the responsiveness of the average tax rate (or ratio of revenue to base) to changes in the tax base. In combination these two factors (the GNP elasticity of the tax base and the base elasticity of the tax rate) make for substantial differences in the revenue elasticity of various taxes.

If we look at built-in flexibility over the business cycle, the corporation profits tax ranks highest, because the base fluctuates more sharply than does GNP. Personal income and sales on the other hand fluctuate in line with GNP or at a somewhat lower level, so that their elasticity tends to be close to or below unity. The property tax, with assessments lagging, tends to have a very low elasticity. Note, however, that built-in flexibility exists provided that the elasticity is positive. The requirement is not that it be in excess of 1.

Over the longer run, proportional-rate taxes tend to have an elasticity coefficient of about 1, because factor shares and output components do not greatly change. The personal income tax, owing to its progressive rate structure, however, has a higher elasticity. As real incomes rise as a result of rising productivity, people move into higher rate brackets so that revenue increases more rapidly than the base. In the past a similar gain in built-in flexibility resulted during periods of inflation, but this is no longer the case now that the income tax has been thoroughly indexed by the tax-reform legislation of 1986.[2]

Is Built-in Flexibility Desirable?

Depending on the circumstances, built-in flexibility may be helpful or harmful to economic stability.

---

[1] Changes in full-employment surplus or deficit as a measure of change in fiscal leverage are helpful but not a perfect index. For one thing, such changes do not take into account the balanced budget multiplier. For another, they do not distinguish between change in real terms and changes in price level only.

[2] See p. 361.

Short-Run Aspects   Built-in flexibility is helpful in that it cushions the amplitude of fluctuations in economic activity. Thus the need for discretionary measures or changes in fiscal parameters is reduced. If the level of expenditures in the private sector falls off and a recession sets in, the decline is dampened automatically. Built-in flexibility is also desirable in an economy which exhibits an inflationary bias, although this potential advantage, as just noted, has been greatly reduced by indexing the income tax. By the same token, however, the built-in response becomes perverse and undesirable if we begin with a position of unemployment. Automatic response now interferes with recovery to full employment and hence increases the burden on discretionary action. Indeed, the magnitude of the required action (e.g., of an increase in government expenditures) is increased because the built-in response dampens the leverage exerted by a given change.[3]

Longer-Run Aspects: Fiscal Drag and Dividend   Turning now to the longer-run aspects of built-in response in a growing economy, we find that the need for discretionary action is increased rather than reduced. Given a passive policy which holds tax rates and expenditure programs unchanged, a built-in increase in revenue leads to a rising surplus at a full-employment level of income, thereby exerting a drag on the economy. The slowdown of the economy in the late 1950s and early 1960s was attributed to this development. A do-nothing policy, which leaves expenditure levels and tax rates unchanged, is in fact a policy of restriction as the economy grows. For policy to be neutral in a growing economy, expansion of demand is needed.

Economic growth may thus be said to yield a fiscal dividend, a concept which played a key role in the "New Economics" of the sixties.[4] This dividend may be used to reduce tax rates, or it may be used to expand public services without having to raise rates. The latter is a tempting option for the administration in office and may lead to the adoption of programs which would not have stood the test of having to meet the additional cost through increased taxation. Moreover, the burden distribution of built-in revenue growth may well differ from that which would have applied with explicit tax adjustments. Built-in revenue growth, therefore, is not an unmitigated blessing.

B.   TIMING OF FISCAL EFFECTS

So far we have traced the effects of fiscal changes upon the level of income by comparing the initial (prechange) level of income with the final (postchange) level. This method of "comparative statics" offers a convenient framework in which to analyze the variables involved, but the actual adjustment process takes time and

---

[3] If the desired income change equals ΔY, we have

$$\Delta Y = \frac{1}{1-c}\,\Delta G = \frac{1}{1-c(1-t)}\,\Delta G' \quad \text{and} \quad \Delta G' = \frac{1-c(1-t)}{1-c}\,\Delta G$$

where ΔG is the required change in G without built-in flexibility, and $\Delta G'$ the required change in G with built-in flexibility. Thus $\Delta G' > \Delta G$ for any positive tax rate t.

[4] See Walter Heller, *New Dimensions of Political Economy*, New York: Norton, 1967.

policy is concerned with how long it takes. If the desired effects come about too slowly, economic conditions may have changed in the meantime and the initial policy may no longer be appropriate. Moreover, depending on lags in the responses of consumers and firms, a fiscal change may give rise to continuous movement rather than lead to a new equilibrium position. In short, analysis of the comparative statics type is useful to bring out certain relationships, but it does not provide a realistic model on which to base actual policy.

Multiplier Time Path

To illustrate the time path of adjustment, we return to the simplest multiplier model of equations (4) to (7) in Table 30-1. In equation (7), we saw that an increase in the annual rate of government purchases ΔG raises equilibrium income by $[1/(1 - c)]\Delta G$. Letting consumption in any one period be a function of income received in the preceding period,[5] we may trace the emergence of this result over successive periods:

Period	Increase in Income above Initial Level
1	ΔG
2	$\Delta G + c\Delta G = (1 + c)\Delta G$
3	$\Delta G + c\Delta G + c^2\Delta G = (1 + c + c^2)\Delta G$
n	$\Delta G + c\Delta G + c^2\Delta G + \ldots + c^{n-1}\Delta G$
	As n increases, this expression approaches
	$\dfrac{1}{1 - c}\Delta G$

In period 1, income rises by ΔG only, since consumers have not as yet had time to respend their additional income. In period 2, such respending occurs and adds $c\Delta G$ to the initial increase. In period 3, the additional income received by persons from respending during the second period is also subject to respending so that a further amount equal to $c \cdot c\Delta G = c^2\Delta G$ is added and so forth. Note that the addition becomes less and less as only a fraction c of the additional earnings is respent with $(1 - c)$ being saved, thereby becoming a "leakage" from the income stream. Finally, the addition approaches zero and the total gains approach $[1/(1 - c)]\Delta G$, as previously shown. In other words, the level of income rises each period as a lengthening chain of respendings from past periods adds to earnings. But as time proceeds, the spillovers from earlier periods peter out and a higher

---

[5] The income determination system may now be rewritten with time subscripts so that (in the absence of taxes)

$$C_t = a + cY_{t-1}$$
$$Y_t = a + cY_{t-1} + I_t + G_t$$

In equilibrium,

$$Y_t = Y_{t-1}$$
$$Y = \frac{1}{1 - c}(a + I + G)$$

level of equilibrium income is reached and maintained, provided, of course, that G continues at its increased annual rate.

Policy makers must know how long this multiplier process takes or what fraction of the total gain is realized within, say, a six- or twelve-month period, which depends on the length of the time lags involved. In our simplified model, the only lag considered is that between income receipt and consumption expenditure by the household. In a more complete model, a variety of lags enter, including the lag between receipts and payments by the firm, drawing down and replacing inventory, and so forth. As we will see presently, the adjustment turns out to be fairly rapid, with a substantial part of the total increase achieved in the first year.

Accelerator

The dynamic nature of the adjustment process was first brought out in connection with the investment function.[6] Whereas in the preceding section investment was shown as a function of the rate of interest, empirical observation has led many observers to depict investment as a function of past changes in income. This is the so-called accelerator type of investment function with investment defined as

$$I_t = b + \beta(Y_{t-1} - Y_{t-2})$$

where t is the time subscript. One interpretation of this formulation views β as a technical coefficient. An increase in GNP or Y calls for increased capacity to produce it, which requires investment.[7] Another interpretation views β as reflecting expectations. Investors take the rise in GNP from one year to the next as an indication of future markets and profit prospects and respond accordingly. Adding this accelerator type of investment function to equations (4) and (5) in Table 30-1, we obtain a dynamic system of income change.[8] Not only does an increase in government purchases result in a rise in income due to the operation of the multiplier effects (as derived from the consumption function), but such income increase generates further changes in investment which in turn are subject to the multiplier, giving rise to new consumption and income changes, and so forth. Depending on the values of the marginal propensity to consume and of the accelerator coefficient β, relating investment to income change, the system will move toward a new equilibrium, follow a steady cyclical pattern, or be explosive.

The lag structure is crucial for the behavior of income as determined by this

---

[6] This relationship was first analyzed by Paul A. Samuelson, "Interactions between the Multiplier Analysis and the Principle of Acceleration," *Review of Economics and Statistics,* May 1939.

[7] The need for expansion depends upon the size of the existing capital stock and its degree of utilization. Thus a term measuring capacity utilization is frequently added to the investment function.

[8] The model of income determination now reads

$$Y_t = a + cY_{t-1} + b + \beta(Y_{t-1} - Y_{t-2}) + G_t$$

Depending on the magnitudes of c and β, the accelerator coefficient, the system when disturbed by an increase in G will return to a stable equilibrium, generate a continuing wavelike movement, or become explosive. With $c < 1$ and a small value of β, a change in G produces a fluctuation which tapers off, leading to a new equilibrium level of Y. This is most in line with what actual behavior of the real economy suggests.

model, and there is no theoretical intuition which tells us just what it should be. Consequently, theorizing becomes difficult once the dynamic nature of the system is allowed for, and empirical evidence must take over. However, observation tells us that the macroeconomic behavior of the economy is not explosive. Built-in stabilizers exist and income changes tend to level off.

Timing of Multiplier Effects in Econometric Models

To estimate the actual time path of the multiplier effect, an econometric model is needed. A change in policy variable may be introduced into such a model and the effects of these changes may be traced over subsequent periods. Such a simulation for the Department of Commerce quarterly econometric model is shown in Table 31-1.

Column I of the table shows the resulting change in GNP as a multiple of the assumed increase in the annual rate of government purchases, with the higher level maintained thereafter. We note that the multiplier reaches about two-thirds of its peak within three quarters and peaks at the end of the second year. Thereafter fluctuations result, reflecting the complex lag structures and interactions of the model. The tax reduction multipliers are somewhat smaller and rise more slowly, whereas the multiplier based on change in money supply responds with a longer lag. These particular multipliers, it should be noted, relate to changes in *nominal* GNP and thus reflect changes in real output as well as in prices, a matter to be examined in detail in the next chapter. The lower is the initial level of unemployment, the lower will be the output and the larger will be the price component in the resulting change

TABLE 31-1
Magnitude and Time Path of GNP Multiplier,
Bureau of Economic Analysis Quarterly Econometric Model*

	SIZE OF MULTIPLIER			
Quarter Following Change	Government Purchases (I)	Personal Taxes (II)	Corporation Profits Tax (III)	Nonborrowed Reserves (IV)
1	1.0	0.3	0.2	0.3
2	1.7	0.6	0.4	0.9
3	2.1	0.8	0.6	1.8
4	2.4	0.9	0.7	2.7
5	2.6	1.1	0.7	3.2
8	3.1	1.4	1.0	4.3
12	3.0	1.7	1.4	5.7
16	2.4	1.5	1.3	5.3
20	2.5	1.7	1.4	5.3

*Column I assumes $5 billion increase in government purchases other than payments to employees. Column II assumes a $5 billion reduction in income tax revenue, sustained at that level thereafter. Column III assumes the same for corporation tax. Column IV assumes a $5 billion change in nonborrowed reserves. Simulations are based on quarterly data for 1971–1975 period. The multiplier coefficients show the resulting increase in nominal GNP reached in the various quarters as a multiple of the postulated increase in government purchases, decrease in tax revenue, or increase in money supply.

Source: See U.S. Department of Commerce, *Survey of Current Business,* June 1977, p. 64.

in nominal GNP. Moreover, these particular multiplier values reflect the economic conditions of the base period (here 1971–1975) over which the results were simulated. Nevertheless, most analyses assume a multiplier of from 2 to 2.5, with full effectiveness largely reached by the end of one year.

Rules versus Discretionary Policy

For policy to be effective, time lags must be allowed for. Not only does it take time to establish that a policy change is needed, but time also passes before policy changes once made become effective. A policy change that seems appropriate when undertaken may thus be outdated when it becomes effective. Ability to look ahead and to project economic conditions becomes of crucial importance. Progress has been made along these lines, but predicting economic events still remains a matter of conjecture.

Consequently, it is evident that stabilization policy is a difficult task and that a perfect solution cannot be achieved. As a result it has been suggested that policy rules be established and then be followed independent of conditions. With regard to fiscal policy in particular, it has been argued that the budget should be set so as to balance at a full or high level of employment and then be left alone, with further reliance limited to built-in changes. Discretionary changes would then be in terms of monetary policy only. While such changes can be implemented more rapidly than can changes in tax rates or expenditure levels, the time period which elapses between policy action and its effectiveness may be even longer. Moreover, the longer-run impact of the two approaches on economic growth will differ. Stabilization policy can therefore hardly afford to forgo the use of fiscal measures, and especially not when it comes to major swings in economic conditions.

C. TAX VERSUS EXPENDITURE CHANGES

Consideration has been given at various points to the appropriate mix of fiscal and of monetary tools in the conduct of stabilization. We now turn to the further question of how the fiscal contribution should be divided between tax and expenditure adjustments. The logic of our discussion in Chapter 1 suggested that the most appropriate instrument for implementing the stabilization function was provided by increases or reductions in the level of taxation. As was noted there, fiscal policy should be conducted so as to satisfy potentially conflicting policy objectives. Efficient expenditure policy or resource allocation among private and public uses was to be based on a full-employment level of output while leaving it to the stabilization branch—acting through tax and transfer measures—to ensure that this level of output is provided. In the case of recession, this procedure will obviate calling for additional expenditures to generate a higher level of employment, if such use of resources would be undesirable at full employment. Under inflationary conditions, it will avoid cutbacks in programs merely to restrain demand. Although the public sector should contribute its share when expansion or restraint in the total level of expenditures is needed, there is no good reason why the entire adjustment should be in that sector. Priority therefore goes to the tax-adjustment route.

Pairing the tax instrument with the stabilization and the expenditure instrument with the allocation target has much merit in principle but must be qualified in practice. The cyclical sensitivity of various industries differs and the level of unemployment varies regionally. Use of expenditure policy may be desirable because it can be focused locally where unemployment exists rather than diffused nationally, as is done with tax reduction. Another reason is that tax reduction, by its very nature, can benefit those who receive income but not the unemployed who are subject to tax. Such at least is so in the absence of a negative income tax or separate transfer programs. There is something to be said for action on both fronts, although, in principle, tax rate and transfer adjustments should be given priority over changes in purchase programs.

D. CAPITAL FORMATION IN THE PUBLIC SECTOR

The effects of fiscal operations on the level of saving and investment in the private sector have been examined in the preceding chapter. What remains to consider is the role of saving and investment by the public sector and its contribution to economic growth.

Public Saving and the Concept of Budget Balance

Two concepts of public saving are distinguished. The appropriateness of one or the other depends on the nature of the economy in which the budget operates.

Saving and the Level of Employment In the preceding discussion of stabilization policy, we viewed saving as a factor which enters into determining the actual level of income and employment. We argued that for income to be at its equilibrium level, saving must be equal to the planned level of investment. If investment falls short of what people wish to save at a full-employment level of income, then income will fall short of what is needed to maintain full employment and capacity utilization. In such a context, government saving is defined as the excess of tax revenue over expenditures. Positive government saving or a budget surplus reflects a withdrawal from aggregate demand and is thus restrictive, just as negative government saving or a deficit reflects an addition to aggregate demand and hence is expansionary. The state of budgetary balance B as given by

$$T - G = B \qquad\qquad (1)$$

thus measures the multiplicand, the amount which, after being subject to the multiplier, offers a crude measure of budgetary leverage, i.e., the effect of the budget (positive if B is negative and negative if B is positive) on the level of GNP.

This concept may then be refined by distinguishing between taxes which fall on consumption and taxes which fall on saving. In the simplest Keynesian model, where investment is held fixed, taxes which fall on saving do not reduce the level of expenditure. Therefore, equation (1) may be rewritten as

$$T_c - G = B \qquad\qquad (2)$$

where T_c stands for taxes which are reflected in reduced consumption.

Saving and the Level of Capacity Output   The role of saving, public or private, differs as we consider an economy which automatically operates at full employment, i.e., where private investment always adjusts to the full-employment level of saving as previously defined. In this case, the level of budget deficit or surplus does not affect the level of employment, because income is always at full employment. It does, however, affect the way in which output is divided between consumption and capital formation.

To focus on this aspect, the concept of government saving may now be redefined as its contribution to capital formation rather than as withdrawal from aggregate demand. This is the role of government saving in a classical model of income determination, as opposed to the Keynesian model underlying the previous paragraph.[9] Whereas the assumption of automatic adjustment to full employment is unrealistic in the short run, this assumption is usually made when it comes to consider the longer-run effects of budget policy upon capacity output and growth.

In such a system, all private savings are invested. Therefore, all government receipts—whether in the form of taxes or borrowing—must be reflected in reduced private spending, whether on consumption or investment. A dollar of tax or loan receipts alike reduces private spending by $1.[10] Government finance, therefore, does not affect the level of aggregate demand. But it will affect the division between consumption and investment.

Suppose that taxes are paid out of income which is otherwise consumed, while loans are drawn from savings which are otherwise directed into private investment. We may then reinterpret the budgetary balance B as measuring the budget's contribution to saving (if $T > G$) or reduction therein (if $T < G$). The budget surplus when used to retire debt increases the funds available for private investment and thus adds to private saving. The opposite holds in the case of deficit, where private saving is diverted into public debt.

Once more, careful consideration would call for a distinction between taxes which fall on consumption and those which fall on saving. The budgetary contribution to saving should then be defined in terms of equation (2) rather than equation (1). Moreover, the assumption that all borrowing goes to reduce saving is too extreme. Loan finance may displace consumption as well as saving. As bonds are issued, the rate of interest is driven up and saving may increase.[11]

---

[9] The terms classical and Keynesian are here used to describe extreme positions. In between there is the neoclassical model which calls for stabilization policy to intervene but assumes that aggregate demand control, by varying the mix of fiscal and monetary policy, permits compliance with both full employment and growth targets.

[10] The underlying assumption is that borrowing is from the public, so as to reduce loanable funds available to private investors. If government expenditures are financed by money creation, the argument does not hold and loan finance becomes inflationary.

[11] Assuming a uniform propensity to save, we may demonstrate this as follows: With full-employment income given at Y_f, the composition of output is given by the system

$$S = a + s(Y_f - T) + bi$$
$$I = d - ei$$
$$I + G = S + T$$

where S = private saving

T = tax revenue

I = private investment

Nevertheless, it is a reasonable first approximation to assume that taxes are drawn largely from private consumption while loan finance draws largely on saving. Tax finance (whether public expenditures are for consumption or capital items) is thus more favorable to economic growth than is loan finance. This conclusion is of considerable importance for development policy, provided again that aggregate demand is sufficient to secure the full utilization of all resources whether in the production of consumer or investment goods.

Allowance for Public Investment   The view of budget surplus as an addition to saving and private capital formation may now be extended to allow for public capital formation. If our concern is with the effects of the budget on economic growth, what matters is the budgetary contribution to total capital formation, public as well as private. Taxes used to finance public capital formation therefore will not be a charge against total capital formation. We may thus rewrite equation (2) as

$$T - G_c = B \tag{3}$$

where G_c stands for government expenditures of the consumption type.

Capital and Current Budget

The various concepts of public saving thus call for different definitions of budgetary balance. If the budget surplus is to measure public saving in the sense of reduction in aggregate demand, the surplus should be defined as the excess of tax revenue over total expenditures, and the same definition holds with a different interpretation, if it is designed to record availability of resources for private capital formation. But if focus is to be on total capital formation, the surplus should be defined as excess of tax revenue over government expenditures for current con-

G = government purchases
i = interest rate

Private investment I adjusts itself to match public saving (or $T - G$) plus private saving S out of full-employment income Y_f.

For the case of tax finance, $\Delta G = \Delta T$ and

$$\frac{dI}{dT} = -\frac{s}{1 + b/e}$$

We find that the investment-depressing effect of tax finance is positively related to the propensity to save, s, because a large s means that a large part of tax revenue comes out of saving. We also note that the investment-depressing effect is large if b is small. A small b means that the positive response of saving to an increase in the interest rate (induced in turn by the decline in investment) is weak. Finally, the resulting decline in investment will be greater if e is larger, since a large e indicates a heavy negative response of I to a rise in the interest rate.

For the case of loan finance, we have $\Delta G = \Delta L$, where $\Delta L = \Delta G - \Delta T$ and

$$\frac{dI}{dL} = -\frac{1}{1 + b/e}$$

Investment-depressing effects again vary directly with e and inversely with b, but s now does not enter. The investment-reducing effect of tax finance thus equals s times that of loan finance. If $b = 0$, the entire loan finance is reflected in reduced private investment.

TABLE 31-2
Estimated Capital Budget for Fiscal Year 1987
(In Billions of Dollars)

I. DEFENSE STRUCTURES AND EQUIPMENT COUNTED AS INVESTMENT

Total budget			
Budget expenditures	1,016	Receipts	842
Depreciation: Nondefense	20	Deficit	254
Defense	60		
Total	1,096		1,096
Current budget			
Current expenditures	796	Revenue	842
Depreciation	80	Current budget deficit	34
Total	876		876
Capital budget			
Capital Expenditures:			
Nondefense	94	Capital budget deficit	220
Defense	126		
Total	220		220

II. DEFENSE INVESTMENT COUNTED AS CONSUMPTION

Total budget			
Budget expenditures	1,016	Revenue	842
Depreciation	80	Deficit	254
Total	1,096		1,096
Current budget			
Current expenditures	922	Revenue	842
Depreciation	60	Current budget deficit	140
Total	982		982
Capital budget			
Capital expenditures: Nondefense	94	Capital budget deficit	94
Total	94		94

Sources: For total expenditures and receipts, see *Budget of the United States Government*, Fiscal Year 1987, p. M-4. For capital expenditures, see *Special Analyses, Budget of the United States Government*, Fiscal Year 1987, p. D-3. Off-budget items are excluded. Figures for depreciation are authors' estimates.

sumption only. In the latter case, the budget may be divided into a current and capital budget, with the surplus in the current budget recording the government's contribution to saving and the latter balanced by definition.

An attempt is made in Table 31-2 to determine how such a budget would look for fiscal 1987. In part I of the table, the acquisition of military equipment and structures is counted as capital formation. We begin with the total budget but add an allowance for depreciation to the overall level of expenditures as reported in the budget. The deficit thus exceeds the conventional deficit which is reported on a cash outlay and receipt basis. With respect to the current budget, only current expenditures are included but depreciation (which is also a current charge) is again allowed for. Balancing these current outlays against current (tax) receipts, we find that the deficit drops to $34 billion, as against $254 billion in the total budget. It is the former amount only that reflects a diversion of resources from consumption to capital formation. If the deficit is reflected in reduced private capital formation, $220 billion thereof is offset by public capital formation, thus leaving a net reduction of only $34 billion. In order to judge the effects of the budget on total capital formation in the economy, it is thus the deficit in the current not that in the total budget that matters.

The construction of a capital budget seems simple enough, but some subtle issues are involved. For one thing, note that depreciation charges are carried as a cost in the current budget, thereby introducing a noncash element into the budget statement. For another, the resulting state of balance in the current budget depends greatly on how capital expenditures are defined. Public acquisition of physical assets (such as an office building) should be included, *not* because the government comes to own a building but because a building is added to the capital stock of the economy. A subsidy to private investment, while adding to the capital stock of the private sector, is just as eligible. As distinct from the balance sheet of a private firm, the purpose of the public capital budget is *not* to test the financial soundness of the government by balancing assets against liabilities (public debt) but to measure the government's contribution to the economy's capital stock. Moreover, there is no good reason why capital formation should be defined in terms of brick and mortar only. Human investment may be as important to productivity growth. Thus, if students increase their skills, which is a form of capital formation, it is a matter of indifference whether the factor input is in the form of teachers' salaries or of increased classroom space. The definition of capital outlays followed in Table 31-2 took this broad approach. If, instead, acquisition of government-owned fixed assets only was included, capital outlays would be reduced by one-half and the current budget deficit would rise to nearly $60 billion. It might also be argued, although questionably so, that outlays on military assets should be counted as consumption, an approach given in the lower part of the table. With this interpretation, the current deficit, as shown in part II of the table, is increased, but it still remains far below that in the total budget.

Although the federal budget could be presented in this form, it is not, and the President's Budget Commission recommended against the use of it for good reason.[12] Since the nature of our economy is not such that full employment is automatically ensured by the private sector, budget policy has a major effect on the level of aggregate demand. Tax and loan finance differ in this effect and the choice between them must be used as an instrument of stabilization policy. Since the responsibility for stabilization policy must rest at the federal level, presentation of a dual budget would divert attention from the more important focus on the aggregate demand effects. These effects are indicated by the state of balance in the total budget as usually shown, i.e., without including depreciation. Nevertheless, the contribution of the federal budget to capital formation might be brought out more strongly by giving prominent attention to the breakdown of federal expenditures between current and capital items, an aspect now dealt with only in the Special Analyses section of the budget, and by allowing for depreciation in assessing the cost of current services. Moreover, a good case can be made for the use of a dual-

---

[12] See *Report of the President's Commission on Budget Concepts,* Washington, 1967.

budget approach at the state-local level, where stabilization policy is less relevant and where considerations of intergeneration equity call for loan finance of investment outlays.[13]

Investment Propensities of Public and Private Sectors

A perspective on the investment propensities of the public and private sectors is given in Table 31-3, which compares the share of public and private resource use going into investment. We find that the share of the public sector (including defense investment) is above that of the private sector. The public sector ratio, however, drops below that of the private sector if defense equipment is viewed as consumption. If a broader view were taken, investment shares would be increased substantially for both levels. However, given the importance of education and health expenditures in public budgets, the public sector share might well gain relative to the private sector. Moreover, the analysis might be extended to allow for the role of tax expenditures in the public budget.

Spillover Effects

Having noted previously the encouragement which tax policy can give to research and development in the private sector, we must note that the role of public investment is also of major importance. Whereas publicly financed research has been largely in the context of weapons technology, there has been a substantial spillover into civilian uses. However, publicly financed civilian research—especially in health—has also been significant, and an expanded input may develop in the search for alternative energy sources.

Viewed more broadly, it is evident that public capital formation—from investment in roads to human investment in education—has important spillover effects on the return to private investment. Cars are useless unless highways are available, and modern technology can be applied only in combination with an educated work force. There are thus two sides to the effects of the public budget on economic growth. On the one side there is concern with the impact of taxation upon private capital formation, but on the other, and no less important, there is the strategic contribution made by capital formation in the public sector.

E.   FISCAL POLICY EXPERIENCE

We complete the discussion of fiscal policy with a brief look at our actual policy experience.

The Early Years

Concern with the budget as an active ingredient of stabilization policy is now fifty years old. It began in the Great Depression of the thirties, when Keynes' *General Theory* and its message of fiscal expansion burst onto the scene. To be sure, little was done during the thirties to apply this approach. Roosevelt's New Deal started out on a platform of budget balance, and such modest recovery as emerged during

---

[13] See p. 554.

TABLE 31-3
Investment Propensities of Public and Private Sector, 1987
(All Levels of Government, in Billions of Dollars)

	Public Sector	Private Sector
1. Consumption	700	2,960
2. Plant and equipment, total	220	705
3. Defense	126	—
4. Nondefense	94	705
5. Total purchases	920	3,665
6. 2 as percentage of 5	23.9	19.2
7. 4 as percentage of (5 − 3)	11.8	19.2

Sources: Line 1, *Survey of Current Business;* Lines 3 and 4, see Table 31-1.

the thirties was largely private-sector based.[14] However, the massive fiscal expansion generated by World War II demonstrated the potential force of such a policy. In the course of the war, the budget rose from 10 to 45 percent of GNP, with half thereof deficit-financed and a supporting monetary policy which held interest rates at 3 percent. Real output rose by 50 percent and unemployment disappeared. While inflationary effects were delayed by price control, even the resulting postwar inflation was moderate by recent standards.

The economy of the fifties and most of the sixties continued a setting of relatively high employment and price-level stability. The rate of unemployment rose above 6 percent in two years only (1958 and 1961), while the inflation rate (from 1952 to 1967) did not go above 3 percent. With this basically strong economy, monetary control recovered its position as a powerful policy tool and the federal budget, operating at a higher share of GNP than before, served as a potent built-in stabilizer. Except for the recession of 1958, the federal deficit was less than 1 percent of GNP, and the full employment budget was in balance throughout. As a sharply rising full employment surplus was permitted to develop in the later fifties, excessive fiscal restraint contributed to the recession of 1958. Expenditure growth during the early sixties, followed by the Kennedy tax cut of 1964, returned the economy to high employment and did so with only moderate inflation pressure. It then appeared that fiscal and monetary policy, working in tandem, could be successful. Stabilization policy, so it seemed, would be able to guide the economy along a path of high employment and noninflationary growth.[15]

These hopes of fine tuning were shattered in the late sixties. Rising expenditures, reflecting the Vietnam war as well as President Johnson's Great Society programs, failed to be matched by additional taxes, thus extending fiscal expansion into an economy which already had arrived at a high level of employment. "Demand-pull" inflation was set in motion, the first step in an inflationary spiral which was to plague the economy for years to come. The setting for fiscal policy had changed with a vengeance. From a situation of unemployment which could be

[14] See E. Cary Brown, "Fiscal Policy in the Thirties: A Reappraisal," *American Economic Review,* December 1956.

[15] This high optimism is reflected in Walter Heller, *New Dimensions of Political Economy,* New York: Norton, 1967.

met by demand expansion without inflation, the task had become one of dealing with the concurrent evils of unemployment *and* inflation.

The Seventies

The economy of the seventies was marred by cyclical instability as well as rising trends of unemployment and inflation. Neither fiscal nor monetary policy could stem the tide.

The decade may be divided into three phases, including the cycle of 1970–73, that of 1973–78, and the downturn of 1979. In each case, the budget deficit as a percentage of GNP fluctuated with the rate of unemployment, thus resulting in countercyclical swings in fiscal leverage. With inflation maintaining or raising the nominal level of income, revenue did not fall even when employment declined, but with revenue lagging behind rising expenditures, built-in swings in the ratio of deficit to GNP nevertheless occurred. These were reinforced by discretionary measures of expansion, including tax reductions in 1971, 1974, and 1978. The high-employment ratio of deficit to GNP also moved with the actual ratio, but swings were less drastic and, with the exception of 1975, rather modest. In all, fiscal variables moved in a countercyclical pattern but built-in responses were inadequate to maintain a stable economy, and discretionary adjustments were not always well-timed. Nor did monetary policy, with its sharp swings in the rate of money growth prove more successful.

More important, stabilization policy failed to stem the upward trend of rising unemployment and inflation. Throughout the decade the rate of unemployment rose from trough to trough of each successive cycle, as did the rate of inflation at the peak of each successive upswing. With the budget in deficit throughout the period, budget policy became the scapegoat of inflation. But it did not deserve such singular blame. While the initial inflation spurt of the late sixties reflected loose budget policy and resulting demand pull, such can hardly be said for the subsequent inflation of the seventies. The periods of most rapid increase in the inflation rate followed the oil price shocks of 1974 and 1978. These were periods of declining ratios of high-employment deficit to GNP and of declining fiscal leverage. Fiscal policy on the whole followed rather than led inflation.

Nor was the period of the seventies one of rapid budget growth. The ratio of budget expenditures to high-employment GNP maintained a level trend, as did our leverage coefficient; and the built-in growth of revenue due to bracket creep was offset in large part by rate reductions. The rising deficit, to be sure, involved increasing needs of finance, but it was not the major cause of increase in money supply. Other forms of indebtedness (including, in particular, the growth of mortgage and consumer credit) were by far the more important claimants on the credit markets. In all, the demand-pull forces of budget policy accounted for only a small part of the inflation.

At the same time, fiscal and monetary policy did sustain the inflation process. Rising prices were supported by expansionary policy in the hopes of thereby avoiding an even sharper drop in real demand in the level of employment. The choice, in the stagflation setting of that period, was among alternative evils, and the longer the process continued, the more difficult it became to escape from it.

The tenuous relationship between budget policy and inflation became apparent especially during the years from 1976 to 1979, when sharply rising inflation was associated with restrictive budget policy, i.e., a declining ratio of high-employment deficit and leverage. But a sharp expansionary shift occurred in 1980 and again in 1981. Driven by rising expenditures and lagging revenue, the deficit and leverage ratios turned up sharply. Demonstrating once more the perverse response of a stagflation economy, unemployment continued to rise while inflation reached a peak rate.

The Eighties

We thus arrive at the setting in which the fiscal policy of the Reagan administration was formulated. Its initial plan, as presented in the Budget Message of January 1981, was to balance the budget via a policy of substantial tax reduction, combined with increased defense and reduced nondefense outlays. Notwithstanding a sharply restrictive monetary policy to check inflation, these measures would so stimulate the economy as to recoup most of the revenue loss from tax reduction. The budget would be balanced by 1984 and the ratio of expenditures to GNP would be reduced from 23 to 19 percent. This response, so the administration argued, would come from the incentive-increasing powers of the tax cut and not from its expansionary effect on aggregate demand.

From 1983 to 1988 the economy indeed enjoyed the comfort of low unemployment and high price stability. But contrary to the earlier 1981 prognosis, the federal budget continued to operate with a large deficit, averaging around 4 percent of GNP, as well as with a sizable trade deficit of about equal magnitude. The two deficits were not accidental partners. Given the large budget deficit, a tighter monetary policy was needed to avoid excessive expansion, and high interest rates attracted an inflow of foreign capital. This helped to finance the deficit but it also strengthened the dollar. That in turn made imports cheap and exports dear, thereby feeding the trade deficit. The trade deficit, finally, provided a leakage which dampened the expansionary effect of the budget deficit.

In building up a trade deficit, the level of available resources was increased and the economy enjoyed a free ride. As shown in Table 31-4, consumption as a percent of GNP held its own while domestic gross investment increased its share somewhat. But acquisition of U.S. assets by foreign investors (reflecting the im-

TABLE 31-4
Economic Patterns, 1982–1987

	1982		1987		Change
	Bill. $	%	Bill. $	%	Bill. $
Consumption	2,051	65	2,966	66	+ 915
Gross domestic investment	447	14	716	16	+ 269
Government purchases	642	20	924	21	+ 282
Net exports	26	1	− 120	− 3	− 146
GNP	3,166	100	4,486	100	+ 1,320

Source: Economic Report of the President, February 1988.

port surplus) also reduced our own claim to national wealth whereby, as noted further below, a burden was placed on future generations.[16]

The lopsided policy mix of fiscal ease and monetary tightness which produced these events denied the hoped-for result of more saving, investment, and faster economic growth. A policy mix involving a tighter budget and greater monetary ease would have been more compatible with those goals. Lower interest rates would have stimulated domestic investment and lessened capital inflow, the dollar would have been cheaper, and the emergence of a large trade deficit would have been checked. There would have been less transfer of U.S. assets to foreign investors.

The problem is why a tighter budget, easier money mix failed to be achieved, be it by expenditure reduction, tax increase, or by both. The intensely political nature of this choice goes far to explain why so unsatisfactory a policy mix was adopted and retained. On the one side, tax increase was ruled out, grounded on the supply-side proposition that this would retard growth and interfere with reducing the size of the public sector. On the other side, there was reluctance to permit further reduction in expenditure programs, especially in the civilian sector. Also, the 1986 tax reform diverted attention from the need for tax increase and raised the political cost of arguing its case. The design of an efficient stabilization mix thus fell victim to the political battle over the size of the budget and taxation.

While the decade of the 1980s succeeded in overcoming serious unemployment and inflation, it also left a disappointing record on economic growth. Personal saving as a percent of disposable income fell from around 7 percent in the 1960s and 1970s to 2 percent, net domestic investment fell from 8 percent of GNP to 2 percent, and the rate of productivity growth declined from 3 to 1 percent. All this happened during the very period when marginal rates of tax were repeatedly and sharply reduced. While many factors other than taxation also contributed to these developments, there is little evidence that domestic supply side effects of tax reduction had played a major role in stimulating growth.

Conclusion

A history of fiscal policy in recent decades cannot be written in a few pages. Indeed, it cannot be undertaken without also examining the changing performance and structure of the economy at large, and without giving equal time to monetary policy as partner in the conduct of stabilization. Nevertheless, the changing role and tasks of fiscal policy have become apparent even from this cursory survey. Bursting on the scene in the Great Depression of the thirties, fiscal policy had its heyday in the war economy of the forties and once more came into its own in the earlier half of the sixties. Thereafter, the problems of stagflation arose, greatly complicating the task of stabilization by aggregate demand management, be it fiscal or monetary in approach. While the danger of rapid inflation had abated and a reasonably high level of employment had been secured, the trade repercussions of a sustained budget deficit continued, and a faulty mix of stabilization policy remained to be corrected.

[16] See p. 554.

F. SUMMARY

This chapter has focused on the fact that fiscal policy operates in a dynamic setting, as against the simpler setting of comparative statics used in the preceding chapter. As a first aspect of fiscal dynamics, the built-in flexibility of the fiscal system was considered:

1. A distinction was drawn between fiscal changes which involve changes in fiscal parameters and others which reflect the response of prevailing parameters to changes in the economic setting.
2. Various ways of measuring changes in the level of fiscal leverage were examined, including automatic changes in deficit as distinct from discretionary changes in deficit at full employment.
3. Differences in the built-in response of various taxes were noted.
4. The desirability of built-in flexibility was appraised.

As a second aspect of fiscal dynamics, the timing of fiscal effects was explored. Consideration was given to:

5. The time path of the multiplier process.
6. The time path of the accelerator effect.
7. The timing of multiplier effects in econometric models.
8. Policy implications of fiscal dynamics.
9. The appropriate role of tax and expenditure changes in the conduct of fiscal policy.

Attention was given to the role of the public sector in capital formation, thus supplementing an earlier discussion of fiscal effects on saving and investment in the private sector:

10. The nature of public saving and the corresponding concepts of budget balance were examined.
11. A dual system of current and capital budgets was explored.
12. Investment propensities in the public and the private sector were compared.
13. Spillover effects of public on private investment were noted.
14. The importance of policy mix for growth was noted once more.

Finally a brief survey of fiscal policy experience was presented:

15. High points in successful macro policy during the decades of the 1940s and 1960s were noted.
16. The impact of sustained budget deficits on the domestic economy and on the trade balance during the 1980s was examined, and the implications of an alternative policy mix were considered.

FURTHER READINGS

Blinder, A., and R. Solow: "Analytical Foundations of Fiscal Policy," in A. Blinder et al. (eds.): *The Economics of Public Finance*, Washington, D.C.: Brookings, 1974.

Friedman, M.: "A Monetary and Fiscal Framework for Economic Stability," in *Essays in Positive Economics*, 2d ed., Chicago: University of Chicago Press, 1959.

Heller, W.: *New Dimensions of Political Economy*, New York: Norton, 1967.

Stein, H.: *The Fiscal Revolution in America,* Chicago: University of Chicago Press, 1969.

Tobin, J.: *The New Economics One Decade Older,* Princeton, N.J.: Princeton University Press, 1974.

A running account of fiscal policy developments and thinking may be found in the successive volumes of the *Economic Report of the President.* For key statements as presented by the Council of Economic Advisors, see especially the reports for 1962, the first report of the Kennedy administration; for 1981, the last report of the Carter administration; and for 1982, the first report of the Reagan administration.

Chapter 32

Economics of the Public Debt*

A. Growth of the Federal Debt: *Level of Interest Payments; Privately Held Debt.* **B. Structure of the Federal Debt:** *Composition of the Debt; Who Holds the Debt?; Maturity Structure; Further Aspects.* **C. Public Debt and Fiscal Solvency:** *Refunding versus Debt Repayment; Tax Burden of Debt Service; Debt Repudiation through Inflation?* **D. Does Debt Finance Burden Future Generations?:** *Transfer through Reduced Capital Formation; Transfer with Generation Overlap; Transfer with Foreign Debt; Borrowing by State and Local Governments; Burden Transfer in Development Finance.* **E. Maturity Mix and Interest Cost:** *Term Structure of Rates; Term Structure and Debt Management.* **F. The Market for State and Local Debt:** *Tax Exemption versus Direct Interest Subsidy; Industrial Revenue Bonds.* **G. Summary.**

The growth of public debt has long been a hot issue in the debate over responsible fiscal policy. Critics not only have faulted deficit finance for its inflationary effects while in process, but have also warned of the future consequences of debt accu-

---

*Reader's Guide to Chapter 32: The first sections of this chapter trace the growth of the federal debt and examine its structure. There follows an analysis of the economics of public debt, including the problem of fiscal solvency and of burden transfer to future generations. A final section explores issues of debt management, in particular the maturity distribution of the debt and its bearing on the cost of debt service.

mulation and its burden upon later generations. All this has been made especially acute by the developments of the 1980s.

A. GROWTH OF THE FEDERAL DEBT

As shown in line 1 of Table 32-1, the federal debt increased greatly during World War II, when the budget exceeded one-half of GNP and was heavily deficit-financed. Growth of the debt continued at a more moderate rate during the fifties and sixties, while the ratio of debt to GNP (see line 7) dropped sharply. This combination of rising debt and declining debt-to-GNP ratio is explained in large part by inflation. Prices doubled from 1946 to 1970 and more than doubled from 1970 to 1982. As prices rise, so does the level of money income, but the par value of the outstanding debt is fixed in money terms, so that the ratio of debt to GNP declines, and so does its real value. Inflation thus appears as a form of debt repudiation, a subject to which we will return shortly. A rising ratio of debt to GNP was resumed in the 1980s when sustained deficits nearly tripled the level of public debt.

Level of Interest Payments

The size of the debt in relation to GNP matters because it affects the liquidity position of the economy and of the investors holding it. But of equal or greater importance is the level of interest service it requires. As shown in line 2, interest payments rose sharply during the 1970s when interest rates soared and during the 1980s when the debt expanded greatly. The federal interest bill has now climbed to 3 percent of GNP and to 13 percent of the federal budget, with the former ratio well above and the latter close to the level which prevailed after World War II.

TABLE 32-1
Growth of Federal Debt, 1941–1987

	1941	1946	1970	1980	1987
Debt data (billions of dollars)					
1. Gross debt	58	259	370	930	2,309
2. Interest	1	5	14	53	140
3. Privately held debt	47	208	217	616	1,658
Reference data (billions of dollars)					
4. GNP	125	210	993	2,632	4,500
5. Budget expenditures	21	36	204	541	1,050
6. Money supply (M2)	73	158	629	1,498	2,900
Ratios (in percent)					
7. Line 1/line 4	46.4	123.3	37.3	35.3	51.3
8. Line 2/line 1	1.7	1.9	3.8	5.6	6.1
9. Line 2/line 4	0.8	2.4	1.4	2.0	3.1
10. Line 2/line 5	4.8	13.9	6.9	9.8	13.3
11. Line 1/line 6	79.4	163.9	58.8	62.1	79.6
12. Line 3/line 4	37.6	99.0	21.8	23.4	36.8
13. Line 3/(line 3 + line 6)	39.2	56.8	25.7	29.1	36.4

Source: Economic Report of the President, January 1983, and *Federal Reserve Bulletin,* January 1988.

Privately Held Debt

With regard to some aspects of public debt (in particular the tax finance of interest payments) it matters little whether the debt is held by the public or by government agencies, such as the Federal Reserve banks or the Social Security Trust Fund. But it is only the publicly held debt that matters when it comes to the role of the debt as a part of the economy's liquidity structure; and it is only the privately held public debt that poses problems of management. The ratio of privately held public debt to GNP is thus given separately in line 12. It lies below the overall ratio in line 7 but follows a generally similar pattern. Whereas the share in the debt held by private investors declined following World War II, it subsequently returned to its traditional level. Line 13, finally, shows the weight of privately held public debt in the overall liquidity structure. Public debt as a percentage of total liquid assets (public debt and money supply) has shown little change over recent decades, with both components rising at about the same rate; and it lies below its post-World War II level.

B. STRUCTURE OF THE FEDERAL DEBT

Before turning to the economics of public debt, some further information regarding its structure is provided.

Composition of the Debt

The composition of the federal debt by type of issue is shown in Table 32-2. The debt is divided into marketable and nonmarketable issues, with the marketable issues accounting for about three-quarters of the total. Marketable issues are traded and are available to all buyers. They include bills, notes, and bonds. The main difference between them is one of maturity. Bills are issued mostly with maturities of twelve months, but the maturities can also be as short as three months. Notes run

TABLE 32-2
Gross Federal Debt by Type of Issue
(Par Values in Billions of Dollars, June 30, 1987)

Marketable	1,644	
Bills		391
Notes		984
Bonds		269
Nonmarketable	650	
Savings bonds and notes		95
Government account series*		422
State and local government series		125
Foreign issues†		5
Other		3
Noninterest bearing	3	
Total	2,297	

*Held by United States agencies and trust funds.
†Issued to foreign governments.
Source: *Federal Reserve Bulletin*, January 1988, p. 930.

from one to ten years and bonds for longer periods. Notes and bonds carry an annual coupon payment and are redeemable at par at the date of maturity. Bills are sold at a discount and pay no interest, with the appreciation in value to maturity representing the investor's return.

Nonmarketable issues are offered to various groups of investors and can be held only by the initial buyer. They are largely designed for holding by the various trust funds of the federal government, but special issues are also provided for state and local governments and for foreign governments. Nonmarketable issues are held by individuals in the form of savings bonds. Introduced as a major source of finance in World War II, these bonds have greatly declined in importance as new and more attractive investment outlets have become available.

Who Holds the Debt?

The distribution of the debt by types of holders is important because it affects the liquidity structure and the position of the capital markets. This distribution of holdings is shown in Table 32-3.

At the close of 1986, 28 percent was held by government trust funds and the Federal Reserve banks. Most important among the former is the OASDI Trust Fund, which acquired these obligations in years when current receipts from payroll taxes exceeded benefit payments. Holdings are in the form of special issues. Federal Reserve Bank holdings in turn are of the marketable type and are acquired in the process of open-market purchases. Given the public nature of the Federal Reserve System, such holdings are, in fact, part of the monetary base rather than part of federal debt owed to the public.

Excluding federally held debt, 80 percent was domestically held, and 20 percent was foreign held. 95 percent of domestic holdings went to private investors, with state and local government holding 5 percent. Much the largest share of private holdings went to savings institutions and corporate trust funds, which ab-

TABLE 32-3
Gross Federal Debt by Type of Holder
(Billions of Dollars, December 31, 1986)

Domestic		
Federal	614	
U.S. government agencies and trust funds		403
Federal Reserve banks		211
Private	1,281	
Commercial banks		232
Insurance companies		107
Other companies		69
Individuals		163
Miscellaneous*		712
State and local governments	69	
Foreign	251	
Total	2,215	

*Includes mutual savings banks, saving and loan associations, corporate trust funds, and so forth.
Source: Treasury Bulletin, December 1987, p. A-36.

sorbed over 50 percent. 18 percent was held by commercial banks, 14 percent by individuals (mostly in the form of savings bonds), and 8 percent by insurance companies.

Maturity Structure

Debt instruments are issued to run for a specified period of time, with payment of the capital made at par at the maturity date. Perpetual bonds, although used in the history of British finances, have not been issued by the U.S. Treasury. Shown in Table 32-4, the maturity structure of the debt was shortened greatly over the 1950s and 1960s. Whereas in 1950, long-term debt in excess of twenty years comprised 16 percent of the total and debt below one year comprised 27 percent, the corresponding ratios for 1970 stood at 5 and 49 percent. Average years to maturity fell from 8.2 to 3.7 years. Debt management during the 1950s and 1960s thus produced a substantial shift toward increased liquidity of the debt and raised the annual volume of refunding. This tendency toward shortening was halted during the 1970s and has been reversed somewhat during the 1980s. The bulk of the debt nevertheless remains heavily concentrated at the short end, with maturities above 10 years accounting for only 16 percent of the total.

Reliance on short debt during an inflationary period has permitted the Treasury to avoid long-term commitment to borrowing at high nominal rates of interest, in the hopes that inflation will be checked and that interest rates will fall in the future. At the same time, investors feel uncertain about the future (inflation may get worse!) and prefer to avoid a long-term commitment. Thus, it is expedient to refund maturing issues on a short-term basis, but in so doing, the liquidity of the claim structure is increased.

Further Aspects

Debt Limitation   The growth of the debt is determined by the underlying tax and expenditure legislation and the levels of surplus or deficit which result. Having

TABLE 32-4
Composition of Marketable Debt by Maturity*

	1950		1960		1970		1987	
	Billions of Dollars	Per-centage	Billions of dollars	Per-centage	Billions of Dollars	Per-centage	Billions of Dollars	Per-centage
Years to maturity								
0–1	42	27	70	38	122	49	483	33
1–5	51	34	73	40	82	33	527	37
5–10	8	5	20	11	23	9	209	14
10–20	28	18	13	7	9	4	73	5
20 and over	25	16	8	4	11	5	153	11
Total	154	100	184	100	247	100	1,445	100
Average years to maturity	8.2		4.8		3.7		5.9	

*Figures for end of year. Includes privately held issues only. Issues are classified by number of years remaining to maturity. Items may not add because of rounding.
Source: *Federal Reserve Bulletin*, March 1979, and *Economic Report of the President*, January 1988.

determined the deficit or surplus and hence changes in the level of debt in this fashion, Congress also sets an explicit debt limit which the Treasury is not allowed to exceed. Whenever current operations call for increases in government borrowing beyond the ceiling, the Secretary of the Treasury must appear before Congress and beg for an increase in the ceiling. The debt ceiling, as most observers agree, is an anachronism because Congress already determines changes in debt through its tax and expenditure legislation. Such is the case especially since the Joint Budget Resolution was provided by the Congressional Budget Act of 1974.

Interest Ceiling   Toward the close of World War I, Congress had enacted an interest ceiling of 4¼ percent on securities in excess of five years, excluding those issued to government agencies. This ceiling remained largely ineffective until the second half of the 1960s when long-term yields in the market rose above this level. Although the ceiling could have been circumvented by selling bonds with a 4¼ percent coupon rate at a price below par, the Treasury chose not to do so, because this would have violated the congressional intention. Thus, no long-term bonds could be sold after 1965 when market yields rose above the ceiling. After repeated Treasury requests, Congress authorized a limited issue of Treasury bonds at above-ceiling yields. This limit has been extended by Congress at various times, and now (1988) lies at $150 billion. It has thus not been a significant factor in limiting the use of longer-term issues.

Agency Debt and Government Lending   In addition to direct Treasury borrowing, the federal government is involved in guaranteeing and sponsoring borrowing by various federal agencies which in turn lend out the proceeds to private borrowers. By June 1987, such direct loans and guarantees amounted to $937 billion, mostly covering issues by the Federal Housing Administration, GNMA, and the Veterans' Administration. In addition, government-sponsored debt of private enterprises amounted to $280 billion, with the Federal National Mortgage Association and the Federal Home Loan Bank Board the main beneficiaries.[1]

As these agencies make use of the funds, government lending (as distinct from spending) enters the scene as an additional instrument of budgetary policy. Lending, like debt retirement, reduces the net debt position of the government. In a perfect capital market, extension of a $100 loan with a ten-year maturity would be equivalent to retirement of a $100 debt issue of similar maturity, assuming that the same tax revenue is used to finance either transaction. But the results of the two transactions may be quite different in an imperfect market. The recipient of the government loan might not have been able to obtain credit elsewhere. Indeed, a major rationale of government lending is to provide funds to borrowers who have not been able to obtain them otherwise but who, for reasons of public policy, should be provided with funds. It is thus typically used as an instrument of allocation rather than as stabilization policy and, as such, is particularly important in the context of developing countries where government-supported investment is an important feature of development policy.

---

[1] See *Treasury Bulletin*, June 1988, p. 54.

C. PUBLIC DEBT AND FISCAL SOLVENCY

Having reviewed the growth and status of the federal debt, we can now turn to its economic implications. The problem is how outstanding debt affects the functioning of the economy, i.e., how the consequences of past policies (e.g., deficits which have added to the debt) bear on future economic conditions. The economic effects of outstanding debt must be distinguished, therefore, from the current effects of deficit finance involving debt creation. Will not continued debt accumulation lead to fiscal bankruptcy?

Refunding versus Debt Repayment

As the debt grows larger and larger, how will it ever be possible to repay it? This frightening question is misplaced: Household debt must be repaid sooner or later, because conduct of the household is a finite affair. Public debt need not be repaid, since the budget and the economy are a continuing undertaking. When a particular debt issue matures, it is paid off; but the necessary funds are obtained by issuing new obligations. The debt is "refunded." With the debt very largely short term, the annual refunding volume is now around $2,500 billion, with the payment of maturing obligations and their replacement by refunding issues a weekly operation. Whereas refunding operations have traditionally involved highly complicated procedures, requiring precise estimation of yields demanded by the market, techniques developed in more recent years have greatly simplified matters. New issues are now sold through an auction system, with closed bids received from the dealers and then met on a first-come, first-served basis. Increased reliance on short-term debt, sold at discount rather than with a coupon, has facilitated this development. In expediting the refunding process, the Federal Reserve Bank of New York, which is closest to the money market, cooperates closely with the Treasury and serves as its agent.

  In short, refunding operations are a management problem and whether we can "repay" the debt is a misdirected question. The issue rather is how interest service will affect the economy and how outstanding debt enters into the liquidity structure of the economy.

Tax Burden of Debt Service

To service the debt, interest must be paid. Taxes raised to finance these payments impose a burden on the economy. This burden does not arise because resources are withdrawn from the economy. Assuming that we are dealing with a domestically held debt, we "owe the debt to ourselves" and taxing to pay interest merely transfers funds from one pocket to another. Nevertheless, the taxes which must be imposed to finance this transfer carry a deadweight loss, just as do other taxes, and this places a burden on the economy.[2] The severity of such effects is likely to rise

---

[2] Note that this problem may arise even though interest payments are included in taxable income. The tax rate t required to finance interest is given by $t = idY/(Y + idY) = id/(1 + id)$, where i is the interest rate and d is the ratio of debt to national income Y. With i equal to 5 percent and d equal to 40 percent, t equals 2 percent. If d rises to, say, 100 percent, t increases to 5 percent, and if d rises to 500 percent, t increases to 20 percent. Suppose that the level of t required for the finance of other services were 30 percent. The corresponding total levels of t would then be 32, 35, and 50 percent, respectively.

as the ratio of tax revenue (needed to service the debt) to GNP increases. Conceivably, it becomes so large as to pose a serious burden and disincentive problem, a factor which is overlooked in the "we owe it to ourselves" proposition. Debt accumulation during wars may be so drastic as to lead to fiscal breakdown and debt repudiation in the postwar period. These events occurred in European countries after both world wars.

Fortunately, there is little reason why such a calamity should occur under peacetime conditions. To be sure, continuing expansion of the debt combined with a constant GNP would lead to an infinite debt-to-GNP ratio. But GNP also expands and it may be shown that a constant ratio of deficit to GNP combined with a constant rate of growth of GNP will cause both the ratio of debt to GNP and the ratio of interest to GNP to approach a constant.[3] Taking the outlook for the next decade, let us suppose that GNP rises at an annual rate of 5 percent (3 percent for inflation and 2 percent for real growth). Also, the annual deficit equals 4 percent of GNP. Under these rather pessimistic assumptions, the ratio of debt to GNP would rise from 51 percent in 1987 to 64 percent in 1997, while the ratio of interest payments to GNP would rise from 4.1 to 5.1. The corresponding levels after a fifty-year period would be 81 and 6.5 percent, respectively. It appears that prospective growth of debt, even under high-deficit assumptions, does not readily assume explosive proportions.[4] The danger inherent in continuing high deficits lies not so much in their effect on the magnitude of debt as in their current impact on the fiscal-monetary mix and thereby on the economy's rate of saving and hence, growth.

Debt Repudiation through Inflation?

Since the par value of outstanding debt is fixed in dollar terms, inflation reduces its value in real terms. Thus the par value of outstanding debt in 1970 was $370 billion. But between 1970 and 1982 prices rose by 150 percent, or at an annual compound rate of 8 percent. The value of this debt in terms of 1970 dollars thus fell to $148 billion, or 40 percent of what it was. Does this mean that inflation resulted in a hidden debt repudiation of 60 percent?

The answer depends on the terms at which the debt was issued. Consider an investor who purchased a three-year government bond in 1970. The yield at that time was 7 percent, so that a bond redeemable at $100 in 1982 and paying $7 per year sold at $100. Assuming a real rate of return on capital of 3 percent, this suggests that our investor expected an inflation rate of 4 percent. At this inflation rate,

---

Thus, the need to tax-finance interest payments *could* come to absorb a substantial share of the economy's taxable capacity and thereby might displace other outlays.

[3] More specifically, the debt-to-GNP ratio approaches α/r, where α is the growth rate of GNP and r is the ratio of deficit to GNP. With $\alpha = 7$ percent and $r = 5$ percent, the debt-to-GNP ratio approaches 1.4. The interest-bill-to-GNP ratio approaches

$$\frac{i}{r/\alpha + i}$$

With i (ratio of interest bill to debt) = 10 percent and r and α as before, the interest-bill-to-GNP ratio approaches 6.7. With $i = 7$ percent, the limit drops to 4.8. See Evsey D. Domar, "The Burden of Debt and the National Income," *American Economic Review*, December 1944.

[4] Thereafter, the ratios approach limits of 83.8 and 6.7 percent, respectively.

the nominal yield of 7 percent would result in a real return of 3 percent. But as it turned out, the inflation rate over the three years ran at 8 percent. If the investor had known this, he or she would have required a yield of 11 percent, i.e., a bond selling at par would have had to carry a coupon payment of \$11 per year. The higher than anticipated rate of inflation left our investor with a real rate of return of -1 percent (7 percent minus 8 percent). This loss to the investor was reflected in a gain to the taxpayer, who benefits from servicing the debt (interest and repayment at maturity) in cheapened dollars. By 1982 yields had risen to 13 percent and caught up with rising inflation expectations. Since then they have fallen to around 8 percent, along with a decline in the inflation rate to below 4 percent.

Whether debt repudiation through inflation occurs therefore depends on how well inflation is anticipated when the debt is issued and on how this anticipation has been reflected in a higher nominal rate of interest. This in turn depends on the maturity of the debt. If the debt is held in the form of short-term claims, say three-month bills, the yield will correspond to the current rate in the money market and will thus tend to reflect the rate of inflation. The situation differs if the debt is long-term and unanticipated high rates of inflation result which were not allowed for when setting the terms at which the debt was issued. With so large a part of the debt in short-term issues, debt repudiation through inflation is no longer a major issue.

D.   DOES DEBT FINANCE BURDEN FUTURE GENERATIONS?

Granted that fears of fiscal bankruptcy are unrealistic, does not debt finance place an unfair burden on future generations? How does such a burden transfer come about and what is its bearing on fiscal equity?

Transfer through Reduced Capital Formation

If resources are fully employed, an increase in public services shifts resources from the private to the public sector, leaving less for the production of private goods. In this sense of resource release, the burden must be borne by the present generation. But not necessarily so if burden transfer is viewed in terms of its current consumption.

A first mechanism of burden transfer is provided through reduced capital formation. To see how this works, we once more return to the framework of a "classical" system where investment adjusts itself automatically to the level of saving forthcoming at a full-employment level of income. Given such a system, any transfer of resources from private to public use leaves the private sector with fewer resources. In this narrow sense, the burden of today's public expenditures must be borne by today's generation. But the resource withdrawal from the private sector may be from consumption or from capital formation. In the first case, the welfare of the present generation, as measured by its consumption, is reduced and the income of the future generation is unaffected. In the second case, the consumption welfare of the present generation is untouched while the future generation will inherit a smaller capital stock and thus enjoy a lower income. In this sense, the future generation is burdened. If we assume further that tax finance comes out of consumption while loan finance comes out of saving (hence, under the assumption of a classical system, out of investment) it then follows that loan finance burdens future generations.

Proceeding on the principle that public services should be financed on a benefit basis, the nature of the expenditure to be financed becomes of crucial importance. In the case of capital expenditures, the benefits will extend into the future, so that burden transfer is called for as a matter of intergeneration equity. As noted before, this is the rationale for dividing the budget into a current and capital component, with the former tax- and the latter loan-financed.[5]

Certain qualifications of the prevailing argument should be noted:

1. Depending on the type of taxes used, tax finance may in part fall on saving. Similarly, loan finance may in part fall on consumption. Nor need all transfer receipts raise consumption. For these reasons, the deficit offers only a rough approximation to resource withdrawal from private capital formation.

2. The rational expectation approach, as noted before, questions whether individuals will respond differently to tax and loan finance. Acting as rational agents, the present generation, when lending to government, is assumed to anticipate the future taxes (payable by their heirs) which will have to be met to service the debt. Because of this, loan finance leaves the first generation in the same position as tax finance. But is not the net worth of taxpayers reduced while lenders are compensated when receiving a government bond? The answer is no, or so the rational expectation school holds, because this gain is canceled by the assumption of future tax obligations. Thus the net worth of the private sector is reduced by the public outlay whichever method of finance is used. Given this "Ricardian Equivalence," it can no longer be argued that loan finance serves to secure burden transfer whereas tax finance does not, but as noted before, this is hardly a realistic assumption.[6]

3. Our reasoning was based on the assumption of a well-behaved, classical system where the level of aggregate demand is not affected by the choice between tax and loan finance. Once this premise is dropped, the choice between tax and loan finance as well as the fiscal-monetary policy mix may have to be determined so as to provide the proper level of aggregate demand, rather than to accommodate considerations of intergeneration equity. This consideration is of particular importance at the federal level, where the responsibility for stabilization policy rests; it is less important at the state-local level where, as noted earlier, the use of a capital budget is more appropriate.

Transfer with Generation Overlap

Absent generation overlap, reduced private capital formation is the only mechanism by which the burden of domestic borrowing can be transferred to a future generation. But such is not a necessary condition if two generations overlap in time. Suppose that generation 1 lives from year one to year fifty, while generation 2 lives from years twenty-five to seventy-five. Also suppose that all taxes come from consumption. Now generation 1, in year one, may be called upon to pay taxes of $200,000 to sustain the cost of a government building with a useful life of fifty years. It must do so at the cost of reducing its own consumption by this amount. But it will then be possible, in years twenty-five to fifty, to collect taxes of $100,000 from generation 2 in order to refund generation 1, thus involving a shift

[5] See p. 534.
[6] See p. 520.

in private consumption from generation 2 to generation 1. In this way generation 1, while initially assuming the entire burden, can transfer part of it to generation 2. For purposes of reassurance generation 1 may be given a promise of repayment in the form of bonds, to be redeemed later out of taxes imposed on generation 2. Such a transfer among overlapping generations can function even though there is no effect on capital formation in the private sector.

In contrast to this case, generation 1 may make a present to generation 2 and assume the entire burden without calling upon generation 2 for repayment later on, which is precisely the mechanism which applied when old-age retirement pensions were introduced and the initially aged were given benefits without having had to contribute.

Transfer with Foreign Debt

Having considered the role of domestic borrowing, we now turn to that of borrowing from outside sources. The mechanism of burden transfer through foreign borrowing differs in several respects. A first difference is that there is now no need for generation 1 to reduce its expenditures. Outlays in the private sector can remain intact because the additional resources needed for the public outlay are acquired abroad via an import supplus.[7] Loan finance now imposes a burden on generation 2 not by leaving it with a reduced capital endowment at home but by saddling it with an obligation to service the foreign debt. Taxes must now be paid to finance interest paid to foreigners rather than to domestic holders of the debt. Generation 2 no longer owes the debt to itself. This foreign debt burden replaces the loss of capital income which generation 2 would have suffered had there been domestic loan finance and a resulting reduction in capital formation.

Compare now our three sources of finance—(1) taxation, (2) domestic borrowing, and (3) foreign borrowing. Assuming 1 to fall on consumption and 2 on capital formation, 1 will burden the present generation while 2 and 3 will burden the future. Even though 2 and 3 are similar in this respect, the choice between them may not be a matter of indifference. The answer depends upon the cost of borrowing at home and abroad. If the cost is the same (if the return on domestic capital is the same as the outside rate of interest), the burden on generation 2 will be the same in each case. But if the domestic cost is higher, foreign borrowing may be preferable.

Reliance on foreign resources need not involve direct placement of the debt abroad but may take indirect form. A similar result comes about if the debt is placed domestically, with raising interest rates inducing capital inflow and once more an import surplus. If channeled into consumption, generation 1 once more escapes the burden while generation 2 now pays the debt service to itself, but it must share part of the national income with its foreign owners. This is essentially the story of the 1980s, a story which was benign while it transpired but which will have to be paid for later on.

Borrowing by State and Local Governments

The problem of intergeneration equity arises most acutely at the state and local levels where the bulk of public investment expenditures are made and financed.

---

[7] Capital inflow will drive up the value of the dollar, thereby cheapening imports and raising the cost of exports.

Suppose that a township is about to construct a school building, the services of which will extend over thirty years. The expenditures thereon call for a sharp, once-and-for-all increase in the total outlays of the township. If it were to be tax-financed, a sharp if temporary increase in the tax rate would be needed. This increase would in itself be undesirable, since taxpayers find it easier to live with a more or less stable tax rate. Moreover, and more important, it would be unfair to place the entire burden on those who pay taxes in this particular year. Since the use of the facility will extend over thirty years, it is only fair to spread the burden among the successive generations of residents which will benefit from the service. The principle of benefit taxation is applied in allocating the burden between generations.

To accomplish benefit taxation, the initial cost is covered by borrowing, typically in outside markets. In subsequent years, future generations, resident and partaking of the benefits, are taxed each year in accordance with their current benefit share. In the process the debt is amortized and repaid by the time the facility is used up. Once more, intergeneration equity is secured, with each generation paying for its own benefit share.[8] A township which finances its school building by borrowing and amortizing the debt over the length of the asset life thus provides for an equitable pattern of burden distribution not only between age groups but also between changing groups of residents as the population of the jurisdiction changes in response to in-migration and out-migration.

Burden Transfer in Development Finance

The preceding discussion has an unhappy application to the problems of development finance and economic growth. Although the mechanism of burden transfer may be used to spread the cost of *public* investment, it cannot be used to spread the cost of a development program, broadly defined, because the very objective of such a program requires that *total* capital formation (public or private) be increased. But no gain is made toward achieving this objective if public capital formation is loan-financed, where this causes an offsetting decline in the rate of private capital formation. Unfortunately, therefore, the mechanism of burden transfer through internal loan finance is inapplicable in the very situation where it would be most appropriate. Such is not the case, however, with regard to foreign borrowing, the role of which will be considered further when development finance is examined.

E. MATURITY MIX AND INTEREST COST

As noted before, debt management involves large annual refunding operations. In conducting these operations, as in financing an increase in total debt, a decision must be made about what type of debt to issue. The major problem here is the choice of maturities. Traditionally, it was held that the public debt should be well "funded," i.e., be in long-term maturities. Thus, the British debt during the nineteenth century was largely in the form of consols or perpetual securities which have no fixed maturity date but can be retired at the government's option provided that

[8] See p. 592.

it is willing to pay the market price. This stipulation would protect the government against the contingency that creditors would demand their money back at an inopportune time. The modern view of national debt and the position of national governments in the debt market is quite different. Debt management proceeds on the assumption that maturing issues can always be refunded. Although the overall level of the debt may be increased at some periods and reduced at others (depending on whether the needs of stabilization policy call for a deficit or a surplus), there is no expectation that accumulated past debts will ever be "paid off." As particular issues mature, they come to be "refunded" into other issues. The shorter the average debt outstanding, the larger will be the annual volume of refunding operations, but this is of no particular concern and not decisive in determining the maturity structure.

Such being the case, what basic guidelines are there to the choice of maturities which the Treasury should offer? One possible answer is that it should select the term structure of the debt so as to minimize interest cost. Since the cost of borrowing tends to differ with the maturity of the debt, those issues should be chosen which investors are willing to absorb at the lowest cost. The same principle of economy which suggests that the government should buy its pencils from the lowest-cost supplier may also suggest that it borrow from the lowest-cost lender. On closer consideration, this proves too simple a rule, but let us first see what it would imply.

Term Structure of Rates

As we look back at the history of interest rates over the course of this century, we find short rates usually have been close to or above long rates. This pattern was reversed during the depression years of the 1930s when the general level of rates declined sharply and short rates fell below long rates. Federal Reserve policy was used to maintain this low level of rates during the war years to permit financing of the war debt at low cost. This required a substantial share of the debt to be absorbed by the commercial banks and a corresponding increase in money supply. Appropriate during the war, this policy was continued until the early fifties. Defended by the Treasury, it came under attack from the Federal Reserve System. The policy proved incompatible with the application of monetary restraint since the Federal Reserve had to stand ready to purchase bonds in the open market when needed to keep their prices from falling and their yields from rising. This constraint proved untenable and the Treasury–Federal Reserve "Accord" of 1951 left the Federal Reserve free to let rates rise. Federal Reserve policy accordingly adopted a "bills only" policy under which all open-market operations would be conducted in Treasury bills. After a gradual transition, the securities markets returned to the earlier pattern of higher rates, with short and long rates moving closer together and with short rates occasionally above long rates.

The development of short and long rates since 1960 is shown in Figure 32-1. It will be seen that the general rate level has been rising, most sharply from 1976 to 1981. Since then, rates have been on a downward trend. Short and long rates have crisscrossed each other at various times but yields on long-term bonds nor-

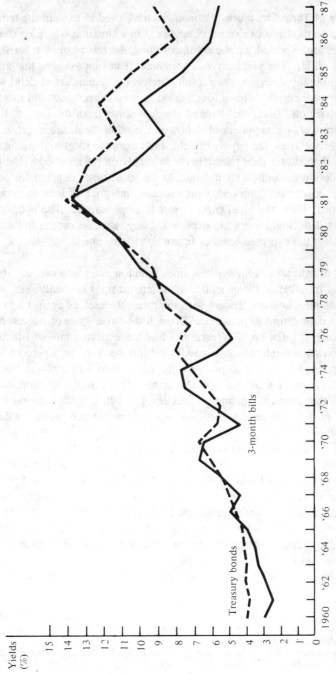

FIGURE 32-1 Short and long rates, 1960–1982. (*Source: Economic Report of the President and Federal Reserve Bulletin.*)

mally remain above those on short-term issues. The "term structure" of yields is said to rise.[9]

Theory of Term Structure Economists have tried to explain the term structure of rates on the basis of rate expectations.[10] In a situation where no changes in interest rates are expected, so the argument goes, there is no reason for short and long rates to differ. The yield curve is horizontal. But suppose now that an expectation of rising rates emerges. As a result, lenders (or demanders of debt) will hesitate to commit themselves for a long period as they expect to obtain more favorable terms later on. Thus, the demand for debt shifts from the long to the short market. Borrowers (or suppliers of debt), on the other hand, are eager to borrow before costs rise. Thus, the supply of debt shifts from the short to the long market. As a result, demand for debt rises relative to supply on the short end. The price of short-term debt rises and yields decline. At the same time, demand for debt falls relative to supply at the long end. Consequently, the price of long-term debt falls and yields rise. Thus, the yield curve comes to slope upward. The opposite result comes about if declining rates are expected. Long rates, according to this theory, come to reflect the expected level of future short-term rates.

Effect of Inflation Finally, how does inflation enter into the rate structure? The effect of inflation on the general level of interest rates is readily seen. Inflation does drive up rates because lenders wish to protect themselves against a loss in the real value of their claims as prices rise. Thus, if the "real" rate of interest or return in the absence of inflation is 3 percent, while the expected rate of inflation is 6 percent, the nominal rate of interest will tend to be $3 + 6$, or 9 percent. The additional 6 percent is needed to maintain the purchasing power of the bond while only the 3 percent is a net gain in real terms. This inflationary adjustment accounted for the sharp rise in the general level of interest rates during the early 1980s, just as the abatement in inflation expectations has accounted for the fall in rates since then.

The relation between inflation and the term structure of rates is less evident. As long as inflation proceeds at a *constant* rate, say 4 percent, and investors expect this rate to be maintained, the "inflation surcharge" will also stay at 4 percent, so that the term structure should not be affected. Only if the expected rate of inflation changes will the term structure be affected. Thus, an expectation that inflation will slow down will tend to make for a decline in future nominal rates and hence lead to a fall in long rates relative to short rates, and vice versa for an expected rise in the rate of inflation.

At various times it has been proposed that both Treasury and taxpayers might

[9] The yield of a bond is the internal rate of discount at which the present value of the redemption payment plus coupon payment equals the purchase price. If the Treasury issues a bond at par (i.e., its redemption value), the yield equals the coupon rate of interest.

[10] For a convenient summary of this theory, see W. L. Smith, "Debt Management in the United States," Study Paper 19, *Study of Employment, Growth, and Price Levels,* Joint Economic Committee, U.S. Congress, June 28, 1960. For the original presentation, see J. R. Hicks, *Value and Capital,* 2d ed., Oxford, England: Clarendon, 1946, chap. 11.

be protected against unforeseen changes in the rate of inflation by issuing longer-term bonds the redemption value of which would be indexed to the price level. Or bonds might be given a fixed par value but carry an annual coupon payment which varies with the rate of inflation. But although these are very plausible ways of dealing with the inflation problem, such securities have not as yet been issued by the Treasury Department.

Term Structure and Debt Management

We can now reconsider the implications of the term structure of interest rates for debt management and ask whether interest cost is minimized by selling those issues which, as measured by current yields, can be placed at the lowest cost to maturity. The answer is clearly no. Suppose that the Treasury can borrow for one year at 5 percent and twenty years at 7 percent. It does not follow that taking the one-year issue is preferable because by year's end the opportunity to borrow at 7 percent may be lost if the level of rates has risen. Or suppose that the Treasury can borrow for twenty years at 5 percent and for one year at 7 percent. The former choice is not necessarily preferable since rates may decline before the twenty years have passed.

What matters most is the *direction* in which the Treasury expects rates to change. If debt managers expect rates to rise, the proper choice is to borrow long; if they expect them to fall, the choice is to stay short. The important point is that once a commitment has been made, there is no way of escape. The interest cost contracted for must be carried for the full period even though rates may fall; and the benefits of a low rate will continue to accrue even though the rates may rise.[11] Debt management is therefore a fine art which requires a shrewd appraisal of market prospects for a considerable time ahead. In the hope that high inflation rates will come to pass, debt managers may be inclined to prefer short issues during an inflationary period.

But even if expected rate changes are allowed for, the criterion of minimum interest cost does not offer a sufficient guide. Differences in the behavior of investors who hold long and short debt must also be taken into account. After all, the central government, with its control over money creation, can regulate the level of interest rates in the market. It can always replace public debt by money, whether crudely through the printing press or more discreetly by borrowing from the central bank. Replacing debt with money would clearly be the cheapest way of handling

---

[11] Suppose that the Treasury borrows $1,000 in a market in which a twenty-year bond, if selling at par, must carry a coupon rate of 6½ percent. After such a bond is sold, suppose that after one year the market yield on a nineteen-year bond falls to 5½ percent. As a result, the price of the old bond will rise to $1,117, i.e., the present value of $1,000 due in nineteen years plus nineteen annual coupon payments of $65 as discounted at 5½ percent. Thus, if the Treasury were to retire the old bond (i.e., that it would repurchase the issue at market price) and to reissue a new nineteen-year bond at 5½ percent, it would have to raise $1,117 rather than $1,000 to replace the outstanding issue. This would leave its position unchanged, since the present values of the two cash flows—i.e., $1,000 in nineteen years plus nineteen annual payments of $65, or $1,117 in nineteen years plus nineteen annual coupon payments of $61.40 discounted at 5½ percent—are the same, and each is equal to $1,117. Similar reasoning applies in a situation where interest rates rise and bond prices fall. Here nothing would be lost by replacing the old bond with a new one. Even though the former could be retired at a lower price, the latter's coupon rate would have to be correspondingly higher.

the matter because it would involve no interest cost at all. Yet it would not be a satisfactory solution because monetizing the debt would result in greatly increased liquidity, giving rise to an excessive level of aggregate demand and inflation.

Viewed this way, the purpose of issuing debt rather than money (or replacing maturing debt outstanding with new debt rather than monetizing it) is to purchase illiquidity. Investors must be convinced to hold debt rather than money, and the way to do this is to pay them. The question arises whether a dollar of short-term debt is as helpful in reducing liquidity as a dollar of long-term debt. If long-term debt makes the holder less liquid, it might pay the Treasury to issue such debt even if the interest cost were somewhat higher. The principle of minimizing interest costs must thus be restated as one of buying illiquidity on the cheapest terms which are compatible with the objectives of stabilization policy.

Lengthening the debt at the time of refunding will tend to be restrictive, and shortening it will tend to be expansionary.[12] Lengthening will raise long rates relative to shorts. Investors who were willing to hold a given supply of longs and shorts at a certain yield spread must now hold more longs and fewer shorts. To do this, they will require more favorable terms on longs and will be willing to accept less favorable terms on shorts. The restrictive effect of the resulting rise in long rates on private investment will outweigh the expansionary effect of decline in short rates, since capital expenditures are usually based on long-term financing.[13] Short-term debt being more like money, a lengthening of the debt is thus restrictive.

The same considerations which apply to refunding (or swapping of debt) also apply with regard to choosing the type of issue or addition to the debt with which a deficit is financed, or the type of issue which is to be withdrawn as the surplus is used for debt reduction.[14] In either case, debt management may be used to support

---

[12] A similar problem arises in open-market operations of the Federal Reserve. However, such operations involve swaps between debt and money only and not between types of debt. Swaps between debt and money are given increased potency by the nature of fractional reserve banking, where (with a reserve ratio of 20 percent) substitution of $100 of debt for $100 of money may force a $500 reduction in money supply. This multiple effect does not arise with swaps between types of debts. However, even here banks may be induced to utilize excess reserves more fully or to extend their use of the discount window if their liquidity is increased by substitution of short-term for long-term debt, thus increasing the holdings of "secondary reserves."

[13] Consider an investor who is confronted with a choice among money, short debt, long debt, and real investment or equity. The individual will balance his or her portfolio among these assets so as to hold the preferred mix at given yields. For the market as a whole, the demand for, and supply of, various types of assets will result in a structure of yields at which both demanders and suppliers are satisfied. If long debt is substituted for short, the market must hold more of the former and less of the latter. Those who absorb additional long-term debt must discard some other assets, whereas those who reduce their holding of short debt must acquire other assets. It seems likely that the former will want to discard equity holdings while the latter will want to shift toward money. The reason for this is that long debt, being less liquid, is a closer substitute for equity, while short debt is a closer substitute for money. As a result, the cost at which equity funds are available will rise and investment will decline. The opposite holds true if the debt is shortened.

[14] It is easy to see that shortening a given debt is expansionary and that a net addition to the debt in short form is more restrictive (or less expansionary) than a similar addition in long form. But it is more difficult to appraise the effects of a net addition of a particular type of debt considered by itself.

Consider a net addition to long-term debt. As a result, the total stock of claims and equity which investors must hold is increased. Since their preferences call for a balanced portfolio, they will not wish to absorb the entire addition in the form of a long debt. They will thus try to substitute other assets. This will increase long-term yields and may thus be expected to be restrictive. However, not only will the

the expansionary or restrictive effects of current stabilization policy. Consequently, short-run policy objectives, rather than long-run expectations of rate change and their implication for interest costs, may be the decisive factor in determining debt management policy.

Short-run adjustments aside, there remains the question of what constitutes a "sound" maturity mix insofar as the body of the outstanding debt is concerned. A long debt, as noted before, calls for a smaller volume of refunding operations, but this is hardly a decisive consideration. A debt of given size, if short, will leave the economy in a more liquid position and thus may tend to increase its volatility. As a result, the task of stabilization policy may be made more difficult. On the other hand, too long a debt may introduce rigidities into the financial structure and fall short of providing the necessary liquidity. In either case, much will depend on the size of the money stock. The effect on liquidity in the private sector of a longer debt combined with a larger money stock may be similar to the effect of a shorter debt with a smaller money supply. In the absence of better reasoning, one is left with the view that a "well-balanced" maturity structure up to, say, fifteen years is to be preferred to one which is almost entirely short or almost entirely long.

F. THE MARKET FOR STATE AND LOCAL DEBT

The problem of debt management for state and local governments is altogether different from that at the federal level and more like that of private investors attempting to secure funds in the market. The difference holds for both the demand and the supply sides of the picture. On the demand side, the occasion for borrowing by state and local governments occurs primarily when substantial capital expenditures are to be financed. For reasons considered in section D, it is prudent that such outlays be loan-financed rather than tax-financed. The rationale for borrowing at the state and local level is thus quite different from that at the federal level where stabilization policy is the primary determinant. On the supply side of the market for funds, a state or local government, unlike the federal government, has no control over the money market conditions under which it must borrow. The best it can do is to obtain funds on as favorable terms as happen to be open to it; and the cost of borrowing differs widely, depending on the fiscal position of the jurisdiction and its "credit rating."

State and local debt now exceeds $500 billion and has risen by an average annual amount of about $15 billion during the past decade. Its percentage rate of increase has been somewhat below that of the federal debt and of GNP. The debt is largely long term and may take various forms, including general obligation bonds and special revenue bonds. The latter are issued by particular agencies or public enterprises, such as water or power companies operated by the state, mu-

---

addition to long-term debt be reflected in an increased demand for short debt and money, but there may also be some desire to substitute equity. To the extent that this occurs, the cost at which equity funds become available is reduced and investment will rise. While less expansionary (or more restrictive) than the net addition of shorter debt, the effect of adding longer debt, taken by itself, may thus go in either direction. See James Tobin, "An Essay on Principles of Debt Management," in Commission on Money and Credit (ed.): *Fiscal and Debt Management Policies*, Englewood Cliffs, N.J.: Prentice-Hall, 1963.

nicipality, or other subdivision, and the profits of the enterprise are pledged for the financing of debt service. The cost at which funds are available to various borrowing jurisdictions enters as an important factor into the provision of those state and local services which involve heavy capital outlays, e.g., highways and school buildings. Such outlays are important from the national as well as the state and local perspective, so that state and local borrowing enters as an additional aspect of fiscal federalism.

Tax Exemption versus Direct Interest Subsidy

As we saw earlier, federal policy gives general support to state and local borrowing by excluding interest on such securities from taxable income under the federal income tax.[15] An investor whose marginal tax rate is 28 percent will be willing (other things being equal) to substitute a municipal bond yielding 4 percent for a corporate bond yielding 5.6 percent. This tax advantage diverts funds into the tax-exempt market, thereby reducing the cost at which state and local governments can borrow. As noted before, this advantage was greatly reduced by the 1986 cut in marginal tax rates.

But this particular form of aid is subject to criticism on two grounds. First, it interferes with the equity of the income tax structure. High-income recipients who receive tax-exempt interest pay less tax than do others with equal income from other sources. Moreover, the value of tax exemption rises with bracket rates so that vertical equity is interfered with. On these grounds alone, it would be preferable to provide such assistance as is desired in a way which does not involve tax preferences. Moreover, tax exemption results in a smaller gain in terms of interest savings to state and local governments than would be provided by a direct subsidy involving the same cost to the federal government.

Apart from the question of how support of interest payments is best given, there is the further question of whether general support for interest payments at the state-local level is called for. With state and local borrowing used for capital expenditure, such support is equivalent to a matching grant for capital outlays. Viewed this way, the question is whether capital expenditures as a group are preferable to current expenditures and hence merit a special subsidy, whether on grounds of spillover effects or of merit-good considerations. The answer seems to be in the negative. Aside from matters of politics and constitutional history (with the earlier view that state-local instrumentalities are to be exempted from federal taxation), the very premise of general interest support seems questionable.

Support for state and local borrowing on a more selective basis, parallel to the case for categorical grants, might be more readily justified. In this connection, the creation of a financial intermediary which would itself borrow in the market and then relend to municipalities is under consideration. Such a bank might be instrumental in overcoming the element of arbitrariness now imposed by the system of credit rating, and it would reduce the cost of borrowing for smaller municipalities by spreading risks. On the other hand, it might also introduce elements of political bias into the availability of funds. In other respects, such an institution might be

---

[15] See p. 335.

helpful in stabilizing cyclical fluctuations in borrowing costs and in modifying the unevenly heavy impact of changes in monetary policy upon this particular sector of the capital market.

Industrial Revenue Bonds

Finally, notice should be taken of the growth of industrial revenue bonds over the last decades. Such bonds are issued by state and local jurisdictions, the proceeds being used to construct industrial facilities which in turn are leased to private firms. More recently, such practice has also been extended into providing mortgage funds. Thus, the reduction in the cost of financing provided through federal tax exemption is passed on to what constitutes essentially private enterprises. From the point of view of a particular municipality, it is seen as a device to attract firms to its location. But such a policy is not defensible from the national point of view, and various limitations have been applied. Under the provision of the 1986 tax reform, such bonds to be eligible for interest reduction do not permit over 25 percent of the proceeds to be used in a trade or business other than the state or local government.

G. SUMMARY

The growth of the federal debt and its implications for the economy has for long been a lively issue of debate, especially so in the current setting of rising federal deficits.

    1.   About 80 percent of the public debt is federal and 20 percent state and local.

    2.   The growth of the federal debt must be seen in relation to GNP. The GNP-to-debt ratio of 128 percent prevailing at the end of World War II subsequently declined to 35 percent in 1980 and subsequently rose to over 50 percent by 1988.

    3.   The ratio of interest payments to GNP fell from 2.4 percent in 1946 to 1.4 percent in 1970, then climbed to 2 percent by 1980, and to over 3 percent by 1988.

    4.   Over 70 percent of the federal debt is in marketable form.

    5.   Commercial banks, insurance companies, and savings institutions are the major holders of federal debt.

    6.   One-third of the outstanding debt has a maturity of less than one year and only 16 percent carries a maturity of over 10 years.

    7.   Federal debt operations include lending by federal agencies largely in the form of mortgage credit.

Having examined the growth and structure of the federal debt, we turn to the economic implications of outstanding debt.

    8.   Fears that the outstanding debt cannot be repaid when it matures are unfounded. By the nature of public debt, maturing issues are refunded, not repaid.

    9.   A rising ratio of interest payments to GNP, however, imposes a burden because taxation is needed to finance the interest payments and imposes a deadweight loss.

    10.   However, prospective growth of this ratio, even under pessimistic assumptions, will be moderate and is not explosive in nature.

    11.   A rising rate of interest payments in the budget tends to crowd out other public programs.

    12.   Inflation may serve as a hidden form of debt repudiation, but this is not a major factor given the fact that the bulk of the federal debt is in very short maturities.

We next note that the role of the federal debt is part of the liquidity structure of the economy.

13. Public debt is an important investment medium for financial institutions, especially commercial banks, insurance companies, and money market funds.

14. The highly short term nature of the debt has rendered it increasingly liquid and a closer money substitute.

Careful examination was given to the question of whether debt finance imposes a burden on future generations.

15. Burden transfer to future generations is appropriate, as a matter of intergeneration equity, for the finance of public capital outlays.

16. Various mechanisms of burden transfer were considered, including (*a*) reduced capital formation, (*b*) transfer with generation overlap, and (*c*) transfer with outside debt.

17. Reliance on outside resources need not involve foreign absorption of the debt but may take the form of capital inflow and an associated import surplus.

The term structure of interest rates and the criteria for an optimal maturity mix were examined.

18. Whether long-term rates are above or below short-term rates depends on whether rates are expected to rise or fall.

19. The choice of maturity structure may be seen as a way of purchasing liquidity at least cost.

Finally, brief consideration was given to the market for state and local debt.

20. The market for state and local debt is highly stratified, with yields depending upon the credit rating of the jurisdiction.

21. The cost of borrowing for state and local governments is reduced, if inefficiently so, by the exclusion of interest payments on such debt from federal income tax.

22. Increasing and questionable use of state and local borrowing is made in the form of revenue bonds, which essentially serve to finance private industry under the umbrella of tax exemption.

FURTHER READINGS

Barro, Robert J.: "Are Government Bonds Net Wealth?" *Journal of Political Economy*, December 1974.

Ferguson, J. M. (ed.): *Public Debt and Future Generations*, Chapel Hill: University of North Carolina Press, 1964. Contains a selection of articles dealing with the problem of intergeneration equity.

Tobin, J.: "An Essay on Principles of Debt Management," in Commission on Money and Credit (ed.): *Fiscal and Debt Management Policies*, Englewood Cliffs, N.J.: Prentice-Hall, 1963.

Part Eight

International Issues

Chapter 33

International Fiscal Coordination*

A. Introduction to Tax Coordination: *Interindividual Equity; Internation Equity; Efficiency.* B. Coordination of Income and Profits Taxes: *Taxation of Earned Income; Taxation of Capital Income; Evaluation; Further Issues in U.S. Policy; International Division of Profits Base.* C. Coordination of Product Taxes: *Efficiency Aspects; Balance-of-Payments Aspects; GATT Rules; Common Market Policy; Revenue Distribution and Burden Export.* D. Expenditure Coordination. E. Coordination of Stabilization Policies: *Trade Effects; Capital Flows.* F. Summary.

Growing interdependence of the world economy has brought increasing concern with the international aspects of public finance. The combining of European economies into the Common Market, the increasing role of multinational corporations, the financing of joint efforts such as the United Nations and NATO, and a rising awareness of the international maldistribution of income have all pointed toward

*Reader's Guide to Chapter 33: The newest and one of the most interesting aspects of the fiscal problem relates to its role in the international setting. Many of the problems which traditionally have been dealt with only in the confines of national finance are becoming increasingly important in their application to international trade, capital flows, international organizations such as the United Nations, and the relationship between poor and rich countries. A brief survey of these new horizons is presented in this chapter.

the need for international fiscal coordination. In principle, these problems are similar to those previously encountered in our discussion of the relationship among member jurisdictions within the confines of a national federation,[1] but they differ in magnitude and international nature of the cooperative effort which is required. Since coordination of stabilization policies has been considered in an earlier context, it will not be reexamined here.[2]

A. INTRODUCTION TO TAX COORDINATION

Tax coordination has been the most discussed part of the problem, and various techniques have been developed to deal with it. Each country must decide how it chooses to tax the foreign income of its residents and the income of foreigners which originates within its borders. Similarly, it must decide how its product and sales taxes are to apply to its exports and imports. These decisions may be made in conjunction with other countries, and international tax treaties are a means of coordinating some of these matters.

As the sphere of tax policy is extended from a national to an international setting, old problems, such as the requirements of interindividual equity and effects on the efficiency of resource use, must be reconsidered, while new problems such as internation equity are added.

Interindividual Equity

If a person receives income which originates in various countries, he or she will be subject to taxation by more than one authority. Mr. A, a resident of the United States, may spend part of the year in the United Kingdom, and pay a United Kingdom tax on his earnings there. Or he may invest in the United Kingdom and derive dividend income on which a United Kingdom tax is paid. At the same time, he receives U.S. income and pays U.S. tax. Does horizontal equity require that he pay the same total of taxes (both domestic and foreign) as Ms. B, who receives the same total income but entirely from U.S. sources? Or should the United States simply consider taxes paid to other countries as a deduction from income and equalize tax burdens in terms of U.S. taxes only? In the first case equity is interpreted in an international sense, and in the second case in a national sense.

Internation Equity

A further and distinct equity problem arises in determining how the tax pie is to be divided among the treasuries of the various countries. This problem arises, although in different ways, with regard to both income and product taxes.

In regard to income and profits taxes, it is generally agreed that the country in which the income originates (also referred to as the "country of source") is entitled to tax that income, but the question is, at what rate? The United Kingdom tax imposed on the earnings of U.S. capital invested in the United Kingdom reduces the net return which accrues to the United States. It differs in this respect from such

---

[1] See p. 458.
[2] See p. 512.

additional taxes as may be imposed by the U.S. Treasury. The latter do not constitute a loss to the United States but are merely a transfer between U.S. residents and the U.S. Treasury. The national loss suffered by the United States thus depends only on the rate at which U.S. capital is taxed in the United Kingdom. One reasonable view of internation equity is that the country of source should be permitted to tax income accruing to foreign investors at the same rate at which foreign countries tax the income which its own residents derive abroad. This may be referred to as the principle of reciprocity.

In the matter of product taxes, the equity issue relates to the possibility of burdening foreigners through changes in price. If country A taxes exports, the cost of exports is increased. If the country dominates the export market, export prices will rise and the foreign consumer will pay more. Thus, part of the tax burden may be shifted abroad. Similarly, if imports are taxed, foreign suppliers may find that they must sell their products at a lower net price. Once more, part of the burden is shifted to the outside. If one accepts the criterion that a country should pay its own taxes, such burden shifting may be considered as running counter to internation equity.

Efficiency

Differential profits tax rates or, as pointed out earlier, differential fiscal net benefits or burdens will affect the location of economic activity and tend to draw resources from their most efficient uses. If Mr. C, an investor, finds his taxes lower if he invests in Italy rather than in the United States, he will send more of his capital to Italy than he would in the absence of the tax differential. The question, then, is how to arrange the taxation of international investment income so as not to disturb the efficiency of capital allocation on a *worldwide* basis. But international tax neutrality is not the only possible criterion. The objective may also be to implement a concept of *national* efficiency (to be explored presently), in which case a different arrangement is called for.

Differential product tax rates also cause inefficiencies but in a different way. If such taxes are imposed at the producer stage (rather than at the retail level), they affect the relative costs of producing a given product in various countries. As a result, the location of production is not determined by comparative advantage (or relative resource cost), which is the requirement for efficient trade, but is modified by differential tax costs.

B. COORDINATION OF INCOME AND PROFITS TAXES

With these general principles in mind, we now consider how they apply to the major taxes, beginning with income and profits taxes.

Taxation of Earned Income

The United States (like most other countries) reserves the right to tax the income of its residents no matter where earned. Ms. D, who spends six months of the year at a job in the United Kingdom and then returns to the United States, will pay United Kingdom tax on her income earned in the United Kingdom. In determining her

U.S. tax, she will include her United Kingdom earnings in her income, but she will credit taxes paid in the United Kingdom against her U.S. tax liability. Her final liability will then be the same as if the entire income had been earned in the United States. Such at least is the procedure so long as her United Kingdom tax does not exceed her U.S. tax on the same (United Kingdom–earned) income. If it does, no refund is given and her total tax is higher than if her income had been earned in the United States. However, a U.S. citizen who is a resident of a foreign country (or spends eleven months abroad) may exclude $90,000 of income earned abroad from U.S. tax.

The general principle thus is to permit income to be taxed in the country of origin with the country of primary residence extending the credit.

This is in line with a concept of internation equity which says that the country of income origin should not discriminate but may apply its own rates to the earnings of foreigners; and the granting of a credit by the country of primary residence, although involving a revenue loss to that country's treasury, is in line with the international view of interindividual equity.[3]

As a result of the increased labor mobility in postwar Europe, the treatment of migrant workers under social security has become a major problem. The usual policy is to extend social security benefits without differentiation, including payment of family allowances where family members remain in the home country. Differentials in social security benefits among countries have thus become a strong factor in attracting labor to high-benefit countries, the effect having been to widen effective wage differentials.

Taxation of Capital Income

The most important and complex part of the problem concerns the tax treatment of foreign investment income, including the treatment of such income received by individuals and corporations, with the latter being the major item.

Present U.S. Practice The major rules in the treatment of foreign investment income as they now apply in the United States are as follows:

1. An individual investor residing in the United States and receiving investment income from abroad pays individual income tax thereon. The government in the country of income origin typically imposes a "withholding tax" of, say, 15 percent, which in turn is credited against U.S. tax. In the reverse case, a similar withholding tax is imposed in the United States, the level of withholding rates generally being agreed upon in international tax treaties.

2. A U.S. corporation operating a branch abroad will find the profits of the branch subject to the foreign corporation tax in the country in which it is located. For purposes of U.S. tax, the profits of the parent corporation and its branch are considered as a unit. Foreign branch profits prior to foreign tax are included in the parent's taxable profits and the foreign tax is then credited against U.S. tax. The foreign country usu-

---

[3] Note that U.S. residents will pay under the same bracket rates whether their income is received here or abroad. However, the tax applicable in the United Kingdom will relate to the rate brackets applicable to United Kingdom income only. Some might argue that the United Kingdom is entitled to tax at rates applicable to the foreigner's total income.

ally imposes no withholding taxes when the profits are repatriated. Provided only that the foreign profits tax does not exceed the U.S. tax, it is a matter of indifference to the U.S. corporation whether profits originate at home or in a foreign branch.

   3.   Neither of these cases compares in importance with that of the foreign incorporated subsidiary. Although owned by the parent corporation in the United States, the foreign subsidiary is incorporated abroad and is legally a separate corporate entity. Its profits are subject to foreign corporation income tax and the U.S. tax is "deferred" until the profits of the subsidiary are repatriated by being paid as dividends to the parent company. At that time, such profits become subject to U.S. corporation tax. Profits gross of foreign profits tax are included in taxable income and the foreign tax is credited against the U.S. tax due.[4] Since the foreign tax (profits tax plus withholding) exceeds the U.S. tax, repatriated foreign earnings pay an extra tax. At the same time, profits which are retained abroad are subject only to foreign profits tax which, depending on location, may be above or below the U.S. tax.

Evaluation

In evaluating these arrangements, we consider the merits of (1) the foreign tax credit, and (2) the deferral provision.

   Credit versus Deduction of Foreign Tax   Crediting the foreign corporation tax against the U.S. corporation tax results in tax neutrality. Such at least is the outcome so long as the foreign tax (i.e., corporation tax plus withholding tax) is not higher than the U.S. tax. Since the U.S. rate applies whether the capital is invested at home or abroad, tax influences on investment choice are neutralized. Thus the efficient allocation of capital resources on a worldwide basis is not interfered with.

   This is an important advantage, but it is not the only way of looking at the matter. Whereas the credit device secures an efficient solution on a worldwide basis, it does not do so from a national point of view. Suppose that investment in both the United States and the United Kingdom yields a pre-tax return of 10 percent. Suppose further that the corporation tax rate in both countries is 34 percent, thus leaving the investor with a net return of 6.6 percent. Yet from the national standpoint, the return on investment made in the United States is 10 percent, with 6.6 percent going to the investor and 3.3 percent going to the U.S. Treasury. The latter share is lost to the investor but not to the country as a whole. However, the return to the United States on investment made in the United Kingdom is only 6.6 percent, the remaining 3.4 percent share which goes to the United Kingdom Exchequer is lost to the United States as a nation. We conclude that from the viewpoint of national efficiency, capital export should be carried to the point where the return *after* foreign tax abroad equals the before-tax return on domestic investment. This

---

[4] Suppose that foreign earnings of $1 million are subject to a foreign corporation tax of 35 percent, or $350,000, leaving $650,000. These earnings are to be repatriated. At the time of repatriation, an additional foreign tax (the "withholding tax") of 15 percent, or $97,500, applies, reducing net profits to $552,500. In the computation of U.S. taxes, the 28 percent rate is applied to $1 million, giving a gross tax of $280,000. Foreign taxes of $350,000 plus $97,500 are then credited, and wipe out the U.S. tax. The investor's total tax equals $350,000 plus $97,500 or $447,500, that is 44.75 percent.

in turn calls for a lower level of capital export than is appropriate under the criterion of world efficiency.

The investor will undertake foreign investment up to the point where the *net* return is the same as from domestic investment. Under the crediting approach, this will be the case where

$$(1 - t_{us})r_{us} = (1 - t_{us})r_f$$

t_{us} and t_f being the U.S. and foreign rates of tax, and r_{us} and r_f the U.S. and foreign rates of return, respectively. Thus, foreign investment is carried up to the point where

$$r_{us} = r_f$$

and the requirement of world efficiency is met. But suppose now that the foreign tax is *deducted* from taxable income rather than *credited* against the U.S. tax. In equating the net return from foreign and domestic investment, the investor will undertake foreign investment to the point where

$$(1 - t_{us})r_{us} = (1 - t_{us})(1 - t_f)r_f$$

that is, where $r_{us} = (1 - t_f)r_f$. Thus, the deduction approach meets the requirement of national efficiency.

Which of the two approaches is to be preferred is an open question. From the point of view of U.S. investors, the credit method is the more favorable since foreign investment income after tax will be larger. In the view of others such as U.S. wage earners, the deduction approach might be preferred. With more capital staying at home, domestic labor will be more productive and wages will be higher. In the matter of U.S. foreign investment, there thus exists a common interest shared by U.S. investors abroad and foreign workers (both of whom benefit) and U.S. workers and foreign owners of capital abroad (both of whom lose).

Deferral   The deferral provision is based on the somewhat fictitious assumption that the foreign subsidiary is a truly separate entity. Thus it seems to contradict the crediting provision which implies that the subsidiary's tax is in fact the parent's tax. To be sure, deferral makes little difference to the parent corporation if the foreign tax does not fall short of what the U.S. tax would be. This tends to be the case for investment in European countries but not for developing countries where tax rates may be substantially lower. Such at least was the case prior to the corporate tax reductions of 1981. Thus corporations were given an incentive not to repatriate and to divert earnings of subsidiaries into investments in low-tax (so-called tax haven) countries. In the 1960s and 1970s various steps were taken to limit such tax avoidance, but it remains a problem.

Further Issues in U.S. Policy

Two further issues relating to U.S. taxation of foreign investment income may be noted. One is posed by the Domestic International Sales Corporation (DISC) provision. Introduced in 1971, the provision is designed to extend the benefit of tax deferral to part of the profits earned by domestic corporations in pursuit of their export activities. Without such an extension, it was argued, domestic exporters would be at a disadvantage when compared with foreign affiliates. The provision has been a controversial one. Not only is it difficult to limit the benefit to production for exports, but limitation of deferral for foreign affiliates may be the better way of restoring balance. Moreover, it has been argued that the provision is in conflict with GATT rules which prohibit export subsidies.

Another controversial issue arises from the treatment of royalty payments by American oil companies to foreign governments. Such royalties, where disguised as profit taxes, are credited against U.S. tax. Since such payments tend to be reflected in price, it would seem appropriate to treat them as indirect taxes, thus allowing them to be treated as a deduction from income but not as a credit against tax.

International Division of Profits Base

We have argued that a country should be entitled to tax such profits as originate within its borders; but implementation of this rule renders it necessary, in the case of multinational corporations, to determine the profit shares which arise in different countries. This is not a simple matter. Suppose a U.S. corporation operates a subsidiary in Canada. Under the rules of internation equity, Canada is entitled to tax the profits of this subsidiary. But how can these profits be separated in a meaningful way from those of the parent company in the United States? If parent and subsidy sell or buy from each other, profits may be easily shifted from one country to another so as to place them where taxes are lower. The difficulties are compounded where tiers of subsidiaries operating in various countries are involved.

Efforts have been made to formulate rules which will preclude profit shifting, such as the requirement that prices be determined on an "arm's-length" basis, i.e., as they would have been if the dealing had been between independent companies. Given these difficulties inherent in conducting separate profit accounting for interrelated entities, it has been suggested that an altogether different approach might be taken. The profits base of multinational corporations might be allocated among countries not by location of subsidiaries but in line with the national origin of profits earned by the business group as a whole. Such origin might be approximated by a formula including both location of value added and sales in its base. Although attractive, this approach would require an international tax administration to implement it, and it therefore remains a rather far-off alternative.[5]

C. COORDINATION OF PRODUCT TAXES

The case for coordination of commodity taxes may be made on various grounds, including efficiency, balance-of-payments, and revenue considerations.

---

[5] See P. B. Musgrave, "The Division of Tax Base and the Multinational Corporation," *Public Finance,* vol. 27, no. 4, 1972. See also the analogous problem posed by the allocation of corporation taxes among states, p. 391.

Efficiency Aspects

Whereas in the case of income taxes the concern was with effects upon capital flows, attention is now directed to effects of product taxes on product flow. The argument is most readily presented under the assumption of flexible exchange rates.

The case for a free flow of international trade is based on the proposition that all trading countries will benefit if each specializes in the production of products in which it has a comparative advantage. Suppose that country A has a comparative advantage in producing product X while country B has an advantage in producing Y. Country A will thus export X and import Y, while country B imports X and exports Y. However, with production subject to increasing costs, A continues to produce some of its own Y and B produces some of its own X. Both A and B will be better off than they would be if there were no trade. By exporting X and importing Y, country A obtains a higher real income than if it produced all its Y at home; and vice versa for B.

Now consider how this situation may be affected by various taxes. For this purpose, we distinguish between consumption, or "destination," taxes which are imposed where the product ends up and is consumed, and production, or "origin," taxes which are imposed where the product originates or is produced. In deciding whether various taxes do or do not interfere with the location of production, the key question is whether the tax affects the relative prices of home-produced and imported goods. If it does, consumers will substitute one for the other and the location of production will differ from what it would be under neutral taxes.

Destination Taxes   Destination taxes do not interfere with the location of production unless there is an outright discrimination between home-produced and imported goods, i.e., unless the tax is in the form of a tariff or customs duty.

Suppose that country A imposes a general tax (e.g., a retail sales tax) on the consumption of all X and Y, including home-produced and imported goods. This will have no trade effects since consumers in A find relative prices of imported and home-produced goods unchanged.[6] Next, assume that the tax applies to Y only but again covers all Y whether imported or produced at home. As a result, consumers will increase their consumption of X and reduce their consumption of Y. This adjustment may affect the level of trade, but the location of production for both products (at their new levels) will still be in line with comparative advantage.[7]

The situation differs drastically if country A applies its tax to imported Y only, i.e., if it imposes a tariff. The tax now enters as a wedge between the relative prices of home-produced and imported goods, leading A's consumers to substitute home-produced Y for imports. As imports fall, the price of A's currency in terms of B's will rise. Thus, exports of X from A will also decline until a new equilib-

---

[6] Nothing else need be said provided that the general sales tax is added to price, leaving factor costs in A unchanged. If, instead, prices stay unchanged while factor costs decline, there will be an exchange rate adjustment so as to increase the price of A's currency in terms of B's, but trade is again unaffected in real terms.

[7] We do not concern ourselves here with inefficiencies which arise from the distortion of *consumption* choices between X and Y; our only concern in this context being with effects on the *location of production*.

rium is established at a lower level of trade and now with a less efficient division of production of X and Y between countries A and B.

Such taxes or tariffs interfere with efficient trade, and substantial efforts have been made in recent decades to reduce trade barriers, although current trends may lead to a reversal.

Origin Taxes   Turning now to the question of origin taxes, we find that distortions may arise although there is no attempt to discriminate against foreign products.

Suppose first that country B imposes a *general* production tax, say a manufacturer's excise tax of 10 percent, on both X and Y. As a result, prices in B rise in line with the tax. B's consumers, finding that the prices of home-produced goods have risen relative to those of imported goods, will import more. A's consumers find themselves in the opposite position. B's exporters will add the tax to their costs, so A's consumers will find import prices increased and will import less. Under flexible exchange rates, the resulting increase in demand for A's currency and decrease in demand for B's currency will cause the price of A's currency to rise relative to that of B's. This will dampen the desire of B's consumers to import more and of A's consumers to import less. Relative prices of exports and imports are unchanged and trade is unaffected in real terms.[8]

The situation differs if B's production tax applies to only one product, say its export good Y. Consumers in A again find the cost of Y increased and will substitute domestically produced Y. As A imports less Y, the price of A's currency in terms of B's rises. B's consumers find the cost of imports increased and B therefore imports less. A new equilibrium is established at a lower level of trade and with a changed distribution in the location of production. Country A now produces more Y and B produces more X than before. Imposition of a selective product tax on Y in country B thus results in a distorting effect similar to that following the imposition of an import duty on Y in country A.

This distorting result would have been avoided if country B had granted a tax rebate on its exported Y. B's move would have forestalled a rise in the price of imported Y in country A, so that there would have been no occasion for substituting home-produced Y. By granting an export rebate B's tax on Y would have been transformed from an origin tax into a destination tax. It would have been made equivalent to a retail sales tax on Y in B, a tax which, as shown before, does not distort the location of production provided only that it covers both imports and home products.

A similar story can be told if B's tax is on X. B's consumers will now substitute imported X, and a corresponding adjustment will follow. In the end, the real level of trade will be increased, but the location of production will again be distorted. More X will be produced in A and more Y will be produced in B than before. The distortion in this case might have been avoided by having B impose a

---

[8] To be precise, trade will remain unchanged if government expenditures are similar to those which would have been made privately in the absence of tax; but even if the pattern of demand changes so as to affect trade, the new pattern of trade will remain efficient in responding to the new structure of demand.

compensating import duty on X. The tax once more would have been transformed into a destination tax (now a tax on all X being consumed in B) without distorting location effects.

Balance-of-Payments Aspects

Similar effects on the location of production result under conditions of fixed exchange rates. However, the equilibrating mechanisms of exchange rate adjustments are then absent, and the additional problem of effects on the balance of payments arises. Taxes which worsen a country's balance of trade by raising imports or lowering exports now lead to a payments deficit.[9] Destination taxes are once more neutral, but origin taxes now worsen a country's balance of payments while tariffs improve it. The introduction of export rebates and of compensating import duties now not only forestalls production inefficiencies but also neutralizes the balance-of-payments effects of origin taxes. During the fifties and sixties when current international practices, such as the General Agreement on Tariffs and Trade (GATT) and Common Market policies, were being worked out, the setting was one of fixed exchange rates. Consequently, both efficiency and balance-of-payments considerations entered the picture, with the latter given primary emphasis. Since then exchange rates have been liberalized, so that balance-of-payments effects have declined in importance.

GATT Rules

In line with these objectives, the GATT provides that a country may grant an export rebate against product taxes which enter into the cost of production and may impose a compensating import duty on imported products.[10] Payroll taxes are not considered eligible for credit nor is the corporation tax, which is assumed to be borne by profits and not to be a component of costs.

United States practice complies with the GATT rules. Manufacturers' excises are reimbursed on exports, but this rebating of taxes is limited because U.S. product taxes are largely imposed at the retail level. Exports are excluded while both imported and home-produced products are subject to retail tax. In European countries, product taxes are typically imposed at an earlier stage or stages, as is the value-added tax. The volume of rebating is correspondingly larger, which has led to the complaint that exporters in European countries are given a competitive advantage because they can credit more tax; and this factor has been cited as supporting the case for a value-added tax in the United States. The argument overlooks

---

[9] Two further differences between the cases of fixed and flexible exchange rates may be noted:

    1.   Whereas a general origin tax has no bearing on trade in the case of flexible exchanges, it *does* matter with fixed rates. If country B imposes a general origin tax, the cost of B's products in A will rise and B will export less. At the same time, domestic prices will rise relative to those of imported goods and B will import more. Thus B develops a balance-of-payments deficit, the result being the same as that of currency appreciation.

    2.   As B imposes a general origin tax, effects on the balance of payments can be neutralized by adding an export rebate and a compensating import duty. This, however, is based on the assumption that prices in B will rise by the amount of tax. If, as is conceivable but not likely, factor prices fall with commodity prices remaining unchanged, no rebate and duty are called for. The GATT rules are based on the premise of rising prices.

[10] See GATT, *The General Agreement on Tariffs and Trade*, Part II, Articles III and XVI.

the fact that higher product taxes also increase costs, so that the benefit of the larger credit is needed as an offset. Without it, European producers would be at a competitive disadvantage.

Common Market Policy

The objectives of the Common Market go beyond those of GATT. Although the rebate and compensating duty devices neutralize trade and balance-of-payments effects of origin taxes, they still call for "fiscal frontiers" in order to determine when rebates or duties are due. Yet it was hoped that with the repeal of internal tariffs, fiscal frontiers could be discarded. To make this possible while maintaining tax neutrality, it has been decided that value-added tax rates should be made uniform across all member countries. This objective, which has not as yet been accomplished, would render export and compensating import duties unnecessary since all products, independent of origin within the market, would pay the same tax. Although elimination of import duties would be accomplished at the price of requiring uniformity in value-added tax rates, countries would continue to set their own rates of retail sales taxes.[11] Some observers who see coordination as a transition to a United States of Europe find the requirement of rate uniformity a desirable step, but others prefer to retain such degrees of freedom for individual countries as are compatible with the achievement of common interests.[12]

Revenue Distribution and Burden Export

In concluding this discussion of product tax coordination, we must again address the question of internation equity. The sensible rule seems to be that a country will be permitted to tax its own consumers but not those of other countries. This approach renders destination taxes (applicable to both imports and exports) but not origin taxes equitable. The latter, in the absence of a rebate, may serve to pass part of the burden to foreign consumers if the tax is on exports; or in the absence of compensating import duties, foreign exporters may benefit if the tax is on import substitutes. Either result runs counter to the rule of self-finance. The rebate and compensating import duty approach is thus in line with internation equity.

An exception arises where government provides intermediate goods which go to reduce the cost of exports, thus rendering the charging of foreign consumers via a destination tax appropriate.[13]

D. EXPENDITURE COORDINATION

Even though most of the attention in the discussion on fiscal coordination has been directed at the tax side, expenditures also enter the picture. They do so with regard to both government purchases and transfer payments.

[11] See the *Report of the Fiscal and Financial Committee on Tax Harmonization in the Common Market.* This report, prepared under the direction of F. Neumark, is reprinted in *Tax Harmonization in the Common Market,* Chicago: Commerce Clearing House, 1963.

[12] For a discussion of various approaches, see D. Dosser, "Economic Analysis of Tax Harmonization," in C. S. Shoup (ed.): *Fiscal Harmonization in Common Markets,* vol. 1, New York: Columbia University Press, 1967, chap. 1.

[13] See p. 169.

Nations, like municipalities, may have common concerns, involving benefit or cost spillovers which lead them to engage in joint projects. The St. Lawrence Seaway, calling for cooperation between the United States and Canada; NATO, involving a joint defense effort among a score of nations; cooperation in reducing pollution in international waterways such as the Rhine; malaria prevention programs conducted by the World Health Organization; Europe's Common Market; and the operation of the United Nations are cases in point.

In all such situations a problem of cost sharing arises. Where the number of participants is small, cost shares may be bargained out in relation to the advantages which each partner hopes to obtain. For the particular case of defense, it has been suggested that cooperation proves of greater net benefit to smaller partners since even a slight strengthening in the defense posture of a large ally provides a large increase in the degree of protection obtained by the small partner.[14] Where numbers are large, the problem is similar to that of interindividual budget determination. Some tax or assessment formula must be used, and ability-to-pay considerations similar to those applied in the domestic context may be employed. If a proportional assessment rate is to be used, each country may be asked to pay the same percentage of its GNP or national income. If progression is to be applied, the question arises whether the rate brackets should be related to the GNP of various countries (with the countries themselves considered the contributors) or whether they should be related to the per capita incomes of the residents in various countries (with individual residents considered the basic units). This problem parallels that of distributing membership votes in a legislative body (e.g., whether the Senate or the House principle of vote apportionment should be followed).

Both types of considerations are involved in determining contributions to the budget of the United Nations. While cost shares are voted upon each year and have been subject to frequent revisions, the procedure is essentially as follows:[15] The total cost is divided among member countries in line with their *contribution base* or GNP. This makes for a proportional tax in relation to GNP, independent of per capita income. This principle is then qualified by further provisions, including a "vanishing exemption" which protects low-income countries, a minimum contribution, and a limitation of the share to be contributed by any one country, with the highest share (now 25 percent) contributed by the United States.[16]

Other organizations have followed different patterns. Contributions to the International Monetary Fund (IMF) were rendered not on an annual basis but as purchase of initial capital stock. The quotas were assigned on a "benefit basis," i.e., related to drawing rights which in turn were determined in line with likely needs for IMF credit. A somewhat similar procedure was followed in assigning subscriptions to the capital stock of the International Bank for Reconstruction and Development. All these contributions, it should be noted, involve relatively small amounts, so

---

[14] See M. Olson, Jr., and R. Zeckhauser, "An Economic Theory of Alliances," *Review of Economics and Statistics,* August 1966; and A. Peacock, "The Public Finances of Inter-Allied Defense Provision," in *Essays in Honor of Antonio de Vito de Marco,* Bari, Italy: Cacucci Editore, 1972.

[15] See John Pincus, *Economic Aid and International Cost Sharing,* Baltimore: Johns Hopkins, 1965; and James E. Price, "The Tax Burden of International Organizations," *Public Finance,* no. 4, 1967.

[16] For further discussion, see *United Nations Yearbook.*

that the stakes for any particular country are not of major importance. Contributions to NATO, which did involve substantial amounts, have not been determined on a fixed formula basis but have been essentially subject to negotiation. The United States has met the largest share of NATO costs, probably exceeding its contribution had assessment been made in relation to the levels of GNP.

E. COORDINATION OF STABILIZATION POLICIES

In an increasingly interdependent world, the economic fate of any one country depends on what happens in other countries. One country, acting alone, is no longer able to control its own affairs. International cooperation in stabilization policy is needed. This is the case especially in closely knit economies such as those in the Common Market, but also holds for countries with lower trade involvement such as the United States. Coordination is particularly needed since interdependence involves not only trade but also capital flows.

Trade Effects

The major lines of interdependence have been noted in our earlier discussion of stabilization policy and need only be restated in summary form.[17] Consider first a setting of fixed exchange rates. As income and employment in country A decline, A's imports fall, thus transmitting the malaise to country B which suffers a decline in exports. As A undertakes an expansionary policy, A's income rises and so do its imports. The import leakage reduces the size of the multiplier and hence the effectiveness of A's policy; but it also spreads recovery to country B whose exports are increased. Policy effects are thus transmitted from one country to another and policy coordination is required to accommodate the needs of both countries. The trade effects of A's expansion will be dampened as we turn to a system of flexible exchange rates. As A's imports rise, the value of its currency will fall. Hence the cost of imports rises, thereby checking A's trade deficit as well as exports by B. Flexible exchange rates thus tend to reduce interdependence.

The same holds under conditions of inflation. Under fixed exchange rates, an inflationary policy in A will adversely affect A's balance of trade and thereby transmit demand pressures to B. Under a system of flexible exchange rates, this transmission is checked by a depreciation in the value of A's currency. Once more, flexible exchange rates reduce trade repercussions. This, however, draws an oversimplified picture. Exchange rates do not adjust at once, and discretionary changes in rates can become disturbing factors. Control over exchange rates itself becomes a policy instrument calling for further cooperation.

Capital Flows

The trade effects of expansionary or restrictive policies tend to be similar, whether undertaken by fiscal or by monetary means. The mix of stabilization policies comes to matter greatly, however, once effects on capital flows are considered. Capital flows respond to rates of return available in various countries. An easy fiscal–tight

[17] See p. 512.

money mix will leave interest rates higher and thus be more attractive to financial capital inflow, just as a tight fiscal–easy money mix will be less attractive. Returning to the former case, typical of U.S. policy during the eighties, capital inflow by strengthening the host country's exchange rate raises imports while reducing exports, thus temporarily raising the level of available resources.

The role of capital inflow becomes more important when considering the effects of stabilization policy on economic growth. Much depends on what form the resulting import surplus will take. If matched by an increase in real investment, there will be an increase in the host country's capital stock, to be reflected in rising productivity of its labor force. Such capital inflow, however, also results in foreign ownership of the host country's capital stock. Future capital income will be diverted to abroad, limiting the host country's own gain to the productivity gain of labor and of other domestic factors.

F. SUMMARY

In this chapter we have dealt with the interaction which results from the coexistence of diverse fiscal systems which are brought in touch with one another through the international flows of capital and trade.

This fact poses problems with regard to both the equity and the efficiency aspects of taxation.

1. With regard to equity among taxpayers, considerations of horizontal and vertical equity may now be extended to include all taxes which a person pays to whatever jurisdiction, as distinct from taxes paid to the individual's jurisdiction of major tax allegiance only.

2. Moreover, there now appears the additional equity question of how the tax base arising from international transactions should be divided among the participating countries, or the problem of internation equity.

3. With regard to efficiency effects, a distinction is now drawn between efficiency as seen from the point of view of worldwide resource use and efficiency as seen from a nation's point of view.

In dealing with the coordination of income and profits taxes, we noted many technical difficulties.

4. A U.S. resident earning income abroad will include such income for purposes of the U.S. income tax, but he or she may credit foreign tax payments against this tax. This provision applies to both wage and investment income.

5. Foreign branches of U.S. corporations are taxed abroad, but their income is included in the income of the parent corporation for purposes of U.S. corporation tax, with the foreign profits tax again credited against the U.S. tax.

6. Much of the largest part of U.S. direct foreign investment is made through subsidiaries of U.S. corporations. Their tax treatment differs from that of branches in that the income of the subsidiary is included in the parent's income for purposes of U.S. tax only when this income is repatriated.

7. An important policy issue is whether foreign taxes should be credited against U.S. tax or deducted from taxable income. The former is in line with world efficiency, the latter with national efficiency.

8. A second important question is whether the U.S. tax on subsidiary income

should be deferred until repatriation, a problem which also involves tax avoidance through tax-haven operations.

9. A further important policy issue relates to the way in which profits arising from international operations should be divided among the taxing authorities of the participating countries. The so-called arm's-length rule is used in this connection.

In dealing with the coordination of product taxes, our major concern was with potential distorting effects on commodity flows.

10. Destination taxes, e.g., retail sales taxes, do not interfere with commodity flows. They do so only if limited to imported goods, that is, if imposed as tariffs.

11. Origin taxes, or product taxes imposed in the country of production, do interfere with the efficient flow of trade since they affect relative costs of production, thus interfering with the flow of trade based on comparative advantage.

12. Such effects are neutralized, however, if product taxes are rebated at the point of export. GATT rules determine which taxes may be thus rebated.

13. Common Market policy in Europe aims at adoption of a uniform value-added tax, thus achieving efficiency without the need for export rebates.

While most attention has been given to fiscal coordination on the revenue side, conditions also arise under which expenditure coordination is called for.

14. Nations, like states or municipalities, may undertake joint provision of public services. This poses the problem of how cost shares should be divided among them.

A final and important aspect of cooperation involves coordination of stabilization policies.

15. Trade effects interfere with the effectiveness of independently undertaken stabilization policies.

16. The response of capital flows depends on the mix of stabilization measures.

17. On both counts policy coordination is called for.

FURTHER READINGS

Cnossen, Sijbren (ed.): *Tax Coordination in the European Community,* Antwerp, Kluwer, 1987.

Dosser, Douglas: "Customs Unions, Tax Unions and Development Unions," in R. M. Bird and J. C. Head (eds.): *Modern Fiscal Issues,* Toronto: University of Toronto Press, 1972.

Musgrave, P. B.: *United States Taxation of Foreign Investment Income: Issues and Arguments,* Cambridge, Mass.: Harvard Law School, International Tax Program, 1969.

Musgrave, R. A.: *Fiscal Systems,* New Haven, Conn.: Yale, 1969.

Chapter 34

Development Finance*

A. Ingredients of Development: *Public Sector Size and Per Capita Income; Capital Formation; Technology, Enterprise, and Efficiency; Social and Political Factors; Foreign Exchange; Balance and Bottlenecks; Role of Fiscal System; Size of Public Sector and Economic Growth.* **B. Fiscal Policy, Stability, and Growth:** *Revenue Requirements; Taxation, Saving, and the Distribution of Income; Foreign Borrowing; Aggregate Demand, Inflation, and Employment.* **C. Tax-Structure Policy:** *Taxable Capacity and Tax Effort; Tax-Structure Development; Individual Income Tax; Business Income Tax; Land Taxes; Wealth and Property Taxes; Commodity Taxes and Tariffs.* **D. Tax Incentives:** *Domestic Incentives; Capital versus Employment Incentives; Incentives to Foreign Capital; Export Incentives.* **E. Expenditure Policy. F. International Aid and Redistribution:** *Magnitude of Transfer Problem; Development Aid.* **G. Summary.**

Public finances, as we have seen throughout this volume, play an important role in the economies of high-income countries such as the United States. The same holds true, perhaps to a greater extent, for developing countries. Some of the difficulties

*Reader's Guide to Chapter 34: Many of the problems discussed in the preceding chapters apply as much to development finance as to the finance of developed countries. However, development finance poses additional problems and some of those previously considered, such as tax-structure design covered in Chapters 19 to 26, appear in a somewhat different light. For this reason, the major aspects of development finance are reviewed in this concluding chapter.

which obstruct the economic progress of low-income countries call for solution by the public sector; yet the institutional and social settings of such countries complicate and constrain the task of budgetary policy. For these reasons, the problems of development finance deserve special and separate consideration.

A.   INGREDIENTS OF DEVELOPMENT

The requirements for economic development in low-income countries include those needed for continued economic growth in the comparatively highly developed countries, but much more besides.[1] To achieve this growth, not only are capital formation (including investment in both physical and human capital) and technological process needed, but also certain changes are required in the social and institutional settings which have been both cause and effect of a low level of economic development. The public sector has an important part to play in all these ingredients of development.

Public Sector Size and Per Capita Income

As noted in our earlier discussion of public sector development in high-income countries, the public sector share has tended to grow with per capita income.[2] A similar picture, including both low- and high-income countries, is given in Figure 34-1. For lack of complete data, only central government expenditures are included. Viewing the picture as a whole, here drawn on a semi-log scale, we again find a positive relationship, especially if the cluster of low-income countries is compared with the high-income group. At the same time, there is no distinct relationship within the group of lower-income countries taken by itself.

Capital Formation

A fundamental requirement of economic development is an adequate rate of capital formation relative to that of population expansion. Such capital formation should be broadly defined to include all expenditures of a productivity-increasing nature. It may take the form of investment in the public or the private sector. Particularly in the early stages of development, the former is of critical importance since in the form of so-called infrastructure (power, communications, port facilities, etc.), it sets the framework for subsequent manufacturing investment whether public (in the socialist economies) or private (in the market economy case). Furthermore, capital formation includes investment in human resources in the form of education and training as well as in physical assets. Indeed, where human productivity is adversely affected by malnutrition and disease, increased food consumption and provision of sanitation and health facilities take on the aspect of investment in human capital. Thus the use of resources for productivity-enhancing purposes may take a wide variety of forms, and the actual mix must be determined in the process of

---

[1] For broad-based discussions of development strategy, see Arnold C. Harberger, "The Fundamentals of Economic Progress in Underdeveloped Countries," *American Economic Review,* May 1959; and Hollis B. Chenery, "Growth and Structural Change," *Finance and Development,* International Monetary Fund and World Bank, November 3, 1971.

[2] See also Ch. 17 above.

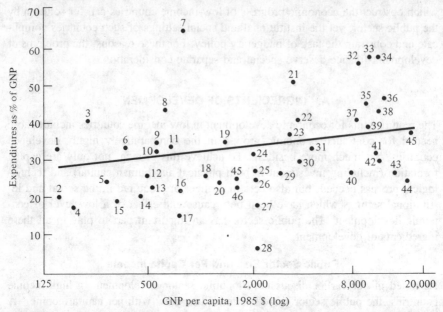

FIGURE 34-1   Per capita GNP and share of central government in GNP, 1985. Number reference to countries as follows: 1, Mali; 2, Nepal; 3, Togo; 4, Burma; 5, Tanzania; 6, Sri Lanka; 7, Nicaragua; 8, Egypt; 9, Morocco; 10, Yemen; 11, Zimbabwe; 12, Liberia; 13, Indonesia; 14, Lesotho; 15, Pakistan; 16, Thailand; 17, Dominican Republic; 18, Turkey; 19, Chile; 20, Costa Rica; 21, Greece; 22, Gabon; 23, Malta; 24, Panama; 25, Mexico; 26, Argentina; 27, Korea; 28, Yugoslavia; 29, Venezuela; 30, Cyprus; 31, Barbados; 32, Italy; 33, Belgium; 34, Netherlands; 35, France; 36, Sweden; 37, Great Britain; 38, Denmark; 39, Australia; 40, Singapore; 41, Ireland; 42, W. Germany; 43, Canada; 44, U.S.A.; 45, Norway. *Source:* IMF Government Finance Statistics and The World Bank, *World Development Report, 1988; Public Finances in Developing Countries,* Washington, D.C., 1988.

expenditure and resource planning. Moreover, priorities change over time and with them the optimum investment mix.

Leaving aside for the time being the problem of investment planning, let us focus on the sources from which these additional resources for investment can be drawn. Unless unutilized resources can be brought into use or additional resources can be procured from abroad, there must be a reduction in current consumption to release the necessary resources for investment purposes. To a certain extent, the mobilization of unused resources should be possible. It has been argued, for example, that many low-income economies possess substantial amounts of underutilized labor which may be put to work on simple forms of public capital formation, such as drainage, irrigation, roads, and dams. The government then enters only as organizer of this improved resource use. But this source of capital formation has its inherent limits; and putting underemployed labor to work may itself require certain supporting investments.

A further possibility is to obtain the needed investment resources from abroad in the form of official loans and grants or as private investment. Neither source, however, is likely to do the whole job, and in any case, will not be forthcoming without supportive "own" effort on the part of the host country. Private investors from abroad, like private investors at home, require the necessary infrastructure investment; and official aid will most likely be conditional upon well-formulated development plans which include provision for substantial tax-financed increases in domestic investment.

Unavoidably, then, a large part of the problem remains one of diverting the needed resources for development from their use in current consumption. In a centrally controlled economy with public enterprise predominating, this shift can be made by holding returns paid to factors of production below their marginal product earnings; but in a decentralized economy, such internal sources of capital formation must come from public or private savings. To some extent, if conditions are rendered congenial, this increased rate of saving may be generated voluntarily in the private sector. Here the government may be helpful in securing reasonable monetary stability so that savings habits are not discouraged by continuing inflation; also, the government may play a part in facilitation, or itself creating, the appropriate financial institutions to attract household savings and direct them into productive uses. The latter is of particular importance for the small saver for whom few uses for personal savings exist beyond high-risk money lending or the collection of valuables like gold. Taxation, as will be seen, has an important role to play in providing savings incentives and/or disincentives to luxury consumption. Business saving may also be encouraged through a system of business income taxation which encourages the retention and reinvestment of earnings.

Voluntary private saving, while useful and important, cannot be expected to be sufficient in itself, particularly at an early stage of development. An economic climate conducive to private saving takes time to develop, and in the meantime, the less developed country must look to the government budget as the most promising source of finance for development purposes. We again define government saving in the classical sense as equal to total revenue minus government consumption expenditures.[3] This public sector saving may be increased by raising total tax revenue and/or reducing current expenditures. Tax revenue must be looked on as a precious and scarce resource, hard to come by, and many a development plan has come to grief as a result of the profligate spending policies of the government, which in turn was often acting under political pressure.

Government saving generated by a surplus in the current budget may be used to finance capital formation in either the public or the private sector. In the latter case, the government saving may be channeled into private investment as debt or equity capital through the medium of government lending agencies or development banks.

Technology, Enterprise, and Efficiency

Improved technology is another important element in the development process, including manufacturing and agriculture. The massive improvements in agricultural productivity in a number of developing countries over the past decade attest to the benefits to be derived from improved technology in that sector. A principal benefit

---

[3] This concept of government saving must be distinguished from the surplus in the *total* budget, i.e., total revenue minus *total* expenditures, which is relevant for the management of aggregate demand. See p. 532.

of private investment from abroad lies in the improved technologies which it brings, although it is important that these be adapted to the particular conditions and resource endowments of the less developed countries (LDCs) themselves. Tax provisions may be designed to stimulate and encourage the use of improved techniques.

Business enterprise is needed if a flourishing private sector is to develop alongside the public sector. In its absence, government enterprise must fill the gap. As with technology, the tax structure can be designed so as to encourage (or at least not to discourage) the willingness to undertake productive investment.

Needless to say, the issue of efficiency in resource use becomes of critical importance in the resource-scarce LDCs, and in the public no less than in the private sector. This factor involves proper expenditure evaluation on the part of the government as well as a development plan which avoids wasteful bottlenecks arising during the development process. Furthermore, distortions arising in the pattern of taxes and tariffs, which in turn induce an inefficient pattern of production in the private sector, should be avoided.

Social and Political Factors

Some of the most intractable problems associated with economic development include the whole range of social attitudes and organizations which have to be modified if development is to proceed. At the same time, a substantial degree of political stability is also needed to allow individual initiative to flourish, development plans to be implemented, and the necessary economic transformation to take place. It is therefore crucial that the fruits of development be bestowed broadly and that extremes of income inequality prevalent in many of the LDCs be dealt with. Whereas certain kinds of redistribution (e.g., land reform) can be undertaken without prejudice to the level of output and indeed may be helpful in this respect, conflicts can arise between policies directed toward a more equitable distribution of income and the objective of increased saving and investment. Whereas public saving can be increased by raising the level of taxation, private incentives to invest may have to be traded off against redistributive tax policies.

Foreign Exchange

Foreign trade plays a critical role in many of the less developed economies. With limited internal markets, foreign trade involvement permits greater specialization, economies of scale, and exercise of comparative advantage. In addition, foreign exchange earnings allow the purchase of certain products (such as machinery and equipment) which are needed for the development process but for which the necessary technology is not available domestically. Yet another contribution of exports to development may be the provision of an expanding market around which "linkage" investments may be made, thereby creating an "export-led" nexus of development.

Thus, public policy must be concerned with the division of resources not only between consumption and investment but also between domestic and traded products; and among traded products that are both import-competing and exported goods. The tax structure, again, has a part to play in the general allocation process embodied in the development plan.

Balance and Bottlenecks

As economic development proceeds, various bottlenecks or limitations to the growth rate may crop up. For example, it has been suggested that in the early stage, the rate of internal saving is the controlling factor. As the rate of saving, and with it the growth of the economy, increases (aided, perhaps, by capital inflow from abroad), the absorptive capacity of the economy becomes the limiting factor, i.e., all the supportive factors which are needed to render the investment productive. Finally, the development process begins to create strains in the balance of payments, outstripping the capacity of the economy to earn foreign exchange to meet imports through exports. Thus, the resources made available for development purposes may go to waste because of these bottlenecks. A sound development plan should therefore endeavor to keep the process running smoothly by a policy of balanced growth. Tax policy in particular may be employed to encourage capital inflow as well as to affect the level of imports and exports.

Role of Fiscal System

It is thus evident that the fiscal system plays a multifold role in the process of economic development:

1. The level of taxation affects the level of public saving and thus the volume of resources available for capital formation.
2. Both the level and the structure of taxation affect the level of private saving.
3. Public investment is needed to provide infrastructure types of investment.
4. A system of tax incentives and penalties may be designed to influence the efficiency of resource utilization.
5. The distribution of tax burdens (along with the distribution of expenditure benefits) plays a large part in promoting an equitable distribution of the fruits of economic development.
6. The tax treatment of investment from abroad may affect the volume of capital inflow and the rate of reinvestment of earnings therefrom.
7. The pattern of taxation on imports and exports relative to that of domestic products will affect the foreign trade balance.

Size of Public Sector and Economic Growth

As is evident from the discussion of this chapter, there are many ways in which the functioning of the public sector bears on economic growth and may do so in both a helpful and a harmful way. A general view of the problem is provided in Figure 34-2, which relates public sector share in GNP to the rate of economic growth. Including a sample of 30 developing countries and covering the decade of 1972–1983, we find little or no evidence of a systematic relationship. This perhaps is as may be expected since so much depends on the content of public expenditures, and many other factors, unrelated to the budget, enter as well. Nevertheless, it is important to note that no ready judgment, pointing one way or the other can be made.

B. FISCAL POLICY, STABILITY, AND GROWTH

The role of fiscal policy in securing stability and growth in the LDCs is of fundamental importance. We begin by considering certain macro aspects of this problem.

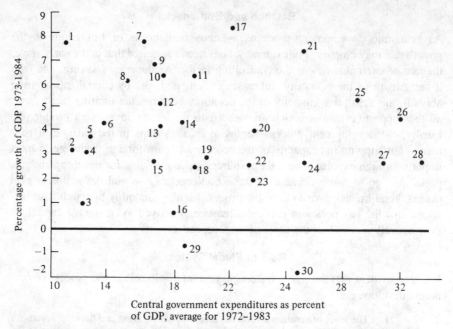

FIGURE 34-2 Government share and economic growth in developing countries.
Number reference to countries as follows: 1, Paraguay; 2, Guatemala; 3, Bolivia; 4,
Nepal; 5, Colombia; 6, Yugoslavia; 7, Korea; 8, Burma; 9, Thailand; 10, Pakistan; 11,
Indonesia; 12, Mexico; 13, Dominican Republic; 14, Brazil; 15, Haiti; 16, Argentina;
17, Singapore; 18, Senegal; 19, Costa Rica; 20, Turkey; 21, Malaysia; 22, Zaire; 23,
Nicaragua; 24, Tanzania; 25, Tunisia; 26, Morocco; 27, Chile; 28, Greece. *Source:*
IMF Government Finance Statistics and The World Bank, *World Development Report,*
1988; Public Finances in Developing Countries, Washington, D.C., 1988.

Revenue Requirements

To begin with, it is helpful to view the problem in terms of a fully employed
economy and to focus on the role of fiscal policy as a means of raising the
domestic savings ratio. In making a first approximation to the amount of tax
revenue needed to achieve a certain target rate of growth, differences between
various sources of tax revenue are disregarded. Suppose that the objective is to
achieve a 2 percent annual rate of growth in income per head. With, say, a 2
percent annual growth rate of population, national income must then grow at
slightly above 4 percent per year. This target rate of growth requires a certain rate
of capital formation, or investment expenditures as a percentage of national income. This ratio z, may be crudely estimated by the use of an incremental capital-
output ratio, and is defined as follows:

$$z = \frac{\Delta K}{\Delta Y} = \frac{I}{\Delta Y}$$

where K = capital stock

I = level of annual investment
Y = national income [4]

If g is the desired rate of growth,

$$g = \frac{\Delta Y}{Y}$$

the required investment rate I/Y may be obtained by substitution as

$$\frac{I}{Y} = \frac{\Delta K}{\Delta Y} \cdot \frac{\Delta Y}{Y} = zg$$

Thus, if $z = 3$, and $g = 4$ percent, $I/Y = 12$ percent. This investment ratio must be matched by a corresponding saving ratio to ensure economic balance. Therefore, the economy must save 12 percent of national income to grow at the desired rate of 4 percent. We must have

$$S_p + S_g = 0.12Y \tag{1}$$

where S_p is private saving and S_g is government saving. The level of private saving is given by

$$S_p = s(Y - T)$$

or

$$S_p = s(1 - t)Y \tag{2}$$

where s = propensity to save out of disposable income
T = tax revenue
t = tax rate

The level of government savings equals

$$S_g = tY - aY \tag{3}$$

where a is current expenditures of government as a fraction of national income.[5] Substituting equations (2) and (3) into (1), we obtain

$$t = \frac{0.12 - s + a}{1 - s} \tag{4}$$

---

[4] In reality, macroplanning of this type would proceed on a disaggregated basis in which a weighted average of incremental capital-output ratios for different sectors of the economy is applied.
[5] Government saving thus defined equals the surplus in the current budget. See p. 534.

TABLE 34-1
Distribution Patterns in Less Developed Countries*

| | PERCENTAGE SHARES IN TOTAL | | |
Ranking by Income	Income (I)	Consumption (II)	Saving (III)
Top 1 percent	20	18	50
Next 9 percent	25	23	50
Next 15 percent	20	22	0
Lowest 75 percent	35	37	0
Total	100	100	100

*The data in column I reflect a typical pattern among available distribution estimates for Latin American countries. Columns II and III include the authors' best guesses designed to reflect the typical situation.

Using a typical value for s of 3 percent and for a of 10 percent, we obtain $t = 19.6$. That is to say, a tax rate of 19.6 percent is needed to obtain a growth rate of 4 percent.[6] With government current expenditures equal to 10 percent of national income, government savings equal to 9.6 percent of national income may be either used to finance public investment or loaned out to finance additional private investment. Having made this first approximation to its revenue needs, the government must then judge whether such a target is feasible and can be attained under any realistic tax reform program. This decision will depend on the institutional framework, the capabilities of tax administration, and the political will to make the necessary tax assessments stick. But two points should be noted. First, a very large effort is required to raise the revenue-income ratio by even one percentage point. Second, a development plan which is too ambitious to be implemented and requires more than the tax system can reasonably be expected to produce may be worse than no development plan at all, because it invites the waste of uncompleted projects and the danger of inflation, not to mention the social repercussions arising from unfulfilled expectations.

Taxation, Saving, and the Distribution of Income

We must now correct the simplifying assumption of the preceding section that all tax dollars are equally useful in raising the level of domestic saving. Indeed, the central problem of tax policy in developing countries is how to obtain the necessary revenue while at the same time providing some correction for a typically high degree of inequality in the distribution of income, but without interfering unduly with private saving and investment.[7]

In Table 34-1, the setting of this problem is presented in more concrete form. The distribution of income, consumption, and saving is shown as it might apply in

---

[6] Since the required savings rate equals zg, equation (4) may be rewritten as

$$t = \frac{zg - s + a}{1 - s}$$

[7] See Richard M. Bird, "Income Redistribution, Economic Growth, and Tax Policy," *Proceedings,* Columbus: National Tax Association, 1969.

a typical LDC, say, a low-income Latin American country. We find that the upper 10 percent of income recipients receive some 45 percent of income and the lowest 75 percent receive 35 percent. The corresponding shares in consumption are estimated at 41 percent and 37 percent while the shares in saving are 100 and 0 percent. The degree of inequality is thus substantially greater than that in developed countries such as the United States, where the corresponding income shares are 30 and 47 percent.

In addition to the highly unequal distribution of income, two other features stand out. First, a very substantial share of total income goes into "luxury" consumption. Defining luxury consumption as per capita consumption in excess of the average per capita consumption and taking total consumption to be 95 percent of total income, it appears that luxury consumption accounts for about 36 percent of income.[8] Consequently, luxury consumption provides a substantial potential reserve for additional taxation. Second, such private savings as there are originate largely in the very high income brackets, including corporate savings in which equity shares are owned. Therefore, highly progressive income taxation as well as high rates of profits tax cut heavily into private sector saving and thereby retard development.[9] Putting the two features together, we note that the key to development finance appears to lie in progressive consumption taxation.[10]

Ideally, this taxation would be applied in the form of a personal consumption tax, but few if any LDCs could do so effectively. As we noted before, effective application of such a tax to higher incomes would require balance-sheet accounting as well as the reporting of earnings, which is difficult even for developed countries.[11] Practical policy must therefore make do with a less perfect approach, i.e., a set of excise taxes which impose higher rates on items that weigh more heavily in the outlays of higher-income households. To this may be added a progressive property tax on residences to deal with housing consumption. In this way, revenue can be obtained by drawing on the pool of luxury consumption, thereby reducing consumption inequality while stimulating rather than depressing saving.

Lest the advantages of this approach be overstated, two shortcomings must be noted. For one thing, there still remains the problem of detrimental effects on work incentives. Such effects may be less in the case of consumption taxation than with progressive income taxation, but they are not eliminated. For another, progressive consumption taxes can reduce inequality of consumption but not inequality of income and wealth. Since the distribution of income and wealth is also significant in securing a broad sharing of development gains, progressive consumption taxes can-

---

[8] From Table 34-1, it can be calculated that the upper 25 percent of the population partake of 63 percent of consumption. Their luxury consumption (defined as that in excess of average per capita consumption) thus represents $63 - 25$, or 38 percent of total consumption. Since consumption as a whole is 95 percent of total income, this "excess" equals $.095 \times 38$, or 36 percent of total income.

[9] For emphasis on the importance of profits in the industrial sector as a source of saving, see W. A. Lewis, *The Theory of Economic Growth,* Homewood, Ill.: Irwin, chap. 5.

[10] See N. Kaldor, "The Expenditure Tax in a System of Personal Taxation," in R. M. Bird and O. Oldman (eds.): *Readings on Taxation in Developing Countries,* 2d ed., Cambridge, Mass.: Harvard Law School, International Tax Program, 1967, pp. 253–273.

[11] See p. 404. A particular difficulty in the case of LDCs is tax avoidance by shifting funds abroad, permitting tax-free spending outside the country. Tight exchange controls may therefore be necessary to close this loophole.

not entirely replace progressive income and wealth taxation. A proper balance between these forms of taxation is called for, such balance being superior to excessive reliance on the income tax approach.

Foreign Borrowing

Prior consideration was given to the role of loan finance in economic development when discussing public debt, but the problem should be noted once more in the present context.[12] The earlier conclusion was that development requires capital formation and that capital formation requires saving. Public investment which is financed by borrowing does not add to capital formation if it merely diverts funds otherwise available for private investment. This recognition also underlies the preceding model on the basis of which the required rate of taxation was determined.

The situation is different, however, if borrowing is from abroad. In this case, additional resources become available, because borrowing is accompanied by increased imports. This borrowing provides additional resources for investment and permits financing a given growth rate with a lower rate of tax and a higher rate of current consumption. Even though the net gain to future generations will be less than it would have been with tax finance, their surrender of consumption (to service the foreign debt) will be less burdensome than tax finance would have been to the initial generation. The reason is that other factors of production, such as labor, share in the productivity gain generated by the increased rate of capital formation. Because of this growth, the future cutback in consumption is made out of a higher level of income, and since the marginal utility of consumption declines with rising consumption levels, the resulting burden will be less severe.

It is thus the income gain to domestic factors which renders foreign borrowing such an important instrument of development policy. Other useful functions of capital import include the provision of foreign exchange and the collateral advantages gained from the introduction of advanced technology and managerial know-how.[13] At the same time, foreign borrowing has its risk, especially when obligations of debt service exceed what can be accommodated with a country's balance of payment constraint. The crisis in which many of the less developed countries now find themselves well illustrates this danger.

Aggregate Demand, Inflation, and Employment

In the above discussion, we proceeded on the assumption of a fully employed economy. In this setting, the appropriate level of aggregate demand is given by the available level of output as valued at current prices. The basic rule for fiscal and monetary policy in this case is to let aggregate expenditures rise with the growth in full-employment output, neither faster nor slower. We now consider two ways in which this conclusion may be qualified.

Inflation as a Source of Saving   It has been argued at times that some degree of inflation will contribute to development because it may impose forced saving

---

[12] See p. 556.

[13] As with all good things in life, there are also disadvantages and dangers. Foreign capital import may bring foreign control and retard the development of domestic managerial talent. For an emphasis on these aspects, see A. O. Hirschman, "How to Divest in Latin America and Why," in A. O. Hirschman (ed.): *A Bias for Hope*, New Haven, Conn.: Yale University Press, 1971, pp. 225–253.

upon consumers. If credit expansion finances increased capital formation (public or private), rising prices reduce the real income of consumers, thus lowering consumption in real terms. In this way, inflation may serve to transfer real resources to capital formation.

Such indeed could be the outcome, but one hesitates to prescribe it as a policy guide. For one thing, inflationary credit creation may be used to finance consumption (especially public consumption) rather than capital formation. For another, the "inflation tax" is among the least equitable of all taxes. Moreover, the inflationary process easily becomes a habit and leads to distortion of investment decisions. Perhaps worst of all, inflationary expectations may lead to a reduction in private saving propensities. For these and other reasons, inflation cannot be recommended as a legitimate approach to development policy.

Underemployment and Unemployment   Apart from avoiding inflation, may aggregate demand management not also be needed to ensure full employment of resources? Put differently, the question is whether unemployment in LDCs is of a kind which can be remedied by an increase in aggregate demand, as is frequently possible in developed countries. This problem arises especially in the context of agriculture and migration to urban areas.

It is widely observed in LDCs that there is a surplus of agricultural labor in the sense that labor is only partially employed, except at harvest time. Cannot such labor be drawn into industrial employment by increased demand based on a higher level of expenditures? The answer depends on the wages which such labor could obtain outside agriculture. If labor productivity is low, the gain might not suffice to offset the increased living costs which are incurred in movement from the farm. The problem may thus be one of low productivity rather than of unemployment; and if this is so, the remedy lies in capital formation and increased productivity rather than in a higher level of expenditures.

The existence of heavy urban unemployment in turn may come about as a result of out-migration, attracted by what appear to be high wages in the industrial or urban sector; but minimum wage legislation or union demands may place a floor below such wages which in turn may make it impossible to absorb the labor influx. As noted below, a remedy lies in tax provisions which counter the overpricing of labor in the market, with increased aggregate demand again an inappropriate measure.

At the same time, these difficulties do not preclude the existence of genuine Keynesian unemployment which can be met by more expansionary demand policy. Some observers have noted that in Latin American countries, existing capital stock is frequently underutilized, so increased employment should be possible. An expansionary fiscal policy, combined with measures to secure the necessary supportive resources, may be helpful in bringing this about.

C. TAX-STRUCTURE POLICY

We now turn to more specific issues of tax policy, beginning with a consideration of tax effort.

Taxable Capacity and Tax Effort

Although it is important, in line with our earlier reasoning, to know what overall level of tax revenue is required to secure a given growth target, the feasibility of achieving that level of taxation is an important consideration which must be allowed for when the target is set. Tax policy must be considered along with other aspects of development policy, but it must not be looked at as the dependent variable in the system which will automatically respond to the requirements placed upon it.

How, then, can one judge what tax effort a country is capable of, and how can its tax performance be measured? As seen earlier, the size of the public sector in developed countries has not only risen with rising per capita income, but the latter has been accompanied by a rising share of the public sector in GNP.[14] As an alternative way of looking at the role of per capita income in explaining the rising share of the public sector, Figure 34-1 above compared the shares for countries with varying levels of per capita income but at the same point in time.[15] We noted the share to be very much smaller for low-income countries as a group, but did not observe a marked relationship within that group. The same pattern also prevails if the ratio of tax revenue to GNP is considered. Once more that ratio in less developed countries is typically quite low, ranging from 8 to 18 percent. Among Latin American countries, the typical ratio is around 14 percent, with some countries as low as 8 percent. The ratios for African and Asian countries with similar per capita incomes tend to be somewhat (though not much) higher. This compares with developed-country ratios of 40 percent and more.

Why is it that the tax effort in developing countries is so much lower, and does the lower ratio in fact signify a lower effort? The answer depends on what the term tax effort is taken to mean. An international lending agency may wish to make its aid con-

---

[14] See p. 584.

[15] For an earlier study see R.J. Chelliah, H.J. Baas, and M.R Kelly, "Tax Ratios and Tax Effort in Developing Countries, 1969–71," *IMF Staff Papers*, International Monetary Fund, 1975.

Writing T for tax revenue and GNP_{pc} for per capita income, the regression equation (based on fifty-three countries) is

$$T/GNP = 14.64 + .006GNP_{pc}$$
$$(11.3) \qquad (8.6)$$

where the figures in parentheses are the ratios of intercept and regression coefficient to their respective standard errors and the R^2 is 0.59.

If social security taxes are excluded, the equation (based on sixty-three countries) becomes

$$T/GNP = 14.11 + .004GNP_{pc}$$
$$(15.2) \qquad (6.7)$$

with an R^2 of 0.41. Thus, per capita income has a high explanatory value in both cases and a good fit is obtained. This picture, however, deteriorates if developing and developed countries are grouped separately. Excluding social security, the equation for forty-seven developing countries is

$$T/GNP = 13.69 + .004GNP_{pc}$$
$$(10.5) \qquad (1.3)$$

With R^2 values of 0.040 and 0.024 respectively. (For source see preceding footnote.)

tingent on the recipient country's making an adequate tax effort of its own. The lending agency may then require a country with a higher per capita income to show a higher revenue ratio in order to demonstrate the same level of tax effort.

A low-income country has less scope for the transfer of resources to public use.[16] At a very low level of per capita income, all private income is needed to meet the very necessities of life, such as food and shelter. Unless the public use of funds is to provide equally basic necessities (e.g., minimal health and sanitation programs), the diversion of funds involves an unsupportably heavy current burden. This conclusion is modified where a highly unequal income distribution results in substantial luxury consumption. As noted before, this factor is frequently of considerable importance as a potential source of taxation.

Apart from the level and distribution of income, the availability of tax handles is related to the economic structure of the country. Thus, the administration of an income tax is much more difficult where employment is in small establishments. Profits taxation is not feasible until accounting practices attain minimal standards, and it is difficult if firms are small and unstable. Product taxes cannot be imposed at the retail level if retail establishments are small and impermanent. Effective land taxation is difficult where food is home-consumed, the agricultural sector is largely nonmonetized, and land surveys are inadequate in providing proper valuations. On the other hand, taxation is simplified in a highly open economy where imports and exports pass through major ports and thus can be readily established by tax authorities.

Finally, the feasibility of taxation depends upon how society views the need for compliance, the extent to which the courts are willing to enforce tax laws, and the availability of a competent and honest staff of tax administrators. Resort to tax farming, i.e., a system where collectors are given a percentage of their tax takes as an incentive, may be a helpful short-run device, as may be the assignment of revenue quotas to tax officials, but these are not methods on which a durable and equitable tax structure can be built.

For these and other reasons, a realistic appraisal of a country's tax effort must allow for the tax handles which are available to it. A comparative measure of tax effort may then be derived by comparing the actual ratio of revenue to GNP of a particular country with the ratio which would apply with an average response to such handles as are available. Using cross-section data from a set of LDCs, we may estimate an equation such as

$$T/Y = a + \alpha Y_p + \frac{\beta X}{Y} + \frac{\gamma E}{Y} + \frac{\delta A}{Y}$$

where T = revenue
$\quad\quad Y$ = GNP
$\quad\quad Y_p$ = per capita GNP
$\quad\quad X$ = exports
$\quad\quad E$ = output of extractive industries
$\quad\quad A$ = output of agriculture

[16] See p. 126, where the relationship of tax handles to economic structure was discussed.

TABLE 34-2
Tax Structure and Level of Per Capita Income*
(1983, as Percentage of Total)

	Low Income	Middle Income	Industrial
Individual income tax	9.6	6.7	26.2
Corporate income tax	8.4	13.5	7.1
Property tax	2.5	2.6	1.8
Payroll tax	2.2	10.1	29.6
Sales tax, turnover tax, VAT	18.8	10.5	16.6
Excises	13.1	13.3	11.1
Import taxes	32.6	16.2	2.7
Export taxes	3.8	1.4	0.2
Total	100.0	100.0	100.0

*Unweighted averages of ratios for countries in the sample.
Source: International Monetary Fund, Government Finance Statistics and The World Bank, *World Development Report, 1988.*

Having estimated the equation, we plug in the values of Y_p, X/Y, E/Y, and A/Y for a particular country to calculate its presumptive tax effort or T/Y ratio. As expected, the values for the α, β, and γ coefficients prove positive while that for δ proves negative. Values of R^2 of over 0.50 are obtained, but due to various variables, are highly interrelated so that their respective impacts are not readily separated.[17] Dividing the presumptive T/Y ratio by the actual T/Y ratio, we then obtain an index by which to compare the effort of this particular country with that of others. Whereas the results of such comparisons must be used with care, they nevertheless offer a framework in which to appraise comparative tax efforts.

Although the setting of particular countries differs, it is usually argued that an LDC should be expected to achieve a tax-to-GNP ratio of at least 18 percent. If one-half of this is spent for current services and a private sector savings rate of 3 percent is added, an overall savings rate of 12 percent would be achieved. This has been postulated by W. A. Lewis as constituting the desirable minimum level.[18]

Tax-Structure Development

The problems associated with the design and administration of various taxes differ with the structure of the economy in which they are applied and with the climate of public attitude about taxation. However, they also differ with respect to stages of economic development, and some general tax-structure characteristics in relation to per capita income may be observed.

Table 34-2 gives tax-structure comparisons for samples of countries at various

---

[17] See Alan A. Tait, Wilfred L. M. Graetz, and Barry J. Eichengreen, "International Comparison of Taxation for Selected Developing Countries, 1972–1976," *International Monetary Fund Staff Papers,* 1977.

For further discussion of such indices, see R. M. Bird, "A Note on Tax Sacrifice Comparisons," *National Tax Journal,* September 1964; H. Aaron, "Some Criticism of Tax Burden Indices," ibid., March 1965; and Bird, "Comment," ibid., September 1965.

[18] See Lewis, *The Theory of Economic Growth,* op. cit.

levels of per capita income. We note the importance of taxes on external trade (mainly customs duties) and of taxes on domestic production and sales for low-income countries, as well as the low share of income taxes. As per capita income rises, the importance of income taxes increases relative to that of customs duties and taxes on domestic sales and production. Payroll taxes also rise in relative importance as per capita income increases.

In addition to changing shares under the major headings of the table, the nature of the various taxes is also subject to change. Thus, taxes classified as income taxes in low-income countries are frequently capitation taxes which bear little resemblance to the personalized individual income tax of developed countries. Similarly, the so-called business income tax is often closer to a sales tax than to a profits tax as applied in the developed countries, and so forth.[19]

Individual Income Tax

Turning now to particular taxes, we begin with the individual income tax. For various reasons, the individual income tax does not and cannot be expected to occupy the central position in the tax structure of LDCs which it typically holds in the developed countries. Nevertheless, the income tax should be established early and strengthened as development proceeds. It is elastic to growth in GNP and therefore a promising revenue source for development finance. Its contribution to total revenue in Latin American countries typically ranges around 20 percent and is thus a significant part of the revenue picture, even though the feasibility of collecting a tax on wage and salary income in LDCs tends to be restricted to government, foreign corporations, and the rather limited group of large local enterprises. Employees of small establishments and the large group of self-employed, especially in agriculture, typically remain outside the orbit of the income tax. In part, this reflects exemption levels which are set high relative to average income, but it is also the result of ineffective enforcement and administration.

Difficulties in reaching capital income are even greater. The principle of self-assessment as followed in the United States is not workable. Official assessments are frequently negotiated rather than objectively based, and there is a substantial lag of final tax payment behind the income year. Use of tax withholding helps to speed up tax collections and is all to the good, but its applicability tends to be limited to the very types of wage and salary income which lend themselves to easy enforcement to begin with. This payment lag enjoyed by capital income is a substantial advantage especially where inadequate interest penalties are charged for delay and the real value of tax debts is eroded by inflation.

Although no reliable estimates are available, it may well be that the taxable income which is in fact reached usually amounts to less than one-half that which should be reached under tight enforcement. There is no magic formula by which these difficulties may be overcome. Source withholding, assignment by taxpayer numbers (especially to high-income returns), computerization and centralized handling of high-income returns, requirements for information returns on interest and

---

[19] For further discussion of various taxes in the LDCs, see R. M. Bird and O. Oldman (eds.): *Readings on Taxation in Developing Countries,* 3d ed., Cambridge, Mass.: Harvard Law School, International Tax Program, 1975.

dividend payments to be filed by corporations and banks, reduction in assessment lags, and higher penalties for delayed payments are all helpful. Yet they are insufficient unless the courts stand behind strict enforcement of the tax laws, a prime requirement which in the cultural and political context of developing countries is frequently difficult to meet.

Income tax administration, moreover, is bedeviled by the problem of inflation. It is not infrequent for developing countries to experience double- or even triple-digit rates of inflation per year. Such has been the case, for instance, in Chile and in Brazil for many years. In adaptation to this, income tax administration may provide for an automatic annual increase in exemption levels and rate brackets as prices rise, so as to keep the relation between marginal rates and real income constant. As a result, the effect of inflation on income tax equity is neutralized, but the built-in inflation check exerted by an unadjusted progressive income tax is reduced.

The problem of capital gains, especially in relation to land and buildings, is of considerable importance in developing countries where rapid urbanization gives rise to increasing land values, much as was observed by Henry George toward the close of the nineteenth century in the United States. To meet this problem, a capital gains tax on real estate, i.e., buildings and land, is administered as a separate tax. As noted below, there is a strong economic, as well as equity, case for such a tax, especially if applied only to gains from land (as distinct from improvements).

Business Income Tax

The most difficult problems arise in the effective taxation of business income, whether under a separate corporation profits tax or as applied to partnership and proprietorship income under the individual income tax. Where business accounting has not been developed to a level sufficient to measure profits with reasonable accuracy, other methods must be applied. Thus, many countries use a presumptive rather than a direct approach to profit determination, which may take the form of a presumptive profit margin on sales, with different margins stipulated for various industries. This method, which is widely used in Asian countries, in fact transforms the profits tax into a type of sales tax. This shift occurs since tax liability is a function of sales and the presumptive rather than actual margin.

In still other situations, the presumptive measure of profits is based on such indices as floor space and location by city block, a practice also to be found in the tax tradition of European countries, especially with regard to professional income. In the case of agriculture, acreage or heads of cattle may be used as the presumptive base. At the same time, ''stick and carrot'' techniques might be used to reward the conscientious taxpayers by the use of so-called blue returns, while penalizing the laggard payers by penalty rates. Again, the process of improvement must be gradual and cannot run too far ahead of improvement in accounting methods. Tax reformers are frequently tempted to overlook the importance of improving the techniques of presumptive taxation in favor of preoccupation with technical refinements of corporation taxation which, although important in developed countries, apply to only a small part of the business sector in the LDCs.

Furthermore, the legal forms of business organization frequently differ. In Latin American countries, for example, continental European rather than common-law traditions prevail, whereas in Asian countries, a quite different system of property law may apply; and practices appropriate for a country such as the United

TABLE 34-3
Net Income from Land at Various Levels of Utilization and Types of Land Tax
(In Dollars)

	PERCENTAGE OF UTILIZATION				
	100	90	50	20	0
No tax					
1. Income	100	90	50	20	0
2. Cost of underutilization to owner	0	10	50	80	100
10 percent tax on actual income					
3. Tax	10	9	5	2	0
4. Net income	90	81	45	18	0
5. Cost of underutilization to owner	0	9	45	72	90
6. Tax	10	10	10	10	10
7. Net income	90	80	40	10	− 10
8. Cost of underutilization to owner	0	10	50	80	100
10 percent tax on potential income plus penalty tax on underutilization					
9. Tax	10	12.5	28.75	42.50	72.50
10. Net income	90	77.5	21.75	− 22.50	− 72.50
11. Cost of underutilization to owner	0	12.5	68.25	112.50	162.50

States may not be applicable to LDCs, given their traditions and current state of development.[20]

Land Taxes

Since the agriculture sector in most LDCs is large, the problem of land taxation remains of major importance. One basic question is whether the tax should be imposed on the value of land, on actual income, or on the potential income which the land could yield under full utilization. In a perfectly competitive system, the three bases would be interchangeable since land values would equal the capitalized value of its income, and actual income would equal the potential. In reality, such is not the case. Land is frequently underutilized and held for speculative purposes or as a matter of social custom. Markets may be thin and current sales values not readily obtainable. Thus, the three bases yield substantially different results. Moreover, the income tax is rarely applied effectively to the agricultural sector, so that land revenue frequently serves as a combined income and land tax, including not only the rent of land but also labor and improvement (capital) income in its base.

With respect to the taxation of income from land only (excluding returns to labor and capital improvements), a strong argument can be made for basing such taxation on potential rather than on actual income.[21] This is shown in Table 34-3. Suppose that a parcel of land at various levels of utilization and in the absence of tax yields the income shown in line 1 of the table. The difference between actual

---

[20] For a discussion of business tax reform proposals, see R. Slitor, "Reform of the Business Tax Structure," in R. A. Musgrave and M. Gillis (eds.): *Fiscal Reform for Colombia*, Cambridge, Mass.: Harvard Law School, International Tax Program, 1971, pp. 463–530.

[21] See J. Hicks and U. Hicks, "The Taxation of the Unimproved Value of Land," in Bird and Oldman, op. cit., pp. 431–442; and R. Bird, *Taxing Agricultural Land in Developing Countries*, Cambridge, Mass.: Harvard Law School, International Tax Program, 1973.

and potential yield is given in line 2 and reflects the cost of underutilization to the owner. After a 10 percent tax on actual income is imposed, the cost of underutilization as shown in line 5 is reduced. Thus, underutilization is encouraged. This effect is avoided and the cost of underutilization is held at its pre-tax level if the tax is imposed on potential rather than actual income, with the result as shown in line 8. The reason is that the tax is independent of actual income so that the marginal tax rate is now zero. In line 9, we go a step further and supplement the 10 percent tax on potential income (line 6) with a penalty charge on underutilization. This charge, for purposes of illustration, rises in rate with the degree of underutilization. Thus, the first 25 percent of shortfall of actual below potential income pays a tax of 25 percent. The next 25 percent (i.e., a shortfall between 25 and 50 percent of potential income) pays at a rate of 50 percent, rising to 75 percent on a shortfall between 50 and 75 percent and to 100 percent on a shortfall between 75 and 100 percent. As shown in line 11, the cost of underutilization is now increased substantially above the pre-tax level, and net income at low levels of utilization becomes negative. The marginal tax rate on additional income turns negative and the tax on deficient income is in fact a tax on idle land.

Whichever approach is taken, the availability of adequate land surveys and their maintenance on an up-to-date basis are an essential requirement for an efficient system of land taxation. Frequently such surveys are not available, so that only haphazard methods of assessment can be applied.

Wealth and Property Taxes

In addition to land revenue, the taxation of urban real estate is an important part of the tax base, especially as urbanization proceeds. As noted before, a good case can be made for progressive taxation of residential property, combining multiple residences in one base so as to supplement the system of commodity taxation on luxury consumption other than housing.

Beyond this, wealth taxation of the net worth type is a frequent component of the tax structure in LDCs. Although such taxes may in the end prove to be little more than part of the system of real property taxation, with intangibles largely escaping the tax base, they are a useful supplement to income taxation as it applies (or rather fails to apply) to capital income. Real capital is visible and, once accounted for under the wealth tax, earnings therefrom may be traced to its owners under the income tax.

Commodity Taxes and Tariffs

The design of commodity taxation involves three major problems: (1) what products should be taxed and at what rates; (2) at what stages such taxes should be imposed; and (3) how taxation of domestic products should be related to import duties.

As noted previously, the twin objectives of protecting savings and of modifying a highly unequal state of distribution point to the taxation of luxury consumption as the most obvious solution. Given that implementation of a personal type of expenditure tax is hardly feasible for LDCs, the situation calls for taxation of luxury consumption. If this view is correct, the basic requirement is not for a comprehensive and flat-rate sales tax but for a system of sales taxation with differing rates.[22] The implementation of progressive consumption taxation by differentiation between products thus depends on the existence of products with sharply different income elasticities, a precondition which appears to be met in developing countries.

The stage or stages at which commodity taxes are to be imposed must be decided on grounds of administrative feasibility and thus depends upon the structure of the particular economy. With a multiple-stage tax of the value-added type, failure to reach the retail stage involves only a partial revenue loss, not the total loss that would be the result under a retail sales tax. Moreover, use of the invoice method contributes to better compliance.[23] On the other hand, taxation of final products at differential rates tends to be more difficult under the value-added approach. Where products comprising an important part of the tax base originate in relatively large manufacturing establishments, manufacturer excises offer the simplest and most direct approach. In any case, there is no need to rely on one or the other approach exclusively. A combination of methods may be applied, depending on what is most expedient in any particular case.[24]

There remains the need for coordinating domestic excises with import duties. In their desire to impose heavier burdens on luxury consumption, LDCs frequently place higher import duties upon luxury products. At the same time, this measure often goes with a failure to match such duties by corresponding excises on home-produced luxury goods. Thus, luxury tariffs tend to provide protection to domestic substitutes. This is clearly poor policy. If protective tariffs are to be used to permit domestic infant industries to develop, such industries should be chosen according to their development potential and not as a side effect of luxury taxation. The best approach may well be to use largely uniform tariff rates while including luxury imports in the tax base of the domestic excise system.

Another aspect of tariff policy which requires critical review is the practice of excluding domestically used capital goods from customs duties.[25] In a situation where, for various reasons, the cost of capital tends to be undervalued relative to the cost of labor, this practice accentuates the price distortion, a matter which will be discussed later.

D. TAX INCENTIVES

We have seen that the twin objectives of economic growth and reduction of inequality can be secured best by reliance on progressive consumption taxes; but we have also seen that equity calls for this approach to be combined with the taxation

---

[22] It should be noted that the distinction is not between types of products which on nutritional or ethical grounds may be considered as essential (e.g., bread) rather than as frills (e.g., butter) but simply between commodities which weigh more heavily in high-income and low-income budgets.

[23] See p. 402.

[24] J. Due, *Indirect Taxation in Developing Countries,* Baltimore: Johns Hopkins, 1970; and M. Gillis, "Objectives and Means of Indirect Tax Reform," R. A. Musgrave and M. Gillis (eds.): *Fiscal Reform for Columbia,* Cambridge, Mass.: Harvard Law School, International Tax Program, September 1971, pp. 559–573.

[25] Exclusion of domestically used capital goods is to be distinguished from the exclusion of raw materials or intermediate products which in turn enter into exports, this being an unobjectionable policy.

of capital income under a progressive income tax. Given the potential conflict of the latter with investment incentives, it is not surprising that much attention has been given to various devices by which detrimental investment effects can be minimized. It is a matter of policy judgment, transcending considerations of tax policy only, how far a country should go in trading distributional equity for growth gains; but it is the task of tax policy to make sure that additions to growth are bought at the least equity cost. Tax relief for investment which does not pay for itself in generating additional growth not only involves revenue loss without gain but worsens the state of income distribution, by giving the relief to high incomes.

Judged on these grounds, tax incentives to investment have been generally wasteful and inequitable, so much so that many observers have been led to reject all incentive devices. But notwithstanding the rather dismal experience, total rejection is not justified. Political pressures for tax incentives will prevail no matter what the tax technician may say; and this being inevitable, the incentives may as well be designed as efficiently as possible. Moreover, some concessions to growth may be in order provided that they are made in the best way.

Domestic Incentives

In dealing with the incentive problem, we find it helpful to distinguish between domestic incentives and the incentive problem as it relates to foreign capital in particular. Domestic incentives might be related to investment in general, or they might be limited to investment in selected industries or regions. Finally, incentives may be designed to stimulate exports and to strengthen the balance of payments.

General Incentives   General investment incentives may take the form of investment credits or accelerated depreciation similar to the devices used in developed countries.[26] In addition, LDCs frequently offer tax holidays during which profits from new enterprises are tax-free for an initial period of, say, five to seven years. This method relates the value of the incentive to high initial profitability, which may run counter to the need for stable and more long-run types of investment. For the case of new investment by existing firms, there is the further difficulty of distinguishing between earnings attributable to the new and old components of their capital stock. Once more this problem is avoided by an investment credit or investment grant approach. Moreover, it is a poor policy for government to make long-run commitments to tax subsidies, especially where it is hoped that there will be a declining need for such subsidies in the future.

Whatever the case may be, general investment incentives cannot be effective in raising the overall level of investment unless equal attention is given to raising the level of saving. This may be done by encouraging retention of profits as well as by giving tax credits for saving under the individual income tax. The problem, of course, is to reach savings which otherwise would not have been made and to avoid their being offset by dissaving in other parts of the taxpayer's accounts. Thus, many of the same difficulties arise as were noted previously in the context of savings incentives.[27]

---

[26] For a discussion of tax incentives in developing countries, see George E. Lent, "Tax Incentives in Developing Countries," in Bird and Oldman, op. cit.

[27] See p. 591.

Growth Industries   Even though the effectiveness of general investment incentives is questionable, there is more reason to expect that incentives limited to particular sectors or industries will be effective in diverting capital to such industries. The big problem here lies in how to select the industries which are to be given preferential treatment.

Presumably, the industries which should be chosen are those which play a strategic role in development and which, without special favor, will remain underexpanded. Undoubtedly there exist external economies in the development process which are not allowed for in private investment decisions; and imperfect capital markets may misdirect investment even without externalities. Wise correction of such investment errors would thus be desirable, but experience has not been encouraging. Frequently the list of eligible industries is so broad as to involve little selection. In other instances, selection reflects political pressure groups; and in still others, incentives are given to sustain the market for public enterprises, such as steel mills, which should not have been constructed in the first place. Although selective use of incentives is good in principle, efficient application is hard to find.

Regional Incentives   Another form of selective incentive arises in regional policy. As we have argued previously, a general case can be made for fiscal neutrality in location decisions, whether for labor or capital.[28] Yet conditions in developing countries may call for departure from this rule. Labor may be immobile, or maintenance of the labor force in particular regions may be preferable either because excessive migration from rural to urban areas is undesirable or because national policy for noneconomic reasons calls for some degree of equalization in regional development rates. Special incentives may then be given to development in such regions.

The question is whether such incentives are given best by subsidizing investment or by subsidizing employment in the target regions. The answer depends upon the policy objective, i.e., whether the focus is on increasing production or value added in the region, or whether the purpose is to increase payrolls and to raise the standard of living of the region's population. With the latter a wage subsidy may well prove more effective, especially if there is a substantial reserve of unemployed (or underemployed) labor in agriculture which can be drawn into industrial employment if labor costs are reduced.[29] Recent evidence on an experiment with a tax credit scheme to develop the Brazilian Northeast, perhaps the most ambitious regional tax credit effort on record, points toward the inability of capital incentives to generate a high degree of labor absorption in the target area.[30]

Capital versus Employment Incentives

The issue of capital versus wage subsidies transcends the regional issue. Whereas incentive policy has been generally directed at increasing the profitability of capi-

[28] See p. 454.

[29] See Charles E. McLure, "The Design of Regional Tax Incentives for Columbia," in Musgrave and Gillis, op. cit., pp. 545–556. See also R. M. Bird, "Tax Subsidy Policies for Regional Development," *National Tax Journal*, June 1966.

[30] For a hopeful early appraisal, see Hirschman, *A Bias for Hope*, op. cit., pp. 124–158. For a less encouraging second look see David E. Goodman, "Industrial Development in the Brazilian Northeast: An Interim Appraisal of the Tax Credit Scheme of Article 34/18," in R. Roett, *Brazil in the Sixties*, Nashville, Tenn.: Vanderbilt University Press, 1972.

tal, recent discussion has pointed toward an alternative approach which would increase the profitability of employing labor. This approach reflects dissatisfaction with an emerging pattern of development which involves increased use of capital without a corresponding increase of employment in the industrial sector. This pattern, which results from the use of highly capital-intensive forms of investment and labor-saving techniques, runs counter to the objective of a broadly based development in which the gains are shared by large sectors of the population.

Use of highly capital-intensive forms of investment is encouraged by price distortions which overprice the cost of labor and underprice the cost of capital. The former tends to result from minimum wage legislation and excessive union demands; the latter reflects preferential exchange rates, tariff exemptions, and ineffective profits taxation. In order to redress the balance, wage subsidies might be given either directly or indirectly through a "wage-bill credit" similar in principle to the investment credit. Alternatively, profits tax relief may be made contingent on the use of more labor-intensive equipment. Such measures might be appropriate in connection with regional incentives where the objective is to raise income levels in backward areas. It might also be appropriate in dealing with unemployment which results from an excessive influx of rural population into urban areas.[31] Another suggestion for inducing more labor-intensive use of capital is to provide tax incentives which reduce the labor cost for night-shift work.[32]

Incentives to Foreign Capital

Foreign capital, as noted previously, plays an important role in development policy, and tax incentives may be helpful in channeling it to the uses which are most desirable for the whole country.

From the national viewpoint, the role of tax incentives to foreign capital differs from that of incentives to domestic capital. The latter merely involve transfers between the treasury (which loses revenue) and the investor (who gains), but tax relief granted to foreign investors reduces the whole country's share in the profits earned by foreign capital. This loss must therefore be compensated for by the gains from additional capital influx if the tax incentive is to pay its way. The design of incentives may be helpful in directing foreign capital into such uses as are advantageous to the host country. The gains to be derived from foreign capital lie in the increased earnings for domestic factors of production to which the foreign capital gives rise. There is little advantage to the host country in foreign capital which brings its own resources with it and uses the foreign location as a production site only.[33] Tax incentives therefore should be linked to domestic value added which the foreign capital induces. Moreover, they should be designed to encourage reinvestment and permanent operation, while discouraging quick-kill types of investments.[34]

---

[31] See A. Harberger, "On Measuring the Social Opportunity Cost of Labor," *International Labor Review*, June 1971.

[32] See D. M. Schydlowsky, "Fiscal Policy for Full Capacity Industrial Growth in Latin America," in *Economic Development in Latin America*, Gainesville: University of Florida Press, 1975.

[33] "Tax haven" types of investments which result in office structures but little local employment, for example, offer little advantage to the host country.

[34] See J. Heller and K. M. Kauffman, *Tax Incentives in Less Developed Countries*, Cambridge, Mass.: Harvard Law School, International Tax Program, 1963.

Whatever the case may be, the LDC needs the cooperation of the investor's country of origin if effective incentives are to be granted. If the country of capital ownership taxes its foreign-earned income at its own rate while giving a foreign tax credit, lower taxation by the LDC merely results in a transfer to the other country's treasury while leaving no advantage to the investor who repatriates profits. Tax deferral, however, becomes of major importance. It not only serves to attract capital to the LDC which offers a tax incentive but also exerts a continuing incentive to reinvest earnings in the LDC. Therefore there is good reason for maintaining deferral on investment in LDCs while terminating it for investment in the developed countries.

Another device which would render incentives effective to foreign investors who intend to repatriate is the so-called tax-sparing arrangement. Under this provision, the country of capital ownership would extend a credit, upon repatriation, equal to the full tax in the LDC even though a lesser tax or no tax is paid under the incentive arrangement. This approach, however, lacks the incentive for reinvestment; and because political pressures call for the incentive to be generalized to all domestic investment, taxation of profits in general is undermined.

A final point arises in connection with competition among LDCs for foreign capital. To the extent that one country outbids another by offering larger incentives, LDCs as a group stand to lose. Some degree of cooperation is desirable to avoid self-defeating tax competition. Avoidance of such competition is one of the important roles of common market arrangements among groups of LDCs, such as are planned for the Andean countries.

Export Incentives

Tax incentives for exports are a popular device to assist in the development of foreign markets and to strengthen the balance of payments. To be effective, such incentives should be related not to total foreign sales or profits therefrom, as is the typical practice, but to domestic value added. It is only the latter component of foreign sales, and not the reexport of imported material or intermediate goods, which adds to a country's foreign exchange earnings.

E. EXPENDITURE POLICY

The role of expenditure policy in economic development has been explored less extensively than that of tax policy, and comparative data are more difficult to obtain. However, in comparing the patterns of African, Latin American, and Asian countries with those of European countries, we obtain some evidence regarding the role of per capita income. Low-income countries direct a higher share of expenditures to education and health services and a lower share to transfers. The higher share for education to some degree reflects the higher cost of educational services in these countries. The higher share of transfers in high-income countries reflects the more developed social security systems.

The strategic role of public investment in economic development has already been noted. This role is based in part on the undeveloped state of private capital markets and in part on local scarcity of entrepreneurial talent; it is also based on the fact that the type of investment needed at the earliest stages of development frequently includes very large outlays, such as those involved in the development of transportation systems or the opening up of undeveloped parts of the country. Moreover, infrastructure investment of this sort carries external benefits which call for public provision.

It is not surprising, therefore, that the development of public investment performs a major function in the design of development plans in LDCs. In this context, the use of cost-benefit analysis is of great importance. Developing countries can ill afford to waste scarce resources, and yet efficient project evaluation is a difficult task. In one respect, cost-benefit analysis is more readily applied in developing than in developed countries, because public investment is typically aimed at the provision of intermediate goods, the value of which may be measured in terms of their effects upon the prices of privately provided goods.[35] Thus the return on transportation or irrigation projects may be appraised in terms of the resulting reduction in the cost of goods as they reach the market—a measure which cannot be applied where public outlays go to provide final goods of the consumption type. But in other respects, the task of evaluation is more difficult.

For one thing, the direct benefits thus made available will be accompanied by indirect or external benefits which are harder to assess. For another, costs are more difficult to determine. Since market prices may not reflect the true social costs involved, shadow prices must be used in their place. If capital is undervalued while labor is overvalued, the use of market prices leads to the previously noted distortion toward excessively capital-intensive technology. Further difficulties arise in the context of dynamic development where relative prices which apply when the project is introduced may give way to a quite different set of prices applicable during the years when the services of the project are rendered. Once more, this possibility points to the importance of longer-run planning and the evaluation of individual projects in the context of an overall development plan.

Another factor of obvious importance is proper determination of the discount rate. With private capital markets not fully developed, use of a "social rate" may be more or less inevitable. Considerations suggesting the presence of external benefits indicate that the social rate should be set below the level of rates prevailing in the market, thus pointing to a higher rate of capital formation and the choice of longer-term projects. Pointing in the other direction is the fact that the cost of forgoing current consumption is very high at low levels of income; yet in the future when the gain from postponement is realized, the marginal utility of consumption will be less since income is higher. This fact tends to be overlooked in individual savings decisions but should be allowed for by government. But here, as in other matters of discount rate determination, cruder approaches are likely to be used. In the typical development context, the government may find itself confronted with the practical necessity of determining the politically acceptable minimum path of consumption over the next five or ten years and may derive the discount rate therefrom.

Human investment, as noted before, deserves particular consideration in the development context. Education programs are important not only with respect to

---

[35] See p. 139.

growth policy but also with regard to their important bearing on how the gains from growth will be distributed both among income groups and among various sectors of the economy. Studies have shown exceedingly high rates of return on educational investment in developing countries, thus pointing to the particular importance of this form of capital formation, but it is essential that the educational inputs be designed to meet the country's need for specific labor skills.

F. INTERNATIONAL AID AND REDISTRIBUTION

Those considerations, humanitarian or political, that provide the basis for concern with the domestic state of income distribution cannot be limited to the confines of one's own nation. Chances are that aspects of international distribution will become an increasingly important element in the world politics of future decades. But important though they may be, distribution issues at the international level are even more difficult to deal with than are their domestic counterparts. Inequalities are larger and the organizational problem is more complex since there is no "central government" to deal with them and policies must be implemented by transfers among nations. Such measures may be in the form of development aid designed to raise the growth rate of low-income countries, this being the approach which has been followed on a modest scale over the past few decades. Or they might in time lead to redistribution out of the existing level of world income similar in nature to a negative income tax as applied to domestic redistribution. Although this approach is not foreseeable at present, it might someday become a central concern for an international system of public finance.

Magnitude of Transfer Problem

In dealing with the problem of distribution on an international basis, the concern may be with differentials in average income among *countries*; or it may be with inequalities in the distribution of income among *individuals* on a worldwide basis without regard for national boundaries. To some extent the two problems overlap, since most poor people are in fact residents of the countries with low per capita income; but where they do not overlap, the basic problem is once more that of redistribution among individuals. Little would be gained if redistribution toward low-income countries were to accrue to a small group of high-income residents. The problem, it appears, is quite similar to that previously dealt with in examining the problem of equalization among jurisdictions in the context of fiscal federalism.[36]

The inequality of interindividual income distribution on a world basis is appalling.[37] Domestic inequalities are compounded with inequalities in average incomes across nations. Assuming that individuals in any one country receive an income equal to the country's average, it may be estimated that the lowest 40 percent of the world's population receives around 3 percent of the world's income, whereas the top 20 percent receives 60 percent. If internal distribution within countries is

---

[36] See p. 460.
[37] S. Andic and A. T. Peacock, "The International Distribution of Income, 1949 and 1957," *Journal of the Royal Statistical Society,* Series A, vol. 124, 1961.

allowed for, the ratios are 2 and 70 percent. This degree of inequality is much greater than that which prevails within countries, especially higher-income countries. The lower half of the world's population, including most of Asia, Africa, and the Middle East, and a good part of South America, subsists on a per capita GNP of around $600 or less, as against an average of $17,000 for the upper 25 percent (1987 levels). Allowing for the difficulties inherent in sweeping comparisons of this sort, the degree of inequality is staggering. Moreover, there is reason to expect that per capita income in the developed countries is rising more rapidly than in low-income countries, so that the situation is worsening rather than (as tends to be occurring with domestic distribution) improving over time.

If total world income could be redistributed to achieve complete equalization, a per capita GNP of over $4,000 could be established. Although such an income would be low compared with the prevailing standards of advanced countries, it would involve a vast improvement for large parts of the world. But obviously, such equalization would be impossible while holding total income constant. The contribution rate required from the higher-income countries to achieve large-scale equalization would be exceedingly high and substantial disincentive effects would arise.

Even apparently modest redistribution targets would involve substantial transfers. To indicate the magnitude of the problem, it may be estimated that in order to raise the floor of per capita GNP in low-income countries to $400 and $800, respectively, tax rates of 2 and 7 percent would have to be imposed in higher-income countries (ratio applies to a GNP base) in order to finance the transfer. Under a proportional rate, the U.S. contribution might account for about one-third of the total, but would be even higher under a progressive rate. If a progressive rate schedule was used, the U.S. contribution might rise above 40 percent.[38] Even a modest redistribution target—leaving minimum levels vastly below those tolerated in the domestic policy of developing countries—would thus require a very substantial increase in the contribution rate of high-income countries.

Development Aid

As has been noted before, distribution policy must not be considered only as a matter of redistributing slices in a given pie. Effects on the size of the pie, in particular the rate of economic growth, must be studied as well. If this viewpoint holds for the case of national redistribution, it holds especially at the international level where the potential scale of distributional adjustment is so much larger. Nothing would be gained if the contribution of developed countries were pushed so far as to interfere with their economic ability to render continued aid.

Indeed it is obvious that a major improvement in the condition of the world's poverty population can be achieved only by raising productivity of workers in low-income countries. An important contribution to this can be made by redirecting capital flows from high-income to low-income countries. As capital is redirected, world output will increase, since capital should be more efficient in countries where the capital-labor ratio is as yet very low. The suppliers of capital in the high-

---

[38] Based on Richard A. Musgrave and Peter Jarrett, "International Redistribution," *Kyklos,* Summer 1979.

income countries stand to gain as larger returns are obtained from investment in low-income countries. However, there would be a redistribution of income from labor in high-income countries (which would then operate with less capital) to labor in low-income countries whose productivity would be increased by the rising capital-labor ratio. An improved distribution of world income might thus be obtained at the cost of increased inequality (although over a much lesser range) in the developed countries. There is also the problem that insertion of foreign management which comes with the capital flow not only adds know-how but may also impede the development of domestic entepreneurship and create conditions of political dependence.

A second important contribution to economic development can be rendered by opening the markets of developed countries more widely to the exports of the less developed countries. This may involve extension of preferential treatment as well as a trend away from (rather than toward) trade restrictions. In this case, labor in developed countries may suffer once more since it is less capable of moving than is the capital factor. However, labor will now gain in its role of consumer from reduced import prices.

Whatever the case may be, policies such as these hold out the hope that developing countries after a successful takeoff can continue their growth independently, thus avoiding the being-on-welfare syndrome, which is as disturbing in the international as in the domestic setting.

G. SUMMARY

Fiscal policy in less developed countries differs in important respects from that in highly developed countries. This variation is owing to the fact that the economic and social setting in LDCs is different.

1. The relation between per capita income and public sector size was examined.
2. The fundamental need for capital formation and the difficulty of generating the required level of saving out of low percapita income are dominant factors.
3. Measures to induce technological improvement, to encourage enterprise, and to develop institutions making for more efficient use of resources are also of major importance.
4. Pursuit of these objectives is made difficult by social and political factors as well as deficient administrative capabilities.
5. Foreign trade is usually of prime importance, as is the need for foreign exchange adequate to secure the necessary imported capital equipment.
6. Sectoral divisions within the economy tend to create bottlenecks and to interfere with balanced growth.

These are only some of the difficulties which arise and which must be considered in the formulation of fiscal policy.

7. Given the target rate of growth, a certain rate of capital formation is needed. The savings rate—public and private—must be set so as to match the needed rate of capital formation.
8. When one measures the contribution of the public sector to overall savings by the surplus in the current budget, the surplus must equal the excess of required total

saving over available private saving. From this figure, the required rate of taxation may be deduced.

9. The requirement for a tax structure which secures an adequate level of saving must be reconciled with the requirement for tax equity.

10. Although severe taxation of saving and investment by individuals and corporations may be counterproductive because it may retard growth, a substantial tax base is available in the consumption of higher-income households.

11. Whereas the primary concern with growth renders the fiscal policy rule applicable in LDCs more akin to those developed in Chapter 17 than to those of Chapters 30 and 31, the contingency of deficient demand with underemployment of the labor force and of inflation nevertheless arises.

12. A cross-section sample shows no simple relation between public sector size and the rate of economic growth.

Turning to the problems of tax policy, we dealt with the general problems of taxable capacity and the composition of the tax structure as well as with the design of particular taxes.

13. The ratio of tax to GNP of LDCs is much below that of developed countries. This fact reflects lower taxable capacity as well as lower tax effort.

14. At low levels of per capita income, tax handles are scarce. The tax structure tends to be dominated by production and sales taxes, especially customs duties, with a low share for profits and income taxes.

15. Effective administration of income and profits taxes is difficult owing to such factors as a high degree of self-employment, the small size of establishments, and inadequate accounting practices. In addition, taxpayer compliance and enforcement tend to be low with large-scale evasion, especially of capital income. Use of presumptive taxes must be relied on.

16. Agricultural taxation is of major importance in most LDCs because of the relatively large scope of their agricultural sectors. However, effective taxation of land and agricultural income is unpopular and difficult to implement.

17. Wealth and property taxes may be a useful supplement to ineffective taxation of capital income.

18. Implementation of a general sales tax at the retail level is difficult because of the small scale of establishments. Typically, taxation at the manufacturer's level is more feasible and may be combined with use of value-added taxation for some products.

19. As distinct from a flat-rate consumption tax, taxation of luxury products at higher rates, with equal treatment of domestically produced and imported goods, permits a more equitable use of consumption taxes.

20. LDCs tend to make widespread use of tax incentives to investment. Frequently, these are not very effective and create tax inequities.

21. Tax incentives to foreign capital should aim at maximizing domestic value added.

22. The incentive structure should be designed to consider effects on employment as well as effects on investment.

Turning, finally, to the role of expenditure policy, we have noted the following:

23. Public investment and public lending play strategic roles in development.

24. The concept of public capital formation should be interpreted to include productivity-increasing investment in human resources.

25. Foreign borrowing increases the current supply of available resources and thus permits development with a lesser burden on the present generation.

FURTHER READINGS ·

For a recent survey of fiscal policy in developing countries see World Bank, *World Development Report, 1988; Public Finances in Developing Countries,* Washington, D.C., 1988. Also see:

Bird, R. M.: *Taxing Agricultural Land in Developing Countries,* Cambridge, Mass.: Harvard Law School, International Tax Program, 1973.

———, and O. Oldman (eds.): *Readings on Taxation in Developing Countries,* 3d ed., Cambridge, Mass.: Harvard Law School, International Tax Program, 1975.

Chenery, Hollis B., et al.: *Redistribution with Growth,* Washington, D.C.: World Bank and Oxford University Press, 1974.

Hinrichs, H.: *A General Theory of Tax Structure Change during Economic Development,* Cambridge, Mass.: Harvard Law School, International Tax Program, 1966.

Musgrave, R. A., and M. Gillis (eds.): *Fiscal Reform for Colombia,* final report and staff papers of the Colombian Commission on Tax Reform, Cambridge, Mass.: Harvard Law School, International Tax Program, September 1971.

———: *Fiscal Systems,* part 2, New Haven, Conn.: Yale, 1969.

NAME INDEX

SUBJECT INDEX